# VALUES AND VOICES

## A College Reader

### BETTY RENSHAW

Holt, Rinehart and Winston, Inc.

New York   Chicago   San Francisco
Atlanta   Dallas

To several persons,
because I value them:
Bunny
Dotsie
Gillian
Nan Chee
Terry
Tompie

**Library of Congress Cataloging in Publication Data**

Renshaw, Betty, comp.
Values and voices, a college reader.

1. College readers. I. Title.
PE1417.R47        808'.04275        74–17200

**ISBN** 0–03–011446–2

Design by: Arthur Ritter

# PREFACE

Students arrive at college bringing sets of values, conscious or unconscious, with them. These values may be inherited, learned, reactive, and may have encountered little real examination; or they may be more consciously chosen, adapted, open-ended beliefs that the individual has deliberately decided to live by.

*Values and Voices* came about because I had been concerned for some years about the desirability of freshman students having an opportunity, very early in college, to begin to examine those values they bring with them. This reader, in nearly 100 selections, invites the student to do just that, through reading, talking, and writing.

*Values and Voices* offers students a wide variety, and balance of statements on values, expressed through a diversity of voices. The book encourages them to discover, to examine, and to choose among, many possible ways of believing and of living. It invites them to question assumptions, to confront dilemmas, and to seek answers and resolutions— at least to whatever degree these latter exist.

The student has the opportunity to read how others have made their "value statements" through a variety of rhetorical modes and voices; the expository essay, the personal narrative, the fable, the interview, critical reviews, satires, letters, speeches, and some fiction. There are both well-known and new pieces: selections by both "wise elder" type voices and younger voices; statements by women as well as by men; a concern with both the tested learnings of the past and the promises— and possible nightmares—of the future; speakers representing several minority voices as well as majority positions.

The book is divided into ten thematic sections. Some of the areas are those traditionally found in freshman readers: Education, Society, Politics, Language and Thought, The Arts and Creativity, Science and Technology, Religion. Many of the traditional essays of a liberal education are provided here, but there are also a number of fresh, up-to-date pieces. The other three sections are somewhat more unusual ones: The Individual, with each selection featuring a uniquely individual voice; New Voices, in which voices from a number of rising segments of America speak up; The Future, covering many aspects of futuristic concern.

The reading selections themselves have been carefully chosen for potential interest to the student and for reading level. Reading length has been controlled; pieces average 4–5 pages. A headnote that introduces each selection offers brief pertinent biographical material and an overview of the piece and, where needed, places the selection in its context. Study questions, of three types, follow each piece: two on content, two on rhetoric, and two that are projects, including writing assignments.

In addition to a basic thematic table of contents, there are an annotated table of contents, with a brief statement about each selection, and a rhetorical table of contents. There is an index, by title and by author.

The instructor will soon discover that many pieces can be used in a cross-reference fashion. Suggestions for so using the book appear in some study questions, and more will be found in the Instructor's Manual, available from the publisher. The Instructor's Manual also offers additional questions for discussion, topics for writing, listings of films and other audio-visual items for use with various pieces, a suggested bibliography to enrich the reading of individual selections, and so on.

In his autobiography, Leonard Woolf has written: " . . . in one's . . . personal life, in terms of humanity and human society, certain things are of immense importance: human relations, happiness, truth, beauty or art, justice and mercy." *Values and Voices* addresses these "certain things . . . of immense importance." Viktor Frankl reminds us: "Man ultimately decides for himself! And . . . education must be education toward the ability to decide." *Values and Voices* wants to help the student learn how to examine alternatives intelligently, to make decisions about them, and to express these decisions in a variety of forms.

## ACKNOWLEDGMENTS

A proper acknowledgment of all the help I have received with this book is indeed impossible. However, I do wish to thank specifically the following persons; *Values and Voices* is without question a better book because of them: John Bodnar, Mary Brown, Charles Buddenhagen, Marlene Carpenter, Bill Fry, Diana Hacker, Joan Murray Naake, Bill Peirce, Ron Powell, Margaret Warner, and Charmaine Yochim, all of Prince George's Community College; Anne King of Prince George's Community College, co-author of the Instructor's Manual; Richard S. Beal of Boston University; Jo Cockelreas of the University of Hawaii; Dixie Goswami of Middlesex Community College; Fred See of SUNY at Buffalo. For invaluable criticisms I must also thank Barbara Bixby of Brevard Community College; Charles Cobb of Los Angeles Pierce College; Frank J. D'Angelo of Arizona State University; Richard Konieczka of Kalamazoo Valley Community College; Nora Leitch of Lamar University; Nina Theiss of Santa Monica College; Robert Zoellner of Colorado State University. I wish also to give special credit for their assistance to Harriett Nolte and Pamela Forcey of Holt, Rinehart and Winston. There is one additional person, whose belief in and help with the book throughout made all the difference: Jane Ross, former English Editor and now Director of Development at Holt, Rinehart and Winston—but, more importantly, friend.

B.R.

# CONTENTS

## 4 Society    Values of Groups and Dissenters

## 5 Politics    Voices of State and Populace

## 6 Language and Thought    Discovering Values Through Words

# 7 The Arts and Creativity Finding Forms for Voices

# 8 Science and Technology Voices of Control and Conscience

# 9 Religion A Search for Values

# 10 The Future Voices of the Imagination

# ANNOTATED CONTENTS

# RHETORICAL CONTENTS

Generally, selections are listed in as many of the six designated categories as possible.

## Argumentation

Certain selections lend themselves particularly well to a discussion of *style:*

A few selections do not fall readily into any category. These special-genre pieces are listed below:

# 1
# Education

# Survival U

## Prospectus for a Really Relevant University

## JOHN FISCHER

John Fischer (1910–    ) has worked as a newspaper reporter in this country and abroad and has served with the Foreign Economics Administration of the U.S. Government. He has written several books, among them *Master Plan, U.S.A.* (1951), and has been editor-in-chief of *Harper's Magazine*, in which the timely essay below first appeared in September, 1969. In his essay, Fischer urges "human ecology" as "the single [coordinating] science" around which his visionary university would be built.

It gets pretty depressing to watch what is going on in the world and realize that your education is not equipping you to do anything about it.
—FROM A LETTER BY A UNIVERSITY OF CALIFORNIA SENIOR

1    She is not a radical, and has never taken part in any demonstration. She will graduate with honors, and profound disillusionment. From listening to her—and a good many like-minded students at California and East Coast campuses—I think I am beginning to understand what they mean when they say that a liberal-arts education isn't relevant.

2    They mean it is incoherent. It doesn't cohere. It consists of bits and pieces which don't stick together, and have no common purpose. One of our leading Negro educators, Arthur Lewis of Princeton, recently summed it up better than I can. America is the only country, he said, where youngsters are required "to fritter away their precious years in meaningless peregrination from subject to subject . . . spending twelve weeks getting some tidbits of religion, twelve weeks learning French, twelve weeks seeing whether the history professor is stimulating, twelve weeks seeking entertainment from the economics professor, twelve weeks confirming that one is not going to be able to master calculus."

3    These fragments are meaningless because they are not organized around any central purpose, or vision of the world. The typical liberal-

arts college has no clearly defined goals. It merely offers a smorgasbord of courses, in hopes that if a student nibbles at a few dishes from the humanities table, plus a snack of science, and a garnish of art or anthropology, he may emerge as "a cultivated man"—whatever that means. Except for a few surviving church schools, no university even pretends to have a unifying philosophy. Individual teachers may have personal ideologies—but since they are likely to range, on any given campus, from Marxism to worship of the scientific method to exaltation of the irrational (à la Norman O. Brown), they don't cohere either. They often leave a student convinced at the end of four years that any given idea is probably about as valid as any other—and that none of them has much relationship to the others, or to the decisions he is going to have to make the day after graduation.

## Attempts at Coherence

4    Education was not always like that. The earliest European universities had a precise purpose: to train an elite for the service of the Church. Everything they taught was focused to that end. Thomas Aquinas had spelled it all out: what subjects had to be mastered, how each connected with every other, and what meaning they had for man and God.

5    Later, for a span of several centuries, Oxford and Cambridge had an equally clear function: to train administrators to run an empire. So too did Harvard and Yale at the time they were founded; their job was to produce the clergymen, lawyers, and doctors that a new country needed. In each case, the curriculum was rigidly prescribed. A student learned what he needed, to prepare himself to be a competent priest, district officer, or surgeon. He had no doubts about the relevance of his courses—and no time to fret about expanding his consciousness or currying his sensual awareness.

6    This is still true of our professional schools. I have yet to hear an engineering or medical student complain that his education is meaningless. Only in the liberal-arts colleges—which boast that "we are not trade schools"—do the youngsters get that feeling that they are drowning in a cloud of feathers.

7    For a long while some of our less complacent academics have been trying to restore coherence to American education. When Robert Hutchins was at Chicago, he tried to use the Great Books to build a comprehensible framework for the main ideas of civilized man. His experiment is still being carried on, with some modifications at St. John's—but it has not proved irresistibly contagious. Sure, the thoughts of Plato and Machiavelli are still pertinent, so far as they go—but somehow they don't seem quite enough armor for a world beset with splitting atoms, urban guerrillas, nineteen varieties of psychotherapists, amplified guitars, na-

palm, computers, astronauts, and an atmosphere polluted simultaneously with auto exhaust and TV commercials.

8     Another strategy for linking together the bits-and-pieces has been attempted at Harvard and at a number of other universities. They require their students to take at least two years of survey courses, known variously as core studies, general education, or world civilization. These too have been something less than triumphantly successful. Most faculty members don't like to teach them, regarding them as superficial and synthetic. (And right they are, since no survey course that I know of has a strong unifying concept to give it focus.) Moreover, the senior professors shun such courses in favor of their own narrow specialties. Consequently, the core studies which are meant to place all human experience—well, at least the brightest nuggets—into One Big Picture usually end up in the perfunctory hands of resentful junior teachers. Naturally the undergraduates don't take them seriously either.

## Guidelines for Reform

9     Any successful reform of American education, I am now convinced, will have to be far more revolutionary than anything yet attempted. At a minimum, it should be:

10     1. Founded on a single guiding concept—an idea capable of knotting together all strands of study, thus giving them both coherence and visible purpose.

11     2. Capable of equipping young people to do something about "what is going on in the world"—notably the things which bother them most, including war, injustice, racial conflict, and the quality of life.

12     Maybe it isn't possible. Perhaps knowledge is proliferating so fast, and in so many directions, that it can never again be ordered into a coherent whole, so that molecular biology, Robert Lowell's poetry, and highway engineering will seem relevant to each other and to the lives of ordinary people. Quite possibly the knowledge explosion, as Peter F. Drucker has called it, dooms us to scholarship which grows steadily more specialized, fragmented, and incomprehensible.

13     The Soviet experience is hardly encouraging. Russian education is built on what is meant to be a unifying ideology: Marxism-Leninism. In theory, it provides an organizing principle for all scholarly activity—whether history, literature, genetics, or military science. Its purpose is explicit: to train a Communist elite for the greater power and glory of the Soviet state, just as the medieval universities trained a priesthood to serve the Church.

14     Yet according to all accounts that I have seen, it doesn't work very well. Soviet intellectuals apparently are almost as restless and unhappy as our own. Increasing numbers of them are finding Marxism-Leninism

too simplistic, too narrowly doctrinaire, too oppressive; the bravest are risking prison in order to pursue their own heretical visions of reality.

## Survival as the Issue

15   Is it conceivable then, that we might hit upon another idea which could serve as the organizing principle for many fields of scholarly inquiry; which is relevant to the urgent needs of our time; and which would not, on the other hand, impose an ideological straitjacket, as both ecclesiastical and Marxist education attempted to do?

16   Just possibly it could be done. For the last two or three years I have been probing around among professors, college administrators, and students—and so far I have come up with only one idea which might fit the specifications. It is simply the idea of survival.

17   For the first time in history, the future of the human race is now in serious question. This fact is hard to believe, or even think about—yet it is the message which a growing number of scientists are trying, almost frantically, to get across to us. Listen, for example, to Professor Richard A. Falk of Princeton and of the Center for Advanced Study in the Behavioral Sciences:

> The planet and mankind are in grave danger of irreversible catastrophe. . . . Man may be skeptical about following the flight of the dodo into extinction, but the evidence points increasingly to just such a pursuit. . . . There are four interconnected threats to the planet—wars of mass destruction, overpopulation, pollution, and the depletion of resources. They have a cumulative effect. A problem in one area renders it more difficult to solve the problems in any other area. . . . The basis of all four problems is the inadequacy of the sovereign states to manage the affairs of mankind in the twentieth century.

18   Similar warnings could be quoted from a long list of other social scientists, biologists, and physicists, among them such distinguished thinkers as René Dubos, Buckminster Fuller, Loren Eiseley, George Wald, and Barry Commoner. They are not hopeless. Most of them believe that we still have a chance to bring our weapons, our population growth, and the destruction of our environment under control before it is too late. But the time is short, and so far there is no evidence that enough people are taking them seriously.

19   That would be the prime aim of the experimental university I'm suggesting here: to look seriously at the interlinking threats to human existence, and to learn what we can do to fight them off.

20   Let's call it Survival U. It will not be a multiversity, offering courses in every conceivable field. Its motto—emblazoned on a life jacket rampant—will be: "What must we do to be saved?" If a course does not help to answer that question, it will not be taught here. Students interested in musicology, junk sculpture, the Theater of the Absurd,

and the literary *dicta* of Leslie Fiedler can go somewhere else.

21    Neither will our professors be detached, dispassionate scholars. To get hired, each will have to demonstrate an emotional commitment to our cause. Moreover, he will be expected to be a moralist; for this generation of students, like no other in my lifetime, is hungering and thirsting after righteousness. What it wants is a moral system it can believe in—and that is what our university will try to provide. In every class it will preach the primordial ethic of survival.

## The Biology Department

22    The biology department, for example, will point out that it is sinful for anybody to have more than two children. It has long since become glaringly evident that unless the earth's cancerous growth of population can be halted, all other problems—poverty, war, racial strife, uninhabitable cities, and the rest—are beyond solution. So the department naturally will teach all known methods of birth control, and much of its research will be aimed at perfecting cheaper and better ones.

23    Its second lesson in biological morality will be: "Nobody has a right to poison the environment we live in." This maxim will be illustrated by a list of public enemies. At the top will stand the politicians, scientists, and military men—of whatever country—who make and deploy atomic weapons; for if these are ever used, even in so-called defensive systems like the ABM, the atmosphere will be so contaminated with strontium 90 and other radioactive isotopes that human survival seems most unlikely. Also on the list will be anybody who makes or tests chemical and biological weapons—or who even attempts to get rid of obsolete nerve gas, as our Army recently proposed, by dumping the stuff in the sea.

24    Only slightly less wicked, our biology profs will indicate, is the farmer who drenches his land with DDT. Such insecticides remain virulent indefinitely, and as they wash into the streams and oceans they poison fish, water fowl, and eventually the people who eat them. Worse yet—as John Hay noted in his recently published *In Defense of Nature*—"The original small, diluted concentrations of these chemicals tend to build up in a food chain so as to end in a concentration that may be thousands of times as strong." It is rapidly spreading throughout the globe. DDT already has been found in the tissues of Eskimos and of Antarctic penguins, so it seems probable that similar deposits are gradually building up in your body and mine. The minimum fatal dosage is still unknown.

25    Before he finishes this course, a student may begin to feel twinges of conscience himself. Is his motorcycle exhaust adding carbon monoxide to the smog we breathe? Is his sewage polluting the nearest river? If so, he will be reminded of two proverbs. From Jesus: "Let him who is without sin among you cast the first stone." From Pogo: "We have met the enemy and he is us."

## Questions in Engineering

26    In like fashion, our engineering students will learn not only how to build dams and highways but where *not* to build them. Unless they understand that it is immoral to flood the Grand Canyon or destroy the Everglades with a jetport, they will never pass the final exam. Indeed, our engineering graduates will be trained to ask a key question about every contract offered them: "What will be its effect on human life?" That obviously will lead to other questions which every engineer ought to comprehend as thoroughly as his slide rule. Is this new highway really necessary? Would it be wiser to use the money for mass transit—or to decongest traffic by building a new city somewhere else? Is an offshore oil well really a good idea, in view of what happened to Santa Barbara?

27    Our engineering faculty also will specialize in training men for a new growth industry: garbage disposal. Americans already are spending $4.5 billion a year to collect and get rid of the garbage which we produce more profusely than any other people (more than five pounds a day for each of us). But unless we are resigned to stifling in our own trash, we are going to have to come up with at least an additional $835 million a year.[1] Any industry with a growth rate of 18 percent offers obvious attractions to a bright young man—and if he can figure out a new way to get rid of our offal, his fortune will be unlimited.

28    Because the old ways no longer work. Every big city in the United States is running out of dumping grounds. Burning won't do either, since the air is dangerously polluted already—and in any case, 75 percent of the incinerators in use are inadequate. For some 150 years Californians happily piled their garbage into San Francisco Bay, but they can't much longer. Dump-and-fill operations already have reduced it to half its original size, and in a few more decades it would be possible to walk dry-shod from Oakland to the Embarcadero. Consequently San Francisco is now planning to ship garbage 375 miles to the yet-uncluttered deserts of Lassen County by special train—known locally as "The Twentieth Stenchery Limited" and "The Excess Express." The city may actually get away with this scheme, since hardly anybody lives in Lassen County except Indians, and who cares about them? But what is the answer for the metropolis that doesn't have an unspoiled desert handy?

29    A few ingenious notions are cropping up here and there. The Japanese are experimenting with a machine which compacts garbage, under great heat and pressure, into building blocks. A New York businessman is thinking of building a garbage mountain somewhere upstate, and equipping it with ski runs to amortize the cost. An aluminum company plans to collect and reprocess used aluminum cans—which, unlike the

---

[1]According to Richard D. Vaughn, chief of the Solid Wastes Program of HEW, in his recent horror story entitled "1968 Survey of Community Solid Waste Practices."

old-fashioned tin can, will not rust away. Our engineering department will try to Think Big along these lines. That way lies not only new careers, but salvation.

## The Earth Sciences—and Crises

30      Survival U's Department of Earth Sciences will be headed—if we are lucky—by Dr. Charles F. Park, Jr., now professor of geology and mineral engineering at Stanford. He knows as well as anybody how fast mankind is using up the world's supply of raw materials. In a paper written for the American Geographical Society he punctured one of America's most engaging (and pernicious) myths: our belief that an ever-expanding economy can keep living standards rising indefinitely.

31      It won't happen; because as Dr. Park demonstrates, the tonnage of metal in the earth's crust won't last indefinitely. Already we are running short of silver, mercury, tin, and cobalt—all in growing demand by the high-technology industries. Even the commoner metals may soon be in short supply. The United States alone is consuming one ton of iron and eighteen pounds of copper every year, for each of its inhabitants. Poorer countries, struggling to industrialize, hope to raise their consumption of these two key materials to something like that level. If they should succeed—and if the globe's population doubles in the next forty years, as it will at present growth rates—then the world will have to produce, somehow, *twelve times* as much iron and copper every year as it does now. Dr. Parks sees little hope that such production levels can ever be reached, much less sustained indefinitely. The same thing, of course—doubled in spades—goes for other raw materials: timber, oil, natural gas, and water, to note only a few.

32      Survival U, therefore, will prepare its students to consume less. This does not necessarily mean an immediate drop in living standards—perhaps only a change in the yardstick by which we measure them. Conceivably Americans might be happier with fewer automobiles, neon signs, beer cans, supersonic jets, barbecue grills, and similar metallic fluff. But happy or not, our students had better learn how to live The Simpler Life, because that is what most of them are likely to have before they reach middle age.

## Math as Social Accounting

33      To help them understand how very precious resources really are, our mathematics department will teach a new kind of bookkeeping: social accounting. It will train people to analyze budgets—both government and corporate—with an eye not merely to immediate dollar costs, but to the long-range costs to society.

34    By conventional bookkepping methods, for example, the coal companies strip-mining away the hillsides of Kentucky and West Virginia show a handsome profit. Their ledgers, however, show only a fraction of the true cost of their operations. They take no account of destroyed land which can never bear another crop; of rivers poisoned by mud and seeping acid from the spoil banks; of floods which sweep over farms and towns downstream, because the ravaged slopes can no longer hold the rainfall. Although these costs are not borne by the mining firms, they are nevertheless real. They fall mostly on the taxpayers, who have to pay for disaster relief, flood-control levees, and the resettlement of Appalachian farm families forced off the land. As soon as our students (the taxpayers of tomorrow) learn to read a social balance sheet, they obviously will throw the strip miners into bankruptcy.

35    Another case study will analyze the proposal of the Inhuman Real Estate Corporation to build a fifty-story skyscraper in the most congested area of midtown Manhattan. If 90 percent of the office space can be rented at $12 per square foot, it looks like a sound investment, according to antique accounting methods. To uncover the true facts, however, our students will investigate the cost of moving 12,000 additional workers in and out of midtown during rush hours. The first (and least) item is $8 million worth of new city buses. When they are crammed into the already clogged avenues, the daily loss of man-hours in traffic jams may run to a couple of million more. The fumes from their diesel engines will cause an estimated 9 percent increase in New York's incidence of emphysema and lung cancer; this requires the construction of three new hospitals. To supply them, plus the new building, with water—already perilously short in the city—a new reservoir has to be built on the headwaters of the Delaware River, 140 miles away. Some of the dairy farmers pushed out of the drowned valley will move promptly into the Bronx and go on relief. The subtraction of their output from the city's supply leads to a price increase of two cents a quart. For a Harlem mother with seven hungry children, that is the last straw. She summons her neighbors to join her in riot, seven blocks go up in flames, and the Mayor demands higher taxes to hire more police. . . .

36    Instead of a sound investment, Inhuman Towers now looks like criminal folly, which would be forbidden by any sensible government. Our students will keep that in mind when they walk across campus to their government class.

## National and International Politics

37    Its main goal will be to discover why our institutions have done so badly in their efforts (as Dr. Falk put it) "to manage the affairs of man-

kind in the twentieth century." This will be a compulsory course for all freshmen, taught by professors who are capable of looking critically at every political artifact, from the Constitution to the local county council. They will start by pointing out that we are living in a state of near-anarchy, because we have no government capable of dealing effectively with public problems.

38    Instead we have a hodgepodge of 80,000 local governments—villages, townships, counties, cities, port authorities, sewer districts, and special purpose agencies. Their authority is so limited, and their jurisdictions so confused and overlapping, that most of them are virtually impotent. The states, which in theory could put this mess into some sort of order, usually have shown little interest and less competence. When Washington is called to help out—as it increasingly has been for the last thirty-five years—it often has proved hamhanded and entangled in its own archaic bureaucracy. The end result is that nobody in authority has been able to take care of the country's mounting needs. Our welfare rolls keep growing, our air and water get dirtier, housing gets scarcer, airports jam up, road traffic clots, railways fall apart, prices rise, ghettos burn, schools turn out more illiterates every year, and a war nobody wants drags on and on. Small wonder that so many young people are losing confidence in American institutions. In their present state, they don't deserve much confidence.

39    The advanced students of government at Survival U will try to find out whether these institutions can be renewed and rebuilt. They will take a hard look at the few places—Jacksonville, Minnesota, Nashville, Appalachia—which are creating new forms of government. Will these work any better, and if so, how can they be duplicated elsewhere? Can the states be brought to life, or should we start thinking about an entirely different kind of arrangement? Ten regional prefectures, perhaps, to replace the fifty states? Or should we take seriously Norman Mailer's suggestion for a new kind of city-state to govern our great metropolises? (He merely called for New York City to secede from its state; but that isn't radical enough. To be truly governable, the new Republic of New York City ought to include chunks of New Jersey and Connecticut as well.) Alternatively, can we find some way to break up Megalopolis, and spread our population into smaller and more livable communities throughout the continent? Why should we keep 70 percent of our people crowded into less than 2 percent of our land area, anyway?

40    Looking beyond our borders, our students will be encouraged to ask even harder questions. Are nation-states actually feasible, now that they have power to destroy each other in a single afternoon? Can we agree on something else to take their place, before the balance of terror becomes unstable? What price would most people be willing to pay for a more durable kind of human organization—more taxes, giving up national flags, perhaps the sacrifice of some of our hard-won liberties?

## Survival U of Human Ecology

41    All these courses (and everything else taught at Survival U) are really branches of a single science. Human ecology is one of the youngest disciplines, and probably the most important. It is the study of the relationship between man and his environment, both natural and technological. It teaches us to understand the consequences of our actions— how sulfur-laden fuel oil burned in England produces an acid rain that damages the forests of Scandinavia, why a well-meant farm subsidy can force millions of Negro tenants off the land and lead to Watts and Hough. A graduate who comprehends ecology will know how to look at "what is going on in the world," and he will be equipped to do something about it. Whether he ends up as a city planner, a politician, an enlightened engineer, a teacher, or a reporter, he will have had a relevant education. All of its parts will hang together in a coherent whole.

42    And if we can get enough such graduates, man and his environment may survive a while longer, against all the odds.

### REVIEW

**Content**

1. What does Fischer see as the central problems in liberal education? Do you agree with him? How do you respond to his proposal to abolish liberal education, in favor of the "survival university"? What arguments can you think of for continuing liberal education, thinking in the context of the problems Fischer lists in paragraph 7?

2. Fischer lists the following kinds of courses for his Survival University, which would offer "a single science . . . human ecology . . . the study of the relationship between man and his environment, both natural and technological": biology, engineering, math (social accounting), earth sciences, political science, and international relations. Do you find any kinds/sources of knowledge missing that would be *essential* for a student, and later a graduate, to deal with what Fischer sees as "key questions"—for example, What must we do to be saved? What will be the effect of a particular decision or action on the quality of human life?

**Rhetoric**

3. One of the techniques for arguing effectively for a new proposal is to first define existing methods and expose their flaws and then anticipate the arguments of a possible opponent to your new idea. Does Fischer do these things adequately in offering his proposal? Explain.

4. The use of humorous touches, where appropriate, is often an effective

technique for keeping a reader involved in reading an argument. Can you find such touches in Fischer's writing?

**Projects**

5. Assume the same reasons for higher education reform that Fischer assumes and decide on the "survival" courses that you would require of *every* student for graduation from *any* institution of higher education. Be ready to defend all your courses in later large-group discussion.
6. Design on paper what you would consider to be the *ideal* education for yourself, in the light of your life goals and plans, and explain why you include the courses you do—and perhaps why you exclude others. Try to avoid giving only vague, abstract reasons; that is, show as direct application as possible of the courses to *your* future.

# The Marks of an Educated Man

## ALAN  SIMPSON

Alan Simpson (1912–    ) is president of Vassar College. In the essay below, featured in the inaugural issue of the magazine *Context*, Spring, 1961, Simpson holds that "any education that matters is liberal" (as contrasted with exclusively practical or professional training). He argues that the truly educated person will be knowledgeable; capable of critical thinking and reading; skillful in expression; sophisticated in the ways of the world; moral; and versatile and flexible enough to survive in today's world.

1   Any education that matters is *liberal*. All the saving truths and healing graces that distinguish a good education from a bad one or a full education from a half-empty one are contained in that word. Whatever ups and downs the term "liberal" suffers in the political vocabulary, it soars above all controversy in the educational world. In the blackest pits of pedagogy the squirming victim has only to ask, "What's liberal about this?" to shame his persecutors. In times past a liberal education set off a free man from a slave or a gentleman from laborers and artisans. It now distinguishes whatever nourishes the mind and spirit from the training which is merely practical or professional or from the trivialities

Reprinted by permission of the author.

which are no training at all. Such an education involves a combination of knowledge, skills, and standards.

2    So far as knowledge is concerned, the record is ambiguous. It is sufficiently confused for the fact-filled freak who excels in quiz shows to have passed himself off in some company as an educated man. More respectable is the notion that there are some things which every educated man ought to know; but many highly educated men would cheerfully admit to a vast ignorance, and the framers of curriculums have differed greatly in the knowledge they prescribe. If there have been times when all the students at school or college studied the same things, as if it were obvious that without exposure to a common body of knowledge they would not be educated at all, there have been other times when specialization ran so wild that it might almost seem as if educated men had abandoned the thought of ever talking to each other once their education was completed.

## Kinds of Knowledge

3    If knowledge is one of our marks, we can hardly be dogmatic about the kind or the amount. A single fertile field tilled with care and imagination can probably develop all the instincts of an educated man. However, if the framer of a curriculum wants to minimize his risks, he can invoke an ancient doctrine which holds that an educated man ought to know a little about everything and a lot about something.

4    The "little about everything" is best interpreted these days by those who have given most thought to the sort of general education an informed individual ought to have. More is required than a sampling of the introductory courses which specialists offer in their own disciplines. Courses are needed in each of the major divisions of knowledge—the humanities, the natural sciences, and social sciences—which are organized with the breadth of view and the imaginative power of competent staffs who understand the needs of interested amateurs. But, over and above this exciting smattering of knowledge, students should bite deeply into at least one subject and taste its full flavor. It is not enough to be dilettantes in everything without striving also to be craftsmen in something.

## Clear Thinking

5    If there is some ambiguity about the knowledge an educated man should have, there is none at all about the skills. The first is simply the training of the mind in the capacity to think clearly. This has always been the business of education, but the way it is done varies enormously.

Marshalling the notes of a lecture is one experience; the opportunity to argue with a teacher is another. Thinking within an accepted tradition is one thing; to challenge the tradition itself is another. The best results are achieved when the idea of the examined life is held firmly before the mind and when the examination is conducted with the zest, rigor, and freedom which really stretches everyone's capacities.

6    The vital aid to clear thought is the habit of approaching everything we hear and everything we are taught to believe with a certain skepticism. The method of using doubt as an examiner is a familiar one among scholars and scientists, but it is also the best protection which a citizen has against the cant and humbug that surround us.

7    To be able to listen to a phony argument and to see its dishonesty is surely one of the marks of an educated man. We may not need to be educated to possess some of this quality. A shrewd peasant was always well enough protected against impostors in the market place, and we have all sorts of businessmen who have made themselves excellent judges of phoniness without the benefit of a high-school diploma; but this kind of shrewdness goes along with a great deal of credulity. Outside the limited field within which experience has taught the peasant or the illiterate businessman his lessons, he is often hopelessly gullible. The educated man, by contrast, has tried to develop a critical faculty for general use, and he likes to think that he is fortified against imposture in all its forms.

8    It does not matter for our purposes whether the impostor is a deliberate liar or not. Some are, but the commonest enemies of mankind are the unconscious frauds. Most salesmen under the intoxication of their own exuberance seem to believe in what they say. Most experts whose *expertise* is only a pretentious sham behave as if they have been solemnly inducted into some kind of priesthood. Very few demagogues are so cynical as to remain undeceived by their own rhetoric, and some of the worst tyrants in history have been fatally sincere. We can leave the disentanglement of motives to the students of fraud and error, but we cannot afford to be taken in by the shams.

9    We are, of course, surrounded by shams. Until recently the schools were full of them—the notion that education can be had without tears, that puffed rice is a better intellectual diet than oatmeal, that adjustment to the group is more important than knowing where the group is going, and that democracy has made it a sin to separate the sheep from the goats. Mercifully, these are much less evident now than they were before Sputnik startled us into our wits.

10    In front of the professor are the shams of the learned fraternity. There is the sham science of the social scientist who first invented a speech for fuddling thought and then proceeded to tell us in his lock-jawed way what we already knew. There is the sham humanism of the humanist who wonders why civilization that once feasted at his table

is repelled by the shredded and desiccated dishes that often lie on it today. There is the sham message of the physical scientist who feels that his mastery of nature has made him an expert in politics and morals, and there are all the other brands of hokum which have furnished material for satire since the first quacks established themselves in the first cloisters.

11    If this is true of universities with their solemn vows and limited temptations, how much truer is it of the naughty world outside, where the prizes are far more dazzling and the only protection against humbug is the skepticism of the ordinary voter, customer, reader, listener, and viewer? Of course, the follies of human nature are not going to be exorcised by anything that the educator can do, and I am not sure that he would want to exorcise them if he could. There is something irresistibly funny about the old Adam, and life would be duller without his antics. But they ought to be kept within bounds. We are none the better for not recognizing a clown when we see one.

## Art of Self-Expression

12    The other basic skill is simply the art of self-expression in speech and on paper. A man is uneducated who has not mastered the elements of clean forcible prose and picked up some relish for style.

13    It is a curious fact that we style everything in this country—our cars, our homes, our clothes—except our minds. They still chug along like a Model T—rugged, persevering, but far from graceful.

14    No doubt this appeal for style, like this appeal for clear thinking, can be carried too far. There was once an American who said that the only important thing in life was "to set a chime of words ringing in a few fastidious minds." As far as can be learned, he left this country in a huff to tinkle his little bell in a foreign land. Most of us would think that he lacked a sense of proportion. After all, the political history of this country is full of good judgment expressed in bad prose, and the business history has smashed through to some of its grandest triumphs across acres of broken syntax. But we can discard some of these frontier manners without becoming absurdly precious.

15    The road ahead bristles with obstacles. There is the reluctance of many people to use one word where they can get away with a half-dozen or a word of one syllable if they can find a longer one. No one has ever told them about the first rule in English composition: every slaughtered syllable is a good deed. The most persuasive teachers of this maxim are undoubtedly the commercial firms that offer a thousand dollars for the completion of a slogan in twenty-five words. They are the only people who are putting a handsome premium on economy of statement.

16    There is the decay of the habit of memorizing good prose and good poetry in the years when tastes are being formed. It is very difficult

to write a bad sentence if the Bible has been a steady companion and very easy to imagine a well-turned phrase if the ear has been tuned on enough poetry.

17    There is the monstrous proliferation of gobbledy-gook in government, business, and the professions. Take this horrible example of verbal smog:

> It is inherent to motivational phenomena that there is a drive for more gratification than is realistically possible, on any level or in any type of personality organization. Likewise it is inherent to the world of objects that not all potentially desirable opportunities can be realized within a human life span. Therefore, any personality must involve an organization that allocates opportunities for gratifications, that systematizes precedence relative to the limited possibilities. The possibilities of gratification, simultaneously or sequentially, of all need dispositons are severely limited by the structure of the object system and by the intrasystemic incompatibility of the consequences of gratifying them all.

18    What this smothered soul is trying to say is simply, "We must pick and choose, because we cannot have everything we want."

19    Finally, there is the universal employment of the objective test as part of the price which has to be paid for mass education. Nothing but the difficulty of finding enough readers to mark essays can condone a system which reduces a literate student to the ignoble necessity of "blackening the answer space" when he might be giving his mind and pen free play. Though we have managed to get some benefits from these examinations, the simple fact remains that the shapely prose of the Declaration of Independence or the Gettysburg Address was never learned under an educational system which employed objective tests. It was mastered by people who took writing seriously, who had good models in front of them, good critics to judge them, and an endless capacity for taking pains. Without that sort of discipline, the arts of self-expression will remain as mutilated as they are now.

## The Educated Person: Three Tests

20    The standards which mark an educated man can be expressed in terms of three tests.

21    The first is a matter of sophistication. Emerson put it nicely when he talked about getting rid of "the nonsense of our wigwams." The wigwam may be an uncultivated home, a suburban conformity, a crass patriotism, or a cramped dogma. Some of this nonsense withers in the classroom. More of it rubs off by simply mixing with people, provided they are drawn from a wide range of backgrounds and exposed within a good college to a civilized tradition. An educated man can be judged by the quality of his prejudices. There is a refined nonsense which survives the raw nonsense which Emerson was talking about.

22    The second test is a matter of moral values. Though we all know individuals who have contrived to be both highly educated and highly immoral, and though we have all heard of periods in history when the subtlest resources of wit and sophistication were employed to make a mockery of simple values, we do not really believe that a college is doing its job when it is simply multiplying the number of educated scoundrels, hucksters, and triflers.

23    The health of society depends on simple virtues like honesty, decency, courage, and public spirit. There are forces in human nature which constantly tend to corrupt them, and every age has its own vices. The worst features of ours is probably the obsession with violence. Up to some such time as 1914, it was possible to believe in a kind of moral progress. The quality which distinguished the Victorian from the Elizabethan was a sensitivity to suffering and a revulsion from cruelty which greatly enlarged the idea of human dignity. Since 1914 we have steadily brutalized ourselves. The horrors of modern war, the bestialities of modern political creeds, the uncontrollable vices of modern cities, the favorite themes of modern novelists—all have conspired to degrade us. Some of the corruption is blatant. The authors of the best sellers, after exhausting all the possibilities of sex in its normal and abnormal forms and all the variations of alcoholism and drug addiction, are about to invade the recesses of the hospitals. A clinical study of a hero undergoing the irrigation of his colon is about all there is left to gratify a morbid appetite.

24    Some of the corruption is insidious. A national columnist recently wrote an article in praise of cockfighting. He had visited a cockfight in the company of Ernest Hemingway. After pointing out that Hemingway had made bullfighting respectable, he proceeded to describe the terrible beauty of fierce indomitable birds trained to kill each other for the excitement of the spectators. Needless to say, there used to be a terrible beauty about Christians defending themselves against lions or about heretics being burned at the stake, and there are still parts of the world where a public execution is regarded as a richly satisfying feast. But for three or four centuries the West taught itself to resist these excitements in the interest of a moral idea.

25    Educators are needlessly squeamish about their duty to uphold moral values and needlessly perplexed about how to implant them. The corruptions of our times are a sufficient warning that we cannot afford to abandon the duty to the homes and the churches, and the capacity which many institutions have shown to do their duty in a liberal spirit is a sufficient guaranty against bigotry.

26    Finally, there is the test imposed by the unique challenge of our own times. We are not unique in suffering from moral confusion—these crises are a familiar story—but we are unique in the tremendous acceleration of the rate of social change and in the tremendous risk of a catastrophic end to all our hopes. We cannot afford educated men who have

every grace except the gift for survival. An indispensable mark of the modern educated man is the kind of versatile, flexible mind that can deal with new and explosive conditions.

## The Whole Person

27    With this reserve, there is little in this profile which has not been familiar for centuries. Unfortunately, the description which once sufficed to suggest its personality has been debased in journalistic currency. The "well-rounded man" has become the organization man, or the man who is so well rounded that he rolls wherever he is pushed. The humanists who invented the idea and preached it for centuries would recoil in contempt from any such notion. They understood the possibilities of the whole man and wanted an educational system which would give the many sides of his nature some chance to develop in harmony. They thought it a good idea to mix the wisdom of the world with the learning of the cloister, to develop the body as well as the mind, to pay a great deal of attention to character, and to neglect no art which could add to the enjoyment of living. It was a spacious idea which offered every hospitality to creative energy. Anyone who is seriously interested in a liberal education must begin by rediscovering it.

### REVIEW

#### Content

1. Simpson cites the traditionally accepted definition of the knowledge needed by an educated person: he should "know a little about everything and a lot about something." Do you find this a feasible definition, in the light of today's "knowledge explosion"? What arguments can you think of for a school's, and a student's, at least striving in this direction—arguments having to do with you as a private individual, as a social being, as a citizen, and in whatever other roles you find yourself?
2. By what three tests does Simpson say we should be able to recognize the educated person? Do you agree with these three criteria? Do they *fully* cover your image of the educated person? Include in your thinking here paragraph 27. How does paragraph 25, about educators dealing with moral values in the classroom, strike you?

#### Rhetoric

3. Simpson discusses the skill of critical thinking rather fully. What relation can you see between being able to think clearly, to read and to listen critically, and to write convincingly? Can you think of writing situations that encourage dishonesty in the writer and that hope for uncritical thinking in the reader?
4. Simpson says, in paragraph 12, that the educated person has "mas-

tered the elements of clean forcible prose and picked up some relish for style." Examine Simpson's own prose, in paragraphs 10 and 11, and see if you can find especially effective (a) choice of precise vocabulary, (b) use of near slang, (c) variety of sentence structure and length, (d) phrasing within sentences, (e) cleverness where appropriate. How well do these paragraphs meet Simpson's own standards?

## Projects

5. Write a paper about something that you care deeply about—as Simpson obviously cares about liberal education. Employ "clean forcible prose." And try to express *your* particular style, remembering that you have a *unique* writing style which is an expression of your own personality in much the same way that your walking and dressing and talking styles are.

6. Try to rewrite one of the following paragraphs from Simpson's essay in gobbledy-gook like the example within paragraph 17: 3, 6, or 26. Use as many pompous, inflated, needless words as you possibly can. Then give someone the original and your rewriting and ask for an explanation of which is better and why.

# What Should College Be For?

## LOUIS W. CARTWRIGHT

Louis Cartwright was 25 when he wrote the informal narrative essay from which the excerpt below is taken. Cartwright had already travelled around this country and in Europe when he enrolled in college. And he found college "stuffy, crowded, tightly scheduled, fast, an authoritarian center where questions were slaughtered"—rather than the "free place" he feels it should be—open to anyone of any age who feels curious at any time about what goes on inside. As spokesman for the student, Cartwright envisions college as a liberating experience.

1    . . . I loathe the notion America is promoting that one has to go to college in order to "make it." How about those who don't want to? Those who have a couple of dreams of their own that they'd like to try out? When a notion like that becomes almost an unwritten law, a

From pp. 16–20 in "With What We Have" by Louis W. Cartwright, in *To Make a Difference*, edited by Otto Butz. Copyright © 1967 by Otto Butz. Reprinted by permission of Harper & Row, Publishers, Inc.

matter of course, then we defeat ourselves: we end up forcing pure character and imagination, our only chance for health and future, into systems of education that return to us a beast who is intelligent only because he has finally been trained to answer with the acceptable notions of our time. Once so potentially brilliant and eager to learn about life, they return to us predictably dull and bored under the oppressive weight of collections of information. We frustrate the creative mind into a desperate submission whereupon it closes up like a clam on the ocean floor and never feels good or free about life again. Some of our young blood isn't meant for college even though it can pass the entrance exams, but where else are they encouraged to go? Into the Army? The parent offers to send him to, and support him through, college only if he goes directly after high school and stays with it for a continuous four years (or is it six, now?). So they go, are never late, are never passionate, sit in classrooms, while the life they felt to be good quietly dies.

2    I first enrolled in college because I wanted to. This was two years after high school, after I had hitchhiked around America, after having cycled a year in Europe, and worked in a missile factory—after, I'd like to say, I felt that I had earned the readiness for learning. I wanted to learn all about the Greeks, especially Odysseus, for he, like me, had traveled. But I wasn't allowed to take Greek Mythology or study the Greek language; I had to take certain *preliminary* courses. I did manage to lie my way into a philosophy class. At the end of that year I felt that I had had enough; I knew that I could learn without having an examination date placed before me for discipline. I still liked learning. So I quit and returned to Europe. My father was astounded and hurt at my courteous refusal of the security of a college degree; he made me feel like I was cheating. But he wished me good luck and a quick return.

3    My first trip to Europe had been a magic carpet tour; I had enough money, and though I cycled I didn't need to work my way, didn't need to stay any place longer than it pleased me. The second trip was the yes-trip: it was yes to everything, and I was broke. I took jobs doing anything, lived anywhere, ate anything, and learned a great deal about freedom. For instance, I learned that you can cycle all day in the rain and not catch cold if you work hard (and if your clothes get washed). I didn't belong in school, anyone could see that. I needed to try myself in life, see if I could learn how to be. From where I was in the south of France, American middle-class security looked like a sickness, one that most got over. When I returned home, in spite of the particular mood I was in or my reason for returning, I was full of life and lean as a coyote. I wanted to sleep, then eat, then think.

4    "But he's got to finish college," I heard my father saying to my mother behind their door that night.

5    "Let him rest awhile," said mother.

6    "Hell, rest, he's twenty-one. When I was his age I was supporting my parents."

7    "We don't need support."

8    "I don't want his support, I want him to get to work. It's not healthy to sit and do nothing."

9    I listened to them. My father was right. So was I. He wouldn't give in and neither would I. The last favor I wanted of my parents was time, time to decide what I wanted to try next. Three months later I introduced him to my fiancée, and within a month, married, I left that time and place of my childhood forever.

10   A year later I wanted to return to school to pursue a new interest, and within a week I hated college. It was stuffy, crowded, tightly scheduled, fast, an authority center where questions were slaughtered quickly and efficiently with brilliant little answers. I had to put away my interests and get in line with the others. It wasn't learning; it was read, memorize and answer, and there wasn't any time for exceptions to the beautiful rules. It was terrible, but I had unwittingly promised myself that I would stick it out. I'd convinced myself that like climbing a long, steep grade there is a personal benefit gained in reaching the top. So here fulfilling my promise was my only reason for remaining. Endurance.

11   My reason for enduring became a chant I whisper to myself when it gets worse than bad: you can make it, you made it over the Alps, you can do anything. Don't I have other reasons? Would I come to watch people? I'd rather stand on Market Street.[1] Would I come to learn from teachers? We all know how unnecessary and redundant many professors are, how they never quite come alive before their classes, as if the administration were controlling their oxygen supply. Most classrooms are holding a recital of the text you read last night. But every now and then, one man sneaks through and holds a class on his own that balances off the entire history of inadequate professors. Yes, for that chance (as long as it doesn't get any slimmer) I'd sign up for a full load and attend. But isn't it so very unfortunate that the clothesline of education droops so low between the occasional giants? To this point I append the twin to the statement that all of us shouldn't go to college: all of those who are teaching shouldn't be. Perhaps half of all who populate a campus should be in a trade school or on a ranch. I feel we have sacrificed learning for education, that, as with missiles, we are competing with Russia to graduate people, hit or miss. No! No no no no. We fail beneath the statistical affidavits of our success: there it is in black and white, but there it ain't in the people.

12   Another aspect of this swelling horror is the soul-shrinking speed at

[1]San Francisco's main business and shopping thoroughfare, running from the Ferry Building to Twin Peaks.

which we educate! Got to hurry, got to meet my future in four years, go go—college à go-go. I imagine an IBM computer graduating twenty thousand cards and there's no one there to claim them. What's the hurry? It reminds me of the Yiddish saying: *Sleep fast, we need the pillows.* Along with this preoccupation with speed develops the feeling that one is supposed to know a few things simply because he is nearing the exit. The poor beast, he knows all the right answers in his field and he is secure. Meantime, as Bob Dylan sings in one of his verses, life goes on all about him.

13    Nope. Our country wants our colleges to do more than they can honestly do, so it forces them to be dishonest. Do anything you have to do but make sure the statistics are ready in time to be published in the July 1 issue of *Time*. One million graduate this June!

14    I'm in no hurry and resent being shoved. A college or university should be slow and easy. It shouldn't have too clear of an idea what an educated man should know. There should be no such system as a major and a minor and so many of each kind of units to sign up for. Curiosity if left alone will fill out a healthy program. And professors should be paid enough to keep them from griping about salaries in the classroom. They sometimes remind me of the street performer who has to send his hat about the crowd.

15    College should be a free place with huge doors that swing open to whomever feels curious about what goes on inside. It shouldn't be a prerequisite to life; it is an aftereffect. I've learned and have been inspired more by my time spent in college bars and cafeterias with others than in the hours I've sat in classrooms. But I get no credit for that time. So maybe classes should be held in the college cafeteria. I want it to be that free and slow. The way I describe how a college should be, it becomes obvious that we have very few colleges in America. We have trade schools where one learns how to do psychology and engineering and creative writing, and where curiosity is called game playing and inefficient. After all, if you keep asking those questions, you'll never get out by June!

16    The university is not an ivory tower without a city to be ivory for; they are inseparable. But America separates them. The American student is in constant conflict between working to earn enough to go to school and studying to earn the grades to stay in school. And most often he can't get a job in the field of his studies. So combine work with school. Give him not only a salary but college credit for his time spent on the job, for isn't experience the best way to learn? The new work-study program sponsored by the government is a timid step in this direction. But it still doesn't reacquaint the city with the college, and this is essential.

17    America devises or chooses so many easy ways out. College is now

an easy way out of worrying about becoming a success. You get a degree and they've got it all worked out for you on an easy-to-understand form which lists how long it will take to be earning twenty-five thousand a year.

## REVIEW

### Content

1. How do you feel about Cartwright's saying that college is not for everyone? *Should* it be? Is there some sort of stigma attached to *not* going to college? If so, what, by whom, why? Should such a stigma exist? What do you see as some good alternatives to the traditionally structured college education—that is, other ways of learning and maturing?
2. What do you think about the college environment Cartwright describes as what he wants to see (paragraphs 14 and 15)? What do *you* expect for the time, money, and energy you are putting into college?

### Rhetoric

3. What particular effect does Cartwright achieve by using an informal, almost conversational tone? What does direct quoting of the dialogue between his father and mother contribute to this effect?
4. Near the beginning of paragraph 11, Cartwright uses three times a device known as the rhetorical question. Explain the purpose of this technique (how it works in the development of this paragraph). Why is it effective? Further on in paragraph 11, Cartwright employs a clever style that works in some instances. Do you find him overcute and/or awkward at any points; that is, does he seem to be striving *too* hard for effect in some places? If so, what happens to you as reader at those points?

### Projects

5. Write a personal essay based on some significant experience in your own life, employing an informal style that is comfortable to you. (It may help you considerably if you "talk through" your paper to another person first; this kind of writing is rather closely related to talking.) Help the reader feel that he/she is there—by making your paper as vivid and lifelike as possible, perhaps through the use of anecdotes, conversation, and the like. Be alert to the pitfalls of humor inappropriately used, too far-out slang, overcuteness, and other such undue "cleverness" that can plague such a style.
6. Write a paper about a course you are taking that you are unhappy with; include your reasons for taking it. How would you restructure

the course to better fit your needs and desires? Be very specific—in both your complaints and your recommendations for change. Or, write about a course you are taking that you wouldn't change very much, and tell why you would not change it.

# ✓The Good Old Medieval Campus

## ARTHUR HOPPE

Arthur Hoppe (1925–    ) is a well-known columnist whose writing is syndicated in more than a hundred newspapers, including the *San Francisco Chronicle,* from which the piece below is taken (December 16, 1968). Hoppe's books include *The Love Everybody Crusade* (1962), *Dreamboat* (1964), and *The Perfect Solution to Absolutely Everything* (1968). Hoppe specializes in satirical writing, often using the parable form, as in the selection here, in which he satirizes the "degree mill" aspect of contemporary higher education.

1   Once upon a time in the country called Wonderfuland there was a 500-year-old institution named Skarewe University. It issued Diplomas.

2   Just about everybody went to Skarewe University. They spent exactly four years studying exactly 16 required courses in thisology and thatology. They did this to get a Diploma.

3   Diplomas were very valuable. If you showed one to a prospective employer he gave you more money. No one knew why.

4   But the country fell on uneasy times. Even the students at Skarewe University caused trouble. They demanded this and they demanded that. And they got everything they demanded. Until, finally, they couldn't think of anything else to demand.

5   "I know," said one student one day, "let's demand that they abolish Diplomas!"

6   And, not having anything else to do, the students went on a Diploma Strike.

7   The President of Skarewe University was stunned. "If we don't issue Diplomas," he said, "we will lose our standing in the academic community."

8   The business community was shocked. "Without diplomas," employers

said, "how can we tell a college graduate from an uneducated man?"

9     Editorial writers viewed with alarm. "These radicals would destroy the very purpose of dear old Skarewe U.," they wrote. "They should be forced to accept their Diplomas whether they like it or not."

10    The Trustees were furious. "Abolishing Diplomas will set our university back 500 years," they thundered. "It will become a medieval institution!"

11    And it did.

12    From the very day that Diplomas were abolished, 64.3 percent of the students quit to go engage in more financially-rewarding pursuits. And those who were left found parking spaces for their cars—for the first time since the Middle Ages.

13    Just as in the Middle Ages, students now attended Skarewe University solely to gain knowledge and wisdom.

14    And as there were no required courses, teachers who imparted knowledge and wisdom gave well-attended lectures. And those who didn't, didn't. Just as in medieval times.

15    Just as in medieval times, students pursued only the studies that interested them and read only the books that stimulated them. And all, being constantly interested and stimulated, were dedicated scholars.

16    Thus it was that Skarewe University became what it had been 500 years before—a vast smorgasbord of knowledge and wisdom from which the student could select that which delighted and enriched him.

17    So everybody was happy. The President was happy to head such a distinguished community of scholars. The trustees were happy there were no more riots. And the taxpayers were happy they no longer had to purchase educations for those who didn't want them.

18    Even prospective employers were happy. For, oddly enough, even without a Diploma, you could still pick out the applicant who had gone through college—because for the first time in 500 years, he was a well-educated man.


## REVIEW

### Content

1. Hoppe's parable works by satire, which has been defined as "holding up a mirror to the world's folly"—for instructive purposes. Discuss specific elements in higher education being satirized in paragraphs 1 through 12.
2. Do you accept Hoppe's apparent conclusion that graduates of Skarewe University, who had been free as students to "select that which delighted and enriched" them, would inevitably be recognizable as "well-educated" persons? Support your answer.

**Rhetoric**

3. Hoppe's style is simple and direct, a relatively informal one. He uses easy words; a number of quite short, direct, simple sentences; and brief paragraphs. Why do you suppose he chooses these elements to relate a satirical parable? What do the words he makes up—thisology, thatology, Wonderfuland, Skarewe University—contribute to his effect?

4. The stylistic device known as parallelism (elements of equal content weight equally expressed in a sequence of two or more) is effectively employed by Hoppe. Find instances of this. And note especially the effect Hoppe achieves by sometimes setting the elements up in separate short paragraphs.

**Projects**

5. If thinking satirically comes relatively easy to you, try your hand at writing a satire on some well-established tradition (institutional or otherwise) that you view as foolish today. Try to find *your own* informal, perhaps rather offhand, voice and style in which to develop your satire, borrowing from Hoppe any techniques (see 3 and 4 above) that *you* can make work. Take care not to overdo the satirization, thereby risking losing your reader; effective satire works partly through subtlety.

6. Write a paper either denouncing or supporting some institution of society—for example, the military, some government agency, organized religion, commercialism. Limit yourself to one or two or three specific elements of your subject, so that you can focus and control your paper. Deliberately use parallelism to achieve some of your effect.

# The Missing Element: Moral Courage

## BARBARA W. TUCHMAN

Barbara W. Tuchman (1912–   ) has achieved intellectual distinction as both historian and journalist. Her care in research, combined with her journalistic skills, resulted in her being awarded the Pulitzer Prize in 1963 for *The Guns of August,* an absorbing account of the historical background of World War I. The selection below is an address by Tuchman in the 1960s to the American Association for Higher Education, in which she deplores the state of moral leadership in a society unwilling to hold up clear standards.

1   What I want to say is concerned less with leadership than with its absence, that is, with the evasion of leadership. Not in the physical sense, for we have, if anything, a superabundance of leaders—hundreds of Pied Pipers, or would-be Pied Pipers, running about, ready and anxious to lead the population. They are scurrying around, collecting consensus, gathering as wide an acceptance as possible. But what they are *not* doing, very notably, is standing still and saying, "*This* is what I believe. This I will do and that I will not do. This is my code of behavior and that is outside it. This is excellent and that is trash." There is an abdication of moral leadership in the sense of a general unwillingness to state standards.

2   Of all the ills that our poor criticized, analyzed, sociologized society is heir to, the focal one, it seems to me, from which so much of our uneasiness and confusion derive is the absence of standards. We are too unsure of ourselves to assert them, to stick by them, or if necessary, in the case of persons who occupy positions of authority, to impose them. We seem to be afflicted by a widespread and eroding reluctance to take any stand on any values, moral, behavioral, or aesthetic.

## Afraid To Fix Blame

3   Everyone is afraid to call anything wrong, or vulgar, or fraudulent, or just bad taste or bad manners. Congress, for example, pussyfooted for months (following years of apathy) before taking action on a member convicted by the courts of illegalities; and when they finally got around to unseating him, one suspects they did it for the wrong motives. In 1922, in England, a man called Horatio Bottomley, a rather flamboyant character and popular demogogue—very similar in type, by the way, to Adam Clayton Powell, with similarly elastic financial ethics—who founded a paper called *John Bull* and got himself elected to Parliament, was found guilty of misappropriating the funds which his readers subscribed to victory bonds and other causes promoted by his paper. The day after the verdict, he was expelled from the House of Commons, with no fuss and very little debate, except for a few friendly farewells, as he was rather an engaging fellow. But no member thought the House had any other course to consider: out he went. I do not suggest that this represents a difference between British and American morality; the difference is in the *times.*

4   Our time is one of disillusion in our species and a resulting lack of

self-confidence—for good historical reasons. Man's recent record has not been reassuring. After engaging in the Great War with all its mud and blood and ravaged ground, its disease, destruction, and death, we allowed ourselves a bare twenty years before going at it all over again. And the second time was accompanied by an episode of man's inhumanity to man of such enormity that its implications for all of us have not yet, I think, been fully measured. A historian has recently stated that for such a phenomenon as the planned and nearly accomplished extermination of a people to take place, one of three preconditions necessary was public indifference.

5    Since then the human species has been busy overbreeding, polluting the air, destroying the balance of nature, and bungling in a variety of directions so that it is no wonder we have begun to doubt man's capacity for good judgment. It is hardly surprising that the self-confidence of the nineteenth century and its belief in human progress has been dissipated. "Every great civilization," said Secretary Gardner last year, "has been characterized by confidence in itself." At mid-twentieth century, the supply is low. As a result, we tend to shy away from all judgments. We hesitate to label anything wrong, and therefore hesitate to require the individual to bear moral responsibility for his acts.

6    We have become afraid to fix blame. Murderers and rapists and muggers and persons who beat up old men and engage in other forms of assault are not guilty; society is guilty; society has wronged them; society beats its breast and says *mea culpa*—it is our fault, not the wrongdoer's. The wrongdoer, poor fellow, could not help himself.

## The Wrongdoer's Neighbor

7    I find this very puzzling because I always ask myself, in these cases, what about the many neighbors of the wrongdoer, equally poor, equally disadvantaged, equally sufferers from society's neglect, who nevertheless maintain certain standards of social behavior, who do *not* commit crimes, who do not murder for money or rape for kicks. How does it happen that they know the difference between right and wrong, and how long will they abide by the difference if the leaders and opinion-makers and pacesetters continue to shy away from bringing home responsibility to the delinquent?

8    Admittedly, the reluctance to condemn stems partly from a worthy instinct—*tout comprendre, c'est tout pardonner*—and from a rejection of what was often the hypocrisy of Victorian moral standards. True, there was a large component of hypocrisy in nineteenth-century morality. Since the advent of Freud, we know more, we understand more about human behavior, we are more reluctant to cast the first stone—to condemn —which is a good thing; but the pendulum has swung to the point where

we are now afraid to place moral responsibility at all. Society, that large amorphous, nonspecific scapegoat, must carry the burden for each of us, relieving us of guilt. We have become so indoctrinated by the terrors lurking in the dark corridors of the guilt complex that guilt has acquired a very bad name. Yet a little guilt is not a dangerous thing; it has a certain social utility.

9    When it comes to guilt, a respected writer—respected in some circles—has told us, as her considered verdict on the Nazi program, that evil is banal—a word that means something so ordinary that you are not bothered by it; the dictionary definition is "commonplace and hackneyed." Somehow that conclusion does not seem adequate or even apt. *Of course,* evil is commonplace; *of course* we all partake of it. Does that mean that we must withhold disapproval, and that when evil appears in dangerous degree or vicious form we must not condemn but only understand? That may be very Christian in intent, but in reality it is an escape from the necessity of exercising judgment—which exercise, I believe, is a prime function of leadership.

## Independent Courage Required

10   What it requires is courage—just a little, not very much—the courage to be independent and stand up for the standard of values one believes in. That kind of courage is the quality most conspicuously missing, I think, in current life. I don't mean the courage to protest and walk around with picket signs or boo Secretary McNamara which, though it may stem from the right instinct, is a group thing that does not require any very stout spirit. I did it myself for Sacco and Vanzetti when I was about twelve and picketed in some now forgotten labor dispute when I was a freshman and even got arrested. There is nothing to that; if you don't do that sort of thing when you are eighteen, then there is something wrong with you. I mean, rather, a kind of lonely moral courage, the quality that attracted me to that odd character, Czar Reed, and to Lord Salisbury, neither of whom cared a rap for the opinion of the public or would have altered his conduct a hair to adapt to it. It is the quality someone said of Lord Palmerston was his "you-be-damnedness." That is the mood we need a little more of.

11   Standards of taste, as well as morality, need continued reaffirmation to stay alive, as liberty needs eternal vigilance. To recognize and to proclaim the difference between the good and the shoddy, the true and the fake, as well as between right and wrong, or what we believe at a given time to be right and wrong, is the obligation, I think, of persons who presume to lead, or are thrust into leadership, or hold positions of authority. That includes—whether they asked for it or not—all educators and even, I regret to say, writers.

12   For educators it has become increasingly the habit in the difficult circumstances of college administration today to find out what the stu-

dents want in the matter of curriculum and deportment and then give it to them. This seems to me another form of abdication, another example of the prevailing reluctance to state a standard and expect, not to say require, performance in accord with it. The permissiveness, the yielding of decision to the student, does not—from what I can tell—promote responsibility in the young so much as uneasiness and a kind of anger at *not* being told what is expected of them, a resentment of their elders' unwillingness to take a position. Recently a student psychiatric patient of the Harvard Health Services was quoted by the director, Dr. Dana Farnsworth, as complaining, "My parents never tell me what to do. They never stop me from doing anything." That is the unheard wail, I think, extended beyond parents to the general absence of a guiding, reassuring pattern, which is behind much of society's current uneasiness.

## Human Beings Want Standards

13    It is human nature to want patterns and standards and a structure of behavior. A pattern to conform to is a kind of shelter. You see it in kindergarten and primary school, at least in those schools where the children when leaving the classroom are required to fall into line. When the teacher gives the signal, they fall in with alacrity; they know where they belong and they instinctively like to *be* where they belong. They like the feeling of being in line.

14    Most people need a structure, not only to fall into but to fall out of. The rebel with a cause is better off than the one without. At least he knows what he is "agin." He is not lost. He does not suffer from an identity crisis. It occurs to me that much of the student protest now may be a testing of authority, a search for that line to fall out of, and when it isn't there students become angrier because they feel more lost, more abandoned than ever. In the late turmoil at Berkeley, at least as regards the filthy speech demonstration, there was a missed opportunity, I think (however great my respect for Clark Kerr) for a hearty, emphatic, and unmistakable "No!" backed up by sanctions. Why? Because the act, even if intended as a demonstration of principle, was in this case, like any indecent exposure, simply offensive, and what is offensive to the greater part of society is anti-social, and what is anti-social, so long as we live in social groups and not each of us on his own island, must be curtailed, like Peeping Toms or obscene telephone calls, as a public nuisance. The issue is really not complicated or difficult but, if we would only look at it with more self-confidence, quite simple.

15    So, it seems to me, is the problem of the CIA.[1] You will say that in this case people have taken a stand, opinion-makers have worked themselves

[1] The Central Intelligence Agency was discovered to be giving secret financial support to the National Student Association (Ed.).

into a moral frenzy. Indeed they have, but over a false issue. The CIA is not, after all, the Viet Cong or the Schutzstaffel in blackshirts. Its initials do not stand for Criminal Indiscretions of America. It is an arm of the American government, our elected, representative government (whatever may be one's feelings toward that body at the moment). Virtually every government in the world subsidizes youth groups, especially in their international relations, not to mention in athletic competitions. (I do not know if the CIA is subsidizing our Equestrian Team, but I know personally a number of people who would be only too delighted if it were.) The difficulty here is simply that the support was clandestine in the first place and not the proper job of the CIA in the second. An intelligence agency should be restricted to the gathering of intelligence and not extend itself into operations. In armies the two functions are distinct: intelligence is G2 and operations is G3. If our government could manage its functions with a little more precision and perform openly those functions that are perfectly respectable, there would be no issue. The recent excitement only shows how easily we succumb when reliable patterns or codes of conduct are absent, to a confusion of values.

## Pornography and Free Speech

16    A similar confusion exists, I think, with regard to the omnipresent pornography that surrounds us like smog. A year ago the organization of my own profession, the Authors League, filed a brief *amicus curiae* in the appeal of Ralph Ginzburg, the publisher of a periodical called *Eros* and other items, who had been convicted of disseminating obscenity through the mails. The League's action was taken on the issue of censorship to which all good liberals automatically respond like Pavlov's dogs. Since at this stage in our culture pornography has so far gotten the upper hand that to do battle in its behalf against the dragon Censorship is rather like doing battle today against the bustle in behalf of short skirts, and since I believe that the proliferation of pornography in its sadistic forms is a greater social danger at the moment than censorship, and since Mr. Ginzburg was not an author anyway but a commercial promoter, I raised an objection, as a member of the Council, to the Authors League's spending its funds in the Ginzburg case. I was, of course, outvoted; in fact, there was no vote. Everyone around the table just sat and looked at me in cold disapproval. Later, after my objection was printed in the *Bulletin,* at my request, two distinguished authors wrote privately to me to express their agreement but did not go so far as to say so publicly.

17    Thereafter, when the Supreme Court upheld Mr. Ginzburg's conviction, everyone in the intellectual community raised a hullaballoo about censorship advancing upon us like some sort of Frankenstein's monster. This seems to me another case of getting excited about the wrong thing.

The cause of pornography is *not* the same as the cause of free speech. There *is* a difference. Ralph Ginzburg is *not* Theodore Dreiser and this is not the 1920's. If one looks around at the movies, especially the movie advertisements, and the novels and the pulp magazines glorifying perversion and the paperbacks that make de Sade available to school children, one does not get the impression that in the 1960's we are being stifled in the Puritan grip of Anthony Comstock. Here again, leaders—in this case authors and critics—seem too unsure of values or too afraid of being unpopular to stand up and assert the perfectly obvious difference between smut and free speech, or to say "Such and such is offensive and can be harmful." Happily, there are signs of awakening. In a *Times* review of a book called *On Iniquity* by Pamela Hansford Johnson, which related pornography to the Moors murders in England, the reviewer concluded that "this may be the opening of a discussion that must come, the opening shot."

## Abdication of Judgment in the Arts

18     In the realm of art, no less important than morals, the abdication of judgment is almost a disease. Last fall when the Lincoln Center opened its glittering new opera house with a glittering new opera on the tragedy of Antony and Cleopatra, the curtain rose on a gaudy crowd engaged in energetic revels around a gold box in the shape of a pyramid, up whose sides (conveniently fitted with toe-holds, I suppose) several sinuous and reasonably nude slave girls were chased by lecherous guards left over from *Aida*. When these preliminaries quieted down, the front of the gold box suddenly dropped open, and guess who was inside? No, it was not Cleopatra, it was Antony, looking, I thought, rather bewildered. What he was doing inside the box was never made clear. Thereafter everything happened—and in crescendos of gold and spangles and sequins, silks and gauzes, feathers, fans, jewels, brocades, and such a quantity of glitter that one began to laugh, thinking that the spectacle was intended as a parody of the old Shubert revue. But no, this was the Metropolitan Opera in the vaunted splendor of its most publicized opening since the Hippodrome. I gather it was Mr. Bing's idea of giving the first night customers a fine splash. What he achieved was simply vulgarity, as at least some reviewers had the courage to say next day. Now, I cannot believe that Mr. Bing and his colleagues do not know the difference between honest artistry in stage design and pretentious ostentation. If they know better, why do they allow themselves to do worse? As leaders in their field of endeavor, they should have been setting standards of beauty and creative design, not debasing them.

19     One finds the same peculiarities in the visual arts. Non-art, as its practitioners describe it—the blob school, the all-black canvasses, the paper

cutouts and Campbell soup tins and plastic hamburgers and pieces of old carpet—is treated as art, not only by dealers whose motive is understandable (they have discovered that shock value sells); not only by a gullible pseudocultural section of the public who are not interested in art but in being "in" and wouldn't, to quote an old joke, know a Renoir from a Jaguar; but also, which I find mystifying, by the museums and the critics. I am sure they know the difference between the genuine and the hoax. But not trusting their own judgment, they seem afraid to say no to anything, for fear, I suppose, of making a mistake and turning down what may be next decade's Matisse.

20    For the museums to exhibit the plastic hamburgers and twists of scrap iron is one thing, but for them to *buy* them for their permanent collections puts an imprimatur on what is fraudulent. Museum curators, too, are leaders who have an obligation to distinguish—I will not say the good from the bad in art because that is an elusive and subjective matter dependent on the eye of the time—but at least honest expression from phony. Most of what fills the galleries on Madison Avenue is simply stuff designed to take advantage of current fads and does not come from an artist's vision or an honest creative impulse. The dealers know it; the critics know it; the purveyors themselves know it; the public suspects it; but no one dares say it because that would be committing oneself to a standard of values and even, heaven forbid, exposing oneself to being called square.

21    In the fairy story, it required a child to cry out that the Emperor was naked. Let us not leave that task to the children. It should be the task of leaders to recognize and state the truth as they see it. It is their task not to be afraid of absolutes.

## The Educated Person Evaluates

22    If the educated man is not willing to express standards, if he cannot show that he has them and applies them, what then is education for? Its purpose, I take it, is to form the civilized man, whom I would define as the person capable of the informed exercise of judgment, taste, and values. If at maturity he is not willing to express judgment on matters of policy or taste or morals, if at fifty he does not believe that he has acquired more wisdom and informed experience than is possessed by the student at twenty, then he is saying in effect that education has been a failure.

**REVIEW**

**Content**

1. Do you agree or disagree with Tuchman's analysis of and conclusions about what students truly want (paragraphs 12 and 13)?

2. Consider Tuchman's definition of the purposes of education, in her final paragraph. What does she mean by "the informed exercise of judgment, taste, and values"? Do you agree with her that unless a person has these capabilities, education has failed him or her?

### Rhetoric

3. Tuchman generally writes long, involved, yet clear sentences. How does she manage to maintain clarity? How much difference does precision of vocabulary make? Are there any wasted words; that is, does she make every word *work,* in clear fashion, for her?
4. Tuchman enriches her address by employing "literary allusions," by referring, either directly or indirectly, to items that her audience, from their reading experience, could be expected to be familiar with. Find three such allusions, two of which are "direct" and one more "hidden" (the latter in paragraph 2).

### Projects

5. If you disagree with Tuchman in paragraphs 12 and 13, write a short paper refuting her. Support your argument by examples, as she has. *OR* If you would define an educated person in terms other than as Tuchman's final paragraph does, write out your definition.
6. Paragraph 21 of Tuchman's speech is made up of four short sentences. Write a brief speech—perhaps 200–250 words—on a subject of interest to you, composed almost entirely of short, relatively simple sentences, and then read your paper aloud to someone so that you can hear how effective such a technique can be for speechwriting. Consider whether the device would become monotonous in a longer speech.

# The Story of Fire
## How To Be Heard
## While Teaching

## A SUFI TALE

The following parable is taken from *Tales of the Dervishes* (1970), collected by Idries Shah, who has been instrumental in introducing the ways of the East to the Western world. Tales like this one come from a wealth of Sufi "teaching stories" used by Sufi masters for the past thousand years that are intended for mulling over by their disciples in the search for insight.

(Sufi is a mystic sect of the Muslim religion.) This particular Sufi tale has to do with teaching and learning—and the difference between merely having knowledge and having the "special capacity to teach."

1    Once upon a time a man was contemplating the ways in which Nature operates, and he discovered, because of his concentration and application, how fire could be made.

2    This man was called Nour. He decided to travel from one community to another, showing people his discovery.

3    Nour passed the secret to many groups of people. Some took advantage of the knowledge. Others drove him away, thinking that he must be dangerous, before they had had time to understand how valuable this discovery could be to them. Finally, a tribe before which he demonstrated became so panic-stricken that they set about him and killed him, being convinced that he was a demon.

4    Centuries passed. The first tribe which had learned about fire reserved the secret for their priests, who remained in affluence and power while the people froze.

5    The second tribe forgot the art and worshipped instead the instruments. The third worshipped a likeness of Nour himself, because it was he who had taught them. The fourth retained the story of the making of fire in their legends: some believed them, some did not. The fifth community really did use fire, and this enabled them to be warmed, to cook their food, and to manufacture all kinds of useful articles.

6    After many, many years, a wise man and a small band of his disciples were traveling through the lands of these tribes. The disciples were amazed at the variety of rituals which they encountered, and one and all said to their teacher: "But all these procedures are in fact related to the making of fire, nothing else. We should reform these people!"

7    The teacher said: "Very well, then. We shall restart our journey. By the end of it, those who survive will know the real problems and how to approach them."

8    When they reached the first tribe, the band was hospitably received. The priests invited the travelers to attend their religious ceremony, the making of fire. When it was over, and the tribe was in a state of excitement at the event which they had witnessed, the master said: "Does anyone wish to speak?"

9    The first disciple said: "In the cause of Truth I feel myself constrained to say something to these people."

10    "If you will do so at your own risk, you may do so," said the master.

11    Now the disciple stepped forward in the presence of the tribal chief and his priests and said: "I can perform the miracle which you take to be a special manifestation of deity. If I do so, will you accept that you have been in error for so many years?"

12    But the priests cried: "Seize him!" and the man was taken away, never to be seen again.

13    The travelers went to the next territory where the second tribe were worshipping the instruments of fire-making. Again a disciple volunteered to try to bring reason to the community.

14    With the permission of the master, he said: "I beg permission to speak to you as reasonable people. You are worshipping the means whereby something may be done, not even the thing itself. Thus you are suspending the advent of its usefulness. I know the reality that lies at the basis of this ceremony."

15    This tribe was composed of more reasonable people. But they said to the disciple: "You are welcome as a traveler and stranger in our midst. But, as a stranger, foreign to our history and customs, you cannot understand what we are doing. You make a mistake. Perhaps, even, you are trying to take away or alter our religion. We therefore decline to listen to you."

16    The travelers moved on.

17    When they arrived in the land of the third tribe, they found before every dwelling an idol representing Nour, the original firemaker. The third disciple addressed the chiefs of the tribe:

18    "This idol represents a man, who represents a capacity, which can be used."

19    "This may be so," answered the Nour-worshippers, "but the penetration of the real secret is only for the few."

20    "It is only for the few who will understand, not for those who refuse to face certain facts," said the third disciple.

21    "This is rank heresy, and from a man who does not even speak our language correctly, and is not a priest ordained in our faith," muttered the priests. And he could make no headway.

22    The band continued their journey, and arrived in the land of the fourth tribe. Now a fourth disciple stepped forward in the assembly of the people.

23    "The story of making fire is true, and I know how it may be done," he said.

24    Confusion broke out within the tribe, which split into various factions. Some said: "This may be true, and if it is, we want to find out how to make fire." When these people were examined by the master and his followers, however, it was found that most of them were anxious to use firemaking for personal advantage, and did not realize that it was something for human progress. So deep had the distorted legends penetrated into the minds of most people that those who thought that they might in fact represent truth were often unbalanced ones, who could not have made fire even if they had been shown how.

25    There was another faction, who said: "Of course the legends are not true. This man is just trying to fool us, to make a place for himself here."

26    And a further faction said: "We prefer the legends as they are, for they are the very mortar of our cohesion. If we abandon them, and

we find that this new interpretation is useless, what will become of our community then?"

27    And there were other points of view, as well.

28    So the party traveled on, until they reached the lands of the fifth community, where firemaking was a commonplace, and where other preoccupations faced them.

29    The master said to his disciples:

30    "You have to learn how to teach, for man does not want to be taught. First of all, you will have to teach people how to learn. And before that you have to teach them that there is still something to be learned. They imagine that they are ready to learn. But they want to learn what they *imagine* is to be learned, not what they have first to learn. When you have learned all this, then you can devise the way to teach. Knowledge without special capacity to teach is not the same as knowledge and capacity."


## REVIEW

### Content

1. Do you agree or disagree with the master's statement that "man does not want to be taught"? If you agree, then can you analyze *why* he does not? If you disagree, then how do you explain what the disciples encounter in the first four villages?
2. What exactly is the tale saying about teaching and learning? Further explain the last paragraph by real examples from your own experience.

### Rhetoric

3. Does the simple, direct style of this tale from the East remind you of any fairy tales, fables, legends, or myths you know from Western literature? If so, what does this similarity tell you about tale-telling and its likely uses, in different cultures? Can you think of more than one possible use?
4. Paragraphs 16 and 27 are very short, to be paragraphs. How do they function in the piece; that is, what kind of paragraphs are they?

### Projects

5. To recapture the spirit and the experience of tale-telling, find another "teaching tale"—from either the East or the West. (Many such tales are much shorter than this one; the college librarian can help you locate a tale.) Memorize the tale, and tell it to others, seeing how well you can make it "work." Immediately after your tale-telling, record both your feelings as you told the tale and the response of your listeners. Then write up the experience as an "observation report."

6. Try to think of some useful knowledge or realization that *you* might fight learning about an account of a barrier similar to one existing in one of the first four villages, and base a paper on the results of your fantasized reaction. Include in your paper something of what you learn about yourself through this experience.

# Teaching and Learning: Person to Person

## MARY CAROLINE RICHARDS

Mary Caroline Richards, after obtaining her doctorate in English in 1942, renounced the exclusive pursuit of intellectual development for a concern with the growth of the whole person—in an attempt to "center" while writing poetry, creating pottery, and teaching and learning in an exchange of her own wholeness with the wholeness of her students. The selection below, from her book *Centering: In Pottery, Poetry and the Person* (1964), reveals how this process works as Richards acts as "teacher."

1  . . . You don't need me to tell you what education is. Everybody really knows that education goes on all the time everywhere all through our lives, and that it is the process of waking up to life. Jean Henri Fabre said something just about like that, I think. He said that to be educated was not to be taught but to wake up. It takes a heap of resolve to keep from going to sleep in the middle of the show. It's not that we want to sleep our lives away. It's that it requires certain kinds of energy, certain capacities for taking the world into our consciousness, certain real powers of body and soul to be a match for reality. That's why knowledge and consciousness are two quite different things. Knowledge is like a product we consume and store. All we need are good closets. By consciousness I mean a state of being "awake" to the world throughout our organism. This kind of consciousness requires not closets but an organism attuned to the finest perceptions and responses. It allows experience to breathe through it as light enters and changes a room. When knowledge is transformed into consciousness and into will, ah then we are on the high road indeed . . .

## Knowledge as Possession

2    That which we consume, with a certain passivity, accepting it for the most part from our teachers, who in turn have accepted it from theirs, is like the food we eat. And food, in order to become energy, or will, is transformed entirely by the processes of metabolism. We do not become the food we eat. Rather the food turns into us. Similarly with knowledge, at best. Hopefully, we do not turn into encyclopedias or propaganda machines or electric brains. Our knowledge, if we allow it to be transformed within us, turns into capacity for lifeserving human deeds. If knowledge does not turn into life, it makes cripples and madmen and dunces. It poisons just as food would if it stayed in the stomach and was never digested, and the waste products never thrown off.

3    It is dangerous to seek to possess knowledge, as if it could be stored. For one thing, it tends to make one impatient with ignorance, as people busy with money-seeking tend to be impatient with idlers. Though ignorance is the prime prerequisite for education, many teachers appear offended by it—or worse, contemptuous. Perhaps it is partly for this reason that many prefer to give advanced courses to select or "gifted" groups.

4    The possession of knowledge may create a materialism of its own. Knowledge becomes property. Teachers compete with each other for status, wealth, influence. A professor of education was speaking to friends of education in the county where I live, and she was urging pay raises as bait for hiring good teachers, "for after all, the standard of success is the salary check." Naturally in this climate professional educators are apt to quarrel over tactics and to engage in pressure politics, motivated by a desire to protect their security and to establish their views as ruling policy. In other words, education may be sacrificed to knowledge-as-commodity. Just as life is sometimes sacrificed to art-as-arrangement. The quest is abandoned. Instead, property is bought at the site of the last dragon killed, and a ruling class is formed out of the heroes. The knights grow fat and lazy and conceited and petulant. They parade in their armor on special occasions to bedazzle the populace. But in their hearts are terror and duplicity. And when difficult times come, they fall upon each other with their rusty axes and try to divide the world into those who know and those who don't. There is nothing to equal in bitterness and gall, childishness and spite, the intramural warfare of the academic community. Where is honor? Where is devotion? Where is responsibility of soul?

## Crippling Brainwashing

5    Such an atmosphere brought me gradually to imagine possible shortcomings in the educational system I had docilely trusted. Initiative and

imagination seemed sorely lacking. Teachers seemed to apply to their students the same pressures that had crippled them. Most of us have been brainwashed to think that knowledge and security make the world go round. And if the world seems to be going round very poorly, we do not think of questioning deeply its education. The need for creative imagination in the intellectually trained person is drastic. Also the need for spontaneous human feeling.

6    Fashionable thinking may dominate the scientist and artist and scholar alike. For them, knowledge is the body of facts currently in fashion. Art is the image and compositional practice now in fashion. Since it is difficult to test the truth of most facts, faculty and students alike settle for "interesting," "original," and "self-consistent" theories. An ability to marshal and interpret "evidence" is highly esteemed, though evidence is often no more than opinions strongly held or secondary research. Very little stress is placed on developing powers of observation or on intuition. Thus, with primary experience held so at a distance, sensory life in particular, I find that my principal task in teaching adults is to win their trust. They tend to be overwhelmingly oriented to manipulation and to effect. It rarely occurs to them to work in a direct way with what they know and are. Their primary motivations are to please, to make a strong impression, to do either what is expected (if they are docile) or what is unexpected (if they are hostile). They assume that pretense and falsity are virtues. The whole thing sometimes seems like a massive confidence game.

7    Like other men, teachers tend to withhold themselves from naked personal contact. They tend to pin their hopes on jargon and style. And this, I have observed, is what many students learn from them: afraid to reveal themselves, burdened with shame and dismay and hopelessness, or expertise and cunning.

8    A theory much in vogue is that Western man is sick with sexual repression and pleasure anxiety. I believe that the squelching of the "person" and his spontaneous intuitive response to experience is as much at the root of our timidity, our falseness. Teachers and students who in the great school markets barter their learning for salaries and grades are hungry for respect, for personal relationship, for warmth. Unfortunately, they have the impression that these are extracurricular (like Newton's secondary qualities of color and so on)—and their capacity for balance between the life within and the world without shrinks or falters, or their desperation turns rank.

9    It is a sensitive matter, of course. I am not going to all these words merely to insult the spirit of true research. But my life as a teacher and as a member of the human community advises me that education may estrange us from life-commitment as well as bind us firmly within it. There are all kinds of things to learn, and we had best learn them all. One of the reasons formal education is in danger today is that a sense of work is split off from human earnestness. How may this split

be healed? Working with our materials as artist-craftsmen may help to engender a new health here.

## An Act of the Self

10    An act of the self, that's what one must make. An act of the self, from me to you. From center to center. We must mean what we say, from our innermost heart to the outermost galaxy. Otherwise we are lost and dizzy in a maze of reflections. We carry light within us. There is no need merely to reflect. Others carry light within them. These lights must wake to each other. My face is real. Yours is. Let us find our way to our initiative.

11    For must we not show ourselves to each other, and will we not know then who are the teachers and who are the students? Do we not all learn from one another? My students at City College are worldly-wise and naïve as lambs. I am sophisticated and uninformed. We make a good combination. They have never heard of e. e. cummings, who lived in their city, nor of the New York painters. They do not know that there are free art galleries where they may see the latest works of modern artists. They do not know very much about contemporary "culture." But they know well the life of the subway, the office, the factory, the union hall, the hassle for employment; they know what they did in the war or in their escape from Hungary or Germany, or in occupied France, or Israel. They know what it is like to be black in America. They are patient with my obtuseness, they check my too quick judgments, my sarcasm which is unperceptive. I help them to unmask, to be openly as tender and hopeful and generous as they inwardly are. I help them to open themselves to knowledge. They help me to open myself to life. We are equal in courage.

## REVIEW

### Content

1. An ancient Greek thinker said that a student is "a lamp to be lighted, not a vessel to be filled." Compare this with Richards' definition of being educated as not being taught but being waked up. Do you agree with these statements? Do you find Richards' distinction between knowledge and consciousness a significant one? How does her analysis of the uses of knowledge—and its potential dangers—strike you?
2. Many representatives of education would quarrel with Richards' saying that teaching requires "an act of the self." Can you see why? How do *you* feel about this philosophy, for both yourself as student and for teachers?

**Rhetoric**

3. Richards' writing reads in many places almost as if she were keeping a journal of her musings about education. What elements can you find that contribute to her informal tone?
4. In paragraph 4 (where she speaks of "the quest"), Richards uses an "extended metaphor" to make her point. Metaphors, as literary devices, work by speaking of unlike things as if they were equal, or the same. Translate Richards' metaphor into what she is actually saying, to show that you understand how it works.

**Projects**

5. Try your hand at writing one or more "journal entries," covering several pages, in which you "talk to yourself" about some area of life that you think a lot about. Find a voice that you feel very comfortable with and then try to make your entry(ies) also appealing to a potential sympathetic reader.
6. Think of a controversial point you would like to make without offending a reader who holds an opposite view. Then try to create an extended metaphor to use in making your point. Will this method help you avoid offense? Write it out, and try it out.

# Anticipating the Future

## ALVIN TOFFLER

Alvin Toffler (1928–    ) has been a Visiting Professor at Cornell University and a Visiting Scholar at the Russell Sage Foundation, an organization primarily concerned with improving social and living conditions. He also has been an editor for *Fortune* magazine. He has written for both *Life* and *Playboy,* in addition to publishing in scholarly journals and producing several books. But by far his greatest impact has come through his book *Future Shock* (1970)—which virtually defined the whole concept of "future shock" in the complex technological, sophisticated, and highly accelerated societies of the world. In the excerpt printed here, Toffler urges education to attend to providing "a sense of the future" for students, by teaching them to "anticipate and project," so that essential adaptability can be developed.

1    ... Three hundred and fifty years after his death, scientists are still finding evidence to support Cervantes' succinct insight into adaptational psychology: "Forewarned, forearmed," Self-evident as it may seem, in most situations we can help individuals adapt better if we simply provide them with advance information about what lies ahead.

2    Studies of the reactions of astronauts, displaced families, and industrial workers almost uniformly point to this conclusion. "Anticipatory information," writes psychologist Hugh Bowen, "allows ... a dramatic change in performance." Whether the problem is that of driving a car down a crowded street, piloting a plane, solving intellectual puzzles, playing a cello or dealing with interpersonal difficulties, performance improves when the individual knows what to expect next.

3    The mental processing of advance data about any subject presumably cuts down on the amount of processing and the reaction time during the actual period of adaptation. It was Freud, I believe, who said: "Thought is action in rehearsal."

## Habit of Anticipation

4    Even more important than any specific bits of advance information, however, is the habit of anticipation. This conditioned ability to look ahead plays a key role in adaptation. Indeed, one of the hidden clues to successful coping may well lie in the individual's sense of the future. The people among us who keep up with change, who manage to adapt well, seem to have a richer, better developed sense of what lies ahead than those who cope poorly. Anticipating the future has become a habit with them. The chess player who anticipates the moves of his opponent, the executive who thinks in long range terms, the student who takes a quick glance at the table of contents before starting to read page one, all seem to fare better.

5    People vary widely in the amount of thought they devote to the future, as distinct from past and present. Some invest far more resources than others in projecting themselves forward—imagining, analyzing and evaluating future possibilities and probabilities. They also vary in how *far* they tend to project. Some habitually think in terms of the "deep future." Others penetrate only into the "shallow future."

6    We have, therefore, at least two dimensions of "futureness"—how much and how far. There is evidence that among normal teenagers maturation is accompanied by what sociologist Stephen L. Klineberg of Princeton describes as "an increasing concern with distant future events." This suggests that people of different ages characteristically devote different amounts of attention to the future. Their "time horizons" may also differ. But age is not the only influence on our futureness. Cultural conditioning affects it, and one of the most important cultural influences of all is the rate of change in the environment.

# Coping with the Future

7    This is why the individual's sense of the future plays so critical a part in his ability to cope. The faster the pace of life, the more rapidly the present environment slips away from us, the more rapidly do future potentialities turn into present reality. As the environment churns faster, we are not only pressured to devote more mental resources to thinking about the future, but to extend our time horizon—to probe further and further ahead. The driver dawdling along an expressway at twenty miles per hour can successfully negotiate a turn into an exit lane, even if the sign indicating the cut-off is very close to the exit. The faster he drives, however, the further back the sign must be placed to give him the time needed to read and react. In quite the same way, the generalized acceleration of life compels us to lengthen our time horizon or risk being overtaken and overwhelmed by events. The faster the environment changes, the more the need for futureness.

8    Some individuals, of course, project themselves so far into the future for such long periods that their anticipations become escapist fantasies. Far more common, however, are those individuals whose anticipations are so thin and short-range that they are continually surprised and flustered by change.

9    The adaptive individual appears to be able to project himself forward just the "right" distance in time, to examine and evaluate alternative courses of action open to him before the need for final decision, and to make tentative decisions beforehand.


# Studies on Projecting

10    Studies by social scientists like Lloyd Warner in the United States and Elliott Jaques in Britain, for example, have shown how important this time element is in management decision-making. The man on the assembly line is given work that requires him to concern himself only with events close to him in time. The men who rise in management are expected, with each successive promotion, to concern themselves with events further in the future.

11    Sociologist Benjamin D. Singer of the University of Western Ontario, whose field is social psychiatry, has gone further. According to Singer, the future plays an enormous, largely unappreciated part in present behavior. He argues, for instance, that "the 'self' of the child is in part feedback from what it is toward what it is becoming." The target toward which the child is moving is his "future focused role image"—a conception of what he or she wishes to be like at various points in the future.

12    This "future focused role image," Singer writes, "tends . . . to organize and give meaning to the pattern of life he is expected to take. Where, however, there is only a hazily defined or functionally non-existent fu-

ture role, then the meaning which is attached to behavior valued by the larger society does not exist; schoolwork becomes meaningless, as do the rules of middle-class society and of parental discipline."

13   Put more simply, Singer asserts that each individual carries in his mind not merely a picture of himself at present, a self-image, but a set of pictures of himself as he wishes to be in the future. "This person of the future provides a focus for the child; it is a magnet toward which he is drawn; the framework for the present, one might say, is created by the future."

## Education to Date

14   One would think that education, concerned with the development of the individual and the enhancement of adaptability, would do all in its power to help children develop the appropriate time-bias, the suitable degree of futureness. Nothing could be more dangerously false.

15   Consider, for example, the contrast between the way schools today treat space and time. Every pupil, in virtually every school, is carefully helped to position himself in space. He is required to study geography. Maps, charts and globes all help pinpoint his spatial location. Not only do we locate him with respect to his city, region, or country, we even try to explain the spatial relationship of the earth to the rest of the solar system and, indeed, to the universe.

16   When it comes to locating the child in time, however, we play a cruel and disabling trick on him. He is steeped, to the extent possible, in his nation's past and that of the world. He studies ancient Greece and Rome, the rise of feudalism, the French Revolution, and so forth. He is introduced to Bible stories and patriotic legends. He is peppered with endless accounts of wars, revolutions and upheavals, each one dutifully tagged with its appropriate date in the past.

17   At some point he is even introduced to "current events." He may be asked to bring in newspaper clippings, and a really enterprising teacher may go so far as to ask him to watch the evening news on television. He is offered, in short, a thin sliver of the present.

18   And then time stops. The school is silent about tomorrow. "Not only do our history courses terminate with the year they are taught," wrote Professor Ossip Flechtheim a generation ago, "but the same situation exists in the study of government and economics, psychology and biology." Time comes racing to an abrupt halt. The student is focused backward instead of forward. The future, banned as it were from the classroom, is banned from his consciousness as well. It is as though there were no future.

## Experiment on Time Sense

19    This violent distortion of his time sense shows up in a revealing experiment conducted by psychologist John Condry, Professor in the Department of Human Development, Cornell University. In separate studies
at Cornell and UCLA, Condry gave groups of students the opening
paragraph of a story. This paragraph described a fictional "Professor
Hoffman," his wife and their adopted Korean daughter. The daughter
is found crying, her clothes torn, a group of other children staring at
her. The students were asked to complete the story.

20    What the subjects did not know is that they had previously been divided into two groups. In the case of one group, the opening paragraph
was set in the past. The characters "heard," "saw" or "ran." The students
were asked to "Tell what Mr. and Mrs. Hoffman did and what was
said by the children." For the second group, the paragraph was set entirely in the future tense. They were asked to "Tell what Mr. and Mrs.
Hoffman will do and what will be said by the children." Apart from
this shift of tense, both paragraphs and instructions were identical.

21    The results of the experiment were sharply etched. One group wrote
comparatively rich and interesting story-endings, peopling their accounts
with many characters, creatively introducing new situations and dialogue.
The other produced extremely sketchy endings, thin, unreal and forced.
The past was richly conceived; the future empty. "It is," Professor Condry commented, "as if we find it easier to talk about the past than the
future."

## Educating for the Future

22    If our children are to adapt more successfully to rapid change, this
distortion of time must be ended. We must sensitize them to the possibilities and probabilities of tomorrow. We must enhance their sense of
the future.

23    Society has many built-in time spanners that help to link the present
generation with the past. Our sense of the past is developed by contact
with the older generation, by our knowledge of history, by the accumu-
lated heritage of art, music, literature, and science passed down to us
through the years. It is enhanced by immediate contact with the objects
that surround us, each of which has a point of origin in the past, each
of which provides us with a trace of identification with the past.

24    No such time spanners enhance our sense of the future. We have
no objects, no friends, no relatives, no works of art, no music or literature that originate in the future. We have, as it were, no heritage of
the future.

25      Despite this, there are ways to send the human mind arching forward
as well as backward. We need to begin by creating a stronger future-
consciousness on the part of the public, and not just by means of Buck
Rogers comic strips, films like *Barbarella*, or articles about the marvels
of space travel or medical research. These make a contribution, but what
is needed is a concentrated focus on the social and personal implications
of the future, not merely on its technological characteristics.

## REVIEW

### Content

1. Toffler defines "future shock" in his book as "what happens to
people when they are overwhelmed by change." Discuss the concept
of "future shock": Do you find the concept a valid one? If so, can
you give examples? And, how do/will *you* adapt?
2. Traditionally education has largely centered on studying the past
(through history, philosophy, literature, for example) and studying
current, "relevant" subject matter (as in the social sciences, ecology,
astronomy), both pursuits intended to help one cope with the present
and, perhaps, one's immediate future. Toffler sees "future studies"
as essential. How do you reconcile the *three* pursuits? Is there *time*
to study all adequately? If not, how, accepting the premise of future
shock, should priorities be established in education?

### Rhetoric

3. Toffler writes in a popularized style common to journalism. From
your acquaintance with what are known as "popular magazines," pick
out elements in the above piece that characterize such a style. That
is, what makes Toffler's writing easy, popular, appealing reading?
4. Toffler cites both scholarly studies and individual "authorities" (e.g.,
Cervantes and Freud) to support his own hypotheses and conclusions.
Select examples of both kinds of citation of expertise and consider
whether each offers relevant, sufficient, and/or provable support, as
used. Can you see any possible dangers in such a technique, possible
traps for a reader to watch for?

### Projects

5. Select some technological invention that is making or that will make
marked changes in the average person's life and try to think through
and write about how *you* will adapt to those changes. Examples: computerized shopping; instant education for all at home through video-
tape cassettes and the like; inexpensive mass transit, possibly accompanied by making the use of cars at certain times and in certain areas
illegal.

6. Write about some sociological or cultural aspect of future shock, other than its implications for education, as if you were on assignment to do the piece for a popular magazine. Appeal to the general reader, presenting carefully established facts in an interesting, readable way. Take care to limit your topic so that you can handle it in a paper of reasonable length—that is, select out the angles you will highlight. You might work with such topics as an individual lifestyle change in light of certain contemporary freedoms; implications of the four-day work week; a way of male-female relating alternative to traditional marriage.

# 2
# The Individual

# The Apology of Socrates

## After He Is Condemned to Death

## PLATO

Socrates (c. 470 B.C.–399 B.C.) was first in the great triad of ancient Greek philosophers: Socrates, Plato, Aristotle. Socrates went about Athens for a number of years asking challenging questions and gaining a reputation as a gadfly on the State. For his insistence on scrutinizing traditional beliefs that were being taken for granted, he was put on trial in 399 B.C. The accusations against him included impiety and corrupting the youth of the city, to whom he had been saying, "The unexamined life is not worth living." The following excerpt is from "The Apology of Socrates"; in this closing passage Socrates explains why a man seeking virtue would choose to die rather than to compromise himself. The Apology has come down to us through its having been later recorded by Plato (c. 427 B.C.–c. 347 B.C.) in his *Dialogues;* Plato apparently was present at the trial.

1 . . . For no great thrift in time, my fellow citizens, you will have from those who wish to vilify the City the name and blame of having put to death the wise man, Socrates; for they will call me wise, even if I am not, they who would defame you. If only you had waited for a little while, the thing would have occurred for you in the course of nature; for you can see my age, that I am far along in life, and near to death. I say this, not to all of you, but only to those who voted for my death. And to them I have also to say this as well. It may be, Gentlemen, that you think I lost my cause for lack of arguments of the sort with which I might have won you over, if I had thought that I ought to say and do all things in order to escape the verdict. Far from it. I lost for a lack, but not of arguments; it was for lack of impudence and daring, and for not being ready to say to you the sort of thing it would have given you most pleasure to hear—me weeping and wailing, and doing and saying any and every sort of thing that I hold

to be unworthy of me, but you are accustomed to hear from the rest. No. I did not then believe that to avoid a danger, I ought to do anything unseemly in a freeman, nor do I now regret my manner of defense. No, far rather would I choose this manner of defense, and die, than follow that, and live. Whether in a court of justice or in war neither I nor any other man should seek by using every means conceivable to escape from death; for in battle you very often see that if you throw away your weapons and beg those who are pursuing you for mercy, you may get out of dying. Indeed, in every sort of danger there are various ways of winning through, if one is ready to do and say anything whatever. No, Gentlemen, that is not the hard thing, to escape from death; ah no, far harder is it to escape from sin, for sin is swifter than death. And so I, being old and slow, am overtaken by the slower enemy; while my accusers, who are strong and swift, have been caught by the swifter, namely wickedness. And so I now depart, by you condemned to pay the penalty of death; and they by the truth convicted of a base injustice. And as I abide the payment, so do they. Who knows? Perhaps it had to be so, and I think that things are as they ought to be.

2    Touching the future, I desire to make for you who voted to condemn me, a prediction; for I am at the point where men foresee the future best—when they are soon to die. Let me tell you then, you men who have condemned me, that after I am gone there will straightway come upon you a chastisement far heavier, by Zeus, than the death you have set for me. You have now done this in the belief that you have freed yourselves from giving any reckoning for your life; but I tell you the result will be the very opposite for you. There will be more inquisitors to sift you, men whom I now hold in check without your knowing it. And they will be more critical as they are younger, and will annoy you more; for if you think that by putting men to death you will prevent the slur from being cast at you that you do not live aright, you are in error. This way of getting freedom is neither very sure nor fine; no, the finest and readiest way is this, not to interfere with other people, but to render oneself as good a man as possible. There is the prophecy I make for you who voted to condemn me. And of them I take my leave.

3    With those of you who voted to acquit me I should be glad to talk about this thing that has occurred, while the magistrates are busy and it is not time for me to go to the place where I must die. So, Gentlemen, please wait with me as long as that. There is nothing to keep us from talking to each other as long as it is allowed. To you as to friends I wish to explain the real meaning of what has just happened to me.

4    Justices, for when I call you that I am naming you aright, the thing that has come to me is wonderful.

5    My customary warning, by the spirit, in previous times has always, up to now, come to me very often to oppose me, even when a matter

was quite important, if ever I was going to do something amiss. But to-day, as you yourselves have witnessed, that thing has happened to me which anybody might suppose, and which is considered, to be the uttermost of evils. Yet neither did the sign from God oppose me when I left my house this morning, nor at the point when I ascended here to the tribunal, nor in my speech at anything I was about to say; though often when I have been talking elsewhere it has stopped me in the middle of a speech. But to-day, with reference to the whole procedure, not once did it oppose me in a thing I did or said. What, then, do I take to be the cause of this? No doubt this thing that has happened to me is good, and it cannot be that our supposition is correct when any of us think that death is a misfortune. For me, the proof of this is telling: it cannot be but that the customary sign would have opposed me, if I had not been about to do a thing that was good. . . . .

6     But, Justices, you also it behoves to have good hope with reference to death, and this one thing you must bear in mind as true, that, living or dead, to a good man there can come no evil, nor are his affairs a matter of indifference to the gods. Nor has my destiny now come about by chance; rather, it is clear to me that it was better for me now to die and to be released from my troubles. That is why the sign did not at any point deter me, and why I am not very bitter at those who voted to condemn me, or at my accusers. It is true they did not have this notion in condemning and accusing me; no, they thought to injure me, and therein they merit blame.

7     One thing, however, I do beg of them. When my sons grow up, then, Gentlemen, I ask you to punish them, you hurting them the same as I hurt you, if they seem to you to care for money, or aught else, more than they care for virtue. And if they pretend to be somewhat when they are nothing, do you upbraid them as I upbraided you, for not regarding as important what they ought to think so, and for thinking they have worth when they do not. If you do that, I shall have received just treatment from you, and my sons as well.

8     And now the time has come for our departure, I to die, and you to live. Which of us goes to meet the better lot is hidden from all unless it be known to God.

## REVIEW

### Content

1. Do you believe, with Socrates, that "the unexamined life is not worth living"? Before you answer, consider the implications of examining one's life. Is doing so easy? Is it painful? If your answer to the original question here is "yes," are you *sure*? If it is "no," what does that answer suggest to you?

2. Socrates says, in paragraph 6, that "to a good man there can come no evil." What does he mean, both in the context of his death trial and for everyday living? Do you agree with this?

**Rhetoric**

3. What techniques are utilized by Socrates to make his speech effective as a direct public address?
4. Can you think of a more effective ending for Socrates' speech than paragraph 7? Why is this paragraph so effective?

**Projects**

5. Be Socrates (male or female, whichever you happen to be). You are elderly; deeply concerned about the condition of the society in which you live; you question some of its assumptions and thereby threaten the power structure; you are tried and condemned to die; you then have the option of naming an alternate sentence (as did Socrates, who was expected to impose upon himself self-exile from Athens, but who chose not to do so because that would suggest his disbelief in the law under which he had enjoyed life). Decide what you would do and write out your rationale, including arguments in addition to Socrates' for choosing death if that is your choice. There are also good arguments for choosing exile, if you choose that alternative.
6. Select some recent incident from the political scene (national or international), from the world of commerce, or in any other of society's institutions—schools, the military—in which an individual has allowed self-serving interests to supersede personal integrity in his/her conduct—or vice versa. Write out for that person a public defense (his/her "apology") for the chosen course of action.

# On Slavery

## FREDERICK DOUGLASS

Frederick Douglass (c. 1817–1895), born into slavery in Maryland, escaped from bondage in 1838 and settled in Massachusetts, where he became a lecturer for the Massachusetts Anti-Slavery Society. He founded a weekly newspaper and became further involved in politics, gaining a reputation for his powerful oratory. Douglass began his autobiography soon after establishing himself as a free man and published it in three volumes, between 1845 and 1892. The first volume, entitled *Narrative of the Life of Frederick Douglass,* contains the passage printed below. The year is 1833 and Douglass has been sent by his master to live with a Mr. Covey, an infamous slave-breaker. Worked into utter exhaustion and poorly fed, Douglass falls sick in the fields and is beaten for not continuing to work. He escapes to his master, who returns him to Covey. The excerpt begins as the slave reports back to Covey's farm.

1    ... I immediately started for home; and upon entering the yard gate, out came Mr. Covey on his way to meeting. He spoke to me very kindly, bade me drive the pigs from a lot near by, and passed on towards the church. ... Long before daylight, I was called to go and rub, curry, and feed the horses. I obeyed, and was glad to obey. But whilst thus engaged, whilst in the act of throwing down some blades from the loft, Mr. Covey entered the stable with a long rope; and just as I was half out of the loft, he caught hold of my legs, and was about tying me. As soon as I found what he was up to, I gave a sudden spring, and as I did so, he holding to my legs, I was brought sprawling on the stable floor. Mr. Covey seemed now to think he had me, and could do what he pleased; but at this moment—from whence came the spirit I don't know—I resolved to fight; and suiting my action to the resolution, I seized Covey hard by the throat; and as I did so, I rose. He held on to me, and I to him. My resistance was so entirely unexpected, that Covey seemed taken all aback. He trembled like a leaf. This gave me assurance, and I held him uneasy, causing the blood to run where I touched him with the ends of my fingers. Mr. Covey soon called out to Hughes for help. Hughes came, and while Covey held me, attempted to tie my right hand. While he was in the act of doing so, I watched my chance, and gave him a heavy kick close under the ribs. This kick fairly sickened Hughes, so that he left me in the hands of Mr. Covey. This kick had the effect of not only weakening Hughes, but Covey also. When he saw Hughes bending over with pain, his courage quailed. He asked me if I meant to persist in my resistance. I told him I did, come what might; that he had used me like a brute for six months, and that I was determined to be used so no longer. With that, he strove to drag me to a stick that was lying just out of the stable door. He meant to knock me down. But just as he was leaning over to get the stick, I seized him with both hands by his collar, and brought him by a sudden snatch to the ground. By this time, Bill came. Covey called upon him for assistance. Bill wanted to know what he could do. Covey said, "Take hold of him, take hold of him!" Bill said his master hired him out to work, and not to help to whip me; so he left Covey and myself to fight our own battle out. We were at it for nearly two hours. Covey at length let me go, puffing and blowing at a great rate, saying that if I had not resisted, he would not have whipped me half so much. The truth was, that he had not whipped me at all. I considered him as getting entirely the worst end of the bargain; for he had drawn no blood from me, but I had from him. The whole six months afterwards,

that I spent with Mr. Covey, he never laid the weight of his finger upon me in anger. He would occasionally say, he didn't want to get hold of me again. "No," thought I, "you need not; for you will come off worse than you did before."

2   This battle with Mr. Covey was the turning-point in my career as a slave. It rekindled the few expiring embers of freedom, and revived within me a sense of my own manhood. It recalled the departed self-confidence, and inspired me again with a determination to be free. The gratification afforded by the triumph was a full compensation for what-ever else might follow, even death itself. He only can understand the deep satisfaction which I experienced, who has himself repelled by force the bloody arm of slavery. I felt as I never felt before. It was a glorious resurrection, from the tomb of slavery, to the heaven of freedom. My long-crushed spirit rose, cowardice departed, bold defiance took its place; and I now resolved that, however long I might remain a slave in form, the day had passed forever when I could be a slave in fact. I did not hesitate to let it be known of me, that the white man who expected to succeed in whipping, must also succeed in killing me.

3   From this time I was never again what might be called fairly whipped, though I remained a slave four years afterwards. I had several fights, but was never whipped.

## REVIEW

### Content

1. What does Douglass mean when he refers to being "a slave in form . . . [but not] in fact"?
2. It is of interest that Douglass was active not only in the struggle for abolition, but also in the mid-nineteenth-century fight for women's rights. The similar titles of two modern-day essays, "Woman as Nigger" and "The Student as Nigger," suggest that if he were alive, he might also be a defender of students' rights. What is the latter concept all about, and what might Douglass have had to say about it?

### Rhetoric

3. The first-person narrative form of autobiography can be a very effective writing voice. What specific elements in paragraph 1 of Douglass' narrative make you feel that "you are there" with Douglass and Covey?
4. Both the tone and the style of paragraph 2 differ radically from those of paragraph 1. What is Douglass trying to achieve with paragraph 2? What choices of diction (vocabulary), phrasing, sentence structures, and so on, help him achieve that effect?

**Projects**

5. Write about some situation in which you were in the position of inferior but did not allow the external *form* to touch the internal *fact* of your own essential freedom and self-dignity. If you cannot think of an actual experience, fantasize one—as good practice for when you may need to stand up.

6. Choose some interesting incident from your life and try to make that bit of your autobiography as vivid on paper as is Douglass'. Get your reader "there" with you.

# Self-Reliance

## RALPH WALDO EMERSON

Ralph Waldo Emerson (1803–1882) was a leading figure in New England's renowned intellectual circle of the mid-1800s. He was known as occasional preacher (Unitarian), lyceum lecturer, and essayist; his famous essays include "Friendship," "Nature," "The Over-Soul," "The American Scholar," and "Self-Reliance." The latter essay (first published in 1841), from which the selection below is taken, states that a human being should be his/her own person, in the face of whatever odds, a principle which Emerson strongly supported.

1   Society everywhere is in conspiracy against the manhood of every one of its members. Society is a joint-stock company, in which the members agree, for the better securing of his bread to each shareholder, to surrender the liberty and culture of the eater. The virtue in most request is conformity. Self-reliance is its aversion. It loves not realities and creators, but names and customs.

## Integrity

2     Whoso would be a man, must be a nonconformist. He who would gather immortal palms must not be hindered by the name of goodness, but must explore if it be goodness. Nothing is at last sacred but the integrity of your own mind. Absolve you to yourself, and you shall have the suffrage of the world. I remember an answer which when quite young I was prompted to make to a valued adviser who was wont to importune me with the dear old doctrines of the church. On my saying,

"What have I to do with the sacredness of traditions, if I live wholly from within?" my friend suggested—"But these impulses may be from below, not from above." I replied, "They do not seem to me to be such; but if I am the Devil's child, I will live then from the Devil." No law can be sacred to me but that of my nature. Good and bad are but names very readily transferable to that or this; the only right is what is after my constitution; the only wrong what is against it. A man is to carry himself in the presence of all opposition as if every thing were titular and ephemeral but he. I am ashamed to think how easily we capitulate to badges and names, to large societies and dead institutions. Every decent and well-spoken individual affects and sways me more than is right. I ought to go upright and vital, and speak the rude truth in all ways. If malice and vanity wear the coat of philanthropy, shall that pass? If an angry bigot assumes this bountiful cause of Abolition, and comes to me with his last news from Barbadoes, why should I not say to him, 'Go love thy infant; love thy wood-chopper; be good-natured and modest; have that grace; and never varnish your hard, uncharitable ambition with this incredible tenderness for black folk a thousand miles off. Thy love afar is spite at home.' Rough and graceless would be such greeting, but truth is handsomer than the affectation of love. Your goodness must have some edge to it—else it is none. The doctrine of hatred must be preached, as the counteraction of the doctrine of love, when that pules and whines. I shun father and mother and wife and brother when my genius calls me. I would write on the lintels of the door-post, *Whim.* I hope it is somewhat better than whim at last, but we cannot spend the day in explanation. Expect me not to show cause why I seek or why I exclude company. Then again, do not tell me, as a good man did today, of my obligation to put all poor men in good situations. Are they *my* poor? I tell thee, thou foolish philanthropist, that I grudge the dollar, the dime, the cent I give to such men as do not belong to me and to whom I do not belong. There is a class of persons to whom by all spiritual affinity I am bought and sold; for them I will go to prison if need be; but your miscellaneous popular charities; the education at college of fools; the building of meeting-houses to the vain end to which many now stand; alms to sots, and the thousand-fold Relief Societies; though I confess with shame I sometimes succumb and give the dollar, it is a wicked dollar, which by and by I shall have the manhood to withhold.

3    Virtues are, in the popular estimate, rather the exception than the rule. There is the man *and* his virtues. Men do what is called a good action, as some piece of courage or charity, much as they would pay a fine in expiation of daily non-appearance on parade. Their works are done as an apology or extenuation of their living in the world—as invalids and the insane pay a high board. Their virtues are penances. I do not wish to expiate, but to live. My life is for itself and not for

a spectacle. I much prefer that it should be of a lower strain, so it be genuine and equal, than that it should be glittering and unsteady. I wish it to be sound and sweet, and not to need diet and bleeding. I ask primary evidence that you are a man, and refuse this appeal from the man to his actions. I know that for myself it makes no difference whether I do or forbear those actions which are reckoned excellent. I cannot consent to pay for a privilege where I have intrinsic right. Few and mean as my gifts may be, I actually am, and do not need for my own assurance or the assurance of my fellows any secondary testimony.

## The World's Opinion

4      What I must do is all that concerns me, not what the people think. This rule, equally arduous in actual and in intellectual life, may serve for the whole disinction between greatness and meanness. It is the harder because you will always find those who think they know what is your duty better than you know it. It is easy in the world to live after the world's opinion; it is easy in solitude to live after our own; but the great man is he who in the midst of the crowd keeps with perfect sweetness the independence of solitude.

5      The objection to conforming to usages that have become dead to you is that it scatters your force. It loses your time and blurs the impression of your character. If you maintain a dead church, contribute to a dead Bible-society, vote with a great party either for the government or against it, spread your table like base housekeepers—under all these screens I have difficulty to detect the precise man you are: and of course so much force is withdrawn from your proper life. But do your work, and I shall know you. Do your work, and you shall reinforce yourself. A man must consider what a blindman's-buff is this game of conformity. If I know your sect I anticipate your argument. I hear a preacher announce for his text and topic the expediency of one of the institutions of his church. Do I not know beforehand that not possibly can he say a new and spontaneous word? Do I not know that with all this ostentation of examining the grounds of the institution he will do no such thing? Do I not know that he is pledged to himself not to look but at one side, the permitted side, not as a man, but as a parish minister? He is a retained attorney, and these airs of the bench are the emptiest affectation. Well, most men have bound their eyes with one or another handkerchief, and attached themselves to some one of these communities of opinion. This conformity makes them not false in a few particulars, authors of a few lies, but false in all particulars. Their every truth is not quite true. Their two is not the real two, their four not the real four; so that every word they say chagrins us and we know not where

to begin to set them right. Meantime nature is not slow to equip us in the prison-uniform of the party to which we adhere. We come to wear one cut of face and figure, and acquire by degrees the gentlest asinine expression. There is a mortifying experience in particular, which does not fail to wreak itself also in the general history; I mean "the foolish face of praise," the forced smile which we put on in company where we do not feel at ease, in answer to conversation which does not interest us. The muscles, not spontaneously moved but moved by a low usurping wilfulness, grow tight about the outline of the face, with the most disagreeable sensation.

6    For nonconformity the world whips you with its displeasure. And therefore a man must know how to estimate a sour face. The bystanders look askance on him in the public street or in the friend's parlor. If this aversion had its origin in contempt and resistance like his own he might well go home with a sad countenance; but the sour faces of the multitude, like their sweet faces, have no deep cause, but are put on and off as the wind blows and a newspaper directs. Yet is the discontent of the multitude more formidable than that of the senate and the college. It is easy enough for a firm man who knows the world to brook the rage of the cultivated classes. Their rage is decorous and prudent, for they are timid, as being very vulnerable themselves. But when to their feminine rage the indignation of the people is added, when the ignorant and the poor are aroused, when the unintelligent brute force that lies at the bottom of society is made to growl and mow, it needs the habit of magnanimity and religion to treat it godlike as a trifle of no concernment.

## Consistency

7    The other terror that scares us from self-trust is our consistency; a reverence for our past act or word because the eyes of others have no other data for computing our orbit than our past acts, and we are loth to disappoint them.

8    But why should you keep your head over your shoulder? Why drag about this corpse of your memory, lest you contradict somewhat you have stated in this or that public place? Suppose you should contradict yourself; what then? It seems to be a rule of wisdom never to rely on your memory alone, scarcely even in acts of pure memory, but to bring the past for judgment into the thousand-eyed present, and live ever in a new day. In your metaphysics you have denied personality to the Deity, yet when the devout motions of the soul come, yield to them heart and life, though they should clothe God with shape and color. Leave your theory, as Joseph his coat in the hand of the harlot, and flee.

9    A foolish consistency is the hobgoblin of little minds, adored by little statesmen and philosophers and divines. With consistency a great soul has simply nothing to do. He may as well concern himself with his shadow on the wall. Speak what you think now in hard words and tomorrow speak what tomorrow thinks in hard words again, though it contradict every thing you said today.—"Ah, so you shall be sure to be misunderstood."—Is it so bad then to be misunderstood? Pythagoras was misunderstood, and Socrates, and Jesus, and Luther, and Copernicus, and Galileo, and Newton, and every pure and wise spirit that ever took flesh. To be great is to be misunderstood.

## REVIEW

### Content

1. Consider such lines of Emerson's as "Nothing is at last sacred but the integrity of your own mind"; "No law can be sacred to me but that of my nature"; ". . . the only right is what is after my constitution; the only wrong what is against it." Would not anarchy result if all persons were to so live? And what about the need for tact and diplomacy, said to be necessary to "oil the wheels of society"?

2. What do you think of Emerson's arguments against consistency? How can the affairs of the world be conducted if what is taken for truth today may not be so seen tomorrow? And what is this about "To be great is to be misunderstood"? Can you think of contemporary examples to add to Emerson's? How do *you* view such persons?

### Rhetoric

3. Emerson's essays continue, a century later, to appeal to readers, not only for what he has to say but also because they are pleasant to read. Why? What various techniques does he use to make his points? Why is his writing vivid/colorful? How does he manage to *involve* his reader?

4. Emerson is known for his "quotable quotes," single-sentence epigrams that can make a powerful point standing alone. Find examples. What creates the effect, in each case?

### Projects

5. Consider yourselves living in a house together. Devise a common living problem to be resolved and agree on a resolution. If one of the group cannot make whatever compromises to individual liberty the common resolution requires, what is to happen to him/her? (Have one of the group role-play this position, if no one is naturally taking it.)

6. Select some important decision in your life, present or likely to come

in the future. Think about and then write about possible consequences *to you* of your clearly taking the responsibility for your own decision versus trying to conform to what you think "Society" is telling you to do.

# The Folsom Prison Letters

## ELDRIDGE CLEAVER and BEVERLY AXELROD

Eldridge Cleaver (1935–   ), Black Revolutionary, and Beverly Axelrod, his white female attorney, exchanged an unorthodox, and intense and poignant, correspondence during Cleaver's confinement in Folsom Prison. (Cleaver was originally arrested on a marijuana charge; Axelrod finally obtained his release at the end of nine years.) While in Folsom, Cleaver wrote *Soul on Ice* (1968), a very powerful "position paper" by a prototype Independent Black Man. The following letters of Cleaver and Axelrod appear in that book.

*Beverly Axelrod*
*Attorney-at-Law*
*San Francisco, California*
*September 10, 1965*

Dear Eldridge Cleaver:

1     . . . The need for expression is now upon me, having finished the legal matters, and I'm getting panicky. I'm not strong enough to take the safest course, which would be to not widen the subject matter of our correspondence, and I'm having a terrible time trying to say what I want knowing it will be read by the censors.

2     Your letter, which I keep rereading, shows you're going through the same turmoil I am; but I bear the onus of having allowed it. You talk about it being lethal, and then about life coming back—and I know that both are true.

3     I'm going purely on instinct now, which is not usual for me, but somehow I know I'm right, or maybe it's just that it's so important that I don't care about the risk of being wrong. Am I coming through to you? I'm writing I know in an obscure kind of way because of the damnable lack of privacy in our communications.

4    Believe this: I accept you. I know you little and I know you much, but whichever way it goes, I accept you. Your manhood comes through in a thousand ways, rare and wonderful. I'm out in the world, with an infinity of choices. You don't have to wonder if I'm grasping at something because I have no real measuring stick. I accept you.

5    About that other side of the record: Did you really think I didn't know? Another facet of the crystal might be an apter term; I have a few facets myself. I do not fear you. I know you will not hurt me. Your hatred is large, but not nearly so vast as you sometimes imagine; it can be used, but it can also be soothed and softened.

6    What an enormous amount of exploring we have to do! I feel as though I'm on the edge of a new world.

7    Memo to me: Be rational. It cannot be resolved. The choices: 1. He believes everything he says, but he cannot know, he has no choice; or 2. It's a beautiful put-on because he doesn't know that you would do exactly what you are doing for him anyway; or 3. It's a game to relieve the monotony, conscious or not. Answer: It doesn't make a damn bit of difference, because I can't find out, he can't find out, and it's too late anyway. The only important thing is to get him out, and that was obvious from the first letter, with all lawyerlike objectivity.

8    What an awesome thing it is to feel oneself on the verge of the possibility of really knowing another person. Can it ever happen? I'm not sure. I don't know that any two people can really strip themselves that naked in front of each other. We're so filled with fears of rejection and pretenses that we scarcely know whether we're being fraudulent or real ourselves.

9    Of all the dangers we share, probably the greatest comes from our fantasizing about each other. Are we making each other up? We have no way of testing the reality of it.

10    I can't write any more. I'm thunderstruck at having written this much. I'm afraid to read it over, because it's likely I would tear it up, so I'll send it as is. Can you imagine how much I haven't said?

Sincerely yours,
Beverly Axelrod

*Eldridge Cleaver*
*Folsom Prison*
*Represa, California*
*September 15, 1965*

Dear Beverly Axelrod:

11    Your letters to me are living pieces—chunks!—of you, and are the most important things in my life. This is fantastic. It only happens in books—or in the dreams of inmates of insane asylums—and with people who are for real. I share with you the awesome feeling of being on the verge of really knowing another person.

12   I place a great deal of emphasis on people really listening to each other, to what the person has to say, because one seldom encounters a person capable of taking either you or themselves seriously. But I was not *really* like this when I was out of prison—although the seeds were there, but there was too much confusion and madness mixed in. I was not too interested in communicating with other people—that is not true. What I mean is, I had a profound desire for communicating with and getting to know other people, but I was incapable of doing so, I didn't know how.

13   Do you know what shameless thought just bullied its way into my consciousness? That I deserve you, that I deserve to know you and to communicate with you, that I deserve to have all this happening. What have I done to merit this? I don't believe in the merit system. I Am That I Am. No, I will not hurt you.

14   Memo to us: 1. He believes everything he says and knows what he is saying; 2. Put-ons are cruel, and how could I be cruel to you? 3. He does not play games, and he does not find life monotonous, conscious or not. He has plans and dreams, and he is deadly serious. Answer: It makes every bit of difference, and I hope to help you find out, he is already finding out; taking it like you find it is a burn, it sells yourself short: be discerning and take only after you spot what you like—but I'm hoping that it is too late for you to flip over on me because it is certainly much too late for me.

15   Your thought, "Of all the dangers we share, probably the greatest comes from our fantasizing about each other. Are we making each other up?" bothers me. It would be very simple if that were the case: I could arrange (and how easy it would be!) to spend the rest of my life in prison and we could live happily ever after. But it is not that easy, is it? I seek a lasting relationship, something permanent in a world of change, in which all is transitory, ephemeral, and full of pain. We humans, we are too frail creatures to handle such titanic emotions and deep magnetic yearnings, strivings and impulses.

16   The reason two people are reluctant to really strip themselves naked in front of each other is because in doing so they make themselves vulnerable and give enormous power over themselves one to the other. How awful, how deadly, how catastrophically they can hurt each other, wreck and ruin each other forever! How often, indeed, they end by inflicting pain and torment upon each other. Better to maintain shallow, superficial affairs; that way the scars are not too deep, no blood is hacked from the soul. You beautifully—O, how beautifully!!—spoke, in your letter, of "What an awesome thing it is to feel oneself on the verge of the possibility of really knowing another person . . ." and "I feel as though I am on the edge of a new world." Getting to know someone, entering that new world, is an ultimate, irretrievable leap into the unknown. The prospect is terrifying. The stakes are high. The emotions are overwhelming. In human experience, only the perennial themes can

move us to such an extent. Death. Birth. The Grave. Love. Hate.

17    I do not believe that a beautiful relationship has to always end in carnage. I do not believe that we have to be fraudulent and pretentious, because that is the source of future difficulties and ultimate failure. If we project fraudulent, pretentious images, or if we fantasize each other into distorted caricatures of what we really are, then, when we awake from the trance and see beyond the sham and front, all will dissolve, all will die and transform into bitterness and hate. I know that sometimes people fake on each other out of genuine motives to hold onto the object of their tenderest feelings. They see themselves as so inadequate that they feel forced to wear a mask in order to continuously impress the other. I do not want to "hold" you, I want you to "stay" out of your own need for me.

18    I seek the profound. Contrary to the advice of the Prophet, I'll take the credit and let the cash go. What I feel for you is profound. Beverly, there is something happening between us that is way out of the ordinary. Ours is one for the books, for the poets to draw new inspiration from, one to silence the cynics, and one to humble us by reminding us of how little we know about human beings, about ourselves. I did not know that I had all these feelings inside me. They have never been aroused before. Now they cascade down upon my head and threaten to beat me down to the ground, into the dust. But because of the strength of the magnetic pull I feel toward you, I am not fazed and I know that I can stand against the tide.

19    I even respect you behind your back. I have a bad habit, when speaking of women while only men are present, of referring to women as bitches. This bitch this and this bitch that, you know. A while back I was speaking of you to a couple of cutthroats and I said, "this bitch . . ." And I felt very ashamed of myself about that. I passed judgment upon myself and suffered spiritually for days afterward. This may seem insignificant, but I attach great importance to it because of the chain of thought kicked off by it. I care about you, I am concerned about you, which is all very new for, and a sharp departure from, Eldridge X.

20    Your persistent query, "How can he tell? He has no choices," deserves an answer. But it is not the type of question that can be answered by words. It takes time and deeds, and this involves trust, it involves making ourselves vulnerable to each other, to strip ourselves naked, to become sitting ducks for each other—and if one of the ducks is shamming, then the sincere duck will pay in pain—but the deceitful duck, I feel, will be the loser. (If both ducks are shamming, what a lark, what a fiasco, what a put-on, what a despicable thought! I laugh at it because it has no power over me, I do not feel vulnerable to it, I feel protected by the flashing eyes of Portia. I extended my trust to you. I am vulnerable and defenseless and I make myself a duck for you.)

21    Listen: Your letter is very beautiful, and you came through with rock-

ets on. You came through and landed on your feet, with spiked shoes on, right on my heart. It is not that we are making each other up and it is not ourselves alone who are involved in what is happening to us. It is really a complex movement taking place of which we are mere parts. We represent historical forces and it is really these forces that are coalescing and moving toward each other. And it is not a fraud, forced out of desperation. We live in a disoriented, deranged social structure, and we have transcended its barriers in our own ways and have stepped psychologically outside its madness and repressions. It is lonely out here. We recognize each other. And, having recognized each other, is it any wonder that our souls hold hands and cling together even while our minds equivocate, hesitate, vacillate, and tremble?

Peace. Don't panic, and don't wake up.

Dream on. I am

Yours,
Eldridge

## REVIEW

### Content

1. Do you agree with paragraphs 8 and 16? Consider also, as you answer, the third sentence in paragraph 11. How does paragraph 19 tie in with this discussion? If you have had negative feelings about the revolutionary/outsider sort of person (like Eldridge Cleaver) in the past, does this paragraph begin to shift your perspective?

2. Paragraph 21 contains some profound ideas. What is Cleaver saying here—about his and Axelrod's contemporary world, about their relationship, and about the relation between that world and their relationship?

### Rhetoric

3. Do you find the correspondence exciting to read? If so, why? Is your response not only to the subject matter and the fact of the black-white relationship, but also to the styles of the two correspondents? What makes their writing powerful?

4. What special effect does Axelrod achieve in paragraph 7 (and Cleaver in 14) by setting up the paragraph as a "memo to me" composed of hypotheses and answers?

### Projects

5. Select some aspect of the relationship between Axelrod and Cleaver as revealed in their correspondence and write out your reaction to this aspect. Do you feel that you *understand* what is happening between them? If not, what puzzles you? What does your reaction to their

relationship tell you about how *you* relate to persons significant to you?

6. Write a letter to a sympathetic receiver in which you express your sincere feelings about something that really matters to you. Try to make the letter as powerful as possible, to help you see how much difference a sense of style can make even in a friendly letter.

# On the Way to Being Real

## BARRY STEVENS

Barry Stevens has contributed to the development of Fritz Perls' well known Gestalt psychology through applying its principles to her own life and then writing about her growth experiences. In 1967 Stevens collaborated with Carl Rogers, the humanistic psychologist, to produce the book *Person to Person: The Problem of Being Human*. In "On the Way to Being Real," Stevens exposes the problems caused by the conflicting role expectations with which we are confronted from childhood onward.

1   In the beginning, I was one person, knowing nothing but my own experience.

2   Then I was told things, and I became two people: the little girl who said how terrible it was that the boys had a fire going in the lot next door where they were roasting apples (which was what the women said)—and the little girl who, when the boys were called by their mothers to go to the store, ran out and tended the fire and the apples because she loved doing it.

3   So then there were two of I.

4   One I always doing something that the other I disapproved of. Or other I said what I disapproved of. All this argument in me so much.

5   In the beginning was I, and I was good.

6   Then came in other I. Outside authority. This was confusing. And then other I became *very* confused because there were so many different outside authorities.

7   Sit nicely. Leave the room to blow your nose. Don't do that, that's silly. Why, the poor child doesn't even know how to pick a bone! Flush

From *Person to Person: The Problem of Being Human* by Carl Rogers and Barry Stevens. Reprinted by permission of Real People Press, Box F, Moab, Utah 84532.

the toilet at night because if you don't it makes it harder to clean. DON'T FLUSH THE TOILET AT NIGHT—you wake people up! Always be nice to people. Even if you don't like them, you mustn't hurt their feelings. Be frank and honest. If you don't tell people what you think of them, that's cowardly. Butter knives. It is important to use butter knives. Butter knives? What foolishness! Speak nicely. Sissy! Kipling is wonderful! Ugh! Kipling (turning away).

8    The most important thing is to have a career. The most important thing is to get married. The hell with everyone. Be nice to everyone. The most important thing is sex. The most important thing is to have money in the bank. The most important thing is to have everyone like you. The most important thing is to dress well. The most important thing is to be sophisticated and say what you don't mean and don't let anyone know what you feel. The most important thing is to be ahead of everyone else. The most important thing is a black seal coat and china and silver. The most important thing is to be clean. The most important thing is to always pay your debts. The most important thing is not to be taken in by anyone else. The most important thing is to love your parents. The most important thing is to work. The most important thing is to be independent. The most important thing is to speak correct English. The most important thing is to be dutiful to your husband. The most important thing is to see that your children behave well. The most important thing is to go to the right plays and read the right books. The most important thing is to do what others say. And others say all these things.

9    All the time, I is saying, live with life. That is what is important.

10    But when I lives with life, other I says no, that's bad. All the different other I's say this. It's dangerous. It isn't practical. You'll come to a bad end. Of course . . . everyone felt that way once, the way you do, but *you'll learn!*

11    Out of all the other I's some are chosen as a pattern that is me. But there are all the other possibilities of patterns within what all the others say which come into me and become other I which is not myself, and sometimes these take over. Then who am I?

12    I does not bother about who am I. I *is,* and is happy being. But when I is happy being, other I says get to work, do something, do something worthwhile. I is happy doing dishes. "You're weird!" I is happy being with people saying nothing. Other I says talk. Talk, talk, talk. I gets lost.

13    I knows that things are to be played with, not possessed. I likes putting things together, lightly. Taking things apart, lightly. "You'll never have anything!" Making things of things in a way that the things themselves take part in, putting themselves together with surprise and delight to I. "There's no money in that!"

14    I is human. If someone needs, I gives. "You can't do that! You'll

never have anything for yourself! We'll have to support you!"

15   I loves. I loves in a way that other I does not know. I loves. "That's too warm for friends!" "That's too cool for lovers!" "Don't feel so bad, he's just a friend. It's not as though you loved him." "How can you let him go? I thought you loved him?" So cool the warm for friends and hot up the love for lovers, and I gets lost.

16   So both I's have a house and a husband and children and all that, and friends and respectability and all that, and security and all that, but both I's are confused because other I says, "You see? You're lucky," while I goes on crying. "What are you crying about? Why are you so ungrateful?" I doesn't know gratitude or ingratitude, and cannot argue. I goes on crying. Other I pushes it out, says "I am happy! I am very lucky to have such a fine family and a nice house and good neighbors and lots of friends who want me to do this, do that." I is not reasonable, either. I goes on crying.

17   Other I gets tired, and goes on smiling, because that is the thing to do. Smile, and you will be rewarded. Like the seal who gets tossed a piece of fish. Be nice to everyone and you will be rewarded. People will be nice to you, and you can be happy with that. You know they like you. Like a dog who gets patted on the head for good behavior. Tell funny stories. Be gay. Smile, smile, smile. . . . I is crying. . . . "Don't be sorry for yourself! Go out and do things for people!" "Go out and be with people!" I is still crying, but now, that is not heard and felt so much.

18   Suddenly: "What am I doing?" "Am I to go through life playing the clown?" "What am I doing, going to parties that I do not enjoy?" "What am I doing, being with people who bore me?" "Why am I so hollow and the hollowness filled with emptiness?" A shell. How has this shell grown around me? Why am I proud of my children and unhappy about their lives which are not good enough? Why am I disappointed? Why do I feel so much waste?

19   I comes through, a little. In moments. And gets pushed back by other I.

20   I refuses to play the clown any more. Which I is that? "She used to be fun, but now she thinks too much about herself." I lets friends drop away. Which I is that? "She's being too much by herself. That's bad. She's losing her mind." Which mind?

## REVIEW

### Content

1. Do you, whether you are female or male, identify with this piece? If so, spot all the specific points at which you identify and do some hard thinking about the implications for yourself in each instance.

2. What is the meaning of "good" in paragraph 5? If you agree with paragraph 5, how *can* paragraphs 5 and 6 be reconciled? To what degree should the individual human being attempt reconciliation? If you find paragraph 5 invalid and/or foolish, then how do you account for the experience of paragraph 6?

**Rhetoric**

3. What special effect does Stevens achieve by having the various I's speak to each other? Do you seem to "overhear" the "conversations"? What other specific devices does she use to achieve special effects?
4. What is the effect of the multi-repetition of "The most important thing is . . ." in paragraph 8? One would expect such repetition to become monotonous, thus losing its effectiveness. If that does not happen here, why not?

**Projects**

5. Write several (two or more) additional paragraphs reflecting various aspects of your own life, to follow Stevens' paragraph 15. Speak through *your* confused I's; that is, write in the first person. Try to make your expression highly personalized, as is Stevens', almost as if you were saying it all aloud. Your style need not imitate Stevens'.
6. Make a list of questions to your own life similar to Stevens' questions to hers in paragraph 18.


# The Woman I Was To Be

## SIMONE DE BEAUVOIR

Simone de Beauvoir, a Frenchwoman, has been writing and publishing her autobiography for a number of years, including *Memoirs of a Dutiful Daughter* (1958), *Force of Circumstance* (1960), and *All Said and Done* (1972). Her other major writings include *The Second Sex* (English edition, 1953), in which Beauvoir attempts to answer a myriad of questions about such issues as the identity of woman and the biological and societal forces that influence her development. In "The Woman I Was To Be," below, from *All Said and Done,* Beauvoir considers how differently her life might have gone had she been of a less independent nature.

1    All through my childhood and my young days, my life had a distinct meaning: its goal and its motive was to reach the adult age. At twenty, living does not mean getting ready to be forty. Yet for me, my duty as a child and an adolescent consisted of forming the woman I was to be tomorrow. My life in those days seemed to me an upward progress. It is true that nothing is gained without something being lost: everyone knows that in fulfilling oneself one necessarily sacrifices some possibilities. The adjustments carried out in a childish mind and body are harmful to those one would like to carry out later. The interests then formed thrust others out; and in me eagerness for knowledge overlaid a great many of them. The possession of an object takes away its newness. Regression in children means that they are sorry to grow up. For my part I lost my mother's caresses, I lost the carefree irresponsibility of my first years and my sense of wonder at the world's mysteries. Sometimes the future frightened me: was I one day to lead my mother's dull, gray kind of existence? Would my sister and I become strangers to one another? But generally speaking the balance was decidedly favorable. The only thing in my young days that was repugnant, scandalous in the strict sense, was death: I liked growing older. I was moving forward. Then later on, I wanted to escape from my family. For me, at that time, growing older meant both ripeness and freedom. Even in my gloomiest days my sanguine nature urged me to put my trust in the future. I believed in my star; I believed that what would happen to me could not but be good.

2    Many children and adolescents long for the grown-up state as they would long for a release. But others dread it. It was far harder for my friend Zaza to grow up than it was for me. The idea of leaving her mother wrung her heart. The magic of her childhood made her look upon her adolescence as gray and dreary, and the prospect of a "prudential" marriage horrified her. For a workingman's son, it is cruel to become a workingman in his turn—that is to say a man condemned to do nothing any more, other than carrying on with the same life. For my part, the idea of earning my own living by work I liked filled me with delight: all the more so since my being a woman seemed to foredoom me to dependence.

## My Family

3    What would have happened if the position of my family had been different? There are many suppositions I could make. Suppose in the first place that my parents, though ruined, had behaved differently: if

my mother had been less tactless and oppressive, the narrowness of her understanding would have troubled me less; resentment would not have overlaid my affection for her and I should have borne my father's withdrawal better. If my father, even without intervening in my struggle with my mother, had continued to interest himself in me, that would have helped a great deal. If he had openly taken my side, demanding that I should be allowed various kinds of freedom—and my mother would in that case have yielded—my life would have been so much the easier. I should still have been against their way of living and thinking, even if both had behaved in a friendly manner; I should still have more or less stifled at home and I should have felt myself isolated; but I should certainly not have felt rejected, thrust out, and betrayed. It would not have changed my destiny; but it would have spared me a great deal of pointless sadness. This is the only period of my life that has left me with regrets. As for the crisis of my awkward age, it was I who stirred it up; and it was fruitful; I tore myself away from the safe comfort of certainties through my love for the truth; and truth rewarded me. Between seventeen and twenty I was deeply hurt by my parents' attitude toward me; and it was a pain from which I derived no benefit whatsoever.

4    If they had kept their money, we should have lived more pleasantly; their mood would have been less gloomy. But I was eleven or twelve when their habit of mind changed for the worse, and by then I was already formed. My mother was so timorous and at the same time so despotic she would never have known how to discover diversions for us and she would have disliked letting us amuse ourselves without her. No doubt I would have spent more of my time in games and sports; the reason why I was so passionately devoted to croquet was that there was no other kind of amusement of that sort in my life. But then it would have been my make-believe games with my sister that would have been more or less sacrificed, certainly not my work or my reading. Even if I had been better dressed and therefore more at my ease, I should have loathed social gatherings. No: money would not have changed much in my childhood nor in my adolescence. And if I had not been obligated to take up a profession, I should still have succeeded in carrying on with my studies.

## Jacques

5    Only in one respect might the course of my life have been turned from its path, but that was an important one. I will not speculate on Jacques having married me without a fortune: he would have had to be so thoroughly unlike himself, so thoroughly another person, that

the hypothesis has no meaning. He would have taken more interest in me if I had been better dressed, more ornamental, and if I had had that ease which money generally gives. My poverty would not have been an impediment to the marriage he thought of at one time. Such as he was, he would willingly have married me if I had had a dowry. If he had proposed marriage before I met Sartre, how should I have reacted?

6    It is difficult to dream retrospectively about one's life: to make the dream valid one would have to control all the variables. Yet had my father been satisfied with his position he would not have seen me as the image of his failure and he would not have withdrawn from me; and even if I had been harassed and badgered by my mother, the house would not have seemed to me a hell nor Jacques a rescuer from it. Perhaps I should only have regarded him as a friend, and one whose faults I should not have overlooked. Even in those days, when I dreamed of sharing his life, that idea sometimes horrified me, I should have hesitated. Yet if he had spoken to me of love, then the emotion and the physical attraction that would have grown up between us would no doubt have persuaded me.

7    What if it had? Would Jacques have drunk less and would he have managed his affairs more intelligently? I do not believe that I should have filled the emptiness in him: he was not ready to receive what I had to bring. I should soon have discovered the poverty of his feelings, and he would not have satisfied me intellectually. I should have been very fond of him, however; and of the children we should have had. I should have experienced the torment that so many young women know, bound hand and foot by love and motherhood without having forgotten their former dreams.

## Studying and Writing

8    There is one thing that I am quite sure of, and that is that I should have dealt with that situation. My first eighteen years had made me into a person who could not possibly have betrayed them. It is impossible to imagine that I should have renounced my ambitions, my hopes, and all that was essential to give my life a meaning. At some given point I should have refused to bog down in the bourgeois way. Separated from Jacques or not, I should have returned to my studies, I should have written, and in the end I should certainly have drifted away from him. I should have had to overcome a great many difficulties; and it may be that confronting them would have been more valuable to me than the easy opportunities that were in fact my lot. More than one future can be imagined for the girl I was, although it is not in the

power of the woman she has now become to conceive herself as other than she is.

9       What real importance did Jacques have in my life? Far less than Zaza. My introduction to modern art and literature would certainly have taken place during my years at the Sorbonne, in any event. Thanks to him I did come to know the "poetry of the bars," and I went to them often; for me it was a valuable relief from pressure, but it was one that did not bring me a great deal. My relationship with Jacques meant more pain than joy. What he stood for in my youth was in fact its share of dreams. Before then I did not daydream much: Zaza, books, nature, and my plans were enough for me. But at eighteen, unhappy at home and maladjusted, I dreamed: not of being someone else but of sharing a life that seemed to me thrilling, like Jacques's. That dream lasted a long while, yet I never really believed in it entirely.

## Blinders

10      I lacked imagination, experience and discernment. I had a childish belief in what people said and I did not wonder at all about what they did not say. It was my own life that was impenetrable to me, and that at a time when I thought I saw the whole of it clear.

11      I was blinder still to the social and political context in which it was being formed. My story was typical of a French bourgeois girl belonging to a poor family. I had access to the consumer goods that my country and my period held out to me, insofar as they suited my parents' budget. What I should learn and what I should read was laid down for me by society.

12      To begin with I knew society only through my parents; then I came to know it more directly, but still without taking any interest in it. This want of concern was conditioned by the state of the world as it then was; it was the security of the years after the War that allowed me to worry so little about what was happening. My companions at the Sorbonne forced me to take at least some notice of current events. I came to understand the disgrace and the shame of colonialism. I was converted to internationalism and antimilitarism. I now accepted to the full the disquiet I had long felt for the fanaticism of the right wing, for racism, for the bourgeois values, and for every form of obscurantism. I was charmed by the idea of Revolution. I slid leftward: every candid intellectual must necessarily, in the name of universalism taught, wish for the abolition of classes. But my personal adventure meant more to me than the adventure of mankind as a whole. I did not realize how much the first depended on the second; and I continued to be very poorly informed about humanity.

# Sartre

13    How should I have developed if I had not met Sartre? The fact is that I did meet him and that was the most important event in my life.

14    I find it hard to decide how far our meeting was owing to chance. It was not entirely fortuitous. By going to the university I had given myself the greatest possible number of opportunities for such a meeting to take place: the ideal companion I dreamed of at fifteen had necessarily to be an intellectual, one who was as intensely eager as I was to understand the world. Then again, from my first days at the Sorbonne, my eyes and my ears had been on the alert to find the fellow student I could sympathize with most fully. And my generally open attitude won me friendly contacts.

15    Yet if Sartre had passed the *agrégation* a year earlier, and if I had sat for it a year later, should we never have known one another? Indeed, it has often occurred to us that if our meeting had not happened in 1929 it might well have come about later: the group of young left-wing teachers to which we belonged was not very large. In any case, I should have taken to writing; I should have seen a great deal of other writers, and because of his books I should have wanted to know Sartre. And because of the solidarity that bound anti-Nazi intellectuals together between 1943 and 1945, my wishes would have been realized. A bond, perhaps different but certainly very strong, would have been created between us.

16    Although to some extent it was chance that brought us into contact, the commitment that has bound our lives together was freely elected: a choice of this kind is not a decree but a long-term undertaking. For me it first came into evidence in the form of a practical decision, that of staying in Paris for two years instead of taking a post. I adopted Sartre's friendships and I moved into his world, not as some people have said because I am a woman, but because it was the world I had longed for for many years.

17    I took great care that our relationship should not deteriorate, gauging just what I should or should not accept from him or from myself, so that our understanding should not be endangered. I would have agreed, unwillingly though not despairingly, to his going to Japan. I am sure that two years later we should have come together again exactly as we had promised. One important decision was that of leaving for Marseilles rather than marrying him. In all other cases my resolutions coincided with my free-springing impulse: but not in this. I very strongly wished not to leave Sartre. I chose what was the hardest course for me at that moment in order to safeguard the future. This was the only time when it seems to me that I gave my life a wholesome change of direction and avoided a danger.

18    What would have happened if I had accepted his proposal? The supposition is meaningless. I was so made that I respected others. I knew Sartre did not want marriage. I could not want it all by myself. I did sometimes exert pressure on him in little things (and he on me), but I should never have been capable, even in thought, of forcing his hand in any serious matter. Supposing that for reasons I can scarcely imagine we had been obliged to marry, I know we should have managed to live our marriage in freedom.

19    Freedom: to what extent did I make use of it during the ten years that followed? How much did chance and circumstance step in? My relationship with Sartre remained living and immediate; I was not chained to a home and household cares; I did not feel myself indissolubly bound to my past. And I kept my eyes steadily on a future full of promise: I was going to be an author.

## Conclusions

20    All in all, my lot has been very fortunate. I have been frightened at times, and at times I have rebelled. But I have never suffered oppression; I have not known exile; nor have I been afflicted with any infirmity. I have not experienced the death of anyone essential to me and since I was twenty-one, I have never been lonely. The opportunities granted to me at the beginning helped me not only to lead a happy life but to be happy in the life I led. I have been aware of my shortcomings and my limits, but I have made the best of them. When I was tormented by what was happening in the world, it was the world I wanted to change, not the place I had in it.

21    "One is born manifold and one dies single," says Paul Valéry, in effect. The philosopher Henri Bergson too emphasizes that in fulfilling ourselves we lose most of our potentialities. That is not at all the way I see myself. Certainly when I was twelve I was tempted by paleontology, astronomy, history, and every fresh branch of learning I chanced upon; but they all formed part of the larger project of discovering the world, a project that I followed steadily. Very early the idea of writing made my future clear and luminous. To begin with I was amorphous, but I was not manifold. On the contrary, what strikes me is the way the little girl of three lived on, grown calmer, in the child of ten, that child in the young woman of twenty, and so forth. Of course, circumstances have caused me to develop in many respects. But through all my changes I still see myself.

22    Mine is a striking example of how dependent the individual is upon childhood. My early years allowed me to make a good start. After that it was my luck that no accident occurred to cut short the unfolding

of my life; another piece of good fortune was that chance favored me extraordinarily in placing Sartre upon my path. My freedom was used to maintain my very first projects; and it has continually devised and contrived ways of remaining faithful to them throughout the variation of circumstance. Sometimes these inventions have assumed the appearance of a decision, but of a decision that always seemed to me self-evident: I have never had to *ponder* important things. My life has been the fulfillment of a primary design; at the same time it has been the product and the expression of the world in which it developed.

# REVIEW

## Content

1. Consider how a single guiding vision helped to shape Beauvoir's life. Do you have such a single vision? If not, what sorts of questions might you ask yourself to help you find such an integrating goal?
2. In paragraph 16, Beauvoir seems very much in command of herself and in control of her own destiny, despite the ambivalence and apparent paradoxes. Is the paragraph in any way helpful to you? If so, why?

## Rhetoric

3. Beauvoir uses rhetorical questions as topic sentences for a number of her paragraphs (examples: 3, 9, 14). How does this device fulfill the purpose of a topic sentence? Is it an engaging device? Explain.
4. Variety in sentence structure and in sentence length is one characteristic that helps to make Beauvoir's style an interesting one and her writing a pleasure to read. Discuss in this context paragraph 2, for example.

## Projects

5. Reflect on several forming factors and/or events that have helped to shape your life to date. Then, get at least some of these down in sketchy outline form so that you can trace them out as influences, in a reflective essay. After you finish writing, think about whether you feel yourself headed in any directions in which you're not sure you want to go and, if so, what you can do about this.
Make a list of a variety of avenues you might try by which to expand your life toward some desired goal. Then tell the group about some of these avenues; if objections are raised to some of your avenues, how well do you persist in defending those avenues? Is this perhaps the same questions as: How independent are you capable of being?

# Awakening

## HERMANN HESSE

Hermann Hesse (1877–1962) was intended to follow in his father's footsteps as a Protestant missionary, but the young student rebelled against academe and became a writer, ultimately winning the Nobel Prize in literature in 1946. His novels deal mostly with the search for meaning in life and the resolution of the conflict between leading the contemplative and the active life. They include *The Journey to the East, Demian* (1919), *Siddhartha* (1922), *Steppenwolf* (1927), *Narcissus and Goldmund* (1930), and *The Glass Bead Game* (1943). As some of his titles suggest, Hesse was considerably influenced by Eastern thought, both through the missionary work of his parents and later during a trip to India in 1911. *Siddhartha,* from which the passage below comes, is the story of an Indian youth in search of answers about life, and especially his own. Siddhartha cannot simply accept the ideas of the adults of his world, but must work through to his own answers.

1   As Siddhartha left the grove in which the Buddha, the Perfect One, remained, in which Govinda remained, he felt that he had also left his former life behind him in the grove. As he slowly went on his way, his head was full of this thought. He reflected deeply, until this feeling completely overwhelmed him and he reached a point where he recognized causes; for to recognize causes, it seemed to him, is to think, and through thought alone feelings become knowledge and are not lost, but become real and begin to mature.

2   Siddhartha reflected deeply as he went on his way. He realized that he was no longer a youth; he was now a man. He realized that something had left him, like the old skin that a snake sheds. Something was no longer in him, something that had accompanied him right through his youth and was part of him: this was the desire to have teachers and to listen to their teachings. He had left the last teacher he had met, even he, the greatest and wisest teacher, the holiest, the Buddha. He had to leave him; he could not accept his teachings.

3   Slowly the thinker went on his way and asked himself: What is it that you wanted to learn from teachings and teachers, and although

they taught you much, what was it they could not teach you? And he thought: It was the Self, the character and nature of which I wished to learn. I wanted to rid myself of the Self, to conquer it, but I could not conquer it, I could only deceive it, could only fly from it, could only hide from it. Truly, nothing in the world has occupied my thoughts as much as the Self, this riddle, that I live, that I am one and am separated and different from everybody else, that I am Siddhartha; and about nothing in the world do I know less than about myself, about Siddhartha.

4    The thinker, slowly going on his way, suddenly stood still, gripped by this thought, and another thought immediately arose from this one. It was: The reason why I do not know anything about myself, the reason why Siddhartha has remained alien and unknown to myself is due to one thing, to one single thing—I was afraid of myself, I was fleeing from myself. I was seeking Brahman, Atman, I wished to destroy myself, to get away from myself, in order to find in the unknown innermost, the nucleus of all things, Atman, Life, the Divine, the Absolute. But by doing so, I lost myself on the way.

5    Siddhartha looked up and around him, a smile crept over his face, and a strong feeling of awakening from a long dream spread right through his being. Immediately he walked on again, quickly, like a man who knows what he has to do.

6    Yes, he thought breathing deeply, I will no longer try to escape from Siddhartha. I will no longer devote my thoughts to Atman and the sorrows of the world. I will no longer mutilate and destroy myself in order to find a secret behind the ruins. I will no longer study Yoga-Veda, Atharva-Veda, or asceticism, or any other teachings. I will learn from myself, be my own pupil; I will learn from myself the secret of Siddhartha.

7    He looked around him as if seeing the world for the first time. The world was beautiful, strange and mysterious. Here was blue, here was yellow, here was green, sky and river, woods and mountains, all beautiful, all mysterious and enchanting, and in the midst of it, he, Siddhartha, the awakened one, on the way to himself. All this, all this yellow and blue, river and wood, passed for the first time across Siddhartha's eyes. It was no longer the magic of Mara, it was no more the veil of Maya, it was no longer meaningless and the chance diversities of the appearances of the world, despised by deep-thinking Brahmins, who scorned diversity, who sought unity. River was river, and if the One and Divine in Siddhartha secretly lived in blue and river, it was just the divine art and intention that there should be yellow and blue, there sky and wood—and here Siddhartha. Meaning and reality were not hidden somewhere behind things, they were in them, in all of them.

8    How deaf and stupid I have been, he thought, walking on quickly.

When anyone reads anything which he wishes to study, he does not despise the letters and punctuation marks, and call them illusion, chance and worthless shells, but he reads them, he studies and loves them, letter by letter. But I, who wished to read the book of the world and the book of my own nature, did presume to despise the letters and signs. I called the world of appearances, illusion. I called my eyes and tongue, chance. Now it is over; I have awakened. I have indeed awakened and have only been born today.

9   But as these thoughts passed through Siddhartha's mind, he suddenly stood still, as if a snake lay in his path.

10   Then suddenly this also was clear to him: he, who was in fact like one who had awakened or was newly born, must begin his life completely afresh. When he left the Jetavana grove that morning, the grove of the Illustrious One, already awakened, already on the way to himself, it was his intention and it seemed the natural course for him after the years of his asceticism to return to his home and his father. Now, however, in that moment as he stood still, as if a snake lay in his path, this thought also came to him: I am no longer what I was, I am no longer an ascetic, no longer a priest, no longer a Brahmin. What then shall I do at home with my father? Study? Offer sacrifices? Practice meditation? All this is over for me now.

11   Siddhartha stood still and for a moment an icy chill stole over him. He shivered inwardly like a small animal, like a bird or a hare, when he realized how alone he was. He had been homeless for years and had not felt like this. Now he did feel it. Previously, when in deepest meditation, he was still his father's son, he was a Brahmin of high standing, a religious man. Now he was only Siddhartha, the awakened; otherwise nothing else. He breathed in deeply and for a moment he shuddered. Nobody was so alone as he. He was no nobleman, belonging to any aristocracy, no artisan belonging to any guild and finding refuge in it, sharing its life and language. He was no Brahmin, sharing the life of the Brahmins, no ascetic belonging to the Samanas. Even the most secluded hermit in the woods was not one and alone; he also belonged to a class of people. Govinda had become a monk and thousands of monks were his brothers, wore the same gown, shared his beliefs and spoke his language. But he, Siddhartha, where did he belong? Whose life would he share? Whose language would he speak?

12   At that moment, when the world around him melted away, when he stood alone like a star in the heavens, he was overwhelmed by a feeling of icy despair, but he was more firmly himself than ever. That was the last shudder of his awakening, the last pains of birth. Immediately he moved on again and began to walk quickly and impatiently, no longer homewards, no longer to his father, no longer looking backwards.

# REVIEW

## Content

1. A Buddhist proverb says: "You yourself must make the effort. The Buddhas are only teachers." When Siddhartha, trained in Buddhism, reaches the awareness stated in this proverb, he realizes he must leave the Master and his beloved friend Govinda. What things, exactly, does he come to realize?
2. Do you agree with Siddhartha that it is a mistake to try to conquer one's self by trying to avoid that self—through repression, self-deception, deliberate turning away from it, and so on? If this does not work, why? How, *exactly*, on the other hand, might Siddhartha henceforth go about "learning from himself the secret of Siddhartha"?

## Rhetoric

3. Hesse writes in a relatively simple, straightforward style. What helps to make his prose easy and pleasant to read? Consider, among other things, his use of questions and of parallelism (equal elements expressed equally, in a series).
4. Paragraphs 7, 11, and 12 begin with vivid description. Analyze these descriptive passages, pointing out particularly effective nouns, adjectives, verbs, and similes (word-pictures created by expressed comparisons).

## Projects

5. Have you experienced such a turning-point moment like Siddhartha's—having to do with any critical decision and/or period in your life? If you have, describe it in a paper; include what you *felt*, as well as what you were thinking as the experience occurred. Some descriptive writing, similar to Hesse's, might help to "set the mood" for your presentation.
6. Are there influences in your life—in the form of individual persons, institutions, or whatever—which you perhaps should be leaving behind? If there are, are you *ready* to move away from them? If so, how will you release yourself from them? Make a paper out of your thinking through of these questions.

# Notes from Underground

## FËDOR DOSTOEVSKI

Fëdor Dostoevski (1821–1881) was a Russian novelist whose works are concerned largely with man's spiritual and psychological sufferings and strivings, as their titles often reflect: *The Double* (1846), *Crime and Punishment* (1866), *The Idiot* (1869), *The Possessed* (1871). His *Memoirs of the House of the Dead* (1861–1862) echo Dostoevski's own experiences during four years in a Siberian prison, where he had been confined for supporting reform socialistic activities. *The Brothers Karamazov* (1879–1880), his final novel, is generally considered his masterpiece. In 1864 Dostoevski published the semi-autobiographical short novel *Notes from Underground*, from which the following passage comes; here Dostoevski argues the conflicts that arise among man's self-interest, his reason, and his will.

1   Who was it that first said that man does nasty things only because he doesn't know where his real interests lie, that if he were enlightened about his true interests, he would immediately stop acting like a pig and become kind and noble? Being enlightened, the argument goes on, and seeing where his real advantage lay, he would realize that it was in acting virtuously. And, since it is well established that a man will not act deliberately against his own interests, it follows that he would have no choice but to become good. Oh, the innocence of it! Since when, in these past thousands of years, has man acted exclusively out of self-interest? What about the millions of facts that show that men, deliberately and in full knowledge of what their real interests were, spurned them and rushed in a different direction? They did so at their own risk without anyone advising them, refusing to follow the safe, well-trodden path and searching for another path, a difficult one, an unreasonable one, stubbornly working their way along it in the darkness. Doesn't this suggest that stubbornness and willfulness were stronger in these people than their interests?

2     Interest! What interest? Can you define exactly what is in the interest of a human being? And suppose the interest of a man is not only consistent with but even demands something harmful rather than advantageous? Of course, if such an instance *is* possible, then the whole rule is nothing but dust. Now you tell me—is such an instance possible? You may laugh if you wish, but I want you to answer me this: is there an accurate scale of human advantages? Aren't there any advantages that

are omitted, that cannot possibly be included in any such scale? As far as I can make out, you've based your scale of advantages on statistical averages and scientific formulas thought up by economists. And since your scale consists of such advantages as happiness, prosperity, freedom, security, and all that, a man who deliberately disregarded that scale would be branded by you—and by me too, as a matter of fact—as an obscurantist and as utterly insane. But what is really remarkable is that all of your statisticians, sages, and humanitarians, when listing human advantages, insist on leaving out one of them. They never even allow for it, thus invalidating all their calculations. One would think it would be easy just to add it to the list. But that's where the trouble lies—it doesn't fit into any scale or chart.

3    You see, ladies and gentlemen, I have a friend—of course, he's your friend, too, and, in fact, everyone's friend. When he's about to do something, this friend explains pompously and in detail how he must act in accordance with the precepts of justice and reason. Moreover, he becomes passionate as he expostulates upon human interests; heaps scorn on the shortsighted fools who don't know what virtue is or what's good for them. Then, exactly fifteen minutes later, without any apparent external cause, but prompted by something inside him that is stronger than every consideration of interest, he pirouettes and starts saying exactly the opposite of what he was saying before; that is, he discredits the laws of logic and his own advantage; in short, he attacks everything. . . .

4    Now, since my friend is a composite type, he cannot be dismissed as an odd individual. So perhaps there is something that every man values above the highest individual advantage, or (not to be illogical) there may exist a human advantage that is the most advantageous (and it is precisely the one that is so consistently left out), which is also more important than the others and for the sake of which a man, if need be, will go against reason, honor, security, and prosperity—in short, against all the beautiful and useful things—just to attain it, the most advantageous advantage of the lot, the one which is the dearest to him.

5    "So," you may interrupt me, "it's an advantage all the same."

6    Wait a minute. Let me make myself clear. It's not a question of words. The remarkable thing about this advantage is that it makes a shambles of all the classifications and tables drawn up by humanitarians for the happiness of mankind. It crowds them out, as it were. But before I name this advantage, let me go on record and declare that all these lovely systems, all these theories that explain to man what is to his true advantage so that, to achieve it, he will forthwith become good and noble—all these are, in my opinion, nothing but sterile exercises in logic. Yes, that's all there is to it. For instance, propounding the theory of human regeneration through the pursuit of self-interest is, in my opin-

ion, almost like . . . well, like saying with H. T. Buckle that man mellows under the influence of civilization and becomes less bloodthirsty and less prone to war. He appears to be following logical reasoning in arriving at that conclusion. But men love abstract reasoning and neat systematization so much that they think nothing of distorting the truth, closing their eyes and ears to contrary evidence to preserve their logical constructions. I'd say the example I've taken here is really too glaring. You have only to look around you and you'll see blood being spilled, and in the most playful way, just as if it were champagne. Look at the United States, that indissoluble union, plunged into civil war! Look at the Schleswig-Holstein farce . . . And what is it in us that is mellowed by civilization? All it does, I'd say, is to develop in man a capacity to feel a greater variety of sensations. And nothing, absolutely nothing else. And through this development, man will yet learn how to enjoy bloodshed. Why, it has already happened. Have you noticed, for instance, that the most refined, bloodthirsty tyrants, compared to whom the Attilas and Stenka Razins are mere choirboys, are often exquisitely civilized? In fact, if they are not overtly conspicuous, it is because there are too many of them and they have become too familiar to us. Civilization has made man, if not always more bloodthirsty, at least more viciously, more horribly bloodthirsty. In the past, he saw justice in bloodshed and slaughtered without any pangs of conscience those he felt had to be slaughtered. Today, though we consider bloodshed terrible, we still practice it—and on a much larger scale than ever before. It was said that Cleopatra—please forgive me this example from ancient history— enjoyed sticking golden pins into the breasts of her slaves, delighting in their screams and writhings. You may object that this happened in relatively barbarous times; or you may say that even now we live in barbarous times (also relatively), that pins are still stuck into people, that even today, although man has learned to be more discerning than in ancient times, he has yet to learn how to follow his reason.

7    Nevertheless, there's no doubt in your mind that he will learn as soon as he's rid of certain bad old habits and when common sense and science have completely reeducated human nature and directed it along the proper channels. You seem certain that man himself will give up erring *of his own free will* and will stop opposing his will to his interests. You say, moreover, that sience itself will teach man (although I say it's a luxury) that he has neither will nor whim—never had as a matter of fact—that he is something like a piano key or an organ stop; that, on the other hand, there are natural laws in the universe, and whatever happens to him happens outside his will, as it were, by itself, in accordance with the laws of nature. Therefore, all there is left to do is to discover these laws and man will no longer be responsible for his acts. Life will be really easy for him then. All human acts will be listed in

something like logarithm tables, say up to the number 108,000, and transferred to a timetable. Or, better still, catalogues will appear, designed to help us in the way our dictionaries and encyclopedias do. They will carry detailed calculations and exact forecasts of everything to come, so that no adventure and no action will remain possible in this world.

8      Then—it is still you talking—new economic relations will arise, relations ready-made and calculated in advance with mathematical precision, so that all possible questions instantaneously disappear because they receive all the possible answers. Then the utopian palace of crystal will be erected; then . . . well, then, those will be the days of bliss.

9      Of course, you can't guarantee (it's me speaking now) that it won't be deadly boring (for what will there be to do when everything is predetermined by timetables?) But, on the other hand, everything will be planned very reasonably.

10      But then, one might do anything out of boredom. Golden pins are stuck into people out of boredom. But that's nothing. What's really bad (this is me speaking again) is that the golden pins will be welcomed then. The trouble with man is that he's stupid. Phenomenally stupid. That is, even if he's not really stupid, he's so ungrateful that another creature as ungrateful cannot be found. I, for one, wouldn't be the least surprised if, in that future age of reason, there suddenly appeared a gentleman with an ungrateful, or shall we say retrogressive smirk, who, arms akimbo, would say:

11      "What do you say, folks, let's send all this reason to hell, just to get all these logarithm tables out from under our feet and go back to our own stupid ways."

12      That isn't so annoying in itself; what's bad is that this gentleman would be sure to find followers. That's the way man is made.

13      And the explanation for it is so simple that there hardly seems to be any need for it—namely, that a man, always and everywhere, prefers to act in the way he feels like acting and not in the way his reason and interest tell him, for it is very possible for a man to feel like acting against his interests and, in some instances, I say that he *positively* wants to act that way—but that's my personal opinion.

14      So one's own free, unrestrained choice, one's own whim, be it the wildest, one's own fancy, sometimes worked up to a frenzy—that is the most advantageous advantage that cannot be fitted into any table or scale and that causes every system and every theory to crumble into dust on contact. And where did these sages pick up the notion that man must have something that they feel is a normal and virtuous set of wishes; what makes them think that man's will must be reasonable and in accordance with his own interests? All man actually needs is *independent* will, at all costs and whatever the consequences.

# REVIEW

## Content

1. Do you agree that a person sometimes acts in ways that would not seem to be in his/her real best interests? If not, why do we sometimes hear, "Now *why* did she do *that?*" or "What a *foolish* thing to do!" ("foolish" meaning "not reasonable")? If you disagree with Dostoevski's argument, then explain nonpsychotic behavior that appears to be bizarre.
2. *Is* "one's own free, unrestrained choice . . . the *independent* will, at all costs and whatever the consequence . . . the most advantageous advantage" a person can have? If so, why? If not, why not?

## Rhetoric

3. Dostoevski writes "Notes" in what reads like the speaking voice—a voice speaking in a forceful rush, almost breathless, that carries the reader headlong toward the conclusion of the argument being developed. Read a passage aloud, to hear this happening. What about Dostoevski's style helps to create this effect?
4. Much of the power of Dostoevski's argument is achieved through the buildup of suspense. By what specific techniques does he develop this suspense and what delaying devices does he use to prolong it?

## Projects

5. Think of a time when you have done what appeared to others—and even perhaps to yourself—something foolish. Did you see yourself then as *choosing* that route? If not, can you now analyze it as chosen behavior? If not, *why* did you so act? Work up your analysis into a paper.
6. Relate some incident in a narrative in which you find *your* "speaking voice" and build suspense through using that voice. Use some delaying devices to heighten the suspense, if you like.

# What I Have Lived For

## BERTRAND RUSSELL

Bertrand Russell (1872–1970) was a well-known British philosopher, author, and mathematician. A humanitarian of liberal and pacifist persuasion, he devoted himself during his long lifetime to many controversial causes, among them free love and conscientious objection to military service. Russell taught in the late 1930s and early 1940s at several American universities, where some of his teaching appointments were later cancelled because of his position on morality. Russell's many books include *An Inquiry into Meaning and Truth* (1940), *Unpopular Essays* (1950), and *New Hopes for a Changing World* (1951); he won the Nobel Prize in literature in 1950. A simple yet profoundly moving statement by Russell about what values have been central to his life follows, in an excerpt from *The Autobiography of Bertrand Russell: 1872–1914.*

1    Three passions, simple but overwhelmingly strong, have governed my life: the longing for love, the search for knowledge, and unbearable pity for the suffering of mankind. These passions, like great winds, have blown me hither and thither, in a wayward course, over a deep ocean of anguish, reaching to the very verge of despair.

2    I have sought love, first, because it brings ecstasy—ecstasy so great that I would often have sacrificed all the rest of life for a few hours of this joy. I have sought it, next, because it relieves loneliness—that terrible loneliness in which one shivering consciousness looks over the rim of the world into the cold unfathomable lifeless abyss. I have sought it, finally, because in the union of love I have seen, in a mystic miniature, the prefiguring vision of the heaven that saints and poets have imagined. This is what I sought, and though it might seem too good for human life, this is what—at last—I have found.

3    With equal passion I have sought knowledge. I have wished to understand the hearts of men. I have wished to know why the stars shine. And I have tried to apprehend the Pythagorean power by which number holds sway above the flux. A little of this, but not much, I have achieved.

4    Love and knowledge, so far as they were possible, led upward toward

the heavens. But always pity brought me back to earth. Echoes of cries of pain reverberate in my heart. Children in famine, victims tortured by oppressors, helpless old people a hated burden to their sons, and the whole world of loneliness, poverty, and pain make a mockery of what human life should be. I long to alleviate the evil, but I cannot, and I too suffer.

5    This has been my life. I have found it worth living, and would gladly live it again if the chance were offered me.

## REVIEW

### Content

1. Why do you suppose both love and knowledge are so important to Russell? Why would not one passion or the other suffice for a man's life?
2. Russell speaks of what might be called two happy passions and one sad one. What does his third passion contribute to his life? Do you think he would have had a better life without it?

### Rhetoric

3. Discuss Russell's essay in the light of the generally accepted definition of a model essay: an introductory paragraph establishing three major points to be developed; the development of those points in three separate paragraphs, making up the body of the essay; and a concluding summary paragraph.
4. Triads (items occurring in threes) are, for some reason, particularly pleasing to the human mind and the human ear. Can you locate a number of triads in Russell's essay? Listen to them aloud as well as thinking about them.

### Projects

5. Write an essay about your own feelings or beliefs—what is central to your life—like Russell's essay, choosing three main points and using the triad device as you develop those points.
6. Discuss with a relative or a friend what is important in life to that person and write an essay statement for him/her, using the same structure as in Question 5. Then, check out the essay with the other person, to discover how well you were listening and how well you can relate what you hear.

# The Rewards of Living a Solitary Life

## MAY SARTON

May Sarton (1912–   ), a poet and author, was born in Belgium, but came to the United States as a child and now lives in Maine. She has won several awards and scholarships in poetry. Sarton has written many books during a long writing career, including *Encounter in April* (1937), *In Time Like Air* (1957), *Shower of Summer Days* (1970), and *Kinds of Love* (1972). The titles of some of her poetry collections suggest the Sarton of the essay below: *Inner Landscape* (1939), *The Land of Silence* (1953), *A Durable Fire* (1972). In 1973 Sarton published the autobiographical *Journal of a Solitude*.

*York, Maine*

1   The other day an acquaintance of mine, a gregarious and charming man, told me he had found himself unexpectedly alone in New York for an hour or two between appointments. He went to the Whitney [Museum of American Art] and spent the "empty" time looking at things in solitary bliss. For him it proved to be a shock nearly as great as falling in love to discover that he could enjoy himself so much alone.

2   What had he been afraid of, I asked myself? That, suddenly alone, he would discover that he bored himself, or that there was, quite simply, no self there to meet? But having taken the plunge, he is now on the brink of adventure; he is about to be launched into his own inner space, space as immense, unexplored and sometimes frightening as outer space to the astronaut.

3   His every perception will come to him with a new freshness and, for a time, seem startlingly original. For anyone who can see things for himself with a naked eye becomes, for a moment or two, something of a genius.

4   With another human being present vision becomes double vision, inevitably. We are busy wondering, what does my companion see or think of this, and what do I think of it? The original impact gets lost, or diffused.

5   "Music I heard with you was more than music." Exactly. And therefore music *itself* can only be heard alone. Solitude is the salt of personhood. It brings out the authentic flavor of every experience.

6   "Alone one is never lonely: the spirit adventures, waking/In a quiet garden in a cool house, abiding single there."

7   Loneliness is most acutely felt with other people, for with others, even with a lover sometimes, we suffer from our differences, differences of taste, temperament, mood. Human intercourse often demands that we soften the edge of perception, or withdraw at the very instant of personal truth for fear of hurting, or of being inappropriately present, which is to say naked, in a social situation. Alone we can afford to be wholly whatever we are, and to feel whatever we feel absolutely. That is a great luxury!

8   For me the most interesting thing about a solitary life, and mine has been that for the last twenty years, is that it becomes increasingly rewarding. When I can wake up and watch the sun rise over the ocean, as I do most days, and know that I have an entire day ahead, uninterrupted, in which to write a few pages, take a walk with my dog, lie down in the afternoon for a long think (why does one think better in a horizontal position?), read and listen to music, I am flooded with happiness.

9   I am lonely only when I am overtired, when I have worked too long without a break, when for the time being I feel empty and need filling up. And I am lonely sometimes when I come back home after a lecture trip, when I have seen a lot of people and talked a lot, and am full to the brim with experience that needs to be sorted out.

10  Then for a little while the house feels huge and empty, and I wonder where my self is hiding. It has to be recaptured slowly by watering the plants, perhaps, and looking again at each one as though it were a person, by feeding the two cats, by cooking a meal.

11  It takes a while, as I watch the surf blowing up in fountains at the end of the field, but the moment comes when the world falls away, and the self emerges again from the deep unconscious, bringing back all I have recently experienced to be explored and slowly understood, when I can converse again with my own hidden powers, and so grow, and so be renewed, till death do us part.

## REVIEW

### Content

1. Did the *title* of the essay startle you? If so, why? Does our culture *encourage* solitude? Do *you* dread "empty" time?
2. Consider especially paragraph 4. And paragraph 7. Do you agree with Sarton's points in these paragraphs?

**Rhetoric**

3. In this reflective personal essay, Sarton seems almost to be thinking certain passages out loud to herself, as she muses. Find some of these passages and analyze what makes them sound "reflective."
4. The poet in Sarton comes through in her prose perhaps most clearly in certain single sentences full of meaning and so memorable that they tend to linger in one's head as good lines of poetry do. Can you find some such lines in this essay?

**Projects**

5. One of the dilemmas the human being has to resolve is the conflict between one's need to be alone and his/her need to be with others (a question Sarton explores at length in her *Journal of a Solitude*). Talk among yourselves about how each of you resolves this conflict. Can you help each other improve your own methods of dealing with the dilemma?
6. Alfred Whitehead once said that "a person's religion is what he does with his solitude." Develop this statement into a paper about yourself, using the word "religion" in the sense of what is important to you.

# The Myth of Sisyphus

## ALBERT CAMUS

Albert Camus (1913–1960), born in French Algiers, was a novelist, dramatist and essayist. During World War II he moved to Paris, where he became active with the French Underground in resisting the Germans, and where he also established himself as a brilliant member of the circle of European Existentialists. He won the Nobel Prize in literature in 1957. Camus' novels include *The Stranger* (1942), *The Plague* (1947), *The Fall* (1956), and *A Happy Death* (1972). In addition, he published short stories and several collections of essays, including *The Rebel* (1952) and *Exile and the Kingdom* (1958). Perhaps his best-known essay, from the book of the same title, *The Myth of Sisyphus* (1942), appears below. Camus once stated that the real philosophical question which man must confront is the question of suicide. And that once man decides against suicide, chooses *not* to give up, his task is to somehow create meaning in the life he has chosen to continue.

1    The gods had condemned Sisyphus to ceaselessly rolling a rock to the top of a mountain, whence the stone would fall back of its own weight. They had thought with some reason that there is no more dreadful punishment than futile and hopeless labor.

2    If one believes Homer, Sisyphus was the wisest and most prudent of mortals. According to another tradition, however, he was disposed to practice the profession of highwayman. I see no contradiction in this. Opinions differ as to the reasons why he became the futile laborer of the underworld. To begin with, he is accused of a certain levity in regard to the gods. He stole their secrets. Aegina, the daughter of Aesopus, was carried off by Jupiter. The father was shocked by that disappearance and complained to Sisyphus. He, who knew of the abduction, offered to tell about it on condition that Aesopus would give water to the citadel of Corinth. To the celestial thunderbolts he preferred the benediction of water. He was punished for this in the underworld. Homer tells us also that Sisyphus had put Death in chains. Pluto could not endure the sight of his deserted, silent empire. He dispatched the god of war, who liberated Death from the hands of her conqueror.

3    It is said also that Sisyphus, being near to death, rashly wanted to test his wife's love. He ordered her to cast his unburied body into the middle of the public square. Sisyphus woke up in the underworld. And there, annoyed by an obedience so contrary to human love, he obtained from Pluto permission to return to earth in order to chastise his wife. But when he had seen again the face of this world, enjoyed water and sun, warm stones and the sea, he no longer wanted to go back to the infernal darkness. Recalls, signs of anger, warnings were of no avail. Many years more he lived facing the curve of the gulf, the sparkling sea, and the smiles of earth. A decree of the gods was necessary. Mercury came and seized the impudent man by the collar and, snatching him from his joys, led him forcibly back to the underworld, where his rock was ready for him.

4    You have already grasped that Sisyphus is the absurd hero. He *is,* as much through his passions as through his torture. His scorn of the gods, his hatred of death, and his passion for life won him that unspeakable penalty in which the whole being is exerted toward accomplishing nothing. This is the price that must be paid for the passions of this earth. Nothing is told us about Sisyphus in the underworld. Myths are made for the imagination to breathe life into them. As for this myth, one sees merely the whole effort of a body straining to raise the huge stone, to roll it and push it up a slope a hundred times over; one sees the face screwed up, the cheek tight against the stone, the shoulder bracing the clay-covered mass, the foot wedging it, the fresh start with arms outstretched, the wholly human security of two earth-clotted hands. At the very end of his long effort measured by skyless space and time without depth, the purpose is achieved. Then Sisyphus watches the stone

rush down in a few moments toward that lower world whence he will have to push it up again toward the summit. He goes back down to the plain.

5    It is during that return, that pause, that Sisyphus interests me. A face that toils so close to stones is already stone itself! I see that man going back down with a heavy yet measured step toward the torment of which he will never know the end. That hour like a breathing-space which returns as surely as his suffering, that is the hour of consciousness. At each of those moments when he leaves the heights and gradually sinks toward the lairs of the gods, he is superior to his fate. He is stronger than his rock.

6    If this myth is tragic, that is because its hero is conscious. Where would his torture be, indeed, if at every step the hope of succeeding upheld him? The workman of today works every day in his life at the same tasks, and this fate is no less absurd. But it is tragic only at the rare moments when it becomes conscious. Sisyphus, proletarian of the gods, powerless and rebellious, knows the whole extent of his wretched condition: it is what he thinks of during his descent. The lucidity that was to constitute his torture at the same time crowns his victory. There is no fate that cannot be surmounted by scorn.

7    If the descent is thus sometimes performed in sorrow, it can also take place in joy. This word is not too much. Again I fancy Sisyphus returning toward his rock, and the sorrow was in the beginning. When the images of earth cling too tightly to memory, when the call of happiness becomes too insistent, it happens that melancholy rises in man's heart: this is the rock's victory, this is the rock itself. The boundless grief is too heavy to bear. These are our nights of Gethsemane. But crushing truths perish from being acknowledged. Thus, Oedipus at the outset obeys fate without knowing it. But from the moment he knows, his tragedy begins. Yet at the same moment, blind and desperate, he realizes that the only bond linking him to the world is the cool hand of a girl. Then a tremendous remark rings out: "Despite so many ordeals, my advanced age and the nobility of my soul make me conclude that all is well." Sophocles' Oedipus, like Dostoevsky's Kirilov, thus gives the recipe for the absurd victory. Ancient wisdom confirms modern heroism.

8    One does not discover the absurd without being tempted to write a manual of happiness. "What! by such narrow ways—?" There is but one world, however. Happiness and the absurd are two sons of the same earth. They are inseparable. It would be a mistake to say that happiness necessarily springs from the absurd discovery. It happens as well as that the feeling of the absurd springs from happiness. "I conclude that all is well," says Oedipus, and that remark is sacred. It echoes in the wild and limited universe of man. It teaches that all is not, has not been, exhausted. It drives out of this world a god who had come into it with

dissatisfaction and a preference for futile sufferings. It makes of fate a human matter, which must be settled among men.

9     All Sisyphus' silent joy is contained therein. His fate belongs to him. His rock is his thing. Likewise, the absurd man, when he contemplates his torment, silences all the idols. In the universe suddenly restored to its silence, the myriad wondering little voices of the earth rise up. Unconscious, secret calls, invitations from all the faces, they are the necessary reverse and price of victory. There is no sun without shadow, and it is essential to know the night. The absurd man says yes and his effort will henceforth be unceasing. If there is a personal fate, there is no higher destiny, or at least there is but one which he concludes is inevitable and despicable. For the rest, he knows himself to be the master of his days. At that subtle moment when man glances backward over his life, Sisyphus returning toward his rock, in that slight pivoting he contemplates that series of unrelated actions which becomes his fate, created by him, combined under his memory's eye and soon sealed by his death. Thus, convinced of the wholly human origin of all that is human, a blind man eager to see who knows that the night has no end, he is still on the go. The rock is still rolling.

10     I leave Sisyphus at the foot of the mountain! One always finds one's burden again. But Sisyphus teaches the higher fidelity that negates the gods and raises rocks. He too concludes that all is well. This universe henceforth without a master seems to him neither sterile nor futile. Each atom of that stone, each mineral flake of that night-filled mountain, in itself forms a world. The struggle itself toward the heights is enough to fill a man's heart. One must imagine Sisyphus happy.

## REVIEW

### Content

1. In sentence 3 of paragraph 4, Camus refers to what kept Sisyphus back on earth, once returned from the underworld, despite the "recalls." How, then, does Camus show Sisyphus *continuing* to prove himself when confronted with the rock? In what sense is the hour of descent down the mountain a "victory"? Why does Camus say that Sisyphus is sometimes "stronger than his rock"? Camus writes elsewhere, "In the midst of winter, I finally learned there was in me an invincible summer." Discuss this statement in the light of "Sisyphus."

2. One purpose of myths is to help human beings live by offering explanations for certain kinds of difficulties they encounter. How can Camus' extension of the original Sisyphus myth help one live?

## Rhetoric

3. Camus is known as a master stylist. How does his interspersing long sentences with short, simple ones contribute to his effectiveness? Locate some good descriptive passages. Consider how he uses humor, both directly and subtly. And how he uses irony.
4. Camus' epigrams (brief, pithy sayings) are often used on posters, quoted by other writers, and so on. Find some epigrams in the above selection that *you* can use in your life. Why are they easy to memorize? What does this fact tell you about Camus' style?

## Projects

5. Try your hand at writing epigrams—which you may prefer to call serious graffiti.
6. Camus ends "The Myth of Sisyphus" with "The struggle itself toward the heights is enough to fill a man's heart." If you agree that this statement is true of life, develop it into a paper; explain what you think the statement means; and use examples of "struggle(s) toward the heights" that appear to be fulfilling for one or more persons you know, including, possibly, yourself.

# 3
# New Voices

# What Is Poverty?

## JO GOODWIN PARKER

Jo Goodwin Parker does not want autobiographical material to accompany her statement about poverty, which appeared in George Henderson's *America's Other Children: Public Schools Outside Suburbia* (1971). Parker offers her searing definition of poverty in very direct terms, supported by her own life experiences.

1  You ask me what is poverty? Listen to me. Here I am, dirty, smelly, and with no "proper" underwear on and with the stench of my rotting teeth near you. I will tell you. Listen to me. Listen without pity. I cannot use your pity. Listen with understanding. Put yourself in my dirty, worn out, ill-fitting shoes, and hear me.

2  Poverty is getting up every morning from a dirt- and illness-stained mattress. The sheets have long since been used for diapers. Poverty is living in a smell that never leaves. This is a smell of urine, sour milk, and spoiling food sometimes joined with the strong smell of long-cooked onions. Onions are cheap. If you have smelled this smell, you did not know how it came. It is the smell of the outdoor privy. It is the smell of young children who cannot walk the long dark way in the night. It is the smell of the mattresses where years of "accidents" have happened. It is the smell of the milk which has gone sour because the refrigerator long has not worked, and it costs money to get it fixed. It is the smell of rotting garbage. I could bury it, but where is the shovel? Shovels cost money.

3  Poverty is being tired. I have always been tired. They told me at the hospital when the last baby came that I had chronic anemia caused from poor diet, a bad case of worms, and that I needed a corrective operation. I listened politely—the poor are always polite. The poor always listen. They don't say that there is no money for iron pills, or better food, or worm medicine. The idea of an operation is frightening and costs so much that, if I had dared, I would have laughed. Who takes care of my children? Recovery from an operation takes a long time. I have three children. When I left them with "Granny" the last time I had a job, I came home to find the baby covered with fly specks,

and a diaper that had not been changed since I left. When the dried diaper came off, bits of my baby's flesh came with it. My other child was playing with a sharp bit of broken glass, and my oldest was playing alone at the edge of a lake. I made twenty-two dollars a week, and a good nursery school costs twenty dollars a week for three children. I quit my job.

4   Poverty is dirt. You can say in your clean clothes coming from your clean house, "Anybody can be clean." Let me explain about housekeeping with no money. For breakfast I give my children grits with no oleo or cornbread without eggs and oleo. This does not use up many dishes. What dishes there are, I wash in cold water and with no soap. Even the cheapest soap has to be saved for the baby's diapers. Look at my hands, so cracked and red. Once I saved for two months to buy a jar of Vaseline for my hands and the baby's diaper rash. When I had saved enough, I went to buy it and the price had gone up two cents. The baby and I suffered on. I have to decide every day if I can bear to put my cracked sore hands into the cold water and strong soap. But you ask, why not hot water? Fuel costs money. If you have a wood fire it costs money. If you burn electricity, it costs money. Hot water is a luxury. I do not have luxuries. I know you will be surprised when I tell you how young I am. I look so much older. My back has been bent over the wash tubs every day for so long, I cannot remember when I ever did anything else. Every night I wash every stitch my school age child has on and just hope her clothes will be dry by morning.

5   Poverty is staying up all night on cold nights to watch the fire knowing one spark on the newspaper covering the walls means your sleeping child dies in flames. In summer poverty is watching gnats and flies devour your baby's tears when he cries. The screens are torn and you pay so little rent you know they will never be fixed. Poverty means insects in your food, in your nose, in your eyes, and crawling over you when you sleep. Poverty is hoping it never rains because diapers won't dry when it rains and soon you are using newspapers. Poverty is seeing your children forever with runny noses. Paper handkerchiefs cost money and all your rags you need for other things. Even more costly are antihistamines. Poverty is cooking without food and cleaning without soap.

6   Poverty is asking for help. Have you ever had to ask for help, knowing your children will suffer unless you get it? Think about asking for a loan from a relative, if this is the only way you can imagine asking for help. I will tell you how it feels. You find out where the office is that you are supposed to visit. You circle that block four or five times. Thinking of your children, you go in. Everyone is very busy. Finally, someone comes out and you tell her that you need help. That never is the person you need to see. You go see another person, and after spilling the whole shame of your poverty all over the desk between you,

you find that this isn't the right office after all—you must repeat the whole process, and it never is any easier at the next place.

7    You have asked for help, and after all it has a cost. You are again told to wait. You are told why, but you don't really hear because of the red cloud of shame and the rising cloud of despair.

8    Poverty is remembering. It is remembering quitting school in junior high because "nice" children had been so cruel about my clothes and my smell. The attendance officer came. My mother told him I was pregnant. I wasn't, but she thought that I could get a job and help out. I had jobs off and on, but never long enough to learn anything. Mostly I remember being married. I was so young then. I am still young. For a time, we had all the things you have. There was a little house in another town, with hot water and everything. Then my husband lost his job. There was unemployment insurance for a while and what few jobs I could get. Soon, all our nice things were repossessed and we moved back here. I was pregnant then. This house didn't look so bad when we first moved in. Every week it gets worse. Nothing is ever fixed. We now had no money. There were a few odd jobs for my husband, but everything went for food then, as it does now. I don't know how we lived through three years and three babies, but we did. I'll tell you something, after the last baby I destroyed my marriage. It had been a good one, but could you keep on bringing children in this dirt? Did you ever think how much it costs for any kind of birth control? I knew my husband was leaving the day he left, but there were no good-bys between us. I hope he has been able to climb out of this mess somewhere. He never could hope with us to drag him down.

9    That's when I asked for help. When I got it, you know how much it was? It was, and is, seventy-eight dollars a month for the four of us; that is all I ever can get. Now you know why there is no soap, no needles and thread, no hot water, no aspirin, no worm medicine, no hand cream, no shampoo. None of these things forever and ever and ever. So that you can see clearly, I pay twenty dollars a month rent, and most of the rest goes for food. For grits and cornmeal, and rice and milk and beans. I try my best to use only the minimum electricity. If I use more, there is that much less for food.

10    Poverty is looking into a black future. Your children won't play with my boys. They will turn to other boys who steal to get what they want. I can already see them behind the bars of their prison instead of behind the bars of my poverty. Or they will turn to the freedom of alcohol or drugs, and find themselves enslaved. And my daughter? At best, there is for her a life like mine.

11    But you say to me, there are schools. Yes, there are schools. My children have no extra books, no magazines, no extra pencils, or crayons, or paper and the most important of all, they do not have health. They

have worms, they have infections, they have pink-eye all summer. They do not sleep well on the floor, or with me in my one bed. They do not suffer from hunger, my seventy-eight dollars keeps us alive, but they do suffer from malnutrition. Oh yes, I do remember what I was taught about health in school. It doesn't do much good. In some places there is a surplus commodities program. Not here. The county said it cost too much. There is a school lunch program. But I have two children who will already be damaged by the time they get to school.

12    But, you say to me, there are health clinics. Yes, there are health clinics and they are in the towns. I live out here eight miles from town. I can walk that far (even if it is sixteen miles both ways), but can my little children? My neighbor will take me when he goes; but he expects to get paid, *one way or another*. I bet you know my neighbor. He is that large man who spends his time at the gas station, the barbershop, and the corner store complaining about the government spending money on the immoral mothers of illegitimate children.

13    Poverty is an acid that drips on pride until all pride is worn away. Poverty is a chisel that chips on honor until honor is worn away. Some of you say that you would do *something* in my situation, and maybe you would, for the first week or the first month, but for year after year after year?

14    Even the poor can dream. A dream of a time when there is money. Money for the right kinds of food, for worm medicine, for iron pills, for toothbrushes, for hand cream, for a hammer and nails and a bit of screening, for a shovel, for a bit of paint, for some sheeting, for needles and thread. Money to pay *in money* for a trip to town. And, oh, money for hot water and money for soap. A dream of when asking for help does not eat away the last bit of pride. When the office you visit is as nice as the offices of other governmental agencies, when there are enough workers to help you quickly, when workers do not quit in defeat and despair. When you have to tell your story to only one person, and that person can send you for other help and you don't have to prove your poverty over and over and over again.

15    I have come out of my despair to tell you this. Remember I did not come from another place or another time. Others like me are all around you. Look at us with an angry heart, anger that will help you help me. Anger that will let you tell of me. The poor are always silent. Can you be silent too?

## REVIEW

### Content

1. Why does Parker say she does not want her hearers' pity, but their understanding?

2. Which paragraph of Parker's speech seems the most tragic to you? Why? How could what is described in that paragraph be remedied?

**Rhetoric**

3. What is the effect of Parker's beginning paragraph after paragraph with "Poverty is . . ."? How does this technique help to hold the reader—or a listener?
4. What elements make Parker's speech a powerful one? Consider her vivid vocabulary, short sentences, descriptions, and especially her directness. She tells of many unpleasant situations and often speaks in very straightforward language. Does her language sound too vulgar, or raw, as she calls a spade a spade? If not, why not? Why is her ending effective?

**Projects**

5. With others, role-play something from one of the following paragraphs: 3, 4, 6, 8. Try very hard to get into the situations and the feelings Parker writes about. How do you feel? Write about what such a fantasizing of poverty meant to you.
6. Choose some social ill or injustice about which you feel indignation, and perhaps some despair, and prepare a speech intended for presentation before a specific audience. State the composition of your audience at the head of your paper, then write with the intent of moving that particular audience. Try to involve your listeners emotionally, as Parker does. Before you begin to write, make a list of the points you might include, then select out the ones most likely to stir your audience, thereby also controlling the length of your paper.

# The Campesinos

## RAYMOND BARRIO

Raymond Barrio (1921–   ), a novelist and an artist, has taught at both the University of California at Santa Barbara and Ventura College. He has written books and articles on art as well as producing fiction. Barrio's novel *The Plum Plum Pickers* (1972) portrays the *campesino* (migrant worker) who follows the crops of the valleys of California. Through the passage below the reader experiences some of the anguish of that life with Manuel, a Chicano *campesino*.

1    The apricots were plump.

2    Smooth.

3    A golden syrupy orange.

4    Manuel popped two into his mouth, enjoying their cool natural sweetness after the bitter coffee. He knew he could not eat too many. His stomach muscles would cramp. Other pickers started pulling rapidly away from him. Let them. Calmly he calculated the struggle. Start the press sure, slow, and keep it going steady. Piecework. Fill the bucket, fill another, and still another. The competition was among a set of savages, as savage for money as himself, savages with machetes, hacking their way through the thickets of modern civilization back to the good old Aztec days, waiting to see who'd be first in line to wrench his heart out. Savage beasts, eager to fill as many buckets as possible in as short a time as possible, cleaning out an entire orchard, picking everything in sight clean, tons of fruit, delivering every bit of ripe fruit to the accountants in their cool air-conditioned orifices.

5    The competition was not between pickers and growers.

6    It was between pickers—Jorge and Guillermo.

7    Between the poor and the hungry, the desperate, and the hunted, the slave and the slave, slob against slob, the depraved and himself. You were your own terrible boss. That was the cleverest part of the whole thing. The picker his own bone picker, his own willing built-in slave driver. God, that was good! That was where they reached into your scrotum and screwed you royally and drained your brain and directed your sinews and nerves and muscles with invisible fingers. To fatten their coffers. And drive you to your coffin. That sure was smart. Meant to be smart. Bookkeepers aren't dumb. You worked hard because you wanted to do that hard work above everything else. Pickfast pickhard pickfurious pick pick pick. They didn't need straw bosses studying your neck to see if you kept bobbing up and down to keep your picking pace up. Like the barn-stupid chicken, you drove yourself to do it. You were your own money monkey foreman, monkey on top of your own back.

8    You over-charged yourself.

9    With your own frenzy.

10   Neat.

11   You pushed your gut and your tired aching arms and your twitching legs pumping adrenalin until your tongue tasted like coarse sandpaper.

12   You didn't even stop to take a drink, let alone a piss, for fear you'd get fined, fired, or bawled out.

13   And then, after all that effort, you got your miserable pay.

14   Would the bobbing boss's-sons stoop to that?

15   His fingers were loose and dexterous now. The plump orange balls plopped pitter patter like heavy drops of golden rain into his swaying, sweaty canvas bucket. His earnings depended entirely on how quickly

he worked and how well he kept the pressure up. The morning sun was high. The sweet shade was fragrant and refreshing and comfortable under the leafy branches. The soil too was still cool and humid. It was going to be another hot one.

16    There.

17    Another row ended.

18    He swung around the end of the row and for a moment he was all alone, all by himself. He looked out far across the neighboring alfalfa field, dark green and rich and ripe. Then he looked at the long low Diablo Range close by, rising up into the misty pale blue air kept cool by the unseen bay nearby. This was all his. For a flowing, deceptive minute, all this rich, enormous terrain was all his. All this warm balmy baby air. All this healthful sunny breeze. All those hills, this rich fertile valley, these orchards, these tiled huertas, these magnificent farms all, all his . . . for his eyes to feast upon. It was a moment he wished he could capture forever and etch permanently on his memory, making it a part of living life for his heart to feast joyously on, forever. Why couldn't he stop? Why? Why couldn't he just put the bucket down and open his arms and walk into the hills and merge himself with the hills and just wander invisibly in the blue?

19    What Manuel couldn't really know was that he was completing yet another arc in the unending circle that had been started by one of his Mexican forebears exactly two hundred years before—for even the memory of history was also robbed from him—when Gaspar de Portola, hugging the coastline, nearing present-day San Francisco, climbed what is now Sweeney Ridge, and looked down upon San Francisco's magnificent land-locked Bay, overlooking what is now the International Airport.

20    Both Don Gaspar and Don Manuel were landlords and landless at precisely the same instant of viewing all this heady beauty. And both were equally dispossessed. Both were also possessed of a keen sense of pride and natural absorption with the ritual and mystery of all life. The living that looked mighty good in a flash to Manuel lasted a good deal longer for Don Gaspar whose stumbling accident swept him into the honored and indelible pages of glorious history.

21    Manuel was now a mere straw among the enormous sludge of humanity flowing past, a creature of limb and his own driving appetites, a creature of heed and need. Swinging around another end run he placed his ladder on the next heavy limb of the next pregnant tree. He reached up. He plucked bunches of small golden fruit with both hands. He worked like a frenzied windmill in slow motion. He cleared away an arc as far as the circumference of his plucking fingers permitted. A living model for da Vinci's outstretched man. Adam heeding God's moving finger. He moved higher. He repeated another circle. Then down and around again to another side of the tree, until he cleared it, cleared it of all visible, viable, delectable, succulent fruit. It was sweet work.

The biggest difference between him and the honeygathering ant was that the ant had a home.

22    Several pickers were halfway down the next row, well in advance of him. He was satisfied he was pacing himself well. Most of the band was still behind him. The moving sun, vaulting the sky dome's crackling earth parting with its bronzing rays, pounded its fierce heat into every dead and living crevice. Perspiration poured down his sideburns, down his forehead, down his cheek, down his neck, into his ears, off his chin. He tasted its saltiness with the tip of his dry tongue. He wished he'd brought some salt tablets. Roberto Morales wasn't about to worry about the pickers, and Manuel wasn't worried either. Despite the heat, he felt some protection from the ocean and bay. It has been much, much worse in Texas, and much hotter in Delano in the San Joaquin valley and worst of all in Satan's own land, the Imperial Valley.

23    No matter which way he turned, he was trapped in an endless maze of apricot trees, as though forever, neat rows of them, neatly planted, row after row, just like the blackest bars on the jails of hell. There had to be an end. There had to be. There—trapped. There had to be a way out. Locked. There had to be a respite. Animal. The buckets and the crates kept piling up higher. Brute. He felt alone. Though surrounded by other pickers. Beast. Though he was perspiring heavily, his shirt was powder dry. Savage. The hot dry air. The hot dry air sucking every drop of living moisture from his brute body. Wreck. He stopped and walked to the farthest end of the first row for some water, raised the dented dipper from the brute tank, drank the holy water in great brute gulps so he wouldn't have to savor its tastelessness, letting it spill down his torn shirt to cool his exhausted body, to replenish his brute cells and animal pores and stinking follicles and pig gristle, a truly refined wreck of an animal, pleased to meetcha. Predator.

24    Lunch.

25    Almost too exhausted to eat, he munched his cheese with tortillas, smoked on ashes, then lay back on the cool ground for half an hour. That short rest in the hot shade replenished some of his humor and resolve. He felt his spirit swell out again like a thirsty sponge in water. Then up again. The trees. The branches again. The briarly branches. The scratching leaves. The twigs tearing at his shirt sleeves. The ladder. The rough bark. The endlessly unending piling up of bucket upon box upon crate upon stack upon rack upon mound upon mountain. He picked a mountain of cots automatically. An automaton. A beast. A ray of enemy sun penetrated the tree that was hiding him and split his forehead open. His mind whirred. He blacked out. Luckily he'd been leaning against a heavy branch. His feet hooked to the ladder's rung. His half-filled bucket slipped from his grasp and fell in slow motion, splattering the fruit he'd so laboriously picked. To the ground. Roberto

happened by and shook his head. "Whatsamatter, can't you see straight, pendejo." Manuel was too tired even to curse. He should have had some salt pills.

26    Midafternoon.

27    The summer's fierce zenith passed overhead. It passed. Then dropped. It started to light the ocean behind him, back of the hills. Sandy dreams. Cool nights. Cold drinks. Soft guitar music with Lupe sitting beside him. All wafting through his feverish moments. Tiredness drained his spirit of will. Exhaustion drained his mind. His fingers burned. His arms flailed the innocent trees. He was slowing down. He could hardly fill his last bucket. Suddenly the whistle blew. The day's work was at last ended.

28    Ended!

29    The contratista Roberto Morales stood there.

30    His feet straddled. Mexican style. A real robber. A Mexican general. A gentlemanly, friendly, polite, grinning, vicious, thieving brute. The worst kind. To his own people. Despite his being a fellow Mexican, despite his torn, old clothing, everyone knew what kind of clever criminal he was. Despite his crude, ignorant manner, showing that he was one of them, that he'd started with them, that he grew up with them, that he'd suffered all the sordid deprivations with them, he was actually the shrewdest, smartest, richest cannibal in forty counties around. They sure couldn't blame the gueros for this miscarriage. He was a crew chief. How could anyone know what he did to his own people? And what did the gueros care? So the anglo growers and guero executives, smiling in their cool filtered offices, puffing their elegant thin cigars, washed their clean blond bloodless dirtless hands of the whole matter. All they did was hire Roberto Morales. Firm, fair, and square. For an agreed-upon price. Good. How he got his people down to the pickings was no concern of theirs. They were honest, those gueros. They could sleep at night. They fulfilled their end of the bargain, and cheated no one. Their only crime, their only soul crime indeed was that they just didn't give a shit how the migratory scum lived. It was no concern of theirs. Their religion said it was no concern of theirs. Their wives said it was no concern of theirs. Their aldermen said it was no concern of theirs. Their—

31    Whenever Roberto Morales spoke, Manuel had to force himself not to answer. He had to keep his temper from flaring.

32    "Now," announced Morales at last, in his friendliest tone. "Now. I must take two cents from every bucket. I am sorry. There was a miscalculation. Everybody understands. Everybody?" He slid his eyes around smiling, palms up.

33    The tired, exhausted pickers gasped as one.

34    Yes. Everyone understood. Freezing in place. After all that hard work.

35   "Any questions, men?"

36   Still grinning, knowing, everyone realizing that he had the upper hand, that that would mean a loss of two or three dollars out of each picker's pay that day, a huge windfall for Morales.

37   "You promised to take nothing!" Manuel heard himself saying. Everyone turned in astonishment to stare at Manuel.

38   "I said two cents, hombre. You got a problem or what?"

39   "You promised."

40   The two men, centered in a huge ring of red-ringed eyes, glared at each other. Reaching for each other's jugular. The other exhausted animals studied the tableau through widening eyes. It was so unequal. Morales remained calm, confident, studying Manuel. As though memorizing his features. He had the whole advantage. Then, with his last remaining energy, Manuel lifted his foot and clumsily tipped over his own last bucket of cots. They rolled away in all directions around everyone's feet.

41   Roberto Morales' eyes blazed. His fists clenched. "You pick them up, Gutierrez."

42   So. He knew his name. After all. For answer, Manuel kicked over another bucket, and again the fruit rolled away in all directions.

43   Then an astonishing thing happened.

44   All the other pickers moved toward their own buckets still standing beside them on the ground awaiting the truck gatherer, and took an ominous position over them, straddling their feet over them. Without looking around, without taking his eyes off Manuel, Roberto Morales said sharply, "All right. All right, men, I shall take nothing this time."

45   Manuel felt a thrill of power course through his nerves.

46   He had never won anything before. He would have to pay for this, for his defiance, somehow, again, later. But he had shown defiance. He had salvaged his money savagely and he had earned respect from his fellow slaves. The gringo hijos de la chingada would never know of this little incident, and would probably be surprised, and perhaps even a little mortified for a few minutes. But they wouldn't give a damn. It was bread, pan y tortillas out of his children's mouths. But they still wouldn't give a single damn. Manuel had wrenched Morales' greedy fingers away and removed a fat slug of a purse from his sticky grasp. And in his slow way, in his stupid, accidental, dangerous way, Manuel had made an extravagant discovery, as Don Gaspar had also made two centuries before, in almost exactly the same spot. And that was—that a man counted for something. For men, Manuel dimly suspected, are built for something more important and less trifling than the mere gathering of prunes and apricots, hour upon hour, decade upon decade, insensibly, mechanically, antlike. Men are built to experience a certain sense of honor and pride.

47   Or else they are dead before they die.

## REVIEW

### Content

1. How did you feel when Manuel kicked over the apricots? Why did he do it? Should he have, in light of his knowing he will have to pay for it later? Explain the last paragraph. How do you feel about Roberto Morales, who is, after all, only a former picker who has "made it" and who now wants his cut? Do you feel *any* identification with him?
2. Explain this sentence in paragraph 7: "You worked hard because you wanted to do that hard work above everything else."

### Rhetoric

3. Barrio writes many very short, sometimes just one-word, paragraphs, as he tells Manuel's story. Why do you suppose he uses this technique? Does it help you get inside Manuel?
4. Although Barrio is writing a narrative (i.e., telling a story), he also uses descriptive writing. What do the descriptive passages contribute to the story?

### Projects

5. Describe some outdoor setting with which you are familiar and which moves you, attempting to make your description as rich, in your own style, as is Barrio's in paragraph 15 or 18. Or, describe a powerful bodily response, as in Barrio's paragraphs 22 and 23.
6. In your writing generally, practice occasionally using very short paragraphs as Barrio does here. Such paragraphs often serve well as transitional devices (between longer, fully developed paragraphs), as well as achieving a certain stylistic effect.

# The Hopes of a Hard-Working Man

## STUDS TERKEL

Studs (Louis) Terkel (1912–   ) studied law, but flunked the bar exam—and so became a writer. His books might be called printed documentaries; he collects his material on a tape recorder, through an informal interviewing technique, and then makes books out of what he has collected to reflect America to herself. His first such effort resulted in *Division Street: America* (1966), about Chicago; his second, in *Hard Times: An Oral History of the Great Depression* (1970). Terkel's third book, entitled *Working: People Talk About What They Do All Day and How They Feel About What They Do* (1973), is a compilation of Terkel interviews with 132 persons. The selection below, from an interview with Mike Lefevre, a factory worker who finds his assembly-line work meaningless, was originally published in a magazine under the title "I got no use for intellectuals, but I want my kid to be an effete snob."

1    *It is a two-flat dwelling, in Cicero, on the outskirts of Chicago. Mike Lefevre sits inside and talks. He is 37, 5'-8" and 180 pounds. He works in a steel mill. On occasion, his wife, Carol, works as a waitress in a neighborhood restaurant; otherwise, she is at home, caring for their two small children, a girl and a boy. Mike says:*

2    I'm a dying breed. A laborer. Strictly muscle work . . . pick it up, put it down, pick it up, put it down. You can't take pride anymore. You remember when a guy could point to a house he built, how many logs he stacked. He built it and he was proud of it. I don't really think I could be proud if a contractor built a home for me. I would be tempted to get in there and kick the carpenter in the ass (laughs) and take the saw away from him. 'Cause I would have to be part of it, you know.

3    It's hard to take pride in a bridge you're never gonna cross, in a door you're never gonna open. You're mass-producing things and you never see the end result of it. I worked for a trucker one time. And I got this tiny satisfaction when I loaded a truck. At least I could see the truck depart loaded. In a steel mill, forget it. You don't see where nothing goes.

4    I got chewed out by my foreman once. He said, "Mike, you're a good worker, but you have a bad attitude." My attitude is that I don't get excited about my job. I do my work, but the day I get excited about my job is the day I go to a head shrinker. How are you gonna get excited about pullin' steel? How are you gonna get excited when you're tired and want to sit down?

5    It's not just the work. Somebody built the pyramids. Pyramids. Empire State Building—these things just don't happen. There's hard work behind it. I would like to see a building, say the Empire State, I would like to see one side of it, a foot-wide strip from top to bottom with the name of every bricklayer, the name of every electrician, with all the names. So when a guy walks by, he could take his son and say: "See, that's me over there on the 45th floor. I put the steel beam in."

Picasso could point to a painting. What can I point to? A writer can point to a book. Everybody should have something to point to.

6    It's the not-recognition by other people. To say a woman is *just* a housewife is degrading, right? O.K. *Just* a housewife. It's also degrading to say *just* a laborer. The difference is that a man goes out and maybe gets smashed.

7    A mule, an old mule, that's the way I feel. Oh, yeah. See (shows black and blue marks on arms and legs, burns). You know what I heard from more than one guy at work? "If my kid wants to work in a factory, I am going to kick the hell out of him." I want my kid to be an effete snob. Yeah, mm-hmm (laughs). I want him to be able to quote Walt Whitman, to be proud of it.

8    If you can't improve yourself, you improve your posterity. Otherwise life isn't worth nothing. I'm sure the first cave man who went over the hill to see what was on the other side—I don't think he went there wholly out of curiosity. He went there because he wanted to get his son out of the cave. Just the same way I want to send my kid to college.

.   .   .

9    You're doing this manual labor and you know that technology can do it (laughs). Automation frightens me if it puts me out on the street. It doesn't frighten me if it shortens my work week. You read that little thing: what are you going to do when this computer replaces you? Blow up computers (laughs). Really. Blow up computers. I'll be god-damned if a computer is gonna eat before I do! I want milk for my kids and beer for me. Machines can either liberate man or enslave 'em, because they're pretty neutral. It's man who has the bias to put the thing one place or another.

10    If I had a 20-hour work week, I'd get to know my kids better, my wife better. Some kid invited me to go on a college campus. On a Saturday. It was summertime. Hell, if I have a choice of taking my wife and kids to a picnic or going to a college campus, it's gonna be the picnic. But if I worked a 20-hour week, I could go do both. Don't you think with that extra 20 hours, people could really expand? Who's to say? There are some people in factories just by force of circumstance. I'm just like the colored people. Potential Einsteins don't have to be white. They could be in cotton fields, in factories.

11    The 20-hour week is a possibility today. The intellectuals, they always say there are potential Lord Byrons, Walt Whitmans, Roosevelts, Picassos working in construction or steel mills or factories. But I don't think they believe it. I think what they're afraid of is the potential Hitlers and Stalins that are there too. The people in power fear the leisure man.

12      What do you think would happen in this country if, for one year, they experimented and gave everybody a 20-hour week? How do they know that the guy who digs Wallace today doesn't try to resurrect Hitler tomorrow? Or the guy who is mildly disturbed at pollution doesn't decide to go to General Motors and shit on the guy's desk? You can become a fanatic, if you had the time. The whole thing is time.

13      It isn't that the average working guy is dumb. He's tired, that's all. I picked up a book on chess one time. That thing laid in the drawer for two or three weeks. You're too tired. During the weekends, you want to take your kids out. You don't want to sit there and the kid comes up, and says, "Daddy, can I go to the park?" and you got your nose in a book. Forget it.

14      I know a guy 57 years old. Know what he tells me? "Mike, I'm old and tired *all* the time." The first thing happens at work is that when the arms start moving, the brain stops. I punch in about 10 minutes to seven in the morning. I say hello to a couple of guys I like, I kid around with them. I put on my hard hat, change into my safety boots, put on my safety glasses, go the the bonderizer. It's the thing I work on. They rake the metal, they wash it, they dip it in a paint solution and we take it off. Put it on, take it off, put it on, take it off, put it on, take it off. . . .

15      I say hello to everybody but my boss. At seven it starts. My arms get tired about the first half hour. After that, they don't get tired any more, until maybe the last half hour, at the end of the day. I work from seven to 3:30. My arms are tired at 7:30 and they're tired at three o'clock. I hope to God I never get broke in, because I always want my arms to be tired at 7:30 and three o'clock (laughs). 'Cause that's when I knew that there's a beginning and there's an end. That I'm not brainwashed. In between, I don't even try to think.

16      Unless a guy's a nut, he never thinks about work or talks about it. Maybe about baseball or about getting drunk yesterday or he got laid or he didn't get laid.

17      Oh yeah, I daydream. I fantasize about a sexy blonde in Miami who's got my union dues (laughs). I think of the head of the union the way I think of the head of my company. Living it up. I think of February in Miami. Warm weather, a place to lay in. When I hear a college kid say, "I'm oppressed," I don't believe him. You know what I'd like to do for one year? Live like a college kid. Wow!

18      Somebody has to do this work. If my kid ever goes to college, I just want him to have a little respect, to realize that his dad is one of those somebodies. This is why even on—yeah, I guess, sure—on the black thing (sighs heavily), I can't really hate the colored fella that's working with me all day. The black intellectual I got no respect for. The white intellectual I got no use for. I got no use for the black militant who's

gonna scream 300 years of slavery to me, while I'm busting my ass. You know what I mean? (laughs) I have one answer for that guy; go see Rockefeller. See Harriman. Don't bother me. We're in the same cotton field.

19    After work, I usually stop off at a tavern. Cold beer. Cold beer right away. When I was single, I used to go into hillbilly bars, get in a lot of brawls. Just to explode. I'm getting older (laughs). I don't explode as much. You might say I'm broken in. No, I'll never be broken in (sighs). When you get a little older, you exchange the words. When you're younger, you exchange the blows.

20    When I get home, I argue with my wife a little bit. Turn on TV, get mad at the news (laughs). I don't even watch the news that much. I watch Jackie Gleason reruns. I look for any alternative to the ten o'clock news. I don't want to go to bed angry.

21    When I come home, know what I do for the first 20 minutes? Fake it. I put on a smile. I got a kid three years old. Sometimes she says, "Daddy, where've you been?" I say, "Work," I could have told her I'd been in Disneyland. What's work to a three-year-old kid? If I feel bad, I can't take it out on the kids. You can't take it out on your wife either. This is why you go to a tavern. You want to release it there rather than do it at home.

22    Weekends, I drink beer, read a book. I've got one there—*Violence in America*. It's one of them studies from Washington. One of them committees they're always appointing. A thing like that I read on a weekend. But during the weekdays, gee—I just thought about it. I don't do that much reading from Monday through Friday. Unless it's a horny book. I'll read it at work and go home and do my homework (laughs). That's what the guys at the plant call it—homework (laughs)

.   .   .

23    I'd like to run a combination bookstore and tavern (laughs). I would like to have a place where college kids and steel workers could sit down and talk. Where a working man would not be ashamed of Walt Whitman and where a college professor would not be ashamed that he painted his house over the weekend.

24    If a carpenter built a cabin for poets, I think the least the poets owe the carpenter is just three or four one-liners on the wall. A little plaque: "Though we labor with our minds, this place we can relax in was built by someone who can work with his hands. And his work is as noble as ours."

25    Sometimes, out of pure meanness, when I make something, I put a dent in it. I like to do something to make it really unique. Hit it with a hammer. I deliberately fuck it up to see if they'll get by, just

so I can say I did it. I want my signature on it. I'd like to make my imprint.

26    This is gonna sound square, but my kid is my imprint. He's my free-dom. You know what I mean? This is why I work. Yes, I want my kid to be an effete snob. Hell, yes, I want my kid to tell me that he's not gonna be like me. Every time I see a young guy walk by with a shirt and tie and dressed up sharp, I'm lookin' at my kid, you know? That's it.

## REVIEW

### Content

1. Discuss how Mike Lefevre feels about his work. Do you sympathize with him? Why does he say, "Unless a guy's a nut, he never thinks about work or talks about it"? How do you respond to the next to last paragraph?
2. Discuss Mike's comments about the 20-hour workweek. List all the advantages, to both the individual and to society, that you can think of for such a week. All the disadvantages. Would such a working schedule be possible in today's world?

### Rhetoric

3. Terkel transcribes Mike's voice from tape onto the printed page so that the reader can almost hear Mike speaking. Would Mike's points be made more effectively if Terkel had "translated" what Mike said, using more big words, restructuring and tightening up sentences, del-eting rough language, and so on?
4. Terkel includes, in parentheses, laughs, sighs, and some body gestures on Mike's part. Does this parenthetical material distract you as you read? If not, why not?

### Projects

5. Write about your present job or some work you have done at some time (including work around the home) as if you were telling Terkel about it. If you have a recorder, talk your paper into that first, then transcribe it into writing. You may find this technique useful for other writing projects, either for school or for other purposes.
6. Fantasize Mike's "combination bookstore and tavern" and write up a conversation that might occur there between two persons from dif-ferent walks of life, as Mike suggests. Include some dialogue about their jobs and/or hobbies, in which they exchange ideas about work.

# The Man Who Killed the Deer

## FRANK WATERS

Frank Waters (1902–    ) is a white man whose empathy with the American Indians is recognized by the Indians themselves. In the passage below from Waters' novel *The Man Who Killed the Deer* (1942), the Indian Martiniano is being tried before the tribal council for failing to observe both the U.S. Government's regulations on the deer-hunting season and the tribe's ritual of recognition of Brother Deer before the kill. Martiniano, who had earlier been sent to the Government "away-school," now finds himself caught between the white man's world and his native Indian pueblo.

1    Martiniano began to speak. He had a cinnamon-sallow, pain-racked face, and a bloody white bandage round his head. He was not as young as Filadelphio and Jesús, or as old as Palemon. He had been to the Government away-school and wore old store clothes and shoes like the former, but hair braids and a blanket like the latter. His face and demeanor showed that he was at once of the old and the new, and that it was not the first time he had been caught between them. His voice was sullen but respectful.

2    "I went to the mountains and I took my rifle. I wanted to kill a deer," he stated defiantly, but with lowered face. "The Council does not give me the privileges of others since I have come back from away-school. It would not give me my turn at the thresher for my oats, my wheat. So I had to thresh them the old way, with my animals' hoofs. It took me a long, long time—what should have taken but a day. Then my friend, the good white trader, loaned me his machine—for one sack out of ten. Yet it was two days after hunting season that I finished. Should my wife be without fresh meat, a skin for boots and moccasins? Should I go without my rights for two days of white man's law? The white man's Government that took me away to school, for which you now do not give me the privileges of others? What is the difference between killing a deer on Tuesday or Thursday? Would I not have killed it anyway?"

3    He paused to twang at the Council the arrow of accusing silence. It missed the mark. Or perhaps the mute impenetrability of those rows

of covered faces was too sturdy a shield to pierce. And completing its arc, like an arrow shot into the sky and which must fall again to earth, it turned home.

4   Martiniano resumed. "This I told the Government man who remained with me as you have heard. I did not have to look up to hear his angry voice, to feel the hate steaming from his body. 'You dirty Indian, who kills deer out of season in the Government's National Forest!' he cried. 'I am going to ride up that old mine for rope to tie you up. Try to run away and I will shoot you like a dog!'

5   "As he went away I laid back the flap of the skin, I cut off a piece of my deer. I had no fear; I had hunger. I had not eaten since the day before. While it cooked over the coals I hid my deer in the bushes. But before I could eat it, he came back. The rope was on his saddle horn, the rifle raised to my breast. He smelled the meat. His face was red with anger.

6   "I turned over the meat. What Indian makes a foolish move before an angry white man's gun? I but raised my hands to wipe off my fingers on my hair.

7   "At that moment he struck. With the iron of his gun. Across my head. I woke up. My head was cracked open. Blood ran down my face. He had taken my knife. My hands were tied behind my back. When he kicked me, I tried to stand up. He lifted me like a sack of meal to the rump of his horse. We started off. I could not sit up, but fell upon his back. Blood ran down his shirt. This made him very angry. He put me in front. Still I bled and kept falling, save for his hand upon my collar.

8   "Now my thoughts returned. I said, 'There is a thing I must do, which every man does, behind a bush. You understand it is this hurt which makes my kidneys weak.'

9   "He stopped the horse. I fell off and stood up. 'Pardon,' I said, 'but my hands are tied behind my back.'

10   " 'Oh no you don't!' he said, and with his rifle butt he swept open the front of my trousers. See? How he tore off the buttons?"

11   His eyes hard as black obsidian, Martiniano stood there, one leg forward, showing the gaping flap of his blood-stained trousers. No one looked. They saw it in his voice.

12   "If he had done more than this," Martiniano stated quietly, "there would be more for this venerated Council to consider. I would have killed him.

13   "But now"—a shade on the apologetic side to balance his unseemly show of passion—"I went noisily into the bushes. Then I quietly waded upstream against the noise of the falls. I hid in water, deep between the logs of a beaver dam. I heard him call. I saw him plunging through the bushes to find me. Suddenly he rode off. Quickly. In a gallop. Fear

pursued him. He had forgotten me, my rifle, my deer.

14    "For a long time I cut at my rope on the sharp rocks. I was too weak to walk when my hands were free. I crawled back up the trail. I was weak, but the thought of the strength of my deer meat made me vomit. I knew I was sick. Too sick to make a fire. So I lay down beside the stream.

15    "I slept sleep, and I slept a sleep that was not a sleep. I thought many thoughts, but there are no words for my thoughts. And strangely, when Morning Star rose, though I was cold and weak and ill, I felt good. I felt good because I knew help would come. It came. It was Palemon.

16    "This I say, with my face and my belly put out before you. And now my heart is empty."

17    Had they all fallen asleep—these rows of old men slumped against the wall, the whitewash rubbing off on their blankets, head down or arm upraised to shut out the last sputtering pulgado of candle? If so, they continued dozing. Only the Cacique sat upright in his chair, a rock jutting into the waves of sleep. Somebody threw another piñon knot on the fire. Somebody spat nosily into one of the little sand boxes. One of the sentinels opened the door and stood inside to get warm. When he went out, the two boys, Filadelphio and Jesús, followed him.

18    Well, here were the facts thrust down the maw of silence. You could hear them being digested. They fitted into the responsibilities of the Governor and Lieutenant-Governor of the pueblo, the "Outside Chief"— the War Captain, the Chiefs of the Kivas, all the officers, all the Council. And so one after another, with proper pause, the guttural Indian voices began to speak.

19    Let us move evenly together, brothers.

20    A young man went into the mountains. He killed a deer out of season. He got arrested, and a knock on the head to boot. He will have to pay a fine, doubtless, for disobeying those Government laws we have sworn to uphold with our canes of office. A simple matter.

21    But wait. Was it so simple?

22    This young man was an Indian, born in our pueblo, belonging to our tribe. Or was he, properly speaking? There was the definition of an Indian by the Government—so much Indian blood, land ownership, all that. But there was the definition of an Indian by the Council according to his conformance to custom, tradition, his participation in ceremonials. Now this young man has been lax, very lax; we have warned him. He has disobeyed us; we have punished him. And now he has disobeyed the laws of the Government outside, likewise. What have we to do with this, that we should interfere?

23    Now there is this. There are good Indians among us, and there are those who look under their eyes. But we are all in one nest. No Indian

is an individual. He is a piece of the pueblo, the tribe. Is it proper to consider that we have done wrong against the Government, our white father, betrayed our canes of office?

24    Yet there was this to consider. All this land was ours—the mountains, the valleys, the desert. Indian land. We have the papers from the Spanish King. The Mexicans came, the white people—the gringos. They built themselves a town on our land, Indian land. We got nothing for it. Now when the Spanish King opened his hand, Our Father at Washington closed his own hand upon the land. He told us, "You will be paid for it. The day will come with compensation." What did we want with money? We wanted land, our land, Indian land. But mostly we wanted the mountains. We wanted the mountains, our mother, between whose breasts lies the little blue eye of faith. The deep turquoise lake of life. Our lake, our church. Where we make our pilgrimages, hold our ceremonials . . . Now what is this? We have waited. The day of compensation has not come. The mountains are Government forests. Not ours. The Mexicans pasture their sheep and goats upon the slopes. Turistas scatter paper bags unseemly upon the ground. They throw old fish bait into our sacred lake. Government men, these rangers, ride through it at will. Is any man safe? Look at this one's broken head. Will our ceremonials long be inviolate from foreign eyes? Now then, is it we who are injured and must seek reparation, demand our rights, our mountains? This is what I say. God knows, will help us, will give strength.

25    The voices kept creeping around the room . . .

26    In the Government office two hundred miles away there is that Indian lawyer, our mouth in many matters. There is the judge in town, a short walk. Are we to turn this young man alone over to the judge? Or are we to call this Indian lawyer? And what are we to tell him? We must move evenly together. We must be one mind, one heart, one body.

27    Silence spoke, and it spoke the loudest of all.

28    *There is no such thing as a simple thing. One drops a pebble into a pool, but ripples travel far. One picks up a little-stone in the mountains, one of the little stones called Lagrimas de Cristo—and look! It is shaped like a star; the sloping mountain is full of stars as the sloping sky. Or take a kernel of corn. Plant it in Our Mother Earth with the sweat of your body, with what you know of the times and seasons, with your proper prayers. And with your strength and manhood Our Father Sun multiplies and gives it back into your flesh. What then is this kernel of corn? It is not a simple thing.*

29    *Nothing is simple and alone. We are not separate and alone. The breathing mountains, the living stones, each blade of grass, the clouds, the rain, each star, the beasts, the birds and the invisible spirits of the air—we are all one, indivisible. Nothing that any of us does but affects us all.*

30    *So I would have you look upon this thing not as a separate simple thing, but as a stone which is a star in the firmament of earth, as a ripple in a pool, as a kernel of corn. I would have you consider how it fits into the pattern*

*of the whole. How far its influence may spread. What it may grow into . . .*

31    *So there is something else to consider. The deer. It is dead. In the old days we all remember, we did not go out on a hunt lightly. We said to the deer we were going to kill, "We know your life is as precious as ours. We know that we are both children of the same Great True Ones. We know that we are all one life on the same Mother Earth, beneath the same plains of the sky. But we also know that one life must sometimes give way to another so that the one great life of all may continue unbroken. So we ask your permission, we obtain your consent to this killing."*

32    *Ceremonially we said this, and we sprinkled meal and corn pollen to Our Father Sun. And when we killed the deer we laid his head toward the East, and sprinkled him with meal and pollen. And we dropped drops of his blood and bits of his flesh on the ground for Our Mother Earth. It was proper so. For then when we too built its flesh into our flesh, when we walked in the moccasins of its skin, when we danced in its robe and antlers, we knew that the life of the deer was continued in our life, as it in turn was continued in the one life all around us, below us and above us.*

33    *We knew the deer knew this and was satisfied.*

34    *But this deer's permission was not obtained. What have we done to this deer, our brother? What have we done to ourselves? For we are all bound together, and our touch upon one travels through all to return to us again. Let us not forget the deer.*

## REVIEW

### Content

1. First, discuss the conflicts within Martiniano which led to his present situation. What would *you* have done in Martiniano's place? Then, discuss the dilemma which Martiniano's plight presents to the Council. How would you advise resolving it if you were sitting on the Council?
2. A basic Indian philosophy is presented in paragraphs 29 through 34. How do *you* respond to this philosophy? Can you tie it in with any contemporary issues on the larger American scene?

### Rhetoric

3. The *tone* of the writing in the story changes several times; it varies when Martiniano is speaking, when the Council is deliberating, when "silence speaks," and in the tribute to the deer. Does your ear catch these variations? What elements contribute to these differences in tone?
4. There are many examples of imagery (word-pictures), especially relating to Nature, in the story; the Indian who lives close to Nature seems to have a special gift for this imagery. Find examples which strike you as particularly effective.

**Projects**

5. Spend some time out-of-doors, away from downtown, look closely at various things in Nature, and try to create some imagery. Does this new way of looking and of putting word-pictures on what you see tend to increase what you see?

6. Try your hand at achieving a dignified tone of expression by composing a tribute. The occasion could be someone's birthday; a farewell party for a friend moving away; an appreciation of your parents on their anniversary; the birth of a godchild. Try to think of a tribute you might actually use at some future date.

# My Cow, She Was Almost Arrested

## TOBIAS LEYBA

Tobias Leyba is a farmer in New Mexico, whose land has come down to him through the land-grants established by treaties between the various governments occupying the Southwest in the early years of this country. The claiming of these lands by the U. S. Government for national parks and forests has persistently encroached on native ownership. In 1970, Leyba's cow, grazing on some land in such jeopardy, skirted arrest by the Forest Service. Bitterness bites through humor in Leyba's account of the near-arrest of his animal.

1    My cow, she was almost arrested last week. The Forest Service was going to arrest her because she walked over the line and ate some grass. She got a little better head, my cow, than the forest ranger, but still she can't read the signs and she doesn't see the lines too pretty good.

2    I keep my cows on private land near the Echo Amphitheatre. This land is private where my cows are and it is across the road from where the Forest Service has its park for the tourists. The State Highway Department has land along both sides of the road and there is a little bit of forest land that goes across the road. Next to where my cows are, there is land that the University of New Mexico says it owns. All this once belonged to the people.

3    Now, mira my cow is eating the grass and it looks the same, and

Originally published in *El Grito del Norte,* April 29, 1970. Reprinted by permission of Chicano Communications Training Project, P. O. Box 12547, Albuquerque, N.M. 87105.

the land looks the same, so I guess she thinks it is still the same—the land still belongs to all of the people. But this ranger, a gauvacho who doesn't know much about the land—or the people—he's watching my cow. And when she steps over the line, he sends me a letter saying he's going to arrest my cow, he's going to "impound" her.

4       This ranger says my cow has walked over onto the University of New Mexico land and over another line of the forest and he is going to arrest her. This land the University of New Mexico has, it is just sitting there, but the university, it doesn't let the people use it. How many taxes does the university pay for the land? I tell you: Nada. But they keep it, and the rangers, they keep the people off of it. Like police. It is the same with the Highway Department land. What is it used for—nada. How many taxes are paid—nada. But the rangers keep the people off.

5       My cow, she doesn't understand such things and she can't read the signs. But the ranger says he saw her cross the lines and I get a letter saying she's going to be arrested in two weeks, she and six other cows I have there. I don't know if they were eating the grass too, because the ranger says he saw only this one walk from the university to the forest and back. But he says he's going to arrest them all.

6       Why do they do this? Why does the University of New Mexico do this? Why can't the people use these lands of the university, which are doing nothing now? Why can't the poor people use the Highway Department land for their cows, when it is just sitting there? Porque? Why does the forest and the university and the highway all work together to hurt our people and keep us off the land?

7       I would laugh at him, but when they do this, they hurt our people. They have the land, and our people have become poor. When they arrest the people's cows, people have to get them back by paying. To get your cow back, it costs $20. Mira, here in the North, that's a lot of money. This ranger, he says he's going to arrest seven of my cows. That would cost $140 to get them back. Hijo, where am I supposed to get that much money? Where would any of the poor people get that much money to pay the rangers?

8       It is like the Presbyterian Ghost Ranch. Why can't the people use the water that's over a little north of Ghost Ranch? It is because all that water, the Forest Service, they give it to the Ghost Ranch for nothing. Only they can use it. The people, they tell the people they can go to hell.

9       The university is doing the same thing. This ranger, he was called by *El Grito* and he told the paper this: "It was the university land that caused this letter (the letter that said they were going to arrest my cows). They were on the forest when we saw them, but they were walking back and forth."

10      How come this ranger is working as a police for the university? Why

can't the people use the university's land? Last week I hear about what they're having called EARTH DAY and at the University of New Mexico they're talking about how much they love the land. They have a big demonstration at the university about loving the earth and the people. At the same time, they're arresting my cow. I don't hear about any demonstrations about my cow being almost arrested.

11    Tobias Leyba and his cattle have lived in Canjilon a long time, all of his life. And this ranger, he is a stranger. What does this ranger know about the land and the people? The way it is, Tobias Leyba and the ranger, they can't never have between each other any real trust. Because Tobias Leyba doesn't have any use for the ranger. The ranger is like he is a policeman for the forest, the university, the highway, the state, the U.S. Government in Washington. The ranger, he is just a police to keep the people off of the land.

12    For my little bit of land, I have to pay taxes. What does the university pay in taxes for our children in the schools in the North—nada. What does the highway pay—nada. What does the forest pay—nada. But they have the land, and these rangers, they are their police. The poor people pay their taxes, and this money is used to keep us poor.

13    I remember once I saw this ranger and another one, two of them, driving one cow. It cost the people more than $20 to get that cow back. They were poor people. They paid because they needed that cow and because they were afraid of the rangers. I don't think the rangers have a right to do this to our people. Now they send me this letter. It seems like they want Tobias Leyba to eat some mierda.

14    And they have put notices in the paper saying they are going to arrest the people's cattle if they cross the lines. It seems like they are saying to our Spanish people—"You just go on and just get out, get out of this land."

15    No, no, no, no, no—not me, not Tobias Leyba, not my people. This land is ours, and we will be here when these rangers, they are all gone.


## REVIEW

### Content

1. Are Tobias Leyba's questions in paragraph 6 reasonable questions? Or is it somewhat unpatriotic of him to pose such questions?
2. How do you respond to paragraph 10? Discuss the various implications of what Leyba is saying here.

### Rhetoric

3. Discuss the effect of your being able to hear Tobias Leyba himself as he tells the story. How does the way he writes contribute to the

impact of his complaint? What is the effect of the occasional Spanish word—"nada," "Porque," "Hijo," "mierda"?

4. Leyba's account of his plight is effective partly because of humor, including absurdity. Discuss the absurdity specifically in relation to the role of the cow.

### Projects

5. Assume an American voice other than the one you usually use in the classroom and narrate some incident in that voice—for example, street talk, jive/hip slang, pidgin English. Do you *feel* any differently when you write this way? If so, how; and does your response tell you anything about language, about how we use it, and about how it affects its users?

6. Leyba's narrative is marked by the irony that he and his fellow poor have to pay to get their cows back, thus having their poverty reinforced. Recall some incident in your life, or one that you have heard about, that contained irony and write about it, playing up the irony. Irony is a sort of upside-down humor; keep this in mind as you present your irony, which should be both laughable and cause for indignation at the same time.

# To All Black Women, from All Black Men

## ELDRIDGE CLEAVER

Eldridge Cleaver (1935–   ), one-time Minister of Information for the Black Panther Party, spoke out in his *Soul on Ice* (1968) in a number of forceful statements about issues his fellow Black Revolutionaries need to confront. Among these is the question of the role—historical and contemporary—of the Black Woman. In the passage below, Cleaver pays tribute to the Black Woman and challenges her toward revolution. (See headnote to "The Folsom Prison Letters" by Eldridge Cleaver and Beverly Axelrod in the preceding section for further background on Cleaver and *Soul on Ice*.)

Queen–Mother–Daughter of Africa
Sister of My Soul
Black Bride of My Passion
My Eternal Love

1   I greet you, my Queen, not in the obsequious whine of a cringing Slave
to which you have become accustomed, neither do I greet you in the
new voice, the unctuous supplications of the sleek Black Bourgeoise,
nor the bullying bellow of the rude Free Slave—but in my own voice
do I greet you, the voice of the Black Man. And although I greet you
*anew,* my greeting is not *new,* but as old as the Sun, Moon, and Stars.
And rather than mark a new beginning, my greeting signifies only my
Return.

2   I have Returned from the dead. I speak to you now from the Here
And Now. I was dead for four hundred years. For four hundred years
you have been a woman alone, bereft of her man, a manless woman.
For four hundred years I was neither your man nor my own man. The
white man stood between us, over us, around us. The white man was
your man and my man. Do not pass lightly over this truth, my Queen,
for even though the fact of it has burned into the marrow of our bones
and diluted our blood, we must bring it to the surface of the mind,
into the realm of knowing, glue our gaze upon it and stare at it as
at a coiled serpent in a baby's playpen or the fresh flowers on a mother's
grave. It is to be pondered and realized in the heart, for the heel of
the white man's boot is our point of departure, our point of Resolve
and Return—the bloodstained pivot of our future. (But I would ask
you to recall, that before we could come up from slavery, we had to
be pulled down from our throne.)

3   Across the naked abyss of negated masculinity, of four hundred years
minus my Balls, we face each other today, my Queen. I feel a deep,
terrifying hurt, the pain of humiliation of the vanquished warrior. The
shame of the fleetfooted sprinter who stumbles at the start of the race.
I feel unjustified. I can't bear to look into your eyes. Don't you know
(surely you must have noticed by now: four hundred years!) that for
four hundred years I have been unable to look squarely into your eyes?
I tremble inside each time you look at me. I can feel . . . in the ray
of your eye, from a deep hiding place, a long-kept secret you harbor.
That is the unadorned truth. Not that I would have felt justified, under
the circumstances, in taking such liberties with you, but I want you to
know that I feared to look into your eyes because I knew I would find
reflected there a merciless Indictment of my impotence and a compelling
challenge to redeem my conquered manhood.

4   My Queen, it is hard for me to tell you what is in my heart for
you today—what is in the heart of all my black brothers for you and

all your black sisters—and I fear I will fail unless you reach out to me, tune in on me with the antenna of your love, the sacred love in ultimate degree which you were unable to give me because I, being dead, was unworthy to receive it; that perfect, radical love of black on which our Fathers thrived. Let me drink from the river of your love at its source, let the lines of force of your love seize my soul by its core and heal the wound of my Castration, let my convex exile end its haunted Odyssey in your concave essence which receives that it may give. Flower of Africa, it is only through the liberating power of your *re*-love that my manhood can be redeemed. For it is in your eyes, before you, that my need is to be justified. Only, only, only you and only you can condemn or set me free.

5    Be convinced, Sable Sister, that the past is no forbidden vista upon which we dare not look, out of a phantom fear of being, as the wife of Lot, turned into pillars of salt. Rather the past is an omniscient mirror: we gaze and see reflected there ourselves and each other—what we used to be, what we are today, how we got this way, and what we are becoming. To decline to look into the Mirror of Then, my heart, is to refuse to view the face of Now.

6    *I have died the ninth death of the cat, have seen Satan face to face and turned my back on God, have dined in the Swine's Trough, and descended to the uttermost echelon of the Pit, have entered the Den and seized my Balls from the teeth of a roaring lion!*

7    Black Beauty, in impotent silence I listened, as if to a symphony of sorrows, to your screams for help, anguished pleas of terror that echo still throughout the Universe and through the mind, a million scattered screams across the painful years that merged into a single sound of pain to haunt and bleed the soul, a white-hot sound to char the brain and blow the fuse of thought, a sound of fangs and teeth sharp to eat the heart, a sound of moving fire, a sound of frozen heat, a sound of licking flames, a fiery-fiery sound, a sound of fire to burn the steel out of my Balls, a sound of Blue fire, a Bluesy sound, the sound of dying, the sound of my woman in pain, *the sound of my woman's pain,* THE SOUND OF MY WOMAN CALLING ME, ME, I HEARD HER CALL FOR HELP, I HEARD THAT MOURNFUL SOUND BUT HUNG MY HEAD AND FAILED TO HEED IT, I HEARD MY WOMAN'S CRY, I HEARD MY WOMAN'S SCREAM, I HEARD MY WOMAN BEG THE BEAST FOR MERCY, I HEARD HER BEG FOR ME, I HEARD MY WOMAN BEG THE BEAST FOR MERCY FOR ME, I HEARD MY WOMAN DIE, I HEARD THE SOUND OF HER DEATH, A SNAPPING SOUND, A BREAKING SOUND, A SOUND THAT SOUNDED FINAL, THE LAST SOUND, THE ULTIMATE SOUND, THE SOUND OF DEATH, ME, I HEARD, I HEAR IT EVERY DAY, I HEAR HER NOW ... I HEAR YOU NOW ... I HEAR YOU. ... I heard you then ... your scream came like a searing bolt of lightning that blazed a white streak down my black back. In a cowardly stupor, with a palpitating

heart and quivering knees, I watched the Slaver's lash of death slash through the opposing air and bite with teeth of fire into your delicate flesh, the black and tender flesh of African Motherhood, forcing the startled Life untimely from your torn and outraged womb, the sacred womb that cradled primal man, the womb that incubated Ethiopia and populated Nubia and gave forth Pharaohs unto Egypt, the womb that painted the Congo black and mothered Zulu, the womb of Mero, the womb of the Nile, of the Niger, the womb of Songhay, of Mali, of Ghana, the womb that felt the might of Chaka before he saw the Sun, the Holy Womb, the womb that knew the future form of Jomo Kenyatta, the womb of Mau Mau, the womb of the blacks, the womb that nurtured Toussaint L'Ouverture, that warmed Nat Turner, and Gabriel Prosser, and Denmark Vesey, the black womb that surrendered up in tears that nameless and endless chain of Africa's Cream, the Black Cream of the Earth, that nameless and endless black chain that sank in heavy groans into oblivion in the great abyss, the womb that received and nourished and held firm the seed and gave back Sojourner Truth, and Sister Tubman, and Rosa Parks, and Bird, and Richard Wright, and your other works of art who wore and wear such names as Marcus Garvey and DuBois and Kwame Nkrumah and Paul Robeson and Malcolm X and Robert Williams, and the one you bore in pain and called Elijah Muhammad, but most of all that nameless one they tore out of your womb in a flood of murdered blood that splashed upon and seeped into the mud. And Patrice Lumumba, and Emmett Till, and Mack Parker.

8      O, My Soul! I became a sniveling craven, a funky punk, a vile, groveling bootlicker, with my will to oppose petrified by a cosmic fear of the Slavemaster. Instead of inciting the Slaves to rebellion with eloquent oratory, I soothed their hurt and eloquently sang the Blues! Instead of hurling my life with contempt into the face of my Tormentor, *I shed your precious blood!* When Nat Turner sought to free me from my Fear, my Fear delivered him up unto the Butcher—a martyred monument to my Emasculation. My spirit was unwilling and my flesh was weak. Ah, eternal ignominy!

9      I, the Black Eunuch, divested of my Balls, walked the earth with my mind locked in Cold Storage. I would kill a black man or woman quicker than I'd smash a fly, while for the white man I would pick a thousand pounds of cotton a day. What profit is there in the blind, frenzied efforts of the (Guilty!) Black Eunuchs (Justifiers!) who hide their wounds and scorn the truth to mitigate their culpability through the pallid sophistry of postulating a Universal Democracy of Cowards, pointing out that in history no one can hide, that if not at one time then surely at another the iron heel of the Conqueror has ground into the mud the Balls of Everyman? Memories of yesterday will not assuage the torrents of blood that flow today from my crotch. Yes, History could pass for a scarlet

text, its jot and tittle graven red in human blood. More armies than shown in the books have planted flags on foreign soil leaving Castration in their wake. But no Slave should die a natural death. There is a point where Caution ends and Cowardice begins. Give me a bullet through the brain from the gun of the beleaguered oppressor on the night of seige. Why is there dancing and singing in the Slave Quarters? A Slave who dies of natural causes cannot balance two dead flies in the Scales of Eternity. Such a one deserves rather to be pitied than mourned.

10   Black woman, without asking how, just say that we survived our forced march and travail through the Valley of Slavery, Suffering, and Death—there, that Valley there beneath us hidden by that drifting mist. Ah, what sights and sounds and pain lie beneath that mist! And we had thought that our hard climb out of that cruel valley led to some cool, green and peaceful, sunlit place—but it's all jungle here, a wild and savage wilderness that's overrun with ruins.

11   But put on your crown, my Queen, and we will build a New City on these ruins.


## REVIEW

### Content

1. What "Return" is Cleaver talking about? Why does Cleaver refer, in paragraph 4, to "being dead"? Do you understand paragraph 3? Tie in here paragraph 8 and the second half of paragraph 9 (from "But no Slave should . . ."). Why does Cleaver say, "The white man was your man and my man" (paragraph 1)?
2. Cleaver is seen by some as being a sexist. Consider paragraph 4. What is *your* position on the often debated question of whether the Black woman's first obligation is to the cause of the Black man (as in the Black Movement) or to her own self-development (as through the Women's Movement)? Is Cleaver's plea a valid one?

### Rhetoric

3. Cleaver's cry needs to be heard, as well as read. Following a reading aloud of part of it, discuss the voice, the tone, the mood. Is the ferocity, the near-violent tone, *over*done? If not, why does so much of it at once, rushing like a great current, not lose its effectiveness? What is the effect of Cleaver's having made the entire last half of paragraph 7 one sentence? Does Cleaver's language put you off? If it would ordinarily, but does not here, why?
4. Why does Cleaver capitalize certain words you would not expect to find capitalized? Why is paragraph 6 in italics, and part of paragraph 7 in all capital letters?

**Projects**

5. Compose a passionate plea for the righting of some wrong in society. Speak with the voice of any group you see as treated unfairly in any way: the prisoner, the student, the underpaid worker, the homosexual, the child not treated with respect as a human being. Make your outcry as strong as possible, perhaps utilizing some of Cleaver's techniques.

6. Write a descriptive paper about something that really moves you— something that you feel passionately enough about that you can muster such vivid phrases as Cleaver uses in paragraph 7.

# The New Racism: Sexism

## ELLEN WILLIS

Ellen Willis is a contributing editor of *Ms.* magazine, writes for *The New Yorker,* and has written a wide variety of articles for the Women's Movement. "The New Racism: Sexism" first appeared in *Mademoiselle,* in September, 1969, as "Whatever Happened to Women?" Willis answers her own question with "Nothing"—on account of the image of "femininity" which society has fostered, locking the female into inactivity and under-achieving. In this article, Willis examines how various institutions—schools, the professional and business worlds, sex-role stereotyping, and marriage and the family—have promoted ineffectiveness in the female and challenges women to unify to fight sexism—on all its fronts.

1   Feminism has revived. It began stirring in 1963, when Betty Friedan deflated the myth of the fulfilled suburban housewife. It got a push from a prankish Southern Senator who, to point up the absurdity of the proposed Civil Rights Act, added a sex-discrimination clause to the fair-employment provision. And it made its first public appearance when a number of professional women founded the National Organization for Women (NOW), a civil-rights group concerned mostly with bread-and-butter issues—discrimination in education, employment, and public accommodations; restrictive abortion laws; lack of day-care facilities. At the same time, younger women involved in the radical movement were

Reprinted by permission of Ellen Willis and International Famous Agency. Copyright ©1970 by Ellen Willis.

discovering that they were second-class revolutionaries. Men who proclaimed the right of all people to control their own lives still expected women to make the coffee, lick the stamps, take typing jobs to support their men's movement work—to do anything, in fact, except help make political decisions on an equal basis. In the past two years, more and more radical women have formed separate groups to discuss their situation as radicals and as women. Out of this separation has come the Women's Liberation Movement, which is growing so fast that some large cities have as many as 20 groups. Although Women's Liberation is also interested in concrete issues, its perspective is very different from NOW's. Radical feminists do not want equal privileges in the existing society; they want to restructure it, changing its definitions of masculine and feminine, of work and the family.

## Women and Blacks

2      Like the early feminist movement, which grew out of the campaign to end slavery, the present-day women's movement has been inspired and influenced by the black liberation struggle. The situation of women and blacks is similar in many ways. Just as blacks live in a world defined by whites, women live in a world defined by males. (The generic term for human being is "man"; "woman" means "wife of man.") To be female or black is to be peculiar; whiteness and maleness are the norm. Newspapers do not have "men's pages," nor would anyone think of discussing the "man problem." Racial and sexual stereotypes also resemble each other: women, like blacks, are said to be childish, incapable of abstract reasoning, innately submissive, biologically suited for menial tasks, emotional, close to nature.

3      Most important, both women and blacks have a history of slavery— only female slavery goes back much further. From the beginnings of civilization until very recently, women in most societies were literally the property of their husbands and fathers. Even now, many vestiges of that chattel status persist in law and custom. Wives are still known by their husbands' names. In many states, a wife is legally required to perform domestic services, have sexual relations on demand if her health permits, and live with her husband wherever *he* chooses or be guilty of desertion. Restaurants, bars, and other public accommodations can legally refuse to admit a woman without a male escort or exclude her altogether. And vote or no vote, politics has remained a male preserve. Women make up more than half the population, but hold less thant 1 percent of elected offices. They also get few political appointments, except for the inevitable "adviser on consumer affairs" (women's place is in the supermarket).

4      In any case, the "emancipated" woman, like the freed slaves, has mere-

ly substituted economic dependence for legal subjection. According to Government statistics, white women workers earn even less than black men. Most women, especially mothers, must depend on men to support them, and that fact alone gives men power over their lives.

## Is Change Needed?

5    By now, almost everyone recognizes racism as an evil. But in spite of all the parallels, most people either defend sexism or deny its existence. "Yes, it's a man's world," some say, "and that's the way it should be. Normal women like the female role." As respected a figure as Dr. Spock recently wrote in a women's magazine, "Biologically and temperamentally, I believe, women were made to be concerned first and foremost with child care, husband care, and home care." Then he explains away the discontent of many women with these roles by saying that their education has confused them! Other antifeminists insist, "Women *are* free. They can vote, work, and have orgasms—what more do they want? In fact, women are too free. They're taking over and robbing men of their masculinity." In between these extremes is the argument that "women can liberate themselves individually; they don't need a movement."

6    The usual response to any mention of feminism is laughter. "Feminists" are little old ladies brandishing umbrellas, square-jawed mannish freaks, or humorless puritans. This prejudice is so strong that even some activists in the women's movement have been reluctant to call themselves feminists or identify in any way with the original women's-rights movement. Because antifeminist sentiment comes from women as well as men, it can't be dismissed out of hand as male propaganda aimed at keeping us in our place. The questions must be taken seriously. Is male supremacy natural and desirable? Are we already as free as we want to be? Do we need a movement?

7    To get an idea of why I'm convinced we *do* need a movement, let's analyze the situation of the most privileged woman in history—the young, educated female who is so often referred to as the "emancipated," or "new," or "modern" woman. This is the woman who wants to enjoy sex, share love and an equal companionship with a man or men, and do engaging work outside the home as well as having children. How likely is she to achieve these not unreasonable goals?

## Training for Femininity

8    In the typical American family, a girl is trained from babyhood to be what the culture defines as feminine. Everyone encourages her to

act cute and charming and flirt with her father, her uncles, and little boys. When she announces that she wants to be a fireman, her mother laughs: girls can't be firemen; you'll be a mother, like me. Or a nurse. Or a teacher. When she roughhouses, parents brag, "She's as tough as a boy." Yet at the same time they warn, "Someday you'll have to stop acting like a boy and be a lady." Most likely her brothers are free to play while she helps with the dishes, and her parents are more tolerant of their noise, dirt, and disobedience—after all, boys will be boys.

9      When she reaches adolescence, she finds that if she wants friendship and approval from other kids she must direct most of her energy toward pleasing boys. That means being preoccupied with clothes and makeup—with how she looks instead of what she does. It means absorbing all the advice about how to have a "good personality" and "build up a boy's ego." (No one worries about her ego.) And it means coming to understand that her status in the world and her worth as a person depend not on what she accomplishes, but on whom she marries. An A in physics is fine, but unless she is also pretty and sought-after, people will pity her and consider her braininess a compensation. She also learns that initiative in social activities belongs to the boys; it is her place to wait by the phone. When she wants a boy's company she can't approach him directly, but must maneuver him into asking her. She steps out of this role at her peril—if she is very pretty and self-assured she may get away with it, but otherwise she faces humiliating snubs. After a while—if, like most girls, she can't measure up to the standards of attractiveness glorified by the mass media and exemplified by the "popular" few—she develops feelings of inferiority that may last a lifetime. Sometimes she rebels and withdraws from the game, but only at the price of loneliness.

## At College

10     Then comes college. If a girl hasn't already lost her incentive to do anything but catch a husband, she is likely to run into new obstacles. Parents will go out of their way to send a boy to the college he prefers; with a girl, they are more reluctant. They may insist that she live at home and go to a public college because it's cheaper, and what difference can it make to a girl? Or put pressure on her to study "something practical that you can fall back on," like teaching. Or make it clear that in return for their investment, she had better snare a professional man.

11     At school she will have to cope with paternalism, condescension, and sometimes outright hostility from male instructors, especially if she takes "masculine" subjects like math or science. If she is particularly bright she may win the highest of all accolades, "You think like a man." She will find that, except in traditionally female fields, professional and grad-

uate schools discriminate in their admissions and financial-aid policies on the grounds that it is a risk to train women who are going to have children and drop out. This becomes a self-fulfilling prophecy. Because of the stubborn prejudice against part-time students and the virtual absence of facilities for communal child care, a woman who gets pregnant accidentally or doesn't want to wait until her childbearing years are half over is often forced to drop out. Theoretically, the husband could stay home instead, but this idea so offends our deepest male-supremacist taboos that few wives would dare even to imagine such an arrangement.

## Discrimination in Employment

12      If a woman does manage to finish graduate school, she faces blatant discrimination in almost every profession, from college teaching and newspaper reporting to medicine and law. In spite of the Civil Rights Act, she has a harder time finding a job and is paid less than a man for the same work. She has to endure nosy personal questions from interviewers who want to know if she's getting married soon; if she's planning to have children; how she'll take care of them if she does. And because of the stigma against women having any authority, she has less freedom on the job. Often, she is afraid to assert herself—all her life she has heard that aggressive women are nasty, man-hating misfits. (Note, for example, a recent ad for a Speedwriting course. Under the caption IS THIS YOUR BOSS? OR IS THIS YOUR BOSS? are two pictures, one of a fat, frowning woman, the other of a clean-cut, smiling man. Guess which we're supposed to prefer?) Her male associates or subordinates are likely to resent her unless she acts "feminine"—i.e., pretends to defer to their superior judgment. (Dr. Mary Meade, a school administrator and recent appointee to the New York Board of Education, has remarked that her technique for getting her suggestions accepted is to convince one of the men she works with to transmit it to the rest.) And she will be inhibited because she knows that a woman has to be twice as good as a man—any mistake will be attributed to female incompetence.

13      The college graduate with no specialized training is even worse off. She will probably end up as a secretary or "gal Friday" with little or no chance of promotion to a policy-making job. The secretary in America is not only a typing-shorthand-telephone-answering machine, but a glorified housewife and quasi geisha girl. She is expected to look pretty and fashionable, have a "good personality," make coffee for the boss, soothe his temper, flatter him, and make him think her ideas are his own. Even if she does, in fact, do original work and make decisions, it is her boss who gets the money and status.

# The "New Woman" and Sex

14     The sexual emancipation of the "new woman" is as illusory as the economic. True, the cruder aspects of the double standard are in disrepute. But real sexual freedom implies that each sex cares equally about the physical and emotional needs of the other. In our sexist society, this is far from the case. Women are brought up to be sensitive to a man's needs, to put him first. Men accept this sensitivity as their due and rarely reciprocate. Rather, they tend to see women as objects, as pretty or ugly, easy to get or a challenge, a good catch or a last resort. In general, women are sexually attracted to men whose whole personality interests them; a man's pursuit of nice legs or breasts or long blond hair may have nothing to do with whether he likes the person they belong to. This naturally makes women more hesitant than men to enter sexual relationships. And their hesitancy then impels men to play more elaborate seduction games, reinforcing the hesitancy.

15     In a way, the relaxation of sexual mores just makes a woman's life more difficult. If she is not cautious about sex, she is likely to get hurt; if she is too cautious, she will lose her man to more obliging women. Either way, her decision is based at least partly on fear and calculation, not on her spontaneous needs and desires. Another myth that needs debunking is that women have won the right to equal sexual enjoyment. Unfortunately, as men have become more sensitive and knowledgeable about female sexuality, they have also begun to *demand* passion from women as an index of their virility. Orgasmic capacity has become another criterion of a desirable object, like good looks. Under such pressure, a woman who cares about a man is increasingly tempted to let him think she is turned on whether she is or not. To refuse him if she's not in the mood or explain to him how to excite her or take the initiative herself is to risk "deflating his ego," provoking accusations of frigidity, and inducing him to look elsewhere for confirmation of his talents.

16     Men want women to be available and responsive, but without making too many demands or challenging their sexual prerogatives. By now it has become a psychiatric cliché that many men have reacted to their wives' new sexual aggressiveness with loss of interest or even impotence. The implication is clear; go back to your passive role, or else. Nearly all the participants in a recent magazine survey of young men's attitudes toward the birth-control pill resented the pill because they felt it made women too independent. Even men who defend the sexual revolution the loudest often display contempt for a woman who has a lot of affairs—not because they really think she is "bad," but because her departure from the traditional role is an implicit threat to their power position.

17      Finally, the sexual double standard can never disappear so long as women are denied contraceptives and abortion on demand. Birth control is not so easily available as is supposed, especially to young, unmarried girls. (Bill Baird, the director of a Long Island birth-control clinic, is currently appealing a three-month sentence for publicly breaking Massachusetts law by handing an unmarried woman a bottle of spermicidal foam.) And thousands of women die or are seriously injured each year as the result of messed-up abortions. Our "new woman" is probably white and middle class and thus unlikely to stick a coat hanger through her uterus or give herself over to a $10-a-job butcher, but even high-class illegal abortions can be dangerous and degrading. Yet, in most cases a woman's only other alternative is to bear a child she doesn't want or cannot afford, emotionally, physically, or financially. One of the ugliest florescences of sexism is the state's power to force a woman to use her body for reproduction. The Constitution prohibits involuntary servitude and guarantees every citizen equal protection of the laws; how can compulsory pregnancy be justified? Politicians and churchmen who moralize about killing the fetus care more about an unconscious clump of cells than about the suffering of living women. Those who say, "She's had her fun, she should take the consequences," are denying women (even married women, who dominate the abortion statistics) the right to sexual happiness on the same basis as men.

## Marriage and Motherhood

18      The institution that affects women's lives most is marriage. For most women, it is a central goal. If a woman wants children, she must marry or suffer social ostracism and economic hardship. Marriage also removes her from the social-sexual rat race and gives her status: she has succeeded as a woman. But does it give her what she wants most—genuine love and companionship? If so, it is only because human tenderness and concern sometimes manage to flourish in the worst of circumstances.

19      Marriage, though disguised as a freely contracted bond between equals, is in fundamental respects a master-slave relationship. It is more necessary to women, but more beneficial to men. A woman's training in being supportive and ego-building is basically practice for the subordinate role in marriage, where she is expected to put her husband's work and interests above her own and provide him with a comfortable domestic environment. A working wife is nonetheless held responsible for the household, though her husband may "help out."

20      The constant celebration of homemaking in the media cannot conceal the fact that most housework is dirty and boring. Most people would prefer just about any job to being a domestic servant; few single women would stand for a female roommate trying to stick them with all the cleaning. But to do the same dirty work for a husband is supposed to be

a privilege. The rationalization is usually that women are inherently altruistic, which makes about as much sense as Senator George Murphy's remark that Mexicans are better suited to stoop labor because they are "built low to the ground."

21     It is equally specious to imagine that because women are uniquely equipped to give birth and nurse infants, they also have a special talent for changing diapers and wiping noses. Much, perhaps most, of child rearing involves routine work that, however necessary for the child, is not particularly edifying for the parent. And Dr. Spock to the contrary, many women have no temperamental gift for relating to children; many men undoubtedly do, or would if they ever had a chance to develop it. Anyway, taking care of children, however rewarding, is not the equivalent of work in the outside world. Children need love, support, someone to stand behind them and put their welfare first—more of what a culturally approved wife is already providing for her husband. A mother cannot use her children as outlets for her creative energies without making them into things that exist for her benefit instead of their own. But if she decides that she needs a vocation of her own, even if she already has one, she comes up against institutionalized sexism. Full-time motherhood is the norm, and the system discourages alternatives. The community refuses to take any responsibility for the children of working mothers. Since most part-time jobs are marginal—both spiritually and economically—it is almost impossible, even when the husband is willing, for most couples to break with the traditional division of labor and share outside work, domestic chores, and child rearing. The only option for a career woman-mother is to hire a poorer woman with fewer choices to take her place in the home. And this is nothing but exploitation, just piling the load on another woman's back.

22     That is the other side of the woman problem. For most women—the millions of file clerks, factory workers, welfare mothers, working-class housewives, daughters of rigid patriarchal families—are not "new women" and have never pretended to be liberated. Citing the pseudo-emancipation of an educated minority as proof that women are free has been one of the crueler sports of postwar sociology and journalism.

## Free Choices?

23     Many women insist that they are happy with things as they are. But would they have chosen the same life if they really had a free choice in the matter or could conceive of an alternative? Male supremacy has existed for so long that it has come to seem an unalterable absolute. What is significant is not that most women are making the best of it, but that more and more women are beginning to rebel, to insist on their primacy as human beings. As for the argument that the emancipation of women has already gone too far, this is akin to the conviction

of many whites that the blacks are taking over. When a group is used to mistaking certain privileges for natural rights, any encroachment on those privileges is regarded as persecution.

24    But the most dangerous illusion is that women can liberate themselves as individuals. Male supremacy is not a problem of individual relationships, but a pervasive social force. No man or woman is unaffected by it. The bohemian and radical subcultures are no less sexist than straight society. In hippie communes, the women still do the cooking and cleaning; the chauvinism of radical men inspired Women's Liberation. A woman cannot hope to find a man who is free of sexist attitudes, nor can she make a man give up his privileges by arguing. He will just find another woman who accepts the *status quo*. We will only begin to solve the problem when women organize and back each other up. That is the immediate goal of Women's Liberation—to get women together, make them see each other as sisters and allies instead of competitors for male favors. As yet we have no clear vision of the new society. That will come later. But we do know that sexism, like racism, is incompatible with human dignity. And we are prepared to fight.

## REVIEW

### Content

1. Willis' article offers many points for debate. Where do you agree with her? Do you disagree at any points? If so, be prepared to defend your position in class discussion.
2. In the several years since Willis' article was first published, some of the situations she writes about have undergone changes. Cite examples. Are you glad, or do you regret these changes? Why do you feel as you do?

### Rhetoric

3. Willis, in this piece of persuasive writing, strives to structure her arguments tightly, to anticipate the opposition, to offer adequate support for her statements. Explain how she tries to make her position a convincing one by pointing to specific techniques of argumentation that she uses.
4. Although she is seriously discussing a subject she obviously cares a great deal about, Willis yet manages to write with clarity and control, and even some humor, if sometimes with a satirical edge. Point to sentences where her sense of style helps to make a highly controversial point at least palatable enough that you are willing to keep reading.

### Projects

5. Write a paper in which you develop one of the following from Willis' article: (a) "Normal women like the female role"; (b) "Women *are*

free. They can vote, work, and have orgasms—what more do they
want?"; (c) "Women are too free. They're taking over and robbing
men of their masculinity."

6. The ERA (Equal Rights Amendment) was passed by Congress in the
early 1970s and then went to the states for the ratification necessary
to make it a part of the Constitution. Get a copy of the Amendment
(from your college library) and consider the implications of its becoming a part of the law of the land. Write a paper either supporting
or opposing the Amendment.

# The Gay Mystique

## PETER FISHER

Peter Fisher writes out of his own experience in his book *The Gay Mystique:
The Myth and Reality of Male Homosexuality* (1972), from which the selection below comes. Fisher's book treats such topics as "Are Some of Your
Best Friends Gay?" "How Do Homosexuals Really Feel About Women?,"
"Is Gay Better Than Straight?," "How Dangerous Is the Gay World?," and
"What Does a Gay Teacher Teach Your Child?" In the excerpt here, Fisher
talks generally about how homosexuals want to be accepted by their straight
friends and, more specifically, about his own parents' perception of him
and his lover Marc. He reminds the reader of the essentially *human* needs
of us all.

1   There are some straight people who use many of the various offensive
slang terms for homosexuals without realizing they are put-downs. Embarrassment about homosexuality is still so common that some people
cannot bring themselves to use the word "homosexual"—they find it
distastefully clinical. Instead they will refer to homos, queers, queens,
fairies, faggots, pansies, and—where gay women are concerned—dykes
and lezzies, not really realizing that gay people find these terms insulting
and demeaning.

2   Some people who would never dream of referring to blacks as niggers
or Jews as kikes will use derogatory terms for gay people casually. Some
don't realize this is in poor taste; others don't think it matters.

3   People who use "nigger" usually will have the sense not to do so
in front of black people. It's not difficult to maintain this minimum
courtesy, because there is seldom any problem in identifying blacks. But

most gay people are invisible, and straights are often unaware that some of their friends are gay. Gay people who are still in the closet often hear people whom they consider friends refer to homosexuals as queers and faggots or tell antihomosexual jokes. This experience is hardly likely to make a gay person feel that he will be well received if he ceases to be secretive about his homosexuality.

## Coming Out

4    Many gay people find the idea of coming out quite terrifying. Aside from the difficulties they can expect to have with their families, they fear that their straight friends will turn against them and no longer want to have anything to do with them. If somebody is a real friend, an admission of homosexuality won't change his or her feelings in the slightest, but many gay people find it difficult to put this to the test.

5    When gay people tell straight friends they are gay, various stock responses are encountered over and over. "But you don't look gay"—as though all homosexuals could be expected to look alike. Some straight people will say that they would have preferred not to know. After all, if the person was able to keep his homosexuality a secret so successfully, why make such a big issue of it now? Nobody really wants to know. The emotional cost of a secret life is enormous.

6    Another common response is "I'm sorry" or "What a shame." After all, some people will say, everyone has his problems, and you just have to learn to live with them. But not many homosexuals enjoy being treated as though they were handicapped or emotionally crippled.

7    The situation is an awkward one. Given the fact that a friend may have felt it necessary to hide his homosexuality for years, it is hard to know how to respond to it in positive terms when it is finally revealed. About the only thing you can say is "Right on!"

8    Once a gay person has made his homosexuality known, even his most sympathetic friends may find it difficult to treat him as he would like to be treated. Who knows how homosexuals like to be treated anyway?

9    It's a lot easier to figure out how gay people do *not* like to be treated, for this requires only a little common sense.

10    The homosexual who has left the closet does not want to be treated like an invalid with an unmentionable disease—he does not want to be treated like a tragic victim of circumstances beyond his control. Things can be bad enough for gay people in our society so that they would prefer not to be constantly reminded of how bad they are, no matter how sympathetic the intentions. It is too easy for a sympathetic attitude to come across as patronizing or condescending. Besides, after a while gay people get thoroughly tired of talking about the problems they encounter as gay people.

11     Straight people sometimes wonder how they should introduce a gay friend to other acquaintances. Do you say that he is gay, and thereby make an issue out of it, or do you avoid mentioning it, thereby creating an impression that his homosexuality is an embarrassment to you? The best thing for a straight person in this position to do is to ask his gay friend what he would prefer. Most gay people see no point in making an issue about the matter with every stranger they meet. They have told their friends about their homosexuality because their friends are important to them. Unless there is some particular reason for introducing someone as a gay friend, what difference does it make?

## The "Good" Homosexual

12     The problem most frequently encountered by gay people who have left the closet is being expected to be on "good" behavior. The "good" homosexual is the gay equivalent of an Uncle Tom. He is supposed to be serious and reticent about his homosexuality. If it comes up as a topic of discussion, he is expected to deal with it in intellectual rather than emotional terms, speak in a sociological vein about the many problems faced by homosexuals. He should be understanding about the hostility he encounters from many straights—after all, they really can't help it, you know, they were brought up that way and they don't know any better. He should never reveal the measure of the anger he sometimes feels.

13     The "good" homosexual is a heterosexual homosexual. He may wear a sign around his neck stating "I am a homosexual," but he should look, act, think, and feel no differently than a straight person would. He should not be an embarrassment. His straight friends should never have to feel uncomfortable about introducing him to people whose respect they want to keep. He should be a tribute to their liberalism, not to their unconventionality.

14     Actually, the "good" homosexual should not even really be a heterosexual homosexual. Heterosexuals are all too open about their sexuality, and the "good" homosexual should avoid giving any hint that he has a sex life. He must be sexually neutral.

15     The "good" homosexual does not mention the affairs he has from time to time or the men he is seeing. If he falls in love, he does not make others uncomfortable by trying to share his joy with them. If an affair comes to a sudden end, he does not embarrass his straight friends by telling them of his unhappiness. He should not mention having sex with other men, because most straight people find the whole idea distasteful. If he has a lover, the two of them should behave like gentlemen—straight gentlemen—in front of other people. This is particularly noticeable when it comes to displays of affection.

## Reactions of Families

16    My lover Marc and I found this to be the case the first time we visited my family as a couple. It had taken a good deal of courage for my parents to even invite us together in the first place. They were anything but pleased about my homosexuality, and it was difficult for them to be confronted with living proof of that homosexuality in the form of my lover. It was an awkward situation for all of us, and yet a vital step in attempting to understand one another better.

17    We sat around having a drink and chatting. Without thinking anything of it, I rested my arm on Marc's shoulder while we talked. Later, my parents told me privately that it had made them very uncomfortable to watch us "making love" right before their eyes. Making love? The same thing happened when we visited Marc's relatives. He happened to put his hand on my knee and was later told how embarrassing it had been to watch us "making out and petting."

18    I could understand and sympathize with our families' reactions. In straight society, men are not supposed to touch. Nor are they supposed to be homosexuals.

19    Many straight people will say "Right on" when it's a matter of leaving the closet, admitting that we are gay, and being ourselves after years of hiding and secrecy. But when we try to really be ourselves, live full and happy lives, search for love, and enjoy it when we find it—they tell us we are going too far. It is all right for us to be homosexuals in name, but we must leave our love in the closet.

20    This is too much to ask.

### REVIEW

#### Content

1. If you were against homosexuality when you began to read this selection, had you been viewing your feelings about it in the context of prejudice? If not, did paragraph 2 disturb you, especially if you consider yourself without prejudice toward Blacks and Jews and other minorities? How did you respond to paragraph 17—both to Peter's and Marc's actions and to their relatives' reactions? What do your responses tell you? Do you think homosexuals should "leave their love in the closet"? If so, why? If not, are you *sure* you are ready for it to come out?

2. Discuss paragraphs 12, 14, and 15. How would the "requirements" of these paragraphs feel to you if you were in Fisher's position? How about paragraphs 6 and 10?

**Rhetoric**

3. What makes the slang terms listed in the last sentence of paragraph 1 so damaging to the feelings of the homosexual? Do you agree with Fisher that it is difficult for people to use the word "homosexual" because "they find it clinically distasteful"? Do you find any irony in the use of the word "gay" in the homosexual community itself? Do you see how this word, used in its literal sense, might damage, rather than enhance, the image of homosexuality? Finally, what does this entire discussion tell you about language and how it affects our lives and persons' self-images?
4. Fisher develops his point partly by analogy with the situation of the Black. Does the analogy work, in each instance where he uses it? Why do you think he chose this particular analogy?

**Projects**

5. Work up your responses to the last three questions in Question 1 into a written argument.
6. Fisher does not develop the point of the last sentence in paragraph 5. Imagine yourself, male or female, in the homosexual situation and write a paper in which you explain this sentence; reinforce your point by specific examples of what "a secret life" could do to you emotionally. Or perhaps you have so lived, or are contemplating so living, in another sort of situation requiring secrecy—a relationship with a married person or living with someone unmarried and trying to keep it hidden. If so, you could write here from your own experience, or from your own projected fantasy.

# Women in Cages

## JESSICA MITFORD

Jessica Mitford (1917–    ) is an Englishwoman who now lives in California. Her books include an autobiography, *Daughters and Rebels* (1960); *The American Way of Death* (1963), an exposé of the business of dying in this country; *The Trial of Dr. Spock* (1969), and *Kind and Usual Punishment: The Prison Business* (1973). The selection below comes from *Kind and Usual Punishment.* As a feature of an eight-day workshop on crime and corrections, Mitford and her fellow participants spent a day and a night as prisoners behind bars. Mitford was sent to the District of Columbia Women's Detention Center. She recounts her disturbingly realistic day and night there in "Women in Cages."

1    . . . The Women's Detention Center is a gloomy pile of masonry at the edge of the ghetto, formerly used by the police department as a temporary lock-up for people taken into custody. Since 1966 it has been used for detention of women awaiting trial and as a reformatory for sentenced women. Once inside, we were taken in charge by several women guards, symbolically clanking real keys.

2    The first step for the newly arrested is called "Reception," although it was unlike any reception I have ever attended. The handcuffs now dispensed with, we were assembled in a large room; our handbags emptied on a counter and the contents catalogued, we were photographed and fingerprinted. Ordered to strip, we were searched for narcotics: "Bend over, spread cheeks." Our heads were examined for lice. From a bin of prison dresses in brightly patterned cottons with unfinished hem and sleeves we chose for approximate fit. (I learned later that these bizarre garments were ordered by Mr. Kenneth Hardy, director of D.C. Corrections, a benign administrator who told me he thought they would restore "a sense of individuality" to women formerly required to wear prison gray.) Cigarettes, lipsticks, paperback books were scrutinized for contraband and then returned to us.

3    From the recesses of the building we heard a disturbing muffled, rhythmic wail. Was it the sound of mechanical equipment, an air-conditioner gone slightly out of kilter? I asked a guard. "Oh, that's just Viola, she's in Adjustment for her nerves."

4    "It doesn't seem to be doing her nerves much good."

5    "Her trouble is she's mental, always bothering the other inmates. So we keep her in Adjustment."


## Waiting for Trial

6    Living quarters at the Detention Center are on two floors, each accommodating some 45 women. About half the women confined there have not been convicted of any crime. Their sole offense: inability to make bail, for which they are imprisoned, often for months on end, waiting for their cases to come to trial. (A recent census report reveals that 52 percent of the nation's jail population are "confined for reasons other than being convicted of a crime," or, to put it more bluntly, because they are too poor to pay the bail bond broker.) Unlike most jails, where the "presumed innocent" are herded in with the guilty, the Detention Center segregates those awaiting trial from the convicted offenders.

7    We were placed with the latter group. Our fellow-inmates were mostly "misdemeanants" serving sentences of less than one year (three months is the average term here), but there were also women sentenced for felonies—robbery, murder, aggravated assault—awaiting transfer to a federal women's penitentiary. More than 90 percent of both inmates and staff of this prison are black, as is 71 percent of the general population of the District. A ghetto within a ghetto.

8    Our domicile was a short and narrow corridor on one side of which are the cells, at the far end a dining room with television set. Women were standing in desultory knots in the corridor, sitting in their cells, or watching TV. The overall impression: a combination of college dorm (silly jokes, putdowns, occasional manifestations of friendliness), lunatic asylum (underlying sense of desolate futility), a scene from *The Threepenny Opera* (graffiti on the walls: "Welcome to the Whores' Paradise!"). I was struck by the number of little-girl faces, kids who except for their funny-looking clothes could be part of a high-school class, and by one or two sad, vacant old faces. The median age here is twenty-five.

## A Cell with Della

9    As we entered, our names were called out, we were handed sheets and led to our assigned cells, tiny cubicles with two beds, a dresser, and a clothesline for hanging coats and dresses (the prison, like most, is fearfully overcrowded and now holds more than twice its intended capacity). My cellmate was a pleasant-faced black woman in her early thirties, named Della. She welcomed me like a good hostess, helped me make my bed, and apologized for the stale, dead smell compounded of people, food, and disinfectant that pervaded our quarters: "We used to have at least some breeze, but they've cut off the air. There's a new rule against opening the corridor window because they claim the inmates were letting down rope to haul up contraband brought by their boyfriends. Now, does that make any sense? With the officers watching you like a hawk every minute of the day and night?"

10    From Della I learned that, as I had suspected, we had been let off lightly at "Reception." The usual routine, she told me, includes a vaginal examination as part of the search for contraband and a Lysol spraying of the head. She had found the experience horrifying, totally degrading. Furthermore some of the guards "get their kicks" from scaring the neophyte inmate by horrendous hints of what to expect from the "bulldaggers" (prison slang for lesbians). Is there actually much homosexuality, I asked? A certain amount, but not as much as the administration seems to think. "They are really hipped on the subject," she said. "They have bed checks all hours of the night, they come around flashing their bright lights, it's hard to get any sleep."

11    Della had been in the section for unsentenced prisoners for nine weeks waiting for her trial. In all that time she never saw her court-appointed lawyer, and her letters to him were unanswered. She met him for the first and only time in court on the day of her trial, where he advised her to plead guilty: "But he never asked me anything about my case, said he didn't want to hear. Said if we tried to fight it, the judge would be hard on me. But I don't see how he could have been any harder—six months for one count of soliciting!"

12    We wandered out into the crowded corridor to join the others. Because of the visitors, Della told me, everyone was on good behavior: "We *scrubbed* this place, girl!" And clean, though dreary, it certainly was.

13    Our group was there to learn, so we started asking questions. The Maryland legislator inquired about recreation facilities. "Re-cre-ation!" an inmate hooted derisively. "Come here, girls, I'll show you." She led us to one of the barred windows, through which we could barely descry a small concrete quadrangle entirely hemmed in by the building. On fine days, she explained, the entire population is sometimes taken down there for an hour or so if the correctional officers have time. Vocational training programs? "There's eight old broken-down typewriters some-where in the building. I don't know if anybody ever uses them, though. Or you can go down to group therapy, but who wants it? A bunch of us bullshitting about our deprived lives?"

## Punishment for Laughter

14    We had been told the authorities had arranged for the visitors to sample various aspects of prison life, that some would spend the night in sickbay, others would be brought before a disciplinary committee, accused of breaking the rules. To fortify myself against the latter even-tuality I asked for a copy of the prison rule book. "No inmate shall engage in loud or boisterous talk, laughter, whistling or other vocal expression," it said in part. "Talking is permitted at all times except in church and in school, but talking must be conducted in a normal voice except on the recreation fields." One of the prisoners, a vivacious young black woman, confided to me that she was due to be disciplined that day for laughing too loud but had been reprieved because of our visit: "It's a dumb thing anyway to be punished for laughing. When you come to think of it, sometimes it's sort of a release to laugh out loud."

15    As in hospitals, food is served at unexpected times. At four thirty we went into the dining room to collect our trays of dinner. The food wasn't bad, but like most institutional cooking it was dull and starchy with a touch of wilted green. We ate tuna casserole, Jell-O, a choice

of weak coffee or a puce-colored synthetic fruit drink. One of the few white prisoners came and sat beside me, a romantic-looking blonde in her early twenties; she reminded me vaguely of prison movies I had seen. Convicted of possession of heroin, she described her first days in the Detention Center as absolute torture: "You come down cold-turkey, they're not equipped here to treat addicts." She proved to be a discriminating connoisseur of the nation's prisons, and twinkled quite merrily as she rated them for me, one-star, two-star, as in a motel guide. "This joint's by no means the worst, but it's not the best, either." Her goal is to be admitted into one of the treatment centers for narcotics addicts, but so far she has been blocked because they are all full up. She has no idea when, or if, there will ever be an opening for her. What does she do all day? "I work some in the kitchen, just to keep from going crazy. There *isn't* anything to do here." Housekeeping jobs, she explained, are available on our floor but not for the unsentenced women on the floor below: "In some ways they're punished worse than we are, although they haven't even been found guilty of anything." Pay ranges from $5 a month to a top of $13, the higher rate being awarded on the basis of performance and "attitude"; there is no compensation for working part of a month.

## To Disciplinary Committee

16     "Jessica ... Mitford ... to the third ... floor." The voice over the intercom was tinny and disembodied. I started to the door of our corridor and was at once intercepted by a correctional officer. "No, no, you can't go down by yourself," she said, shocked, and, siezing my arm, led me to the elevator. "You're wanted by the disciplinary committee," she said severely. Lock, double-lock all the way, from our fourth-floor abode to the elevator and down. A third-floor guard took over and led me to the small office where I was to be tried.

17     My prosecutors, jury, and judges (for the disciplinary committee incorporates all three functions) were the prison psychologist and two correctional officers. They were trying to look suitably stern, to make it all as "real" as possible. One of the officers read off the charges: "At 17.05 hours, Officer Smith opened the door to your cell and found you locked in a passionate embrace with Maureen [the reporter from the Washington *Post*]. As you know, this is an extremely serious offense. What have you to say?"

18     What, indeed. I could of course deny all (insist she wasn't my type?), but, mindful of my assignment for the ACLU, I decided to go another route. What if I challenged the whole legality of this "trial"? I took a deep breath.

## Prison Rules vs. Prison Crimes

19      "First, I should like to draw your attention to the prison rule book."
(The trio seemed surprised; the rule book, it seems, is not generally
available to prisoners.) "I see you have infractions broken down into
two categories: *crimes* such as assault, theft, possession of narcotics, and
failure to obey *rules*—wasting food, vulgar conversation, not making
one's bed. Homosexual acts between inmates are listed here as a crime.
Before I plead guilty or not guilty to the charge, I should like to see
a copy of the statute under which homosexuality between consenting
females is a crime. I don't believe it is a crime in any jurisdiction. I'm
already in here for one crime. If you find me guilty of another, it will
go very hard with me when my case comes before the parole board."

20      My inquisitors exchanged uncertain looks. "It's not a *statute,* it's a
rule," said one.

21      "But as you've listed it as a *crime,* I want a lawyer to represent me.
I want to cross-examine the officer who accused me, and to call witnesses
who'll verify that I was in the dining room watching TV at 17.05 hours."

22      Nonplussed, the chief correctional officer said she thought they should
send for Mrs. Patricia Taylor, the director of the Detention Center. This
was done, and I repeated my request.

23      "Jessica, you must realize we're only trying to help you," said Mrs.
Taylor.

24      "Well, thanks a lot. But I should still like to assert my right to the
same procedural safeguards that should apply to any citizen accused
of crime."

25      "You don't understand, Jessica, you are in an institution now, you're
an inmate, you haven't a right to a trial. *We'll* decide who's telling the
truth. Now, if Officer Smith hadn't seen that, why would she say she
had?"

26      "But I say she's lying, I'm not guilty and I want a chance to prove
it. Why don't you bring her down here so I can question her, and clear
myself?"

27      "Jessica, do you realize what would happen to discipline if we permitted the inmates to cross-examine the officers?"

28      We went over this a few times; I had made my point, but since it
was only a charade (and I knew Maureen was waiting for her turn before
the disciplinary committee) I soon gave up, and was duly sentenced to
"ten days in Adjustment."

29      What if the situation had been real, I kept thinking? Instead of making this well-reasoned little speech about my constitutional rights I would
have been shouting furiously, perhaps in tears. And instead of listening
and answering calmly, would not my captors have responded in kind—
put me down as a troublemaker or psycho for asserting my rights, and

treated me accordingly? Now I was beginning to "feel." The governessy young criminology student would be proud of me!

## To Adjustment

30    Accompanied by the chief correctional officer, who firmly gripped my arm (did she think I might try to escape?), I traversed several corridors and those eerie wails gradually came closer. The officer in charge of Adjustment took me over. Here the stripping of individuality is turned up a notch. I am given a gray cotton shift in place of the patterned dress from the bin. Bra, shoes, cigarettes, wristwatch, wedding ring, paperback books are confiscated. To her chagrin, the officer discovers that all eight solitary cells are occupied (which means that about one in ten of the inmates is locked up there). I will have to double up with a thief who was put in Adjustment for beating up other women. Not a terribly reassuring thought. The door giving onto the corridor of solitary cells is immensely thick, opened by my keeper with several huge keys. Now we hear the screams full force—not just from Viola, they seem to be coming from several cells. *"Let me out!" "I want out!"* Women are moaning, shrieking, pounding with their fists against their doors. This is "Adjustment"? To what are they being adjusted?

31    "You have company," the officer announces tersely to my cellmate, and she double-locks the door behind us. Mindful of my companion's alleged infraction I flash her a conciliatory smile, but she is pleased to see me, makes me welcome, we sit on the bed (sole furnishing except for an open toilet that flushes only from the outside) and talk.

32    The Thief's Tale was well larded with fantasy, or so it seemed to me. A tall, attractive black woman about thirty years old, she was essentially "state-raised": orphaned at the age of eight, in and out of trouble, in and out of juvenile detention (but mostly in) until her middle twenties. "I tried to go straight for a spell, but I don't really dig it. On welfare, with two little kids to raise—what kind of life is that?" She turned to pickpocketing, a discipline in which she had received much theoretical instruction during her many years in reformatories. "The best place is near the Americana Hotel in New York, that's where lots of businessmen hang out." She told me she could clear upward of $500 on a good night and that once she netted $14,000 from the wallet of an unsuspecting passerby. Yet, in view of her expanding needs, she found it slow going: "My boyfriend and I wanted to start a nightclub in Atlantic City, we figured on $100,000 to open it. So I told him leave it to me, I'd raise it." The quickest way, she decided, was to travel around the country from motel to motel cashing bad checks in amounts of $500 to $1,000. She had got up to $40,000 of the needed capital when the feds caught up with her.

## 17-Year-Old Screams

33    Our corridor had all but quieted down after the guard left. Now the screams started up again, coming apparently from the cell directly opposite ours, a terrible outcry of rage and misery, shrieks and obscenities interspersed with deep, racking sobs. We peered through the tiny grill in our door and could dimly see movement behind the opposite grill, hands clawing, head wildly shaking. My cellmate shouted soothing words across the corridor: "Now, honey, hush up, won't you? If you be a good girl and stop all that noise, I'll speak to Mrs. Taylor, and I'll see that she lets you out of there. If I say to let you out, she'll do it."

34    "Who is she?" I asked.

35    "She's a juvenile, she's down here because she's too young to go up-stairs."

36    *"Too young?* How old is she?"

37    "Seventeen."

38    Of course I didn't believe a word of it. Just another of her delusions, I thought, like the $14,000 wallet, the obliging motel managers who cash $1,000 checks for strangers, her role as confidante and adviser to Mrs. Taylor.

39    Soon—in an hour and a half, to be exact—my "ten days" were up. For further clarification I sought out Mrs. Taylor, a highly qualified black administrator with a long background in social work and Corrections. No longer an "inmate," I was formally ushered into her office, where we discussed what I had heard and seen that day.


## Prostitution and Narcotics

40    First, as to the general prison scene, what are the women here being punished for? The great majority, about 85 percent, are in for a combination of prostitution and narcotics (as one inmate had told me, "They go together like salt and pepper; once you're hooked on the stuff, you have to hustle to support your habit"). Does Mrs. Taylor think prostitution is a crime? No, she believes many women are driven to it by circumstances outside their control. What about drug addiction? That's not a crime either, it's a sickness and should be treated as such.

41    Checking Mrs. Taylor's opinions against those of others in authority, from correctional officers to Mr. Kenneth Hardy, director of the department, I found unanimity on these points. *None* believed that prostitution and drug addiction are "crimes." Thus the patently crazy situation in which the keepers themselves, up and down the line, believe their man-date to imprison these women rests on a fundamentally unsound prem-ise. But, they all point out, they are merely doing the job required

of them by the courts, the legislature, the public: "We don't choose the inmates, we have to take whoever the judges send us."

42    In our discussion of the Adjustment setup, this sense of total irrationality deepened.

43    The case of Viola: she is a diagnosed schizophrenic, Mrs. Taylor explained. Because of a recent court decision, she cannot be transferred to a mental institution without a sanity hearing; but the courts are so clogged with cases that no date for such a hearing has been set. How long will she stay locked away in Adjustment? Nobody knows.

44    The screaming girl across the corridor? My cellmate was right after all, she really *is* only seventeen, she really *is* there because she is too young to go upstairs—in solitary because of a mistake of the Juvenile Court. Finding that she was incorrigible in the children's prison, the judge sentenced her to Women's Detention. But the law says that juvenile offenders may not mix with the adult prison population, so she was put in Adjustment. At first she was allowed "privileges"—mail, books, cigarettes. After several days of total solitude she set her mattress on fire (perhaps, Mrs. Taylor surmised, "to draw attention to herself?"). Consequently she is now considered a "disciplinary case" and all privileges have been withdrawn. How long will she have to stay there? For about three months, until she turns eighteen.

## Risk of Insanity?

45    "Aren't you afraid she'll go completely insane by that time?"

46    "Well . . . there is that danger . . ."

47    Why, I wanted to know, is the inmate who is being punished for some infraction denied books, newspapers, games—*anything* that might make solitary confinement more tolerable?

48    "The idea is to remove her completely from the environment. You heard those women screaming in there. If we'd kept you in there for twenty-four hours, you would have been screaming, too."

49    "Then—is that your purpose, to destroy my self-control, to reduce me to a helpless, howling infant?"

50    "That's a risk we have to take," said Mrs. Taylor with a faint smile.

51    What of homosexuality, recognized by everyone in Corrections as an inevitable consequence of long-term segregation of the sexes? Having driven them to it, why punish for it? "Love affairs" between women inmates, born out of loneliness, longing for human affection, lack of male companionship—does Mrs. Taylor consider this sort of behavior criminal? "No, but if permitted it might lead to jealousy and fights. Besides, I am responsible for their morals while they are in here." *Their* morals? Yet Mrs. Taylor had something there, I thought. Is this not the essence of women's prisons, the punishment of unchaste, unwomanly

behavior, a grotesque bow to long-outmoded nineteenth-century notions of feminine morality?

## No Training or Education

52    There is, Mrs. Taylor regretfully conceded, barely even the pretense of a useful trade or educational program for the women, most of whom she expects to see back again in her custody shortly after they are let out. They exit and reenter as through a revolving door, three quarters of those who are in now have been here before. Chances of getting a decent job when they leave, slim enough for ghetto women in any circumstances, are almost nonexistent for those with prison records, so inevitably they turn to their old ways when released.

53    This, then, is an American women's prison of the 1970's—and "not the worst," as my dinner companion said. A life of planned, unrelieved inactivity and boredom . . . no overt brutality but plenty of random, largely unintentional cruelty . . . a pervasive sense of helplessness and frustration engulfing not only the inmates but their keepers, themselves prisoners trapped in the weird complex of paradoxes that is the prison world.

## REVIEW

### Content

1. A frequent complaint by both prisoners and advocates of prison reform has to do with the loss of individuality and the affronts to human dignity encountered in jails and prisons. Discuss Mitford's account above in this context, citing specific examples. Do you see these as *serious* concerns? If so, what can/should be done about them, inside our present institutions?
2. Mitford refers several times to the "irrationality" and the "paradoxes" of what she observes in the Women's Detention Center. Can you think of other ways in which our present system of punishment fails to make sense? Why is it continued? If you think change is needed, what can *you* do to help change the situation?

### Rhetoric

3. Mitford often quotes directly and at length from conversations she was a part of while in the Detention Center. Does this detract from the points she is trying to make elsewhere through citing statistics and describing conditions?
4. Gertrude Stein is reported to have said to Ernest Hemingway, who frequently used parentheses in his writing: "My dear Ernest, parenthet-

ical remarks are *not* literature." Mitford uses parenthetical remarks often in the above selection. For what various purposes does she use them? Do you find the technique distracting?

**Projects**

5. Based on the "vocal expressions" rule quoted in paragraph 14 and the rules mentioned in paragraph 19, compose a list of rules you feel might be found in the prison rule book at the Detention Center. Then imagine yourself living under these rules. How does this make you feel?

6. It is possible to carry on a "pen pal" correspondence with persons in many jails and prisons. A student in the class can find out how and where through the college library and report back to the class, for those who want to pursue this activity. *OR* Write a letter to your Congressman (and/or your representative in your state legislature) or a letter-to-the-editor protesting prison conditions and pushing for reform; send the letter.

# McMurphy's First Therapy Session

## KEN KESEY

Ken Kesey (1935–   ) is known not only for his own writing, but also as the real-life leader of the Merry Pranksters, a group that travelled about in a psychedelic bus staging happenings, in *The Electric Kool-Aid Acid Test* by Tom Wolfe. The following passage is from Kesey's *One Flew Over the Cuckoo's Nest* (1962), a fictional exposé of life in a mental institution. McMurphy, an independent spirit, is in the hospital because he had gotten fed up with weeding peas on a penal farm and had decided to pretend madness as an escape. He "escapes" into the arms of Big Nurse Ratched, who rules her ward with an iron thumb, breaking the spirit of her charges in the process. The novel itself follows out the struggle between the dauntless McMurphy and the relentless Big Nurse.

1   The nurse takes off her wrist watch and looks at the ward clock and winds the watch and sets it face toward her in the basket. She takes a folder from the basket.

2    "Now. Shall we get into the meeting?"

3    She looks around to see if anybody else is about to interrupt her, smiling steady as her head turns in her collar. The guys won't meet her look; they're all looking for hangnails. Except McMurphy. He's got himself an armchair in the corner, sits in it like he's claimed it for good, and he's watching her every move. He's still got his cap on, jammed tight down on his red head like he's a motorcycle racer. A deck of cards in his lap opens for a one-handed cut, then clacks shut with a sound blown up loud by the silence. The nurse's swinging eyes hang on him for a second. She's been watching him play poker all morning and though she hasn't seen any money pass hands she suspects he's not exactly the type that is going to be happy with the ward rule of gambling for matches only. The deck whispers open and clacks shut again and then disappears somewhere in one of those big palms.

4    The nurse looks at her watch again and pulls a slip of paper out of the folder she's holding, looks at it, and returns it to the folder. She puts the folder down and picks up the log book. Ellis coughs from his place on the wall; she waits until he stops.

5    "Now. At the close of Friday's meeting . . . we were discussing Mr. Harding's problem . . . concerning his young wife. He had stated that his wife was extremely well endowed in the bosom and that this made him uneasy because she drew stares from men on the street." She starts opening to places in the log book; little slips of paper stick out of the top of the book to mark the pages. "According to the notes listed by various patients in the log, Mr. Harding has been heard to say that she 'damn well gives the bastards reason to stare.' He has also been heard to say that he may give *her* reason to seek further sexual attention. He has been heard to say, 'My dear sweet but illiterate wife thinks any word or gesture that does not smack of brickyard brawn and brutality is a word or gesture of weak dandyism.' "

6    She continues reading silently from the book for a while, then closes it.

7    "He has also stated that his wife's ample bosom at times gives him a feeling of inferiority. So. Does anyone care to touch upon this subject further?"

8    Harding shuts his eyes, and nobody else says anything. McMurphy looks around at the other guys, waiting to see if anybody is going to answer the nurse, then holds his hand up and snaps his fingers, like a school kid in class; the nurse nods at him.

9    "Mr.—ah—McMurry?"

10    "Touch upon what?"

11    "What? Touch—"

12    "You ask, I believe, 'Does anyone care to touch upon—' "

13    "Touch upon the—subject, Mr. McMurry, the subject of Mr. Harding's problem with his wife."

14    "Oh. I thought you mean touch upon her—something else."

15    "Now what could you—"

16    But she stops. She was almost flustered for a second there. Some of the Acutes hide grins, and McMurphy takes a huge stretch, yawns, winks at Harding. Then the nurse, calm as anything, puts the log book back in the basket and takes out another folder and opens it and starts reading.

17    "McMurry, Randle Patrick. Committed by the state from the Pendleton Farm for Correction. For diagnosis and possible treatment. Thirty-five years old. Never married. Distinguished Service Cross in Korea, for leading an escape from a Communist prison camp. A dishonorable discharge, afterward, for insubordination. Followed by a history of street brawls and barroom fights and a series of arrests for Drunkenness, Assault and Battery, Disturbing the Peace, *repeated* gambling, and one arrest—for Rape."

18    "Rape?" The doctor perks up.

19    "Statutory, with a girl of—"

20    "Whoa. Couldn't make that stick," McMurphy says to the doctor. "Girl wouldn't testify."

21    "With a child of fifteen."

22    "Said she was *seven*teen, Doc, and she was *plenty* willin'."

23    "A court doctor's examination of the child proved entry, re*peated* entry, the record states—"

24    "So willin', in fact, I took to sewing my pants shut."

25    "The child refused to testify in spite of the doctor's findings. There seemed to be intimidation. Defendant left town shortly after the trial."

26    "Hoo boy, I *had* to leave. Doc, let me tell you"—he leans forward with an elbow on a knee, lowering his voice to the doctor across the room—"that little hustler would of actually burnt me to a frazzle by the time she reached legal sixteen. She got to where she was tripping me and beating me to the floor."

27    The nurse closes up the folder and passes it across the doorway to the doctor. "Our new Admission, Doctor Spivey," just like she's got a man folded up inside that yellow paper and can pass him on to be looked over. "I thought I might brief you on his record later today, but as he seems to insist on asserting himself in the Group Meeting, we might as well dispense with him now."

28    The doctor fishes his glasses from his coat pocket by pulling on the string, works them on his nose in front of his eyes. They're tipped a little to the right, but he leans his head to the left and brings them level. He's smiling a little as he turns through the folder, just as tickled by this new man's brassy way of talking right up as the rest of us, but, just like the rest of us, he's careful not to let himself come right out and laugh. The doctor closes the folder when he gets to the end, and puts his glasses back in his pocket. He looks to where McMurphy is still leaned out at him from across the day room.

29    "You've—it seems—no other psychiatric history, Mr. McMurry?"

30   "Mc*Murphy*, Doc."

31   "Oh? But I thought—the nurse was saying—"

32   He opens the folder again, fishes out those glasses, looks the record over for another minute before he closes it, and puts his glasses back in his pocket. "Yes. McMurphy. That is correct. I beg your pardon."

33   "It's okay, Doc. It was the lady there that started it, made the mistake. I've known some people inclined to do that. I had this uncle whose name was Hallahan, and he went with a woman once who kept acting like she couldn't remember his name right and calling him Hooligan just to get his goat. It went on for months before he stopped her. Stopped her good, too."

34   "Oh? How did he stop her?" the doctor asks.

35   McMurphy grins and rubs his nose with his thumb. "Ah-ah, now, I can't be tellin' that. I keep Unk Hallahan's method a strict secret, you see, in case I need to use it myself someday."

36   He says it right at the nurse. She smiles right back at him, and he looks over at the doctor. "Now; what was you asking about my record, Doc?"

37   "Yes, I was wondering if you've any previous psychiatric history. Any analysis, any time spent in any other institution?"

38   "Well, counting state *and* county coolers—"

39   "*Mental* institutions."

40   "Ah. No, if that's the case. This is my first trip. But I am crazy, Doc. I swear I am. Well here—let me show you here. I believe that other doctor at the work farm . . ."

41   He gets up, slips the deck of cards in the pocket of his jacket, and comes across the room to lean over the doctor's shoulder and thumb through the folder in his lap. "Believe he wrote something, back at the back here somewhere . . ."

42   "Yes? I missed that. Just a moment." The doctor fishes his glasses out again and puts them on and looks to where McMurphy is pointing.

43   "Right here, Doc. The nurse left this part out while she was *summarizing* my record. Where it says, 'Mr. McMurphy has evidenced re*peated*'—I just want to make sure I'm understood completely, Doc—'*repeated* outbreaks of passion that suggest the possible diagnosis of psychopath.' He told me that 'psychopath' means I fight and fuh—pardon me, ladies—means I am he put it *over*zealous in my sexual relations. Doctor, is that real serious?"

44   He asks it with such a little-boy look of worry and concern all over his broad, tough face that the doctor can't help bending his head to hide another little snicker in his collar, and his glasses fall from his nose dead center back in his pocket. All of the Acutes are smiling too, now, and even some of the Chronics.

45   "I mean that overzealousness, Doc, have you ever been troubled by it?"

46 The doctor wipes his eyes. "No, Mr. McMurphy, I'll admit I haven't. I am interested, however, that the doctor at the work farm added this statement: 'Don't overlook the possibility that this man might be feigning psychosis to escape the drudgery of the work farm.' " He looks up at McMurphy. "And what about that, Mr. McMurphy?"

47 "Doctor"—he stands up to his full height, wrinkles his forehead, and holds out both arms, open and honest to all the wide world—"do I look like a sane man?"

48 The doctor is working so hard to keep from giggling again he can't answer. McMurphy pivots away from the doctor and asks the same thing of the Big Nurse: *"Do* I?" Instead of answering she stands up and takes the manila folder away from the doctor and puts it back in the basket under her watch. She sits back down.

49 "Perhaps, Doctor, you should advise Mr. McMurry on the protocol of these Group Meetings."

50 "Ma'am," McMurphy says, "have I told you about my uncle Hallahan and the woman who used to screw up his name?"

51 She looks at him for a long time without her smile. She has the ability to turn her smile into whatever expression she wants to use on somebody, but the look she turns it into is no different, just a calculated and mechanical expression to serve her purpose. Finally she says, "I beg your pardon. Mack-Murph-y." She turns back to the doctor. "Now, Doctor, if you would explain . . ."

52 The doctor folds his hands and leans back. "Yes, I suppose what I should do is explain the complete *theory* of our Therapeutic Community, while we're at it. Though I usually save it until later. Yes. A good idea, Miss Ratched, a fine idea."

53 "Certainly the theory too, doctor, but what I had in mind was the rule that the patients remain seated during the course of the meeting."

54 "Yes. Of course. Then I will explain the theory. Mr. McMurphy, one of the first things is that the patients remain seated during the course of the meeting. It's the only way, you see, for us to maintain order."

55 "Sure, Doctor. I just got up to show you that thing in my record book."

56 He goes over to his chair, gives another big stretch and yawn, sits down, and moves around for a while like a dog coming to rest. When he's comfortable, he looks over at the doctor, waiting.

## REVIEW

### Content

1. Do you find the scene believable? How do you feel toward McMurphy? Toward Nurse Ratched? Is your response here disturbing in any way, when you consider that Nurse Ratched has the authority of the State

behind her? What does the ongoing struggle between McMurphy and Nurse Ratched say to you about the perspective on human dignity of the patients—sometimes called inmates—in such a hospital? Does anything about paragraphs 53 and 54 particularly bother you?
2. How are diagnoses of the kind of sickness that places one in a mental hospital arrived at—barring McMurphy's kind of trick admission? What are the implications of your answer?

### Rhetoric

3. *One Flew over the Cuckoo's Nest* has been made into a very successful stage play. What elements of the single incident printed here suggest to you why the entire novel might work well on stage?
4. Kesey keeps the battle between McMurphy and Nurse Ratched going in a number of effective ways, sometimes by having quite subtle things happen. Point out how he keeps things moving by what he has them say, how they move, their gestures, their tone of voice, how they lay traps for each other, and so on. What is the particular significance of Nurse Ratched's persisting in miscalling McMurphy's name? Why does one's name matter so much? What is the role of Dr. Spivey in what's going on here?

### Projects

5. To get the full effect of the incident, role-play it in the classroom. If you cannot handle it on your own, invite some students from speech and/or drama courses to help you.
6. In a paper analyze Nurse Ratched as a person in a position of authority who has allowed her power to go to her head. *OR* Write a straight prose description of McMurphy, giving your reader a sense of his appearance, his movements, his style, and so on.

# The Esalen Foundation
## "Joy Is the Prize"

## LEO LITWAK

Leo Litwak (1924–   ) is a novelist whose works include *To The Hanging Gardens* and *In O'Brien's House*. "The Esalen Foundation: 'Joy Is the

Prize' " was first published in *The New York Times Magazine* in 1967. Esalen, at Big Sur, California, fronting the Pacific Ocean, is the home base of the Human Potential Movement in the United States. Persons seeking "growth experiences," through encountering and other techniques developed by humanistic psychology, migrate there year 'round. Litwak writes below of his personal experience at Esalen.

1 ... Esalen has changed considerably since my previous visit. Rows of new cabins are ranged along terraces on the hillside. The lodge is located at the bottom of a steep incline, in a meadow. The meadow is perhaps 200 yards deep and ends at the cliff edge. The Pacific Ocean is 150 feet below. A staff of fifty operates the kitchen, supervises the baths, cleans the cabins and garden, and works on construction.

2 I passed hippy laborers, stripped to the waist, long hair flowing, operating with pick and shovel. Dreamy girls in long gowns played flutes near the pool.

3 I was somewhat put off by what I considered to be an excessive show of affection. Men hugged men. Men hugged women. Women hugged women. These were not hippies, but older folks, like myself, who had come for the workshop. People flew into one another's arms, and it wasn't my style at all.

4 After dinner, thirty of us met in the gallery for our first session. We began our excursion toward joy at 9 P.M. of a Sunday in a woodsy room on a balmy, starry night.

5 William Schutz, solidly built, with bald head and muzzle beard, began by telling us that in the course of the workshop we would come to dangerous ground. At such times we ought not to resist entering, for in this area lay our greatest prospect for self-transcendence. He told us to avoid verbal manipulations and to concentrate on our feelings.

## Absurd Exercises

6 We began with exercises. A fat lady in a leotard directed us to be absurd. We touched our noses with our tongues. We jumped. We ran. We clutched one another, made faces at one another. Afterward, we gathered in groups of five and were given an ambiguous instruction to discover one another by touching in any way we found agreeable. I crouched in front of a strange-looking young man with an underslung jaw and powerful shoulders. I tried unlocking his legs and he glared at me.

7 When Schutz asked each group of five to select one couple that seemed least close, the young man with the underslung jaw selected me. The hostile pairs were then requested to stand at opposite diagonals

of the room and approach each other. They were to do whatever they felt like doing when they met in the center of the room. A burly middle-aged man marched toward a petite lady. They met, they paused, stared, then suddenly embraced. The next couple, two husky men, both frozen rigid, confronted each other, stared, then also embraced. The young man and I came next. We started at opposite diagonals. We met in the center of the room. I found myself looking into the meanest, coldest eyes I had ever seen. he pressed his hands to his sides, and it was clear to me that we were not going to embrace. I reached for his hand to shake it. He jerked free. I put my hand on his shoulder; he shrugged me off. We continued staring and finally returned to our group.

8    There was a general discussion of this encounter. Some feared we might start fighting. Nothing, of course, was farther from my mind. I had gone out, intending to play their game and suddenly found myself staring at a lunatic. He had very mean, cold eyes, a crazy shape to his jaw, lips so grim that his ill-feeling was unmistakable. Back in our group he said to me, in a raspy, shrill voice: "You thought I was going to bat you in the face; that's why you turned away." There was a slurred quality to his speech, and it occurred to me that I might have triggered off a madman. I denied that I had turned away and I was challenged to stare him down. I was annoyed that I had been forced into something so silly.

## Name-Giving

9    We proceeded, on the basis of our first impressions, to give one another names, which we kept for the duration of the workshop. My nemesis accepted the name of Rebel. There was a plump, lovely girl we called Kate. A silent, powerful man with spectacles we named Clark. Our fat group leader received the name of Brigitte. A lumpy, solemn man with thick spectacles we named Gary. An elegant, trim middle-aged woman we named Sheba. A buxom, mournful woman with long hair became Joan. A jovial middle-aged pipe smoker with a Jean Hersholt manner we named Hans. A fierce, mustached swaggerer in Bermuda shorts was Daniel. A quiet man with a little boy's face we named Victor. I was named Lionel. We were addressed by these names at all times.

10    I considered this renaming of ourselves a naive attempt to create an atmosphere free of any outside reference. Many of the techniques impressed me as naive. It seemed tactless and obvious to ask so blunt and vague a question as: "What are you feeling?" Yet what happened in the course of five days was that the obvious became clarified. Clichés became significant.

11    I found myself discovering what had always been under my nose. I had not known how my body felt under conditions of tension or fear

or grief. I discovered that I was numb. I had all sorts of tricks for avoiding encounter. I didn't particularly like to be touched. I avoided looking strangers in the eye. I took pride in my coolness and trickery. I didn't believe one should give oneself away. It seemed to me a virtue to appear cool, to be relatively immune to feeling, so that I could receive shocks without appearing to. I considered it important to keep up appearances. I'm no longer proud of what I now believe to be an incapacity rather that a talent.

12    I thought my group rather dull. I saw no great beauty and a great deal of weakness. I felt somewhat superior, since I was there on assignment, not by choice. I hated and feared Reb.

13    But in the next five days, I became enormously fond of these apparently uninteresting strangers. We encountered one another in violent and intimate ways, and I could no longer dismiss them.


# Rebel

14    I was convinced that Rebel was insane. He opened our second meeting with gratuitous insults. He referred to me as "Charley Goodguy." When Brigitte, the leader of our group, told him not to think in stereotypes, he sneered at her: "Why don't you shut up, Fats?" It is difficult to convey the nastiness of his tone—an abrasive, jeering quality.

15    Daniel exploded. He called Rebel a shark and a rattlesnake. He said he wanted to quit the group because he despised this frightening, violent kid. "You scare me," he told Reb. "It's people like you who are responsible for Vietnam and Auschwitz. You're a monster and you're going to suck up all the energy of this group and it's not worth it. I want to get out."

16    I told Daniel his response seemed excessive. Vietnam and Auschwitz? "He's a little hostile," I said.

17    Reb didn't want any favors from me. "Hostile?" he sneered. "Say, I bet I know what you are. You sound to me like a professor. Or a pawnbroker. Which are you, a professor or a pawnbroker?"

18    Schutz intervened. He said to me and Rebel: "I feel you have something going. Why don't you have it out?" He suggested that we arm wrestle, an innocuous contest, but, under the circumstances, there seemed to be a great deal invested in winning or losing. My arm felt numb, and there was some trembling in my thighs. I feared I might not have all my strength, and Rebel appeared to be a powerful kid.

19    I pinned him so easily, however, that the group accused him of having quit. Daniel was jubilant: "You're a loser. You're trying to get clobbered."

20    Rebel was teased into trying again. On the second trial, he pressed my left arm down and demanded a rematch with the right hand. We remained locked together for close to twenty minutes. It was unbearable.

I lost all sensation in my hand and arm. I willed my hand not to yield. Finally, I hoped he would press me down and get it over with. It ended when Rebel squirmed around and braced his foot against the wall and the contest was called.

21      Daniel was delighted by the outcome. He felt as though I had won something for him. Schutz asked: "Why don't *you* wrestle Reb?" Daniel despised violence. He probably would lose and he didn't want to give that monster the satisfaction of a victory. Violence was right up that shark's alley. He refused to play his games. Nonetheless, Daniel was on the ground with Rebel a moment later, beet red with strain, trembling down to his calves. Rebel raised his elbow, pressed Daniel down, and the match was called off. Daniel leaped to his feet, circled the room. He suddenly charged Rebel, who was seated, and knocked him from his chair. He then rushed at Schutz, yelling: "It's you I hate, you bastard, for making me do this." Schutz did not flinch, and Daniel backed off. I could see that his impulse was histrionic. I felt sorry for Reb, who mumbled: "I copped out. I should have hit him."

## A Different Rebel

22      Reb later presented a different guise. Far from being an idiot, he was an extremely precocious twenty-year-old computer engineer, self-taught in the humanities. His father had abandoned the family when he was a child. His mother was a cold customer—never a sign of feeling. He didn't know where he stood with her. She taunted him in the same abrasive style which he tried with us.

23      Reb suffered sexual agonies that had brought him several hundred miles in search of a solution. He considered himself perverse and contemptible, the only impotent twenty-year-old kid in the world. He admitted he found women repugnant as sexual objects, and it was hardly surprising that his crude advances were rebuffed. He admitted that his strategy had been to strike out in hope that someone would strike back so that he might *feel*. He was boyish and affectionate outside the group.

24      My feeling for him underwent a complete reversal. He began to impress me as an intelligent kid, trying with great courage to repair terrible injuries. The monster I had seen simply vanished.

## Wanting To Let Go

25      I never anticipated the effect of these revelations, as one after another of these strangers expressed his grief and was eased. I woke up one night and felt as if everything were changed. I felt as if I were about to weep. The following morning the feeling was even more intense.

26      Brigitte and I walked down to the cliff edge. We lay beneath a tree.

She could see that I was close to weeping. I told her that I'd been thinking about my numbness, which I had traced to the war. I tried to keep the tears down. I felt vulnerable and unguarded. I felt that I was about to lose all my secrets and I was ready to let them go. Not being guarded, I had no need to put anyone down, and I felt what it was to be unarmed. I could look anyone in the eyes and my eyes were open.

27    That night I said to Daniel: "Why do you keep diverting us with intellectual arguments? I see suffering in your eyes. You give me a glimpse of it, then you turn it off. Your eyes go dead and the intellectual stuff bores me. I feel that's part of your strategy."

28    Schutz suggested that the two of us sit in the center of the room and talk to each other. I told Daniel that I was close to surrender. I wanted to let go. I felt near to my grief. I wanted to release it and be purged. Daniel asked about my marriage and my work. Just when he hit a nerve, bringing me near the release I wanted, he began to speculate on the tragedy of the human condition. I told him: "You're letting me off and I don't want to be let off."

29    Schutz asked if I would be willing to take a fantasy trip.

## A Fantasy Trip

30    It was late afternoon and the room was already dark. I lay down, Schultz beside me, and the group gathered around. I closed my eyes. Schultz asked me to imagine myself very tiny and to imagine that tiny self entering my own body. He wanted me to describe the trip.

31    I saw an enormous statue of myself, lying in a desert, mouth open as if I were dead. I entered my mouth. I climbed down my gullet, entering it as if it were a manhole. I climbed into my chest cavity. Schutz asked me what I saw. "It's empty," I said. "There's nothing here." I was totally absorbed by the effort to visualize entering myself and lost all sense of the group. I told Schutz there was no heart in my body. Suddenly, I felt tremendous pressure in my chest, as if tears were going to explode. He told me to go to the vicinity of the heart and report what I saw. There, on a ledge of the chest wall, near where the heart should have been, I saw a baby buggy. He asked me to look into it. I didn't want to, because I feared I might weep, but I looked, and I saw a doll. He asked me to touch it. I was relieved to discover that it was only a doll. Schutz asked me if I could bring a heart into my body. And suddenly there it was, a heart sheathed in slime, hung with blood vessels. And that heart broke me up. I felt my chest convulse. I exploded. I *burst* into tears.

32    I recognized the heart. The incident had occurred more than twenty years before and had left me cold. I had written about it in a story published long ago in *Esquire*. The point of the story was that such

events should have affected me but never did. The war in Germany was about over. We had just taken a German village without resistance. We had fine billets in German houses. The cellars were loaded with jams and sausages and wine. I was the aid man with the outfit, and was usually summoned by the call of "Aid man!" When I heard that call I became numb, and when I was numb I could go anywhere and do anything. I figured the battles were over. It came as a shock when I heard the call this time. There were rifle shots, then: "Aid man!" I ran to the guards and they pointed to bushes ten yards from where they had been posted. They had spotted a German soldier and called for him to surrender. He didn't answer and they fired. I went to the bushes and turned him over. He was a kid about sixteen, blond, his hair strung out in the bushes, still alive. The .30-caliber bullets had scooped out his chest and I saw his heart. It was the same heart I put in my chest twenty-three years later. He was still alive, gray with shock, going fast. He stared up at me—a mournful, little boy's face. He asked: "Why did you shoot? I wanted to surrender." I told him we didn't know.

## The Prize of Joy

33     Now, twenty-three years later, I wailed for that German boy who had never mattered to me and I heaved up my numbness. The trip through my body lasted more than an hour. I found wounds everywhere. I re membered a wounded friend whimpering: "Help me, Leo," which I did—a close friend, yet after he was hit no friend at all, not missed a second after I heard of his death, numb to him as I was to everyone else, preparing for losses by anesthetizing myself. And in the course of that trip through my body I started to feel again, and discovered what I'd missed. I felt wide open, lightened, ready to meet others simply and directly. No need for lies, no need to fear humiliation. I was ready to be a fool. I experienced the joy Schutz had promised to deliver. I'm grateful to him. Not even the offer of love could threaten me.

34     This was the transformation I underwent in the course of that fantasy trip. The force of the experience began to fade quickly, and now, writing two weeks later, I find that little remains. But I still have a vision of a possibility I had not been aware of—a simple, easy connection with my own feeling and, consequently, with others'.

## REVIEW

### Content

1. If you shared Litwak's and Daniel's dislike for Rebel through paragraph 21, did your feeling toward him change as you continued to

read about him, beginning, perhaps, at the end of paragraph 21? If so, did this surprise you? Had you *meant* to continue to dislike him? What does your answer here tell you about this kind of encountering?

2. How well did you understand what Litwak was talking about as you read paragraph 11? And paragraphs 26 and 28? Why had he been "anesthetizing" himself (paragraph 33)? What does he mean, finally, when he says, at the end of paragraph 33, "Not even the offer of love could threaten me"?

## Rhetoric

3. There is a certain immediacy to Litwak's account of his time at Esalen, so that the reader seems to be experiencing it all with him. What elements of his style help to establish this effect? Think about such factors as vocabulary, sentence structure and length, description.

4. Reread paragraph 9. Do the names the members of the group give each other seem in specific ways to fit the persons as described? Does what we are called by other persons—either our christened names and/or nicknames—affect how we see ourselves? Consider what your thinking here tells you about the, often subtle, effects on us of language.

## Projects

5. Give each other names. Is anyone surprised at what the others want to name him/her; that is, does how others see you match how you see yourself? Continue to work until each person accepts his/her name. Then, continue to talk among yourselves about anything in Litwak's piece that especially strikes you, using your new names. Do you feel any differently about a name you have helped give yourself than you did about your "old" one?

6. Have someone you trust read the above selection. Then both of you try to help each other get in touch with some area of your emotional life that you have kept yourself cut off from. Can you? Write an account of your attempt and how it made you feel. If you feel you succeeded, include that; if not, can you think through why not? Did you find the experience a valuable one? If so, why? If not, why not?

# Twin Oaks: A Walden-Two Experiment

## KATHLEEN KINKADE

Kathleen Kinkade (1931–   ) was one of the original members of Twin Oaks, a rural commune in the hills of Virginia. Twin Oaks is modeled on *Walden Two*, B. F. Skinner's fictional account of a utopian community founded on the principles of behavioral conditioning for which Skinner is well known. Kinkade has chronicled the growth of Twin Oaks in *A Walden Two Experiment: The First Five Years of Twin Oaks Community* (1973). In the section of her book printed below, she tells of various behavior modification techniques that have been tried for eliminating undesirable traits in Twin Oaks members. An explanation of the labor credit system, used by the commune for getting needed work done, and the Twin Oaks Code are also included here.

1   When we founded Twin Oaks in 1967, we limited our social planning to equality, with emphasis on economic equality. Today our labor and property systems are fair. We all get a fair share of the community's wealth, such as it is, and the managers and planners make the best decisions they can for the benefit of the whole group—they have no reason to do anything else. At first I thought that this thorough and determined economic equality, plus a little common sense, would insure good human relations. Most quarrels arise out of envy, and if we removed the causes of envy, I thought, we would be removing the causes of the quarrels.

2   I now think that I was naive. We removed a lot of the causes for discord, but there is more to human antagonism than envy, and we cannot even do away with envy.

3   *Problems*   We had no way of dealing with envy caused by superior social talents or disgruntlement over appointment to public office. Our systems did not touch the problems of loneliness, rejection, and unrequited love. Dissatisfaction over the failure of members to agree on standards of workmanship, cleanliness, or courtesy plague us. There were problems in human behavior that our institutions just didn't reach. They were problems, we would say to each other with wry humor, for "behavioral engineering."

4   We have never been hindered by the silly prejudices that picture behavioral engineering as the manipulation of people's desires and preferences by scientists in white coats. But we were hindered, nevertheless; our equality ethic complicated the problem.

5   Behaviorists have made great strides with token economies in mental hospitals and schools. Students or patients earn tokens for certain desirable behaviors—homework, taking a bath, cleaning a room. The tokens can be traded for sweets or privileges. Behavior quickly conforms to desired norms without the use of punishment. Fine. But Twin Oaks is different from these institutions in a fundamental way: there is no staff, and there are no students or patients.

6   We are all on the same level. In a token economy someone must hand out tokens. If the planners at Twin Oaks began to dispense tokens, resentment over their blatant presumption and authority would topple the government.

7   We have experimented with behavior shaping at Twin Oaks, but these experiments have remained peripheral to our basic cultural planning. Behavior graphs became a fad for a while at Twin Oaks and there are still small seizures of graphing now and then. Our procedure was simple—take temper control for an example. If I were doing this I would first define what I meant by temper—popping off with sarcastic comments or nasty putdowns, or impatient, exasperated outbursts. The first week or so, I would simply count the number of times in a day that I caught myself saying nasty things and mark the number on graph paper. A week or two of counting would give me a baseline. In the third week I would start trying to control my behavior and watch it on the graph.

8   At one time about eight of us were graphing various behaviors—Brian once recorded the number of drinking glasses he used and the number that he returned to the kitchen to be washed. This was in response to a criticism that he left dirty glasses all over the community.

9   To keep track we have used expensive golf counters, worn on the wrist, and knitting-stitch counters, but the simplest and cheapest thing is a string of beads.

10   The reward is largely the new behavior itself: if I learn to control my temper I probably will have more friends, and if Brian brings all his drinking glasses back to the kitchen he will stop feeling guilty. But most of us found that the graph itself was a reward. It was reinforcing to watch the rate go down in response to our efforts. Graphing has proved to be successful for only a few of us. Almost everyone has tried it, but most persons do not care enough to be reinforced by it.

11   *M & Ms*   Self-control projects are more interesting when several persons are involved. Our neatness program (known as the M&M project) is an example. It started when some of us agreed to learn to pick up after ourselves and thus keep the house neat. It is easy to notice sloppy

behavior in other persons, so we agreed to monitor each other's behavior. If I got up from the lunch table and left my pudding dish there, another member would say to me, "Hey, give me an M&M for your pudding dish." I would return to the table, pick up my pudding dish and put it away, and give my reminding friend an M&M candy. Of course participants had to buy M&MS out of their tiny allowances and the project encouraged excessive candy-eating, but it worked for a while. This project, like all the others, was entirely voluntary, a circumstance that insures cooperation but can miss the mark if the sloppiest persons won't play.

12     We gave the name BITS (Behavior-Improvement Token System) to another behavior-change game. Community members awarded paper tokens to members who were trying to modify behaviors. One participant got a token every time he smiled; another got one each time we heard him bitch in public. Both used the tokens in keeping graphs; the tokens had no exchange value.

13     *Games*   We know very well that the games we make up are simplistic ways to deal with complicated behavior and that we do not control the genuine reinforcers at all. I suspect that what really goes on behind these projects is the desire to be liked and approved of. If someone successfully changes an undesirable behavior, splendid; if he doesn't, at least the group knows that he trying to change.

14     Aside from these simplistic games, we still use serious techniques of behavior engineering. The approval of our peers is a powerful reinforcer; peaceful and pleasant human relations are reinforcing, as is the solution of sticky problems.

15     We can try anything that looks as though it might help—law, admonition, persuasion, criticism, encounter groups—and we can quite legitimately call it behavioral engineering. Thus, we can use the encounter techniques that B.F. Skinner's theoretical opponents advocate, without abating our admiration for behaviorism. We, like Frazier in Skinner's *Walden Two,* comb the literature for techniques.

16     *Gossip*   Rules are the simplest and perhaps the oldest of all techniques of social control. Walden Two had them. We have them. Item four of the Twin Oaks behavior code says that we will not speak negatively about other members behind their backs. This was our interpretation of the hint in *Walden Two* that the Walden code prohibited "gossip." Actually, we interpreted gossip in an unusual way. Commenting on someone's love affairs is not considered gossip at Twin Oaks. To call it so is to imply there is something wrong or shameful about sexual relations, which we did not want to do even indirectly. "Gossip" in our definition is talk that does damage. Exasperated comment on the quality of someone's work is gossip, as is a disparaging remark about personal characteristics. If you have something negative to say, our rule is that

you must say it to the person's face—and when nobody else is listening. (For this reason the words, "May I speak to you alone?" have an ominous sound.)

17    We learned unsurprisingly that we could not do away with negative speech by writing a rule against it. But we did curb it. We wrote the rule; we signed a contract saying we would try to live by it; we generally approve of it. Sometimes we violate our agreement, but we can try again tomorrow.

18    That leaves us with unresolved frustration over the unacceptable behavior of others—someone lets the cows get out again, the kitchen is dirty, or someone breaks the gossip rule.

19    We have tried several ways to deal with legitimate criticism, all with some success.

20    *Bastard*    First we appointed a "generalized bastard." It was Brian's idea, and we appointed him. If I wanted to tell Quincy that he wasn't doing his share of the work, I was supposed to tell Brian, and Brian would relay the unpleasant information without mentioning my name. Brian quickly found that he lacked the stomach for face-to-face encounters and he reduced the system to note-writing. We lived with variations of this system for over three years. Now we have the "bitch box," into which we can drop our grievances, in writing, if we lack the courage to confront the offender.

21    Suppose I am unhappy about money wasted on automobile trips to Richmond. I notice that one person in particular seems to make extra trips. I write a note for the bitch box, and can sign it or not. My note might go something like this: "I am Goddamned sick and tired of seeing community cars being run back and forth to Richmond for nothing. Three trips have been made this week, in addition to the regularly scheduled one, two of them by John. John doesn't seem to care whether he wastes community money, community time, and community automobiles. He just likes to go for rides. His excuses for this week's trips are pretty weak ones, considering that it costs us 10 dollars a trip in wear and tear and gasoline. I tried to talk to him about it, and he just said he needed to get some things. I say he doesn't need to get those things. He could wait for a regular Richmond trip."

22    *Trips*    The bitch manager gets my note, but does not deliver it directly to John. He probably speaks to John about automobile trips in general and says something like this: "Some people have been noticing that we have been putting a lot of automobile mileage into trips to Richmond, and someone mentioned your name in this connection, questioning whether the value of the trips was really worth the 10 dollars per trip it costs us." John will explain why he thought the trips were necessary, and the bitch manager will respond sympathetically. He may or may not relay this information back to me, depending on whether it is likely

to mollify me or just make me madder. In any case several things have been accomplished: I have expressed myself vehemently to someone who cares, without having gossiped in public and made others uncomfortable; John now knows that trips to Richmond really do cost 10 dollars each, which he may not have thought of; and John now realizes that his driving does not go unnoticed, a form of gentle pressure that probably helps the situation if he is indeed driving more than he ought to.

23   The bitch box helps a little. But it isn't enough. Some persons have overriding personality traits that engender interpersonal friction; what they do is not illegal and one cannot legitimately bitch about it, but the traits need to be discussed. It was to solve this problem that we started group-criticism sessions.

24   *Critics*   In 1969 we had an educational project called "utopia class." It amounted to a weekly group meeting to read about communities of the past and to discuss possible applications of their systems, ideas, successes and failures to Twin Oaks. A great many ideas came out of these sessions. One of them was group criticism, which we borrowed from the Oneida Community.

25   During this period, I wrote in my journal: "Criticism of Penn tonight. Jenny, Penn and I had all volunteered to be the first subject for group criticism, so we tossed a coin, and Penn 'won.' There was some feeling that this was a bad place to begin, because it was obvious that there wasn't much to criticize in Penn's behavior. He is good, kind, considerate, and fun to be with. What can you say about somebody like that?

26   "Everybody in the community attended, including the little kids. We read the ground rules aloud. Then we started around the group clockwise. Everybody said that he couldn't think of anything to criticize.

27   "Penn was pleased and embarrassed by so much oblique praise, and he said he had learned that he hid his faults well. This meeting made other people want to be 'it,' and set a tone of helpfulness and courtesy for the meetings that followed. But no meeting since has been so well attended."

28   Here's more from my journal: "*Me.* About 10 people present. Brian said I ought to get the newsletter out oftener than I do. Also that I am too easily bored, which I interpret to mean that I show my boredom openly. Simon said that I ought to drink a little beer and hang around and party a little—loosen up and be part of the social life instead of worrying about the community all the time. I understand what he is trying to say, but it amounted to telling me to be somebody else.

29   *Duchess*   "Dwight, from whom I feared the sharpest criticism, confessed that he was unprepared. He said "I feel that I should have a great deal to say, but I haven't thought it out.' I was disappointed. But later he wrote me a letter of criticism. It was devastating, and I wish it had been said in public, where I could hear other people comment on it.

Dwight concentrated on what he called 'imperial attitudes.' He said that I exhibit a 'condescension toward the group—a certain regal airiness,' that I sometimes act as if Twin Oaks were my 'duchy.' I sense that Dwight is saying (at last) something a lot of people have felt but won't say, and I feel a mixture of defensiveness and gratitude. He cited incidents and quoted comments of mine that I recall with embarrassment. He completely misinterpreted the things I said. But, then, probably everybody else misinterpreted them, too. That's the point, I have got to change my verbal behavior. . ."

30    Criticism sessions went on for a year and a half and have fallen into disuse only during the last few months. I never missed a session, and I feel that I ought to have a better idea than I do of whether they did good or harm. The truth is that I still feel ambivalent about them. They seemed to reassure timid and modest persons that they were appreciated and liked by the group. They also allowed some of us to let off steam about annoying character traits. Occasionally we even noticed behavior changes after a criticism.

31    *Peers*    But the major benefit of the method in my opinion was the attitude it induced in us. We became aware of imperfection and were willing to listen to the opinions of our peers about our conduct. We said, in effect, *I am not defending my bad behavior; I want to know how I come across; I care what you all think about me.* I found myself more tolerant of a person's foibles if I had told him or her about them.

32    I am glad that I went through the experience. I know more about my social self than I did before I came here, and I am much more sensitive to group opinion.

33    Nevertheless, criticism did not achieve its major goal, which was to impart to every group member the consciousness of his responsibility to the others. It worked only for volunteers. Dissenters did not attend; they asserted that public criticism was nothing more than authorized gossip and that it had the same bad effects that the unauthorized kind had.

34    The right not to attend is fundamental to Twin Oak's sense of liberty. As the number of nonparticipants grew in 1971, subjecting one's ego to official criticism ceased to be the norm. The persons who volunteered for criticism just weren't the ones we were mad at. There was little to say, and interest flagged.

35    In the last year or so some of our new members have not been content with our social aims. It is not enough, they say, simply to reduce interpersonal friction. If we all just loved and trusted one another, they say, we could dispense with the bitch box, the gossip rule, and group criticism.

36    *Antagonisms*    Young persons who have joined the community during the last two years refuse to believe that mutual love and trust are out of our reach. They think that hatred and suspicion and jealousy are

functions of misunderstanding, and that increased understanding would bring increased affection. I find this difficult to swallow. I can see that a great many antagonisms rise out of clear perceptions of conflict of interest.

37    Many of the new members are interested in group-encounter techniques. A few months ago we got a lot of help from a pair of professional group-encounter leaders, who lived at Twin Oaks for several days, asked us in depth about our internal conflicts, and used their skills deftly and effectively in lively group sessions. We accomplished a lot: exposing and discarding old hostility. It was like a religious revival, and the effects still linger.

---

### Inside Twin Oaks

We operate on a labor-credit system that evolved from the one proposed in *Walden Two*. The purpose of the system is to give as much free choice of work as possible to every member and to adjust the amount of labor to the desirability of the job. We receive more credit per hour for aversive work and less credit per hour for enjoyable work. We all do work mostly of our own choosing. We sign up for a week's work at a time and may vary our schedules as much as we like. Work to be done includes construction, milking, and cattle care, making hammocks (which helps to support the commune), working in our other manufacturing projects, printing, auto maintenance, general farm maintenance, gardening, and field work. The work quota varies from week to week. It has been as high as 49 credits, and as low as 25. Each credit is for one hour of work.

*Polity*   Twin Oaks uses the planner-manager system of government outlined in *Walden Two*. We have three planners who have overall responsibility and decision-making power as well as judicial and arbitrative functions. They have appointed managers over all the areas of community life that need supervision (e.g., health manager, hammock manager, animal manager, garden manager). There are a score or more such areas, and sometimes one person holds more than one position. Planners and managers receive no extra credits or privileges for their administrative duties. The only reward for this work is the satisfaction of getting involved and seeing one's ideas carried out. Planners are in office one and a half years.

Twin Oaks always needs managerial ability. It is always true that those of us who want to be involved in important ways can get as much responsibility as we can handle.

There is no voting at Twin Oaks except in occasional emergencies. The membership as a whole makes its will felt through open planners' meetings, polls, and group-feedback sessions. Our bylaws contain provisions for the over-rule of planners' decisions by a two thirds majority of the full membership. However it is very rare that disagreement reaches the point that such measures become necessary.

*Rules*   Our code is borrowed from *Walden Two*. We don't go around quoting it to each other; most of the time we forget we have it. Nor do we live up to it—but it shows some of the norms we are trying to establish.

1) We don't use titles. All members are equal in the sense that all are entitled to the same privileges, advantages, and respect.

2) All members are expected to explain their work to any other members who desire to learn it. The purpose of this is to insure the opportunity to learn any available and appropriate work.

3) We don't discuss the personal affairs of other members; we don't speak negatively of other members when they are not present, or in the presence of third parties.

4) We don't publicly complain about things we think are wrong within the community. Gripes are best taken up with the appropriate manager.

5) Members who may have unconventional or unorthodox views on politics, religion, or national policies stay clear of such topics when it is prudent.

6) Seniority is not discussed among us. We wish to avoid prestige groups of any kind.

7) We try to exercise consideration and tolerance of each others' individual habits.

8) We don't boast of individual accomplishments. We are trying to create a society without heroes.

9) We try to clean up after ourselves after any private or individual project; we try not to keep articles longer than we need them, and to return them to their proper places so that other members can enjoy them.

10) Individual rooms are inviolate. No member enters another's room without permission.

From: "Twin Oaks" published by Twin Oaks, Louisa, Virginia 23093

## REVIEW

### Content

1. Discuss paragraphs 35 and 36. Do you think the young new members are right? If your answer is no, then why would one *want* to live in a group setting that needed "the bitch box, the gossip rule, and group criticism"? Would not the difficulties outweigh the advantages? How do you feel about rule 5? Rule 10?

2. Kinkade begins her discussion with a reference to equality. And three of the ten rules of the Twin Oaks Code speak to this question (1, 6, and 8). How would *you* feel about living in a society in which special recognition was against the rules?

### Rhetoric

3. Do you find Kinkade's style interesting to read? How might it be improved so that you would feel more involved with the commune as you read?

4. Paragraphs 25 through 29 are from Kinkade's personal journal. From their content, what would you guess to be her reasons for keeping

a journal? Do you find any differences between her journal style and her writing for publication?

## Projects

5. A potential new member of Twin Oaks has been to the commune for a trial visit. He/she would like to join, but is having difficulty accepting one of the rules. Write a letter to him/her further explaining, and supporting, the rule (choose the rule you want to work with). *OR* You are the potential new member. Write a letter back to the commune explaining your opposition to the rule.

6. Read in B. F. Skinner's *Walden Two* about some aspect of his projected utopia other than those covered in the above selection from Kinkade's book. Make a paper out of your reactions to what you read.

# 4
# Society

# Babbitt Speaks

## SINCLAIR LEWIS

Sinclair Lewis (1885–1951) was an outstanding—and outspoken—novelist and satirist during the first third of the twentieth century. Born in Minnesota, Lewis knew well the provincialism of the insular American mind, and its inherent dangers, and exposed these in his novels. Among the best known of these are *Main Street* (1920), *Babbitt* (1922), *Arrowsmith* (1925), *Elmer Gantry* (1927), and *It Can't Happen Here* (1935). Lewis was recognized internationally when he won the Nobel Prize in literature in 1930. The passage below is a speech to the Real Estate Board of Zenith, in Midwestern America, by Babbitt, in which he damns individualism and promotes what the Establishment of the 1920s saw as "the ideal of American manhood and culture."

1 . . . "Gentlemen, it strikes me that each year at this annual occasion when friend and foe get together and lay down the battle-ax and let the waves of good-fellowship waft them up the flowery slopes of amity, it behooves us, standing together eye to eye and shoulder to shoulder as fellow-citizens of the best city in the world, to consider where we are both as regards ourselves and the common weal.

2 "It is true that even with our 361,000 or practically 362,000 population, there are, by the last census, almost a score of larger cities in the United States. But, gentlemen, if by the next census we do not stand at least tenth, then I'll be the first to request any knocker to remove my shirt and to eat the same, with the compliments of G. F. Babbitt, Esquire! It may be true that New York, Chicago, and Philadelphia will continue to keep ahead of us in size. But aside from these three cities, which are notoriously so overgrown that no decent white man, nobody who loves his wife and kiddies and God's good out-o'-doors and likes to shake the hand of his neighbor in greeting, would want to live in them—and let me tell you right here and now, I wouldn't trade a high-class Zenith acreage development for the whole length and breadth of Broadway or State Street!—aside from these three, it's evident to any one with a head for facts that Zenith is the finest example of American life and prosperity to be found anywhere.

3     "I don't mean to say we're perfect. We've got a lot to do in the way
of extending the paving of motor boulevards, for, believe me, it's the
fellow with four to ten thousand a year, say, and an automobile and
a nice little family in a bungalow on the edge of town, that makes the
wheels of progress go round!

4     "That's the type of fellow that's ruling America to-day; in fact, it's
the ideal type to which the entire world must tend, if there's to be
a decent, well-balanced, Christian, go-ahead future for this little old
planet! Once in a while I just naturally sit back and size up this Solid
American Citizen, with a whale of a lot of satisfaction.

## Our Ideal Citizen

5     "Our Ideal Citizen—I picture him first and foremost as being busier
than a bird-dog, not wasting a lot of good time in day-dreaming or
going to sassiety teas or kicking about things that are none of his business, but putting the zip into some store or profession or art. At night
he lights up a good cigar, and climbs into the little old bus, and maybe
cusses the carburetor, and shoots out home. He mows the lawn, or
sneaks in some practice putting, and then he's ready for dinner. After
dinner he tells the kiddies a story, or takes the family to the movies,
or plays a few fists of bridge, or reads the evening paper, and a chapter
or two of some good lively Western novel if he has a taste for literature,
and maybe the folks next-door drop in and they sit and visit about
their friends and the topics of the day. Then he goes happily to bed,
his conscience clear, having contributed his mite to the prosperity of
the city and to his own bank-account.

6     "In politics and religion this Sane Citizen is the canniest man on earth;
and in the arts he invariably has a natural taste which makes him pick
out the best, every time. In no country in the world will you find so
many reproductions of the Old Masters and of well-known paintings
on parlor walls as in these United States. No country has anything like
our number of phonographs, with not only dance records and comic
but also the best operas, such as Verdi, rendered by the world's highest-
paid singers.

7     "In other countries, art and literature are left to a lot of shabby bums
living in attics and feeding on booze and spaghetti, but in America the
successful writer or picture-painter is indistinguishable from any other
decent business man; and I, for one, am only too glad that the man
who has the rare skill to season his message with interesting reading
matter and who shows both purpose and pep in handling his literary
wares has a chance to drag down his fifty thousand bucks a year, to
mingle with the biggest executives on terms of perfect equality, and
to show as big a house and as swell a car as any Captain of Industry!

But, mind you, it's the appreciation of the Regular Guy who I have been depicting which has made this possible, and you got to hand as much credit to him as to the authors themselves.

## Superior to Europe

8    "Finally, but most important, our Standardized Citizen, even if he is a bachelor, is a lover of the Little Ones, a supporter of the hearthstone which is the basic foundation of our civilization, first, last, and all the time, and the thing that most distinguishes us from the decayed nations of Europe.

9    "I have never yet toured Europe—and as a matter of fact, I don't know that I care to such an awful lot, as long as there's our own mighty cities and mountains to be seen—but, the way I figure it out, there must be a good many of our own sort of folks abroad. Indeed, one of the most enthusiastic Rotarians I ever met boosted the tenets of one-hundred-percent pep in a burr that smacked o' bonny Scotland and all ye bonny braes o' Bobby Burns. But same time, one thing that distinguishes us from our good brothers, the hustlers over there, is that they're willing to take a lot off the snobs and journalists and politicians, while the modern American business man knows how to talk right up for himself, knows how to make it good and plenty clear that he intends to run the works. He doesn't have to call in some highbrow hired-man when it's necessary for him to answer the crooked critics of the sane and efficient life. He's not dumb, like the old-fashioned merchant. He's got a vocabulary and a punch.

10   "With all modesty, I want to stand up here as a representative business man and gently whisper, 'Here's our kind of folks! Here's the specifications of the Standardized American Citizen! Here's the new generation of Americans: fellows with hair on their chests and smiles in their eyes and adding-machines in their offices. We're not doing any boasting, but we like ourselves first-rate, and if you don't like us, look out—better get under cover before the cyclone hits town!'

11   "So! In my clumsy way I have tried to sketch the Real He-man, the fellow with Zip and Bang. And it's because Zenith has so large a proportion of such men that it's the most stable, the greatest of our cities. New York also has its thousands of Real Folks, but New York is cursed with unnumbered foreigners. So are Chicago and San Francisco. Oh, we have a golden roster of cities—Detroit and Cleveland with their renowned factories, Cincinnati with its great machine-tool and soap products. Pittsburgh and Birmingham with their steel, Kansas City and Minneapolis and Omaha that open their bountiful gates on the bosom of the ocean-like wheatlands, and countless other magnificent sister-cities, for, by the last census, there were no less than sixty-eight glorious Ameri-

can burgs with a population of over one hundred thousand! And all these cities stand together for power and purity, and against foreign ideas and communism—Atlanta with Hartford, Rochester with Denver, Milwaukee with Indianapolis, Los Angeles with Scranton, Portland, Maine, with Portland, Oregon. A good live wire from Baltimore or Seattle or Duluth is the twin-brother of every like fellow booster from Buffalo or Akron, Fort Worth or Oskaloosa!

## Zenith

12    "But it's here in Zenith, the home for manly men and womanly women and bright kids, that you find the largest proportion of these Regular Guys, and that's what sets it in a class by itself; that's why Zenith will be remembered in history as having set the pace for a civilization that shall endure when the old time-killing ways are gone forever and the day of earnest efficient endeavor shall have dawned all round the world!

13    "Some time I hope folks will quit handing all the credit to a lot of moth-eaten, mildewed, out-of-date, old, European dumps, and give proper credit to the famous Zenith spirit, that clean fighting determination to win Success that has made the little old Zip City celebrated in every land and clime, wherever condensed milk and pasteboard cartons are known! Believe me, the world has fallen too long for these worn-out countries that aren't producing anything but bootblacks and scenery and booze, that haven't got one bathroom per hundred people, and that don't know a loose-leaf ledger from a slipcover; and it's just about time for some Zenithite to get his back up and holler for a showdown!

14    "I tell you, Zenith and her sister-cities are producing a new type of civilization. There are many resemblances between Zenith and these other burgs, and I'm darn glad of it! The extraordinary, growing, and sane standardization of stores, offices, streets, hotels, clothes, and newspapers throughout the United States shows how strong and enduring a type is ours.

## A Classic Poem

15    "I always like to remember a piece that Chum Frink wrote for the newspapers about his lecture-tours. It is doubtless familiar to many of you, but if you will permit me, I'll take a chance and read it. It's one of the classic poems, like 'If' by Kipling, or Ella Wheeler Wilcox's 'The Man Worth While'; and I always carry this clipping of it in my notebook:

When I am out upon the road, a poet with a pedler's load, I mostly sing a hearty song, and take a chew and hike along, a-handing out my samples fine of Cheero Brand of sweet sunshine, and peddling optimistic pokes and stable lines of japes and jokes to Lyceums and other folks, to Rotarys, Kiwanis' Clubs, and feel I ain't like other dubs. And then old Major Silas Satan, a brainy cuss who's always waitin', he gives his tail a lively quirk, and gets in quick his dirty work. He fills me up with mullygrubs; my hair the backward way he rubs; he makes me lonelier than a hound, on Sunday when the folks ain't round. And then b' gosh, I would prefer to never be a lecturer, a-ridin' round in classy cars and smoking fifty-cent cigars, and never more I want to roam; I simply want to be back home, a-eatin' flap-jacks, hash, and ham, with folks who savvy whom I am!

But when I get that lonely spell, I simply seek the best hotel, no matter in what town I be—St. Paul, Toledo, or K.C., in Washington, Schenectady, in Louisville or Albany. And at that inn it hits my dome that I again am right at home. If I should stand a lengthy spell in front of that first-class hotel, that to the drummers loves to cater, across from some big film theayter; if I should look around and buzz, and wonder in what town I was, I swear that I could never tell! For all the crowd would be so swell, in just the same fine sort of jeans they wear at home, and all the queens with spiffy bonnets on their beans, and all the fellows standing round a-talkin' always, I'll be bound, the same good jolly kind of guff, 'bout autos, politics and stuff and baseball players of renown that Nice Guys talk in my home town!

Then when I entered that hotel, I'd look around and say, "Well, well!" For there would be the same news-stand, same magazines and candies grand, same smokes of famous standard brand, I'd find at home, I'll tell! And when I saw the jolly bunch come waltzing in for eats at lunch, and squaring up in natty duds to platters large of French Fried spuds, why then I'd stand right up and bawl, "I've never left my home at all!" And all replete I'd sit me down beside some guy in derby brown upon a lobby chair of plush, and murmur to him in a rush, "Hello, Bill, tell me, good old scout, how is your stock a-holdin' out?" Then we'd be off, two solid pals, a-chatterin' like giddy gals of flivvers, weather, home, and wives, lodge-brothers then for all our lives! So when Sam Satan makes you blue, good friend, that's what I'd up and do, for in these States where'er you roam, you never leave your home sweet home.

## Milk, Boxes, and Light Fixtures

16      "Yes, sir these other burgs are our true partners in the great game of vital living. But let's not have any mistake about this. I claim that Zenith is the best partner and the fastest-growing partner of the whole caboodle. I trust I may be pardoned if I give a few statistics to back up my claims. If they are old stuff to any of you, yet the tidings of prosperity, like the good news of the Bible, never become tedious to the ears of a real hustler, no matter how oft the sweet story is told! Every intelligent person knows that Zenith manufactures more condensed milk and evaporated cream, more paper boxes, and more lighting-fixtures, than any other city in the United States, if not in the

world. But it is not so universally known that we also stand second in the manufacture of package-butter, sixth in the giant realm of motors and automobiles, and somewhere about third in cheese, leather findings, tar roofing, breakfast food, and overalls!

17    Our greatness, however, lies not alone in punchful prosperity but equally in that public spirit, that forward-looking idealism and brotherhood, which has marked Zenith ever since its foundation by the Fathers. We have a right, indeed we have a duty toward our fair city, to announce broadcast the facts about our high schools, characterized by their complete plants and the finest school-ventilating systems in the country, bar none; our magnificent new hotels and banks and the paintings and carved marble in their lobbies; and the Second National Tower, the second highest business building in any inland city in the entire country. When I add that we have an unparalleled number of miles of paved streets, bathrooms, vacuum cleaners, and all the other signs of civilization; that our library and art museum are well supported and housed in convenient and roomy buildings; that our park system is more than up to par, with its handsome driveways adorned with grass, shrubs, and statuary, then I give but a hint of the all-round unlimited greatness of Zenith!

18    "I believe, however, in keeping the best to the last. When I remind you that we have one motor car for every five and seven-eights persons in the city, then I give a rock-ribbed practical indication of the kind of progress and braininess which is synonymous with the name Zenith!

## Dangers of Radical Professors

19    "But the way of the righteous is not all roses. Before I close I must call your attention to a problem we have to face, this coming year. The worst menace to sound government is not the avowed socialists but a lot of cowards who work under cover—the long-haired gentry who call themselves 'liberals' and 'radicals' and 'non-partisan' and 'intelligentsia' and God only knows how many other trick names! Irresponsible teachers and professors constitute the worst of this whole gang, and I am ashamed to say that several of them are on the faculty of our great State University! The U. is my own Alma Mater, and I am proud to be known as an alumni, but there are certain instructors there who seem to think we ought to turn the conduct of the nation over to hoboes and roustabouts.

20    "Those profs are the snakes to be scotched—they and all their milk-and-water ilk! The American business man is generous to a fault, but one thing he does demand of all teachers and lecturers and journalists: if we're going to pay them our good money, they've got to help us by selling efficiency and whooping it up for rational prosperity! And when it comes to these blab-mouth, fault-finding, pessimistic, cynical

University teachers, let me tell you that during this golden coming year it's just as much our duty to bring influence to have those cusses fired as it is to sell all the real estate and gather in all the good shekels we can.

21    "Not till that is done will our sons and daughters see that the ideal of American manhood and culture isn't a lot of cranks sitting around chewing the rag about their Rights and their Wrongs, but a God-fearing, hustling, successful, two-fisted Regular Guy, who belongs to some church with pep and piety to it, who belongs to the Boosters or the Rotarians or the Kiwanis, to the Elks or Moose or Red Men or Knights of Columbus or any one of a score of organizations of good, jolly, kidding, laughing, sweating, upstanding, lend-a-handing Royal Good Fellows, who plays hard and works hard, and whose answer to his critics is a square-toed boot that'll teach the grouches and smart alecks to respect the He-man and get out and root for Uncle Samuel, U.S.A.!"

## REVIEW

### Content

1. The headnote to this selection refers to Lewis' familiarity with "the provincialism of the insular American mind." What is "provincialism"? What evidences of it do you find in Babbitt's speech? What dangers can you see in this kind of perspective on the world?

2. How do *you* respond to Babbitt's definition of the "Ideal, Sane, Standardized American Citizen" (paragraphs 3 through 8)? And to his view of Zenith, the home of "the sane and efficient life," as the model American city? How about paragraphs 19 and 20?

### Rhetoric

3. Much of Babbitt's speech is composed of what is known as "purple prose"—pompous, inflated, flowery diction. Point to some especially choice examples of this. Can you compare it with any recent utterances of contemporary public figures?

4. The novel *Babbitt* is a *satire*. How does Lewis accomplish his satirization? Does frequent capitalization of words contribute here? What about the name of the city? The word "Babbitt" itself has become a part of our language, listed in dictionaries; how is it used today?

### Projects

5. Try to get a pro and con debate going about some particular facet of Zenith and/or its inhabitants.

6. Write a paper of several paragraphs in which you update paragraph 5, to depict today's Ideal (meaning here "Standardized") American Citizen.

# The Adjusted American

## SNELL PUTNEY
## and GAIL PUTNEY

Snell and Gail Putney are a husband-and-wife team of sociologists, who completed their Ph.D.s in sociology together at the University of Oregon in 1954. Teaching has taken them to San Jose State College, Drake University, and Florida State University. In 1964 they coauthored *The Adjusted Americans: Normal Neuroses in the Individual and Society*. In the section of that book printed below, the Putneys expose the problem of deep-seated conformity to "the unquestioned assumptions of [one's] culture" (in contrast to what is usually designated conformity, in dress, manners, and so on); they then pose the question of whether the "adjusted" individual who readily fits his society's norms is necessarily the psychologically healthy individual.

## The Invisible Strait Jacket

1   The dilemma in which the dissatisfied conformist finds himself is a false dilemma, deriving from a narrow conception of conformity. The typical American thinks of conformity as involving taste, dress, manners, and opinion. But such superficial and conscious conformity is not the real source of his discontent. At the heart of the problem lies a deeper conformity of which he is hardly aware: conformity to the unquestioned assumptions of his culture.

2       In every society certain things are regarded as "self-evident truths." Different societies make different assumptions about man and the universe, but within each society the great majority of the people conform unwittingly to the prevailing set of beliefs. Louis Wirth observed that "the most important thing . . . we can know about a man is what he takes for granted, and the most elemental and important facts about the society are those that are seldom debated and generally regarded as settled." Such implicit assumptions are the premises from which thought begins, the starting point for any course of action.

3       For example, in a society in which the power of evil spirits is "obvious" beyond debate, the average man employs devices to placate or confuse evil spirits. He may conform rigidly to local custom or he may innovate

and experiment with various types of demon baffles, but it would be literally unthinkable to him to try doing without them altogether. His thought and action start from the premise that demons exist. And he finds proof of the influence of evil spirits on men's lives, for he interprets every stroke of misfortune, from a hailstorm that ruins his crop to the sudden death of a friend, as *prima facie* evidence of the power of malevolent spirits.

4     Similarly, in a society where war is taken for granted, the average man applauds the development of increasingly destructive weapons systems. He may recognize that the use of these weapons would probably mean the destruction of himself, his society, and perhaps the human race. but his thought starts from the premise that military force is essential to survival and he cannot conceive of other alternatives. It is literally unthinkable to him that disarmament may be the only solution, so he can only laud every development in weaponry and hope that somehow the weapons will never be used.

5     So long as the individual takes for granted the assumptions that prevail in his society, he is limited to those thoughts and actions which are conceivable in terms of these assumptions. To perceive other alternatives he must first break free of the preconceptions which limit his imagination.

6     The prerequisite to such a breakthrough is to become fully conscious of those beliefs which are so familiar that they are seldom remarked. The best chance of recognizing and questioning such basic preconceptions occurs when some fortuitous exception to the "obvious" draws attention to a hitherto unchallenged belief. The person who is able to resist the temptation to ignore such evidence is rewarded with sudden insight and a new perspective.

## The Yellow-Eyed Cat

7     This process of insight through surprise can be seen in a humble example. Our son grew up with a Siamese cat and when he was about three the only other cat in his limited world was also Siamese. Both had blue eyes, like all their breed. One day he saw a Persian cat padding toward him, and in the manner of three-year-olds he squatted down on the sidewalk to get a better look. The Persian also sat, wrapped her tail around her feet and regarded the boy. Suddenly he jumped up and ran into the house shouting, "I saw a cat with yellow eyes, Mommy! A cat with yellow eyes!"

8     In the moment when our small son and the Persian cat were face to face, two things had occurred to the boy: he became aware that all cats do not have blue eyes and he also became aware that until that moment he had believed that they did. *He became conscious of the belief*

*he had taken for granted only in the moment of perceiving that it was false.* Excited with his new insight and struggling with its implications, he bombarded his mother with questions about the eyes of cats—questions that would never have occurred to him before. Precisely the same process of challenging exception, breakthrough, and stimulation can occur with profound and consequential beliefs.

9    But unless or until some "yellow-eyed cat" challenges the beliefs men take for granted, these beliefs remain unremarked and unassailable. They constitute the most basic and restraining type of conformity, an invisible strait jacket on thought and thus ultimately on action.

10    The American who is chagrined about his conformity in matters of taste and consumption remains generally oblivious of his conformity to preconceptions regarding human needs and human nature. Yet the pattern of his life is predicated on these assumptions, and the ultimate cause of his discontent is his uncritical conformance to inaccurate assumptions concerning what he is and what he needs.

## Normalcy and Adjustment

11    Somewhat inconsistently, the very Americans who chafe at conformity are likely to seek adjustment. One of the prevailing assumptions which Americans have learned to take for granted is that anxiety is a product of inadequate adjustment. This may be the case, but it is equally likely that anxiety reflects inadequacies in the pattern to which the individual attempts to adjust. *The adjusted individual is one who is able to fit readily into the normal patterns of his society,* but *it cannot be taken for granted that one who is adjusted is psychologically healthy.* He can be superbly adjusted to his culture, normal in every respect, and yet not lead a full and satisfying life.

12    The word "normal" is used by Americans in several senses. It means average or typical, as in the observation that the normal age at high school graduation is eighteen. It is also used to mean natural, as when one says that it is normal for boys to be interested in girls. This dual usage reflects the assumption that the customary patterns of one's culture are the natural ways of humanity.

13    However, the typical behaviors of a human society are not natural in the sense that the typical behaviors of an anthill are natural. For instance, the ant satisfies its hunger by unlearned behaviors which are built into the very structure of its nervous system. It does not need to learn how to find food, or what it can eat. It simply acts on the basis of its instincts and need satisfaction generally results. An ant's behavior is natural: that is, it is inherent in the nature of the ant.

14    In contrast, the behaviors that seem natural to men are usually only habitual. Man has a great capacity to learn, precisely because he is not

limited to inflexible instinctive responses. Because man lacks such built-in response patterns, however, he has no inherent natural way of behaving.

15    Normal human behavior, then, is not natural, but rather habitual behavior that over a period of time has become typical in a particular society. The person who seeks to adjust more fully to the normal behavior of his society in the belief that he is moving toward fulfillment is only wriggling inside a strait jacket of conventional assumptions. He is only becoming more typical.

16    In no society are the normal behaviors perfectly adapted to the satisfaction of all human needs. The adjusted members of any given society will satisfy some needs effectively, others inadequately. The extent to which the adjusted individual is capable of satisfying his needs depends on the efficacy of the normal means of need satisfaction to which he has adjusted. And his well-being depends on the degree to which he is able to satisfy his needs.

17    When normal behaviors leave him deprived, the adjusted individual is relatively helpless. In the first place, he does not have a clear idea of what he is seeking; he has learned a set of customs, not an understanding of human needs. In the second place, he has learned to take for granted deprivation in certain areas of his life.

## Deprivation Accepted

18    Just as the behaviors the adjusted individual employs are nearly universal in his society, so also are the consequences of these behaviors. In societies where the traditional means of securing food are inadequate, hunger may be accepted as an inevitable part of life. To be hungry is unpleasant, but the adjusted member of such a society cannot imagine a world without hunger—unless it be some mythical land or heaven where the hungry ones of this existence will find ultimate fulfillment. The adjusted man in such a society may struggle to secure sufficient food by traditional means, but he is unlikely to devise radically different means which might bring an end to hunger, or even to adopt radically new techniques if someone points them out to him. (The difficulty of introducing new agricultural techniques, for example, is attested by agronomists in most underdeveloped countries.) In short, those deprivations which are normal (that is, typical of most of the population) assume the stature of an inevitably recurring fact of life.

19    The adjusted American regards famine as an unusual crisis, a problem which can and must be resolved immediately. But in other areas of human need he is resigned to deprivation. For example, he accepts as a natural and inevitable part of life debilitating self-doubts and fears of personal inadequacy which are no more inevitable than starvation.

He experiences this chronic deprivation simply because the normal behaviors and understandings of his society do not lead to fulfillment of
his need for self-acceptance.

20      Neurosis may be defined as an internal, nonorganic barrier to need
fulfillment. The adjusted American's difficulties in satisfying his emotional needs are not external, nor are they based in his organic nature;
they are simply neuroses. These neuroses which plague the adjusted
American and give a distinctive cast to American society are normal,
just as "normal" malnutrition plagues and shapes other societies. It is
the abnormal (i.e., nontypical) neuroses which invite attention and analysis because of their novelty; the normal neuroses are generally endured,
precisely because of their prevalence in a society.

## Autonomy

21      Given sufficient self-understanding to make a valid choice, most
people would presumably choose to act in ways which lead to satisfaction.
They would hardly be opposed to conformance *per se,* but they would
seek to transcend adjustment to those beliefs and behaviors which leave
their compatriots unsatisfied.

22      Those who are capable of conforming when conformance is functional, and also capable of real innovation (rather than mere nonconform-
ance) when normal behaviors would leave them deprived, are *autonomous* in the fullest sense of the word. *Autonomy means the capacity of the
individual to make valid choices of his behavior in the light of his needs.* To
the extent that his choices are limited externally (by coercion) or internally (by normal neurosis or sterile rebellion) the individual is incapable
of autonomy. In the case of most Americans, the internal limitations
far outweigh the external ones.

23      In *The Lonely Crowd,* David Riesman uses the term *autonomy* in a similar
sense. Pointing to autonomy as an ultimate goal, Riesman offers scant
hope that it can be readily achieved. The institutional barriers "false
personalization" and "enforced privatization" appear to be too great,
the way to autonomy too ill defined. But he does see some evidence
of progress toward autonomy in the "other-directed" American who is
concerned with being acceptable to the "jury of his peers" and thus
is led to be increasingly self-conscious. According to Riesman, this awareness of self may ultimately lead to an "organic development of autonomy
out of other-direction."

24      If awareness of self is to lead toward autonomy, it must begin with
awareness of the needs which motivate the self and of the normal neuroses which inhibit satisfaction of these needs. Such awareness may have
the effect of an encounter with a "yellow-eyed cat" in suggesting alterna-

tive understandings and alternative means by which the individual can find satisfaction. Through such a process, self-awareness may enable the individual to transcend adjustment and move toward autonomy.

## REVIEW

### Content

1. Try to think of several "unquestioned assumptions" that create an "invisible strait jacket" for *you*. What are their implications and consequences? Would you like to move outside any of them? If so, *will* you?
2. Discuss the Putneys' conclusion that "the adjusted individual" is not necessarily the "psychologically healthy individual." Do you agree or disagree? If you disagree, and if you accept their reference, in the last sentence of paragraph 10, to the "discontent" of Americans, then how do you explain that discontent? Consider here especially paragraphs 15, 17, 19, and 20. Do you think Americans *want* autonomy? Do you? Do the people you know? Why might one *not*?

### Rhetoric

3. The Putneys often write long, rather involved sentences. Where these are quite clear, what contributes to that clarity? How precise is their vocabulary? Do you find them lapsing at any points into a style known as "social sciencese"—which often uses more words than necessary? If you find any such passages, how do you as reader respond to their style in these instances?
4. How well does the yellow-eyed cat story work to make the Putneys' point about unquestioned assumptions and sudden revelations?

### Projects

5. Try to recall one of *your* yellow-eyed cat experiences and write about it. Make your account vivid enough so that your reader will relive the experience with you. State clearly what "sudden insight and . . . new perspective" the experience gave you.
6. Can you think of some assumption you have been taking for granted that you would like to move beyond? How tight is the "invisible strait jacket" in this instance? If you want to get past the assumption, can you do so by squarely confronting it and reasoning/willing your way out of the strait jacket, or will you require a yellow-eyed cat experience here? How *ready* are you to relinquish the assumption? Make a paper out of your thinking about all this.

# Why We Need
# a Self-Renewing
# Society

## JOHN W. GARDNER

John W. Gardner (1912–   ) has gained a reputation as "the citizen's citizen." He has given an unusually wide and varied range of public service to this country, notably as Secretary of Health, Education and Welfare (1965–1968) and, beginning in 1968, as head of the Urban Coalition, a private organization founded to help solve the problems of our cities. During the 1960s Gardner established Common Cause, a "citizens' lobby." Gardner's books include *Excellence* (1961), *Self-Renewal* (1963), and *The Recovery of Confidence* (1970). The following selection is from the 1962 Annual Report of the Carnegie Corporation, which Gardner served as president of the Carnegie Foundation for the Advancement of Teaching for ten years (1955–1965). In this section Gardner analyzes what causes a society to stagnate, and goes on to discuss how to build into a society certain self-renewing devices, as well as how to encourage creative self-renewal in the individuals making up that society.

1    Education looks to the future, and is inevitably an attempt to shape the future. Today the road ahead is clouded by the danger of nuclear war, and the enormity of the threat blocks our vision. We have the difficult task of facing the threat and at the same time looking beyond it. If we fail to look beyond it, if the long-term future loses all reality for us, then educational strategies degenerate into spasmodic responses to the alarms of the moment—as they have today.

2    If we free ourselves for a moment from preoccupation with the nuclear problem, we encounter another specter that haunts the modern mind. A generation of critics has dismantled the idea of Progress, and every few years the archaeologists unearth another ancient civilization that flourished for a time and then died. The modern mind, acutely conscious of the sweep of history and chronically apprehensive, is quick to ask, "Is it our turn now?"

3    Rather than debate that overworked topic, I am going to ask another kind of question: Suppose one tried to imagine a society that would be relatively immune to decay—an ever-renewing society. What would it be like? What would be the ingredients that provided the immunity?

4    The skeptic may ask whether any society should last forever, even ours. It is not a crucial question. If longevity were the only virtue of the continuously renewing society, the whole exercise might turn out to be numbingly dull. But a society that has learned the secret of continuous renewal will be a more interesting and a more vital society—not in some distant future but in the present. Since continuous renewal depends on conditions that permit the growth and fulfillment of individuals, it will also be a society fit for free men.

## Obstacles to Renewal

5    To accomplish renewal, we need to understand what prevents it.

6    When we talk about revitalizing a society, we tend to put exclusive emphasis on finding new ideas. But there is usually no shortage of new ideas; the problem is to get a hearing for them. And that means breaking through the crusty rigidity and stubborn complacency of the *status quo*. The aging society develops elaborate defenses against new ideas —"mind-forged manacles," in William Blake's vivid phrase.

7    The development of resistance to new ideas is a familiar process in the individual. The infant is a model of openness to new experience—receptive, curious, eager, unafraid, willing to try anything. As the years pass these priceless qualities fade. He becomes more cautious, less eager, and accumulates deeply rooted habits and fixed attitudes.

8    The same process may be observed in organizations. The young organization is willing to experiment with a variety of ways to solve its problems. It is not bowed by the weight of tradition. It rushes in where angels fear to tread. As it matures it develops settled policies and habitual modes of solving problems. In doing so it becomes more efficient, but also less flexible, less willing to look freshly at each day's experience. Its increasingly fixed routines and practices are congealed in an elaborate body of written rules. In the final stage of organizational senility there is a rule or precedent for everything. Someone has said that the last act of a dying organization is to get out a new and enlarged edition of the rule book.

## Customs and Precedents

9    And written rules are the least of the problem. In mature societies and organizations there grows a choking underbrush of customs and precedents. There comes to be an accepted way to do everything. Eccentric experimentation and radical departures from past practice are ruled out. The more pervasive this conventionality, the less likely is the innovator to flourish. The inventor of the Bessemer process for steel-making, Sir Henry Bessemer, wrote:

I had an immense advantage over many others dealing with the problem inasmuch as I had no fixed ideas derived from long-established practice to control and bias my mind, and did not suffer from the general belief that whatever is, is right.

10     As a society becomes more concerned with precedent and custom, it comes to care more about *how* things are done and less about *whether* they are done. The man who wins acclaim is not the one who "gets things done" but the one who has an ingrained knowledge of the rules and accepted practices. Whether he accomplishes anything is less important than whether he conducts himself in an "appropriate" manner. Thus do men become the prisoners of their procedures.

11     The body of custom, convention, and "reputable" standards exercises such an oppressive effect on creative minds that new developments in a field often originate outside the area of respectable practice. The break with traditional art was not fostered within the Academy. Jazz did not spring from the bosom of the respectable music world. The land-grant colleges, possibly the most impressive innovation in the history of American higher education, did not spring from the inner circle of higher education as it then existed. Motels, the most significant development of this generation in innkeeping, were at first regarded with scorn by reputable hotel people.

12     Vested interests constitute another problem for the aging society. The phrase "vested interests" has been associated with individuals or organizations of wealth and power, but the vested interests of workers may be as strong as those of the top executives. In any society many established ways of doing things are held in place, not by logic nor even by habit, but by the enormous restraining force of vested interests. In an organization certain things remain unchanged for the simple reason that changing them would jeopardize the rights, privileges, and advantages of specific individuals—perhaps the president, perhaps the maintenance men.

13     The more democratic an organization—or a society—the more clearly it will reflect the interests of its members. So a democratic group may be particularly susceptible to the rigidifying force of vested interest.

## Loss of Motivation

14     Still another reason for the loss of vitality and momentum in a society is a lowered level of motivation. It is not always easy to say why motivation deteriorates. Perhaps people stop believing in the things they once believed in—the things that gave meaning to their efforts. Perhaps they grow soft from easy living. Perhaps they fall into the decadent habit of imagining that intense effort is somehow unsophisticated, that dedication is naive, that ambition is a bit crude. Or perhaps a rule-ridden

society has bottled up their energy, or channeled it into all the tiny rivulets of conformity.

15    One may argue, as Toynbee does, that a society needs challenge. It is true. But societies differ notably in their capacity to see the challenge that exists. No society has ever so mastered the environment and itself that no challenge remained; but a good many have gone to sleep because they failed to understand the challenge that was undeniably there.

16    Whatever the reason for loss of motivation, the consequences are apt to be devastating. Nothing—neither wealth nor technology, neither talent nor wisdom—will save a society in which motivation continues to deteriorate.

17    So much for the factors that contribute to loss of vitality in a society. What can be done about them?

18    Many of the qualities crucial to a society's continued vitality are qualities of youth: vigor, flexibility, enthusiasm, readiness to learn. This could lead us to imagine that the critical question is how to stay young. But youth implies immaturity. And though everyone wants to be young, no one wants to be immature.

## Framework for Self-Renewal

19    Every society must mature, but much depends on how this process takes place. A society whose maturing consists simply of acquiring more firmly established ways of doing things is headed for the graveyard— even if it learns to do those things with greater and greater skill. *In the ever-renewing society what matures is a system or framework within which continuous innovation, renewal, and rebirth can occur.*

20    Concern with decay and renewal in societies must give due emphasis to both continuity and change. Peter Drucker has wisely said that in a world buffeted by change the only way to conserve is by innovating. We can turn the saying around and assert that innovation would be impossible without certain kinds of conserving. The scientist in his laboratory may seem to be the personification of innovation and change, yet he functions effectively because of certain deeply established continuities in his life. As a scientist he is living out a tradition several centuries old in its modern incarnation, thousands of years old in its deeper roots. Every move that he makes reflects skills, attitudes, and habits of mind that were years in the making. He is part of an enduring tradition and a firmly established intellectual system; but it is *a tradition and a system designed to accomplish its own continuous renewal.*

21    The free society is not the only kind that can accomplish change. Far from it. A totalitarian regime coming to power on the heels of a revolution may be well fitted to accomplish one great burst of change. But in the long run its spurt of energy is not only in danger of dying

out but of being replaced by deadly rigidity. Compared to the free society, it is not well fitted for continuous renewal, generation after generation.

22     One crucial respect in which the ever-renewing society parts company with all totalitarianism is that it is pluralistic. There is a willingness to entertain diverse views. There are many sources of initiative rather than one. Power is widely dispersed rather than tightly held. There are multiple channels through which the individual may gain information and express his views.

23     It would be hard to overemphasize the importance of pluralism in helping a society to escape the cycle of growth and decay. The ever-renewing society is not convinced that it enjoys eternal youth. It knows that it is forever growing old and must do something about it. It knows that it is always producing deadwood and must, for that reason, look to its seed beds. If a society is dominated by one official point of view, the tentative beginnings of a new point of view may be a matter of devastating strain and conflict. In a pluralistic society, where there are already various points of view, the emergence of another is hardly noticed. In an open society, freedom of communication ensures that the new ideas will be brought into confrontation with the old.

## Provisions for Criticism

24     Perhaps the most important characteristic of an ever-renewing system is that it has built-in provisions for vigorous criticism. It protects the dissenter and the nonconformist. It knows that from the ranks of the critics come not only cranks and troublemakers but saviors and innovators. And since the spirit that welcomes nonconformity is a fragile thing, the ever-renewing society does not depend on that spirit alone. It devises explicit legal and constitutional arrangements to protect the critic.

25     And that brings us to another requirement for the continuously renewing society. It must have some capacity to resolve conflicts, both internal and external. Without such capacity, it either will be destroyed or will dissipate its energies in the maintenance of fiercely entrenched feuds. The peace that it seeks is not a state of passivity and uneventfulness. It knows that without the ebb and flow of conflict and tension progress will not be made in eradicating old evils or opening new frontiers; but it is committed to the orderly "management of tensions." Thus in its internal affairs it deliberately makes possible certain kinds of conflict, e.g., by protecting dissenters and assuring them a hearing; but it creates a framework of rules which will assure that the conflict is resolved in an orderly fashion. It devises institutional arrangements that provide a harmless outlet for minor tensions and resolve some of the worst tensions before they reach the point of explosion.

26    In the last analysis, no society will be capable of continuous renewal unless it produces the kind of men who can further that process. It will need innovative men and men with the capacity for self-renewal.

27    Faced as we are with problems that put a constant strain on our adaptive powers, it is hardly surprising that the word *creativity* has achieved a dizzying popularity. It is more than a word today, it is an incantation. It is a kind of psychic wonder drug, powerful and presumably painless; and everyone wants a prescription. But the fact that the word has become a slogan should not make us antagonistic to the thing itself. What is implied in the word creativity, rightly conceived, is something that the continuously renewing society needs very much.

28    Only a handful of men and women in any population will achieve the highest levels of creativity and innovation. But a good many can be moderately creative, and even more can show some spark of creativity at some time in their lives. The number of men and women who exhibit some measure of creativity, and the extent to which they exhibit it, may depend very much on the climate in which they find themselves.

29    From all that we know of the creative individual—and we now know a good deal—he thrives on freedom. Recent research shows that he is not the capricious and disorderly spirit some romantics have imagined him to be. He may be quite conventional with respect to all the trivial customs and niceties of life. But in the area of his creative work he must be free to believe or doubt, agree or disagree. He must be free to ask the unsettling questions, and free to come up with disturbing answers.

## Climate for Self-Renewal

30    When Alexander the Great visited Diogenes and asked whether he could do anything for the famed teacher, Diogenes replied, "Only stand out of my light." Perhaps some day we shall know how to heighten creativity. Until then, one of the best things we can do for creative men and women is to stand out of their light.

31    No one knows why some individuals seem capable of self-renewal while others do not. The people interested in adult education have struggled heroically to increase the *opportunities* for self-development, and they have succeeded remarkably. Now they had better turn to the thing that is really blocking self-development—the individual's own intricately designed, self-constructed prison; or to put it another way, the individual's incapacity for self-renewal.

32    It is not unusual to find that the major changes in life—marriage, a move to a new city, a new job, or a national emergency—reveal to us quite suddenly how much we had been imprisoned by the comfortable web we had woven around ourselves. Unlike the jailbird, we don't know

that we have been imprisoned until after we have broken out. It was a common experience during World War II that men and women who had been forced to break the pattern of their lives often discovered within themselves resources and abilities they had not known to exist. How ironic that it should take war and disaster to bring about self-renewal on a large scale.

33    When we have learned to accomplish such self-renewal without wars and other disasters, we shall have discovered one of the most important secrets a society can learn, a secret that will unlock new resources of vitality throughout the society. And we shall have done something to avert the hardening of the arteries that attacks so many societies. Men who have lost their adaptiveness naturally resist change. The most stubborn protector of his own vested interest is the man who has lost the capacity for self-renewal.

## REVIEW

### Content

1. How *important* do you find Gardner's hypothesis about stagnation in a society and the need for self-renewal? Do you agree with paragraph 10? What other factors can you think of that might contribute to the decay of a society beyond those Gardner discusses?
2. In what ways is the American society a self-renewing one? In what ways is it not? What measures can you recommend to make it more self-renewing? How much do you find America encouraging self-renewal and creativity in her citizens? What ways, short of those Gardner discusses in paragraph 32, can you think of to help yourself and others develop the capacity for self-renewal?

### Rhetoric

3. Gardner's books have found a large reading public. Discuss what makes his style a readable one. Note his effective use of varied sentence structure, the sentence fragment, and short sentences in paragraphs 21 and 22.
4. Gardner writes the following generalization: "The most stubborn protector of his own vested interest is the man who has lost the capacity for self-renewal." Does his statement need development to convince you of his point? If so, how would you help him develop it, assuming that you agree with him here?

### Projects

5. Consider yourself, someone you know, or some group or organization you are familiar with in the light of blocks to self-renewal in what Gardner calls "intricately designed, self-constructed prisons." Write a

paper in which you describe the block(s) and then recommend steps for their removal.

6. Gardner is the founder of Common Cause (see headnote). Investigate, through your college library's resources, how Common Cause works as a self-renewing device and write a paper about its methods and at least one specific issue it has addressed and has influenced.

# Work in an Alienated Society

## ERICH FROMM

Erich Fromm (1900–   ) is a German social psychologist who fled Germany for the United States in 1934. In this country he has taught at several universities and has written a number of widely read books, among them *Escape from Freedom* (1941), *Man for Himself* (1947), *The Art of Loving* (1956), and *The Anatomy of Human Destructiveness* (1973). Among Fromm's central concerns have been the effect on Americans of a sociological environment which exalts success through dog-eat-dog competition, and the human alienation that accompanies technological development which isolates the workman from the finished product. Fromm deals with these questions in *The Sane Society* (1955), from which the excerpt below is taken.

1   What becomes the meaning of *work* in an alienated society?

2   We have already made some brief comments about this question in the general discussion of alienation. But since this problem is of utmoost importance, not only for the understanding of present-day society, but also for any attempt to create a saner society, I want to deal with the nature of work separately and more extensively in the following pages.

3   Unless man exploits others, he has to work in order to live. However primitive and simple his method of work may be, by the very fact of production, he has risen above the animal kingdom; rightly has he been defined as "the animal that produces." But work is not only an inescapable necessity for man. Work is also his liberator from nature, his creator as a social and independent being. *In the process of work, that is, the molding and changing of nature outside of himself, man molds and changes himself.*

He emerges from nature by mastering her; he develops his powers of cooperation, of reason, his sense of beauty. He separates himself from nature, from the original unity with her, but at the same time unites himself with her again as her master and builder. The more his works develops, the more his individuality develops. In molding nature and re-creating her, he learns to make use of his powers, increasing his skill and creativeness. Whether we think of the beautiful paintings in the caves of Southern France, the ornaments on weapons among primitive people, the statues and temples of Greece, the cathedrals of the Middle Ages, the chairs and tables made by skilled craftsmen, or the cultivation of flowers, trees or corn by peasants—all are expressions of the creative transformation of nature by man's reason and skill.

## Craftsmanship

4      In Western history, craftsmanship, especially as it developed in the thirteenth and fourteenth centuries, constitutes one of the peaks in the evolution of creative work. Work was not only a useful activity, but one which carried with it a profound satisfaction. The main features of craftsmanship have been very lucidly expressed by C. W. Mills. "There is no ulterior motive in work other than the product being made and the processes of its creation. The details of daily work are meaningful because they are not detached in the worker's mind from the product of the work. The worker is free to control his own working action. The craftsman is thus able to learn from his work; and to use and develop his capacities and skills in its prosecution. There is no split of work and play, or work and culture. The craftsman's way of livelihood determines and infuses his entire mode of living."[1]

5      With the collapse of the medieval structure, and the beginning of the modern mode of production, the meaning and function of work changed fundamentally, especially in the Protestant countries. Man, being afraid of his newly won freedom, was obsessed by the need to subdue his doubts and fears by developing a feverish activity. The outcome of this activity, success or failure, decided his salvation, indicating whether he was among the saved or the lost souls. *Work, instead of being an activity satisfying in itself and pleasureable, became a duty and an obsession.* The more it was possible to gain riches by work, the more it became a pure means to the aim of wealth and success. Work became, in Max Weber's terms, the chief factor in a system of "inner-worldly asceticism," an answer to man's sense of aloneness and isolation.

6      However, work in this sense existed only for the upper and middle classes, those who could amass some capital and employ the work of

[1]C. W. Mills, *White Collar*, Oxford University Press, New York, 1951, p. 220.

others. For the vast majority of those who had only their physical energy to sell, work became nothing but forced labor. The worker in the eighteenth or nineteenth century who had to work sixteen hours if he did not want to starve was not doing it because he served the Lord in this way, nor because his success would show that he was among the "chosen" ones, but because he was forced to sell his energy to those who had the means of exploiting it. The first centuries of the modern era find the meaning of work divided into that of *duty* among the middle class, and that of *forced labor* among those without property.

## Alienating Work

7   The religious attitude toward work as a duty, which was still so prevalent in the nineteenth century, has been changing considerably in the last decades. Modern man does not know what to do with himself, how to spend his lifetime meaningfully, and he is driven to work in order to avoid an unbearable boredom. But work has ceased to be a moral and religious obligation in the sense of the middle-class attitude of the eighteenth and nineteenth centuries. Something new has emerged. Ever-increasing production, the drive to make bigger and better things, have become aims in themselves, new ideals. Work has become alienated from the working person.

8   What happens to the industrial worker? He spends his best energy for seven or eight hours a day in producing "something." He needs his work in order to make a living, but his role is essentially a passive one. He fulfills a small isolated function in a complicated and highly organized process of production, and is never confronted with "his" product as a whole, at least not as a producer, but only as a consumer, provided he has the money to buy "his" product in a store. He is concerned neither with the whole product in its physical aspects nor with its wider economic and social aspects. He is put in a certain place, has to carry out a certain task, but does not participate in the organization or management of the work. He is not interested, nor does he know why one produces this, instead of another commodity—what relation it has to the needs of society as a whole. The shoes, the cars, the electric bulbs, are produced by "the enterprise," using the machines. He is a part of the machine, rather than its master as an active agent. The machine, instead of being in his service to do work for him which once had to be performed by sheer physical energy, has become his master. Instead of the machine being the substitute for human energy, man has become a substitute for the machine. *His work can be defined as the performance of acts which cannot yet be performed by machines.*

9   Work is a means of getting money, not in itself a meaningful human activity. P. Drucker, observing workers in the automobile industry, ex-

presses this idea very succinctly: "For the great majority of automobile workers, the only meaning of the job is in the pay check, not in anything connected with the work or the product. Work appears as something unnatural, a disagreeable, meaningless and stultifying condition of getting the pay check, devoid of dignity as well as of importance. No wonder that this puts a premium on slovenly work, on slowdowns, and on other tricks to get the same pay check with less work. No wonder that this results in an unhappy and discontented worker—because a pay check is not enough to base one's self-respect on."[2]

## Human Engineering

10    This relationship of the worker to his work is an outcome of the whole social organization of which he is a part. Being "employed,"[3] he is not an active agent, has no responsibility except the proper performance of the isolated piece of work he is doing, and has little interest except the one of bringing home enough money to support himself and his family. Nothing more is expected of him, or wanted from him. He is part of the equipment hired by capital, and his role and function are determined by this quality of being a piece of equipment. In recent decades, increasing attention has been paid to the psychology of the worker, and to his attitude toward his work, to the "human problem of industry"; but this very formulation is indicative of the underlying attitude; there is a human being spending most of his lifetime at work, and what should be discussed is the *"industrial problem of human beings,"* rather than *"the human problem of industry."*

11    Most investigations in the field of industrial psychology are concerned with the question of how the productivity of the individual worker can be increased, and how he can be made to work with less friction; psychology has lent its services to "human engineering," an attempt to treat the worker and employee like a machine which runs better when it is well oiled. While Taylor was primarily concerned with a better organization of the technical use of the worker's physical powers, most industrial psychologists are mainly concerned with the manipulation of the worker's psyche. The underlying idea can be formulated like this: if he works better when he is happy, then let us make him happy, secure, satisfied, or anything else, provided it raises his output and diminishes friction. In the name of "human relations," the worker is treated with all devices which suit a completely alienated person; even happiness and human values are recommended in the interest of better relations with the pub-

[2]Cf. Peter F. Drucker, *Concept of the Corporation,* The John Day Company, New York, 1946, p. 179.

[3]The English "employed" like the German *angestellt* are terms which refer to things rather than to human beings.

lic. Thus, for instance, according to *Time* magazine, one of the best-known American psychiatrists said to a group of fifteen hundred Supermarket executives: "It's going to be an increased satisfaction to our customers if we are happy. . . . It is going to pay off in cold dollars and cents to management, if we could put some of these general principles of values, human relationships, really into practice." One speaks of "human relations" and one means the most inhuman relations, those between alienated automatons; one speaks of happiness and means the perfect routinization which has driven out the last doubt and all spontaneity.

## Laziness and Hostility

12    The alienated and profoundly unsatisfactory character of work results in two reactions: one, the ideal of complete *laziness;* the other a deep-seated, though often unconscious *hostility* toward work and everything and everybody connected with it.

13    It is not difficult to recognize the widespread longing for the state of complete laziness and passivity. Our advertising appeals to it even more than to sex. There are, of course, many useful and labor saving gadgets. But this usefulness often serves only as a rationalization for the appeal to complete passivity and receptivity. A package of breakfast cereal is being advertised as *"new—easier to eat."* An electric toaster is advertised with these words: ". . . the most distinctly different toaster in the world! Everything is done *for* you with this new toaster. You need not even bother to lower the bread. Power-action, through a unique electric motor, *gently takes the bread right out of your fingers!"* How many courses in languages, or other subjects are announced with the slogan "effortless learning, no more of the old drudgery." Everybody knows the picture of the elderly couple in the advertisement of a life insurance company, who have retired at the age of sixty, and spend their life in the complete bliss of having nothing to do except just travel.

14    Radio and television exhibit another element of this yearning for laziness: the idea of "push-button power"; by pushing a button, or turning a knob on my machine, I have the power to produce music, speeches, ball games, and on the television set, to command events of the world to appear before my eyes. The pleasure of driving cars certainly rests partly upon this same satisfaction of the wish for push-button power. By the effortless pushing of a button, a powerful machine is set in motion; little skill and effort is needed to make the driver feel that he is the ruler of space.

15    But there is far more serious and deep-seated reaction to the meaninglessness and boredom of work. It is a hostility toward work which is much less conscious than our craving for laziness and inactivity. Many

a businessman feels himself the prisoner of his business and the commodities he sells; he has a feeling of fraudulency about his product and a secret contempt for it. He hates his customers, who force him to put up a show in order to sell. He hates his customers because they are a threat; his employees as well as his superiors, because he is in a constant competitive fight with them. Most important of all, he hates himself, because he sees his life passing by, without making any sense beyond the momentary intoxication of success. Of course, this hate and contempt for others and for oneself, and for the very things one produces, is mainly unconscious, and only occasionally comes up to awareness in a fleeting thought, which is sufficiently disturbing to be set aside as quickly as possible.

## REVIEW

### Content

1. Discuss Fromm's thesis of the modern worker as a "piece of equipment" and a being alienated from the activity of his work. Do you agree with him? Consider especially the implications of Fromm's definition of such work as "the performance of acts which cannot yet be performed by machines."
2. Do you agree with what Fromm says about "the ideal of complete laziness" and "a deepseated hostility toward work" in paragraphs 12 through 15? What other evidence do you find in our society to support the first point beyond Fromm's examples in paragraphs 13 and 14? Does Fromm's discussion of hostility in paragraph 15 seem a *logical* analysis of the point?

### Rhetoric

3. In paragraph 11, Fromm is dealing in irony. What is the irony here, and how well does Fromm expose it?
4. Fromm quotes three scholars who have written about economics and its influences on mankind: C. Wright Mills, Max Weber, and Peter Drucker. What effect does this technique of citation of recognized authorities have on Fromm's own argument?

### Projects

5. Have you ever been, or are you, employed in "meaningless work"— either at home or elsewhere? If so, write about what you did/do, and your feelings toward the work. Or write a paper based on having talked with someone else in this position.
6. Develop one of the following statements from the above selection into an essay:
   (a) "A pay check is not enough to base one's self-respect on." (paragraph 9)

(b) "Modern man does not know what to do with himself, how to spend his lifetime meaningfully, and he is driven to work in order to avoid an unbearable boredom." (paragraph 7)

(c) "There is no split of work and play [for the craftsman]." (paragraph 4)

Support, or refute, the statement through the use of examples.

# A Crisis,
# a Challenge:
# Energy and Ecology

## MARGARET MEAD

Margaret Mead (1901–   ), a cultural anthropologist, has gained worldwide recognition as author and lecturer in her field. She has lived among natives in various parts of the world, to conduct her studies firsthand, resulting in such books as *Coming of Age in Samoa* (1928), *Growing Up in New Guinea* (1930), and *Male and Female* (1949). But Mead has served her profession more widely yet, teaching at both Fordham and Columbia universities, as well as serving as Curator at the American Museum of Natural History in New York City. In December, 1973, Mead presented to the New York Academy of Sciences the address printed below, in which she calls on her fellow citizens to make a creative challenge out of the energy crisis.

1   The energy crunch being felt around the world forces us to take stock of our reckless despoiling of the earth's resources. It also provides the United States with a magnificent opportunity to initiate a transformation in our present way of life.

2   Our present way was conceived in a spirit of progress, in an attempt to improve the standard of living of all Americans, in the increasing capability of technological development to bring previously undreamed of amenities within reach of the common man. But this search has taken a form which this planet cannot support. The overdevelopment of motor transport has contributed to the near destruction of our great cities, the disintegration of the family, the isolation of the old, the young and the poor, the pollution of local air, and the poisoning of the earth's atmosphere. Our wasteful use of electricity, and our waste rather than

recycling of nonrenewable resources are likewise endangering our rivers and oceans and the atmosphere which protects the planet.

3   The realization that a drastic transformation was needed has steadily increased, but the problem was how to turn around? How to alter our dependence on motor transport? How to stop building enormous, uneconomical buildings which waste electricity night and day, all year round? How to break the deadlock between environmentalists bent upon enacting immediate measures to protect an endangered environment, and industry caught in the toils of a relentness compulsion to expand? How to turn around in our own course and not injure the young economies of the developing countries, desperate to obtain the barest necessities of food and water and light for their hungry millions? It had seemed almost impossible to turn around short of some major catastrophe which would destroy millions of lives.

4   The catastrophe has now arrived, in the energy crunch. The causes may and will be debated: How much blame to assign to government mismanagement, how much to the recent war in the Mideast, and so on. But in a more basic sense, these triggering events do not matter. They could in fact divert our attention from a much more important issue—how we are to take advantage of the crisis to move toward a way of life which will not destroy the environment and use up irreplaceable resources.

## Responsibility for Transformation

5   We can use the crisis to lead in a transformation which is needed around the world, to aim not for a shallow independence but for genuine responsibility. We must not be content with half measures, following the administration's assurance that the crisis will mean only fewer Sunday drives to visit a mother-in-law, and lowered lights on Christmas trees—to be followed by an early return to normal waste and pollution.

6   During the inevitable disorganization of everyday life, we will be making decisions, learning new habits, initiating new research. It is vital that these activities move us forward into a new era, in which the entire nation is involved in a search for a new standard of living, a new quality of life, based on conservation not waste, on protection not destruction, on human values rather than built-in obsolescence and waste.

7   As scientists who know the importance of accurate information we can press immediately for the establishment of an inquiry with subpoena power to ascertain from the energy industries the exact state of supplies and reserves in this country. We can press for a massive project on alternative and environmentally safe forms of energy. It should be as ambitious as the Manhattan Project or NASA, but it would have no need to secrecy. It would not be aimed at destroying or outdistancing

other countries, but at ways of conserving our resources, in new technologies which would themselves provide new activities for those industries whose present prosperity is based on oil and motor transport and energy-expensive synthetic materials.

8     Those of us who are social scientists have a special responsibility for the relationship between measures that are to be taken and the way in which the American people and American institutions will respond. If there is to be gasoline rationing, we have to consider the importance of built-in flexibility and choice. In the United States, a rationing system will only be experienced as fair and just if it discriminates among the needs of different users, recognizes that workers have to get to work, that many people work on Sundays, that different regions of the country will need different measures. Without rationing, we will set one set of users against another, one part of the country against another, encouraging such narrowly partisan measures as severance taxes through which oil rich states will benefit at the expense of the residents of oil-less states. Rationing is a way of making the situation genuinely national, involving each American in the fate of all Americans.

9     It will be important to consider that the American people have only experienced rationing as a temporary measure in war time. There will be danger that rationing may simply accentuate the desire to get back to normal again, with normal defined as where we were when the shortages hit us. But what we need to do is to define all measures taken, not as temporary but as *transitional,* to a saner, safer, more human lifestyle.

## Planetary Interdependence

10     In the past, war, revolution and depressions have been the dire circumstances within which society's technologies and social institutions have been transformed. But wars are won, or lost, revolutions succeed or fail, depressions grind to an end. The situation we are in is profoundly different. An interdependent, planetary man-made system of resource exploitation and energy use has brought us to a state where long-range planning is essential, where what we need is not a return to our present parlous state, which endangers the future of our country, our children and our earth, but movement forward to a new norm, where the developed and the developing countries will be able to help each other. The developing countries have less obsolescence, fewer entrenched 19th century industrial forms to overcome; the developed countries have the scientists and the technologists to work rapidly and effectively on planetary problems.

11     In the past it has been only in war, in defense of one's own country or one's ideals, that any people have been able to invoke total commit-

ment. Then it has always been on behalf of one group against another. This is the first time in history, that American people have been asked to defend ourselves and everything that we hold dear, *in cooperation* with all the other inhabitants of this planet, who share with us the same endangered air and oceans. This time there is no enemy. There is only a common need to reassess our present course, to change course, to devise methods by which we can survive.

## REVIEW

### Content

1. Mead is talking here of the need for Americans to feel a sense of *private responsibility* for *public welfare* on a planetary scale. To what extent do *you* believe her pleas justifiable; that is, how far would you be willing to go in doing *your* part here? Is her hope a feasible, practicable (workable) one?
2. The United States experienced the initial "energy crunch" in the oil crisis of late 1973. Did *your* lifestyle change any then? Did these changes last, or did you return to earlier habits once the crisis began to subside? Does Mead's address make you do any *further* thinking here?

### Rhetoric

3. Paragraph 3 of Mead's speech is composed almost entirely of questions, each beginning "How to . . ." Discuss the two techniques she employs, question-posing and parallel construction, as especially effective sentence-structure devices for a public address.
4. How does the use of the word "catastrophe" at the end of paragraph 3 and again at the beginning of paragraph 4 help Mead make her point about the energy crunch?

### Projects

5. Write a paper based on your responses to Question 2 above.
6. Mead sees the energy crunch as "a magnificent opportunity to initiate a transformation in our present way of life," a transformation in which she hopes that all measures taken will be seen "not as temporary but as *transitional,* to a saner, safer, more human lifestyle" (paragraph 9). Fantasize some changes for the better that you can imagine as a part of such a transformation and write a paper describing what you envision; limit yourself to developing few enough ideas so that you can say enough about each one to make it appealing.

# The New Puritanism

## ROLLO MAY

Rollo May (1909–    ) is a New York psychotherapist and a leading figure in humanistic or Third Force psychology, as contrasted with the Freudian and the behavioristic schools. He has written a number of popular books to help modern man understand himself: *The Meaning of Anxiety* (1950), *Man's Search for Himself* (1953), *Love and Will* (1969), and *Power and Innocence* (1972). The selection below is from an essay that appeared originally in the *Saturday Review* during the 1960s, some of it later becoming part of *Love and Will*. In this piece, May examines the implications and consequences of "uncommitted" sex, arguing that total permissiveness combined with mechanical performance criteria is hardly a healthier attitude toward sex than was Puritan and Victorian repression.

1    There are several strange and interesting dilemmas in which we find ourselves with respect to sex and love in our culture. When psychoanalysis was born in Victorian times half a century ago, repression of sexual impulses, feelings, and drives was the accepted mode. It was not nice to feel sexual, one would not talk about sex in polite company, and an aura of sanctifying repulsiveness surrounded the whole topic. Freud was right in pointing out the varied neurotic symptoms to which this repression of sex gave birth.

2    Then, in the 1920s, a radical change occurred almost overnight. The belief became a militant conviction in liberal circles that the opposite of repression—sex education, freedom of talking, feeling, and expression—would have healthy effects, and was obviously the only stand for the enlightened person. According to Max Lerner, our society shifted from acting as though sex did not exist to placing the most emphasis on sex of any society since the Roman.

3    Partly as a result of this radical change, we therapists rarely get nowadays in our offices patients who exhibit repression of sex in the pre-World War I Freudian sense. In fact we find just the opposite in the people who come for help: a great deal of talk about sex, a great deal of sexual activity, practically no one complaining of any cultural prohibitions over his going to bed as often or with as many partners as he wishes.

## Guilty If Not Sexual

4      But what our patients *do* complain of is lack of feeling and passion—so much sex and so little meaning or even fun in it! Whereas the Victorian person didn't want anyone to know that he or she had sexual feelings, now we are ashamed if we do not. Before 1910 if you called a lady "sexy," you insulted her; nowadays the lady accepts the adjective as a prized compliment. Our patients often have problems of impotence or frigidity, but they struggle desperately not to let anyone know they *don't* feel sexually. The Victorian nice man or woman was guilty if he or she did perform sexually; now we are guilty if we *don't*.

5      One dilemma, therefore, is that enlightenment has not at all solved the sexual problems in our culture. To be sure, there are important positive results of the new enlightenment, chiefly in increased freedom for the individual. And some external problems are eased—sexual knowledge can be bought in any bookstore, contraception is available almost everywhere outside Boston, and external societal anxiety has lessened. *But internalized anxiety and guilt have increased.* And in some ways these are more morbid, harder to handle, and impose a heavier burden upon the individual man and woman than external anxiety and guilt.

6      A second dilemma is that the new emphasis on technique in sex and love-making backfires. It often seems to me that there is an inverse relationship between the number of how-to-do-it books perused by a person, or rolling off the presses in a society, and the amount of sexual passion or even pleasure experienced by the persons involved. Nothing is wrong with technique as such, in playing golf or acting or making love. But the emphasis beyond a certain point on technique in sex makes for a mechanistic attitude toward love-making, and goes along with alienation, feelings of loneliness, and depersonalization.

7      The third dilemma I propose is that our highly vaunted sexual freedom has turned out to be a new form of puritanism. I define puritanism as a state of alienation from the body, separation of emotion from reason, and use of the body as a machine. These were the elements of moralistic puritanism in Victorian times; industrialism expressed these same characteristics of puritanism in economic guise. Our modern sexual attitudes have a new content, namely, full sexual expression, but in the same old puritan form—alienation from the body and feeling, and exploitation of the body as though it were a machine.

## "Sin"

8      In our new puritanism bad health is equated with sin. Sin used to be "to give in to one's sexual desires"; now it is "not to have full sexual expression." A woman used to be guilty if she went to bed with a man;

now she feels vaguely guilty if after a certain number of dates she still refrains. And her partner, who is always completely enlightened—or at least pretends to be—refuses to allay her guilt and does not get overtly angry at her sin of "morbid repression," her refusal to "give." This, of course, makes her "no" all the more guilt-producing for her.

9    All this means, of course, that people have to learn to perform sexually but at the same time not to let themselves go in passion or unseemly commitment—which latter may be interpreted as exerting an unhealthy demand on the partner. *The Victorian person sought to have love without falling into sex; the modern person seeks to have sex without falling into love.*

10   Recently I amused myself by drawing an impressionistic picture of the attitude of the contemporary enlightened person toward sex and love. I call it the portrait of the new sophisticate:

> The new sophisticate is not castrated by society but, like Origen, is self-castrated. Sex and the body are for him not something to be and live out, but tools to be cultivated like a TV announcer's voice. And like all genuine Puritans (very passionate men underneath) the new sophisticate does it by devoting himself passionately to the moral principle of dispersing all passion, loving everybody until love has no power left to scare anyone. He is deathly afraid of his passions unless they are kept under leash, and the theory of total expression is precisely his leash. His dogma of liberty is his repression; and his principle of full libidinal health, full sexual satisfaction, are his puritanism and amount to the same thing as his New England forefathers' denial of sex. The first Puritans repressed sex and were passionate; our new man represses passion and is sexual. Both have the purpose of holding back the body, both are ways of trying to make nature a slave. The modern man's rigid principle of full freedom is not freedom at all but a new straitjacket, in some ways as compulsive as the old. He does all this because he is afraid of his body and his compassionate roots in nature, afraid of the soil and his procreative power. He is our latter-day Baconian devoted to gaining power *over* nature, gaining knowledge in order to get more power. And you gain power over sexuality (like working the slave until all zest for revolt is squeezed out of him) precisely by the role of full expression. Sex becomes our tool like the caveman's wheel, crowbar, or adz. Sex, the new machine, the *Machina Ultima.*

11   It is not surprising that, confronted by these dilemmas, people become more and more concerned about the technical, mechanical aspects of the sexual act. The questions typically asked about the act of lovemaking are not whether there was passion or meaning or even pleasure, but how well did one perform? Even the sexologists, whose attitude is generally the more the merrier, are raising their eyebrows these days about the anxious overemphasis on achieving the orgasm and the great importance attached to "satisfying" the partner. The man makes a point of asking the woman if she "made it," or is she "all right," or uses some other such euphemism for an experience for which obviously no euphemism is possible. We men are reminded by Simone de Beauvoir and

other women who try to interpret the love act to us, that this is the last thing in the world a woman wants to be asked at that moment.

## Motives of the Game

12    I often get the impression, amid the male flexing of sexual biceps, that men are in training to become sexual athletes. But what is the great prize of the game? Now it is well known in psychotherapeutic circles that the overconcern with potency is generally a compensation for feelings of impotence. Men and women both are struggling to prove their sexual power. Another motive of the game is to overcome their own solitariness. A third motive is often the desperate endeavor to escape feelings of emptiness and the threat of apathy: they pant and quiver to find an answering quiver in someone else's body to prove their own is not dead. Out of an ancient conceit we call this love.

13    The struggle to find an identity is also a central motive in acting out these sexual roles—a goal present in women as well as men, as Betty Friedan in *The Feminine Mystique* made clear. The point I wish to emphasize here is the connection between this dilemma about potency and the tendency in our society for us to become machines or ledger books even in bed. A psychiatrist colleague of mine tells me that one of his patients brought in the following dream. "I was in bed with my wife. Between us was my accountant. He was going to make love to my wife. Somehow it seemed all right."

14    Along with the overemphasis upon mechanism there goes, understandably enough, a lessening of passion and of feeling itself, which seems to take the form of a kind of anaesthesia in people who otherwise can perform the mechanical aspects of the sexual act very capably. This is one reason we therapists get a good number of patients these days with problems of impotence, frigidity, and simple lack of feeling in the sexual act. We psychiatrists often hear the disappointed refrain, "We made love, but it wasn't much good."

15    Sex is the "last frontier," David Riesman meaningfully wrote fifteen years ago in *The Lonely Crowd*. Gerald Sykes in the same vein spoke of sex as the "last green thing." It is surely true that the zest, adventure, the discovering of vast new areas of feeling and passion in one's self, the trying out of one's power to arouse feelings in others—these are indeed "frontier experiences." They are normally present as part of the psychosexual development of every individual, and the young person rightly gets a validation of himself from such experiences. Sex in our society did in fact have this power in the several recent decades since the 1920s, when almost every other activity was becoming "other-directed," jaded, emptied of zest and adventure.

16    But for various reasons—one of them being that sex had to carry by itself the weight for the validation of the personality on practically

all other levels as well—the frontier freshness and newness and challenge of sex were more and more lost. We are now living in the post-Riesman age, and are experiencing the difficult implications of the "other-directed," radar behavior. The "last frontier" has become a teeming Las Vegas and no frontier at all.

## Youth and Revolt

17    Young people can no longer get a bootlegged feeling of personal identity out of the sexual revolt, since there is nothing left to revolt against. A study of drug addiction among young people, published recently in the *New York Times*, reports the young people are saying that the revolt against parents and society, the "kick" of feeling their own "oats" which they used to get from sex, they now have to get from drugs. It is not surprising that for many youngsters what used to be called love-making is now so often experienced as a futile "panting palm to palm," in Aldous Huxley's predictive phrase, and that they tell us that it is hard for them to understand what the poets were talking about.

18    Nothing to revolt against, did I say? Well, there is obviously one thing left to revolt against, and that is sex itself. The frontier, the establishing of identity, can be, and not infrequently is for the young people, a revolt against sexuality entirely. A modern Lysistrata in robot's dress is rumbling at the gates of our cities, or if not rumbling, at least hovering. As sex becomes more machine-like, with passion irrelevant and then even pleasure diminishing, the problem comes full circle, and we find, *mirabile dictu*, a progression from an *anaesthetic* attitude to an *antiseptic* one. Sexual contact itself then tends to be avoided. The sexual revolution comes finally back on itself not with a bang but a whimper.

19    This is another and surely least constructive aspect of the new puritanism: it returns, finally, to an ascetic attitude. This is said graphically in a charming limerick that seems to have sprung up on some sophisticated campus:

> The word has come down from the Dean,
> That with the aid of the teaching machine,
>      King Oedipus Rex
>      Could have learned about sex
> Without ever touching the Queen.

## REVIEW

### Content

1. As a psychotherapist of many years' practice, May has worked with many clients. Do you agree with his conclusions at the following points in his essay: paragraphs 4 and 8; the last sentence of paragraph 6

and the motives listed in paragraph 12; his reference to "exploitation of the body as though it were a machine" in paragraph 7? If you do not, be prepared to support a refutation of May in class discussion.
2. Think carefully about the first sentence in paragraph 9. May does not develop this point. Does your trying to think further about it carry you toward any surprising and/or disturbing possibilities?

**Rhetoric**

3. May develops his "portrait of the new sophisticate" (paragraph 10) by drawing an analogy between "the first Puritans" and what he sees as "the new Puritans." How clear is the analogy?
4. Does May's use of a limerick at the end of this selection reinforce or diminish the effectiveness of his point in paragraph 18?

**Projects**

5. Discuss one of the following paragraphs: 5, 6, 9, 11, 15. Does your experience and/or that of your friends validate May's points here?
6. Develop one of the following sentences from May's essay into a paper:
   (a) "The Victorian person sought to have love without falling into sex; the modern person seeks to have sex without falling into love."
   (b) "The first Puritans repressed sex and were passionate; our new man represses passion and is sexual."

OR If any part of May's essay offends you as sexist, write out and defend your protest.

# New Directions of Marriage

## VANCE PACKARD

Vance Packard (1914–   ) has had a varied and full journalistic career, reporting and writing columns for newspapers, free-lancing magazine articles, and producing a number of very popular book-length surveys of the American sociological scene. The titles of some of his books suggest the aspects of that scene he has dealt with: *The Hidden Persuaders* (1957), *The Status Seekers* (1959), *The Waste Makers* (1960), *The Pyramid Climbers* (1962), *The Sexual Wilderness* (1968). In the selection below, from *The Sexual Wilderness*, Packard states that there are two basic needs traditionally fulfilled

From *The Sexual Wilderness* by Vance Packard, Copyright © 1968 by Vance Packard. Used by permission of the publisher, David McKay Company, Inc., New York.

by conventional marriage, and then examines eight possible male-female relationships as he sees their potential for meeting those needs.

1 Most of the rules regulating marriages and their dissolution were made in eras when the bride and groom could look forward to fewer than half the number of years together that the couples marrying in the next few years can anticipate. For that reason alone, entering into wedlock calls for a new high level of prudence. There is now obviously a greater chance the partners will outgrow each other, lose interest, or become restless. In the past quarter-century, instead of greater prudence, however, we have seen a considerable increase in imprudent embarkations upon marriage.

2 Wives in the future surely will spend an increasing proportion of their married life as equal partners of the husband free of the "motherhood-service role," and so will have more options for the outlet of their surplus energy. They can no longer view marriage as a haven where they will be looked after by a husband in return for traditional services rendered.

3 Instead, more than ever before, women will have not only the opportunity but the expectation to push out for themselves and function as autonomous individuals who happen to have marriage partners. Marriages will apparently continue to be brittle for some time. Families in the immediate future will be expected to be highly mobile, and ever smaller in size.

## Two Reasons for Marriage

4 While, as noted, the traditional economic functions of marriage have shrunk, there are two particularly compelling reasons looming why people will be marrying in the coming decade despite the relatively free availability of unmarried sexual partners:

5 1. The warm, all-embracing companionship that in marriage can endure through the confusion, mobility, and rapid social change of our times.

6 2. The opportunity to obtain immortality and personal growth for married individuals who perpetuate themselves through reproduction as they help mold personalities of their children and proudly induct them into the larger community.

7 This opportunity is so profoundly desired by most adult humans who are capable of reproduction that childlessness by choice would seem to be almost as difficult to popularize on any large scale as singleness by choice. Both would probably require intensive, prolonged social conditioning.

8    The institution of marriage is obviously in need of modifications to fit the modern needs. Author Jerome Weidman made an important point in his book *Your Daughter Iris* when he wrote of today's marriages: "Human beings do not obtain permanent possession of each other when they marry. All they obtain is the right to work at the job of holding on to each other." In pressing for modification of marriage as an institution we should seek above all to assure that the two functions of marriage just stated be fulfilled.

## Eight Possible Liaison Patterns

9    A variety of predictions and proposals are being heard today as to how the male-female liaison will or should evolve in the next few decades to meet the changing conditions of modern life. Here, for example, are eight possible patterns of marriage or near-marriage that are being discussed:

10    1. *Serial mating.* Sometimes it is called serial monogamy, sometimes serial polygamy, sometimes consecutive polygamy. But the basic idea is pretty much the same for all. It would assume a turnover of partners over the 50-odd years that a man and a woman can expect to live after they first consider marriage. Swedish sociologist Joachim Israel suggested that four or five marriages might be about par for a lifetime. The mood behind such proposals was summed up by a New York model when she said, "Why lie to yourself? We know we're not going to love one man all our lives." Among others, a psychologist-social worker in California, Virginia Star, has advocated the adoption of renewable marriage contracts. She suggests the contract lapse unless renewed every five years.

11    2. *Unstructured cohabitation.* These are the prolonged affairs without any assumption of permanence or responsibility. Such so-called unstructured liaisons—long popular in the lower classes—have been springing up in many of the larger universities in the off-campus housing. A psychiatrist at the University of California in Berkeley has suggested these liaisons may be the shape of the future. He said, "Stable, open non-marital relationships are pushing the border of what society is going to face in 10 years."[1]

12    A man's magazine in the mid-1960s presented some unconventional views of a woman who had been involved in a national controversy. During the presentation, she was asked, "How many lovers have you had, if you don't mind our asking?"

13    She responded, "You've got a helluva nerve, but I really don't mind. I've had five, if you count my marriage as an affair . . . five affairs, all of them really wing-dings."

[1]"Unstructured Relations," *Newsweek,* July 4, 1966.

14    3. *Mutual polygamy.* At a conference of marriage specialists in 1966 one expert from a Midwestern university speculated, "If we are moving into a new pattern where we are not claiming that marriage can do all the things that have been assumed, we may be moving into a kind of situation where there will be more than one partner. A compartmentalizing." Each partner in any particular marriage might have several mates, each chosen for a special purpose—for example, economic, recreational, procreational. A more informal variant of this would be "flexible monogamy," which in the view of Phyllis and Eberhard Kronhausen would frankly allow "for variety, friendships, and even sexual experiences with other individuals, if these are desired."[2]

15    4. *Single-parent marriages by intent.* These, on the Swedish model, would be the females—and occasional males—who yearn for parenthood ·without the burdens of wedlock.

16    5. *Specialists in parenthood.* Anthropologist Margaret Mead, in looking a few decades ahead, suggests the time may come when pressures to keep the birth rate low will produce a social style "in which parenthood would be limited to a smaller number of families whose principal function would be child-rearing; the rest of the population would be free to function—for the first time in history—as individuals."[3]

17    6. *Communal living.* In such a situation, several adult females and several adult males might live together in the same large dwelling and consider themselves an enlarged communal family, much as the hippies and other unconventional family groups have already been doing for some time.

18    7. *Legalized polygamy for senior citizens.* This is a form of polygamy that enables a man to have several wives at the same time. It has been advanced as a way to ease the demographic problem created by the fact that after the age of 60 there are increasingly more females than males in the population. One such proposal was advanced in the magazine *Geriatrics* by Dr. Victor Kassel, of Salt Lake City (the Mormon capital). The idea was taken seriously enough to be debated and unofficially turned down by the National Council of the Aging. A widow in South Carolina gave one feminine viewpoint when she said, "I am lonesome—but not that lonesome!"

19    8. *A variety of liaison patterns functioning in society simultaneously.* David Mace suggests we are moving toward a three-layer cake type of society as far as male-female liaisons are concerned. He speculated that there may be a coexistence of several patterns. One pattern, as he sees it, will be that a proportion of the people will settle for sex freedom. They will not marry, but will drift into liaisons of long and short terms. There

[2]Phyllis and Eberhard Kronhausen, *The Sexually Responsive Woman* (New York: Grove Press, 1964), p. 236.

[3]Margaret Mead, "The Life Cycle and Its Variants: The Division of Roles," *Daedalus,* Summer, 1967.

will be no attempt to punish or suppress such persons. He suggested that the second layer of this cake would involve somewhat more structuring, with a number of people choosing to go in and out of marriage and probably having several marriages in a lifetime, as in the common Hollywood pattern. Probably in this second layer there will be an attitude of freedom regarding extramarital sex while the couples are married. He suggested that in the third layer of the cake will be those who accept the concept of exclusive monogamy, preceded in at least some cases by premarital chastity.

## Marriage Still Needed

20    Moral standards aside, one complication of most of the eight possible patterns cited above is that they do not allow sufficiently for the intense desire that most women have for a secure arrangement—or at least women have had this intense desire until very recent times. They have had greater difficulty accepting fluid arrangements, especially after they pass the age of 30, than males.

21    An even bigger complication is that while most of these arrangements might seem attractive in terms of providing the companionship so important to male-female partnerships today, they do not come to terms with the second crucial ingredient of modern marriages: a partnership where there is a sound environment for reaching for immortality through the rearing of children. Thus most should be rejected from serious consideration as socially unfeasible—at least for people interested in having children, and we suspect that those who don't will remain a small minority.

### REVIEW

#### Content

1. How do *you* view Packard's "compelling reasons" for marriage? Can you think of others? Do you see these reasons, his and/or yours, as capable of fulfillment outside of marriage? Consider here the last sentence in paragraph 15 and paragraph 19.
2. Do any of Packard's eight proposals especially appeal to you? Do any of them shock you, or otherwise upset you? What do your reactions here suggest to you about your own mating needs? About your respect for the varying needs of others?

#### Rhetoric

3. The prose in Packard's books reads like that of newsmagazines, with points made rapidly and succinctly, for "popular reading." How does

his method of presentation and development of his points help you
to follow what he is saying?

4. Does Packard's use of humorous quotations about various kinds of
liaisons, from different people (a New York model, the woman he
refers to in paragraph 12, a South Carolina widow) distract you from
his serious intent? Explain whatever effect this device has.

**Projects**

5. Develop a paper out of one of the following from the selection:
   (a) "Human beings do not obtain permanent possession of each other
       when they marry. All they obtain is the right to work at the job
       of holding on to each other." (paragraph 8)
   (b) Virginia Star's proposal about renewable marriage contracts (para-
       graph 10)
   (c) the Kronhausens' ideas about "flexible monogamy" (paragraph 14)
   (d) Margaret Mead's statement that, with parenthood limited to a
       small number of families, "the rest of the population would be
       free to function—for the first time in history—as individuals."
       (paragraph 16)
   (e) paragraph 2, plus the first sentence in paragraph 3
   (f) paragraph 20

6. Fantasize an ideal "mating projection" for yourself. Try to be aware
   of your *real needs* (perhaps by contrast with those Society has suggested
   to you that you should have?). Make a paper out of your projection.

# Twice-Minded
# About
# Population Growth

## MARTHA KENT WILLING

Martha Kent Willing (1920–   ) has worked as medical assistant to a doctor
in Seattle, where she is also associated with Population Dynamics. For Population Dynamics she has created several educational films, and she says
that the idea for her book, *Beyond Conception: Our Children's Children*
(1971), came to her during her filming experience in clinics. In *Beyond
Conception,* from which the excerpt below is taken, Willing expresses her

concern about the "twice-minded" about population growth: those people who admit that population is growing too fast for housing, food, jobs, pollution control, and other necessities for survival to keep up with it—and who yet think, with another part of their minds, that more houses, more jobs, more industrial production can and should be provided to resolve the population problem.

1   Many of the people most interested in discussing population are twice-minded about it. Population is growing too fast for housing, food, jobs, pollution control, and so on. These people readily admit this and then say with another part of their minds, "So we will grow more food, develop new jobs, build houses faster." They do not realize that population is a problem in itself requiring single-minded population solutions. Housing problems can be solved by housing, job problems by jobs, food problems by food. But none of these by themselves nor all together, will solve population problems.

2   For any population, there is an absolute upper limit, and an absolute lower limit. There are optimum levels, and conditions of density above and below optimum. These vary with the intrinsic energy-relations between people: the point where cooperation falls off and competition rises to an unhealthy level. The values which are threatened by population above a certain density are not merely related to higher material living standards. They are related to kinds of living. But we have no simple, well-understood names for these values. Because we have had to hunt, eat, burn, chop, build, our languages for these activities are well developed. We understand each other when we talk food and shelter and money. But we have only just come to the point where density bothers us, where the irritations of noise, voice, presence have penetrated our collective awareness. We are irresponsible in new ways, angry in new ways which are hard for us to understand. Our language is not well developed for explaining why we are irritated. It is still in the textbooks and laboratories, and not yet coined on the street.

3   The generation gap is partly a function of density. The young no longer have a place to move into because the old are not yet ready to move out. But the gap is of language too. Lack of communication is noticed by everyone, as though it were somebody's fault. Common language, shared experience can develop over time, and under pressure of consensus. In the greatly specialized densities of urban living, common experience and consensus on meaning is harder to come by. We are all somewhat like a four-year-old who is convinced that tears and shouting, smashing and smearing will somehow make up for the fact that others lack understanding of his private language. He has not yet developed enough notion of "others" to use their public language. We seem to be shouting at each other in private languages about the unfamiliar pressures of a too-crowded world.

## Calhoun's Experiment with Rats

4    Many unpleasant feelings: anxiety, loneliness, a sense of uselessness, of not belonging have become more common, more unpleasant. But the direct relation between these feelings and the density experience of modern man has not been well investigated. Striking experiments by John Calhoun (1962) have demonstrated it in rats. Calhoun's experimental series provides a genuine analogy to our population experience: a limited space, an unlimited food supply, and a small initial population. Given enough food, the animals breed up to and beyond the optimum density. They continue to breed while all normal patterns of social relations break down. Young are deserted, males are sterile, adults die of stress. Leaving much of the cage empty they crowd into a central mass.

5    Rat-man and rat behavior is a fact of our scene, and these experiments in themselves tell us less perhaps than do the aversion and denial reactions they arouse in the general public. No one likes to think about rat-man but we must, for sincere humans believe that we can and should develop unlimited food supplies, and that this will solve our problems. The pope in his speech on population said just this: because governments have not yet done enough to supply their peoples, they must not limit peoples.

6    We know that we are not going to increase food supplies as fast as we increase ourselves. The World Congress of Botanists said this most clearly in 1969. If we were to increase food by the amount necessary to avert the famines predicted for the seventies world reaction would be one of intense relief. We would look upon the varieties of hybrid Mexican wheat which might make this possible as lifesaving, wonderful. But solving a specific shortage of food with a specific increase in grain harvest is the single-minded solving of a food problem. It will not lead to optimum density. People will still have to occupy houses, find work, drink water, and produce waste. They still have to live near each other in densities fixed by the nature of landownership and farm-village relations. Too many people is too many whether they are hungry or not. Where human life is cheap, and fate is all-powerful, bias toward life is less acute. In such countries reduction in population is more easily recognized as a desirable goal in itself, just as producing more food is a desirable goal.

## The Chalicodoma Bees

7    We are angry and have no proper language for our new experiences. Also it seems as though there were a special fixity in human attitudes. The four-year-old who cannot figure out what another is telling him becomes extremely intense. He repeats his efforts and concentrates on

shouting out a single word or idea as the clue. Perhaps we are as new as four-year-olds in dealing with such massive human numbers; perhaps to realize how difficult we are, we need to observe ourselves from another perspective.

8    The Chalicodoma of the walls is a handsome bee of the Camarque, the delta of the Rhone Valley near Marseilles. She builds a little mud pot for her eggs, carrying the clay mouthful by mouthful and smoothing it inside and out. When the masonry is finished, she becomes a supplier of honey and not of houses.

9    A tiny hole pierced in the underside of the mud while she is building causes her to fly off and mend it immediately with fresh clay. But if she has already started to fill the nest with honey, so that the honey flows out when it is pierced, the bee will carry honey to the jar for some time without finding the hole. Then she finds it. She inspects it carefully, seems excited and flies off quickly, to return with more honey!

10   This resembles the behavior of human population specialists. They propose solutions and improve crops and housing enormously. But people are still crowded and still hungry. In consternation the experts rush around in consultation and go off to develop new programs of?— more food and more housing! Their progress, their vital energies are draining away through the flaw of too-rapid population increase. They never suspect they are like the Chalicodoma of the walls. The honey flows unplugged from the nest of the bee. Her efforts are useless. Her instincts are too inflexible to permit her to go back and repair the hole. We, too, seem to have become inflexible experts. When our remedies fail to work, we, too, are excited and anxious, and rush around with new efforts to produce more of everything except a new solution. Like the bee we cannot recognize that our answers are no answers at all to the real problem. We are twice-minded, staring population problems in the face, and producing everything except a population remedy.

## Childbearing Choices

11   Permissive liberality defeats its own purpose, for we cannot have un-limited people and limited resources! We could devise suitable experiments and expect significant, if not final, answers to the question of how many people we ought to have. But family planning experts are like the cancer patient who fears diagnosis and surgery. We are afraid to discover that we have already passed the optimum density for humans even in America, and cannot bear the thought of the remedy. We have no option except to produce fewer children, yet even people who sincerely accept the evidence of crowding are not able to make this single-minded decision. As Americans, we hate to admit there may

be no options for us since we are especially critical of other governments whose citizens have none. We like to imagine that choice is a vital part of our social system.

12    Yet day after day we are moving toward less and less choice because we are twice-minded. We are boxing ourselves into ugliness, deficits, unemployment and deteriorating education in the name of freedom to breed as we please. Millions of citizens are unable to understand what is happening to them. Others who are beginning to understand feel trapped in the grip of an unresponsive bureaucracy. It is difficult to pursue even one thought to its faraway conclusion, without being distracted many times on the way. It is difficult to pin responsibility on any official for anything he has done or refuses to do. Seeing both sides can become a national weakness as well as a political skill. As a nation, we can rarely scrape ourselves up over the energy-top to the high level of performance that results from being single-minded.

## REVIEW

### Content

1. Do you agree with Willing that many persons are "twice-minded" about population growth? Are *you* "single-minded" about it? If your answer here is "yes," do your actions support your words? If you want, or are in the midst of having, children, will you and your partner be able to limit yourselves to the "two for replacement" that is generally recommended by population specialists?
2. Have you experienced the "irritations" caused by density to which Willing refers in paragraphs 2 and 4? If so, do you *yet* respond with the "denial reactions" of their existence which she cites in paragraph 5? If you do, *why* do you? And how can you bring your reactions into more logical conjunction with your experience? Why do you suppose Calhoun's remaining rats crowded into "a central mass . . . leaving much of the cage empty"?

### Rhetoric

3. Do you agree with Willing that one problem surrounding the population growth question is that most of us do not yet have the language to discuss it adequately? Consider in this context the relation between problem-solving and language. Can you think of other critical contemporary issues for which the general public does not have adequate thinking and talking language?
4. Willing illustrates how "inflexible experts" approach the population problem with a story about the Chalicodoma of the walls. Does the story help you better understand her point? In what way does imagery support her explanation here?

**Projects**

5. Take sides, as being either single-minded or twice-minded about population growth, and debate. Search out statistics, statements by experts, laboratory studies (there has been at least one that suggests that humans *prefer* crowding), and all other support you can possibly find for your position.

6. Develop one of the following statements into a paper:

   (a) "[There is a] point where cooperation falls off and competition rises to an unhealthy level." (paragraph 2)

   (b) "The young no longer have a place to move into because the old are not yet ready to move out." (paragraph 3)

   (c) "Too many people is too many whether they are hungry or not." (paragraph 6)

   (d) "Where human life is cheap, and fate is all-powerful, bias toward life is less acute." (paragraph 6)

   Try to use "another perspective" to illustrate your point as Willing does with the story of the bees; you might think of analogies from the animal world, from some other culture, or from another time in history.

# A Living Will

The Living Will is a creation of the Euthanasia Educational Council, which has its headquarters in New York City. The word "euthanasia" comes from two Greek words: *eu*—good, and *thanatos*—death; thus it means "a good death." The Council states as its purpose: "To establish the right to die with dignity." In an age when one can be kept alive beyond what some persons think a reasonable point, "death with dignity" has become more and more difficult to achieve. As one means of encouraging the possibility, the EEC distributes free of charge, on request, copies of the Living Will. The Will, printed below, speaks for itself.

### To My Family, My Physician, My Clergyman, My Lawyer—

If the time comes when I can no longer take part in decisions for my own future, let this statement stand as the testament of my wishes:

If there is no reasonable expectation of my recovery from physical or mental disability,

I, _____
request that I be allowed to die and not be kept alive by artificial means or heroic measures. Death is as much a reality as birth, growth, maturity and

old age—it is the one certainty. I do not fear death as much as I fear the indignity of deterioration, dependence and hopeless pain. I ask that drugs be mercifully administered to me for terminal suffering even if they hasten the moment of death.

This request is made after careful consideration. Although this document is not legally binding, you who care for me will, I hope, feel morally bound to follow its mandate. I recognize that it places a heavy burden of responsibility upon you, and it is with the intention of sharing that responsibility and of mitigating any feelings of guilt that this statement is made.

Signed _____    _____

Date _____    _____

Witnessed by:

_____

_____

## REVIEW

### Content

1. How do *you* feel about the content of the sentence in the Living Will that begins "I do not . . ."?
2. The Living Will addresses the possibility of both active euthanasia (the administration of drugs to terminate suffering even if they hasten death) and passive euthanasia (being allowed to die; i.e., not being kept alive). Do you feel differently about the two forms? If so, why? Who is to make the determination implied in the clause "If there is no reasonable expectation of my recovery from physical or mental disability"? How does the last paragraph of the Will strike you? Is the request a *fair* one?

### Rhetoric

3. Euthanasia is sometimes referred to as "mercy-killing." Consider how the two terms affect you, recalling the origin of the word "euthanasia" (see headnote). What does all this tell you about language?
4. Think about the phrase "no reasonable expectation of my recovery from physical or mental disability." Is there enough precision of vocabulary here, and is the point fully enough explained, to satisfy *you*? If not, how would you rephrase this part?

**Projects**

5. Debate the question of euthanasia, pro versus con. Limit the context of your debate by choosing a specific situation: for example, a terminally ill patient in considerable pain; a very old person no longer able to attend to his/her life needs; a baby born with irreparable defects.
6. Write a paper in which you explain either your consent or your refusal to sign as a witness to a living will which someone very close to you has asked you to sign; designate the person as you begin your paper. Write the paper as a letter to that person, if you prefer.

# Coffee Break

## LANGSTON HUGHES

Langston Hughes (1902–1967) was a poet, novelist, short story writer, playwright, teacher, and lecturer. He traveled widely, including making a poetry-reading tour of the southern United States. Hughes' writing consistently reflects his concern with the development of a social conscience in relation to his people. Among his published works are ten volumes of poetry and a two-volume autobiography. During the 1950s, his contribution to America's folk humor, the Simple stories, came out. One of those stories follows.

1    "My boss is white," said Simple.

2    "Most bosses are," I said.

3    "And being white and curious, my boss keeps asking me just what does THE Negro want. Yesterday he tackled me during the coffee break, talking about THE Negro. He always says 'THE Negro,' as if there was not 50–11 different kinds of Negroes in the U.S.A.," complained Simple. "My boss says, 'Now that you-all have got the Civil Rights Bill and the Supreme Court, Adam Powell in Congress, Ralph Bunche in the United Nations, and Leontyne Price singing in the Metropolitan Opera, plus Dr. Martin Luther King getting the Nobel Prize, what more do you want? I am asking you, just what does THE Negro want?' "

4    " 'I am not THE Negro,' I says, 'I am *me*.'

5    " 'Well,' says my boss, 'you represent THE Negro.'

6    " 'I do not,' I says. 'I represent my own self.'

7    " 'Ralph Bunche represents you, then,' says my boss, and Thurgood Marshall and Martin Luther King. Do they not?'

8    " 'I am proud to be represented by such men, if you say they represent me,' I said. 'But all them men you name are *way* up there, and they do not drink beer in my bar. I have never seen a single one of them mens on Lenox Avenue in my natural life. So far as I know, they do not even live in Harlem. I cannot find them in the telephone book. They all got private numbers. But since you say they represent THE Negro, why do you not ask them what THE Negro wants?'

9    " 'I cannot get to them,' says my boss.

10   " 'Neither can I,' I says, 'so we both is in the same boat.'

11   " 'Well then, to come nearer home,' says my boss, 'Roy Wilkins fights your battles, also James Farmer.'

12   " 'They do not drink in my bar neither,' I said.

13   " 'Don't Wilkins and Farmer live in Harlem?' he asked.

14   " 'Not to my knowledge,' I said. 'And I bet they have not been to the Apollo since Jackie Mabley cracked the first joke.'

15   " 'I do not know him,' said my boss, 'but I see Nipsey Russell and Bill Cosby on TV.'

16   " 'Jackie Mabley is no *him*,' I said. She is a *she*—better known as Moms.'

17   " 'Oh,' said my boss.

18   " 'And Moms Mabley has a story on one of her records about Little Cindy Ella and the magic slippers going to the Junior Prom at Ole Miss which tells all about what THE Negro wants.'

19   " 'What's its conclusion?' asked my boss.

20   " 'When the clock strikes midnight, Little Cindy Ella is dancing with the President of the Ku Klux Klan, says Moms, but at the stroke of twelve, Cindy Ella turns back to her natural self, black, and her blonde wig turns to a stocking cap—and her trial comes up next week.'

21   " 'A symbolic tale,' says my boss, 'meaning, I take it, that THE Negro is in jail. But you are not in jail.'

22   " 'That's what you think,' I said.

23   " 'Anyhow, you claim you are not THE Negro,' said my boss.

24   " 'I am not,' I said. 'I am *this* Negro.'

25   " 'Then what do *you* want?' asked my boss.

26   " 'To get out of jail,' I said.

27   " 'What jail?'

28   " 'The jail you got me in.'

29   " 'Me?' yells my boss. 'I have not got you in jail. Why, boy, I like you. I am a liberal. I voted for Kennedy. And this time for Johnson. I believe in integration. Now that you got it, though, what more do you want?'

30   " 'Reintegration,' I said.

31   " 'Meaning by that, what?'

32   " 'That you be integrated with *me*, not me with you.'

33   " 'Do you mean that I come and live in Harlem?' asked my boss. 'Never!'

34   " 'I live in Harlem,' I said.

35    " 'You are adjusted to it,' said my boss. 'But there is so much crime in Harlem.'

36    " 'There are no two-hundred-thousand dollar bank robberies, though,' I said, 'of which there was three lately *elsewhere*—all done by white folks, and nary one in Harlem. The biggest and best crime is outside of Harlem. We never has no half-million-dollar jewelry robberies, no missing star sapphires. You better come uptown with me and reintegrate.'

37    " 'Negroes are the ones who want to be integrated,' said my boss.

38    " 'And white folks are the ones who do *not* want to be,' I said.

39    " 'Up to a point, we do,' said my boss.

40    " 'That is what THE Negro wants,' I said, to remove that *point.*'

41    " 'The coffee break is over,' said my boss."

**REVIEW**

**Content**

1. Why do the boss' references to "THE Negro" bother Simple so much? Why does the boss perceive as he does? Why does Simple say he is "in jail"? Can you make a list of the things that "go wrong" in paragraph 29? What does Simple mean by "reintegration"? What do you think is the *key* line in the story?

2. Compare this story with "The Gay Mystique" in Section 3 and with "On the Art of Stealing Human Rights" in Section 5.

**Rhetoric**

3. What techniques does Hughes use to make the Simple tales funny? Is there *irony* in this tale? What does the use of the dialect contribute? Is it demeaning here?

4. Do you find the ending effective? If so, why?

**Projects**

5 One way of "keeping a person in his/her place" is by treating him/her like a non-person; that is, saying and doing—or not saying and doing—various things that make the person realize you do not *really see* him/her. Talk about ways in which this can be done, whether deliberately or unconsciously. Do *you* ever do it?

6. A number of Black writers deal with various themes that come up in this story. To increase your appreciation of the perceptions and the dilemmas of the Black person, read in one of the following: *The Invisible Man* by Ralph Ellison; *Native Son* by Richard Wright; *I Know Why the Caged Bird Sings* by Maya Angelou; *Manchild in the Promised Land* by Claude Brown; *The Fire Next Time* or *Notes of a Native Son* by James Baldwin. Write a brief review of what you have read—and your own reaction to it, as one human being responding to the life of another human being.

# Address

## CHIEF SEATTLE

Chief Seattle was a chief of the Duwampo tribe in the Washington Territory during the nineteenth century. In 1854 the United States Government sent Governor Isaac Stevens, Commissioner of Indian Affairs for the Washington Territory, out to the Indians with a treaty that included federal purchase of 2 million acres of Indian land. Chief Seattle, a giant of a man with a majestic voice, responded for the Indians in the following eloquent address, translated from Duwamish into English by Henry A. Smith.

1 Yonder sky that has wept tears of compassion upon my people for centuries untold, and which to us appears changeless and eternal, may change. Today is fair. Tomorrow may be overcast with clouds. My words are like the stars that never change. Whatever Seattle says the great chief at Washington can rely upon with as much certainty as he can upon the return of the sun or the seasons. The White Chief says that Big Chief at Washington sends us greetings of friendship and goodwill. That is kind of him for we know he has little need of our friendship in return. His people are many. They are like the grass that covers vast prairies. My people are few. They resemble the scattering trees of a storm-swept plain. The great, and—I presume—good, White Chief sends us word that he wishes to buy our lands but is willing to allow us enough to live comfortably. This indeed appears just, even generous, for the Red Man no longer has rights that he need respect, and the offer may be wise also, as we are no longer in need of an extensive country. . . . I will not dwell on, nor mourn over, our untimely decay, nor reproach our paleface brothers with hastening it, as we too may have been somewhat to blame.

2 Youth is impulsive. When our young men grow angry at some real or imaginary wrong, and disfigure their faces with black paint, it denotes that their hearts are black, and then they are often cruel and relentless, and our old men and old women are unable to restrain them. Thus it has ever been. Thus it was when the white men first began to push our forefathers further westward. But let us hope that the hostilities between us may never return. We would have everything to lose and nothing to gain. Revenge by young men is considered gain, even at the cost of their own lives, but old men who stay at home in times of war, and mothers who have sons to lose, know better.

3 Our good father at Washington—for I presume he is now our father

From *Northwest Gateway* by Archie Binns, published by Doubleday & Company. Reprinted by permission of Ellen F. Binns.

as well as yours, since King George has moved his boundaries further north—our great good father, I say, sends us word that if we do as he desires he will protect us. His brave warriors will be to us a bristling wall of strength, and his wonderful ships of war will fill our harbors so that our ancient enemies far to the northward—the Hydas and Tsimpsians—will cease to frighten our women, children, and old men. Then in reality will he be our father and we his children. But can that ever be? Your God is not our God! Your God loves your people and hates mine. He folds his strong and protecting arms lovingly about the paleface and leads him by the hand as a father leads his infant son—but He has forsaken His red children—if they really are his. Our God, the Great Spirit, seems also to have forsaken us. Your God makes your people wax strong every day. Soon they will fill the land. Our people are ebbing away like a rapidly receding tide that will never return. The white man's God cannot love our people or He would protect them. They seem to be orphans who can look nowhere for help. How then can we be brothers? How can your God become our God and renew our prosperity and awaken in us dreams of returning greatness? If we have a common heavenly father He must be partial—for He came to his paleface children. We never saw Him. He gave you laws but He had no word for His red children whose teeming multitudes once filled this vast continent as stars fill the firmament. No; we are two distinct races with separate origins and separate destinies. There is little in common between us.

4       To us the ashes of our ancestors are sacred and their resting place is hallowed ground. You wander far from the graves of your ancestors and seemingly without regret. Your religion was written upon tables of stone by the iron finger of your God so that you could not forget. The Red Man could never comprehend nor remember it. Our religion is the traditions of our ancestors—the dreams of our old men, given them in solemn hours of night by the Great Spirit; and the visions of our sachems; and it is written in the hearts of our people.

5       Your dead cease to love you and the land of their nativity as soon as they pass the portals of the tomb and wander way beyond the stars. They are soon forgotten and never return. Our dead never forget the beautiful world that gave them being.

6       Day and night cannot dwell together. The Red Man has ever fled the approach of the White Man, as the morning mist flees before the morning sun. However, your proposition seems fair and I think that my people will accept it and will retire to the reservation you offer them. Then we will dwell apart in peace, for the words of the Great White Chief seem to be the words of nature speaking to my people out of dense darkness.

7       It matters little where we pass the remnant of our days. They will not be many. A few more moons; a few more winters—and not one of the descendants of the mighty hosts that once moved over this broad

land or lived in happy homes, protected by the Great Spirit, will remain to mourn over the graves of a people once more powerful and hopeful than yours. But why should I mourn at the untimely fate of my people? Tribe follows tribe, and nation follows nation, like the waves of the sea. It is the order of nature, and regret is useless. Your time of decay may be distant, but it will surely come, for even the White Man whose God walked and talked with him as friend with friend, cannot be exempt from the common destiny. We may be brothers after all. We will see.

8    We will ponder your proposition, and when we decide we will let you know. But should we accept it, I here and now make this condition that we will not be denied the privilege without molestation of visiting at any time the tombs of our ancestors, friends and children. Every part of this soil is sacred in the estimation of my people. Every hillside, every valley, every plain and grove, has been hallowed by some sad or happy event in days long vanished. . . . The very dust upon which you now stand responds more lovingly to their footsteps than to yours, because it is rich with the blood of our ancestors and our bare feet are conscious of the sympathetic touch. . . . Even the little children who lived here and rejoiced here for a brief season will love these somber solitudes and at eventide they greet shadowy returning spirits. And when the last Red Man shall have perished, and the memory of my tribe shall have become a myth among the White Men, these shores will swarm with the invisible dead of my tribe, and when your children's children think themselves alone in the field, the store, the shop, upon the highway, or in the silence of the pathless woods, they will not be alone. . . . At night when the streets of your cities and villages are silent and you think them deserted, they will throng with the returning hosts that once filled and still love this beautiful land. The White Man will never be alone.

9    Let him be just and deal kindly with my people, for the dead are not powerless. Dead, did I say? There is no death, only a change of worlds.

## REVIEW

### Content

1. How did you *feel* while reading Seattle's address? Discuss your emotional response to *specific* passages. Has anything happened to your sense of human kinship with the Indian?
2. Seattle's address is marked by a wide variety of traits and tones: a sense of fairness, compassion, reflective wisdom, irony, righteous indignation, feelings of human fellowship, a kinship with Nature, a sense of history and sustaining tradition. How do you regard *him* as you finish reading the speech?

**Rhetoric**

3. Do you find Seattle's arguments in paragraph 3 *logical*—so that the conclusions of the final sentences in that paragraph are *inevitable*?

4. Seattle seems to speak with several voices: that of a poet, a philosopher, a religious spokesman, a judge. In what passages can you "hear" these varying voices, and how do they differ?

**Projects**

5. Seattle's address needs to be heard, as well as read. Listen while a classmate orates it and consider the effect, on both the other Indians and the White listeners, on that day in 1854.

6. Be Governor Isaac Stevens and write your response to Seattle's address, following the signing of the treaty—to which Seattle has agreed in paragraph 6.

# 5
# Politics

# Law as the Means to Freedom

## A. DELAFIELD SMITH

A. Delafield Smith (1893–   ) was a practicing lawyer for a number of years. In 1937 he began a long term of service as an attorney in the United States Government, working with the Department of Health, Education and Welfare among other agencies. The following is from Smith's book *The Right to Life* (1955). In this excerpt, Smith attempts to explain the purpose of law, through the analogy of games—in sports or cards. Without "ground rules"—in either law or game-playing—no one is free, because neither the environment nor the behavior of other persons is predictable.

1   We need to see what the true meaning and function of law is, not in terms of authority, which is so commonly mistaken for law, but in terms of the rule of law in the ideal sense as a guide and challenge to the human will.

2   The best example of how law, in the ideal sense, works, how it evokes the sense of freedom and stimulates the individual is the survey of a game. Have you ever asked yourself why the participation in a game is so excellent a medium for self-expression and character development? This question is often superficially answered in terms of the rein given to the competitive instincts of the individual and his "zest" for conquest. But have you ever considered that here, in a game, and perhaps here alone, we human beings really do act almost completely under the aegis of law? That, rather than competition, is the real source of the game's restorative value for the human spirit. Analyze the process step by step and you must be convinced that this is the truth.

3   Your first step upon entering a game is the assumption of a distinct personality. You become clothed in a personality defined by the rules of the game. You assume a legal or game personality. You may describe yourself as a first baseman, as a right guard, or as a dealer. But however you describe yourself you will see that what you have described is a legal status—one of the focal points in a legal pattern with rights and obligations suitable to the position. These rights and duties are defined

Reprinted by permission of The University of North Carolina Press from A. Delafield Smith, *The Right to Life*.

by the rules under whose empery you have thus put both yourself and all others with whom you have dealings. Your status, your rights, your obligations, all are secure, for the rules of the game are almost sure to be followed. The game indeed is defined by its rules. These are purely abstract. They are wholly free of will and dictation. They are pure rules of action composed usually in some physical setting which they serve to interpret and fashion till it becomes an arena of human action, just as, for example, the rules of the highway, in relation to the highway pattern itself, provide individuals with an arena on which they can operate successfully. Now the rules of the game have many functions. They, in fact, define the very goals that the players seek. One wins only in the context of the rules of the game. They determine inexorably the consequences of the player's action, every play that he makes. He acts solely in relation to the rules. Their empery is accepted like a fact or a circumstance. Finally, they challenge and stimulate him for he uses the rules to win. The game is otherwise unmanaged. An umpire or a referee is but an interpreter of the rules. He *can* be wrong. Such is the conception. This, then, may furnish an introduction to the real function of law in society.

4    Law gave birth to the concept of freedom. True it is that you can have no security in a situation in which every person and everything around you acts capriciously, unpredictably, or, in other words, lawlessly; but the point I wish to make is that while you would have no security in such an environment, it is more significant that you would have no freedom in such an environment. The reason you could not be free in such a situation is that you could not get anywhere you wanted to go or successfully do anything you wanted to do. You could make no plan in the expectation of carrying it out. You cannot possibly carry out any aim or goal of your own unless you have some basis for calculating what results may follow from any given act or activity of your own. Unless you can determine in advance what are the prospects and limitations of a given course of behavior, you cannot act intelligently. Whatever intelligence you may have will do you no good. You cannot adjust your own step to anyone else's step nor can you relate your conduct to any series of events or occurrences outside yourself except to the extent that they follow a pattern that you can learn about in advance of your action.

5    The only way to promote freedom is to devise a set of rules and thus construct a pattern which the various members of that society can follow. Each can then determine his own acts in the light of his knowledge of the rules. On this basis each can predict his field of action in advance and what results are likely to ensue from his acts; and so he gains freedom to plan and to carry out his plans. The more you attempt to administer society, however, the less free it becomes. There is opportunity for freedom of choice only in acting subject to the rules,

and then only if the rules are freed of any element of will or dictation. If these rules are just rules that tell you what method or act will yield what results, like the rules of a game, you can then freely determine your own play. You can use the rules to win the game. The more abstract and objective the rule, the freer is the individual in the choice of his alternatives. The rules must be so written as to cover every possible eventuality of choice and action.

## REVIEW

### Content

1. Smith wants his reader to consider law, not as "authority," but "as a guide and challenge to the human will." Explain what he means by the latter phrase. Do you so view law? If not, how does your view differ from Smith's?
2. Do you agree with Smith, in paragraph 4, that security and freedom are possible only in an environment where the law—the rules of the game—is clearly defined? Expand in class discussion the next to last sentence in paragraph 5. Is the requirement Smith sets forth in the final sentence here *possible*? If not, how should a society resolve this problem?

### Rhetoric

3. Smith structures a tight argument, to prove his points. Follow his argument through carefully and explain how, both through what he says and how he says it (stylistic devices), he leads you through the argument.
4. Smith develops his points about the purposes of law by direct and rather exhaustive analogy with the purposes of the game. The validity, and hence the usefulness, of an analogy is determined by how *completely* it works; that is, how *specifically* the analogy can be drawn. Does this particular analogy work exactly throughout? Can you think of any possible points at which it might break down?

### Projects

5. Think of some facet of law which you are tempted to break from time to time: for example, traffic laws, laws infringing on property rights, laws about petty theft. Prepare a role-playing scene showing what happens when *several* persons decide to break the law you are dealing with. Have some others role-play non-lawbreakers.
6. Write a paper explaining either why you did or did not, at some time in your life, break some law you regard as a minor one. Can you relate the reasoning behind that decision to Smith's discussion of law?

# On the Duty of Civil Disobedience

## HENRY DAVID THOREAU

Henry David Thoreau (1817–1862) was one of the group of writers in the "New England Awakening" in this country in the mid-1800s. One of the best known works of this philosopher and naturalist is *Walden; or, Life in the Woods* (1854). Another is the famous essay entitled "On the Duty of Civil Disobedience" (1849), in which Thoreau argues for following one's own conscience above mindless conformity to civil law. Thoreau himself refused to pay his poll tax to support the Mexican War he did not believe in—and landed in jail. It is said that his friend Ralph Waldo Emerson came to see him in jail and asked, "Henry, *what* are you doing in there?" And that Thoreau replied: "Ralph, what are *you* doing out there?"

1   I heartily accept the motto—"That government is best which governs least"; and I should like to see it acted up to more rapidly and systematically. Carried out, it finally amounts to this, which also I believe,—"That government is best which governs not at all"; and when men are prepared for it, that will be the kind of government which they will have. Government is at best but an expedient; but most governments are usually, and all governments are sometimes, inexpedient. The objections which have been brought against a standing army, and they are many and weighty, and deserve to prevail, may also at last be brought against a standing government. The standing army is only an arm of the standing government. The government itself, which is only the mode which the people have chosen to execute their will, is equally liable to be abused and perverted before the people can act through it. Witness the present Mexican war, the work of comparatively a few individuals using the standing government as their tool; for, in the outset, the people would not have consented to this measure.

2       This American government —what is it but a tradition, though a recent one, endeavoring to transmit itself unimpaired to posterity, but each instant losing some of its integrity? It has not the vitality and force of a single living man; for a single man can bend it to his will. It is a sort of wooden gun to the people themselves. But it is not the less necessary for this; for the people must have some complicated machinery or other, and hear its din, to satisfy that idea of government which they have. Governments show us how successfully men can be imposed on, even impose on themselves, for their own advantage. It is excellent, we must all allow. Yet this government never of itself furthered any

enterprise, but by the alacrity with which it got out of its way. *It* does not keep the country free. *It* does not settle the West. *It* does not educate. The character inherent in the American people has done all that has been accomplished; and it would have done somewhat more, if the government had not sometimes got in its way. For government is an expedient by which men would fain succeed in letting one another alone; and, as has been said, when it is most expedient, the governed are most let alone by it. Trade and commerce, if they were not made of India-rubber, would never manage to bounce over the obstacles which legislators are continually putting in their way; and, if one were to judge these men wholly by the effects of their actions and not partly by their intentions, they would deserve to be classed and punished with those mischievous persons who put obstructions on the railroads.

3      But, to speak practically and as a citizen, unlike those who call themselves no-government men, I ask for, not at once no government, but *at once* a better government. Let every man make known what kind of government would command his respect, and that will be one step toward obtaining it.

## Individual Conscience

4      After all, the practical reason why, when the power is once in the hands of the people, a majority are permitted, and for a long period continue, to rule is not because they are most likely to be in the right, nor because this seems fairest to the minority, but because they are physically the strongest. But a government in which the majority rule in all cases cannot be based on justice, even as far as men understand it. Can there not be a government in which majorities do not virtually decide right and wrong, but conscience—in which majorities decide only those questions to which the rule of expediency is applicable? Must the citizen ever for a moment, or in the last degree, resign his conscience to the legislator? Why has every man a conscience, then? I think that we should be men first, and subjects afterward. It is not desirable to cultivate a respect for the law, so much as for the right. The only obligation which I have a right to assume is to do at any time what I think right. It is truly enough said, that a corporation has no conscience; but a corporation of conscientious men is a corporation *with* a conscience. Law never made men a whit more just; and, by means of their respect for it, even the well-disposed are daily made the agents of injustice. A common and natural result of an undue respect for law is, that you may see a file of soldiers, colonel, captain, corporal, privates, powder-monkeys, and all, marching in admirable order over hill and dale to the war, against their will, ay, against their common sense and consciences, which makes it very steep marching indeed, and produces a palpitation of the heart.

They have no doubt that it is a damnable business in which they are concerned; they are all peaceably inclined. Now, what are they? Men at all? or small movable forts and magazines, at the service of some unscrupulous man in power? Visit the Navy-Yard, and behold a marine, such a man as an American government can make, or such as it can make a man with its black arts—a mere shadow and reminiscence of humanity, a man laid out alive and standing, and already, as one may say, buried under arms with funeral accompaniments, though it may be,—

> Not a drum was heard, not a funeral note,
>   As his corpse to the rampart we hurried;
> Not a soldier discharged his farewell shot
>   O'er the grave where our hero we buried.

5     The mass of men serve the state thus, not as men mainly, but as machines, with their bodies. They are the standing army, and the militia, jailors, constables, posse comitatus, etc. In most cases there is no free exercise whatever of the judgment or of the moral sense; but they put themselves on a level with wood and earth and stones; and wooden men can perhaps be manufactured that will serve the purpose as well. Such command no more respect than men of straw or a lump of dirt. They have the same sort of worth only as horses and dogs. Yet such as these even are commonly esteemed good citizens. Others—as most legislators, politicians, lawyers, ministers, and office-holders—serve the state chiefly with their heads: and, as they rarely make any moral distinctions, they are as likely to serve the Devil, without *intending* it, as God. A very few, as heroes, patriots, martyrs, reformers in the great sense, and *men*, serve the state with their consciences also, and so necessarily resist it for the most part; and they are commonly treated as enemies by it. A wise man will only be useful as a man, and will not submit to be "clay," and "stop a hole to keep the wind away," but leave that office to his dust at least:—

> I am too high-born to be propertied,
> To be a secondary at control,
> Or useful serving-man and instrument
> To any sovereign state throughout the world.

6     He who gives himself entirely to his fellow-men appears to them useless and selfish; but he who gives himself partially to them is pronounced a benefactor and philanthropist.

## The Slave's Government

7     How does it become a man to behave toward this American government to-day? I answer, that he cannot without disgrace be associated

with it. I cannot for an instant recognize that political organization as *my* government which is the *slave's* government also.

8     All men recognize the right of revolution; that is, the right to refuse allegiance to, and to resist, the government, when its tyranny or its inefficiency are great and unendurable. But almost all say that such is not the case now. But such was the case, they think, in the Revolution of '75. If one were to tell me that this was a bad government because it taxed certain foreign commodities brought to its ports, it is most probable that I should not make an ado about it, for I can do without them. All machines have their friction; and possibly this does enough good to counterbalance the evil. At any rate, it is a great evil to make a stir about it. But when the friction comes to have its machine, and oppression and robbery are organized, I say, let us not have such a machine any longer. In other words, when a sixth of the population of a nation which has undertaken to be the refuge of liberty are slaves, and a whole country is unjustly overrun and conquered by a foreign army, and subjected to military law, I think that it is not too soon for honest men to rebel and revolutionize. What makes this duty the more urgent is the fact that the country so overrun is not our own, but ours is the invading army. . . .

> A drab of state, a cloth-o'-silver slut,
>     To have her train borne up, and her soul trail in the dirt

Practically speaking, the opponents to a reform in Massachusetts are not a hundred thousand politicians at the South, but a hundred thousand merchants and farmers here, who are more interested in commerce and agriculture than they are in humanity, and are not prepared to do justice to the slave and to Mexico, *cost what it may.* I quarrel not with far-off foes, but with those who, near at home, cooperate with, and do the bidding of, those far away, and without whom the latter would be harmless. We are accustomed to say, that the mass of men are unprepared; but improvement is slow, because the few are not materially wiser or better than the many. It is not so important that many should be as good as you, as that there be some absolute goodness somewhere; for that will leaven the whole lump. There are thousands who are *in opinion* opposed to slavery and to the war, who yet in effect do nothing to put an end to them; who, esteeming themselves children of Washington and Franklin, sit down with their hands in their pockets, and say that they know not what to do, and do nothing; who even postpone the question of freedom to the question of free-trade, and quietly read the prices-current along with the latest advices from Mexico, after dinner, and, it may be, fall asleep over them both. What is the price-current of an honest man and patriot to-day? They hesitate, and they regret, and sometimes they petition; but they do nothing in earnest and with effect. They will wait, well disposed, for others to remedy the evil, that they may no longer have it to regret. At most, they give only a cheap vote, and a feeble countenance and God-speed, to the right, as it goes by them. There are nine hundred and ninety-nine patrons of virtue to one virtuous man. But it is easier to deal with the real possessor of a thing than with the temporary guardian of it.

## Voting and Doing

9      All voting is a sort of gaming, like checkers or backgammon, with a slight moral tinge to it, a playing with right and wrong, with moral questions; and betting naturally accompanies it. The character of the voters is not staked. I cast my vote, perchance, as I think right; but I am not vitally concerned that that right should prevail. I am willing to leave it to the majority. Its obligation, therefore, never exceeds that of expediency. Even voting *for the right* is *doing* nothing for it. It is only expressing to men feebly your desire that it should prevail. A wise man will not leave the right to the mercy of chance, nor wish it to prevail through the power of the majority. There is but little virtue in the action of masses of men. When the majority shall at length vote for the abolition of slavery, it will be because they are indifferent to slavery, or because there is but little slavery left to be abolished by their vote. *They* will then be the only slaves. Only *his* vote can hasten the abolition of slavery who asserts his own freedom by his vote.

10     I hear of a convention to be held at Baltimore, or elsewhere, for the selection of a candidate for the Presidency, made up chiefly of editors, and men who are politicians by profession; but I think, what is it to any independent, intelligent, and respectable man what decision they may come to? Shall we not have the advantage of his wisdom and honesty, nevertheless? Can we not count upon some independent votes? Are there not many individuals in the country who do not attend conventions? But no: I find that the respectable man, so called, has immediately drifted from his position, and despairs of his country, when his country has more reason to despair of him. He forthwith adopts one of the candidates thus selected as the only *available* one, thus proving that he is himself *available* for any purposes of the demagogue. His vote is of no more worth than that of any unprincipled foreigner or hireling native, who may have been bought. O for a man who is a *man,* and, as my neighbor says, has a bone in his back which you cannot pass your hand through! Our statistics are at fault: the population has been returned too large. How many *men* are there to a square thousand miles in this country? Hardly one. Does not America offer any inducement for men to settle here? The American has dwindled into an Odd Fellow,—one who may be known by the development of his organ of gregariousness, and a manifest lack of intellect and cheerful self-reliance; whose first and chief concern, on coming into the world, is to see that

the Almshouses are in good repair; and, before yet he has lawfully donned the virile garb, to collect a fund for the support of the widows and orphans that may be; who, in short, ventures to live only by the aid of the Mutual Insurance Company, which has promised to bury him decently.

## Indirect Support

11    It is not a man's duty, as a matter of course, to devote himself to the eradication of any, even the most enormous wrong; he may still properly have other concerns to engage him; but it is his duty, at least, to wash his hands of it, and, if he gives it no thought longer, not to give it practically his support. If I devote myself to other pursuits and contemplations, I must first see, at least, that I do not pursue them sitting upon another man's shoulders. I must get off him first, that he may pursue his contemplations too. See what gross inconsistency is tolerated. I have heard some of my townsmen say, "I should like to have them order me out to help put down an insurrection of the slaves, or to march to Mexico;—see if I would go"; and yet these very men have each, directly by their allegiance, and so indirectly, at least, by their money, furnished a substitute. The soldier is applauded who refuses to serve in an unjust war by those who do not refuse to sustain the unjust government which makes the war; is applauded by those whose own act and authority he disregards and sets at naught; as if the state were penitent to that degree that it hired one to scourge it while it sinned, but not to that degree that it left off sinning for a moment. Thus, under the name of Order and Civil Government, we are all made at last to pay homage to and support our own meanness. After the first blush of sin comes its indifference; and from immoral it becomes, as it were, *un*moral, and not quite unnecessary to that life which we have made.

12    The broadest and most prevalent error requires the most disinterested virtue to sustain it. The slight reproach to which the virtue of patriotism is commonly liable, the noble are most likely to incur. Those who, while they disapprove of the character and measures of a government, yield to it their allegiance and support are undoubtedly its most conscientious supporters, and so frequently the most serious obstacles to reform. Some are petitioning the state to dissolve the Union, to disregard the requisitions of the President. Why do they not dissolve it themselves—the union between themselves and the state,—and refuse to pay their quota into its treasury? Do not they stand in the same relation to the state that the state does to the Union? And have not the same reasons prevented the state from resisting the Union which have prevented them from resisting the state?

13      How can a man be satisfied to entertain an opinion merely, and enjoy
*it*? Is there any enjoyment in it, if his opinion is that he is aggrieved?
If you are cheated out of a single dollar by your neighbor, you do
not rest satisfied with knowing that you are cheated, or with saying
that you are cheated, or even with petitioning him to pay you your
due; but you take effectual steps at once to obtain the full amount,
and see that you are never cheated again. Action from principle, the
perception and the performance of right, changes things and relations;
it is essentially revolutionary, and does not consist wholly with anything
which was. It not only divides states and churches, it divides families;
ay, it divides the *individual*, separating the diabolical in him from the
divine.

## REVIEW

### Content

1. Thoreau says that the best government is that which governs least
   and that, indeed, government sometimes deters progress by needlessly
   setting up obstructions. Can you think of contemporary examples to
   illustrate his point? To what extent *shoud* government participate, in
   each instance? What results would you predict if government stayed
   completely out, in each instance?
2. Paragraph 4 of Thoreau's essay is an appeal to individual conscience.
   Do you agree with him that "We should be men first, and subjects
   afterward"? Why does he title his essay "On the *Duty* of Civil Disobedience"? Do you agree with the last part of the sentence that begins
   "A very few . . .," in paragraph 5? Compare Thoreau's essay on
   civil disobedience with the one by his friend Ralph Waldo Emerson
   on "Self-Reliance" in Section 2 of this book.

### Rhetoric

3. Part of the appeal of Thoreau's style lies in his frequent references
   to the everyday life of his contemporaries and in his ability to express
   his points in a homespun way. Point to particularly effective examples
   of both these elements in the essay.
4. Thoreau was a poet, as well as an essayist. Evaluate how the poetry
   he intersperses with his prose either strengthens or weakens his essay.

### Projects

5. Develop one of the following lines from Thoreau's essay into a paper
   in which you either support or refute the statement:
   (a) "The government itself . . . is . . . liable to be abused and perverted
       before the people can act through it." (paragraph 1)
   (b) "It is not desirable to cultivate a respect for the law, so much as
       for the right." (paragraph 4)

(c) "Law never made men a whit more just." (paragraph 4)
(d) "He who gives himself entirely to his fellow-men appears to them useless and selfish; but he who gives himself partially to them is pronounced a benefactor and philanthropist." (paragraph 6)
(e) "Even voting *for the right* is *doing* nothing for it." (paragraph 9)
   Illustrate your point by the use of examples where appropriate.
6. Thoreau's essay has inspired a number of posters and graffiti; for example, "Suppose they gave a war and nobody came." Create some others, from your reading of the essay.

# And Aren't I a Woman?

## SOJOURNER TRUTH

Sojourner Truth (1797?–1883) was named Isabella at her birth as a slave in New York state. Winning her freedom in the late 1820s—by fleeing her owner who refused to honor the 1827 New York emancipation law—she said the Lord had given her the name Sojourner Truth. Sojourner began to preach for the cause of freedom at camp meetings and in private homes in New England and the West. Later, a white friend, Olive Gilbert, compiled *The Narrative of Sojourner Truth* (subtitled *Drawn from Her Book of Life*), which includes the following speech. The occasion for the speech was a Women's Rights Convention in Akron, Ohio, and Sojourner's simple but incisive arguments are said to have turned the tide of the meeting in favor of the women.

1   Well, children, where this is so much racket, there must be somethin' out of kilter. I think between the Negroes of the South and the white women of the North—all talkin' about rights—the white men will be in a hell of a fix pretty soon. But what's all this about anyway?

2   That man over there. He says women need to be helped into carriages and lifted over ditches and to have the best everywhere. Nobody ever helps me into carriages, over mud puddles, or gets me any best place.

3   Aren't I a woman? Look at me! Look at my arm. I have ploughed. And I have planted. And I have gathered into barns. And no man could head me. *And aren't I a woman?*

4   I could work as much, and eat as much as any man—when I could

Reprinted from *Journey Toward Freedom: The Story of Sojourner Truth* by Jacqueline Bernard. Copyright © 1967 by Jacqueline Bernard. Published by Grosset & Dunlap, Inc.

get it—and bear the lash as well. And aren't I a woman? I have borne thirteen children and seen them sold into slavery, and when I cried out with a mother's grief, none but Jesus heard me. *And aren't I a woman?*

5    He talks about this thing in the head. What's that they call it?

6    That's it, honey. Intellect. What's intellect got to do with women's rights or black folk's rights? If my cup won't hold but a pint, and yours holds a quart, wouldn't you be mean not to let me have my little half-measure full?

7    That little man in black there! He says women can't have as much rights as men, 'cause Christ wasn't a woman. Where did your Christ come from?

8    Where did he come from? From God and a woman. Man had nothing to do with him.

9    If the first woman God ever made was strong enough to turn the world upside down all alone, these women together ought to be able to turn it back and get it right-side up again.

10    Obliged to you for hearin' me.

## REVIEW

### Content

1. Can you *refute* any of Sojourner Truth's points in her speech? If not, what does this tell you about *her*?
2. Why do you suppose Sojourner Truth, Black and a former slave, chose to speak at a women's rights convention for White women who had never known slavery?

### Rhetoric

3. What is the effect of Sojourner Truth's repetition of "[And] aren't I a woman?"?
4. If your answer to the first question in Question 1 was "no," can you now explain *why* Sojourner Truth's speech is so effective, both in content and in style? How does she accomplish her purposes?

### Projects

5. The speech is exciting and fun to hear. If someone in the class will memorize and recite it, try to imagine yourself at the convention in Akron in 1851. Fantasize the effect on the audience—made up of White women engaged in the struggle for their rights and a number of White men, including clergymen, who opposed that struggle.
6. If you are taking a course in speech, begin to use some of Sojourner Truth's stylistic devices in the speeches you compose: repetition of a short, especially meaningful question; parallel structure (see para-

graph 3); use of direct questions intended to make your audience think (paragraphs 6 and 7); a concluding challenge and/or the suggestion of a promise (as in paragraph 9).

# Of Power, Worth, Dignity, Honor, and Worthiness

## THOMAS HOBBES

Thomas Hobbes (1588–1679) was an English political philosopher, whose master work was *Leviathan, or the Matter, Form and Power of a Commonwealth, Ecclesiastical and Civil,* published in 1651. It was so controversial, in its support of the divine right of kings and other critical elements in what Hobbes saw as the essential interdependence of Church and State, that it was proscribed by the church and burned at Oxford. *Leviathan* was divided into four major parts, one of which was "Of Man"; the following is excerpted from that section. In this passage Hobbes defines the terms of the essay's title, and delineates, with remarkable conciseness, their sources and circumstances. He cites those manifestations of the listed qualities that lead to a man's deserving recognition in politics.

1   The *power of a man,* to take it universally, is his present means, to obtain some future apparent good; and is either *original* or *instrumental.*

2   *Natural power,* is the eminence of the faculties of body, or mind: as extraordinary strength, form, prudence, arts, eloquence, liberality, nobility. *Instrumental* are those powers, which acquired by these, or by fortune, are means and instruments to acquire more: as riches, reputation, friends, and the secret working of God, which men call good luck. For the nature of power, is in this point, like to fame, increasing as it proceeds; or like the motion of heavy bodies, which the further they go, make still the more haste.

3   The greatest of human powers, is that which is compounded of the powers of most men, united by consent, in one person, natural, or civil, that has the use of all their powers depending on his will; such as is the power of a commonwealth: or depending on the wills of each particular; such as is the power of a faction or of divers factions leagued. Therefore to have servants, is power; to have friends, is power: for they are strengths united.

4    Also riches joined with liberality, is power; because it procureth friends, and servants: without liberality, not so; because in this case they defend not; but expose men to envy, as a prey.

5    Reputation of power, is power; because it draweth with it the adherence of those that need protection.

6    So is reputation of love of a man's country, called popularity, for the same reason.

7    Also, what quality soever maketh a man beloved, or feared of many; or the reputation of such quality, is power; because it is a means to have the assistance and service of many.

8    Good success is power; because it maketh reputation of wisdom, or good fortune; which makes men either fear him, or rely on him.

9    Affability of men already in power, is increase of power; because it gaineth love.

10    Reputation of prudence in the conduct of peace or war, is power; because to prudent men, we commit the government of ourselves, more willingly than to others.

11    Nobility is power, not in all places, but only in those commonwealths, where it has privileges: for in such privileges, consisteth their power.

12    Eloquence is power, because it is seeming prudence.

13    Form is power; because being a promise of good, it recommendeth men to the favor of women and strangers.

14    The sciences, are small power; because not eminent; and therefore, not acknowledged in any man; nor are at all, but in a few, and in them, but of a few things. For science is of that nature, as none can understand it to be, but such as in a good measure have attained it.

15    Arts of public use, as fortification, making of engines, and other instruments of war; because they confer to defense, and victory, are power: and though the true mother of them, be science, namely the mathematics; yet, because they are brought into the light, by the hand of the artificer, they be esteemed, the midwife passing with the vulgar for the mother, as his issue.

## Worth

16    The *value,* or WORTH of a man, is as of all other things, his price; that is to say, so much as would be given for the use of his power: and therefore is not absolute; but a thing dependant on the need and judgment of another. An able conductor of soldiers, is of great price in time of war present, or imminent; but in peace not so. A learned and uncorrupt judge, is much worth in time of peace; but not so much in war. And as in other things, so in men, not the seller, but the buyer determines the price. For let a man, as most men do, rate themselves at the highest value they can; yet their true value is no more than it is esteemed by others.

17     The manifestation of the value we set on one another, is that which is commonly called honoring, and dishonoring. To value a man at a high rate, is to *honor* him; at a low rate, is to *dishonor* him. But high, and low, in this case, is to be understood by comparison to the rate that each man setteth on himself.

## Dignity

18     The public worth of a man, which is the value set on him by the commonwealth, is that which men commonly call DIGNITY, And this value of him by the commonwealth, is understood, by offices of command, judicature, public employment; or by names and titles, introduced for distinction of such value.

19     To pray to another, for aid of any kind, is *to* HONOR; because a sign we have an opinion he has power to help; and the more difficult the aid is, the more is the honor.

## To Honor and Dishonor

20     To obey, is to honor, because no man obeys them, whom they think have no power to help, or hurt them. And consequently to disobey, is to *dishonor*.

21     To give great gifts to a man, is to honor him; because it is buying of protection, and acknowledging of power. To give little gifts, is to dishonor; because it is but alms, and signifies an opinion of the need of small helps.

22     To be sedulous in promoting another's good; also to flatter, is to honor; as a sign we seek his protection or aid. To neglect, is to dishonor.

23     To give way, or place to another, in any commodity, is to honor; being a confession of greater power. To arrogate, is to dishonor.

24     To show any sign of love, or fear of another, is to honor; for both to love, and to fear, is to value. To contemn, or less to love or fear, than he expects, is to dishonor; for it is undervaluing.

25     To praise, magnify, or call happy, is to honor; because nothing but goodness, power, and felicity is valued. To revile, mock, or pity, is to dishonor.

26     To speak to another with consideration, to appear before him with decency, and humility, is to honor him; as signs of fear to offend. To speak to him rashly, to do any thing before him obscenely, slovenly, impudently, is to dishonor.

27     To believe, to trust, to rely on another, is to honor him; sign of opinion of his virtue and power. To distrust, or not believe, is to dishonor.

28    To hearken to a man's counsel, or discourse of what kind soever is to honor; as a sign we think him wise, or eloquent, or witty. To sleep, or go forth, or talk the while, is to dishonor.

29    To do those things to another, which he takes for signs of honor, or which the law or custom makes so, is to honor; because in approving the honor done by others, he acknowledgeth the power which others acknowledge. To refuse to do them, is to dishonor.

30    To agree with in opinion, is to honor; as being a sign of approving his judgment, and wisdom. To dissent, is dishonor, and an upbraiding of error; and, if the dissent be in many things, of folly.

31    To imitate, is to honor; for it is vehemently to approve. To imitate one's enemy, is to dishonor.

32    To honor those another honors, is to honor him; as a sign of approbation of his judgment. To honor his enemies, is to dishonor him.

33    To employ in counsel, or in actions of difficulty, is to honor; as a sign of opinion of his wisdom, or other power. To deny employment in the same cases, to those that seek it, is to dishonor.

## REVIEW

### Content

1. Do you agree with Hobbes in paragraph 16?
2. Are you inclined to challenge Hobbes at any point in his discourse on honoring and dishonoring, as these occur in relation to civil (political) leaders? Can you think of examples from recent American history of "honoring" overdone, so to speak, for some individual's self-serving purposes? How about "dishonoring" deliberately done in order to expose the ills of government?

### Rhetoric

3. Hobbes' English is that of the mid-1600s. What are some adjectives to describe the *tone* of the English Hobbes writes? Can you find both single words and phrasing that one no longer hears today? Words whose meanings have changed? What does this exercise tell you about language?
4. Hobbes says "Eloquence is power, because it is seeming prudence" (paragraph 12). What does he mean here? Can you apply his point to your own writing?

### Projects

5. Write a paragraph explaining one of the following paragraphs from Hobbes, to show that you understand what he is saying: 4, 8, 13, 14. (Be sure you are clear about how Hobbes is using the word "form" in 13.) Illustrate the point of the paragraph as vividly as possible;

that is, don't try to explain Hobbes' relatively abstract language merely by further abstraction.

6. Choose some other abstract principle and explain it by the method Hobbes uses for honoring and dishonoring: define various actions by how they do or do not fulfill the principle; set up each paragraph in parallel construction, as does Hobbes, in order to further heighten and clarify the contrast. Example: To . . . is to be *fair* (or *just*). To . . . is to be *unfair* (or *unjust*). Other possible principles: honesty vs. dishonesty; thrift vs. extravagance; sincerity vs. insincerity.

# All the King's Men

## ROBERT PENN WARREN

Robert Penn Warren (1905– ) is poet, novelist, teacher, critic, editor, and anthologist. Born in Kentucky, he attended Vanderbilt University in Tennessee and has made a considerable contribution to the rise of Southern writing in this country in the twentieth century. Warren's novel *All the King's Men* (1946), from which the following is taken, won for him the Pulitzer Prize. Governor Huey Long of Louisiana is generally thought to have been the prototype for Willie Stark, "the Boss" (the King, all of whose men are controlled by him). In the scene below, between the Boss and the State's Attorney-General, the two men are discussing Byram White, who had just swung a money-making deal. The deal had been exposed to "the McMurfee boys in the Legislature," by someone wanting a cut. The boss has just "arranged" White's resignation, in order to avert a challenge by the McMurfee boys.

1   . . . Sadie stuck her head in. "Mr. Miller would like to see you," she said to the Boss, and didn't give the impression of glad tidings.

2   "Send him in," the Boss ordered, and I could tell that, no matter what he had on his mind to say to me a second before, he had something else on it now. He had Hugh Miller, Harvard Law School, Lafayette Escadrille, Croix de Guerre, clean hands, pure heart, Attorney General, on his mind.

3   "He won't like it," I said.

4   "No," he said, "he won't."

5    And then in the doorway stood the tall, lean, somewhat stooped man, with swarthy face and unkempt dark hair and sad eyes under black brows, and with a Phi Beta Kappa key slung across his untidy blue serge. He stood there for a second, blinking the sad eyes, as though he had come out of darkness into a sudden light, or had stumbled into the wrong room. He looked like the wrong thing to be coming through that door, all right.

6    The Boss had stood up and padded across in his sock-feet, holding out his hand, saying, "Hello, Hugh."

7    Hugh Miller shook hands, and stepped into the room, and I started to edge out the door. Then I caught the Boss's eye, and he nodded, quick, toward my chair. So I shook hands with Hugh Miller, too, and sat back down.

8    "Have a seat," the Boss said to Hugh Miller.

9    "No, thanks, Willie," Hugh Miller replied in his slow solemn way. "But you sit down, Willie."

10   The Boss dropped back into his chair, cocked his feet up again, and demanded, "What's on your mind?"

11   "I reckon you know," Hugh Miller said.

12   "I reckon I do," the Boss said.

13   "You are saving White's hide, aren't you?"

14   "I don't give a damn about White's hide," the Boss said. "I'm saving something else."

15   "He's guilty."

16   "As hell," the Boss agreed cheerfully. "If the category of guilt and innocence can be said to have any relevance to something like Byram B. White."

17   "He's guilty," Hugh Miller said.

18   "My God, you talk like Byram was human! He's a thing! You don't prosecute an adding machine if a spring goes bust and makes a mistake. You fix it. Well, I fixed Byram. I fixed him so his unborn great-grandchildren will wet their pants on this anniversary and not know why. Boy, it will be the shock in the genes. Hell, Byram is just something you use, and he'll sure be useful from now on."

19   "That sounds fine, Willie, but it just boils down to the fact you're saving White's hide."

20   "White's hide be damned," the Boss said, "I'm saving something else. You let that gang of MacMurfee's boys in the Legislature get the notion they can pull something like this and there's no telling where they'd stop. Do you think they like anything that's been done? The extraction tax? Raising the royalty rate on state land? The income tax? The highway program? The Public Health Bill?"

21   "No, they don't," Hugh Miller admitted. "Or rather, the people behind MacMurfee don't like it."

22   "Do you like it?"

23    "Yes," Hugh Miller said, "I like *it*. But I can't say I like some of the stuff around it."

24    "Hugh," the Boss said, and grinned, "the trouble with you is you are a lawyer. You are a damned fine lawyer."

25    "You're a lawyer," Hugh Miller said.

26    "No," the Boss corrected, "I'm not a lawyer. I know some law. In fact, I know a lot of law. And I made me some money out of law. But I'm not a lawyer. That's why I can see what the law is like. It's like a single-bed blanket on a double bed and three folks in the bed and a cold night. There ain't ever enough blanket to cover the case, no matter how much pulling and hauling, and somebody is always going to nigh catch pneumonia. Hell, the law is like the pants you bought last year for a growing boy, but it is always this year and the seams are popped and the shankbone's to the breeze. The law is always too short and too tight for growing humankind. The best you can do is do something and then make up some law to fit and by the time that law gets on the books you would have done something different. Do you think half the things I've ever done were clear, distinct, and simple in the constitution of this state?"

27    "The Supreme Court has ruled—" Hugh Miller began.

28    "Yeah, and they ruled because I put 'em there to rule it, and they saw what had to be done. Half the things *weren't* in the constitution but they are now, by God. And how did they get there? Simply because somebody did 'em."

29    The blood began to climb up in Hugh Miller's face, and he shook his head just a little, just barely, the way a slow animal does when a fly skims by. Then he said, "There's nothing in the constitution says that Byram B. White can commit a felony with impunity."

30    "Hugh," the Boss began, soft, "don't you see that Byram doesn't mean a thing? Not in this situation. What they're after is to break the administration. They don't care about Byram, except so far as it's human nature to hate to think somebody else is getting something when you aren't. What they care about is undoing what this administration has done. And now is the time to stomp 'em. And when you start out to do something—" he sat up straight in the chair now, with his hands on the overstuffed sides, and thrust his head forward at Hugh Miller—"you got to use what you've got. You got to use fellows like Byram, and Tiny Duffy, and that scum down in the Legislature. You can't make bricks without straw, and most of the time all the straw you got is second-hand straw from the cowpen. And if you think you can make it any different, you're crazy as a hoot owl."

31    Hugh Miller straightened his shoulders a little. He did not look at the Boss but at the wall beyond the Boss. "I am offering my resignation as Attorney General," he said. "You will have it in writing, by messenger, in the morning."

32   "You took a long time to do it," the Boss said softly. "A long time. Hugh. What made you take such a long time?"

## REVIEW

### Content

1. Do you agree with how the Boss defines the law in the passage "It's like a . . . for growing humankind," paragraph 26? How do you respond to the rest of that paragraph through paragraph 29? Someone has called politics "the art of the possible." Apply that definition here. What is the "something else" that the Boss wants to save?
2. How did paragraphs 16, 18, and 30 affect you?

### Rhetoric

3. Warren makes his writing more vivid by the use of similes (describing by comparison) several times in the above passage. Point to some.
4. Does this scene from a novel seem *real* to you? If so, why? How does Warren get you inside the Boss' office and into the action?

### Projects

5. Write a paragraph describing the Boss, based on what you have observed of him from this passage. Make it as lifelike as possible.
6. Select some abstract concept and make it understandable in a paper by comparing it with elements of everyday common experience, as the Boss does with the law. Some possibilities: democracy, philanthropy, mercy, fidelity.

# On the Art
# of Stealing
# Human Rights

## JERRY GAMBILL (RARIHOKWATS)

Jerry Gambill, who is now known as Rarihokwats, is a Mohawk Indian scholar. When he made a satirical speech at a human rights conference at Tobique Reserve, in New Brunswick, Canada, in the summer of 1968, he listed the steps for usurping an Indian's human rights. The speech was later recorded, in 1969, in *Akwesasne Notes*, of which Gambill is editor.

From *The Way: An Anthology of American Indian Literature*, edited by Shirley Hill Witt and Stan Steiner, published by Alfred A. Knopf, Inc. Reprinted by permission of the author.

1   The art of denying Indians their human rights has been refined to a science. The following list of commonly used techniques will be helpful in "burglar-proofing" your reserves and *your rights.*

2   GAIN THE INDIANS' CO-OPERATION—It is much easier to steal someone's human rights if you can do it with his OWN co-operation.
SO. . . .

3   1. Make him a non-person. Human rights are for people. Convince Indians their ancestors were savages, that they were pagan, that Indians are drunkards. Make them wards of the government. Make a legal distinction, as in the Indian Act, between Indians and persons. Write history books that tell half the story.

4   2. Convince the Indian that he should be patient, that these things take time. Tell him that we are making progress, and that progress takes time.

5   3. Make him believe that things are being done for his own good. Tell him that you're sure that after he has experienced your laws and actions that he will realize how good they have been. Tell the Indian he has to take a little of the bad in order to enjoy the benefits you are conferring on him.

6   4. Get some Indian people to do the dirty work. There are always those who will act for you to the disadvantage of their own people. Just give them a little honor and praise. This is generally the function of band councils, chiefs, and advisory councils: They have little legal power, but can handle the tough decisions such as welfare, allocation of housing, etc.

7   5. Consult the Indian, but do not act on the basis of what you hear. Tell the Indian he has a voice and go through the motions of listening. Then interpret what you have heard to suit your own needs.

8   5. Insist that the Indian "GOES THROUGH THE PROPER CHANNELS." Make the channels and the procedures so difficult that he won't bother to do anything. When he discovers what the proper channels are and becomes proficient at the procedures. change them.

9   7. Make the Indian believe that you are working hard for him, putting in much overtime and at a great sacrifice, and imply that he should be appreciative. This is the ultimate in skills in stealing human rights. When you obtain the thanks of your victim.

10   8. Allow a few individuals to "MAKE THE GRADE" and then point to them as examples. Say that the "HARDWORKERS" and the "GOOD" Indians have made it, and that therefore it is a person's own fault if he doesn't succeed.

11   9. Appeal to the Indian's sense of fairness, and tell him that, even though things are pretty bad, it is not right for him to make strong protests. Keep the argument going on his form of protest and avoid talking about the real issue. Refuse to deal with him while he is protesting. Take all the fire out of his efforts.

12   10. Encourage the Indian to take his case to court. This is very expensive, takes lots of time and energy, and is very safe because the laws

are stacked against him. The court's ruling will defeat the Indian's cause, but makes him think he has obtained justice.

13    11. Make the Indian believe that things could be worse, and that, instead of complaining about the loss of human rights, to be grateful for the human rights we do have. In fact, convince him that to attempt to regain a right he has lost is likely to jeopardize the rights that he still has.

14    12. Set yourself up as the protector of the Indian's human rights, and then you can choose to act on only those violations you wish to act upon. By getting successful action on a few minor violations of human rights, you can point to these as examples of your devotion to his cause. The burglar who is also the doorman is the perfect combination.

15    13. Pretend that the reason for the loss of human rights is for some other reason than that the person is an Indian. Tell him some of your best friends are Indians, and that his loss of rights is because of his housekeeping, his drinking, his clothing. If he improves in these areas, it will be necessary for you to adopt another technique of stealing his rights.

16    14. Make the situation more complicated than is necessary. Tell the Indian you will have to take a survey to find out just how many other Indians are being discriminated against. Hire a group of professors to make a year-long research project.

17    15. Insist on unanimity. Let the Indian know that when all the Indians in Canada can make up their minds about just what they want as a group, then you will act. Play one group's special situation against another group's wishes.

18    16. Select very limited alternatives, neither of which has much merit, and then tell the Indian that he indeed has a choice. Ask, for instance, if he could or would rather have council elections in June or December, instead of asking if he wants them at all.

19    17. Convince the Indian that the leaders who are the most beneficial and powerful are dangerous and not to be trusted. Or simply lock them up on some charge like driving with no lights. Or refuse to listen to the real leaders and spend much time with the weak ones. Keep the people split from their leaders by sowing rumor. Attempt to get the best leaders into high-paying jobs where they have to keep quiet to keep their paycheck coming in.

20    18. Speak of the common good. Tell the Indian that you can't consider yourselves when there is the whole nation to think of. Tell him that he can't think only of himself. For instance, in regard to hunting rights, tell him we have to think of all the hunters, or the sporting-goods industry.

21    19. Remove rights so gradually that people don't realize what has happened until it is too late. Again, in regard to hunting rights, first

restrict the geographical area where hunting is permitted, then cut the season to certain times of the year, then cut the limits down gradually, then insist on licensing, and then Indians will be on the same grounds as white sportsmen.

22    20. Rely on reason and logic (your reason and logic) instead of rightness and morality. Give thousands of reasons for things, but do not get trapped into arguments about what is right.

23    21. Hold a conference on HUMAN RIGHTS, have everyone blow off steam and tension, and go home feeling that things are well in hand.

## REVIEW

### Content

1. Do you understand the rights-stealing psychology that is operating in each of the points Gambill makes? Do you find his analysis of each technique valid?
2. Explain how the various techniques Gambill cites could make an Indian feel like a "non-person." Can you empathize with the Indian here, from similar experiences that have made you feel like a non-person? What does non-personhood feel like?

### Rhetoric

3. Although he is discussing serious matters, Gambill speaks in a very direct style, with no flowery verbiage. Why?
4. Much of the satirical tone of Gambill's speech is achieved through the use of irony. What are some particularly effective ironical passages?

### Projects

5. Role-play something from Gambill's speech, to illustrate how one of the methods he talks about works. Take turns being the Indian(s) and then write up how you *felt* in the Indian role.
6. Do some reading about the Bureau of Indian Affairs, the federal agency in charge of Indian concerns, and about the agency's relationship with the Indians themselves. Report your findings in a brief documented paper.

# The Crime of Punishment

## KARL MENNINGER

Karl Menninger (1893–    ), psychiatrist, is associated with the Menninger Clinic and Foundation, a center for research and education in psychiatry, in Topeka, Kansas. Menninger has been a controversial—and humane—crusader for a wide range of causes, among them ecology, the humanistic practice of psychiatry, and an enlightened approach to dealing with the lawbreaker. His books include *Man Against Himself* (1938), *Love Against Hate* (1942), and *A Psychiatrist's World* (1959). In *The Crime of Punishment* (1966), widely used in courses in sociology, psychology, and criminology, Menninger reveals what he sees as the underlying need for vengeance by the punisher—the public. This, he says, is *"our* crime against criminals—and . . . against ourselves."

1   The great secret, the deeply buried mystery of the apparent public apathy to crime and to proposals for better controlling crime, lies in the persistent, intrusive wish for vengeance.

2   We are ashamed of it; we deny to ourselves and to others that we are influenced by it. Our morals, our religious teachings, even our laws repudiate it. But behind what we do to the offender is the desire for revenge on someone—and the unknown villain proved guilty of wrongdoing is a good scapegoat. We call it a wish to see justice done, i.e., to have him "punished." But in the last analysis this turns out to be a thin cloak for vengeful feelings directed against a legitimized object.

3   It is natural to resent a hurt, and all of us have many unfulfilled wishes to hurt back. But in our civilization that just is not done—openly. Personal revenge we have renounced, but official legalized revenge we can still enjoy. Once someone has been labeled an offender and proved guilty of an offense he is fair game, and our feelings come out in the form of a conviction that a hurt to society should be "repaid."

4   This sentiment of retaliation is, of course, exactly what impels most offenders to do what they do. Except for racketeers, robbers, and professional criminals, the men who are arrested, convicted, and sentenced are usually out to avenge a wrong, assuage a sense of injury, or correct an injustice as they see it. Their victims are individuals whom they be-

lieve to be assailants, false friends, rivals, unfaithful spouses, cruel parents—or symbolic figures representing these individuals. . . .

5   Today criminals rather than witches and peasants have become the official wrongdoers, eligible for punitive repayment. Prosecuting attorneys have become *our* agents, if not God's, and often seem to embody the very spirit of revenge and punition. They are expected to be tough, and to strike hard. . . .

## Imprisonment

6   The idea of punishment as the law interprets it seems to be that inasmuch as a man has offended society, society must officially offend him. It must deliver him a tit for the tat that he committed. This tit must not be impulsive retaliation; not mob action. It must be done dispassionately, by agency, by stipulation, and by statute. It must be something that will make the offender sorry (or sorrier) for what he did and resolve to do it no more.

7   Let no one deceive himself about the intention of the prison to be a terrible place. When the Maine State Prison was opened, its first warden proclaimed:

> Prisons should be so constructed that even their aspect might be terrific and appear like what they should be—dark and comfortless abodes of guilt and wretchedness. No more of degree of punishment . . . is in its nature so well adapted to purposes of preventing crime or reforming a criminal as close confinement in a solitary cell, in which, cut off from all hope of relief, the convict shall be furnished a hammock on which he may sleep, a block of wood on which he may sit, and with such coarse and wholesome food as may best be suited to a person in a situation designed for grief and penitence, and shall be favored with so much light from the firmament as may enable him to read the New Testament which will be given him as his sole companion and guide to a better life. There his vices and crimes shall become personified, and appear to his frightened imagination as co-tenants of his dark and dismal cell. They will surround him as so many hideous spectres and overwhelm him with horror and remorse.[1]

8   The Constitutional prohibition against "cruel and unusual" punishment implies that in some way or other the hurting done by the state must be a familiar garden variety and not something unexpected. For inexplicable reasons, to deprive a man of decent social relationships, palatable food, normal friendships and sexual relations, and constructive communication is not—in the eyes of the law—cruel and unusual. Im-

---

[1]Ulmer, Walter F.: "History of Maine Correctional Institutions." *Amer. J. Correction,* 27:33, July-August 1965.

prisonment, it will be recalled, was not originally considered punishment; it was only a method of detention prior to sentence, banishment, or execution. Hard labor extracted from the individual, presumably disagreeable, monotonous, menial, and often pointless, was the other type of punishment available.

9    And so, on the basis of this philosophy, the convicted prisoner, now officially a "criminal," is remanded to the local jail after sentence until the sheriff or his deputy can get around to making the trip to the state prison. . . . He is herded about by men half afraid and half contemptuous of him, toward whom all offenders early learn to present a steadfast attitude of hostility. An atmosphere of monotony, futility, hate, loneliness, and sexual frustration pervades the dank dungeons and cold hangars like a miasma, while time grinds out weary months and years. (Not every prison is like this, but too many are.)

10    When General Grant entered Richmond he found in operation a prison that had been opened in 1797; the prison is still in use (1967). According to former Federal Commissioner James V. Bennett, more than one hundred prisons still in operation were built before Grant took Richmond. . . .

## Our Crime Against Ourselves

11    The public has a fascination for violence, and clings tenaciously to its yen for vengeance, blind and deaf to the expense, futility, and dangerousness of the resulting penal system. But we are bound to hope that this will yield in time to the persistent, penetrating light of intelligence and accumulating scientific knowledge. The public will grow increasingly ashamed of its cry for retaliation, its persistent demand to punish. This is its crime, *our* crime against criminals—and incidentally our crime against ourselves. For before we can diminish our sufferings from the ill-controlled aggressive assaults of fellow citizens, we must renounce the philosophy of punishment, the obsolete, vengeful penal attitude. In its place we would seek a comprehensive, constructive social attitude—therapeutic in some instances, restraining in some instances, but preventive in its total social impact.

12    In the last analysis this becomes a question of personal morals and values. No matter how glorified or how piously disguised, vengeance as a human motive must be personally repudiated by each and every one of us. This is the message of old religions and new psychiatries. Unless this message is heard, unless we, the people—the man on the street, the housewife in the home—can give up our delicious satisfactions in opportunities for vengeful retaliation on scapegoats, we cannot expect to preserve our peace, our public safety, or our mental health.

# REVIEW

## Content

1. Had *you* ever thought before of America's system of punishment as vengeance? Does Menninger's explanation disturb you? Do you agree with it? If not, why not? Why does Menninger say, in paragraph 11, that the public's "persistent demand to punish" is "our crime against ourselves"? Explain his reference to mental health in paragraph 12.
2. What evidence of the realization of the hope Menninger expresses in paragraph 11 do you find today? What proposals can you recommend?

## Rhetoric

3. Menninger is writing about an issue of deep concern to him. How does he involve *you* in it? Are there specific word usages, ways of phrasing, descriptive elements, that are especially effective?
4. Note the language of the first warden of the Maine State Prison. From your familiarity with American literature and American historical documents, can you put a likely date on this passage, considering both its content and its style?

## Projects

5. Visit a jail or prison facility nearby and write a paper describing the experience and/or comparing the conditions of that facility with the description in paragraph 7. Include the date of construction in your description. If you are not allowed into the facility, find out *why* and write a paper about your attempt and the explanation for the refusal.
6. Capital punishment is the ultimate scapegoating technique of punishment. In June, 1972, the Supreme Court struck down certain state laws allowing capital punishment, but did not absolutely ban death sentences. By June, 1974, the death penalty had been reestablished, in some form, in more than half the states. Write a paper in which you review the arguments both for and against capital punishment and conclude with your own position on this question.

# We Need a
# New Kind of
# Patriotism

## RALPH NADER

Ralph Nader (1934–    ) is best known as America's "consumer advocate."
Trained in law, he and his "Nader's Raiders" have taken on a wide range
of vested interests on behalf of the consumer public—including General
Motors, coal mine owners, the medical profession, the Federal Trade Commission, and the Food and Drug Administration. Nader's book, *Unsafe at
Any Speed: The Designed-in Dangers of the American Automobile* (1965)
first brought him to wide public attention. Since then, he and his associates
have published a number of other books, including *You and Your Pension*
(1972), *Action for Change: A Student's Manual for Public Interest Organizing* (1972), and *Corporate Power in America* (1973). Nader has also published many articles, including the one below, written for *Life* (July 9, 1971).
In this piece, Nader denounces the "my country—right or wrong" brand
of "patriotism" and opts for a new patriotism characterized by greater concern for human welfare on the domestic front.

1    . . . It is time to talk of patriotism, not as an abstraction steeped in
nostalgia, but as behavior that can be judged by the standard of "liberty
and justice for all."

2    Patriotism can be a great asset for any organized society, but it can
also be a tool manipulated by unscrupulous or cowardly leaders and
elites. The development of a sense of patriotism was a strong unifying
force during our Revolution and its insecure aftermath. Defined then
and now as "love of country," patriotism was an extremely important
motivating force with which to confront foreign threats to the young
nation. It was no happenstance that *The Star Spangled Banner* was composed during the War of 1812 when the Redcoats were not only coming
but already here. For a weak frontier country beset by the competitions
and aggressions of European powers in the New World, the martial
virtues were those of sheer survival. America produced patriots who
never moved beyond the borders of their country. They were literally
defenders of their home.

3    As the United States moved into the 20th century and became a world
power, far-flung alliances and wars fought thousands of miles away

From *Life*, July 9, 1971. Reprinted by permission of the author.

stretched the boundaries of patriotism. "Making the world safe for democracy" was the grandiose way Woodrow Wilson put it. At other times and places (such as Latin America) it became distorted into "jingoism." World War II was the last war that all Americans fought with conviction. Thereafter, when "bombs bursting in air" would be atomic bombs, world war became a suicidal risk. Wars that could be so final and swift lost their glamour even for the most militaristically minded. When we became the most powerful nation on earth, the old insecurity that made patriotism into a conditioned reflex of "my country right or wrong" should have given way to a thinking process; as expressed by Carl Schurz: "Our country . . . when right, to be kept right. When wrong, to be put right." It was not until the Indochina war that we began the search for a new kind of patriotism.

4      If we are to find true and concrete meaning in patriotism, I suggest these starting points. First, in order that a free and just consensus be formed, patriotism must once again be rooted in the individual's own conscience and beliefs. Love is conceived by the giver (citizens) when merited by the receiver (the governmental authorities). If "consent of the governed" is to have any meaning, the abstract ideal of country has to be separated from those who direct it; otherwise the government cannot be evaluated by its citizens. The authorities in the State Department, the Pentagon, or the White House are not infallible; they have been and often are wrong, vain, misleading, shortsighted or authoritarian. When they are, leaders like these are shortchanging, not representing, America. To identify America with them is to abandon hope and settle for tragedy. Americans who consider themselves patriotic in the traditional sense do not usually hesitate to heap criticism in domestic matters over what they believe is oppressive or wasteful or unresponsive government handling of their rights and dignity. They should be just as vigilant in weighing similar government action which harnesses domestic resources for foreign involvements. Citizenship has an obligation to cleanse patriotism of the misdeeds done in its name abroad.

5      The flag, as the Pledge of Allegiance makes clear, takes its meaning from that "for which it stands"; it should not and cannot stand for shame, injustice and tyranny. It must not be used as a bandanna or a fig leaf by those unworthy of this country's leadership.

6      Second, patriotism begins at home. Love of country in fact is inseparable from citizen action to make the country more lovable. This means working to end poverty, discrimination, corruption, greed and other conditions that weaken the promise and potential of America.

7      Third, if it is unpatriotic to tear down the flag (which is a symbol of the country), why isn't it more unpatriotic to desecrate the country itself—to pollute, despoil and ravage the air, land and water? Such environmental degradation makes the "pursuit of happiness" ragged indeed. Why isn't it unpatriotic to engage in the colossal waste that characterizes

so many defense contracts? Why isn't it unpatriotic to draw our country into a mistaken war and then keep extending the involvement, with untold casualties to soldiers and innocents, while not telling Americans the truth? Why isn't the deplorable treatment of returning veterans by government and industry evaluated by the same standards as is their dispatch to war? Why isn't the systematic contravention of the U.S. Constitution and the Declaration of Independence in our treatment of minority groups, the poor, the young, the old and other disadvantaged or helpless people crassly unpatriotic? Isn't all such behavior contradicting the innate worth and the dignity of the individual in America? Is it not time to end the tragic twisting of patriotism whereby those who work to expose and correct deep injustices, and who take intolerable risks while doing it, are accused of running down America by the very forces doing just that? Our country and its ideals are something for us to uphold as individuals and together, not something to drape, as a deceptive cloak, around activities that mar or destroy these ideals.

8    Fourth, there is no reason why patriotism has to be so heavily associated, in the minds of the young as well as adults, with military exploits, jets and missiles. Citizenship must include the duty to advance our ideals actively into practice for a better community, country and world, if peace is to prevail over war. And this obligation stems not just from a secular concern for humanity but from a belief in the brotherhood of man—"I am my brother's keeper"—that is common to all major religions. It is the classic confrontation—barbarism *vs.* the holy ones. If patriotism has no room for deliberation, for acknowledging an individual's sense of justice and his religious principles, it will continue to close minds, stifle the dissent that has made us strong, and deter the participation of Americans who challenge in order to correct, and who question in order to answer. We need only to recall recent history in other countries where patriotism was converted into an epidemic of collective madness and destruction. A patriotism manipulated by the government asks only for a servile nod from its subjects. A new patriotism requires a thinking assent from its citizens. If patriotism is to have any "manifest destiny," it is in building a world where all mankind is our bond in peace.

## REVIEW

### Content

1. How did *you* define "patriotism" before reading this essay? How do you react to Nader's definition of it? Do you view the practices he cites in paragraph 7 as "unpatriotic"?
2. Cite specific examples in American life where the standard of "liberty and justice for all" Nader holds up as the criterion for patriotic behavior is not being fulfilled. What "patriotic" measures would you recommend, in each instance?

## Rhetoric

3. Nader devotes two long paragraphs of a nine-paragraph essay entitled "We Need a New Kind of Patriotism" to tracing the concept of "patriotism" through American history. Why?
4. What is the effect of Nader's use of quotations from *The Star Spangled Banner*, the Declaration of Independence, the Pledge of Allegiance, and the Bible?

## Projects

5. Select some other political concept and define it in reverse by a series of questions, as Nader defines lack of patriotism in paragraph 7. Examples: Why isn't it undemocratic to . . . ? Why isn't it against civil (or human) rights to . . . ?
6. Nader's Raiders are engaged in efforts to expose and right a number of America's ills. Read about one of their crusades and report about it in a paper.

# Privacy

## ALAN F. WESTIN

Alan Westin (1929–   ) has served on the board of the American Civil Liberties Union, while pursuing his career as professor of public law and government at Columbia University. His publications include books about the Supreme Court and on constitutional law, and he has been heard as "expert witness" for constitutional rights during Senate hearings on wiretapping. Westin's essay below considers the paradoxical question of the most appropriate balance between the individual citizen's right to privacy and a government's legitimate need for certain information in order to function in an ever more complex society.

1   Are Americans worried today about invasion of their privacy? If so, just what intrusions do they fear, by whom, and are these worries real or imaginary? In August 1970, Louis Harris and Associates, Inc., a leading public opinion survey organization, published the results of a national poll of American attitudes toward invasion of privacy. The survey asked each respondent whether he felt that people are trying to find out things about him that "are not any of their business." Sixty-two percent of those queried said they did not feel that their privacy was

From the 1971 *Year Book*, Macmillan Educational Corporation. Reprinted by permission of the author.

being invaded in this way, 34 percent said that they felt it was, and 4 percent said they were "not sure."

2    One can interpret these findings in two opposite ways. On the one hand, almost two-thirds of those polled reported that they did not feel that they were being subjected to intrusive and prying practices. On the other hand, one in every three persons felt that his privacy was being invaded, and that represents a lot of people in the United States.

## Offensive Intrusions

3    What kinds of intrusions are one in three Americans worried about? When the Harris poll asked respondents to check off specific violations of privacy that concerned them, part of the list reflected issues of neighborhood and personal life, such as "people looking in your windows"; "people overhearing your conversations with other people"; "neighbors who gossip about your family"; "hotel and motel phone operators"; and even "public opinion poll-takers."

4    But the main fears—those which 10 to 19 percent of the respondents identified as their particular worries—were intrusions with a more political and institutional basis, issues that have been primary topics of public debate during the past decade. Specifically, one in every five respondents listed "computers which collect a lot of information about you" and "business which sells you things on credit" as intrusive practices. Other "violations" respondents checked off were "the government when it collects tax returns"; "people listening in to your telephone conversations"; "the government when it takes a census"; and, finally, "employment interviewing."

5    The Harris poll tends to confirm what much other evidence also suggests: concern over intrusive practices by government agencies and private organizations represents a growing issue in contemporary American political and cultural life. This concern has been heightened by the development of advanced surveillance technology, from microminiaturized listening and watching devices and new eye-blink emotion-reading sensors to giant computerized data banks. For many Americans, George Orwell's *1984* seems to be rushing in ahead of schedule with its portrait of the ultimate loss of privacy.

## Levels of Privacy

6    To sort out facts from nightmare fiction in this area, some basic definitions, concepts, history, and social analysis must be sketched in as background. First, the norms of privacy in any society will be set at three basic levels—political, sociocultural, and personal.

7    At the political level, every society sets a distinctive balance between the private sphere and the public order, based on the political philosophy of the state. In authoritarian societies, where public life is celebrated as the highest good and the fulfillment of man's purpose on earth, the concept of legally or socially protected privacy for the individual, family, social group, and private association is rejected as hedonistic and immoral. It is also politically dangerous to the regime. Such governments keep extensive records on people to watch for "deviationist" behavior and use a wide range of physical surveillance techniques to watch and listen secretly to elite groups. In contrast, constitutional democracies, with a strong commitment to individualism and freedom of association, regard the private sector as a major force for social progress and morality. The public order, government, is seen as a useful and necessary mechanism for providing services and protection, but one that is expressly barred by bills of rights and other guarantees of civil liberty from interfering with the citizen's private beliefs, associations, and acts, except in extraordinary situations and then only through tightly controlled procedures.

8    This political balance is the framework for a second level of privacy—the sociocultural level. Environmental factors, such as crowded cities, and class factors of wealth and race shape the real opportunities people have to claim freedom from the observation of others. In this sense, privacy is frequently determined by the individual's power and status. The rich can withdraw from society when they wish; the lower classes cannot.

9    Finally, within the political and sociocultural limits just described there are levels of privacy set by each individual as he seeks an "intrapsychic balance" between his needs for privacy and his needs for disclosure and communication. This balance is generally a function of one's family life, education, and psychological makeup and reflects each individual's particular needs and desires.

## Degrees of Personal Privacy

10    The extent of personal privacy varies, but there are four degrees that can be identified. Sometimes the individual wants to be completely out of the sight and hearing of anyone else, in solitude; alone, he is in the most relaxed state of privacy. In a second situation the individual seeks the intimacy of his confidants—his family, friends, or trusted associates with whom he chooses to share his ideas and emotions. But there are still some things that he does not want to disclose, whether he is with intimates or in public. Either by personal explanation or by social convention, the individual may indicate that he does not wish certain aspects of himself discussed or noticed, at least at that particular mo-

ment. When his claim is respected by those around him, he achieves a third degree of privacy, the state of reserve. Finally, an individual sometimes goes out in public to seek privacy, for by joining groups of people who do not recognize him, he achieves anonymity, being seen but not known. Such relaxation on the street, in bars or movies or in the park constitutes still another dimension of the individual's quest for privacy.

11    In all these states of privacy the individual's needs usually change from time to time. At one moment, he may desperately want to be alone. At another, aloneness can be so frightening that he desperately seeks the companionship either of an intimate friend or of a complete stranger, a one-time acquaintance who will listen to his problems but who will not be encountered again.

12    The fundamental element of choice involved in personal privacy is embodied in every definition of privacy used today in law, social science, or common understanding. With some variation in terminology, these definitions all agree that privacy is the claim of an individual to determine for himself whether and how he will communicate with others—what he will reveal, when, and to whom.

13    The importance of the right to choose, both to the individual's self-development and to the exercise of responsible citizenship, makes the claim to privacy a fundamental part of civil liberty in a constitutional society. Without the power to decide when to remain private, we cannot exercise many other basic freedoms. If we are switched "on" without our knowledge or consent, we have lost our constitutional rights to decide when and with whom we speak, publish, worship, and associate. We have been made glass men.

## Necessary Surveillance

14    So far, we have stressed the importance of privacy to the individual in a democracy. But every society must also provide for the disclosure of information necessary to the rational conduct of public affairs and must engage in some surveillance of individual and group activity in order to control illegal or antisocial acts. From the earliest periods of Western society, these disclosure-surveillance functions have been vested in five authorities: the employer-landlord, the church, the heads of other associations to which the individual belongs, local governmental officials, and the national regime. In every historical era, as conflicts for primacy raged between church and state, town and guild, or king and baron, the individual's immunity from unwanted surveillance or disclosure has been a part of these basic power struggles.

15    In fact, looking back over 2,000 years of Western political history, we can identify two basic patterns of privacy and disclosure-surveillance.

In the authoritarian tradition—exemplified by Sparta, the Roman Empire, early France, and modern totalitarian regimes—unlimited or very extensive powers to compel disclosure and carry on surveillance have been an essential part of the system. In the libertarian tradition—typified by Periclean Athens, the Roman Republic, the English constitutional state, the American republic, and modern democratic nations—basic limits have been placed on the powers of the authorities to put individuals or groups under surveillance or to compel their disclosure of information considered private or privileged. While the issue of privacy is complicated historically—it has often been enmeshed in rival claims to power by the contesting authorities—it is fair to say that no political system with a reputation for liberty in its time failed to provide important legal and social limits on surveillance by authorities.

16     This is the broad background for the issue of privacy in the 1970s. Until the post–World War II era, American law and social norms provided an effective libertarian balance of privacy. Because the presence of walls and doors provided people with a shelter within which to speak and act in private, American society forbade physical entry into the "constitutional castle" by uninvited private persons or by government officials unless the latter met the requirements of probable cause and specificity in warrants provided for in state and federal constitutions. Because torture and compulsory test oaths were the only ways to penetrate the thoughts and mind of an individual, such practices were forbidden. And because daily life in a mobile, frontier society was beyond the monitoring capacity of record-keepers, the federal government concentrated on forbidding or minimizing the practice of spying, the maintenance of dossiers by police, and the use of internal passport systems that marked the autocratic regimes of royal Europe, to all of which the American republic was fundamentally opposed.

## Shift in Balance of Privacy

17     In the past two decades, however, a combination of new technology and sociopolitical changes has overturned the classic balance of privacy in the United States. On the technological front, microminiaturized bugs, television monitors, and devices capable of penetrating solid surfaces to listen or photograph have dissolved the physical barriers of walls and doors. Polygraph devices to measure emotional states have been improved as a result of space research, and increased use has been made of personality tests for personnel selection. The development of electronic computers and long-distance communication networks has made it possible to collect, store, and process far more information about an individual's life and transactions than was practical in the era of typewriter and file cabinet.

18      These dramatic advances in technology—revolutionizing the means of conducting physical, psychological, and data surveillance over the citizenry—were accompanied by equally critical changes in American society. As the industrial economy became more complex and interconnected; as government took on giant programs in social welfare; as the social sciences moved toward behavioral, data-dependent theories of social explanation; and as both criminal and revolutionary groups made use of modern technology, a whole new framework for data collection and use by authorities had to be defined, and a new balance of privacy had to be worked into American law and social practice.

19      Just how this new balance should be set for the 1970's is the heart of the privacy issue today. Whether the specific concern is government power to eavesdrop on conversations, compulsory questions on the decennial census, or computerized data banks, what is really at issue is how to have both effective government and organizational life *and* protected zones of individual and group privacy. If the United States must choose between these equally compelling aspects of civilized social life, the nation will have failed in the art of democracy.

## Three Approaches

20      With this perspective, we can identify three important suggestions that have been made for setting a new balance of privacy in the electronic age. The first suggestion, a total ban approach, calls for the use of legislation, judicial decisions, and organizational rules to forbid the use of new technological measures which intrude too deeply into personal privacy. A second approach, administrative discretion, favors letting the authorities use new methods under their own regulations and safeguards until a clear case is made that the intervention of law is needed to set standards and control abuses. The third approach calls for a variety of policy responses—bans, regulations, and nonintervention—according to the particular state of the technological art, the need for information collection, the impact on the individuals concerned, and the effect on society as a whole.

21      In my view, neither a total ban or administrative discretion is the answer, since each misunderstands both the nature of sociotechnological development and the essence of constitutional government. Let me illustrate with some current controversies. Why shouldn't we simply outlaw intrusive public opinion polling, electronic eavesdropping, and computerized data banks? The answer lies in a careful assessment of what is really at stake in each situation.

22      As long as the individual is free to refuse to answer private and government opinion surveys, to close the door with a firm "I do not want to reply," it is the height of legalized puritanism to forbid Americans

to speak out voluntarily and make their individual wishes, needs, and fears known to leaders of government and private institutions. Indeed, some critical changes in mores and laws have come about as a result of facts learned by such opinion surveys as the Kinsey reports, in which people willingly revealed their intimate sexual behavior. Because what is told to a legitimate opinion surveyor is kept confidential—identities are not revealed and the respondent's disclosure does not result in his being regulated—total bans on such polling are unwarranted and dangerous. On the other hand, some regulation may well be needed to forbid salesmen from posing as pollsters to push their wares, voluntary government questionnaires from being presented as though responses were legally required, or governmental agencies from violating the confidential nature of survey research data for investigative or regulatory purposes or from selling lists or information to private business firms.

23    The issue of electronic eavesdropping is harder to resolve, since the specter of federal or local law enforcement agents overhearing conversations and building transcript files is not one to reassure citizens of a democratic nation. But the bedrock facts brought out by many legislative hearings and legal studies reveal that there are criminal and revolutionary conspiracies which do engage in violence, theft, and murder and that these groups are shrewd enough so that traditional methods of investigation are inadequate. In an era of rapid communication and mobility, no government in the world refrains from all use of electronic eavesdropping. And if any nation were to enact a total ban, it is almost certain that police working on kidnapping, bombing, and similar cases would use such techniques covertly and that the public would approve.

## Administrative Discretion

24    But if total bans are unrealistic, so are counsels for administrative discretion. Law enforcement agencies cannot be left to decide within executive department ranks when to eavesdrop, for how long, and what uses to make of the material they obtain. For this, a constitutional system requires legislative definition of a highly limited set of crimes for which this intrusive technique is to be permitted, judicial procedures to assess the need for eavesdropping in each case, and extensive controls over the process and products of eavesdropping. While this was the basic policy adopted by the federal Omnibus Crime Control and Safe Streets Act of 1968 and by many state legislatures under the guidelines of that act, there are still serious issues arising from that legislation. Broad powers are given the attorney general to eavesdrop without court authorization on organizations that he decides pose a threat to internal security. It was under this provision that wiretaps and bugs were used to get information on new left groups involved in the 1968 demonstrations

in Chicago and on such organizations as the Black Panthers. Similarly, under the 1968 federal law, state police powers were broadened to allow electronic eavesdropping in any crime punishable under state law by more than a year's imprisonment; in some states this would allow eavesdropping for such offenses as defacing a cemetery. Either judicial interpretation or legislative amendment of such provisions seems necessary to prevent abuse.

25    A final example involves computerized data banks, one of the two issues with which the Harris poll found one-third of the population to be most concerned. At every level of government today—in city, county, state, and federal agencies—written records are gradually being converted into computer-stored material. The same is true in business, universities, hospitals, churches, and voluntary associations. As such organizations consolidate their records about each client, patient, parishioner, customer, or member and as it becomes possible to exchange data files among organizations by machine-to-machine communication, the possibility of a complete record on every citizen arises. His educational, medical, military, employment, governmental, and civic activities could be so assembled and circulated that he would confront an "official" portrait of himself everywhere he turned, at each critical stage of his life. Not only would this close off escapes from past mistakes or failures and give unprecedented powers to the authorities who compiled and used such dossiers, but it also would raise fundamental issues as to what information should be collected at all, how errors could be caught and subjective evaluations challenged, and how such files could be prevented from suffocating free expression and political dissent.

26    Confronted with these technological possibilities for the future, some critics have called for a total ban, urging that the creation of all such data banks be outlawed. Others say that no public intervention is needed at this time; aware that any total consolidation of information within agencies is unrealistic today and aware that the assembling of life dossiers using data from many organizations is even more remote, they believe that existing regulations about the confidential nature of information are enough to protect rights to privacy or to individual review of file contents.

## Varied Policy Responses

27    Again, I believe it is the variety of responses that are most effective in dealing with the real social dilemmas. We need extensive information to manage a rational and humane society—to make judgments about individuals, programs, and policies. The computer cannot be stuffed back in the bottle of undiscovered technology, nor should we have to

do so to preserve civil liberties. What is needed is a ban by law on any computerized data banks that are so dangerous per se that they should not be allowed (such as a proposal that the California national guard compile a data bank on political protesters). Among other possible responses, we might convene hearings before legislatures and regulatory commissions so that government agencies and interstate organizations may present their plans for computerized systems and demonstrate necessary safeguards before they are allowed to computerize sensitive files containing personal information. Within the computerized systems, we can reexamine existing rules, such as those which pertain to the confidential nature of data, and then formulate rules that are fully responsible to norms of privacy and due process.

28      As these examples of policy choices suggest, what confronts us is the age-old problem of how man uses the tools that nature or science make available to him. If we mean to preserve and update the right of privacy in the electronic age, there are ways to do so intelligently.

29      What may well be the underlying question for the 1970's is whether American society as a whole is able to provide the racial and economic justice and able to provide the paths to world peace which will allow the nation to become unified again, pursuing the goals of a humane democracy. If we move along those paths, we can work out the problems of balancing privacy, disclosure, and surveillance. If we do not, if the internal struggles of American society deepen, then those who oppose the structure of the society will challenge any measures that would make elected government or private institutions more effective; the claim to privacy will then become open defiance and a withdrawal from organized society. At the same time, authorities facing such challenges are likely to seek greater surveillance powers to cope with the sharpening conflict. What this tells us is that privacy is not an end in itself, for either the individual or society. It is a means for helping to achieve a healthy personality in a healthy social system. As in the time of Athens, Rome, and the early European nation-states, the enjoyment of privacy will, in the United States, depend for its vitality on the state of the nation.


# REVIEW

## Content

1. Based on Westin's summary definition of privacy in the second half of paragraph 12, do you feel that your privacy is being unduly invaded? If so, in what specific ways?
2. Discuss recommendations for establishing an appropriate balance of privacy between the public and private sectors of our society. Expand your thinking beyond Westin's proposals.

**Rhetoric**

3. In paragraphs 6 through 13, Westin carefully defines privacy in terms of the individual. Trace how he develops this discussion and how he moves from one paragraph into the next.
4. Westin supports his statements, arguments, and proposals with substantial detail. Analyze how this practice helps to command respect for what he has to say.

**Projects**

5. Represent the government or some other public entity (a business, the police, a bank) and ask someone else to be a private citizen. Role-play a discussion about a specific proposal for surveillance which the former sees as essential and to which the latter violently objects as unnecessary invasion of privacy.
6. The surveillance devices Westin mentions—and others—are in rather widespread use for various purposes. Select one of them and write a paper about a use of it that you consider an abuse, either an actual account or one you fantasize.

# The Day the Computers Got Waldon Ashenfelter

## BOB ELLIOTT and RAY GOULDING

Bob Elliott and Ray Goulding are better known as Bob and Ray, a radio and television comedy team. Their skits satirize a wide range of persons and institutions in this country. In the script below, Bob and Ray take off, in devastating fashion, on a projected night in the Basement General Headquarters of the Central Data Bank—a government "servant" which eventually victimizes its own "masters."

1    A presidental commission has recommended approval of plans for establishing a computerized data center where all personal information on individual Americans compiled by some twenty scattered agencies would

be assembled in one place and made available to the federal government as a whole.

2      Backers of the proposal contend that it would lead to greater efficiency, and insist that the cradle-to-grave dossiers on the nation's citizens would be used only in a generalized way to help deal with broad issues. Opponents argue that the ready availability of so much confidential data at the push of a computer button could pose a dangerous threat to the privacy of the individual by enabling the federal bureaucracy to become a monstrous, snooping Big Brother.

3      Obviously, the plan elicits reactions that are emotional, and cooler heads are needed to envision the aura of quiet, uneventful routine certain to pervade the Central Data Bank once it becomes accepted as just another minor government agency.

4      Fade in:

5      *Interior–Basement GHQ of the Central Data Bank–Night. (At stage right, 950 sophisticated third-generation computers may be seen stretching off into the distance. At stage left, the CDB graveyard-shift chargé d'affaires, Nimrod Gippard, is seated behind a desk. He is thirty-five-ish and attired in socks that don't match. At the open, Gippard is efficiently stuffing mimeographed extortion letters to Omaha's 3277 suspected sex deviates into envelopes. He glances up as Waldon Ashenfelter, an indoorsy type of questionable ancestry, enters.)*

6      GIPPARD   Yes, sir?

7      ASHENFELTER   *(flashing ID card)* Ashenfelter. Bureau of Indian Affairs. Like to have you run a check on a key figure named Y. Claude Garfunkel.

8      GIPPARD   *(reaching for pad and pencil)* Sure thing. What's his Social Security number?

9      ASHENFELTER   I dunno.

10     GIPPARD   Hmmm. How about his zip code? Or maybe a cross-reference to some banks where he may have been turned down for a loan. Just any clue at all to his identity.

11     ASHENFELTER   Well, as I say, his name is Y. Claude Garfunkel.

12     GIPPARD   *(after a weary sigh)*   It's not much to go on, but I'll see what I can do.

13     *(Gippard rises and crosses to the master data-recall panel. Ashenfelter strolls to a nearby computer and casually begins checking the confidential reports on his four small children to learn how many are known extremists.)*

14     ASHENFELTER   You're new here, aren't you?

15     GIPPARD   No. Just my first week on the night shift. Everybody got moved around after we lost McElhenny.

16     ASHENFELTER   Wasn't he that heavy-set fellow with beady eyes who drove the Hudson?

17     GIPPARD   Yeah. Terrible thing. Pulled his own dossier one night when things were quiet and found out he was a swish. Kind of made him go all to pieces.

18      ASHENFELTER   That's a shame. And now I suppose he's gone into analysis and gotten himself cross-filed as a loony.

19      GIPPARD   No. He blew his brains out right away. But having a suicide on your record can make things tough, too.

20      ASHENFELTER   Yeah. Shows a strong trend toward instability.

21      *(The computer informs Ashenfelter that his oldest boy was detained by police in 1963 for roller-skating on municipal property, and that the five-year-old probably founded the Farmer-Labor Party in Minnesota.)*

22      ASHENFELTER *(cont.) (mutters in despair)*   Where did I fail them as a father?

23      GIPPARD   Didn't you tell me you're with Indian Affairs?

24      ASHENFELTER   Yeah. Why?

25      GIPPARD   I think I'm onto something hot. Is that like India Indians or whoop-it-up Indians?

27      GIPPARD   Well, either way, no Indian named Garfunkel has ever complied with the Alien Registration Law.

28      ASHENFELTER   I never said he was an Indian. He's Jewish, and I think he's playing around with my wife.

29      GIPPARD   Gee, that's too bad.

30      ASHENFELTER *(dramatically)*   Oh, I blame myself really. I guess I'd started taking LaVerne for granted and—

31      GIPPARD   No. I mean it's too bad he's only Jewish. The computers aren't programmed to feed back home-wreckers by religious affiliation.

32      ASHENFELTER   Oh.

33      GIPPARD   Can you think of anything kinky that's traditional with Jews? You know. Like draft dodging . . . smoking pot . . . something a computer could really hang its hat on.

34      ASHENFELTER   No. They just seem to feed each other a lot of chicken soup. And they do something around Christmastime with candles. But I'm not sure any of it's illegal.

35      GIPPARD   We'll soon see. If the curve on known poultry processors correlates geographically with a year-end upswing in tallow rendering— Well, you can appreciate what that kind of data would mean to the bird dogs at the ICC and the FDA. They'd be able to pinpoint exactly where it was all happening and when.

36      ASHENFELTER   Uh-huh—Where and when what?

37      GIPPARD   That's exactly what I intend to find out.

38      *(Gippard turns back to the panel and resumes work with a sense of destiny. Ashenfelter, whistling softly to himself, absently begins plunking the basic melody of "Mexicali Rose" on the keyboard of a nearby computer. The machine responds by furnishing him with Howard Hughes's 1965 income tax return and the unlisted phone numbers of eight members of a New Orleans wife-swapping club who may have known Lee Harvey Oswald. As Ashenfelter pockets the information, Major General Courtney ("Old Napalm and Guts") Nimshaw enters. He has a riding crop but no mustache.)*

39      NIMSHAW   Yoohoo! Anybody home?

40    GIPPARD  Back here at the main console.

41    (*Nimshaw moves to join Gippard, then sees Ashenfelter for the first time and freezes. The two stand eyeing each other suspiciously as Gippard re-enters the scene.*)

42    GIPPARD  Oh, forgive me. General Nimshaw, I'd like for you to meet Ashenfelter from Indian Affairs.

43    (*Nimshaw and Ashenfelter ad-lib warm greetings as they shake hands. Then each rushes off to pull the dossier of the other. Ashenfelter learns that Nimshaw was a notorious bed wetter during his days at West Point and that his heavy drinking later caused an entire airborne division to be parachuted into Ireland on D-Day. Nimshaw learns that Ashenfelter owns 200 shares of stock in a Canadian steel mill that trades with Communist China and that he has been considered a bad credit risk since 1949, when he refused to pay a Cincinnati dance studio for $5500 worth of tango lessons. Apparently satisfied, both men return to join Gippard, who has been checking out a possible similarity in the patterns of poultry-buying by key Jewish housewives and reported sighting of Soviet fishing trawlers off the Alaskan coast.*)

44    ASHENFELTER  Working late tonight, eh, General?

45    NIMSHAW  (*nervously*)  Well, I just stumbled across a little military hardware transport thing. We seem to have mislaid an eighty-six-car trainload of munitions between here and the West Coast. Can't very well write it off as normal pilferage. So I thought maybe Gippard could run a check for me on the engineer and brakeman. You know. Where they hang out in their spare time. Whether they might take a freight train with them. What do you think, Gipp?

46    GIPPARD  Sure. Just have a few more things to run through for Ashenfelter first. He's seeking a final solution to the Jewish problem.

47    ASHENFELTER  (*blanching*)   Well, not exactly the whole—

48    NIMSHAW  Oh, has all that come up again?

49    (*Two janitors carrying lunch pails enter and cross directly to the computer programmed for medical case histories of nymphomaniacs. They pull several dossiers at random and then cross directly to a far corner, unwrapping bacon, lettuce, and tomato sandwiches as they go. They spread a picnic cloth on the floor and begin reading the dossiers as they eat. They emit occasional guffaws, but the others pay no attention to them.*)

50    GIPPARD  (*as he compares graph curves*)  No doubt about it. Whatever those Russian trawlers are up to, it's good for the delicatessen business. This could be the break we've been hoping for.

51    NIMSHAW  Hating Jews been a big thing with you for quite a while, Ashenfelter?

52    ASHENFELTER  (*coldly*)  About as long as you've been losing government property by the trainload, I imagine.

53    (*Nimshaw and Ashenfelter eye each other uneasily for a moment. Then they quickly exchange hush money in the form of drafts drawn against secret Swiss bank accounts as Gippard's assistant, Llewelyn Fordyce, enters. Fordyce is a typical brilliant young career civil servant who has been lost for several hours*)

*trying to find his way back from the men's room. He appears haggard, but is in satisfactory condition otherwise.)*

54    FORDYCE   Are you gentlemen being taken care of?

55    *(Ashenfelter and Nimshaw nod affirmatively. Fordyce hurriedly roots through the desk drawers, pausing only to take a quick, compulsive inventory of paper clips and map pins as he does so.)*

56    FORDYCE *(cont.) (shouts)*   Hey, Gipp! I can't find the registry cards for these two idiots out here.

57    GIPPARD *(faintly, from a distance)*   I've been too busy to sign 'em in yet. Take care of it, will you?

58    *(Fordyce gives a curt, efficient nod, inefficiently failing to realize that Gippard is too far away to see him nodding. Fordyce then brings forth two large pink cards and hands them to Nimshaw and Ashenfelter.)*

59    FORDYCE   If you'd just fill these out please. We're trying to accumulate data on everybody who uses the data bank so we can eventually tie it all in with something or other.

60    *(Nimshaw studies the section of his card dealing with maximum fines and imprisonment for giving false information, while Ashenfelter skips over the hard part and goes directly to the multiple-choice questions.)*

61    FORDYCE *(cont.)*   And try to be as specific as you can about religious beliefs and your affiliation with subversive groups. We're beginning to think there's more to this business of Quakers denying they belong to the Minutemen than meets the eye.

62    *(Nimshaw and Ashenfelter squirm uneasily as they sense the implication. Ashenfelter hurriedly changes his answer regarding prayer in public schools from "undecided" to "not necessarily" as Nimshaw perjures himself by listing the principal activity at the Forest Hills Tennis Club as tennis. Meantime, Gippard has rejoined the group, carrying four rolls of computer tape carefully stacked in no particular sequence.)*

63    GIPPARD   I know I'm onto something here, Fordyce, but I'm not sure what to make of it. Surveillance reports on kosher poultry dealers indicate that most of them don't even show up for work on Saturday. And that timing correlates with an unexplained increase in activity at golf courses near key military installations. But the big thing is that drunken drivers tend to get nabbed most often on Saturday night, and that's exactly when organized groups are endangering national security by deliberately staying up late with their lights turned on to overload public power plants.

64    FORDYCE *(whistles softly in amazement)*   We're really going to catch a covey of them in this net. How'd you happen to stumble across it all?

65    GIPPARD   Well, it seemed pretty innocent at first. This clown from Indian Affairs just asked me to dig up what I could so he'd have some excuse for exterminating the Jews.

66    *(Ashenfelter emits a burbling throat noise as an apparent prelude to something more coherent, but he is quickly shushed.)*

67    GIPPARD *(cont.)*   But you know how one correlation always leads to

another. Now we've got a grizzly by the tail, Fordyce, and I can see "organized conspiracy" written all over it.

68     FORDYCE   Beyond question. And somewhere among those 192 million dossiers is the ID number of the Mister Big we're after. Do the machines compute a cause-and-effect relationship that might help narrow things down?

69     GIPPARD   Well, frankly, the computers have gotten into a pretty nasty argument among themselves over that. Most of them see how golf could lead to drunken driving. But the one that's programmed to chart moral decay and leisure time fun is pretty sure that drunken driving causes golf.

70     *(Nimshaw glances up from the job of filling out his registry card.)*

71     NIMSHAW   That's the most ridiculous thing I ever heard in my life.

72     FORDYCE  *(with forced restraint)*   General, would you please stick to whatever people like you are supposed to know about and leave computer-finding interpretation to analysts who are trained for the job?

73     *(Nimshaw starts to reply, but then recalls the fate of a fellow officer who was broken to corporal for insubordination. He meekly resumes pondering question No. 153, unable to decide whether admitting or denying the purchase of Girl Scout cookies will weigh most heavily against him in years to come.)*

74     FORDYCE  *(cont.)*   Any other cause-and-effect computations that we ought to consider in depth, Gipp?

75     GIPPARD   Not really. Of course, Number 327's been out of step with the others ever since it had that circuitry trouble. It just keeps saying, "Malcolm W. Biggs causes kosher poultry." Types out the same damned thing over and over: "Malcolm W. Biggs causes kosher poultry."

76     FORDYCE   Who's Malcolm W. Biggs?

77     GIPPARD   I think he was a juror at one of the Jimmy Hoffa trials. Number 327 was running a check on him when the circuits blew, and it's had kind of an obsession about him ever since.

78     FORDYCE   Mmmm. Well, personally, I've never paid much attention to the opinions of paranoids. They can get your thinking as screwed up as theirs is.

79     *(Fordyce notices Ashenfelter making an erasure on his card to change the data regarding his shoe size from 9½ C to something less likely to pinch across the instep.)*

80     FORDYCE  *(cont.) (shrieks at Ashenfelter)*   What do you think you're doing there? You're trying to hide something from me. I've met your kind before.

81     *(Ashenfelter wearily goes back to a 9½ C, even though they make his feet hurt, and Fordyce reacts with a look of smug satisfaction.)*

82     GIPPARD   Maybe if I fed this junk back into the machine, it could name some people who fit the pattern.

83     FORDYCE   Why don't you just reprocess the computations in an effort to gain individualized data that correlates?

84     *(Gippard stares thoughtfully at Fordyce for a long moment and then exits*

*to nail the ringleaders through incriminating association with the key words "drunk," "poultry," "golf," and "kilowatt.")*

85    NIMSHAW   I think maybe I'd better come back sometime when you're not so busy.

86    *(He slips his registry card into his pocket and starts toward the door, but Fordyce grabs him firmly by the wrist.)*

87    FORDYCE  Just a minute. You can't take that card out of here with you. It may contain classified information you shouldn't even have access to.

88    NIMSHAW   But it's about me. I'm the one who just filled it out.

89    FORDYCE  Don't try to muddy up the issue. Nobody walks out of this department with government property. Let's have it.

90    *(Nimshaw relunctantly surrenders the card. Fordyce glances at it and reacts with a look of horror.)*

91    FORDYCE *(cont.)*   You've filled this whole thing out in longhand! The instructions clearly state, "Type or print legibly." You'll have to do it over again.

92    *(Fordyce tears up the card and hands Nimshaw a new one. Nimshaw, suddenly aware that a display of bad conduct could cost him his good conduct medal, goes back to work, sobbing quietly to himself.)*

93    GIPPARD *(faintly, from a distance)*   Eureka! Hot damn!

94    FORDYCE *(happily)*   He's hit paydirt. I know old Gippard, and he hasn't cut loose like that since he linked Ralph Nader with the trouble at Berkeley.

95    *(Gippard enters on the dead run, unmindful of the computer tape streaming out behind him.)*

96    GIPPARD   It all correlates beautifully. *(ticks off points on his fingers)* A chicken plucker. Three arrests for common drunk. FBI's observed him playing golf with a known Cuban. Psychiatric report shows he sleeps with all the lights on.

97    FORDYCE  All wrapped up in one neat bundle. Who is he?

98    GIPPARD   A virtual unknown. Never been tagged as anything worse than possibly disloyal until I found him. He uses the name Y. Claude Garfunkel.

99    ASHENFELTER   Y. Claude Garfunkel!

100    FORDYCE *(menacingly)*   Touch a raw nerve, Ashenfelter?

101    *(The two janitors, who are really undercover sophomores majoring in forestry at Kansas State on CIA scholarships, rise and slowly converge on Ashenfelter.)*

102    GIPPARD   Want to tell us about it, Ashenfelter? We have our own methods of computing the truth out of you anyway, you know.

103    FORDYCE  No point in stalling. What's the connection? The two of you conspired to give false opinions to the Harris Poll, didn't you?

104    ASHENFELTER *(pitifully)*   No! Nothing like that. I swear.

105    GIPPARD   Then what, man? What? Have you tried to sabotage the Data Bank by forging each other's Social Security numbers?

106    ASHENFELTER *(a barely audible whisper)*   No. Please don't build a treason

case against me. I'll tell. A neighbor saw him with my wife at a luau in Baltimore.

107 *(The CIA men posing as college students posing as janitors react intuitively to jab Ashenfelter with a sodiumpentothol injection. Gippard rushes to a computer, where he begins cross-checking Garfunkel and Ashenfelter in the Urban Affairs file on "Polynesian power" advocates in Baltimore's Hawaiian ghetto and Interstate Commerce Commission reports on suspected participants in interstate hankypanky. Fordyce grabs the red "hot line" telephone on his desk and reacts with annoyance as he gets a busy signal. General Nimshaw, sensing himself caught up in a tide of events which he can neither turn back nor understand, hastily erases the computer tape containing his own dossier and then slashes his wrists under an assumed name.)*

108 Fade Out.

## REVIEW

### Content

1. What happens during this night in the GHQ of the Central Data Bank is Kafkasesque; that is, nothing makes truly logical sense; one cannot at all predict what will happen in an absurd world such as the one represented here. Cite some of the absurdities, the exaggerations, the mad associations and projections inspired by random pieces of data, the apparently pointless collection of information.
2. What does Bob and Ray's satire say about the potential power of "analysts . . . trained for . . . computer-finding interpretations"?

### Rhetoric

3. Part of the effect of the satire is achieved through the characterizations of the persons involved. Explore how this works by considering their names, how they look, how they talk, what they do, and so on.
4. Satire works partly through humor. How many different kinds of humor can you find in Bob and Ray's satire?

### Projects

5. In the summer of 1974, Congress learned of a $100-million computer network called FEDNET on which a government agency, the General Services Administration, had been working for two years without consulting Congress, which would be expected to set guidelines for such a potential data bank. Congressional hearings began immediately. Read about FEDNET in your college library's resources and write a paper about the current status of this project.
6. It has been said of the Watergate affair that government wiretappers caught themselves in their own network. Do some reading about this facet of Watergate and write a satire about one instance of this.

# 6
# Language and Thought

# Man at the Mercy of His Language

## PETER FARB

Peter Farb (1929–    ) is an author and naturalist who lives in Massachusetts. He has been Curator for American Indian Cultures at Riverside Museum in New York City and a feature editor for *Argosy* magazine. In 1974 he published the book *Word Play: What Happens When People Talk.* In the essay printed here, Farb illustrates, through Navaho and Eskimo vocabularies, what is known as the Sapir–Whorf Hypothesis: That man lives only in that part of the world that his language lets him know. So that, in a sense, our language creates our reality, and our cultures are language-bound. The selection comes from Farbs's *Man's Rise to Civilization as Shown by the Indians of North America from Primeval Times to the Coming of the Industrial State* (1968).

1    Linguistically speaking, man is not born free. He inherits a language full of quaint sayings, archaisms, and a ponderous grammar; even more important, he inherits certain fixed ways of expression that may shackle his thoughts. Language becomes man's shaper of ideas rather than simply his tool for reporting ideas. An American's conventional words for directions often limit his ability to read maps: It is an apt youngster indeed who can immediately grasp that the *Upper* Nile is in the *south* of Egypt and the *Lower* Nile is in the *north* of Egypt. Another example: English has only two demonstrative pronouns ("this" and "that," together with their plurals) to refer either to something near or to something far away. The Tlingit Indians of the Northwest Coast can be much more specific. If they want to refer to an object very near and always present, they say *he; ya* means an object also near and present, but a little farther away; *yu* refers to something still farther away, while *we* is used only for an object so far away that it is out of sight. So the question arises

whether even the most outspoken member of American society can "speak his mind." Actually, he has very little control over the possible channels into which his thoughts can flow. His grammatical mind was made up for him by his culture before he was born.

## English and Hopi "Water"

2     The way in which culture affects language becomes clear by comparing how the English and Hopi languages refer to $H_2O$ in its liquid state. English, like most other European languages, has only one word—"water"—and it pays no attention to what the substance is used for or its quantity. The Hopi of Arizona, on the other hand, use *pahe* to mean the large amounts of water present in natural lakes or rivers, and *keyi* for the small amounts in domestic jugs and canteens. English, though, makes other distinctions that Hopi does not. The speaker of English is careful to distinguish between a lake and a stream, between a waterfall and a geyser; but *pahe* makes no distinction among lakes, ponds, rivers, streams, waterfalls, and springs.

3     A Hopi speaker, of course, knows that there is a difference between a geyser, which spurts upward, and a waterfall, which plunges downward, even though his vocabulary makes no such distinction. Similarly, a speaker of English knows that a canteen of water differs from a river of water. But the real point of this comparison is that neither the Hopi nor the American uses anywhere near the possible number of words that could be applied to water in all of its states, quantities, forms, and functions. The number of such words is in the hundreds and they would hopelessly encumber the language. So, to prevent the language from becoming unwieldy, different kinds of water are grouped into a small number of categories. Each culture defines the categories in terms of the similarities it detects; it channels a multitude of ideas into the few categories that it considers important. The culture of every speaker of English tells him that it is important to distinguish between oceans, lakes, rivers, fountains, and waterfalls—but relatively unimportant to make the distinction between the water in a canteen in his canoe and the water underneath the same canoe. Each culture has categorized experience through language in a quite unconscious way—at the same time offering anthropologists commentaries on the differences and similarities that exist in societies.

## Sapir–Whorf Hypothesis

4     The possibility of such a relationship between language and culture has been formulated into a hypothesis by two American linguists, Sapir and Whorf. According to Sapir, man does not live in the midst of the

whole world, but only in a part of it, the part that his language lets him know. He is, says Sapir, "very much at the mercy of the particular language which has become the medium of expression" for his group. The real world is therefore "to a large extent unconsciously built up on the language habits of the group . . . The worlds in which different societies live are distinct worlds, not merely the same world with different labels attached." To Sapir and Whorf, language provides a different network of tracks for each society, which, as a result, concentrates on only certain aspects of reality.

5    According to the hypothesis, the differences between languages are much more than mere obstacles to communication; they represent basic differences in the "world view" of the various peoples and in what they understand about their environment. The Eskimo can draw upon an inventory of about twenty very precise words for the subtle differences in a snowfall. The best a speaker of English can manage are distinctions between sticky snow, sleet, hail, and ice. Similarly, to most speakers of English, a seal is simply a seal, and they have only that one word to describe it; if they want to say anything else about the seal, such as its sex or its color, then they have to put an adjective before the word "seal." But the Eskimo has a number of words with which to express various kinds of sealdom: "a young swimming seal," "a male harbor seal," "an old harbor seal," and so forth. A somewhat similar situation exists in English with the word "horse." This animal may be referred to as "chestnut," "bay mare," "stallion," and other names that one would not expect to find in the vocabulary of the horseless Eskimo.

6    The Eskimo, of course, is preoccupied with seals, a primary food source for him, whereas some speakers of English seem to be taken up with the exact particulars of the domesticated horse. The real question is: Do these different vocabularies restrict the Eskimo and the speaker of English, and do they force the speakers of different languages to conceptualize and classify information in different ways? Can an Eskimo look at a horse and in his own mind classify it as "a bay mare"? Or, because he lacks the words, is he forever blind to the fact that this kind of animal exists? The answer is that with a little practice an Eskimo can learn to tell apart the different kinds of horses, just as an American can learn about the various seals, even though the respective languages lack the necessary vocabularies. So vocabulary alone does not reveal the cultural thinking of a people.

## Navaho and English "Grab"

7    But does the *totality* of the language tell anything about the people who speak it? To answer that, look at the English very "grab." An English speaker says, "I grab it," "I grabbed it," "I will grab it," and so on. Only the context of the situation tells the listener what it is that

is being grabbed and how it is being done. "I grab it" is a vague sentence—except in one way. English is remarkably concerned about the tense of the verb. It insists on knowing whether I grab it now, or grabbed it some time in the past, or will grab it at a future time. The English language is preoccupied with time, and so is the culture of its speakers, who take considerable interest in calendars, record-keeping, diaries, history, almanacs, stock-market forecasts, astrological predictions, and always, every minute of the waking day, the precise time.

8    No such statement as "I grab it" would be possible in Navaho. To the Navaho, tense is of little importance, but the language is considerably more discriminating in other ways. The Navaho language would describe much more about the pronoun "I" of this sentence; it would tell whether the "I" initiated the action by reaching out to grab the thing, or whether the "I" merely grabbed at a horse that raced by. Nor would the Navaho be content merely with "grab"; the verb would have to tell him whether the thing being grabbed is big or little, animate or inanimate. Finally, a Navaho could not say simply "it"; the thing being grabbed would have to be described much more precisely and put in a category. (If you get the feeling that Navaho is an exceedingly difficult language, you are correct. During World War II in the Pacific, Navaho Indians were used as senders and receivers of secret radio messages because a language, unlike a code, cannot be broken; it must be learned.)

9    Judging by this example and by other linguistic studies of Navaho, a picture of its speakers emerges: They are very exacting in their perception of the elements that make up their universe. But is this a true picture of the Navaho? Does he perceive his world any differently from a White American? Anthropological and psychological studies of the Navaho show that he does. He visualizes himself as living in an eternal and unchanging universe made up of physical, social, and supernatural forces, among which he tries to maintain a balance. Any accidental failure to observe rules or rituals can disturb this balance and result in some misfortune. Navaho curing ceremonies, which include the well-known sandpainting, are designed to put the individual back into harmony with the universe. To the Navaho, the good life consists of maintaining intact all the complex relationships of the universe. It is obvious that to do so demands a language that makes the most exacting discriminations.

## Navaho and Hopi Differences

10    Several words of caution, though, about possible misinterpretations of the Sapir–Whorf Hypothesis. It does not say that the Navaho holds such a world view because of the structure of his language. It merely states that there is an interaction between his language and his culture.

Nor does the hypothesis maintain that two cultures with different languages and different world views cannot be in communication with each other (the Navaho and the White American are very much in communication today in Arizona and New Mexico). Instead, the hypothesis suggests that language is more than a way of communicating. It is a living system that is a part of the cultural equipment of a group, and it reveals a culture at least as much as do spear points, kinship groups, or political institutions. Look at just one of the clues to culture that the Sapir–Whorf Hypothesis has already provided: Shortly after the hypothesis was proposed, it was attacked on the basis that the Navaho speak an Athabaskan language and the Hopi a Uto-Aztecan one, yet they live side by side in the Southwest and share a culture. So, after all, asked the critics, what difference can language make in culture? Instead of demolishing the hypothesis, this comparison actually served to reveal its value. It forced anthropologists to take another look at the Navaho and the Hopi. As the hypothesis had predicted, their world views are quite far apart— and so are their cultures.

11    The Sapir–Whorf Hypothesis has alerted anthropologists to the fact that language is keyed to the total culture, and that it reveals a people's view of its total environment. Language directs the perceptions of its speakers to certain things; it gives them ways to analyze and to categorize experience. Such perceptions are unconscious and outside the control of the speaker. The ultimate value of the Sapir–Whorf Hypothesis is that it offers hints to cultural differences and similarities among peoples.

## REVIEW

### Content

1. Do you agree with Farb that a person "has very little control over the possible channels into which his [or her] thoughts can flow"? What happens to your everyday perception of the world as you learn about new things, often accompanied by an increase in your vocabulary? Does your answer here suggest that you can increase the control Farb refers to?

2. Think of a color discrimination that you just happened to learn—or suddenly realized—one day: for instance, fuchsia, from the flower of that name; cochineal, from learning about the insect in biology. Do such experiences enrich your *seeing*, from that time forth? What happens when you discover that you can use direct borrowings from other languages for more exact expression in English of certain concepts for which we lack adequate phrasing; examples: *joie de vivre*, from French; *weltanschauung*, from German; *querencia*, from Spanish? (If you do not know these words, look them up in a dictionary, perhaps an unabridged one.) How do we happen to have these words in our language: teepee (from Dakota Indian *ti pi*); igloo (Eskimo *iglu*)?

**Rhetoric**

3. Farb uses many examples to illustrate his thesis about a person's culture and his/her language. How well could you have followed his argument *without* such examples? Would you have remained interested in his presentation of linguistic theory without examples?

4. Farb writes on a serious subject in a relatively informal style. Is his style appropriate? Can you respect what he has to say at the same time that you can enjoy how he says it? What do direct questions (paragraphs 6 and 9) contribute here? How about the parenthetical aside at the end of paragraph 8?

**Projects**

5. Think of English words for which we need a wide range of discrimination (like "horse," in paragraph 5), and list all the discriminations you can.

6. If members of the class have lived in various parts of the United States, bring in examples of *regional* designations that vary, and see if fellow students can "de-code" them; examples: seesaw, teeter-totter; merry-go-round, carousel. OR Do the same sort of thing with "street" talk versus "straight" talk.

# Prejudice: Linguistic Factors

## GORDON W. ALLPORT

Gordon W. Allport (1897–1967) was a professor of psychology at Harvard and a major figure in humanistic psychology. His books include *Becoming* (1955), *The Nature of Prejudice* (1958), *Personality and Social Encounter* (1960), and *The Person in Psychology* (1968). In "Prejudice: Linguistic Factors," Allport explains how classifiers (stereotyping group labels) help both to create and spread prejudice.

1   Without words we should scarcely be able to form categories at all. A dog perhaps forms rudimentary generalizations, such as small-boys-are-to-be-avoided—but this concept runs its course on the conditioned reflex level, and does not become the object of thought as such. In order

Reprinted from *The Nature of Prejudice* by Gordon W. Allport by permission of Addison-Wesley Publishing Company, Inc. Copyright 1954.

to hold a generalization in mind for reflection and recall, for identification and for action, we need to fix it in words. Without words our world would be, as William James said, an "empirical sand-heap."

2    In the empirical world of human beings there are some two and a half billion grains of sand corresponding to our category "the human race." We cannot possibly deal with so many separate entities in our thought, nor can we individualize even among the hundreds whom we encounter in our daily round. We must group them, form clusters. We welcome, therefore, the names that help us to perform the clustering.

3    The most important property of a noun is that it brings many grains of sand into a single pail, disregarding the fact that the same grains might have fitted just as appropriately into another pail. To state the matter technically, a noun *abstracts* from a concrete reality some one feature and assembles different concrete realities only with respect to this one feature. The very act of classifying forces us to overlook all other features, many of which might offer a sounder basis than the rubric we select. Irving Lee gives the following example:

> I knew a man who had lost the use of both eyes. He was called a "blind man." He could also be called an expert typist, a conscientious worker, a good student, a careful listener, a man who wanted a job. But he couldn't get a job in the department store order room where employees sat and typed orders which came over the telephone. The personnel man was impatient to get the interview over. "But you're a blind man," he kept saying, and one could almost feel his silent assumption that somehow the incapacity in one aspect made the man incapable in every other. So blinded by the label was the interviewer that he could not be persuaded to look beyond it.[1]

## Labels of Primary Potency

4    Some labels, such as "blind man," are exceedingly salient and powerful. They tend to prevent alternative classification, or even cross-classification. Ethnic labels are often of this type, particularly if they refer to some highly visible feature, e.g., Negro, Oriental. They resemble the labels that point to some outstanding incapacity—*feeble-minded, cripple, blind man.* Let us call such symbols "labels of primary potency." These symbols act like shrieking sirens, deafening us to all finer discriminations that we might otherwise perceive. Even though the blindness of one man and the darkness of pigmentation of another may be defining attributes for some purposes, they are irrelevant and "noisy" for others.

5    Most people are unaware of this basic law of language—that every label applied to a given person refers properly only to one aspect of his nature. You may correctly say that a certain man is *human, a philan-*

[1] I. J. Lee, *How Do You Talk about People?*, Freedom Pamphlet (New York, Anti-Defamation League, 1950), p. 15.

*thropist, a Chinese, a physician, an athlete.* A given person may be all of these; but the chances are that *Chinese* stands out in your mind as the symbol of primary potency. Yet neither this nor any other classificatory label can refer to the whole of a man's nature. (Only his proper name can do so.)

6    Thus each label we use, especially those of primary potency, distracts our attention from concrete reality. The living, breathing, complex individual—the ultimate unit of human nature—is lost to sight. As in the figure following, the label magnifies one attribute out of all proportion to its true significance, and masks other important attributes of the individual.

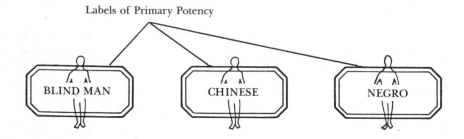

Labels of Primary Potency

BLIND MAN          CHINESE          NEGRO

7    . . . a category, once formed with the aid of a symbol of primary potency, tends to attract more attributes than it should. The category labeled *Chinese* comes to signify not only ethnic membership but also reticence, impassivity, poverty, treachery. To be sure, . . . there may be genuine ethnic-linked traits making for a certain *probability* that the member of an ethnic stock may have these attributes. But our cognitive process is not cautious. The labeled category, . . . includes indiscriminately the defining attribute, probable attributes, and wholly fanciful, nonexistent attributes.

8    Even proper names—which ought to invite us to look at the individual person—may act like symbols of primary potency, especially if they arouse ethnic associations. Mr. Greenberg is a person, but since his name is Jewish, it activates in the hearer his entire category of Jews-as-a-whole.

9    The anthropologist Margaret Mead has suggested that labels of primary potency lose some of their force when they are changed from nouns into adjectives. To speak of a Negro soldier, a Catholic teacher, or a Jewish artist calls attention to the fact that some other group classifications are just as legitimate as the racial or religious. If George Johnson is spoken of not only as a Negro but also as a *soldier,* we have at least two attributes to know him by, and two are more accurate than one. To depict him truly as an individual, of course, we should have to name many more attributes. It is a useful suggestion that we designate ethnic and religious membership where possible with *adjectives* rather than with *nouns.*

# Emotionally Toned Labels

10      Many categories have two kinds of labels—one less emotional and one more emotional. Ask yourself how you feel, and what thoughts you have, when you read the words *school teacher,* and then *school marm.* Certainly the second phrase calls up something more strict, more ridiculous, more disagreeable than the former. Here are four innocent letters: m-a-r-m. But they make us shudder a bit, laugh a bit, and scorn a bit. They call up an image of a spare, humorless, irritable old maid. They do not tell us that she is an individual human being with sorrows and troubles of her own. They force her instantly into a rejective category.

11      In the ethnic sphere even plain labels such as Negro, Italian, Jew, Catholic, Irish-American, French-Canadian may have emotional tone for a reason that we shall soon explain. But they all have their higher key equivalents: nigger, wop, kike, papist, harp, cannuck. When these labels are employed we can be almost certain that the speaker *intends* not only to characterize the person's membership, but also to disparage and reject him.

12      Quite apart from the insulting intent that lies behind the use of certain labels, there is also an inherent ("physiognomic") handicap in many terms designating ethnic membership. For example, the proper names characteristic of certain ethnic memberships strike us as absurd. (We compare them, of course, with what is familiar and therefore "right.") Chinese names are short and silly; Polish names intrinsically difficult and outlandish. Unfamiliar dialects strike us as ludicrous. Foreign dress (which, of course, is a visual ethnic symbol) seems unnecessarily queer.

13      But of all of these "physiognomic" handicaps the reference to color, clearly implied in certain symbols, is the greatest. The word Negro comes from the Latin *niger,* meaning black. In point of fact, no Negro has a black complexion, but by comparison with other blonder stocks, he has come to be known as a "black man." Unfortunately *black* in the English language is a word having a preponderance of sinister connotations: the outlook is black, blackball, blackguard, blackhearted, black death, blacklist, blackmail, Black Hand. . . .

14      There is thus an implied value-judgment in the very concept of *white race* and *black race.* One might also study the numerous unpleasant connotations of *yellow,* and their possible bearing on our conception of the people of the Orient.

15      Such reasoning should not be carried too far, since there are undoubtedly, in various contexts, pleasant associations with both black and yellow. Black velvet is agreeable, so too are chocolate and coffee. Yellow tulips are well liked; the sun and moon are radiantly yellow. Yet it is true that "color" words are used with chauvinistic overtones more than most people realize. There is certainly condescension indicated in many familiar phrases: dark as a nigger's pocket, darktown strutters, white hope (a term originated when a white contender was sought against

the Negro heavyweight champion, Jack Johnson), the white man's burden, the yellow peril, black boy. Scores of everyday phrases are stamped
with the flavor of prejudice, whether the user knows it or not.[2]

16     Members of minority groups are often understandably sensitive to
names given them. Not only do they object to deliberately insulting epi-
thets, but sometimes see evil intent where none exists. Often the word
Negro is spelled with a small *n*, occasionally as a studied insult, more
often from ignorance. (The term is not cognate with white, which is
not capitalized, but rather with Caucasian, which is.) Terms like "mulat-
to" or "octoroon" cause hard feeling because of the condescension with
which they have often been used in the past. Sex differentiations are
objectionable, since they seem doubly to emphasize ethnic difference:
why speak of Jewess and not of Protestantess, or of Negress and not
of whiteness? Similar overemphasis is implied in terms like Chinaman
or Scotchman; why not American man? Grounds for misunderstanding
lie in the fact that minority group members are sensitive to such shadings, while majority members may employ them unthinkingly.

## REVIEW

### Content

1. Have you had "blind man" experiences like the one Allport reports
   in paragraph 3? Through your thus limited perception, did you miss
   qualities in a person that you perhaps later came to appreciate? Is
   the range of your friendships limited by frequent such experiences?
   How might your life change if you were to eliminate *all* stereotype
   thinking you may now do about other persons?
2. In paragraph 16 Allport gives one reason why sex differentiations
   are objectionable. Can you think of others? Compare what Allport
   says with what Peter Fisher has to say about language and homosexuality in his selection (Section 3 of this book).

### Rhetoric

3. For what purpose does Allport compare the human race to a sand-
   heap? Does this analogy help you to grasp why we categorize human
   beings?
4. Allport refers to "labels of primary potency". How does this phrase
   help to carry his points about what happens when we stereotype individuals?

[2]L. L. Brown, "Words and White Chauvinism," *Masses and Mainstream* (1950), 3, pp.
3–11. See also *Prejudice Won't Hide! A Guide for Developing a Language of Equality* (San
Francisco, California Federation for Civic Unity, 1950).

**Projects**

5. Think of other "labels of primary potency" like those Allport cites in paragraphs 3 through 6, and discuss the way in which each is negatively limiting. Think of a list of emotionally toned uses of the word "white," like Allport's list for "black." Then, list all the positive associations for "black," and all the negative ones for "white," that you can think of. Begin to use the latter two lists in your everyday conversation, to help counterbalance the prejudice our language ordinarily suggests.
6. Write a paper developed from some of the questioning in 1 above.

# Male Perspective in Language

## JESSICA MURRAY

Jessica Murray (1951–   ) was a painting major at Brown University in Providence, Rhode Island, with a minor in linguistics. In her senior year, however, she proposed and had approved an independent concentration in Feminist Studies for herself, and eventually established an official interdisciplinary Feminist Studies major at Brown. In 1972 Murray wrote "Male Perspective in Language," which was printed in *Women: A Journal of Liberation*. The article, from which the following has been excerpted, argues that our language *assumes* that "human" means "male." Murray cites various sex-oriented distinctions which language reinforces. She urges, first, awareness of this phenomenon, and then, efforts toward change.

1   . . . It seems to me that there is something much more far-reaching about the sexism in language than the offensive words themselves. There is something inherently disturbing about the fact that the word *man* means both "the human race" and "male(s)"; about the fact that we as women must unconsciously switch sexes in order to identify with the unmarked human pronouns *his* and *him*, which are supposed to be understood as neuter. There is something going on above and beyond the linguistic level when, in my Spanish lab at school, I am called *amigo* (masculine form for "friend") by a pre-recorded voice that cannot see that I am female.

2     I will argue that the male bias of language, exemplified above, is an indication of a male outlook that pervades human culture; that the grammar is only a reflection of a phenomenon which goes so deep as to be concerned with our very definitions of Humanity; that the language we use, like everything else that reflects our culture, is based on the archetypal assumption that *human* means *male*.

. . .

## Female Specification in Language

3     A . . . familiar example of female specification in language is the prefixing of *lady-* or *woman-* or *female-* to occupational terms. A poem written by a friend of mine illustrates this phenomenon quite succinctly, I think:

> When I grow up I want to be a female vocalist.
> When I grow up I want to be a lady veterinarian.
> When I grow up I want to be a woman lawyer.
> When I grow up I want to be a boy doctor.
>     . . . and they'll say that's redundant.[1]

Part of the connotation behind the term which has been thus feminized, for instance *lady doctor,* is that this doctor is not an ordinary, proper doctor. The subtly derisive tone to this expression also has to do with the ironic presence of the chivalrous compliment "lady" in the context of a kind of put-down.

4     Even when they are being flattered, women are usually treated as a special case. Varda One of *Everywoman* magazine quotes a situation where a woman is complimented for having a trait that men are simply assumed to possess:

> After a recent radio interview the male host complimented Madalyn Murray O'Hair for being "an articulate and intelligent woman." When I asked him if he ever had complimented a male guest for intelligence, he admitted he never had. This is the perfect example of a left-handed compliment, telling a woman she has the qualities you take for granted in an average man.[2]

. . .

## Sexualization in Language

5     The most conspicuous example of woman-as-special-case, in language and without, is the sexualization of women: the tendency to view them as beings whose whole characterization is their femaleness. In language, in writing (fiction and fact), in the media, one finds that a woman's gender is the most significant thing about her. . . . One of the most interesting examples of the sexualization of women in language is the word

---

[1]Elsa King, unpublished manuscript; Toronto feminist.
[2]Varda One, "Manglish," *Everywoman*, April 1972, p. 25.

*girl*. Literally it means "young woman," but it is often applied indiscriminately as to age. A parallel can be found in the use of *boy* again indiscriminately as to age to refer to male blacks in the Old South. The motive behind this juvenilization is clearly disrespect. Yet there seems to be another level to the use of the word *girl* to refer to full-grown women: in some instances the term carries a sexual connotation which is not so emphatic in the word *woman*. For instance, I was once told that so-and-so (male) had once had "a girl in the Philippines." I immediately understood the term as it had been meant: the guy had had a mistress. The term was not marked for age; I wasn't necessarily to think that the woman had been young. The factor of age explicit in the term serves the implicit sexual meaning only in that it is younger women who are the more sexually desirable to men (besides good looks, youth suggests vulnerability and innocence, both of which traits are sexually desirable in woman, and not in men). Hence, reference to a woman's (metaphorical) youth seems to titillate men: from the affectionate term "baby" to the hyperbole of the Beatles' song "Little Child."

6    Because women are actually thought of as sex objects, they are linguistically treated as such ("Wine, Women, and Song"). And because a sexual tone is so deeply embedded in the word, a euphemism had to be invented as a polite substitute. *Lady* fulfills this service, protecting the user from the uncomfortable, oversexed connotations of the word *woman*. Linguist Robin Lakoff points this out:

> *Lady* is really a euphemism for *woman*, but *gentleman* is not nearly frequent enough to classify as a euphemism for *man*. Just as we do not call whites "Caucasian-Americans," there is no felt need to refer to men commonly as "gentlemen." And just as there is a felt need for such terms as Afro-Americans, there is similarly a felt need for "lady." One might even say that when a derogatory epithet exists, *broad*, etc., a parallel euphemism is deemed necessary.[3]

. . .

## Words Carry Messages

7    Language is a powerful conceptual force, and, as a transmitter of society's deep biases, it can be a means of conditioning our thoughts. I think it has been amply demonstrated that words are not mere empty vessels of syntax and semantics: they can fairly overflow with implicit opinion, and they can and do perpetuate prejudice. The terminology

[3]Robin Lakoff, "Language and Woman's Place," unpublished manuscript. I am grateful to her for many original and insightful ideas I've included in this paper. Besides dealing in depth with linguistic sexualization of women and women's language, discussed here, she suggests applications of these ideas to the realm of theoretical linguistics, language teaching, and the movement itself. Lakoff has been doing research at the Center for Advanced Study in the Behavioral Sciences, 202 Junipero Boulevard, Stanford, California.

applied to our movement by a hostile press is a prime example. Eschewing the proper term "feminism," the media coined the curt abbreviaton "Women's Lib," a phrase which connotes, needless to say, a whole different set of associations in people's minds. The connotation of Feminism as a historical movement, with a chronological continuity, suffrage, property rights . . . all that is forgotten: "Women's Lib" can only be a fad. It's no accident that the new media-ized term came into being: an antidote was needed for the painful questions feminism was raising.

8    Words can carry messages that their denotations only hint at. Take the phrase "career woman": it has an ugly ring. Definitions, invented by society and imposed on a subordinate group, may have little or nothing to do with the nature of that group. For instance, since the word "feminine" means "weak-and-female," is a woman who is strong- and-female allowed to call herself "feminine"? Technically no, since what women are, in our language and in our culture, is what the men in our society think of us.

9    It is true that language only represents a phenomenon that is almost too vast to contemplate changing. But the role of language in perpetuating the archetype of women-as-extra-human could be changed, it seems to me, by adopting new language conventions. Congresswoman Abzug's "Ms." proposal, for instance, could not fail to make a difference: people would simply not know, with the new title, whether the woman was married or not, and their immediate image of her would not be completely clouded by the fact of her marital status, as it is with "Miss" or "Mrs." The thing that I consider most important, however, is change in the English pronoun system. Consider the following blurb from an advertisement for dictionaries:

> You spent four thousand dollars to send your child to college this fall. Now spend sixty more to keep him there.

When people read that sentence they do not just brush over the male pronoun, *him,* as if it were a meaningless place-holder. I think people inevitably call up a mental image of a male student. In their unconscious semantic systems, the *him* really does represent a male. The picture underneath the blurb could never have been incongruous with the *him* in the sentence. It seems to me that an egalitarian pronoun system, *her-or-him,* for instance, could cause people to call up a mental image of a woman student presumably half the time, and give women—for the first time—the opportunity to identify with the concept of unmarked humanness.

## Awareness of Male Orientation

10    For a change of any depth to occur, however, male perspective must be understood, in all its depth. I think we should take a good look

at what insight language offers us into our basic concepts: consider the attitude revealed by that seemingly innocuous word *Man,* for instance . . . an attitude that is hidden in that it has for so long gone unquestioned. In this sense, then, we should keep phrases like "The history of Man" intact, for they actually mean what they say: the history we know has always been a history of *men.*

11     Let us not do away with male-initiated terminology until we fully understand from whence it came. Once women are into the habit of noticing male outlook in what we read and hear, the linguistic exclusions such as the ones I've mentioned will no longer be tolerable. The first step, then, in solving the inequity is ridiculously logical: it requires that we see the male orientation of phenomena such as language for what it is.

## REVIEW

### Content

1. Do you agree with Murray that our language is male-biased and that "what women are, in our language and in our culture, is what the men in our society think of us." (paragraph 8)? Does *your* language usage, whether you are male or female, suggest that *you* view women as "extra-human"? Do you think it is more important to keep our language as it is and hence clear and graceful in traditional ways than to start using words and expressions that sound strange and awkward: for instance, chairperson, mailwoman, he or she has left his or her scarf at my house? Do you agree with the second sentence in Murray's final paragraph?
2. Discuss these words: girl, lady, woman, femininity. What associations exactly does each bring up to you? Are any of them ever used in a *limiting* way? Which of the first three words would you guess is generally preferred by feminists? Why?

### Rhetoric

3. Murray supports her arguments with examples. Point to some particularly effective instances of her use of such support. Do you find any examples which are not especially valid?
4. What is the effect of Murray's final sentence? Do you hear a challenge in it? Would it profit from being more strongly expressed?

### Projects

5. Observe newspaper and magazine advertisements for about a week and collect two kinds: those that reinforce sexism (stereotyping either men or women, in pictures and/or words); and those that suggest a new awareness that moves beyond such stereotyping. Make a collage of each set of ads, pasting one set on one side of a piece of cardboard

and the other on the reverse side. Bring the result to class and discuss the effect created by the concentration of sexism in the one collage and the absence of it in the other. Perhaps you could also use the collage in other courses—speech, psychology, sociology, philosophy.

6. Listen carefully for a day or two to the talk that goes on around you. Then write a paper about anything you hear that bears out points Murray makes. Include what you yourself say.

# The Language of Soul

## CLAUDE BROWN

Claude Brown (1937–   ) grew up in New York City, later attending Howard University in Washington, D.C. His *Manchild in the Promised Land* (1965), an autobiographical novel, was among the outstanding books produced by the new wave of Black writers of the period. Brown's article below, first published in *Esquire* in April, 1968, traces the development of soul language and its meaning to its users.

1   Perhaps the most soulful word in the world is "nigger." Despite its very definite fundamental meaning (the Negro man), and disregarding the deprecatory connotation of the term, "nigger" has a multiplicity of nuances when used by soul people. Dictionaries define the term as being synonymous with Negro, and they generally point out that it is regarded as a vulgar expression. Nevertheless, to those of chitlins-and-neck-bones background the word nigger is neither a synonym for Negro nor an obscene expression.

2   "Nigger" has virtually as many shades of meaning in Colored English as the demonstrative pronoun "that," prior to application to a noun. To some Americans of African ancestry (I avoid using the term Negro whenever feasible, for fear of offending the Brothers X, a pressure group to be reckoned with), nigger seems preferable to Negro and has a unique kind of sentiment attached to it. This is exemplified in the frequent—and perhaps even excessive—usage of the term to denote either fondness or hostility.

3   It is probable that numerous transitional niggers and even established ex-soul brothers can—with pangs of nostalgia—reflect upon a day in

the lollipop epoch of lives when an adorable lady named Mama bemoaned her spouse's fastidiousness with the strictly secular utterance: "Lord, how can one nigger be so hard to please?" Others are likely to recall a time when that drastically lovable colored woman, who was forever wiping our noses and darning our clothing, bellowed in a moment of exasperation: "Nigger, you gonna be the death o' me." And some of the brethren who have had the precarious fortune to be raised up, wised up, thrown up, or simply left alone to get up as best they could, on one of the nation's South Streets or Lenox Avenues, might remember having affectionately referred to a best friend as "My nigger."

## Nigger More Soulful

4    The vast majority of "back-door Americans" are apt to agree with Webster—a nigger is simply a Negro or black man. But the really profound contemporary thinkers of this distinguished ethnic group—Dick Gregory, Redd Foxx, Moms Mabley, Slappy White, etc.—are likely to differ with Mr. Webster and define nigger as "something else"—a soulful "something else." The major difference between the nigger and the Negro, who have many traits in common, is that the nigger is the more soulful.

5    Certain foods, customs, and artistic expressions are associated almost solely with the nigger: collard greens, neck bones, hog maws, black-eyed peas, pigs' feet, etc. A nigger has no desire to conceal or disavow any of these favorite dishes or restrain other behavioral practices such as bobbing his head, patting his feet to funky jazz, and shouting and jumping in church. This is not to be construed that all niggers eat chitlins and shout in church, nor that only niggers eat the aforementioned dishes and exhibit this type of behavior. It is to say, however, that the soulful usage of the term nigger implies all of the foregoing and considerably more.

6    The Language of Soul—or, as it might also be called, Spoken Soul or Colored English—is simply an honest vocal portrayal of black America. The roots of it are more than three hundred years old.

7    Before the Civil War there were numerous restrictions placed on the speech of slaves. The newly arrived Africans had the problem of learning to speak a new language, but also there were inhibitions placed on the topics of the slaves' conversation by slave masters and overseers. The slaves made up songs to inform one another of, say, the underground railroads' activity. When they sang *Steal Away* they were planning to steal away to the North, not to heaven. Slaves who dared to speak of rebellion or even freedom usually were severely punished. Consequently, Negro slaves were compelled to create a semi-clandestine vernacular in the way that the criminal underworld had historically created

words to confound law-enforcement agents. It is said that numerous Negro spirituals were inspired by the hardships of slavery, and that what later became songs were initially moanings and coded cotton-field lyrics. To hear these songs sung today by a talented soul brother or sister or by a group is to be reminded of an historical spiritual bond that cannot be satisfactorily described by the mere spoken word.

8      The American Negro, for virtually all of his history, has constituted a vastly disproportionate number of the country's illiterates. Illiteracy has a way of showing itself in all attempts at vocal expression by the uneducated. With the aid of colloquialisms, malapropisms, battered and fractured grammar, and a considerable amount of creativity, Colored English, the sound of soul, evolved.

## Hip Blacks vs. Unhip Whites

9      The progress has been cyclical. Often terms that have been discarded from the soul people's vocabulary for one reason or another are reaccepted years later, but usually with completely different meaning. In the Thirties and Forties "stuff" was used to mean vagina. In the middle Fifties it was revived and used to refer to heroin. Why certain expressions are thus reactivated is practically an indeterminable question. But it is not difficult to see why certain terms are dropped from the soul language. Whenever a soul term becomes popular with whites it is common practice for the soul folks to relinquish it. The reasoning is that "if white people can use it, it isn't hip enough for me." To many soul brothers there is just no such creature as a genuinely hip white person. And there is nothing more detrimental to anything hip than to have it fall into the square hands of the hopelessly unhip.

10      White Americans wrecked the expression "something else." It was bad enough that they couldn't say "sump'n else," but they weren't even able to get out "somethin' else." They had to go around saying *something else* with perfect or nearly perfect enunciation. The white folks invariably fail to perceive the soul sound in soulful terms. They get hung up in diction and grammar, and when they vocalize the expression it's no longer a soulful thing. In fact, it can be asserted that spoken soul is more of a sound than a language. It generally possesses a pronounced lyrical quality which is frequently incompatible to any music other than that ceaseless and relentlessly driving rhythm that flows from poignantly spent lives. Spoken soul has a way of coming out metered without the intention of the speaker to invoke it. There are specific phonetic traits. To the soulless ear the vast majority of these sounds are dismissed as incorrect usage of the English language and, not infrequently, as speech impediments. To those so blessed as to have had bestowed upon them

at birth the lifetime gift of soul, these are the most communicative and meaningful sounds ever to fall upon human ears: the familiar "mah" instead of "my," "gonna" for "going to," "yo" for "your." "Ain't" is pronounced "ain' "; "bread" and "bed," "bray-ud" and "bay-ud"; "baby" is never "bay-bee" but "bay-buh"; Sammy Davis, Jr., is not "samme" but a kind of "sam-eh"; the same goes for "Eddeh" Jefferson. No matter how many "man's" you put into your talk, it isn't soulful unless the word has the proper plaintive, nasal "maee-yun."

## Soul vs. Slang

11    Spoken soul is distinguished from slang primarily by the fact that the former lends itself easily to conventional English, and the latter is diametrically opposed to adaptations within the realm of conventional English. Police (pronounced pō 'lice) is a soul term, whereas "The Man" is merely slang for the same thing. Negroes seldom adopt slang terms from the white world and when they do the terms are usually given a different meaning. Such was the case with the term "bag." White racketeers used it in the Thirties to refer to the graft that was paid to the police. For the past five years soul people have used it when referring to a person's vocation, hobby, fancy, etc. And once the appropriate term is given the treatment (soul vocalization) it becomes soulful.

12    However, borrowings from spoken soul by white men's slang— particularly teen-age slang—are plentiful. Perhaps because soul is probably the most graphic language of modern times, everybody who is excluded from Soulville wants to usurp it, ignoring the formidable fettering to the soul folks that has brought the language about. Consider "uptight," "strung-out," "cop," "boss," "kill 'em," all now widely used outside Soulville. Soul people never question the origin of a slang term; they either dig it and make it a part of their vocabulary or don't and forget it. The expression "uptight," which meant being in financial straits, appeared on the soul scene in the general vicinity of 1953. Junkies were very fond of the word and used it literally to describe what was a perpetual condition with them. The word was pictorial and pointed; therefore it caught on quickly in Soulville across the country. In the early Sixties when "uptight" was on the move, a younger generation of soul people in the black urban communities along the Eastern Seaboard regenerated it with a new meaning: "everything is cool, under control, going my way." At present the term has the former meaning for the older generation and the latter construction for those under thirty years of age.

13    It is difficult to ascertain if the term "strung-out" was coined by junkies or just applied to them and accepted without protest. Like the term

"uptight" in its initial interpretation, "strung-out" aptly described the constant plight of the junkie. "Strung-out" had a connotation of hopeless finality about it. "Uptight" implied a temporary situation and lacked the overwhelming despair of "strung-out."

14    The term "cop" (meaning "to get") is an abbreviation of the word "copulation." "Cop," as originally used by soulful teen-agers in the early Fifties, was deciphered to mean sexual coition, nothing more. By 1955 "cop" was being uttered throughout national Soulville as a synonym for the verb "to get," especially in reference to illegal purchases, drugs, pot, hot goods, pistols, etc. ("Man, where can I cop now?") But by 1955 the meaning was all-encompassing. Anything that could be obtained could be "copped."

15    The word "boss," denoting something extraordinarily good or great, was a redefined term that had been popular in Soulville during the Forties and Fifties as a complimentary remark from one soul brother to another. Later it was replaced by several terms such as "groovy," "tough," "beautiful," and, most recently, "out of sight." This last expression is an outgrowth of the former term "way out," the meaning of which was equivocal. "Way out" had an ad hoc hickish ring to it which made it intolerably unsoulful and consequently it was soon replaced by "out of sight," which is also likely to experience a relatively brief period of popular usage. "Out of sight" is better than "way out," but it has some of the same negative, childish taint of its predecessor.

16    The expression, "kill 'em," has neither a violent nor a malicious interpretation. It means "good luck," "give 'em hell," or "I'm pulling for you," and originated in Harlem from six to nine years ago.

## Classic Soul Terms

17    There are certain classic soul terms which, no matter how often borrowed, remain in the canon and are reactivated every so often, just as standard jazz tunes are continuously experiencing renaissances. Among the classical expressions are: "solid," "cool," "jive" (generally as a noun), "stuff," "thing," "swing" (or "swinging"), "pimp," "dirt," "freak," "heat," "larceny," "busted," "okee doke," "piece," "sheet" (a jail record), "squat," "square," "stash," "lay," "sting," "mire," "gone," "smooth," "joint," "blow," "play," "shot," and there are many more.

18    Soul language can be heard in practically all communities throughout the country, but for pure, undiluted spoken soul one must go to Soul Street. There are several. Soul is located at Seventh and "T" in Washington, D.C., on One Two Five Street in New York City; on Springfield Avenue in Newark; on South Street in Philadelphia; on Tremont Street in Boston; on Forty-seventh Street in Chicago, on Fillmore in San Francisco, and dozens of similar locations in dozens of other cities.

# Abandonment of Soul

19    As increasingly more Negroes desert Soulville for honorary membership in the Establishment clique, they experience a metamorphosis, the
repercussions of which have a marked influence on the young and impressionable citizens of Soulville. The expatriates of Soulville are often
greatly admired by the youth of Soulville, who emulate the behavior
of such expatriates as Nancy Wilson, Ella Fitzgerald, Eartha Kitt, Lena
Horne, Diahann Carroll, Billy Daniels, or Leslie Uggams. The result—
more often than not—is a trend away from spoken soul among the young
soul folks. This abandonment of the soul language is facilitated by the fact
that more Negro youngsters than ever are acquiring college educations
(which, incidentally, is not the best treatment for the continued good
health and growth of soul); integration and television, too, are contributing significantly to the gradual demise of spoken soul.

20    Perhaps colleges in America should commence to teach a course in
spoken soul. It could be entitled the Vocal History of Black America,
or simply Spoken Soul. Undoubtedly there would be no difficulty
finding teachers. There are literally thousands of these experts throughout the country whose talents lie idle while they await the call to duty.

21    Meanwhile the picture looks dark for soul. The two extremities in
the Negro spectrum—the conservative and the militant—are both trying
diligently to relinquish and repudiate whatever vestige they may still
possess of soul. The semi-Negro—the soul brother intent on gaining
admission to the Establishment even on an honorary basis—is anxiously
embracing and assuming conventional English. The other extremity, the
Ultra-Blacks, are frantically adopting everything from a Western version
of Islam that would shock the Caliph right out of his snugly fitting
shintiyan to anything that vaguely hints of that big, beautiful, bountiful
black bitch lying in the arms of the Indian and Atlantic Oceans and
crowned by the majestic Mediterranean Sea. Whatever the Ultra-Black
is after, it's anything but soulful.

## REVIEW

### Content

1. How aware were you, before reading this article, of how many expressions quite common in this country originated as soul talk: for instance, uptight, cool, strung-out, beautiful, square, out of sight? *Why*
   are these words appealing enough to become popularized? Does the
   imagery behind them have anything to do with our liking them?
2. Can you think of other situations which develop a language of their
   own: for instance, the love relationship, a mother with her children?
   Explore this question, thinking of situations and their vocabularies.

What does this exercise suggest to you about our relationship with language?

**Rhetoric**

3. Brown uses a number of terms basic to a discussion of language. If you do not already know the following words, look them up, to help you discuss the essay in class: connotation (paragraphs 1, 13); nuance (1); synonym (1); vernacular (7); colloquialism (8); malapropism (8).

4. What is the effect of the next to last sentence of Brown's final paragraph? What is he trying to do here?

**Projects**

5. "Soul," often referred to as "street talk," is very vivid and colorful. Make a list of all the additional "street talk" you can think of that has become everyday English. If you are lucky enough to have in your group someone who knows street talk firsthand, try to learn some new expressions. OR Discuss the first half of the last sentence in paragraph 19, along with paragraph 21. Debate whether what Brown says here is a good or a bad thing to be happening.

6. If you know street talk, write an account of something interesting that happened to you, in street talk. Make it as much *your own* as you can. OR Write a paper based on the second half of 5 above.

# Posture of Pomposity: Gobbledygook

## BUREAU OF LAND MANAGEMENT

The Bureau of Land Management of the U. S. Department of the Interior produced during the 1960s a little booklet entitled *Gobbledygook Has Gotta Go,* written by John O'Hayre, an employee in Denver, Colorado. The book was intended to promote "better written communications on the part of all Bureau employees." However, it is instructive for us all, as it cites the pompous, often ridiculous, and sometimes dangerously evasive diction all too frequently used by representatives of the institutions of our society—in government, in industry, in the military, in education, and elsewhere. A passage from *Gobbledygook* is printed below.

1   Predicated on the irrefragable evidence manifested in ruminating over the efficient causes of the innumerable devastating effects that were ponderously present in the multifarious exemplifications of available written communications vertically representative of the Bureau of Land Management, it is judicious and feasible to establish categorically that these BLM writings have been more banefully enervated by the omnipresence of reticulated pomposity than by any other deleterious factor that is contributory to their obfuscated yet embellished condition of utter ennui.

2   And that is simply a very pompous way of saying that one of the deadliest, most contagious diseases infecting BLM writing today is pomposity.

3   Remember we said pompous writing is writing that is NOT natural . . . is stuffy . . . stilted. And some of the other terms the experts use to describe it are . . . ornate . . . elegant . . . exquisite . . . ostentatious . . . affective not effective . . . puffed up . . . falsely dignified . . . overly formalistic . . . scared stiff of being human . . .

4   But we think the best way to describe pompous writing is by saying it's just plain *phony, filigreed flapdoodle*. Dictionary-defined it comes out this way:

   (a) *Phony*—not genuine . . . counterfeit . . . faked
   (b) *Filigreed*—fanciful . . . curlicued . . . merely decorative
   (c) *Flapdoodle*—oily talk having a false look of genuineness . . . unctuous prattle.

5   And in that definition we have a perfect description of pompous writing.

6   But what causes pomposity in writing? Or, better still, what causes BLM people to get pompous when they write?

7   Two things mostly: (1) An error in judgment; and (2) an almost maniacal madness for using big words.

8   Error No. 1: When you write pompously, you judge wrongly that readers appreciate elegant writing; that they expect you as an educated person to sound elegant and impressive and will think you undignified if you don't. This may have been true years ago, when 5 percent of the people had social position and educational status and the other 95 percent had neither. But that isn't the way things are any more and readers don't like you to write like they were. In short, parading elegant words is no longer a suitable ceremony for the educated to use to IMPRESS the less educated.

9   Nor was this puffed up elegance appreciated in Europe even in the roughness of the fifth century when semi-Christianized barbarian hordes roamed a rude world with rock and ax. Even then, a Latinized Frankish bishop was warning his priests about pomposity:

   Be neither ornate nor flowery in your speech . . . or the educated will think you a boor and you will fail to impress the peasants.

10    As for Error No. 2—the maniacal madness for big words—H. W. Fowler says that those writers who run to long words are mainly the unskillful and tasteless; they confuse pomposity with dignity, flaccidity with ease, and bulk with force.

11    Big words are not always and necessarily bad. They are bad when the writer is obsessed with them, when he uses them for their own sake, when he uses them to the exclusion of plain words. Then they are pompous.

12    Of course there's one way of killing this big word bug, and that's to stop talking like a mechanical nobleman who has been stuffed to overflowing with impressive, exotic words, and start talking like the genuine, natural human being you are. It's that simple.

13    Another writing evil caused by big word pomposity is the evil of falling into error. The more pompous and profound we get, the more we're apt to make mistakes. This pops up in our next sample from a monthly progress report by a state fire officer:

> FIRE REPORT: Heavy rains throughout most of the State have given an optimistic outlook for lessened fire danger for the rest of the season. However, an abundance of lightning maintains a certain amount of hazard in isolated areas that have not received an excessive amount of rain. We were pleased to have been able to help Nevada with the suppression of their conflagration.

14    The curious thing about this stilted, stuffy, unnatural, puffed up and pompous piece is that the fire officer who wrote it is an educated, dignified, uncomplicated, easy-going, unpretentious, plain-talking fellow, who wouldn't be caught dead talking like he writes.

15    But what happened to him is the same thing that happens to many of us when we pick up a pencil. We become somebody else—and usually that somebody else is an aristocratic dandy of some past century. We just never really look at ourselves as we actually appear in print. If we did, we'd either quit writing or we'd quit writing like we do.

16    Now let's see how our fog-fighting secretary wrote the pomposity out of the fire officer's memo:

> Fire readings are down throughout most of the State. But a few rain-skipped areas are dry, and lightning is a hazard there. We are glad we could send some of our people to help Nevada put out their recent range fire.

17    The important point here is NOT that our secretary cut down from 60 pompous words to 42 rather simple ones; mere word-cutting is never an end in itself: but that she did make the item simple, natural, and accurate.

18    As for its accuracy: Our fire officer didn't mean . . . "lightning maintains a hazard in areas that have NOT received an EXCESSIVE amount of rain!" He probably meant . . . "lightning is a hazard in areas that have not received a SUFFICIENT amount of rain"; or, ". . . in areas

that ARE EXCESSIVELY dry." Whatever he meant to say, he didn't say it, and he used big, elegant words not saying it.

19    He did not know how to handle the negative "not." This led him to pick the wrong word in "excessive." However, even this is no real explanation, for you can't explain away a 60-word passel of pomposity by the wrong use of one "not" and one "excessive."

20    Pomposity isn't that simple. You can't "select it out" by changing a big word here and there; you've got to write it out by rewriting the whole thing. That's because pomposity is more than mere words; it's false tone as well.

21    It was this false tone that angered Franklin D. Roosevelt when he happened across it. He was convinced that the simple, personal style of writing was the most dignified style for men of importance in government and everywhere else.

22    Here's a pompous memo that rankled F.D.R. so much he rewrote it and shot it back to the man who pomped it up in the first place. This memo dealt with what Federal workers were to do in case of an air raid:

> Such preparations shall be made as will completely obscure all Federal buildings and non-Federal buildings occupied by the Federal Government during an air raid for any period of time from visibility by reason of internal or external illumination. Such obscuration may be obtained either by blackout construction or by termination of the illumination.

23    Here's how F.D.R. dignified the memo by giving it simplicity:

> Tell them that in buildings where they have to keep the work going to put something over the windows; and, in buildings where they can let the work stop for a while, turn out the lights.

24    If this kind of unpompous, simple writing means a loss of dignity, then we know a whole lot of readers who wish a lot of writers would lose a lot of "dignity" writing this way. F.D.R. did it all the time. Once, when Frances Perkins was getting a speech ready for him, she wrote this line:

> We are endeavoring to construct a more inclusive society.

25    That night when F.D.R. read the line on the radio, it came out this way:

> We are going to make a country in which no one is left out.

26    Nor did presidential simplicity go out of style with F.D.R.

·  ·  ·

27    And then there's the kind of pomposity that comes from using what we call *persuader* words, words that are nothing more than airy symbols.

They are usually used in BLM writing to "important-up" the Bureau or one of its routine jobs. These persuader words are fluff, not fact, air, not action, impressive, not expressive.

> The publication of this attractive map is an outstanding example of . . . etc.
>
> This patent was presented at impressive ceremonies held in the Bureau of Land Management State Office . . . etc.
>
> The Board will discuss all of the very difficult problems they will encounter next year . . . etc.
>
> The lease was won after several rounds of spirited bidding, which was highly competitive . . . etc.
>
> As a result, the hearings were completed in record-breaking time and with great savings to the public . . . etc.
>
> The Bureau's case was presented in practically a flawless manner . . . etc.
>
> A huge crowd attended the special installation ceremonies . . .
>
> Fire rehabilitation plans will have to be coordinated very closely with other agencies . . . etc. (You could write the rest of your natural life and not use the word very again. At least not very often!)
>
> Before BLM takes such serious steps, careful consideration is given to . . . etc.
>
> In a move denoting close cooperation between Federal and State agencies, BLM . . . etc.
>
> Mr. So and So retired after giving 33 years of faithful and dedicated service to the Department of the Interior . . . etc.
>
> The distinguished visitors were guests at a BLM orientation meeting this morning in the . . . etc.

28    And then there's the kind of pomposity that comes from trying to sound "important" when we write "talk." In many ways, this is the worst kind of pomp, for more than anything else, written talk should sound like spoken talk. If it doesn't, if it's pomped up above and beyond naturalness, kill it; then rewrite it. This quote, from a BLM news release, emphasizes the point:

> Because the heavy mistletoe infestation in the Kringle Creek area has rendered the residual timber useless for timber production, the ultimate goal is to establish a healthy new stand of Douglas Fir.

29    That isn't anywhere near plain talk; it's plain pomposity. And it's about time somebody said so.

30    The mistletoe quote isn't out of the ordinary in BLM writing. Out of 100 BLM quotes we found only 1 that sounded like it might have been said by somebody who talks the way most of us do:

> We got everything lined up this morning. Now all we have to take care of is the paper work. Like always, that'll take more time than it should. But we're all set to push it through as fast as we can. I think we'll be able to wrap it up sometime late next week.

# REVIEW

## Content

1. Had you ever encountered gobbledygook before reading this selection? If so, where? How did you feel about both it and its user? Have *you* ever written gobbledygook? Why?
2. Discuss H. W. Fowler's characterization of persons with a "maniacal madness for big words" (paragraph 10). Analyze the fire report in paragraph 13 on the basis of Fowler's description.

## Rhetoric

3. Some of the experts' definitions of gobbledygook quoted in paragraph 3 are themselves examples of that plague on language, especially by comparison with other phrases in the list. Which defining words/phrases are the most descriptive—and why? What does this tell you about gobbledygook?
4. The booklet from which this excerpt was taken was written as a manual for BLM employees. In what ways does O'Hayre's style especially fit both the topic of his argument and his audience?

## Projects

5. Try to analyze all the reasons you can think of for anybody's indulging in gobbledygook, written or spoken. Some possibilities: a wholesaler to a retailer; a teacher to students; a parent to a child (of a specific age); an employer to an employee. Discuss how and why language is often abused in such relationships.
6. Rewrite the sentences in paragraph 27, removing as much "fluff" and "air" as possible without changing the apparent intended meaning. OR Textbooks sometimes contain gobbledygook. Copy such a passage from a text and then try to rewrite it, more succinctly and clearly.

# Love Is a
# Fallacy

## MAX SHULMAN

Max Shulman (1919–   ) is an American humorist, and creator of the very popular Dobie Gillis (*The Many Loves of Dobie Gillis,* 1951), who went on to become a character on television. "Love Is a Fallacy" is taken from *The Many Loves . . .,* and in this section Shulman instructs as well as entertains, as Dobie undertakes to teach logic to Polly Espy, friend of his roommate Petey. Through Dobie and Polly, Shulman introduces the reader to a wide range of logical fallacies.

1    Cool was I and logical. Keen, calculating, perspicacious, acute and astute—I was all of these. My brain was as powerful as a dynamo, as precise as a chemist's scales, as penetrating as a scalpel. And—think of it!—I was only eighteen.

2    It is not often that one so young has such a giant intellect. Take, for example, Petey Burch, my roommate at the University of Minnesota. Same age, same background, but dumb as an ox. A nice enough fellow, you understand, but nothing upstairs. Emotional type. Unstable. Impressionable. Worst of all, a faddist. Fads, I submit, are the very negation of reason. To be swept up in every new craze that comes along, to surrender yourself to idiocy just because everybody else is doing it—this, to me, is the acme of mindlessness. Not, however, to Petey.

3    One afternoon I found Petey lying on his bed with an expression of such distress on his face that I immediately diagnosed appendicitis. "Don't move," I said. "Don't take a laxative. I'll get a doctor."

4    "Raccoon," he mumbled thickly.

5    "Raccoon?" I said, pausing in my flight.

6    "I want a raccoon coat," he wailed.

7    I perceived that his trouble was not physical, but mental. "Why do you want a raccoon coat?"

8    "I should have known it," he cried, pounding his temples. "I should have known they'd come back when the Charleston came back. Like a fool I spent all my money for textbooks, and now I can't get a raccoon coat."

9    "Can you mean," I said incredulously, "that people are actually wearing raccoon coats again?"

10     "All the Big Men on Campus are wearing them. Where've you been?"

11     "In the library," I said, naming a place not frequented by Big Men on Campus.

12     He leaped from the bed and paced the room. "I've got to have a raccoon coat," he said passionately. "I've got to!"

13     "Petey, why? Look at it rationally. Raccoon coats are unsanitary. They shed. They smell bad. They weigh too much. They're unsightly. They——"

14     "You don't understand," he interrupted impatiently. "It's the thing to do. Don't you want to be in the swim?"

15     "No," I said truthfully.

16     "Well, I do," he declared. "I'd give anything for a raccoon coat. Anything!"

17     My brain, that precision instrument, slipped into high gear. "Anything?" I asked, looking at him narrowly.

18     "Anything," he affirmed in ringing tones.

19     I stroked my chin thoughtfully. It so happened that I knew where to get my hands on a raccoon coat. My father had had one in his undergraduate days; it lay now in a trunk in the attic back home. It also happened that Petey had something I wanted. He didn't *have* it exactly, but at least he had first rights on it. I refer to his girl, Polly Espy.

20     I had long coveted Polly Espy. Let me emphasize that my desire for this young woman was not emotional in nature. She was, to be sure, a girl who excited the emotions, but I was not one to let my heart rule my head. I wanted Polly for a shrewdly calculated, entirely cerebral reason.

21     I was a freshman in law school. In a few years I would be out in practice. I was well aware of the importance of the right kind of wife in furthering a lawyer's career. The successful lawyers I had observed were, almost without exception, married to beautiful, gracious, intelligent women. With one omission, Polly fitted these specifications perfectly.

22     Beautiful she was. She was not yet of pin-up proportions, but I felt sure that time would supply the lack. She already had the makings.

23     Gracious she was. By gracious I mean full of graces. She had an erectness of carriage, an ease of bearing, a poise that clearly indicated the best of breeding. At table her manners were exquisite. I had seen her at the Kozy Kampus Korner eating the specialty of the house—a sandwich that contained scraps of pot roast, gravy, chopped nuts, and a dipper of sauerkraut—without even getting her fingers moist.

24     Intelligent she was not. In fact, she veered in the opposite direction. But I believed that under my guidance she would smarten up. At any rate, it was worth a try. It is, after all, easier to make a beautiful dumb girl smart than to make an ugly smart girl beautiful.

25     "Petey," I said, "are you in love with Polly Espy?"

26    "I think she's a keen kid," he replied, "but I don't know if you'd call it love. Why?"

27    "Do you," I asked, "have any kind of formal arrangement with her? I mean are you going steady or anything like that?"

28    "No. We see each other quite a bit, but we both have other dates. Why?"

29    "Is there," I asked,. "any other man for whom she has a particular fondness?"

30    "Not that I know of. Why?"

31    I nodded with satisfaction. "In other words, if you were out of the picture, the field would be open. Is that right?"

32    "I guess so. What are you getting at?"

33    "Nothing, nothing," I said innocently, and took my suitcase out of the closet.

34    "Where are you going?" asked Petey.

35    "Home for the weekend." I threw a few things into the bag.

36    "Listen," he said, clutching my arm eagerly, "while you're home, you couldn't get some money from your old man, could you, and lend it to me so I can buy a raccoon coat?"

37    "I may do better than that," I said with a mysterious wink and closed my bag and left.

38    "Look," I said to Petey when I got back Monday morning. I threw open the suitcase and revealed the huge, hairy, gamy object that my father had worn in his Stutz Bearcat in 1925.

39    "Holy Toledo!" said Petey reverently. He plunged his hands into the raccoon coat and then his face. "Holy Toledo!" he repeated fifteen or twenty times.

40    "Would you like it?" I asked.

41    "Oh yes!" he cried, clutching the greasy pelt to him. Then a canny look came into his eyes. "What do you want for it?"

42    "Your girl," I said, mincing no words.

43    "Polly?" he said in a horrified whisper. "You want Polly?"

44    "That's right."

45    He flung the coat from him. "Never," he said stoutly.

46    I shrugged. "Okay. If you don't want to be in the swim, I guess it's your business."

47    I sat down in a chair and pretended to read a book, but out of the corner of my eye I kept watching Petey. He was a torn man. First he looked at the coat with the expression of a waif at a bakery window. Then he turned away and set his jaw resolutely. Then he looked back at the coat, with even more longing in his face. Then he turned away, but with not so much resolution this time. Back and forth his head swiveled, desire waxing, resolution waning. Finally he didn't turn away at all; he just stood and stared with mad lust at the coat.

48     "It isn't as though I was in love with Polly," he said thickly. "Or going steady or anything like that."

49     "That's right," I murmured.

50     "What's Polly to me, or me to Polly?"

51     "Not a thing," said I.

52     "It's just been a casual kick—just a few laughs, that's all."

53     "Try on the coat," said I.

54     He complied. The coat bunched high over his ears and dropped all the way down to his shoe tops. He looked like a mound of dead raccoons. "Fits fine," he said happily.

55     I rose from my chair. "Is it a deal?" I asked, extending my hand.

56     He swallowed. "It's a deal," he said and shook my hand.

57     I had my first date with Polly the following evening. This was in the nature of a survey; I wanted to find out just how much work I had to do to get her mind up to the standard I required. I took her first to dinner. "Gee, that was a delish dinner," she said as we left the restaurant. Then I took her to a movie. "Gee, that was a marvy movie," she said as we left the theater. And then I took her home. "Gee, I had a sensaysh time," she said as she bade me good night.

58     I went back to my room with a heavy heart. I had gravely underestimated the size of my task. This girl's lack of information was terrifying. Nor would it be enough merely to supply her with information. First she had to be taught to *think*. This loomed as a project of no small dimensions, and at first I was tempted to give her back to Petey. But then I got to thinking about her abundant physical charms and about the way she entered a room and the way she handled a knife and fork, and I decided to make an effort.

59     I went about it, as in all things, systematically. I gave her a course in logic. It happened that I, as a law student, was taking a course in logic myself, so I had all the facts at my finger tips. "Polly," I said to her when I picked her up on our next date, "tonight we are going over to the Knoll and talk."

60     "Oo, terrif," she replied. One thing I will say for this girl: you would go far to find another so agreeable.

61     We went to the Knoll, the campus trysting place, and we sat down under an old oak, and she looked at me expectantly. "What are we going to talk about?" she asked.

62     "Logic."

63     She thought this over for a minute and decided she liked it. "Magnif," she said.

64     "Logic," I said, clearing my throat, "is the science of thinking. Before we can think correctly, we must first learn to recognize the common fallacies of logic. These we will take up tonight."

65     "Wow-dow!" she cried, clapping her hands delightedly.

66    I winced, but went bravely on. "First let us examine the fallacy called Dicto Simpliciter."

67    "By all means," she urged, batting her lashes eagerly.

68    "Dicto Simpliciter means an argument based on an unqualified generalization. For example: Exercise is good. Therefore everybody should exercise."

69    "I agree," said Polly earnestly. "I mean exercise is wonderful. I mean it builds the body and everything."

70    "Polly," I said gently, "the argument is a fallacy. *Exercise is good* is an unqualified generalization. For instance, if you have heart disease, exercise is bad, not good. Many people are ordered by their doctors *not* to exercise. You must *qualify* the generalization. You must say exercise is *usually* good, or exercise is good *for most people*. Otherwise you have committed a Dicto Simpliciter. Do you see?"

71    "No," she confessed. "But this is marvy. Do more! Do more!"

72    "It will be better if you stop tugging at my sleeve," I told her, and when she desisted, I continued. "Next we take up a fallacy called Hasty Generalization. Listen carefully: You can't speak French. I can't speak French. Petey Burch can't speak French. I must therefore conclude that nobody at the University of Minnesota can speak French."

73    "Really?" said Polly, amazed. *"Nobody?"*

74    I hid my exasperation. "Polly, it's a fallacy. The generalization is reached too hastily. There are too few instances to support such a conclusion."

75    "Know any more fallacies?" she asked breathlessly. "This is more fun than dancing even."

76    I fought off a wave of despair. I was getting nowhere with this girl, absolutely nowhere. Still, I am nothing if not persistent. I continued. "Next comes Post Hoc. Listen to this: Let's not take Bill on our picnic. Every time we take him out with us, it rains."

77    "I know somebody just like that," she exclaimed. "A girl back home—Eula Becker, her name is. It never fails. Every single time we take her on a picnic—"

78    "Polly," I said sharply, "it's a fallacy. Eula Becker doesn't *cause* the rain. She has no connection with the rain. You are guilty of Post Hoc if you blame Eula Becker."

79    "I'll never do it again," she promised contritely. "Are you mad at me?"

80    I sighed deeply. "No, Polly, I'm not mad."

81    "Then tell me some more fallacies."

82    "All right. Let's try Contradictory Premises."

83    "Yes, let's," she chirped, blinking her eyes happily.

84    I frowned, but plunged ahead. "Here's an example of Contradictory Premises: If God can do anything, can He make a stone so heavy that He won't be able to lift it?"

85      "Of course," she replied promptly.

86      "But if He can do anything, He can lift the stone," I pointed out.

87      "Yeah," she said thoughtfully. "Well, then I guess He can't make the stone."

88      "But He can do anything," I reminded her.

89      She scratched her pretty, empty head. "I'm all confused," she admitted.

90      "Of course you are. Because when the premises of an argument contradict each other, there can be no argument. If there is an irresistible force, there can be no immovable object. If there is an immovable object, there can be no irresistible force. Get it?"

91      "Tell me some more of this keen stuff," she said eagerly.

92      I consulted my watch. "I think we'd better call it a night. I'll take you home now, and you go over all the things you've learned. We'll have another session tomorrow night."

93      I deposited her at the girls' dormitory, where she assured me that she had had a perfectly terrif' evening and I went glumly home to my room. Petey lay snoring in his bed, the raccoon coat huddled like a great hairy beast at his feet. For a moment I considered waking him and telling him that he could have his girl back. It seemed clear that my project was doomed to failure. The girl simply had a logic-proof head.

94      But then I reconsidered. I had wasted one evening; I might as well waste another. Who knew? Maybe somewhere in the extinct crater of her mind, a few embers still smoldered. Maybe somehow I could fan them into flame. Admittedly it was not a prospect fraught with hope, but I decided to give it one more try.

95      Seated under the oak the next evening I said, "Our first fallacy tonight is called Ad Misericordiam."

96      She quivered with delight.

97      "Listen closely," I said. "A man applies for a job. When the boss asks him what his qualifications are, he replies that he has a wife and six children at home, the wife is a helpless cripple, the children have nothing to eat, no clothes to wear, no shoes on their feet, there are no beds in the house, no coal in the cellar, and winter is coming."

98      A tear rolled down each of Polly's pink cheeks. "Oh, this is awful, awful," she sobbed.

99      "Yes, it's awful," I agreed, "but it's no argument. The man never answered the boss's question about his qualifications. Instead he appealed to the boss's sympathy. He committed the fallacy of Ad Misericordiam. Do you understand?"

100      "Have you got a handkerchief?" she blubbered.

101      I handed her a handkerchief and tried to keep from screaming while she wiped her eyes. "Next," I said in a carefully controlled tone, "we will discuss False Analogy. Here is an example: Students should be al-

lowed to look at their textbooks during examinations. After all, surgeons have X-rays to guide them during an operation, lawyers have briefs to guide them during a trial, carpenters have blueprints to guide them when they are building a house. Why, then, shouldn't students be allowed to look at their textbooks during an examination?"

102   "There now," she said enthusiastically, "is the most marvy idea I've heard in years."

103   "Polly," I said testily, "the argument is all wrong. Doctors, lawyers, and carpenters aren't taking a test to see how much they have learned, but students are. The situations are altogether different, and you can't make an analogy between them."

104   "I still think it's a good idea," said Polly.

105   "Nuts," I muttered. Doggedly I pressed on. "Next we'll try Hypothesis Contrary to Fact."

106   "Sounds yummy," was Polly's reaction.

107   "Listen: If Madame Curie had not happened to leave a photographic plate in a drawer with a chunk of pitchblende, the world today would not know about radium."

108   "True, true," said Polly, nodding her head. "Did you see the movie? Oh, it just knocked me out. That Walter Pidgeon is so dreamy. I mean he fractures me."

109   "If you can forget Mr. Pidgeon for a moment," I said coldly, "I would like to point out that the statement is a fallacy. Maybe Madame Curie would have discovered radium at some later date. Maybe somebody else would have discovered it. Maybe any number of things would have happened. You can't start with a hypothesis that is not true and then draw any supportable conclusions from it."

110   "They ought to put Walter Pidgeon in more pictures," said Polly. "I hardly ever see him any more."

111   One more chance, I decided. But just one more. There is a limit to what flesh and blood can bear. "The next fallacy is called Poisoning the Well."

112   "How cute!" she gurgled.

113   "Two men are having a debate. The first one gets up and says, 'My opponent is a notorious liar. You can't believe a word that he is going to say.' . . . Now, Polly, think. Think hard. What's wrong?"

114   I watched her closely as she knit her creamy brow in concentration. Suddenly a glimmer of intelligence—the first I had seen—came into her eyes. "It's not fair," she said with indignation. "It's not a bit fair. What chance has the second man got if the first man calls him a liar before he even begins talking?"

115   "Right!" I cried exultantly. "One hundred percent right. It's not fair. The first man has *poisoned the well* before anybody could drink from it. He has hamstrung his opponent before he could even start. . . . Polly, I'm proud of you."

116   "Pshaw," she murmured, blushing with pleasure.

117    "You see, my dear, these things aren't so hard. All you have to do is concentrate. Think—examine—evaluate. Come now, let's review everything we have learned."

118    "Fire away," she said with an airy wave of her hand.

119    Heartened by the knowledge that Polly was not altogether a cretin, I began a long, patient review of all I had told her. Over and over and over again I cited instances, pointed out flaws, kept hammering away without letup. It was like digging a tunnel. At first everything was work, sweat, and darkness. I had no idea when I would reach the light, or even *if* I would. But I persisted. I pounded and clawed and scraped, and finally I was rewarded. I saw a chink of light. And then the chink got bigger and the sun came pouring in and all was bright.

120    Five grueling nights this took, but it was worth it. I had made a logician out of Polly; I had taught her to think. My job was done. She was worthy of me at last. She was a fit wife for me, a proper hostess for my many mansions, a suitable mother for my well-heeled children.

121    It must not be thought that I was without love for this girl. Quite the contrary. Just as Pygmalion loved the perfect woman he had fashioned, so I loved mine. I determined to acquaint her with my feelings at our very next meeting. The time had come to change our relationship from academic to romantic.

122    "Polly," I said when next we sat beneath our oak, "tonight we will not discuss fallacies."

123    "Aw, gee," she said, disappointed.

124    "My dear," I said, favoring her with a smile, "we have now spent five evenings together. We have gotten along splendidly. It is clear that we are well matched."

125    "Hasty Generalization," said Polly brightly.

126    "I beg your pardon," said I.

127    "Hasty Generalization," she repeated. "How can you say that we are well matched on the basis of only five dates?"

128    I chuckled with amusement. The dear child had learned her lessons well. "My dear," I said, patting her hand in a tolerant manner, "five dates is plenty. After all, you don't have to eat a whole cake to know that it's good."

129    "False Analogy," said Polly promptly. "I'm not a cake. I'm a girl."

130    I chuckled with somewhat less amusement. The dear child had learned her lessons perhaps too well. I decided to change tactics. Obviously the best approach was a simple, strong, direct declaration of love. I paused for a moment while my massive brain chose the proper words. Then I began:

131    "Polly, I love you. You are the whole world to me, and the moon and the stars and the constellations of outer space. Please, my darling, say that you will go steady with me, for if you will not, life will be meaningless. I will languish. I will refuse my meals. I will wander the face of the earth, a shambling, hollow-eyed hulk."

132    There, I thought, folding my arms, that ought to do it.

133    "Ad Misericordiam," said Polly.

134    I ground my teeth. I was not Pygmalion; I was Frankenstein, and my monster had me by the throat. Frantically I fought back the tide of panic surging through me. At all costs I had to keep cool.

135    "Well, Polly," I said, forcing a smile, "you certainly have learned your fallacies."

136    "You're darn right," she said with a vigorous nod.

137    "And who taught them to you, Polly?"

138    "You did."

139    "That's right. So you do owe me something, don't you, my dear? If I hadn't come along you never would have learned about fallacies."

140    "Hypothesis Contrary to Fact," she said instantly.

141    I dashed perspiration from my brow. "Polly," I croaked, "you mustn't take all these things so literally. I mean this is just classroom stuff. You know that the things you learn in school don't have anything to do with life."

142    "Dicto Simpliciter," she said, wagging her finger at me playfully.

143    That did it. I leaped to my feet, bellowing like a bull. "Will you or will you not go steady with me?"

144    "I will not," she replied.

145    "Why not?" I demanded.

146    "Because this afternoon I promised Petey Burch that I would go steady with him."

147    I reeled back, overcome with the infamy of it. After he promised, after he made a deal, after he shook my hand! "The rat!" I shrieked, kicking up great chunks of turf. "You can't go with him, Polly. He's a liar. He's a cheat. He's a rat."

148    "Poisoning the Well," said Polly, "and stop shouting. I think shouting must be a fallacy too."

149    With an immense effort of will, I modulated my voice. "All right," I said. "You're a logician. Let's look at this thing logically. How could you choose Petey Burch over me? Look at me—a brilliant student, a tremendous intellectual, a man with an assured future. Look at Petey—a knothead, a jitterbug, a guy who'll never know where his next meal is coming from. Can you give me one logical reason why you should go steady with Petey Burch?"

150    "I certainly can," declared Polly. "He's got a raccoon coat."


**REVIEW**

**Content**

1. Characterize Dobie. Through what various means does Shulman "show" him to you? Then characterize Petey. Does your picture of Petey in any way heighten your picture of Dobie?

2. Note the stereotyped "beautiful but dumb" Polly—in a stereotyped situation. Then note how quickly she finds her wits when it becomes to her advantage to be smart. What does all this suggest to you about feminine role-playing? *Is* Polly dumb? If not, why has she acted dumb? Should she have done so?

## Rhetoric

3. Besides the clever plot, how does Shulman use style to make his story funny?
4. Shulman employs a wide variety of verbs to convey specific ways of speaking, inquiring, responding, and so on. Take any passage and find examples, noting the vivid effect of the language. Compare with what the result might have been had he simply written "he said," "she said," over and over in the lengthy dialogue. Shulman's use of adverbs with speaking verbs works in the same way; again, find examples.

## Projects

5. Work with a fallacy from Shulman's story and make up as many examples of that fallacy as you can in a given period of time, testing out your examples against classmates as you work (some fallacies can be *very* tricky!).
6. Select one fallacy that especially intrigues you and "explain" it through a written anecdote, thereby showing your own understanding of the fallacy.

# Newspeak

## GEORGE ORWELL

George Orwell was a pen name for Eric Blair (1903–1950), a British novelist and satirist. Orwell, born in India, educated in England, and later assigned by the British Civil Service back to India, was particularly sensitive concerning human beings' treating each other humanely. This concern is clearly and movingly reflected in his many essays, collected in such books as *Shooting an Elephant* (1950) and two other anthologies (1946 and 1953). The same sentiment, in a satirical vein, comes through in Orwell's two famous novels, *Animal Farm* (1945) and *1984* (1949). *1984*, a vivid portrayal of a future society in Oceania, where "Big Brother watches your every move," contains the following passage on Newspeak. Newspeak steadily reduces the vocabulary of the "old" society until the "language" left makes possible only very simplistic thinking.

1    Newspeak was the official language of Oceania and had been devised to meet the ideological needs of Ingsoc, or English Socialism. In the year 1984 there was not as yet anyone who used Newspeak as his sole means of communication, either in speech or writing. The leading articles in the *Times* were written in it, but this was a tour de force which could only be carried out by a specialist. It was expected that Newspeak would have finally superseded Oldspeak (or Standard English, as we should call it) by about the year 2050. Meanwhile it gained ground steadily, all Party members tending to use Newspeak words and grammatical constructions more and more in their everyday speech. The version in use in 1984, and embodied in the Ninth and Tenth Editions of the Newspeak dictionary, was a provisional one, and contained many superfluous words and archaic formations which were due to be suppressed later. It is with the final, perfected version, as embodied in the Eleventh Edition of the dictionary, that we are concerned here.

2    The purpose of Newspeak was not only to provide a medium of expression for the world-view and mental habits proper to the devotees of Ingsoc, but to make all other modes of thought impossible. It was intended that when Newspeak had been adopted once and for all and Oldspeak forgotten, a heretical thought—that is, a thought diverging from the principles of Ingsoc—should be literally unthinkable, at least so far as thought is dependent on words. Its vocabulary was so constructed as to give exact and often very subtle expression to every meaning that a Party member could properly wish to express, while excluding all other meanings and also the possibility of arriving at them by indirect methods. This was done partly by the invention of new words, but chiefly by eliminating undesirable words and by stripping such words as remained of unorthodox meanings, and so far as possible of all secondary meanings whatever. To give a simple example. The word *free* still existed in Newspeak, but it could only be used in such statements as "This dog is free from lice" or "This field is free from weeds." It could not be used in its old sense of "politically free" or "intellectually free," since political and intellectual freedom no longer existed even as concepts, and were therefore of necessity nameless. Quite apart from the suppression of definitely heretical words, reduction of vocabulary was regarded as an end in itself, and no word that could be dispensed with was allowed to survive. Newspeak was designated not to extend but to *diminish* the range of thought, and this purpose was indirectly assisted by cutting the choice of words down to a minimum.

3    Newspeak was founded on the English language as we now know it, though many Newspeak sentences, even when not containing newly

created words, would be barely intelligible to an English-speaker of our own day. Newspeak words were divided into three distinct classes, known as the A vocabulary, the B vocabulary (also called compound words), and the C vocabulary. It will be simpler to discuss each class separately, but the grammatical peculiarities of the language can be dealt with in the section devoted to the A vocabulary, since the same rules held good for all three categories.

## Words for Everyday Life

4    *The A vocabulary*   The A vocabulary consisted of the words needed for the business of everyday life—for such things as eating, drinking, working, putting on one's clothes, going up and down stairs, riding in vehicles, gardening, cooking, and the like. It was composed almost entirely of words that we already possess—words like *hit, run, dog, tree, sugar, house, field*–but in comparison with the present-day English vocabulary, their number was extremely small, while their meanings were far more rigidly defined. All ambiguities and shades of meaning had been purged out of them. So far as it could be achieved, a Newspeak word of this class was simply a staccato sound expressing *one* clearly understood concept. It would have been quite impossible to use the A vocabulary for literary purposes or for political or philosophical discussion. It was intended only to express simple, purposive thoughts, usually involving concrete objects or physical actions.

5    The grammar of Newspeak had two outstanding peculiarities. The first of these was an almost complete interchangeability between different parts of speech. Any word in the language (in principle this applied even to very abstract words such as *if* or *when*) could be used either as verb, noun, adjective, or adverb. Between the verb and the noun form, when they were of the same root, there was never any variation, this rule of itself involving the destruction of many archaic forms. The word *thought*, for example, did not exist in Newspeak. Its place was taken by *think*, which did duty for both noun and verb. No etymological principle was followed here; in some cases it was the original noun that was chosen for retention, in other cases the verb. Even where a noun and verb of kindred meaning were not etymologically connected, one or other of them was frequently suppressed. There was, for example, no such word as *cut*, its meaning being sufficiently covered by the noun-verb *knife*. Adjectives were formed by adding the suffix *-ful* to the noun-verb, and adverbs by adding *-wise*. Thus, for example, *speedful* meant "rapid" and *speedwise* meant "quickly." Certain of our present-day adjectives, such as *good, strong, big, black, soft*, were retained, but their total number was very small. There was little need for them, since almost any adjectival meaning could be arrived at by adding *-ful* to a noun

verb. None of the now-existing adverbs was retained, except for a very few already ending in *-wise;* the *-wise* termination was invariable. The word *well,* for example, was replaced by *goodwise.*

6    In addition, any word—this again applied in principle to every word in the language—could be negatived by adding the affix *un-,* or could be strengthened by the affix, *plus-,* or, for still greater emphasis, *doubleplus-.* Thus, for example, *uncold* meant "warm," while *pluscold* and *doublepluscold* meant, respectively, "very cold" and "superlatively cold." It was also possible, as in present-day English, to modify the meaning of almost any word by prepositional affixes such as *ante-, post-, up-, down-,* etc. By such methods it was found possible to bring about an enormous diminution of vocabulary. Given, for instance, the word *good,* there was no need for such a word as *bad,* since the required meaning was equally well—indeed, better—expressed by *ungood.* All that was necessary, in any case where two words formed a natural pair of opposites, was to decide which of them to suppress. *Dark,* for example, could be replaced by *unlight,* or *light* by *undark,* according to preference.

7    The second distinguishing mark of Newspeak grammar was its regularity. Subject to a few exceptions which are mentioned below, all inflections followed the same rules. Thus, in all verbs the preterite and the past participle were the same and ended in *-ed.* The preterite of *steal* was *stealed,* the preterite of *think* was *thinked,* and so on throughout the language, all such forms as *swam, gave, brought, spoke, taken,* etc., being abolished. All plurals were made by adding *-s* or *-es* as the case might be. The plurals of *man, ox, life* were *mans, oxes, lifes.* Comparisons of adjectives was invariably made by adding *-er, est (good, gooder, goodest),* irregular forms and the *more, most* information being suppressed.

8    The only classes of words that were still allowed to inflect irregularly were the pronouns, the relatives, the demonstrative adjectives, and the auxiliary verbs. All of these followed their ancient usage, except that *whom* had been scrapped as unnecessary, and the *shall, should* tenses had been dropped, all their uses being covered by *will* and *would.* There were also certain irregularities in word-forming arising out of the need for rapid and easy speech. A word which was difficult to utter, or was liable to be incorrectly heard, was held to be ipso facto a bad word; occasionally, therefore, for the sake of euphony, extra letters were inserted into a word or an archaic formation was retained. But this need made itself felt chiefly in connection with the B vocabulary. *Why* so great an importance was attached to ease of pronunciation will be made clear later in this essay.

## Words for Political Usage

9    *The B vocabulary*    The B vocabulary consisted of words that had been deliberately constructed for political purposes: words, that is to say,

which not only had in every case a political implication, but were intended to impose a desirable mental attitude upon the person using them. Without a full understanding of the principles of Ingsoc it was difficult to use these words correctly. In some cases they could be translated into Oldspeak, or even into words taken from the A vocabulary, but this usually demanded a long paraphrase and always involved the loss of certain overtones. The B words were a sort of verbal shorthand, often packing whole ranges of ideas into a few syllables, and at the same time more accurate and forcible than ordinary language.

10    The B words were in all cases compound words.[1] They consisted of two or more words, or portions of words, welded together in an easily pronounceable form. The resulting amalgam was always a noun-verb, and inflected according to the ordinary rules. To take a single example: the word *goodthink*, meaning, very roughly, "orthodoxy," or, if one chose to regard it as a verb, "to think in an orthodox manner." This inflected as follows: noun-verb, *goodthink;* past tense and past participle, *goodthinked;* present participle, *goodthinking;* adjective, *goodthinkful;* adverb, *goodthinkwise;* verbal noun, *goodthinker.*

11    The B words were not constructed on any etymological plan. The words of which they were made up could be any parts of speech, and could be placed in any order and mutilated in any way which made them easy to pronounce while indicating their derivation. In the word *crimethink* (thoughtcrime), for instance, the *think* came second, whereas in *thinkpol* (Thought Police) it came first, and in the latter word *police* had lost its second syllable. Because of the greater difficulty in securing euphony, irregular formations were commoner in the B vocabulary than in the A vocabulary. For example, the adjectival forms of *Minitrue, Minipax,* and *Miniluv* were, respectively, *Minitruthful, Minipeaceful,* and *Minilovely,* simply because *-trueful, -paxful,* and *-loveful* were slightly awkward to pronounce. In principle, however, all B words could inflect, and all inflected in exactly the same way.

12    Some of the B words had highly subtilized meanings, barely intelligible to anyone who had not mastered the language as a whole. Consider, for example, such a typical sentence from a *Times* leading article as *Oldthinkers unbellyfeel Ingsoc.* The shortest rendering that one could make of this in Oldspeak would be: "Those whose ideas were formed before the Revolution cannot have a full emotional understanding of the principles of English Socialism." But this is not an adequate translation. To begin with, in order to grasp the full meaning of the Newspeak sentence quoted above, one would have to have a clear idea of what is meant by *Ingsoc.* And, in addition, only a person thoroughly grounded in Ingsoc could appreciate the full force of the word *bellyfeel,* which implied a blind, enthusiastic acceptance difficult to imagine today; or of the word

---

[1]Compound words, such as *speakwrite,* were of course to be found in the A vocabulary, but these were merely convenient abbreviations and had no special ideological color.

*oldthink,* which was inextricably mixed up with the idea of wickedness and decadence. But the special function of certain Newspeak words, of which *oldthink* was one, was not so much to express meanings as to destroy them. These words, necessarily few in number, had had their meanings extended until they contained within themselves whole batteries of words which, as they were sufficiently covered by a single comprehensive term, could now be scrapped and forgotten. The greatest difficulty facing the compilers of the Newspeak dictionary was not to invent new words, but, having invented them, to make sure what they meant: to make sure, that is to say, what ranges of words they canceled by their existence.

## Purging of Heretical Words

13    As we have already seen in the case of the word *free,* words which had once borne a heretical meaning were sometimes retained for the sake of convenience, but only with the undesirable meanings purged out of them. Countless other words such as *honor, justice, morality, internationalism, democracy, science,* and *religion* had simply ceased to exist. A few blanket words covered them, and, in covering them, abolished them. All words grouping themselves round the concepts of liberty and equality, for instance, were contained in the single word *crimethink,* while all words grouping themselves round the concepts of objectivity and rationalism were contained in the single word *oldthink.* Greater precision would have been dangerous. What was required in a Party member was an outlook similar to that of the ancient Hebrew who knew, without knowing much else, that all nations other than his own worshiped "false gods." He did not need to know that these gods were called Baal, Osiris, Moloch, Ashtaroth, and the like; probably the less he knew about them the better for his orthodoxy. He knew Jehovah and the commandments of Jehovah; he knew, therefore, that all gods with other names or other attributes were false gods. In somewhat the same way, the Party member knew what constituted right conduct, and in exceedingly vague, generalized terms he knew what kinds of departure from it were possible. His sexual life, for example, was entirely regulated by the two Newspeak words *sexcrime* (sexual immorality) and *goodsex* (chastity). *Sexcrime* covered all sexual misdeeds whatever. It covered fornication, adultery, homosexuality, and other perversions, and, in addition, normal intercourse practiced for its own sake. There was no need to enumerate them separately, since they were all equally culpable, and, in principle, all punishable by death. In the C vocabulary, which consisted of scientific and technical words, it might be necessary to give specialized names to certain sexual aberrations, but the ordinary citizen had no need of them. He knew what was meant by *goodsex*—that is to say, normal intercourse between

man and wife, for the sole purpose of begetting children, and without physical pleasure on the part of the woman; all else was *sexcrime*. In Newspeak it was seldom possible to follow a heretical thought further than the perception that it *was* heretical; beyond that point the necessary words were nonexistent.

14    No word in the B vocabulary was ideologically neutral. A great many were euphemisms. Such words, for instance, as *joycamp* (forced-labor camp) or *Minipax* (Ministry of Peace, i.e., Ministry of War) meant almost the exact opposite of what they appeared to mean. Some words, on the other hand, displayed a frank and contemptuous understanding of the real nature of Oceanic society. An example was *prolefeed*, meaning the rubbishy entertainment and spurious news which the Party handed out to the masses. Other words, again, were ambivalent, having the connotation "good" when applied to the Party and "bad" when applied to its enemies. But in addition there were great numbers of words which at first sight appeared to be mere abbreviations and which derived their ideological color not from meaning but from their structure.

## Abbreviated Words

15    So far as it could be contrived, everything that had or might have political significance of any kind was fitted into the B vocabulary. The name of every organization, or body of people, or doctrine, or country, or institution, or public building, was invariably cut down into the familiar shape; that is, a single easily pronounced word with the smallest number of syllables that would preserve the original derivation. In the Ministry of Truth, for example, the Records Department, in which Winston Smith worked, was called *Recdep*, the Fiction Department was called *Ficdep*, the Teleprograms Department was called *Teledep*, and so on. This was done solely with the object of saving time. Even in the early decades of the twentieth century, telescoped words and phrases had been one of the characteristic features of political language; and it had been noticed that the tendency to use abbreviations of this kind was most marked in totalitarian countries and totalitarian organizations. Examples were such words as *Nazi, Gestapo, Comintern, Inprecorr, Agitprop*. In the beginning the practice had been adopted as it were instinctively, but in Newspeak it was used with a conscious purpose. It was perceived that in thus abbreviating a name one narrowed and subtly altered its meaning, by cutting out most of the associations that would otherwise cling to it. The words *Communist International*, for instance, call up a composite picture of universal human brotherhood, red flags, barricades, Karl Marx, and the Paris Commune. The word Comintern, on the other hand, suggests merely a tightly knit organization and a well-defined body of doctrine. It refers to something almost as easily recognized, and as

limited in purpose, as a chair or a table. *Comintern* is a word that can be uttered almost without taking thought, whereas *Communist International* is a phrase over which one is obliged to linger at least momentarily. In the same way, the associations called up by a word like *Minitrue* are fewer and more controllable than those called up by *Ministry of Truth*. This accounted not only for the habit of abbreviating whenever possible, but also for the almost exaggerated care that was taken to make every word easily pronounceable.

16    In Newspeak, euphony outweighed every consideration other than exactitude of meaning. Regularity of grammar was always sacrificed to it when it seemed necessary. And rightly so, since what was required, above all for political purposes, were short clipped words of unmistakable meaning which could be uttered rapidly and which roused the minimum of echoes in the speaker's mind. The words of the B vocabulary even gained in force from the fact that nearly all of them were very much alike. Almost invariably these words—*goodthink, Minipax, prolefeed, sexcrime, joycamp, Ingsoc, bellyfeel, thinkpol,* and countless others—were words of two or three syllables, with the stress distributed equally between the first syllable and the last. The use of them encouraged a gabbling style of speech, at once staccato and monotonous. And this was exactly what was aimed at. The intention was to make speech, and especially speech on any subject not ideologically neutral, as nearly as possible independent of consciousness. For the purposes of everyday life it was no doubt necessary, or sometimes necessary, to reflect before speaking, but a Party member called upon to make a political or ethical judgment should be able to spray forth the correct opinions as automatically as a machine gun spraying forth bullets. His training fitted him to do this, the language gave him an almost foolproof instrument, and the texture of the words, with their harsh sound and a certain willful ugliness which was in accord with the spirit of Ingsoc, assisted the process still further.

17    So did the fact of having very few words to choose from. Relative to our own, the Newspeak vocabulary was tiny, and new ways of reducing it were constantly being devised. Newspeak, indeed, differed from almost all other languages in that its vocabulary grew smaller instead of larger every year. Each reduction was a gain, since the smaller the area of choice, the smaller the temptation to take thought. Ultimately it was hoped to make articulate speech issue from the larynx without involving the higher brain centers at all. This aim was frankly admitted in the Newspeak word *duckspeak,* meaning "to quack like a duck." Like various other words in the B vocabulary, *duckspeak* was ambivalent in meaning. Provided that the opinions which were quacked out were orthodox ones, it implied nothing but praise, and when the *Times* referred to one of the orators of the Party as a *doubleplusgood duckspeaker* it was paying a warm and valued compliment.

## Scientific and Technical Words

18    *The C vocabulary*    The C vocabulary was supplementary to the others and consisted entirely of scientific and technical terms. These resembled the scientific terms in use today, and were constructed from the same roots, but the usual care was taken to define them rigidly and strip them of undesirable meanings. They followed the same grammatical rules as the words in the other two vocabularies. Very few of the C words had any currency either in everyday speech or in political speech. Any scientific worker or technician could find all the words he needed in the list devoted to his own specialty, but he seldom had more than a smattering of the words occurring in the other lists. Only a very few words were common to all lists, and there was no vocabulary expressing the function of Science as a habit of mind, or a method of thought, irrespective of its particular branches. There was, indeed, no word for "Science," any meaning that it could possibly bear being already sufficiently covered by the word *Ingsoc.*

19    From the foregoing account it will be seen that in Newspeak the expression of unorthodox opinions, above a very low level, was well-nigh impossible. It was of course possible to utter heresies of a very crude kind, a species of blasphemy. It would have been possible, for example, to say *Big Brother is ungood.* But this statement, which to an orthodox ear merely conveyed a self-evident absurdity, could not have been sustained by reasoned argument, because the necessary words were not available. Ideas inimical to Ingsoc could only be entertained in a vague wordless form, and could only be named in very broad terms which lumped together and condemned whole groups of heresies without defining them in doing so. One could, in fact, only use Newspeak for unorthodox purposes by illegitimately translating some of the words back into Oldspeak. For example, *All mans are equal* was a possible Newspeak sentence, but only in the same sense in which *All men are redhaired* is a possible Oldspeak sentence. It did not contain a grammatical error, but it expressed a palpable untruth, i.e., that all men are of equal size, weight, or strength. The concept of political equality no longer existed, and this secondary meaning had accordingly been purged out of the word *equal.* In 1984, when Oldspeak was still the normal means of communication, the danger theoretically existed that in using Newspeak words one might remember their original meanings. In practice it was not difficult for any person well grounded in *doublethink* to avoid doing this, but within a couple of generations even the possibility of such a lapse would have vanished. A person growing up with Newspeak as his sole language would no more know that *equal* had once had the secondary meaning of "politically equal," or that *free* had once meant "intellectually free," than, for instance, a person who had never heard of chess would be aware of the secondary meanings attached to *queen*

and *rook*. There would be many crimes and errors which it would be beyond his power to commit, simply because they were nameless and therefore unimaginable. And it was to be foreseen that with the passage of time the distinguishing characteristics of Newspeak would become more and more pronounced—its words growing fewer and fewer, their meanings more and more rigid, and the chance of putting them to improper uses always diminishing.

## History and Literature Rewritten

20    When Oldspeak had been once and for all superseded, the last link with the past would have been severed. History had already been rewritten, but fragments of the literature of the past survived here and there, imperfectly censored, and so long as one retained one's knowledge of Oldspeak it was possible to read them. In the future such fragments, even if they chanced to survive, would be unintelligible and untranslatable. It was impossible to translate any passage of Oldspeak into Newspeak unless it either referred to some technical process or some very simple everyday action, or was already orthodox (*goodthinkful* would be the Newspeak expression) in tendency. In practice this meant that no book written before approximately 1960 could be translated as a whole. Prerevolutionary literature could only be subjected to ideological translation—that is, alteration in sense as well as language. Take for example the well-known passage from the Declaration of Independence:

> We hold these truths to be self-evident, that all men are created equal, that they are endowed by their Creator with certain inalienable rights, that among these are life, liberty and the pursuit of happiness. That to secure these rights, Governments are instituted among men, deriving their powers from the consent of the governed. That whenever any form of Government becomes destructive of those ends, it is the right of the People to alter or abolish it, and to institute new Government . . .

21    It would have been quite impossible to render this into Newspeak while keeping to the sense of the original. The nearest one could come to doing so would be to swallow the whole passage up in the single word *crimethink*. A full translation could only be an ideological translation, whereby Jefferson's words would be changed into a panegyric on absolute government.

22    A good deal of the literature of the past was, indeed, already being transformed in this way. Considerations of prestige made it desirable to preserve the memory of certain historical figures, while at the same time bringing their achievements into line with the philosophy of Ingsoc. Various writers, such as Shakespeare, Milton, Swift, Byron, Dickens and some others were therefore in process of translation; when the task had been completed, their original writings, with all else that survived of

the literatire of the past, would be destroyed. These translations were a slow and difficult business and it was not expected that they would be finished before the first or second decade of the twenty-first century. There were also large quantities of merely utilitarian literature—indispensable technical manuals and the like—that had to be treated in the same way. It was chiefly in order to allow time for the preliminary work of translation that the final adoption of Newspeak had been fixed for so late a date as 2050.

## REVIEW

### Content

1. Discuss paragraph 2 of Orwell's explanation of Newspeak in the light of Farb's essay "Man at the Mercy of His Language," at the beginning of this section of the book.
2. Why does Orwell say, in paragraph 13, that "greater precision [than that of "blanket words" for certain ideological principles] would have been dangerous"? Did you foresee, at the end of paragraph 8, why *ease of pronunciation* was to be so important in Newspeak? Had the effect of *abbreviating* which Orwell discusses in paragraph 15 ever occurred to you before? Look up "doublethink" (paragraph 19) in the dictionary. Why would it *be possible* in Newspeak?

### Rhetoric

3. *1984*, Orwell's novel from which the above passage comes, is a satire. Does this part of the book sound *untrue* to you? If not, what does this suggest to you about effective satire?
4. Orwell is generally recognized as a master stylist of English prose. Can you see why? What about his writing especially appeals to you?

### Projects

5. Translate a paragraph of British or American fiction into Newspeak, making up the words you need as you go along, basing your creations as much as possible on the principles of Newspeak Orwell has explained. Some writers you might work with: Dickens, Emily Brontë, Hawthorne, Hemingway, Fielding, Willa Cather. What happens to the original as you translate?
6. Explain in a paper the rationale behind and the implications of one of the following statements about Newspeak:
   a. "Ultimately it was hoped to make articulate speech issue from the larynx without involving the higher brain centers at all."
   b. "There was, indeed, no word for 'Science,' any meaning that it could possibly bear being already sufficiently covered by the word *Ingsoc*."

c. "When Oldspeak had been once and for all superseded, the last link with the past would have been severed. History had already been rewritten."

OR Follow the same instructions in developing this sentence from *The Adjusted American*, by Snell and Gail Putney: "A [person] is not free to do that which [he/she] cannot imagine." OR Write a poem in Newspeak.

# 7
# The Arts
# and
# Creativity

# Where Do Those Bright Ideas Come From?

## LANCELOT LAW WHYTE

Lancelot Law Whyte (1896–   ) is a British philosopher as well as an engineer, scientist, and social scientist, especially interested in the creative process. That interest is reflected in his books—among them, *Archimedes, or the Future of Physics* (1927), *The Next Development in Man* (1948), and *Aspects of Form* (1954). In the excerpt below, from an essay first published in *Harper's Magazine* in July, 1951, Whyte tells the reader how Wagner conceived of the prelude to "The Rhinegold" in his great operatic cycle of *The Ring of the Nibelung;* how the French mathematician Poincaré developed the mathematical method known today as Fuchsian functions; and how Descartes came upon his famous declaration, "Cogito ergo sum" ("I think, therefore I am").

> . . . as imagination bodies forth
> The forms of things unknown, . . .
>
> —A MIDSUMMER NIGHT'S DREAM

1    There are few experiences quite so satisfactory as getting a good idea. You've had a problem, you've thought about it till you were tired, forgotten it and perhaps slept on it, and then flash! when you weren't thinking about it suddenly the answer has come to you, as a gift from the gods. You're pleased with it, and feel good. It may not be right, but at least you can try it out.

2    Of course all ideas don't come like that, but the interesting thing is that so many do, particularly the most important ones. They burst into the mind, glowing with the heat of creation. How they do it is a mystery. Psychology does not yet understand even the ordinary processes of conscious thought, but the emergence of new ideas by a "leap in thought," as Dewey put it, is particularly intriguing, because they

must have come from somewhere. For the moment let us assume that they come from the "unconscious." This is reasonable, for the psychologists use this term to describe mental processes which are unknown to the subject, and creative thought consists precisely in what was unknown becoming known.

3   We have all experienced this sudden arrival of a happy idea, but it is easiest to examine it in the great creative figures, many of whom experienced it in an intensified form and have put it on record in their memoirs and letters. One can draw examples from genius in any realm, from religious mysticism, philosophy, and literature to art and music, and even in mathematics, science, and technical invention, though these are often thought to rest solely on logic and experiment. It seems that all truly creative activity depends in some degree on these signals from the unconscious, and the more highly intuitive the person, the sharper and more dramatic the signals become.

4   Here, for example, is Richard Wagner conceiving the prelude to "Rhinegold," as told by Wagner himself and recounted by Newman in his biography. Wagner had been occupied with the general idea of the "Ring" for several years, and for many weary months had been struggling to make a start with the actual composition. On September 4, 1863, he reached Spezia sick with dysentery, crawled to a hotel, could not sleep for noise without and fever within, took a long walk the next day, and in the afternoon flung himself on a couch intending to sleep. And then at last the miracle happened for which his subconscious mind had been crying out for so many months. Falling into a trance-like state, he suddenly felt, he says, as though he were sinking in a mighty flood of water:

> The rush and roar soon took musical shape within my brain as the chord of E-flat major, surging incessantly in broken chords. . . . Yet the pure triad of E-flat major never changed, but seemed by its steady persistence to impart infinite significance to the element in which I was sinking. I awoke from my half-sleep in terror, feeling as though the waves were rushing high above my head. I at once recognized that the orchestral prelude to the "Rhinegold," which for a long time I must have carried about within me, yet had never been able to fix definitely, had at last come to being within me; and I quickly understood the very essence of my own nature: the stream of life was not to flow to me from without, but from within.

5   In this example, which is exceptional only in the violence of the emotions, the conscious mind at the moment of creation knew nothing of the actual processes by which the solution was found. As a contrast we may take a famous story: the discovery by Henri Poincaré, the great French mathematician, of a new mathematical method called the Fuchsian functions. For here we see the conscious mind, in a person of the highest ability, actually watching the unconscious at work, if that paradox may be allowed. Poincaré describes how he came to write his first treatise on these functions.

For a fortnight I had been attempting to prove that there could not be any function analogous to what I have since called the Fuchsian functions. I was at that time very ignorant. Every day I sat down at my table and spent an hour or two trying a great number of combinations, and I arrived at no result. One night I took some black coffee, contrary to my custom, and was unable to sleep. A host of ideas kept surging in my head; I could almost feel them jostling one another, until two of them coalesced, so to speak, to form a stable combination. When morning came, I had established the existence of one class of Fuchsian functions. . . . I had only to verify the results, which took only a few hours.

6    While the Wagner story illustrates the sudden explosion of a new conception into consciousness, in this one we see the conscious mind observing the new combinations being formed in that part of the mind whose operations are normally beyond the range of conscious attention. A third type of creative experience is exemplified by the dreams which came to Descartes at the age of twenty-three and determined the path he was to follow for the rest of his life. Descartes tells how he had vainly searched for certainty, first in the world of books, and then in the world of men, and how in a triple dream on November 10, 1619, he made the crucial discovery that he could only find certainty in his own thoughts, *cogito ergo sum.* This dream filled him with intense religious enthusiasm, because it had brought to him the "simple and fertile idea, all sparkling with angelic luster" (Maritain), which provided the foundation of the "admirable science" which it was his mission to create. Freud classified this dream as one of those whose content is very close to conscious thought.

7    Wagner's, Poincaré's, and Descartes' experiences are representative of countless others in every realm of culture. The unconscious is certainly the source of instinctive activity and therefore sometimes of conflict with the demands of reason, as Freud emphasized. But in creative thought the unconscious is responsible, not for conflict, but for the production of new organized forms from relatively disorganized elements.

## REVIEW

### Content

1. Did you recognize from your own experience what Whyte is talking about in paragraph 1?
2. Discuss the last two sentences of paragraph 7, contrasting the implications of their content.

### Rhetoric

3. What does Whyte achieve by speaking directly to you as reader in paragraph 1?
4. Is Whyte's commentary on the psychological processes involved in creativity, in paragraph 2, adequate to introduce the discussion that

follows? Would he have gained or lost effect had he attempted a
fuller explanation here?

**Projects**

5. Write a paper based on your answer to 1 above. Recount the experience as vividly as you can.
6. If you are not as creative as you would like to be, try to think through
*why*, what obstacles you may place in your own way, in what ways
you may not be as open to creative thought as you might be; and
write a paper based on this thinking through. Read further in your
college library on the creative process before you write, if you like.

# How Do You
# Know It's Good?

## MARYA MANNES

Marya Mannes (1904–    ), a native New Yorker, has been observing and
commenting candidly and concisely upon the American scene for a number
of years. She offers her cogent remarks both through magazine articles and
on the lecture circuit. Her most recent major publications include an
autobiographical volume, *Out of My Time* (1971); *Uncoupling* (1972),
about divorce and related subjects; and *Last Rights* (1973), about dying
and the right to die with dignity. In the following essay, Mannes, herself
brought up in a cultured household, deplores the failure of contemporary
art critics to express and uphold standards—and what she sees as the consequent decline of the arts in this country into anarchy. She then encourages
individual responsibility for establishing artistic standards.

1    Suppose there were no critics to tell us how to react to a picture, a
play, or a new composition of music. Suppose we wandered innocent
as the dawn into an art exhibition of unsigned paintings. By what
standards, by what values would we decide whether they were good
or bad, talented or untalented, successes or failures? How can we ever
know that what we think is right?

2        For the last fifteen or twenty years the fashion in criticism or appreciation of the arts has been to deny the existence of any valid criteria

and to make the words "good" or "bad" irrelevant, immaterial, and inapplicable. There is no such thing, we are told, as a set of standards, first acquired through experience and knowledge and later imposed on the subject under discussion. This has been a popular approach, for it relieves the critic of the responsibility of judgment and the public of the necessity of knowledge. It pleases those resentful of disciplines, it flatters the empty-minded by calling them open-minded, it comforts the confused. Under the banner of democracy and the kind of equality which our forefathers did *not* mean, it says, in effect, "Who are you to tell us what is good or bad?" This is the same cry used so long and so effectively by the producers of mass media who insist that it is the public, not they, who decides what it wants to hear and see, and that for a critic to say that *this* program is bad and *this* program is good is purely a reflection of personal taste. Nobody recently has expressed this philosophy more succinctly than Dr. Frank Stanton, the highly intelligent president of CBS television. At a hearing before the Federal Communications Commission, this phrase escaped him under questioning: "One man's mediocrity is another man's good program."

3    There is no better way of saying "No values are absolute." There is another important aspect to this philosophy of *laissez faire:* It is the fear, in all observers of all forms of art, of guessing wrong. This fear is well come by, for who has not heard of the contemporary outcries against artists who later were called great? Every age has its arbiters who do not grow with their times, who cannot tell evolution from revolution or the difference between frivolous faddism, amateurish experimentation, and profound and necessary change. Who wants to be caught *flagrante delicto* with an error of judgment as serious as this? It is far safer, and certainly easier, to look at a picture or a play or a poem and to say "This is hard to understand, but it may be good," or simply to welcome it as a new form. The word "new"—in our country especially—has magical connotations. What is new must be good; what is old is probably bad, and if a critic can describe the new in language that nobody can understand, he's safer still. If he has mastered the art of saying nothing with exquisite complexity, nobody can quote him later as saying anything.

## The Audience's Responsibility

4    But all these, I maintain, are forms of abdication from the responsibility of judgment. In creating, the artist commits himself; in appreciating, you have a commitment of your own. For after all, it is the audience which makes the arts. A climate of appreciation is essential to its flowering, and the higher the expectations of the public, the better the performance of the artist. Conversely, only a public ill-served by its critics could have accepted as art and literature so much in these last years

that has been neither. If anything goes, everything goes; and at the bottom of the junkpile lie the discarded standards too.

5    But what are these standards? How do you get them? How do you know they're the right ones? How can you make a clear pattern out of so many intangibles, including that greatest one, the very private I?

6    Well for one thing, it's fairly obvious that the more you read and see and hear, the more equipped you'll be to practice that art of association which is at the basis of all understanding and judgment. The more you live and the more you look, the more aware you are of a consistent pattern—as universal as the stars, as the tides, as breathing, as night and day—underlying everything. I would call this pattern and this rhythm an order. Not order—*an* order. Within it exists an incredible diversity of forms. Without it lies chaos. I would further call this order— this incredible diversity held within one pattern— health. And I would call chaos—the wild cells of destruction—sickness. It is in the end up to you to distinguish between the diversity that is health and the chaos that is sickness, and you can't do this without a process of association that can link a bar of Mozart with the corner of a Vermeer painting, or a Stravinsky score with a Picasso abstraction; or that can relate an aggressive act with a Franz Kline painting and a fit of coughing with a John Cage composition.

7    There is no accident in the fact that certain expressions of art live for all time and that others die with the moment, and although you may not always define the reasons, you can ask the questions. What does an artist say that is timeless; how does he say it? How much is fashion, how much is merely reflection? Why is Sir Walter Scott so hard to read now, and Jane Austen not? Why is baroque right for one age and too effulgent for another?

8    Can a standard of craftsmanship apply to art of all ages, or does each have its own, and different, definitions? You may have been aware, inadvertently, that craftsmanship has become a dirty word these years because, again, it implies standard—something done well or done badly. The result of this convenient avoidance is a plenitude of actors who can't project their voices, singers who can't phrase their songs, poets who can't communicate emotion, and writers who have no vocabulary— not to speak of painters who can't draw. The dogma now is that craftsmanship gets in the way of expression. You can do better if you don't know *how* you do it, let alone *what* you're doing.

## Contemporary Painting

9    I think it is time you helped reverse this trend by trying to rediscover craft: the command of the chosen instrument, whether it is a brush, a word, or a voice. When you begin to detect the difference between freedom and sloppiness, between serious experimentation and ego-

therapy, between skill and slickness, between strength and violence, you are on your way to separating the sheep from the goats, a form of segregation denied us for quite a while. All you need to restore it is a small bundle of standards and a Geiger counter that detects fraud, and we might begin our tour of the arts in an area where both are urgently needed: contemporary painting.

10    I don't know what's worse: to have to look at acres of bad art to find the little good, or to read what the critics say about it all. In no other field of expression has so much double-talk flourished, so much confusion prevailed, and so much nonsense been circulated: further evidence of the close interdependence between the arts and the critical climate they inhabit. It will be my pleasure to share with you some of this double-talk so typical of our times.

11    Item one: preface for a catalogue of an abstract painter:

12    "Time-bound meditation experiencing a life; sincere with plastic piety at the threshold of hallowed arcana; a striving for pure ideation giving shape to inner drive; formalized patterns where neural balances reach a fiction." End of quote. Know what this artist paints like now?

13    Item two: a review in the *Art News:*

14    ". . . a weird and disparate assortment of material, but the monstrosity which bloomed into his most recent cancer of aggregations is present in some form everywhere. . . ." Then, later, "A gluttony of things and processes terminated by a glorious constipation."

15    Item three, same magazine, review of an artist who welds automobile fragments into abstract shapes:

16    "Each fragment . . . is made an extreme of human exasperation, torn at and fought all the way, and has its rightness of form as if by accident. *Any technique that requires order or discipline would just be the human ego.* No, these must be egoless, uncontrolled, undesigned and different enough to give you a bang—fifty miles an hour around a telephone pole. . . ."

17    "Any technique that requires order or discipline would just be the human ego." What does he mean—"just be"? What are they really talking about? Is this journalism? Is it criticism? Or is it that other convenient abdication from standards of performance and judgment practiced by so many artists and critics that they, like certain writers who deal only in sickness and depravity, "reflect the chaos about them"? Again, whose chaos? Whose depravity?

18    I had always thought that the prime function of art was to create order *out* of chaos—again, not the order of neatness or rigidity or convention or artifice, but the order of clarity by which one will and one vision could draw the essential truth out of apparent confusion. I still do. It is not enough to use parts of a car to convey the brutality of the machine. This is as slavishly representative, and just as easy, as arranging dried flowers under glass to convey nature.

19    Speaking of which, i.e., the use of real materials (burlap, old gloves,

bottletops) in lieu of pigment, this is what one critic had to say about an exhibition of Assemblage at the Museum of Modern Art last year:

20   "Spotted throughout the show are indisputable works of art, accounting for a quarter or even half of the total display. But the remainder are works of non-art, anti-art, and art substitutes that are the aesthetic counterparts of the social deficiencies that land people in the clink on charges of vagrancy. These aesthetic bankrupts . . . have no legitimate ideological roof over their heads and not the price of a square intellectual meal, much less a spiritual sandwich, in their pockets."

21   I quote these words of John Canaday of *The New York Times* as an example of the kind of criticism which puts responsibility to an intelligent public above popularity with an intellectual coterie. Canaday has the courage to say what he thinks and the capacity to say it clearly: two qualities notably absent from his profession.

## Music, Poetry, and Drama

22   Next to art, I would say that appreciation and evaluation in the field of music is the most difficult. For it is rarely possible to judge a new composition at one hearing only. What seems confusing or fragmented at first might well become clear and organic a third time. Or it might not. The only salvation here for the listener is, again, an instinct born of experience and association which allows him to separate intent from accident, design from experimentation, and pretense from conviction. Much of contemporary music is, like its sister art, merely a reflection of the composer's own fragmentation: an absorption in self and symbols at the expense of communication with others. The artist, in short, says to the public: If you don't understand this, it's because you're dumb. I maintain that you are not. You may have to go part way or even halfway to meet the artist, but if you must go the whole way, it's his fault, not yours. Hold fast to that. And remember it too when you read new poetry, that estranged sister of music.

23   "A multitude of causes, unknown to former times, are now acting with a combined force to blunt the discriminating powers of the mind, and, unfitting it for all voluntary exertion, to reduce it to a state of almost savage torpor. The most effective of these causes are the great national events which are daily taking place and the increasing accumulation of men in cities, where the uniformity of their occupations produces a craving for extraordinary incident, which the rapid communication of intelligence hourly gratifies. To this tendency of life and manners, the literature and theatrical exhibitions of the country have conformed themselves."

24   This startingly applicable comment was written in the year 1800 by William Wordsworth in the preface to his "Lyrical Ballads"; and it has

been cited by Edwin Muir in his recently published book, *The Estate of Poetry*. Muir states that poetry's effective range and influence have diminished alarmingly in the modern world. He believes in the inherent and indestructible qualities of the human mind and the great and permanent objects that act upon it, and suggests that the audience will increase when "poetry loses what obscurity is left in it by attempting greater themes, for great themes have to be stated clearly." If you keep that firmly in mind and resist, in Muir's words, "the vast dissemination of secondary objects that isolate us from the natural world," you have gone a long way toward equipping yourself for the examination of any work of art.

25    When you come to theatre, in this extremely hasty tour of the arts, you can approach it on two different levels. You can bring to it anticipation and innocence, giving yourself up, as it were, to the life on the stage and reacting to it emotionally, if the play is good, or listlessly, if the play is boring; a part of the audience organism that expresses its favor by silence or laughter and its disfavor by coughing and rustling. Or you can bring to it certain critical faculties that may heighten, rather than diminish, your enjoyment.

26    You can ask yourselves whether the actors are truly in their parts or merely projecting themselves; whether the scenery helps or hurts the mood; whether the playwright is honest with himself, the characters, and you. Somewhere along the line you can learn to distinguish between the true creative act and the false arbitrary gesture; between fresh observation and stale cliché; between the avant-garde play that is pretentious drivel and the avant-garde play that finds new ways to say old truths.

## Keys to Judgment

27    Purpose and craftsmanship—end and means—these are the keys to your judgment in all the arts. What is this painter trying to say when he slashes a broad band of black across a white canvas and lets the edges dribble down? Is it a statement of violence? Is it a self-portrait? If it is *one* of these, has he made you believe it? Or is this a gesture of the ego or a form of therapy? If it shocks you, what does it shock you into?

28    And what of this tight little painting of bright flowers in a vase? Is the painter saying anything new about flowers? Is it different from a million other canvases of flowers? Has it any life, any meaning, beyond its statement? Is there any pleasure in its forms or texture? The question is not whether a thing is abstract or representational, whether it is "modern" or conventional. The question, inexorably, is whether it is good. And this is a decision which only you, on the basis of instinct, experience, and association, can make for yourself. It takes independence and cour-

age. It involves, moreover, the risk of wrong decision and the humility, after the passage of time, of recognizing it as such. As we grow and change and learn, our attitudes can change too, and what we once thought obscure or "difficult" can later emerge as coherent and illuminating. Entrenched prejudices, obdurate opinions are as sterile as no opinions at all.

29    Yet standards there are, timeless as the universe itself. And when you have committed yourself to them, you have acquired a passport to that elusive but immutable realm of truth. Keep it with you in the forests of bewilderment. And never be afraid to speak up.


## REVIEW

### Content

1. Do you agree with sentences 2, 3, and 4 in paragraph 4?
2. Discuss paragraph 6, along with the first sentence in paragraph 7, and the following in paragraph 22: "The artist . . . not yours."

### Rhetoric

3. What does Mannes achieve by making her entire introductory paragraph a series of questions?
4. A device which Mannes uses often and with considerable effect is parallel structure (equal elements equally expressed). Analyze paragraph 6 for examples of this device.

### Projects

5. Visit some department of your college concerned with the arts—painting, sculpture, music, poetry, drama—and ask to see, hear, or read something very modern. Then, write two brief reviews of the experience: the first like paragraphs 12, 14, 16 above, and a second in which you try to be as clear and helpful as possible to someone who has not shared your experience. Be honest in both reviews.
6. If you go to see avant garde films, write a review of one. OR Try your hand at satirizing such a film, if you prefer.

# Architecture in Akron

## ADA LOUISE HUXTABLE

Ada Louise Huxtable is architecture critic for *The New York Times*. Her critiques are models of good writing, as she delineates detail after detail of a structure in clear, succinct, and vivid prose. Her books include *Classic New York* (1964) and *Will They Ever Finish Bruckner Boulevard?* (1970). One of Huxtable's central concerns, as she considers a building, is what should ever be a central concern of architecture itself, the question of form and function: Does the building fulfill the purpose for which it is intended? That concern is demonstrated in the following piece about a performing arts hall in the Midwest.

1  They got it all together in Akron. The trials and errors of a 15-year performing arts center building boom in the United States have finally produced a superb structure—the Edwin J. Thomas Performing Arts Hall, which had its gala opening last week.

2  It happened in Akron, not in New York, where the performance halls of Lincoln Center look, and are, provincial by comparison, or in any of the cities that call themselves the country's cultural capitals. This is a building of which any world capital could be proud.

. . .

3  It is a big, as well as an expensive, building, providing a 3,000-seat auditorium. Like other big performance halls in smaller cities—Greater Akron numbers about 250,000—it is designed as a multi-use, multi-form facility.

## Counterweights as Sculpture

4  A striking hung ceiling of steel sections that move in mitered catenary curves can cut off parts of the house to make it serve smaller audiences of 2,400 or 900 people. It takes an incredibly short 15 minutes to make one of these changes; we know, we watched. The cables from which the ceiling is hung are counterweighted to lighten it, so that the 44-ton ceiling is balanced by 47 tons of weights, which hang, as 27 massive

chrome-plated steel cylinders, in the soaring lobby. Their polished geometric forms, suspended in 90 feet of space, surpass any sculpture.

5   The building is poured concrete, its weighty mass lightened by entrance walls of glass on two sides, butted and joined without metal, in the European fashion. This crystalline delicacy juxtaposed to solid walls makes a facade of great visual elegance, in which boldness and delicacy strike a breathtaking balance.

6   From the outside, the angled structure—the result of an asymmetrical plan—appears to be folded into terraced steps and plantings which lift people from a foundation below to entrances on several levels above, with parking tucked underneath. Nothing is static. The upper and lower plazas, banked tiers of flowers and patterns of movement, turn this architecture into a multidimensional solution through extremely skillful site planning and the treatment of the act of entrance as a complex and ceremonial sequence of spatial experiences.

7   Inside, the lobbies are also a spatial experience. This is just about the handsomest public area to be seen anywhere, barring some not-quite-appropriate furniture. Three continuous lobbies flank the auditorium and stage house, and they can accommodate all 3,000 occupants of the hall at one time.

8   The focus of this splendid space is the clerestory-lit main lobby that rises to the full height of the 90-foot wall which contains and insulates the whole complex against the bordering railroad. Bridges, balconies and stairs lead to this great room from orchestra, grand tier and balcony levels, and the movement of people is like an architectural fugue. Dominating the space are the shining giant cylinders of the counterweights with their intricate pattern of wires and pulleys. A lower lobby continues down steps, under the grand tier, and up again to open full height on the other side.

## Sensitively Controlled Space

9   It is space—functional and formal space sensitively controlled—that is the chief ingredient here; beyond that there is the restrained effect of white plaster, discreetly used pale gumwood facing, and vermilion red (not "theater" red) carpeting that sends a warm reflective glow to all surfaces, including the splendid steel "sculpture." See this play of scale, movement and color and sense the public and esthetic presence here, and then think of the big, banal box that stretches across the Kennedy Center's halls as a public foyer for depressing contrast. And if you haven't had enough, think of the kitsch of New York's Metropolitan Opera House.

10   Inside, the auditorium breaks many rules. It is fanshaped, rather than the more conventional rectangle, a 30-degree hall in which no seat is

more than 132 feet from the stage. How the far side seats will work in terms of vision and intimacy for drama is still to be tested. There is a noticeable lack of traditional acoustic treatment of broken surfaces, wood and fabric.

11 What one sees is a three-level sweep of vermilion seats in so-called "continental" arrangement, topped by a floating abstraction of a ceiling consisting of 3,700 steel sections hung invisibly on 20 miles of wire and cable in natural catenary curves, looking like an undulating black-veined white mosaic. Computers control the movement that cuts off the hall's back sections. Lighting, indirect except over the stage, shines up from balcony and tier edges, reflecting softly from the irregular ceiling.

12 Below the patterned white ceiling, and surrounding the vermilion seats, are plain, straight, undecorated walls of a soft brownish tone, and what one does not see is everything that goes on behind them. They are made of heavy bronze mesh screen, through which sound travels. In back of this screen are the curves, baffles, absorptive surfaces and adjustable felt curtains that respond to computerized directions for "tuning." The stage walls, of the same composition, are moveable.

13 It must be noted that there is not one "glamour" cliché, and this is a genuinely glamorous house. There are none of the expected touches of "theater" nostalgia; no one has fruited it up with mock-modern chandeliers or gift-shop crystal and colored it conventional red. This technique never works anyway; the result always has a cheesiness that looks second-rate even when the stuff has been turned out by royal factories and supplied by government gift. Elegance is not a handful of beads or gold trim. It is drama and sensuosity, as practiced here.

## REVIEW

### Content

1. Huxtable refers, in paragraph 3, to Thomas Hall as a "multi-use, multi-form facility." Most of the rest of her critique concerns itself with the hall's form. From her description of the form, can you envision the hall's adaptability to a variety of uses?
2. Discuss paragraph 13. Do you agree with Huxtable here? If not, how do *you* define "elegance"?

### Rhetoric

3. Can you *visualize* Thomas Hall from Huxtable's descriptive prose? Note her attention to very specific detail. How does she make verbs help you see what she is describing in sentence 1 of paragraph 6? Note the last sentence of paragraph 5 for Huxtable's sense of style.
4. Does Huxtable make you want to see Thomas Hall?

**Projects**

5. Closely observe some building on your campus and then write either a positive or a negative critique of its *form*.      OR
6. Study some building on your campus and review it in terms of the appropriateness of its form, exterior and/or interior, to its intended function.

# Listening to Music

## AARON COPLAND

Aaron Copland (1900–   ) is known as composer and conductor, and as teacher and lecturer about music. A distinctively modern composer, Copland is responsible for the music for three popular contemporary ballets: *Appalachian Spring, Billy the Kid,* and *Rodeo.* He has also written the musical scores for several films. The titles of Copland's books reflect his interest in making music accessible to us all: *What To Listen for in Music* (1939), *Our New Music* (1941), *Music and Imagination* (1952). The excerpt below is from the 1957 revised edition of the first title. Here Copland encourages the listener toward responding to music on three planes: the sensuous (the plane of sound); the expressive (the plane of meaning); and the sheerly musical (the plane of "the notes themselves").

1   We all listen to music according to our separate capacities. But, for the sake of analysis, the whole listening process may become clearer if we break it up into its component parts, so to speak. In a certain sense we all listen to music on three separate planes. For lack of a better terminology, one might name these: (1) the sensuous plane, (2) the expressive plane, (3) the sheerly musical plane. The only advantage to be gained from mechanically splitting up the listening process into these hypothetical planes is the clearer view to be had of the way in which we listen.

## The Sensuous Plane

2      The simplest way of listening to music is to listen for the sheer pleasure of the musical sound itself. That is the sensuous plane. It is the

plane on which we hear music without thinking, without considering it in any way. One turns on the radio while doing something else and absentmindedly bathes in the sound. A kind of brainless but attractive state of mind is engendered by the mere sound appeal of the music.

3    You may be sitting in a room reading this book. Imagine one note struck on the piano. Immediately that one note is enough to change the atmosphere of the room—proving that the sound element in music is a powerful and mysterious agent, which it would be foolish to deride or belittle.

4    The surprising thing is that many people who consider themselves qualified music lovers abuse that plane in listening. They go to concerts in order to lose themselves. They use music as a consolation or an escape. They enter an ideal world where one doesn't have to think of the realities of everyday life. Of course they aren't thinking about the music either. Music allows them to leave it, and they go off to a place to dream, dreaming because of and apropos of the music yet never quite listening to it.

5    Yes, the sound appeal of music is a potent and primitive force, but you must not allow it to usurp a disproportionate share of your interest. The sensuous plane is an important one in music, a very important one, but it does not constitute the whole story.

6    There is no need to digress further on the sensuous plane. Its appeal to every normal human being is self-evident. There is, however, such a thing as becoming more sensitive to the different kinds of sound stuff as used by various composers. For all composers do not use that sound stuff in the same way. Don't get the idea that the value of music is commensurate with its sensuous appeal or that the loveliest sounding music is made by the greatest composer. If that were so, Ravel would be a greater creator than Beethoven. The point is that the sound element varies with each composer, that his usage of sound forms an integral part of his style and must be taken into account when listening. The reader can see, therefore, that a more conscious approach is valuable even on this primary plane of music listening.

## The Expressive Plane

7    The second plane on which music exists is what I have called the expressive one. Here, immediately, we tread on controversial ground. Composers have a way of shying away from any discussion of music's expressive side. Did not Stravinsky himself proclaim that his music was an "object," a "thing," with a life of its own, and with no other meaning than its own purely musical existence? This intransigent attitude of Stravinsky's may be due to the fact that so many people have tried to read different meanings into so many pieces. Heaven knows it is difficult

enough to say precisely what it is that a piece of music means, to say it definitely, to say it finally so that everyone is satisfied with your explanation. But that should not lead one to the other extreme of denying to music the right to be "expressive."

8    My own belief is that all music has an expressive power, some more and some less, but that all music has a certain meaning behind the notes and that that meaning behind the notes constitutes, after all, what the piece is saying, what the piece is about. This whole problem can be stated quite simply by asking, "Is there a meaning to music?" My answer to that would be, "Yes." And "Can you state in so many words what the meaning is?" My answer to that would be, "No." Therein lies the difficulty.

9    Simple-minded souls will never be satisfied with the answer to the second of these questions. They always want music to have a meaning, and the more concrete it is the better they like it. The more the music reminds them of a train, a storm, a funeral, or any other familiar conception the more expressive it appears to be to them. This popular idea of music's meaning—stimulated and abetted by the usual run of musical commentator—should be discouraged wherever and whenever it is met. One timid lady once confessed to me that she suspected something seriously lacking in her appreciation of music because of her inability to connect it with anything definite. That is getting the whole thing backward, of course.

10    Still, the question remains, How close should the intelligent music lover wish to come to pinning a definite meaning to any particular work? No closer than a general concept, I should say. Music expresses, at different moments, serenity or exuberance, regret or triumph, fury or delight. It expresses each of these moods, and many others, in a numberless variety of subtle shadings and differences. It may even express a state of meaning for which there exists no adequate word in any language. In that case, musicians often like to say that it has only a purely musical meaning. They sometimes go farther and say that *all* music has only a purely musical meaning. What they really mean is that no appropriate word can be found to express the music's meaning and that, even if it could, they do not feel the need of finding it.

## Searching for Words

11    But whatever the professional musician may hold, most musical novices still search for specific words with which to pin down their musical reactions. That is why they always find Tchaikovsky easier to "understand" than Beethoven. In the first place, it is easier to pin a meaning-word on a Tchaikovsky piece than on a Beethoven one. Much easier. Moreover, with the Russian composer, every time you come back to a piece of his it almost always says the same thing to you, whereas with

Beethoven it is often quite difficult to put your finger right on what he is saying. And any musician will tell you that that is why Beethoven is the greater composer. Because music which always says the same thing to you will necessarily soon become dull music, but music whose meaning is slightly different with each hearing has a greater chance of remaining alive.

12    Listen, if you can, to the forty-eight fugue themes of Bach's *Well-Tempered Clavichord*. Listen to each theme, one after another. You will soon realize that each theme mirrors a different world of feeling. You will also soon realize that the more beautiful a theme seems to you the harder it is to find any word that will describe it to your complete satisfaction. Yes, you will certainly know whether it is a gay theme or a sad one. You will be able, in other words, in your own mind, to draw a frame of emotional feeling around your theme. Now study the sad one a little closer. Try to pin down the exact quality of its sadness. Is it pessimistically sad or resignedly sad; is it fatefully sad or smilingly sad?

13    Let us suppose that you are fortunate and can describe to your own satisfaction in so many words the exact meaning of your chosen theme. There is still no guarantee that anyone else will be satisfied. Nor need they be. The important thing is that each one feel for himself the specific expressive quality of a theme or, similarly, an entire piece of music. And if it is a great work of art, don't expect it to mean exactly the same thing to you each time you return to it.

14    Themes or pieces need not express only one emotion, of course. Take such a theme as the first main one of the *Ninth Symphony*, for example. It is clearly made up of different elements. It does not say only one thing. Yet anyone hearing it immediately gets a feeling of strength, a feeling of power. It isn't a power that comes simply because the theme is played loudly. It is a power inherent in the theme itself. The extraordinary strength and vigor of the theme results in the listener's receiving an impression that a forceful statement has been made. But one should never try to boil it down to "the fateful hammer of life," etc. That is where the trouble begins. The musician, in his exasperation, says it means nothing but the notes themselves, whereas the nonprofessional is only too anxious to hang on to any explanation that gives him the illusion of getting closer to the music's meaning.

15    Now, perhaps, the reader will know better what I mean when I say that music does have an expressive meaning but that we cannot say in so many words what that meaning is.

## The Sheerly Musical Plane

16    The third plane on which music exists is the sheerly musical plane. Besides the pleasurable sound of music and the expressive feeling that

it gives off, music does exist in terms of the notes themselves and of their manipulation. Most listeners are not sufficiently conscious of this third plane. It will be largely the business of this book to make them more aware of music on this plane.

17    Professional musicians, on the other hand, are, if anything, too conscious of the mere notes themselves. They often fall into the error of becoming so engrossed with their arpeggios and staccatos that they forget the deeper aspects of the music they are performing. But from the layman's standpoint, it is not so much a matter of getting over bad habits on the sheerly musical plane as of increasing one's awareness of what is going on, in so far as the notes are concerned.

18    When the man in the street listens to the "notes themselves" with any degree of concentration, he is most likely to make some mention of the melody. Either he hears a pretty melody or he does not, and he generally lets it go at that. Rhythm is likely to gain his attention next, particularly if it seems exciting. But harmony and tone color are generally taken for granted, if they are thought of consciously at all. As for music's having a definite form of some kind, that idea seems never to have occurred to him.

19    It is very important for all of us to become more alive to music on its sheerly musical plane. After all, an actual musical material is being used. The intelligent listener must be prepared to increase his awareness of the musical material and what happens to it. He must hear the melodies, the rhythms, the harmonies, the tone colors in a more conscious fashion. But above all he must, in order to follow the line of the composer's thought, know something of the principles of musical form. Listening to all of these elements is listening on the sheerly musical plane.

20    Let me repeat that I have split up mechanically the three separate planes on which we listen merely for the sake of greater clarity. Actually, we never listen to one or the other of these planes. What we do is to correlate them—listening in all three ways at the same time. It takes no mental effort, for we do it instinctively.

## Like Theatergoing

21    Perhaps an analogy with what happens to us when we visit the theater will make this instinctive correlation clearer. In the theater, you are aware of the actors and actresses, costumes and sets, sounds and movements. All these give one the sense that the theater is a pleasant place to be in. They constitute the sensuous plane in our theatrical reactions.

22    The expressive plane in the theater would be derived from the feeling that you get from what is happening on the stage. You are moved to pity, excitement, or gayety. It is this general feeling, generated aside from the particular words being spoken, a certain emotional something

which exists on the stage, that is analogous to the expressive quality in music.

23    The plot and plot development is equivalent to our sheerly musical plane. The playwright creates and develops a character in just the same way that a composer creates and develops a theme. According to the degree of your awareness of the way in which the artist in either field handles his material will you become a more intelligent listener.

24    It is easy enough to see that the theatergoer never is conscious of any of these elements separately. He is aware of them all at the same time. The same is true of music listening. We simultaneously and without thinking listen on all three planes.

25    In a sense, the ideal listener is both inside and outside the music at the moment, judging it and enjoying it, wishing it would go one way and watching it go another—almost like the composer at the moment he composes it; because in order to write his music, the composer must also be inside and outside his music, carried away by it and yet coldly critical of it. A subjective and objective attitude is implied in both creating and listening to music.

26    What the reader should strive for, then, is a more *active* kind of listening. Whether you listen to Mozart or Duke Ellington, you can deepen your understanding of music only by being a more conscious and aware listener—not someone who is just listening, but someone who is listening *for* something.

## REVIEW

### Content

1. Do you agree with Copland in paragraph 4 that listening to music "as a consolation or an escape" is an "abuse" of the sensuous plane?
2. Copland says, in his last paragraph, that one should not just listen, but listen *for* something. What specific things does he encourage you to listen for as he develops his essay?

### Rhetoric

3. Copland's essay is an example of development of a subject by analysis. Why does he use this mode of development? What does your answer tell you about the purposes of analytical writing?
4. The tone of Copland's writing is relatively informal. What makes it so? How does his writing as if speaking directly to you as reader affect you? What does his analogy of music-listening with theatergoing add here? Does this "visualization" of the three planes help you better comprehend them?

**Projects**

5. Listen to a piece of music and consider it in the light of paragraphs 18 and 19. From Copland's discussion of listening on the "sheerly musical plane," were you able to hear more in this music than you probably would have in the past?

6. Listen to a piece of classical music you have never heard before (listen in your college library or in the music department, if you do not have recordings at home). Then try very hard to write about its meaning for you (the expressive plane)—what you experienced and what you felt the music was trying to say. Did you have difficulty finding *words* here—as Copland suggests you would?

# Dance to the Piper

## AGNES DE MILLE

Agnes de Mille grew up in a theatrical family in the early days of Hollywood. The young Agnes' own talent for dance became crystallized toward ballet when, at the age of eight, she saw the great Russian ballerina Pavlova. De Mille herself was to go on to create, against a heavy international tradition of old Russian classical ballet, the first truly American ballet, *Rodeo* (1942). She has choreographed numerous other popular scores, among them *Oklahoma* (1943) and *Carousel* (1945). The selection below is from de Mille's delightful autobiography, *Dance to the Piper* (1952); in this passage she tells how she sets about composing a dance, a technique she says she developed while choreographing *Rodeo*.

1    . . . To make up a dance, I still need, as I needed then, a pot of tea, walking space, privacy and an idea. Although every piece I have done so far for a ballet company is a *ballet d'action* or story ballet, I have no preference for this type—quite the contrary—I think the lyric or abstract ballets more pleasing and much more enduring, but my knack has been for dramatics.

2    When I first visualize the dance, I see the characters moving in color and costume. Before I go into rehearsal, I know what costumes the people wear and generally what color and texture. I also, to a large extent, hear the orchestral effects. Since I can have ideas only under the stress of emotion, I must create artificially an atmosphere which will induce this excitement. I shut myself in a studio and play gramo-

phone music, Bach, Mozart, Smetana, or almost any folk music in interesting arrangements. At this point I avoid using the score because it could easily become threadbare.

## On the Floor

3    I start sitting with my feet up and drinking pots of strong tea, but as I am taken into the subject I begin to move and before I know it I am walking the length of the studio and acting full out the gestures and scenes. The key dramatic scenes come this way. I never forget a single nuance of them afterwards; I do usually forget dance sequences.

4    The next step is to find the style of gesture. This is done standing and moving, again behind locked doors and again with a gramophone. Before I find how a character dances, I must know how he walks and stands. If I can discover the basic rhythms of his natural gesture, I will know how to expand them into dance movement.

5    It takes hours daily of blind instinctive moving and fumbling to find the revealing gesture, and the process goes on for weeks before I am ready to start composing. Nor can I think any of this out sitting down. My body does it for me. It happens. That is why the choreographic process is exhausting. It happens on one's feet after hours of work, and the energy required is roughly the equivalent of writing a novel and winning a tennis match simultaneously. This is the kernel, the nucleus of the dance. All the design develops from this.

## At the Desk

6    Having established a scenario and discovered the style and key steps, I then sit down at my desk and work out the pattern of the dances. If the score is already composed, the dance pattern is naturally suggested by and derived from the pattern of the music. If it remains to be composed as it does in all musical comedies, the choreographer goes it alone. This, of course, is harder. Music has an enormous suggestive power and the design of the composer offers a helpful blueprint.

7    All I know about dance composition I learned from folk dances. These are trustworthy models because they are the residuum of what has worked; there is no folk dance extant that did not work. I had first become aware of the importance of folk dancing when Dr. Lily Campbell asked me to reconstruct medieval singing games for her class in English Drama. I have studied folk forms since where possible. It must be remembered that outside of Louis Horst's classes in preclassic dance forms, choreography is taught nowhere and there are no texts on the subject. I learned by trial and error as did all my colleagues.

8    Through practice I have learned to project a whole composition in

rough outline mentally and to know exactly how the dancers will look at any given moment moving in counterpoint in as many as five groups. As an aid in concentration, I make detailed diagrams and notes of my own arbitrary invention, intelligible only to me and only for about a week, but they are not comparable in exactness to music notation.

## To the Rehearsal Hall

9   At this point, I am ready, God help me, to enter the rehearsal hall.

10   I don't believe any choreographer ever overcomes his terror of the waiting company. Imagine a composer facing the New York Philharmonic with his score projected in his head, not a note on paper, and the task before him of teaching the symphony by rote to the waiting men. He could start by whistling the main theme to the first violins.

11   Well, there they stand, the material of your craft, patient, disciplined, neat and hopeful in their black woolens. They will offer you their bodies for the next several weeks to milk the stuff of your ideas out of their muscles. They will submit to endless experimentation. They will find technique that has never been tried before; they will submerge their personalities and minds to the blindest, feeblest flutterings of yours. They will remember what you forget. They are pinning all the hopes of their past practices and future performings on the state of your brains. There they stand and consider you as you walk into the room. If they know you and are fond of you, it's easier. But at best, it's a soul-challenging moment.

12   The choreographer is apt to be short-tempered and jumpy at these times; he has not only to face the psychological problems of mastering and guiding a group of human beings, but all the problems of composition simultaneously. I take comfort in hot coffee. With the friendly warmth of a carton between my hands and the steaming rim to hide my face in, and the piping hot reassurance in my stomach, I can just manage to step out on the floor and make a suggestion. Dancers very quickly learn to hand me coffee before they ask a taxing question such as "What do we do next over here?" I find a ring of cartons waiting around my chair in the morning.

## With the Dancers

13   It's a good idea to give the company for a beginning something definite and technically difficult to get their feet down on. The minute they start to sweat they feel busy and useful. Like [Antony] Tudor, I always try to start with two or three dancers I know who are sympathetic to my suggestion, and I have learned to have the rehearsal planned

through to the end, preferably on a piece of paper in case I dry up mentally. Standing and scratching one's head while the dancers cool off in their tights, and then put on extra sweaters, and then sit down on the floor, and then light cigarettes and start to talk, is what one wishes to avoid. No group of workers in the world is slower to lose faith or interest, but they are human. While you are struggling to find the exact phrasing they get tired in the back of their knees. And when you ask them to get off the floor and try the jump in the eighteenth variation they rise creaking. Then you grow hot with anger that you cannot solve the problem and punish their bodies for your own stupidity, forcing them to do it again and again and again, pretending that it is their lack of performance quality that invalidates the idea. But no one is fooled. Neither you nor they. You scold them. And your company quietly grows to hate you. They are now more or less useless for your purposes. If you were working with marble you could hack at it for a year without any deterioration of material. If you were writing a book you could lay down your pen, take a walk, take a nap, have some coffee and come back to find your manuscript just as you left it. But dancers stand with patient drawn faces waiting for your brains to click.

14    One could simply terminate a rehearsal and wait for a more fruitful moment. But after all, the dancers are there to work, the hall is rented, the pianist hired and attentive.

## Critical Moments

15    There are, however, the times when one scrapes absolute bottom. The manner in which he deals with these moments is the exact measure of a choreographer's experience. Balanchine dismisses a rehearsal without any ado at all and goes home. If, on the other hand, he likes what he is doing, hell can break loose around him and he pays not the slightest mind. Short of hell he nearly always is surrounded by a roomful of chattering, knitting, practicing dancers and visitors. Massine holds the entire company in the room. They sit for hours sometimes while he wrestles with one or two soloists. If he gets stuck he keeps it to himself as he never explains a single thing he is doing to anyone he is working with. Martha Graham sends her group from the room and has it out with God. I cannot endure the sight of one person sitting down waiting. A sense of guilt and tedium oppresses me exactly as though I were failing a guest. I, therefore, allow in the room with me only the people I am working with, never any visitors, and inside the rehearsal room no one may sit down or chew gum or smoke. I have to keep myself geared to such a pitch that if I relax or allow the dancers to relax the rehearsal for all effective purposes is over. Outside in the waiting room or hall they may do as they like—drink, chew, eat, gossip,

play cards. This pertains to the beginning weeks. When the composition stands by itself on the floor and is no longer a matter of hypnotism between me and the group, everything is easier.

16    But with all the good planning possible, there comes sooner or later the inevitable point of agony when the clock dictates and one must just set one's teeth and get on with it. Then one wrings the ultimate out of one's marrow. The astonishing fact is that it is there to be wrung.


## REVIEW

### Content

1. Can you compare paragraphs 2 through 5 of the de Mille excerpt with the selection on creativity by Whyte which opens this section of the book?
2. It is often said of good ballet, "It looks as though they just come out on the stage and dance; it all looks *so easy*." One choreographer is said to have responded to such a remark: "It's *supposed* to look that way." After reading de Mille on choreography, can you see why it "looks so easy"?

### Rhetoric

3. What is the effect of the single-sentence paragraph 9?
4. In paragraph 11, de Mille employs parallel structure, beginning several succeeding sentences, "They will . . ." What effect does she achieve by this device? And what does her use of the second person pronoun "you" contribute to the effect of this paragraph?

### Projects

5. Try to see a dance sequence—modern dance or ballet on stage, a television performance, a movie with dance scenes, a film in your college library; recall as you watch de Mille's discussion of choreography. Then write about what you saw, referring to as many distinct elements of the performance as you can.
6. If you have ever taught a skill to someone else (for instance, swimming, bowling, drawing, sewing, driving), write about the experience. Intersperse some humor if you can to make your account more appealing to the reader, as de Mille does at the end of paragraph 12.

# The Raw Material of Poetry

## RAINER MARIA RILKE

Rainer Maria Rilke (1875–1926) was an Austrian poet. His best-known work is *Duino Elegies*, a long cycle of poems that Rilke worked on for ten years (1912–1922), having been first inspired to the work while at Schloss Duino on the Adriatic Sea near Trieste, Italy. In the diary-like passage below, from *The Notebooks of Malte Laurids Brigge* (1910), Rilke speaks of the many and long years of living—the "raw material"—that must occur before such inspiration as that of Duino can produce a poem.

I think I ought to begin to do some work, now that I am learning to see. I am twenty-eight years old, and almost nothing has been done. To recapitulate: I have written a study on Carpaccio which is bad, a drama entitled "Marriage," which sets out to demonstrate something false by equivocal means, and some verses. Ah! but verses amount to so little when one writes them young. One ought to wait and gather sense and sweetness a whole life long, and a long life if possible, and then, quite at the end, one might perhaps be able to write ten lines that were good. For verses are not, as people imagine, simple feelings (those one has early enough),—they are experiences. For the sake of a single verse, one must see many cities, men and things, one must know the animals, one must feel how the birds fly and know the gesture with which the little flowers open in the morning. One must be able to think back to roads in unknown regions, to unexpected meetings and to partings one had long seen coming; to days of childhood that are still unexplained, to parents whom one had to hurt when they brought one some joy and one did not grasp it (it was a joy for someone else); to childhood illnesses that so strangely begin with such a number of profound and grave transformations; to days in rooms withdrawn and quiet and to mornings by the sea, to the sea itself, to seas, to nights of travel that rushed along on high and flew with all the stars—and it is not yet enough if one may think of all this. One must have memories of many nights of love, none of which was like the others, of the screams of women in labor, and of light, white, sleeping women in childbed, closing again. But one must also have been beside the dying, must have sat beside the dead in the room with the open window and the fitful noises. And still it is not yet enough to have memories. One must be able to forget them when they are many and one must have the great patience to wait until they come again. For it is not yet the memories themselves. Not till they have turned to blood within us, to glance and gesture, nameless and no longer to be distinguished from ourselves—not till then can it happen that in a most rare hour the first word of a verse arises in their midst and goes forth from them.

## REVIEW

### Content

1. Where does Rilke say poetry comes from? What does he mean, in the first sentence, when he says "now that I am learning to see"? Explain "And still it is not yet enough . . . goes forth from them."
2. With what experiences Rilke mentions do *you* identify? Can you see how these could later become "the raw material of poetry"?

### Rhetoric

3. Parts of this passage of prose by Rilke sound like poetry. Can you point to such passages? What makes them poetic?
4. In sentence 3, Rilke seems to be mocking himself. How does his phrasing here create that effect?

### Projects

5. Make a list of things that have made enough of an impression on you that you think they might one day provide "raw material for poetry."
6. Rilke says that "verses are not, as people imagine, simple feelings . . . they are experiences." Have you experiences that you have lived with long enough, that have become enough a part of you, that "a verse [can] arise . . . and go forth"? If you think you have, try to write down that poem.

# Reflections on Writing

## HENRY MILLER

Henry Miller (1891–   ) is an American writer who was among the avant garde in twentieth-century explicitness in literature. Two of his best known works, which uninhibitedly relate his own sexual experience, *Tropic of Cancer* (1934) and *Tropic of Capricorn* (1939), were banned in this country until the Supreme Court ruled in their favor in 1964 following a series of obscenity trials. The fact that Miller refused to compromise his life on paper will not surprise you as you read his "Reflections on Writing." Here Miller relates where his material comes from and how the writing occurs. He says, "Every line and word is vitally connected with my life, *my* life only, be it in the form of deed . . . emotion . . . revery. . . ."

. . . I have often thought that I should like one day to write a book explaining how I wrote certain passages in my books, or perhaps just one passage. I believe I could write a good-sized book on just one small paragraph selected at random from my work. A book about its inception, its genesis, its metamorphosis, its accouchement, of the time which elapsed between the birth of the idea and its recording, the time it took to write it, the thoughts I had between times while writing it, the day of the week, the state of my health, the condition of my nerves, the interruptions that occurred, those of my own volition and those which were forced upon me, the multifarious varieties of expression which occurred to me in the process of writing, the alterations, the point where I left off and in returning, completely altered the original trend, or the point where I skillfully left off, like a surgeon making the best of a bad job, intending to return and resume some time later, but never doing so, or else returning and continuing the trend unconsciously some few books later when the memory of it had completely vanished. Or I might take one passage against another, passages which the cold eye of the critic seizes on as examples of this or that, and utterly confound them, the analytical-minded critics, by demonstrating how a seemingly effortless piece of writing was achieved under great duress whereas another difficult, labyrinthian passage was written like a breeze, like a geyser erupting. Or I could show how a passage originally shaped itself when in bed, how it became transformed upon arising, and again transformed at the moment of sitting down to record it. Or I could produce my scratch pad to show how the most remote, the most artificial stimulus produced a warm, life-like human flower. I could produce certain words discovered by hazard while riffling the pages of a book, show how they set me off—but who on earth could ever guess how, in what manner, they were to set me off? All that the critics write about a work of art, even at the best, even when most sound, convincing, plausible, even when done with love, which is seldom, is as nothing compared to the actual mechanics, the real genetics of a work of art. I remember my work, not word for word, to be sure, but in some more accurate, trust-worthy way; my whole work has come to resemble a terrain of which I have made a thorough, geodetic survey, not from a desk, with pen and ruler, but by touch, by getting down on all fours, on my stomach, and crawling over the ground inch by inch, and this over an endless period of time in all conditions of weather. In short, I am as close to the work now as when I was in the act of executing it—closer perhaps. The conclusion of a book was never anything more than a shift of bodily position. It might have ended in a thousand different ways. No single part of it is finished off: I could resume the narrative at any point, carry on, lay canals, tunnels, bridges, houses, factories, stud it with other inhabitants, other fauna and flora, all equally true to fact. I have no beginning and no ending, actually. Just as life begins at any moment, through an act of realization, so the work. But each beginning, whether of book, page, paragraph, sentence or phrase, marks a vital connection, and it is in the vitality, the durability, the timelessness and changelessness of the thoughts and events that I plunge anew each time. Every line and word is vitally connected with my life, *my* life only, be it in the form of deed, event, fact, thought, emotion, desire, evasion, frustration, dream, revery, vagary, even the unfinished nothings which float listlessly in the brain like the snapped filaments of a spider's web. There is noth-ing really vague or tenuous—even the nothingnesses are sharp, tough, definite, durable. Like the spider I return again and again to the task, conscious that the web I am spinning is made of my own substance, that it will never fail me, never run dry.

## REVIEW

### Content

1. Compare what Miller says about his writing with what Rilke says, in the preceding selection, about "the raw material of poetry."
2. What does Miller mean when he says, "I could produce my scratch pad to show how the most remote, the most artificial stimulus pro-duced a warm, life-like human flower"? And, discuss the passage, "No single part . . . so the work."

**Rhetoric**

3. This excerpt from Miller reads somewhat like stream-of-consciousness writing. What would you guess that term to mean?
4. Judging from both the style and the content of this selection, what would you expect to find Miller's novels like?

**Projects**

5. In class: Do some "free writing"—in which you simply begin to write and let flow whatever comes. Then, with classmates, discuss both what this writing experience felt like and where the content of your writing came from.
6. Write about something that has happened to you, as if another part of you were standing off observing it all. Write in a stream-of-consciousness style. If you need further examples of this mode to help you get started, read some in Virginia Woolf's novels or in James Joyce's *Portrait of the Artist as a Young Man.*

# Film-Making

## INGMAR BERGMAN

Ingmar Bergman (1918–    ) is a well-known Swedish director of films noted for their starkness, their subtle use of black and white and "shades" of those extremes, the ambiguity of their content, and a certain brooding presence that seems to pervade them all. The list of Bergman films is long; his best known include *The Seventh Seal* (1957), *Wild Strawberries* (1958), *The Virgin Spring* (1960), *The Silence* (1963), *Persona* (1967), *The Passion of Anna* (1970), and *Cries and Whispers* (1973)—this last film in color, though emphasizing red in all its shadings. In the following selection, the Introduction to *Four Screenplays by Ingmar Bergman* (1960), Bergman discusses how he views the art of film-making.

1    During the shooting of *The Virgin Spring,* we were up in the northern province of Dalarna in May and it was early in the morning, about half past seven. The landscape there is rugged, and our company was working by a little lake in the forest. It was very cold, about 30 degrees, and from time to time a few snowflakes fell through the gray, rain-dimmed sky. The company was dressed in a strange variety of clothing—raincoats, oil slickers, Icelandic sweaters, leather jackets, old blankets,

coachmen's coats, medieval robes. Our men had laid some ninety feet of rusty, buckling rail over the difficult terrain, to dolly the camera on. We were all helping with the equipment—actors, electricians, make-up men, script girl, sound crew—mainly to keep warm. Suddenly someone shouted and pointed toward the sky. Then we saw a crane floating high above the fir trees, and then another, and then several cranes, floating majestically in a circle above us. We all dropped what we were doing and ran to the top of a nearby hill to see the cranes better. We stood there for a long time, until they turned westward and disappeared over the forest. And suddenly I thought: this is what it means to make a movie in Sweden. This is what can happen, this is how we work together with our old equipment and little money, and this is how we can suddenly drop everything for the love of four cranes floating above the tree tops.

## Childhood Foretells Future

2    My association with film goes back to the world of childhood.

3    My grandmother had a very large old apartment in Uppsala. I used to sit under the dining-room table there, "listening" to the sunshine which came in through the gigantic windows. The cathedral bells went ding-dong, and the sunlight moved about and "sounded" in a special way. One day, when winter was giving way to spring and I was five years old, a piano was being played in the next apartment. It played waltzes, nothing but waltzes. On the wall hung a large picture of Venice. As the sunlight moved across the picture the water in the canal began to flow, the pigeons flew up from the square, people talked and gesticulated. Bells sounded, not those of Uppsala Cathedral but from the picture itself. And the piano music also came from that remarkable picture of Venice.

4    A child who is born and brought up in a vicarage acquires an early familiarity with life and death behind the scenes. Father performed funerals, marriages, baptisms, gave advice and prepared sermons. The devil was an early acquaintance, and in the child's mind there was a need to personify him. This is where my magic lantern came in. It consisted of a small metal box with a carbide lamp—I can still remember the smell of the hot metal—and colored glass slides: Red Riding Hood and the Wolf, and all the others. And the Wolf was the Devil, without horns but with a tail and a gaping red mouth, strangely real yet incomprehensible, a picture of wickedness and temptation on the flowered wall of the nursery.

5    When I was ten years old I received my first, rattling film projector, with its chimney and lamp. I found it both mystifying and fascinating. The first film I had was nine feet long and brown in color. It showed

a girl lying asleep in a meadow, who woke up and stretched out her arms, then disappeared to the right. That was all there was to it. The film was a great success and was projected every night until it broke and could not be mended any more.

6    This little rickety machine was my first conjuring set. And even today I remind myself with childish excitement that I am really a conjurer, since cinematography is based on deception of the human eye. I have worked it out that if I see a film which has a running time of one hour, I sit through twenty-seven minutes of complete darkness—the blankness between frames. When I show a film I am guilty of deceit. I use an apparatus which is constructed to take advantage of a certain human weakness, an apparatus with which I can sway my audience in a highly emotional manner—make them laugh, scream with fright, smile, believe in fairy stories, become indignant, feel shocked, charmed, deeply moved or perhaps yawn with boredom. Thus I am either an impostor or, when the audience is willing to be taken in, a conjurer. I perform conjuring tricks with apparatus so expensive and so wonderful that any entertainer in history would have given anything to have it.

## Split-Second Impressions

7    A film for me begins with something very vague—a chance remark or a bit of conversation, a hazy but agreeable event unrelated to any particular situation. It can be a few bars of music, a shaft of light across the street. Sometimes in my work at the theater I have envisioned actors made up for yet unplayed roles.

8    These are split-second impressions that disappear as quickly as they come, yet leave behind a mood—like pleasant dreams. It is a mental state, not an actual story, but one abounding in fertile associations and images. Most of all, it is a brightly colored thread sticking out of the dark sack of the unconscious. If I begin to wind up this thread, and do it carefully, a complete film will emerge.

9    This primitive nucleus strives to achieve definite form, moving in a way that may be lazy and half asleep at first. Its stirring is accompanied by vibrations and rhythms which are very special and unique to each film. The picture sequences then assume a pattern in accordance with these rhythms, obeying laws born out of and conditioned by my original stimulus.

10    If that embryonic substance seems to have enough strength to be made into a film, I decide to materialize it. Then comes something very complicated and difficult: the transformation of rhythms, moods, atmosphere, tensions, sequences, tones and scents into words and sentences, into an understandable screenplay.

11    This is an almost impossible task.

12    The only thing that can be satisfactorily transferred from that original complex of rhythms and moods is the dialogue, and even dialogue is a sensitive substance which may offer resistance. Written dialogue is like a musical score, almost incomprehensible to the average person. Its interpretation demands a technical knack plus a certain kind of imagination and feeling—qualities which are so often lacking, even among actors. One can write dialogue, but how it should be delivered, its rhythm and tempo, what is to take place between lines—all this must be omitted for practical reasons. Such a detailed script would be unreadable. I try to squeeze instructions as to location, characterization and atmosphere into my screenplays in understandable terms, but the success of this depends on my writing ability and the perceptiveness of the reader, which are not always predictable.

## The Rhythm of a Film

13    Now we come to essentials, by which I mean montage, rhythm and the relation of one picture to another—the vital third dimension without which the film is merely a dead product from a factory. Here I cannot clearly give a key, as in a musical score, nor a specific idea of the tempo which determines the relationship of the elements involved. It is quite impossible for me to indicate the way in which the film "breathes" and pulsates.

14    I have often wished for a kind of notation which would enable me to put on paper all the shades and tones of my vision, to record distinctly the inner structure of a film. For when I stand in the artistically devastating atmosphere of the studio, my hands and head full of all the trivial and irritating details that go with motion-picture production, it often takes a tremendous effort to remember how I originally saw and thought out this or that sequence, or what was the relation between the scene of four weeks ago and that of today. If I could express myself clearly, in explicit symbols, then this problem would be almost eliminated and I could work with absolute confidence that whenever I liked I could prove the relationship between the part and the whole and put my finger on the rhythm, the continuity of the film.

15    Thus the script is a very imperfect *technical* basis for a film. And there is another important point in this connection which I should like to mention. Film has nothing to do with literature; the character and substance of the two art forms are usually in conflict. This probably has something to do with the receptive process of the mind. The written word is read and assimilated by a conscious act of the will in alliance with the intellect; little by little it affects the imagination and the emotions. The process is different with a motion picture. When we experience a film, we consciously prime ourselves for illusion. Putting aside

will and intellect, we make way for it in our imagination. The sequence of pictures plays directly on our feelings.

16    Music works in the same fashion; I would say that there is no art form that has so much in common with film as music. Both affect our emotions directly, not via the intellect. And film is mainly rhythm; it is inhalation and exhalation in continuous sequence. Ever since childhood, music has been my great source of recreation and stimulation, and I often experience a film or play musically.

## Film and Written Literature

17    It is mainly because of this difference between film and literature that we should avoid making films out of books. The irrational dimension of a literary work, the germ of its existence, is often untranslatable into visual terms—and it, in turn, destroys the special, irrational dimension of the film. If, despite this, we wish to translate something literary into film terms, we must make an infinite number of complicated adjustments which often bear little or no fruit in proportion to the effort expended.

18    I myself have never had any ambition to be an author. I do not want to write novels, short stories, essays, biographies, or even plays for the theater. I only want to make films—films about conditions, tensions, pictures, rhythms and characters which are in one way or another important to me. The motion picture, with its complicated process of birth, is my method of saying what I want to my fellow men. I am a film-maker, not an author.

19    Thus the writing of the script is a difficult period but a useful one, for it compels me to prove logically the validity of my ideas. In doing this, I am caught in a conflict—a conflict between my need to transmit a complicated situation through visual images, and my desire for absolute clarity. I do not intend my work to be solely for the benefit of myself or the few, but for the entertainment of the general public. The wishes of the public are imperative. But sometimes I risk following my own impulse, and it has been shown that the public can respond with surprising sensitivity to the most unconventional line of development.

20    When shooting begins, the most important thing is that those who work with me feel a definite contact, that all of us somehow cancel out our conflicts through working together. We must pull in one direction for the sake of the work at hand. Sometimes this leads to dispute, but the more definite and clear the "marching orders," the easier it is to reach the goal which has been set. This is the basis for my conduct as director, and perhaps the explanation of much of the nonsense that has been written about me.

21    While I cannot let myself be concerned with what people think and

say about me personally, I believe that reviewers and critics have every right to interpret my films as they like. I refuse to interpret my work to others, and I cannot tell the critic what to think; each person has the right to understand a film as he sees it. Either he is attracted or repelled. A film is made to create reaction. If the audience does not react one way or another, it is an indifferent work and worthless.

22    I do not mean by this that I believe in being "different" at any price. A lot has been said about the value of originality, and I find this foolish. Either you are original or you are not. It is completely natural for artists to take from and give to each other, to borrow from and experience one another. In my own life, my great literary experience was Strindberg. There are works of his which can still make my hair stand on end—*The People of Hemsö*, for example. And it is my dream to produce *Dream Play* some day. Olof Molander's production of it in 1934 was for me a fundamental dramatic experience.

## Significant Persons

23    On a personal level, there are many people who have meant a great deal to me. My father and mother were certainly of vital importance, not only in themselves but because they created a world for me to revolt against. In my family there was an atmosphere of hearty wholesomeness which I, a sensitive young plant, scorned and rebelled against. But that strict middle-class home gave me a wall to pound on, something to sharpen myself against. At the same time they taught me a number of values—efficiency, punctuality, a sense of financial responsibility—which may be "bourgeois" but are nevertheless important to the artist. They are part of the process of setting oneself severe standards. Today as a film-maker I am conscientious, hard-working and extremely careful; my films involve good craftsmanship, and my pride is the pride of a good craftsman.

24    Among the people who have meant something in my professional development is Torsten Hammaren of Gothenburg. I went there from Hälsingborg, where I had been head of the municipal theater for two years. I had no conception of what theater was; Hammaren taught me during the four years I stayed in Gothenburg. Then, when I made my first attempts at film, Alf Sjöberg—who directed *Torment*—taught me a great deal. And there was Lorens Marmstedt, who really taught me film-making from scratch after my first unsuccessful movie. Among other things I learned from Marmstedt is the one unbreakable rule: you must look at your own work very coldly and clearly; you must be a devil to yourself in the screening room when watching the day's rushes. Then there is Herbert Grevenius, one of the few who believed in me as a writer. I had trouble with script-writing, and was reaching out more

and more to the drama, to dialogue, as a means of expression. He gave me great encouragement.

25    Finally, there is Carl Anders Dymling, my producer. He is crazy enough to place more faith in the sense of responsibility of a creative artist than in calculations of profit and loss. I am thus able to work with an integrity that has become the very air I breathe, and one of the main reasons I do not want to work outside of Sweden. The moment I lose this freedom I will cease to be a film-maker, because I have no skill in the art of compromise. My only significance in the world of film lies in the freedom of my creativity.

## The Tightrope of Film-Making

26    Today, the ambitious film-maker is obliged to walk a tightrope without a net. He may be a conjurer, but no one conjures the producer, the bank director or the theater owners when the public refuses to go see a film and lay down the money by which producer, bank director, theater owner and conjurer can live. The conjurer may then be deprived of his magic wand; I would like to be able to measure the amount of talent, initiative and creative ability which has been destroyed by the film industry in its ruthlessly efficient sausage machine. What was play to me once has now become a struggle. Failure, criticism, public indifference all hurt more today than yesterday. The brutality of the industry is undisguised—yet that can be an advantage.

27    So much for people and the film business. I have been asked, as a clergyman's son, about the role of religion in my thinking and film-making. To me, religious problems are continuously alive. I never cease to concern myself with them; it goes on every hour of every day. Yet this does not take place on the emotional level, but on an intellectual one. Religious emotion, religious sentimentality, is something I got rid of long ago—I hope. The religious problem is an intellectual one to me: the relationship of my mind to my intuition. The result of this conflict is usually some kind of tower of Babel.

28    Philosophically, there is a book which was a tremendous experience for me: Eiono Kaila's *Psychology of the Personality*. His thesis that man lives strictly according to his needs—negative and positive—was shattering to me, but terribly true. And I built on this ground.

## Cathedral-Building

29    People ask what are my intentions with my films—my aims. It is a difficult and dangerous question, and I usually give an evasive answer: I try to tell the truth about the human condition, the truth as I see

it. This answer seems to satisfy everyone, but it is not quite correct. I prefer to describe what I *would like* my aim to be.

30    There is an old story of how the cathedral of Chartres was struck by lightning and burned to the ground. Then thousands of people came from all points of the compass, like a giant procession of ants, and together they began to rebuild the cathedral on its old site. They worked until the building was completed—master builders, artists, laborers, clowns, noblemen, priests, burghers. But they all remained anonymous, and no one knows to this day who built the cathedral of Chartres.

31    Regardless of my own beliefs and my own doubts, which are unimportant in this connection, it is my opinion that art lost its basic creative drive the moment it was separated from worship. It severed an umbilical cord and now lives its own sterile life, generating and degenerating itself. In former days the artist remained unknown and his work was to the glory of God. He lived and died without being more or less important than other artisans; "eternal values," "immortality" and "masterpiece" were terms not applicable in his case. The ability to create was a gift. In such a world flourished invulnerable assurance and natural humility.

32    Today the individual has become the highest form and the greatest bane of artistic creation. The smallest wound or pain of the ego is examined under a microscope as if it were of eternal importance. The artist considers his isolation, his subjectivity, his individualism almost holy. Thus we finally gather in one large pen, where we stand and bleat about our loneliness without listening to each other and without realizing that we are smothering each other to death. The individualists stare into each other's eyes and yet deny the existence of each other. We walk in circles, so limited by our anxieties that we can no longer distinguish between true and false, between the gangster's whim and the purest ideal.

33    Thus if I am asked what I would like the general purpose of my films to be, I would reply that I want to be one of the artists in the cathedral on the great plain. I want to make a dragon's head, an angel, a devil—or perhaps a saint—out of stone. It does not matter which; it is the sense of satisfaction that counts. Regardless of whether I believe or not, whether I am a Christian or not, I would play my part in the collective building of the cathedral.

## REVIEW

### Content

1. Compare Bergman's experience when he was five, recounted in paragraph 3, with what he says in paragraph 7. Why does he refer to himself as a "conjurer"?
2. Discuss paragraphs 27 and 28, and the first two sentences of para-

graph 29. How do Bergman's concerns here relate to the part he wants to play "in the collective building of the cathedral"?

## Rhetoric

3. What is the effect of the descriptive passage with which Bergman begins his introduction? What sense of *him* do you get when he and all his crew stop work to watch the cranes?
4. Did you hear the *visual artist's* voice speaking in specific passages by Bergman? Point to particularly effective use of imagery, for example, in his prose.

## Projects

5. Bergman talks about a number of persons who were important to his development as a film-maker. Write a paper about someone who has been important to some facet of your development and explain that person's significance in your life.
6. In a sense, we are all creative artists—of our own lives, if in no other mode. And to a degree, "individualism" has become the fashion today. Re-read paragraph 32 and write a paper about how too heavy a focus on individualism might serve to diminish rather than to enrich the life *you* are creating for yourself.

# Blessed Profanity:
# *M*A*S*H*

## PAULINE KAEL

Pauline Kael (1919–   ), movie reviewer for *The New Yorker,* is generally recognized as an outstanding film critic. Her pointed, often witty, and always intelligent reviews and essays have been collected into several volumes: *I Lost It at the Movies* (1965), *Kiss Kiss Bang Bang* (1968), *Going Steady* (1970), *The Citizen Kane Book* (1971), and *Deeper into Movies* (1972). The latter collection reviews more than 150 American and foreign films, among them *M*A*S*H*, the original source for the popular television series of the same name. Kael sees the movies as "our national theatre"— and she reports with unerring verve on how that particular theatre reflects its society, as theatre ever tends to do.

1    *M\*A\*S\*H* is a marvellously unstable comedy, a tough, funny, and sophisticated burlesque of military attitudes that is at the same time a tale of chivalry. It's a sick joke, but it's also generous and romantic—an erratic, episodic film, full of the pleasures of the unexpected. I think it's the closest an American movie has come to the kind of constantly surprising mixture in *Shoot the Piano Player*, though *M\*A\*S\*H* moves so fast that it's over before you have time to think of comparisons. While it's going on, you're busy listening to some of the best overlapping comic dialogue ever recorded. The picture has so much spirit that you keep laughing—and without discomfort, because all the targets *should* be laughed at. The laughter is at the horrors and absurdities of war, and, specifically, at people who flourish in the military bureaucracy. The title letters stand for Mobile Army Surgical Hospital: the heroes, played by Donald Sutherland and Elliott Gould, are combat surgeons patching up casualties a few miles from the front during the Korean war. They do their surgery in style, with humor: they're hip Galahads, saving lives while ragging the military bureaucracy. They are so quick to react to bull—and in startling, unpredictable ways—that the comedy is, at times, almost a poetic fantasy. There's a surreal innocence about the movie; though the setting makes it seem a "black" comedy, it's a cheery "black" comedy. The heroes win at everything. It's a modern kid's dream of glory: Holden Caulfield would, I think, approve of them. They're great surgeons, athletes, dashing men of the world, sexy, full of noblesse oblige, but ruthless to those with pretensions and lethal to hypocrites. They're so good at what they do that even the military brass admires them. They're winners in the war with the Army.

2    War comedies in the past have usually been about the little guys who foul things up and become heroes by accident (Chaplin in *Shoulder Arms*, Danny Kaye in *Up in Arms*). In that comedy tradition, the sad-sack recruit is too stupid to comprehend military ritual. These heroes are too smart to put up with it. Sutherland and Gould are more like an updated version of Edmund Lowe's and Victor McLaglen's Sergeant Quirt and Captain Flagg from *What Price Glory* and *The Cockeyed World*—movies in which the heroes retain their personal style and their camaraderie in the midst of blood and muck and the general insanity of war. One knows that though what goes on at this surgical station seems utterly crazy, it's only a small distortion of actual wartime situations. The pretty little helicopters delivering the bloody casualties are a surreal image, all right, but part of the authentic surrealism of modern warfare. The jokes the surgeons make about their butchershop work are a form of plain talk. The movie isn't naïve, but it isn't nihilistic, either. The surgery room looks insane and is presented as insane, but as the insanity in which we must preserve the values of sanity and function as sane men. An incompetent doctor is treated as a foul object; competence is one of the values the movie respects—even when it is demonstrated by a nurse

(Sally Kellerman) who is a pompous fool. The heroes are always on the side of decency and sanity—that's why they're contemptuous of the bureaucracy. They are heroes *because* they're competent and sane and gallant, and in this insane situation their gallantry takes the form of scabrous comedy. The Quirt and Flagg films were considered highly profane in their day, and I am happy to say that *M\*A\*S\*H*, taking full advantage of the new permissive rating system, is blessedly profane. I've rarely heard four-letter words used so exquisitely well in a movie, used with such efficacy and glee. I salute *M\*A\*S\*H* for its contribution to the art of talking dirty.

## Silliness and Sanity

3    The profanity, which is an extension of adolescent humor, is central to the idea of the movie. The silliness of adolescents—compulsively making jokes, seeing the ridiculous in everything—is what makes sanity possible here. The doctor who rejects adolescent behavior flips out. Adolescent pride in skills and games—in mixing a Martini or in devising a fishing lure or in golfing—keeps the men from becoming maniacs. Sutherland and Gould, and Tom Skerritt, as a third surgeon, and a lot of freakishly talented new-to-movies actors are relaxed and loose in their roles. Their style of acting underscores the point of the picture, which is that people who aren't hung up by pretensions, people who are loose and profane and have some empathy—people who can joke about anything—can function, and maybe even do something useful, in what may appear to be insane circumstances.

4    There's also a lot of slapstick in the movie, some of it a little like *Operation Mad Ball,* a fifties service comedy that had some great moments but was still tied to a sanctimonious approach to life and love. What holds the disparate elements of *M\*A\*S\*H* together in the precarious balance that is the movie's chief charm is a free-for-all, throwaway attitude. The picture looks as if the people who made it had a good time, as if they played with it and improvised and took some chances. It's elegantly made, and yet it doesn't have that overplanned rigidity of so many Hollywood movies. The cinematography, by Harold E. Stine, is very fine—full of dust and muddy olive-green tones; it has immediacy and the clarity possible in Panavision. The editing and the sound engineering are surprisingly quick-witted. When the dialogue overlaps, you hear just what you should, but it doesn't seem all worked out and set; the sound seems to bounce off things so that the words just catch your ear. The throwaway stuff isn't really thrown away; it all helps to create the free, graceful atmosphere that sustains the movie and keeps it consistently funny. The director, Robert Altman, has a great feel for low-keyed American humor. With the help of Ring Lardner, Jr.'s script (from a

novel by a combat surgeon), Altman has made a real sport of a movie which combines traditional roustabout comedy with modern attitudes. As in other good comedies, there's often a mixture of what seems perfectly straight stuff and what seems incredible fantasy, and yet when we try to say which is which we can't. *M\*A\*S\*H* affects us on a bewildering number of levels, like the Radio Tokyo versions of American songs on the camp loudspeaker system. All this may sound more like a testimonial than a review, but I don't know when I've had such a good time at a movie. Many of the best recent American movies leave you feeling that there's nothing to do but get stoned and die, that that's your proper fate as an American. This movie heals a breach in American movies: it's hip but it isn't hopeless. A surgical hospital where the doctors' hands are lost in chests and guts is certainly an unlikely subject for a comedy, but I think *M\*A\*S\*H* is the best American war comedy since sound came in, and the sanest American movie of recent years.

## REVIEW

### Content

1. Kael uses several terms common to drama- and film-reviewing. What is a burlesque? "Black" comedy? Surrealism? Slapstick? "Throwaway stuff"?
2. One responsibility of the critic may be said to be as a guide for the public, encouraging it to support what the critic evaluates as superior and to avoid what he or she judges to be inferior. Does Kael make *you* want to see M*A*S*H?

### Rhetoric

3. Kael's two opening sentences are packed. Evaluate them for how much they manage to say. What is especially effective about Kael's vocabulary here? About how she structures the sentences?
4. Kael is known for her rousing style. What makes her prose so lively and readable? Point to especially apt expressions.

### Projects

5. If you were in the service, write a firsthand account in which you treat some facet of the military experience. Tell it in the way Kael says *M\*A\*S\*H* takes off on medical aid at the front.
6. Do you know someone who reminds you of Kael's description in the last sentence of paragraph 3? If you do, write a paper about that person, applying the description.

# Pornography
# and
# Censorship

## STANLEY KAUFFMANN

Stanley Kauffmann (1916–    ) has worked as an actor and a director, as well as serving as film critic for *The New Republic* and drama critic for *The New York Times*. His collections of essays and film reviews include *A World on Film* (1958). In the statement below, printed in *The Public Interest*, Winter, 1971, Kauffmann announces that he dislikes both pornography and censorship—and explains why. He then goes on to recognize that "people want pornography," however, and to argue against attempts to "legislate taste."

1    One pleasant aspect of pornography discussions is that they never end, even within oneself. No set of arguments can be air-tight, and one can always think of points to be added or changed in one's own arguments. But here are some of my present views:

2    I dislike pornography; and I dislike censorship laws.

3    I dislike pornography because after the excitements, there comes tedium; and with the tedium comes a sense of imperfection. After sex itself comes no such tedium (languor is something else) and no such basic sense of inappropriateness. Porno excites me because all my neural systems seem to be adequately hooked up, but after the shock of crossing the threshold into that "world" wears off, which doesn't take so long, I begin to think that porno represents an ideal—essentially male—of sexual freedom and power, unrelated to reality as is, or as is desirable. I am an anti-idealist; ideals seem morally and functionally corruptive. I am against this ideal as well.

4    I dislike censorship laws because they intrude on personal rights. Most laws operate between at least two people: they protect me from you and vice-versa. Laws against pornography, like laws against drinking and drug-taking and suicide, come between me and myself. I object to the state's arrogance.

5    People want pornography.

6    This has been true of many cultures, especially for men, in many areas. Porno producers are not philanthropists or missionaries; they're

in business because people want what they produce. What right have some of us to tell others that they may not have what they want? (I know some intelligent, cultivated men—and a few such women—who delight in porno.) I disbelieve in the legislation of taste.

## Defense Against Repression

7    The question of theatrical productions like *Oh! Calcutta!* is self-solving. If you want to go, go; if not, don't. The concept of "the dram of eale" is a puritan delusion. Gresham's Law doesn't operate in art. If bad art drove out good, there would not be any good art at all because for centuries there has been more bad art than good.

8    Most films are now clearly labeled by the ratings system of the Motion Picture Association of America. That system has manifest defects, but I have argued for it—and would still—as the best defense against repression. The X rating is, as is often said, a license for opportunists, but numbers of people want what the opportunists offer and I don't recognize anyone's right to deny it to them. More important, the X rating is a license for the serious film maker who wants to deal with sexual subjects. I'm glad that *Midnight Cowboy* (whatever its faults) was made and widely distributed, something that was difficult anyway and would have been nearly impossible without the protection of the X rating.

## Danish Survey

9    The concept of the state's interest in pornography, possibly related to the Roman concept of the republic of virtue, is gradually being eroded by scientific research. The researches in the Lockhart report, incomplete though they are, support the belief that there is no connection between porno and sexual crime. A Danish study *(New York Times, Nov. 9, 1970)* finds that sex crimes have sharply declined in Denmark—coincidentally?—in the three years since censorship laws have been eased there. The data and conclusions of the British Arts Council report on obscenity laws (full text in the *New Statesman,* August 8, 1969) support a recommendation for repeal of the Obscene Publications Acts. The state surely has a legitimate interest in the moral welfare of the community, but every ground for including porno in that interest is weakening.

10    The only real legal question is the protection of children. And it is a *question.* I can't define what a child is—six, yes, but sixteen?—and I can't define what "protection" is. I'm simply not convinced that a young person without sexual experience and some maturity of judgment can see pornography as pornography: that is—aside from understanding the

acts themselves and understanding the unconventionality (even impossibility) of some of them—can see the relation of porno to experience, as commentary and stimulant and revenge. "Depravity and corruption" are supposed to be considerations, too, though no one seems to know much about them. I have no wish to be blithe about parents' concern for a child (particularly since I have no children), but my guess is that a parent's attitude toward his child's exposure to porno is as much secret embarrassment at revelation of his own fantasies as it is protection of the young.

## Protection for Minors

11   Censorship legislation for minors, however, only moves the semantic and moral problem to a different locus. Two sociologists on the Lockhart commission recommended the abolition of *all* statutory legislation, for young persons as well as adults, on the ground that obscenity and pornography have long proved undefinable. They would rather rely on "informal social controls" and "improvements in sex education and better understanding of human sexual behavior" than on "ambiguous and arbitrarily administered laws."

12   Nevertheless I confess that, even without scientific data to prove harm, I'm uneasy at the thought of children being exposed to pornography before those "improvements" are realized.

13   Porno is of two distinct kinds.

14   I don't mean the difference between porno and erotic art nor the argument that sections of recognized classics—Rabelais, Joyce, etc.—are pornographic. (An argument I cannot accept. A sexual portion of a genuine artwork cannot—in my understanding—be pornographic. The latter means, for me, material devised *only* for sexual stimulation.)

15   The real difference is between imagined porno—written or drawn or painted—and performed porno, done in actuality or on film or in still photographs. The latter entails the degradation of human beings. It doesn't seem to me to matter that these performing men and women always seem cheerful and busily engaged, or that (reportedly) some of the occupants enjoy it or that some of them perform public sex acts as part of lives that are otherwise quite conventional. Obviously conditionings and rationales can vary widely, but I cannot believe that the use of human beings for these purposes is socially beneficial or morally liberating. On the contrary, I think it socially stultifying and morally warped.

16   I'm not talking about nudity and simulated intercourse in such plays as *Che!*, which are frequently done quite self-righteously as an attempt to *épater le bourgeois*. I mean (currently available in person and on film

in New York and other cities) the public performance of coition, fellatio, cunnilingus, and mutual masturbation—with the coition usually interrupted so that the male ejaculation can be seen.

## Acts of Vindictiveness

17   I've been as excited by watching some of those films as a human being ought presumably to be. But essentially those films seem to me acts of vindictiveness by men against women in return for the sexual restrictions and taboos of our society and for the cruelties of women toward men that those restrictions have produced. The vindictiveness is essentially mean-spirited and exploitative. I would hope that the socio-sexual improvements on which the Lockhart sociologists rely may affect performed porno first.

18   In any event, I think that the lumping-together of all porno—imagined and performed—is a conceptual error. The one-to-one relation of writer and reader is a different matter, in psychic and social senses, from the employment of people to enact fantasies.

19   Conclusions, *pro tem.*

20   I am not a swinger. I don't believe in pornography as a healthful reminder of the full genital life amidst a pallid and poky society, or as an extender of consciousness in any beneficial way. These views seem to me phony emancipation—in fact, a negation of the very fullness of life that is ostensibly being affirmed. Much better to concentrate on our silliness about the romanticized restrictions of love and the shortcomings of marriage, on the humiliations of both men and women in our rituals of courtship and bedding and wedding, that make pornography such a popular form of vengeance.

21   But the legal suppression of pornography seems to me anticivil and anticivilized (because it misses the anticivilizing reasons for porno), and also shows a failure in sense of humor. (If the idea of sex is funny, as it often is, the idea of porno is funniness multiplied.) I'm against censorship laws just as I'm against laws against certain kinds of sexual practice, or against any sexual practice between unmarried people, that still exist in many parts of this country. I want to be able to have porno if I want it. The purely personal opinion that I don't happen to want it very often should not be made the law of the land.

22   To put it entirely subjectively, I think that one way to cure my uneasiness on the subject of porno is to repeal all the laws restricting it, except possibly the ones forbidding the advertising and sale to minors. The more mature the individual, the more he resents the idea of being forbidden something that affects him alone; and the more mature individuals there are, the better the polity.

# REVIEW

## Content

1. Do you agree with Kauffmann's definition of pornography at the end of paragraph 14? Apply this definition to various items you have heard challenged as being pornographic: books, films, plays, poetry, the visual arts (paintings, sculpture, and so on). If Kauffmann's definition does not fit your conception of pornography, how do you define it?
2. Would you support Kauffmann in a drive to repeal all the laws restricting pornography, with the possible qualification he notes in sentence 1 of paragraph 22? If so, why? If not, why not?

## Rhetoric

3. There are several very short, one-sentence paragraphs in Kauffmann's essay. What is their effect? In what varying ways does Kauffmann use them? In addition, he ends paragraphs 3, 4, and 6 with very short sentences, all set up in the same structure. What is the effect of both the short sentences and the use of parallel structure here?
4. Kauffmann writes in a distinctive, highly readable style. Characterize his style and his readability by an analysis of paragraphs 20 and 21.

## Projects

5. Read in your college's library about the current status of debate on pornography and censorship in the United States and write up your findings in a paper.
6. Develop one of the following from Kauffmann's argument into a paper in which you either explain the quoted material or argue it, pro or con.
   (a) "Censorship laws . . . intrude on personal rights . . . . Laws against pornography, like laws against drinking and drug-taking and suicide, come between me and myself." (paragraph 4)
   (b) "Performed porno . . . entails the degradation of human beings." (paragraph 15)
   (c) films of performed porno as "acts of vindictiveness by men against women in return for the sexual restrictions and taboos of our society and for the cruelties of women toward men that those restrictions have produced." (paragraph 17)
   (d) "The legal suppression of pornography . . . shows a failure in sense of humor." (paragraph 21)
   (e) "The more mature the individual, the more he resents the idea of being forbidden something that affects him alone." (paragraph 22)

# Man Will Prevail

## WILLIAM FAULKNER

William Faulkner (1897–1962) is considered one of America's greatest twentieth-century novelists. A Southerner from Mississippi, Faulkner created, throughout a series of novels, Yoknapatawpha County, Mississippi, a fictitious locale that involves the reader in a Southern saga. Faulkner portrayed all levels of Southern society, as he delineated a region he viewed as doomed. And yet William Faulkner had great faith in the endurance of man against tremendous odds, as rings out in his famous Nobel Prize Acceptance Speech of 1950. In that address, Faulkner also reminds his fellow writers of their duty to help man "endure and prevail."

1   I feel that this award was not made to me as a man, but to my work—a life's work in the agony and sweat of the human spirit, not for glory and least of all for profit, but to create out of the materials of the human spirit something which did not exist before. So this award is only mine in trust. It will not be difficult to find a dedication for the money part of it commensurate with the purpose and significance of its origin. But I would like to do the same with the acclaim too, by using this moment as a pinnacle from which I might be listened to by the young men and women already dedicated to the same anguish and travail, among whom is already that one who will some day stand here where I am standing.

2   Our tragedy today is a general and universal physical fear so long sustained by now that we can even bear it. There are no longer problems of the spirit. There is only the question: When will I be blown up? Because of this, the young man or woman writing today has forgotten the problems of the human heart in conflict with itself which alone can make good writing because only that is worth writing about, worth the agony and the sweat.

3   He must learn them again. He must teach himself that the basest of all things is to be afraid; and, teaching himself that, forget it forever, leaving no room in his workshop for anything but the old verities and truths of the heart, the old universal truths lacking which any story is ephemeral and doomed—love and honor and pity and pride and compassion and sacrifice. Until he does so, he labors under a curse. He writes not of love but of lust, of defeats in which nobody loses anything

of value, of victories without hope and, worst of all, without pity or compassion. His griefs grieve on no universal bones, leaving no scars. He writes not of the heart but of the glands.

4      Until he relearns these things, he will write as though he stood alone and watched the end of man. I decline to accept the end of man. It is easy enough to say that man is immortal simply because he will endure: that when the last ding-dong of doom has clanged and faded from the last worthless rock hanging tideless in the last red and dying evening, that even then there will still be one more sound: that of his puny inexhaustible voice, still talking. I refuse to accept this. I believe that man will not merely endure: he will prevail. He is immortal, not because he alone among creatures has an inexhaustible voice, but because he has a soul, a spirit capable of compassion and sacrifice and endurance. The poet's, the writer's, duty is to write about these things. It is his privilege to help man endure by lifting his heart, by reminding him of the courage and honor and hope and pride and compassion and pity and sacrifice which have been the glory of his past. The poet's voice need not merely be the record of man, it can be one of the props, the pillars to help him endure and prevail.

## REVIEW

### Content

1. The Nobel Prize in Literature is received with an acceptance speech each year—but few such speeches become as memorable and as widely anthologized as has Faulkner's. Why, based on its *content,* do you guess this has happened?
2. Do you agree with Faulkner, in paragraph 2, that "the problems of the human heart in conflict with itself . . . alone can make good writing"? Do you agree that it is "the writer's duty" to help sustain the rest of the human race?

### Rhetoric

3. Apply the question in 1 above to the *style* of the speech.
4. Faulkner's speech is highly dramatic. What makes it so? Hear it read aloud, if possible. Do you hear any passages that you feel are *overdone,* where effect is sacrificed to eloquence?

### Projects

5. Write a paper about some instance in which *your* heart was "in conflict with itself." How do you *feel* toward such writing as compared with, say, analyzing a problem on a sociology test?
6. If you are taking a course in speech, can you apply some of Faulkner's stylistic techniques to your speeches?

# 8
# Science
# and
# Technology

# The Scientific Method

## PETER RITCHIE-CALDER

Peter Ritchie-Calder, Baron Ritchie-Calder of Balmashannar (1906–   ), was born in Scotland. A career in journalism took him to London, where he worked for several publications. He returned to Scotland as a professor of international relations at Edinburgh University (1961–1967). Since 1972, Ritchie-Calder has been a senior fellow at the Center for the Study of Democratic Institutions at Santa Barbara, California. His books include *After the Seventh Day* (1960), *Living with the Atom* (1962), *Common Sense About a Starving World* (1962), and *Man and the Cosmos: The Nature of Science Today* (1968). In the following excerpt from *Man and the Cosmos*, Ritchie-Calder explains the methods of "pure" science and contrasts that discipline with both "applied" science and "technology."

1    Sir Francis Bacon can be fairly said to have resurrected the scientific method by insisting on experimental investigation. He himself was scarcely a laboratory scientist, although he died as a result of an experiment (anticipating refrigeration); at the age of 65, he went out to stuff a goose with snow and contracted pneumonia. His writings (*Advancement of Learning, Novum organum,* and *New Atlantis*) spell out what now are widely accepted principles of modern science, rejecting the *deductive,* or thinking-off-the-top-of-the-head principle, in favor of *inductive,* or take-off-your-coat principle. He insisted that the man of science must *observe* and choose his facts; he must form a *hypothesis* that links them together and provides a plausible explanation of them; and he must carry out numerous checks or repeated *experiments* to support or deny his hypothesis. Trained as a lawyer, Bacon applied to science the laws of evidence and the burden of proof.

2    The scientific method, as ideally practiced today, is an exacting discipline, demanding that the man of science lay aside all his preconceptions. As Claude Bernard enjoined his students, "When you enter the laboratory, put off your imagination, as you take off your overcoat;

but put it on again as you do your overcoat when you leave the laboratory. Before the experiment and between whiles, let your imagination
wrap you round; put it right away from you during the experiment
itself lest it hinder your observatory power."

## Science and Precision

3      The man of science strives to attain the perfection of reducing everything to precise measurements. He will doubt the very sensory data that
constitute his observations, often relying on sensing devices that appear
more reliable and sensitive than he. Sharing the beauties of the rainbow
with the poet, he also will spell it out in angstrom units (of wavelength).
His olfactory nerves and tastebuds help him enjoy the bouquet and flav-
or of a wine, but his stern mistress, Science, expects him to express
it by chromatography as aromatics. He may revel in beautiful music,
but to make sound more scientifically meaningful he will reduce it to
pitch, frequency, and amplitude of sound waves. He observes that the
upper limit of human hearing is about 20,000 cycles per second while
his instruments seem to detect frequencies of 100,000,000 cycles per
second. His experiences of hot and cold often are inadequate to deal
with the range and precision of temperature with which he may·work
in his experiments.

4      Precise measurements are essential because every experiment has to
be repeatable, not only by him but by other men of science, anywhere
and everywhere. He has to justify, not only by argument by by proof
(empirically repeatable evidence), any hypothesis he tries to establish.
Exact science is quantitative and not qualitative.

5      The observant reader will have noticed the labored use of "man of
science." This has been deliberate. The word "scientist" did not appear
in the English language nor, as far as one knows, in any language until
1840. As late as 1895 the London *Daily News* was still complaining about
this term as "an American innovation." And H. G. Wells always preferred "man of science" to "scientist." The distinction is important because the "-ist" meant the arrival of the career investigator and the development of specializations (each with its inbred terminology). Previously
a "man of science" had meant a person of learning, especially inquisitive
about nature—but not bulkheaded within narrow interests—and capable
of sharing his inquiries and findings with other educated men. Even
his terminology was common ground. It was descriptively derived from
Greek or Latin roots; *e.g., protozoon* (1834) meant just what it said—first
form of living things. Today the terms become more and more cryptic.
From the point of departure symbolized by "scientist," experimental
science deviated from natural philosophy and other forms of learning.
The tendency was confirmed when in 1901 the influential Royal Society

of London dissociated itself from the concept of the Academy as the forum of all learning. Promoting the establishment of the British Academy to take care of "moral and political sciences, including history, philosophy, law, politics and economics, archaelogy and philology," the Royal Society assumed custody of the experimental sciences.

## The Hierarchy of Science

6    Another process had been going on—what A. N. Whitehead called "the greatest invention of the 19th-century . . . the invention of the method of invention." This was technology that increasingly brought science into the industrial arts and crafts. So there came about a hierarchy of science—"pure" or academic science, seeking knowledge for its own sake; oriented fundamental science, research within a frame of reference; "applied" or programmed science, which is research with a practical or manipulative purpose; and "technology," which is the transfer of scientific knowledge into technical practice. Within such a hierarchy scientific practitioners might be distinguished as The Makers Possible, The Makers to Happen, and The Makers to Pay. But the growing tendency is to minimize such distinctions; indeed, there is an interrelationship so pervasive that it amounts to what cyberneticists call feedback: stimulation, response, and adjustment.

7    The theoretician adjusts his parameters to experimental evidence; the experimentalist responds to the theory; the technologist reacts to both in creating his "hardware," and the "hardware" itself stimulates the experimentalist and the theoretician. (Just as academic science would be crippled significantly without the computer, so the computer was derived from mathematical principles that the electronics engineers activated.) With its rapid accumulation of knowledge, with its aggregation of new discoveries, and with its impetuous conversion of desk-and-laboratory findings into practical innovations, the fantastic acceleration of scientific progress has arisen through feedback.

8    The result has been that the volume of knowledge—six million published scientific communications, increasing at the rate of half-a-million a year—has become a Niagara of information; that the number of scientists is doubling every ten years; and that science is becoming more and more fragmented into specializations, barely able to communicate with each other because of the unique language each has invented for its convenience. And "natural philosophy" has been swamped by experimental results. No wonder, then, that the ordinary intelligent layman finds himself overawed and feels that scientists have become a priesthood, creating and conserving their own mysteries.

9    The object of this discussion is not to qualify the reader to join the priesthood. It is hoped that it will offer an insight into the processes

of science that will help the reader take part in an open-ended debate, rather than eavesdrop on a closed seminar, and help him form his own judgments as to what may happen and where Science is going.

## Scientific Principles Applied

10   As a reminder that the scientific method, on which all the arguments depend, is not at all intimidating, let us recapitulate with a simple example of Baconian principles:

11   You are interested in animals and you notice that some have long tails; some have short; and some (to wit: human beings) have no tails. (You never have seen the occasional infant who is born with one.) Some have toes; some have claws; and some have hooves. Some eat meat; some eat herbage; and some eat both. And so on. . . . But you notice that a whole group of them, including human beings, have one thing in common—they all suckle their young. So you classify them as "milk-giving animals" or, if you know Latin, you call them "mammals" (*mamma* — breast). Something else strikes you as significant: you have observed no mammals that lay eggs. From your data you say: "Animals that suckle their young *apparently* do not lay eggs." That is your hypothesis, a provisional statement on which you proceed to do more research (which means search and search again). In the woods, farms, and zoos, and wherever you search, you continue to verify your impression that mammals do not lay eggs. You even find swimming animals, like whales and seals, that, unlike other sea creatures, do not lay eggs, but suckle their young. Now you are getting somewhere. Your *hypothesis* can be promoted into a *theory*, which is a well-established hypothesis that can be related to other accepted principles. You drop the word "apparently." But you are still not satisfied. You travel through North America, South America, Europe, Africa, and Asia, observing and comparing notes with others. Always it is the same: "Animals that suckle their young do not lay eggs." Now you may think you can state it as a universal *"Law* of Nature." You say categorically, "No animals that suckle their young lay eggs." But no scientific "law" ever is proved ultimately, one reason being that it is not feasible to observe *all* the individual cases to which it is held to apply. Any "law" in science is tentative, probabilistic, and uncertain; it is always subject to revision in the light of new evidence. Thus no scientific inquiry is ever complete, and you go off to the Australian continent to continue testing your theory. There you meet the duck-billed platypus, or duck mole, and find that this curious animal not only lays eggs but also suckles its young. All that trouble just to find yourself wrong in the end! This may be disappointing, but it is not disastrous. You can restate your *law* more precisely: "No animals (with the exception of, etc.) that suckle their young lay eggs."

12    A physiologist then may remind you that the human egg (ovum) is "laid" in a nest formed by a fold in the wall of the womb. You accept this observation of internal incubation and restate your law adding the word "externally." A scientific law, like judicial law, can define the conditions in which it will apply. This mutability of scientific law is important: it is "case law," not dogma. That is what contrasts the modern and medieval conception of science.

## REVIEW

### Content

1. Why does imagination not belong in the laboratory? Why does Ritchie-Calder say, "Exact science is quantitative and not qualitative"?
2. Why is no scientific "law" ultimately "true"? Why does Ritchie-Calder call it "case law"—versus dogma?

### Rhetoric

3. Ritchie-Calder has been a journalist as well as a scholar. In what way does his early journalistic career seem to have influenced his writing on scholarly subjects, as here? Do you find his writing interesting to read?
4. Ritchie-Calder presents his sample "experiment" (paragraph 11) in a different style from that of the rest of the essay. Why? Contrast the styles. What does he achieve by using "you" in paragraph 11?

### Projects

5. Relate some interesting experience you have had in the same way Ritchie-Calder relates the experiment in paragraph 11; that is, involve your reader as if it were happening directly to him/her by using "you." Write short, direct sentences, to give a sense of immediacy to what is happening. Make the narrative as much a "you-are-there" one as you can.
6. The various branches of science organize their knowledge by classification; that is, by searching out distinguishing characteristics and then creating a word to become a classifying label—as "mammal" designates animals that suckle their young and that generally do not lay eggs externally. Look up in the dictionary and figure out how the following designating words were arrived at: conifer(ous), alkaline, tuberous, amphibian, legume, igneous, deciduous, reptilian, mollusk, Lepidoptera, rodent—and others that interest you from some science course.

# We Scientists Have the Right To Play God

## EDMUND R. LEACH

Edmund R. Leach (1910–    ) is a noted British anthropologist and educator who has served as provost of King's College, Cambridge. He has done considerable anthropological field research and has held professional posts in America as well as in England. Leach has written, among other books, *Rethinking Anthropology* (1961), *A Runaway World?* (1968), and *Genesis as a Myth* (1970). "We Scientists Have the Right To Play God" first appeared in *The Saturday Evening Post,* November 16, 1968. In his essay, Leach argues that, as the powers of man more and more replace the power of God as controller of the natural universe, scientists must assume moral responsibility for the quality of life on earth.

1    Human scientists now have it in their power to redesign the face of the earth, and to decide what kind of species shall survive to inherit it. How they actually use this terrible potentiality must depend on moral judgments, not on reason. But who shall decide, and how shall we judge? The answer to these questions seems to me repugnant but quite plain: There can be no source for these moral judgments except the scientist himself. In traditional religion, morality was held to derive from God, but God was only credited with the authority to establish and enforce moral rules because He was also credited with supernatural powers of creation and destruction. Those powers have now been usurped by man, and he must take on the moral responsibility that goes with them.

2    Our idea of God is a product of history. What I now believe about the supernatural is derived from what I was taught by my parents, and what they taught me was derived from what they were taught, and so on. But such beliefs are justified by·faith alone, never by reason, and the true believer is expected to go on reaffirming his faith in the same verbal formula, even if the passage of history and the growth of scientific knowledge should have turned the words into plain nonsense. Everyone now knows that the cosmology that is presupposed by the language of Christian utterance is quite unrelated to any empirical reality. This explains why so many religious-minded people exhibit an extreme reluctance to inquire at all closely into the meaning of basic religious concepts.

## Traditional Roles of God

3      But just what *do* we mean by the word God? In Christian mythology, as represented by the Bible, God is credited with a variety of functions. He is the creator who first set the cosmological clock in motion; He is the lawgiver who establishes the principles of the moral code; He is the judge who punishes sinners even when human law fails to do so; He is also a kind of trickster who intervenes in human affairs in a quite arbitrary way so as to test the faith of the righteous; and, finally, He is a mediator between sinful man and his destiny. He is not only the judge of sinners but their salvation. These attributes of God are by definition "superhuman," but they are nevertheless qualities of an essentially human kind. The God of Judeo-Christianity is, in all His aspects, whether creator, judge, trickster or mediator, quite explicitly anthropomorphic. And the converse is equally true: There is necessarily something godlike about every human being.

4      Anthropologists, who make it their business to discover just how human beings perceive themselves as differing from one another and from other natural species, will tell you that every community conceives of itself as being uniquely "human." This humanity is always felt to be a quality of civilization and orderliness that "we" alone share; "other" creatures, whether they be foreigners or animals, are members of inferior species and are described by labels such as "savage," "wild," "lawless," "heathen," "dangerous," "mysterious."

5      There is a paradox here: When we affirm that *we* are civilized and that the *others* are savage, we are claiming superiority over the others, but the mythology always explains the origin of this superiority by a story of the Adam and Eve type. "In the beginning God created our first ancestors and gave them the moral rules that are the basis of our present civilization." But this "God" himself belongs to the category of "others": He is nonhuman, He is above the law, He is dangerous and mysterious, He existed even before the beginning, He is Nature itself. So we find that, in religious terms, culture—that is, civilization—stands in a curiously ambivalent relationship to nonculture—that is, nature. At one level we, the men of culture, are dominant over nature, but at another level God and nature merge together and become dominant over us.

6      All this is more relevant to my title than might at first appear, for scientists, like God, have now become mediators between culture and nature. Modern science grew out of medieval alchemy, and the alchemists were quite explicitly men who sought to do what only gods might properly do—to transform one element into another and to discover the elixir of immortal life. They pursued these revolutionary objectives in the atmosphere of a very conservative society. Official doctrine held that the order of nature had been established once and for all in the first six days of the Creation, and that the proper station and destiny

of every individual had been preordained by God. The alchemists, therefore, were very properly regarded as blasphemous heretics, for they were
attempting to tamper with God's handiwork, they were claiming that
"laws of nature" could be altered by human intervention, they were
playing at being God. Moreover, they lived in a world of fantasy: The
heretical miracles that they claimed to perform were imaginary.

## "Supernatural" Achievements of Science

7    But at the present time the ordinary everyday achievements of science,
which we take quite for granted, are of precisely the kind that our medieval forebears considered to be supernatural. We can fly through the
air, we can look in on events that are taking place on the other side
of the earth, we can transplant organs from corpses to living bodies,
we can change one element into another, we can even produce a chemical mimicry of living tissue itself.

8    In the traditional mythology, the performance of miracles is only a
part (and on the whole a minor part) of God's function. God's major
role is moral—He is the source of the rules, He punishes (or redeems)
the wicked. The scientist can now play God in his role, as wonder-
worker, but can he—and should he—also play God as moral arbiter?
If you put this question to any group of actual scientists, the great majority will answer it with an unhesitating "No," for it is one of the most
passionately held formal dogmas of modern science that research procedure should be objective and not tendentious. The scientist must seek
to establish the truth for truth's sake, and not as an advocate of any
particular creed. And on the face of it, this principle is self-evident:
If we are to attain scientific objectivity, moral detachment is absolutely
essential.

9    Yet this viewpoint, too, is a product of history. Modern science can
be said to have begun when Copernicus and Galileo established the fundamental bases of modern astronomy. In order to do this, they had
to achieve moral detachment and deny the truth of the Ptolemaic cosmology, which at that time had the official sanction of the Church. As
both these men were good Catholics, and several of the cardinals, including Galileo's Pope, were excellent scientists, the conflict of values led
to the utmost tribulation on all sides. And so it has continued even
down to the present. Again and again leaders of the Church have felt
themselves compelled to declare that some finding of science—such as
evolution by natural selection, or the chemical origin of life, or the capacity of the human race to reproduce itself beyond the limits of its
food supply—is contrary to religious doctrine, and they have demanded
that the scientists recant. Against this coercion the scientists have created

their own counterdogma: The prusuit of scientific truth must be free of all moral or religious restraints.

## Drawing the Line

10    But the claim to moral detachment is not absolute. In actual practice all scientists draw the line somewhere, and they usually draw it between culture and nature. Freedom from moral restraint applies only to the study of nature, not to the study of culture. Even the Nazi scientists who experimented with human beings as if they were monkeys, rats or guinea pigs, would not have challenged this distinction. They merely drew their line in a different place: From their point of view the Jews were not really human, but just a part of nature.

11    But discriminations of this sort are very ungodlike. God is the creator and protector of *all* things: He does not destroy one part of His creation in order to give benefit to another; creation is a totality, one and indivisible. In contrast, we human beings habitually act as if all other living species, whether animals or plants, exist only for our own convenience; we feel free to exploit or destroy them as we think fit. It is true that some sentimental laymen have moral qualms about vivisection, but no orthodox scientist could ever have any hesitation about experiments involving "mere animals." All the same, there are always some kinds of experiments that any particular research worker would *not* be prepared to carry out. Each individual does, in practice, "draw the line somewhere," so the question arises whether he might not with advantage draw it somewhere else.

12    The moral doubts of those who helped to design the first atomic bombs have become notorious, and today there must be thousands of highly qualified scientists engaged on hundreds of different chemical and biological research projects who face similar difficulties. It is not simply a matter of trying to measure the positive value of a gain in human knowledge against the negative value of powers of military destruction; the merits and demerits of our whole biological history are at stake. It is no good for the scientist to suppose that there is some outside authority who can decide whether his experiments are legitimate or illegitimate. It has become useless to appeal to God against the Devil; the scientist must be the source of his own morality.

13    Because God traditionally had unlimited power to intervene and alter the natural course of events, it made sense to treat Him as the ultimate moral authority as well. But today when the molecular biologists are rapidly unraveling the genetic chemistry of all living things—while the radio astronomers are deciphering the program of an evolving cosmos—all the marvels of creation are seen to be mechanisms rather than mys-

teries. Since even the human brain is nothing more than an immensely complicated computer, it is no longer necessary to invoke metaphysics to explain how it works. In the resulting mechanistic universe all that remains of the divine will is the moral consciousness of man himself.

## Assuming God's Moral Role

14    So we must now learn to play God in a moral as well as in a creative or destructive sense. To do this effectively, we shall have to educate our children in quite a different way. In the past, education has always been designed to inculcate a respect for the wisdom and experience of the older generation, whose members have been credited with an intuitive understanding of the wishes of an omniscient God. From this point of view, the dogmas of religion represent the sum of our historical experience. So long as it appeared that "natural law" was eternal and unalterable—except by God—it was quite sensible to use history in this way as a guide to virtue. But in our changed circumstances, when we ourselves can alter all the ground rules of the game, excessive deference to established authority could well be an invitation to disaster. For example, as long as medical science was virtually impotent—as it was until the beginning of this century—it made perfect sense to accept the traditional theological principle that it is always virtuous to save a life. But today the doctors, provided they are given sufficient resources, can preserve alive all manner of deformed infants and senile invalids who would, in the natural course of events, have been dead long ago. But the cost of preserving these defective lives is ultimately borne by those who are normal and healthy, and at some point the burden will become intolerable, and saving life will become morally evil. When we are faced with moral paradoxes of this kind—and science presents us with new ones every day—it is useless to console ourselves with the conventional religious formulas. We ourselves have to decide what is sin and what is virtue, and we must do so on the basis of our modern knowledge and not on the basis of traditional categories. This implies that we must all share in a kind of immediate collective responsibility for any action that any one individual performs. Perhaps this all sounds like a pie-in-the-sky doctrine. But unless we teach those of the next generation that they can afford to be atheists only if they assume the moral responsibilities of God, the prospects for the human race are decidedly bleak.

## REVIEW

### Content

1. What was *your* feeling, before reading the essay, about science and the question of "moral responsibility" that Leach speaks of in paragraph 1? Did the essay make you think further here? *Should* scientists become

"the source of [their] own morality"? If you say "no" here, then what do you see as *preferable* guidelines for science as it becomes more and more powerful in relation to human life?

2. Leach makes some very broad statements in paragraph 13: "all the marvels . . . man himself." Do you agree with him here? Discuss.

## Rhetoric

3. Although Leach has constructed a carefully woven argument on a highly controversial subject, the writing flows smoothly and is quite readable. What structural devices contribute to this? How do the following help? Opening paragraph 3 with a question; parallel structure in paragraphs 3, 5, and 7; beginning paragraphs with short sentences (paragraphs 2, 10, and 11); the use of "But" to begin 3, 10 and 11; dividing sentences with a colon (first sentence, paragraph 5; final sentence, paragraphs 3, 6, 8, 9, 10).

4. Leach uses a number of words that would be useful in any discussion about science and religion. What do the following mean? Define them from their context here, if you can, using the dictionary only secondarily or to check your meaning: cosmology (paragraph 2); empirical (2), anthropomorphic (3); paradox (5 and 14); alchemy (6); heretical (6); vivisection (12); metaphysics (13); omniscient (14).

## Projects

5. Make a paper out of some of your thinking in relation to 1 above. Try to use some of Leach's writing devices (see 3 above). Try also to compose a first paragraph that is strong and carefully reasoned, as is Leach's opening paragraph, in order to command at once your reader's respect for your argument.

6. Develop a paper from one of the following statements by Leach, *if* you agree with him:

   (a) "The scientist must seek to establish the truth for truth's sake, and not as an advocate of any particular creed." (paragraph 8)

   (b) "It is no good [any longer] for the scientist to suppose that there is some outside authority who can decide whether his experiments are legitimate or illegitimate." (12)

   (c) "Since . . . the human brain is nothing more than an immensely complicated computer, it is no longer necessary to invoke metaphysics to explain how it works." (13)

   (d) ". . . the cost of preserving . . . defective lives is ultimately borne by those who are normal and healthy, and at some point the burden will become intolerable, and saving life will become morally evil." (14) (Argue either pro or con on this one.)

   (e) "[Given the level of development of science today] we ourselves have to decide what is sin and what is virtue, and we must do so on the basis of our modern knowledge and not on the basis of traditional categories." (14)

# The Land Pyramid

## ALDO LEOPOLD

Aldo Leopold (1886–1948) began a career in conservation and forestry with the U.S. Forest Service in New Mexico and Arizona in 1909. After helping to develop National Forest policies, Leopold moved into wildlife management in 1928. A chair of game management was created for him in 1933 at the University of Wisconsin. The following selection, from Leopold's *A Sand County Almanac* (1948), outlines the chain of dependency in Nature and takes note of the consequences of man's interference in that delicate balance.

1   An ethic to supplement and guide the economic relation to land presupposes the existence of some mental image of land as a biotic mechanism. We can be ethical only in relation to something we can see, feel, understand, love, or otherwise have faith in.

2   The image commonly employed in conservation education is "the balance of nature." For reasons too lengthy to detail here, this figure of speech fails to describe accurately what little we know about the land mechanism. A much truer image is the one employed in ecology: the biotic pyramid. I shall first sketch the pyramid as a symbol of land, and later develop some of its implications in terms of land-use.

3   Plants absorb energy from the sun. This energy flows through a circuit called the biota, which may be represented by a pyramid consisting of layers. The bottom layer is the soil. A plant layer rests on the soil, an insect layer on the plants, a bird and rodent layer on the insects, and so on up through various animal groups to the apex layer, which consists of the larger carnivores.

4   The species of a layer are alike not in where they came from, or in what they look like, but rather in what they eat. Each successive layer depends on those below it for food and often for other services, and each in turn furnishes food and services to those above. Proceeding upward, each successive layer decreases in numerical abundance. Thus, for every carnivore there are hundreds of his prey, thousands of their prey, millions of insects, uncountable plants. The pyramidal form of the system reflects this numerical progression from apex to base. Man shares an intermediate layer with the bears, raccoons, and squirrels which eat both meat and vegetables.

# The Energy Circuit

5    The lines of dependency for food and other services are called food chains. Thus soil-oak-deer-Indian is a chain that has now been largely converted to soil-corn-cow-farmer. Each species, including ourselves, is a link in many chains. The deer eats a hundred plants other than oak, and the cow a hundred plants other than corn. Both, then, are links in a hundred chains. The pyramid is a tangle of chains so complex as to seem disorderly, yet the stability of the system proves it ot be a highly organized structure. Its functioning depends on the co-operation and competion of its diverse parts.

6    In the beginning, the pyramid of life was low and squat; the food chains short and simple. Evolution has added layer after layer, link after link. Man is one of thousands of accretions to the height and complexity of the pyramid. Science has given us many doubts, but it has given us at least one certainty: the trend of evolution is to elaborate and diversify the biota.

7    Land, then, is not merely soil; it is a fountain of energy flowing through a circuit of soils, plants, and animals. Food chains are the living channels which conduct energy upward; death and decay return it to the soil. The circuit is not closed; some energy is dissipated in decay, some is added by absorption from the air, some is stored in soils, peats, and long-lived forests; but it is a sustained circuit, like a slowly augmented revolving fund of life. There is always a net loss by downhill wash, but this is normally small and offset by the decay of rocks. It is deposited in the ocean and, in the course of geological time, raised to form new lands and new pyramids.

8    The velocity and character of the upward flow of energy depend on the complex structure of the plant and animal community, much as the upward flow of sap in a tree depends on its complex cellular organization. Without this complexity, normal circulation would presumably not occur. Structure means the characteristic numbers, as well as the characteristic kinds and functions, of the component species. This interdependence between the complex structure of the land and its smooth functioning as an energy unit is one of its basic attributes.

# Changes in Circuit—Subsequent Adjustments

9    When a change occurs in one part of the circuit, many other parts must adjust themselves to it. Change does not necessarily obstruct or divert the flow of energy; evolution is a long series of self-induced changes, the net result of which has been to elaborate the flow mechanism and to lengthen the circuit. Evolutionary changes, however, are

usually slow and local. Man's invention of tools has enabled him to make changes of unprecedented violence, rapidity, and scope.

10      One change is in the composition of floras and faunas. The larger predators are lopped off the apex of the pyramid; food chains, for the first time in history, become shorter rather than longer. Domesticated species from other lands are substituted for wild ones, and wild ones are moved to new habitats. In this world-wide pooling of faunas and floras, some species get out of bounds as pests and diseases, others are extinguished. Such effects are seldom intended or foreseen; they represent unpredicted and often untraceable readjustments in the structure. Agricultural science is largely a race between the emergence of new pests and the emergence of new techniques for their control.

11      Another change touches the flow of energy through plants and animals and its return to the soil. Fertility is the ability of soil to receive, store, and release energy. Agriculture, by overdrafts on the soil, or by too radical a substitution of domestic for native species in the superstructure, may derange the channels of flow or deplete storage. Soils depleted of their storage, or of the organic matter which anchors it, wash away faster than they form. This is erosion.

12      Waters, like soil, are part of the energy circuit. Industry, by polluting waters or obstructing them with dams, may exclude the plants and animals necessary to keep energy in circulation.

13      Transportation brings about another basic change: the plants or animals grown in one region are now consumed and returned to the soil in another. Transportation taps the energy stored in rocks, and in the air, and uses it elsewhere; thus we fertilize the garden with nitrogen gleaned by the guano birds from the fishes of seas on the other side of the Equator. Thus the formerly localized and self-contained circuits are pooled on a world-wide scale.

14      The process of altering the pyramid for human occupation releases stored energy, and this often gives rise, during the pioneering period, to a deceptive exuberance of plant and animal life, both wild and tame. These releases of biotic capital tend to becloud or postpone the penalties of violence.

## REVIEW

### Content

1. Does setting up a biotic pyramid, with food chains representing the upward flow of energy and death and decay representing its downward flow, seem to you a logical and useful way to describe "the land mechanism"? Had you ever thought of the overriding importance of *land* before reading this selection?

2. Develop through discussion Leopold's last sentence in paragraph 5: both how this point "works" ecologically and the implications of *ignor-*

*ing* it. Elaborate on the energy circuit Leopold describes in paragraph 7 by filling in the specific details of various "layers" as the energy is both utilized upward and dissipated, or otherwise re-converted, downward.

## Rhetoric

3. Leopold has chosen to use a geometric figure, subdivided, to help you follow his analysis of the energy chain originating in land. Does this "diagramming analogy" help you understand the points he makes?
4. Leopold is trying to explain a complex system by analytically breaking it down into its component parts. One might have expected that this could be accomplished only in long, involved, very densely structured sentences. Analyze Leopold's prose to see how he structures sentences to promote clarity.

## Projects

5. Draw and label the land pyramid, to help you "visualize" Leopold's analysis; try to make your diagram as specific as needed to demonstrate something of how the "cooperation and competition" Leopold refers to in paragraph 5 occurs.
6. Write a paper developed by one detailed example related to one of the following;
   (a) "One change . . . are extinguished." (paragraph 10)
   (b) "Agricultural science . . . for their control." (1)
   (c) a cause of erosion (11)
   (d) interference with the water component of the energy circuit (12)
   (e) paragraph 14

# Observation and Discovery
## Chimpanzees Make Tools
### JANE VAN LAWICK-GOODALL

Jane van Lawick-Goodall is an anthropologist who specializes in the study of animal behavior. She is Scientific Director of the Gombe Stream Research Centre at Tanzania in East Africa. Lawick-Goodall and her photographer husband, Baron Hugo van Lawick, who work as a team, were awarded

the Louis S. B. Leakey Foundation's 1974 Ethology Award for their achievements. They are coauthors of *Innocent Killers* (1971) and *Grub: The Bush
Baby* (1972). In 1971, Lawick-Goodall published *In the Shadow of Man*,
about her field observations of chimpanzees in the Gombe Stream National
Park. The following selection from that book recounts the excitement of
her initial observation of meat-eating habits and tool-making techniques
among the chimpanzees.

1    . . . As the weeks went by the chimpanzees became less and less afraid.
Quite often when I was on one of my food-collecting expeditions I came
across chimpanzees unexpectedly, and after a time I found that some
of them would tolerate my presence provided they were in fairly thick
forest and I sat still and did not try to move closer than sixty to eighty
yards. And so, during my second month of watching from the peak,
when I saw a group settle down to feed I sometimes moved closer and
was thus able to make more detailed observations.

2    It was at this time that I began to recognize a number of different
individuals. As soon as I was sure of knowing a chimpanzee if I saw
it again, I named it. Some scientists feel that animals should be labeled
by numbers—that to name them is anthropomorphic—but I have always
been interested in the *differences* between individuals, and a name is not
only more individual than a number but also far easier to remember.
Most names were simply those which, for some reason or other, seemed
to suit the individuals to whom I attached them. A few chimps were
named because some facial expression or mannerism reminded me of
human acquaintances.

## Old Mr. McGregor and Friends

3    The easiest individual to recognize was old Mr. McGregor. The crown
of his head, his neck, and his shoulders were almost entirely devoid
of hair, but a slight frill remained around his head rather like a monk's
tonsure. He was an old male—perhaps between thirty and forty years
of age (the longevity record for a captive chimp is forty-seven years).
During the early months of my acquaintance with him, Mr. McGregor
was somewhat belligerent. If I accidentally came across him at close quarters he would threaten me with an upward and backward jerk of his
head and a shaking of branches before climbing down and vanishing
from my sight. He reminded me, for some reason, of Beatrix Potter's
old gardener in *The Tale of Peter Rabbit*.

4    Ancient Flo with her deformed, bulbous nose and ragged ears was
equally easy to recognize. Her youngest offspring at that time were two-
year-old Fifi, who still rode everywhere on her mother's back, and her

juvenile son, Figan, who was always to be seen wandering around with his mother and little sister. He was then about six years old; it was approximately a year before he would attain puberty. Flo often traveled with another old mother, Olly. Olly's long face was also distinctive; the fluff of hair on the back of her head—though no other feature—reminded me of my aunt, Olwen. Olly, like Flo, was accompanied by two children, a daughter younger than Fifi, and an adolescent son about a year older than Figan.

5    Then there was William, who, I am certain, must have been Olly's blood brother. I never saw any special signs of friendship between them, but their faces were amazingly alike. They both had long upper lips that wobbled when they suddenly turned their heads. William had the added distinction of several thin, deeply etched scar marks running down his upper lip from his nose.

6    Two of the other chimpanzees I knew well by sight at that time were David Graybeard and Goliath. Like David and Goliath in the Bible, these two individuals were closely associated in my mind because they were very often together. Goliath, even in those days of his prime, was not a giant, but he had a splendid physique and the springy movements of an athlete. He probably weighed about one hundred pounds. David Graybeard was less afraid of me from the start than were any of the other chimps. I was always pleased when I picked out his handsome face and well-marked silvery beard in a chimpanzee group, for with David to calm the others, I had a better chance of approaching to observe them more closely.

7    Before the end of my trial period in the field I made two really exciting discoveries—discoveries that made the previous months of frustration well worth while. And for both of them I had David Graybeard to thank.

## Chimpanzees Eating Piglet

8    One day I arrived on the Peak and found a small group of chimps just below me in the upper branches of a thick tree. As I watched I saw that one of them was holding a pink-looking object from which he was from time to time pulling pieces with his teeth. There was a female and a youngster and they were both reaching out toward the male, their hands actually touching his mouth. Presently the female picked up a piece of the pink thing and put it to her mouth: it was at this moment that I realized the chimps were eating meat.

9    After each bite of meat the male picked off some leaves with his lips and chewed them with the flesh. Often, when he had chewed for several minutes on this leafy wad, he spat out the remains into the waiting hands of the female. Suddenly he dropped a small piece of meat,

and like a flash the youngster swung after it to the ground. Even as he reached to pick it up the undergrowth exploded and an adult bushpig charged toward him. Screaming, the juvenile leaped back into the tree. The pig remained in the open, snorting and moving backward and forward. Soon I made out the shapes of three small striped piglets. Obviously the chimps were eating a baby pig. The size was right and later, when I realized that the male was David Graybeard, I moved closer and saw that he was indeed eating piglet.

10    For three hours I watched the chimps feeding. David occasionally let the female bite pieces from the carcass and once he actually detached a small piece of flesh and placed it in her outstretched hand. When he finally climbed down there was still meat left on the carcass; he carried it away in one hand, followed by the others.

11    Of course I was not sure, then, that David Graybeard had caught the pig for himself, but even so, it was tremendously exciting to know that these chimpanzees actually ate meat. Previously scientists had believed that although these apes might occasionally supplement their diet with a few insects or small rodents and the like they were primarily vegetarians and fruit eaters. No one had suspected that they might hunt larger mammals.

12    It was within two weeks of this observation that I saw something that excited me even more. By then it was October and the short rains had begun. The blackened slopes were softened by feathery new grass shoots and in some places the ground was carpeted by a variety of flowers. The Chimpanzees' Spring, I called it. I had had a frustrating morning, tramping up and down three valleys with never a sign or sound of a chimpanzee. Hauling myself up the steep slope of Mlinda Valley I headed for the peak, not only weary but soaking wet from crawling through dense undergrowth. Suddenly I stopped, for I saw a slight movement in the long grass about sixty yards away. Quickly focusing my binoculars I saw that it was a single chimpanzee, and just then he turned in my direction. I recognized David Graybeard.

## David Graybeard Uses a Tool

13    Cautiously I moved around so that I could see what he was doing. He was squatting beside the red earth mound of a termite nest, and as I watched I saw him carefully push a long grass stem down into a hole in the mound. After a moment he withdrew it and picked something from the end with his mouth. I was too far away to make out what he was eating, but it was obvious that he was actually using a grass stem as a tool.

14    I knew that on two occasions casual observers in West Africa had seen chimpanzees using objects as tools: one had broken open palm-nut

kernels by using a rock as a hammer, and a group of chimps had been observed pushing sticks into an underground bees' nest and licking off the honey. Somehow I had never dreamed of seeing anything so exciting myself.

15    For an hour David feasted at the termite mound and then he wandered slowly away. When I was sure he had gone I went over to examine the mound. I found a few crushed insects strewn about, and a swarm of worker termites sealing the entrances of the nest passages into which David had obviously been poking his stems. I picked up one of his discarded tools and carefully pushed it into a hole myself. Immediately I felt the pull of several termites as they seized the grass, and when I pulled it out there were a number of worker termites and a few soldiers, with big red heads, clinging on with their mandibles. There they remained, sticking out at right angles to the stem with their legs waving in the air.

16    Before I left I trampled down some of the tall dry grass and constructed a rough hide—just a few palm fronds leaned up against the low branch of a tree and tied together at the top. I planned to wait there the next day. But it was another week before I was able to watch a chimpanzee "fishing" for termites again. Twice chimps arrived, but each time they saw me and moved off immediately. Once a swarm of fertile winged termites—the princes and princesses, as they are called—flew off on their nuptial flight, their huge white wings fluttering frantically as they carried the insects higher and higher. Later I realized that it is at this time of year, during the short rains, when the worker termites extend the passages of the nest to the surface, preparing for these emigrations. Several such swarms emerge between October and January. It is principally during these months that the chimpanzees feed on termites.

17    On the eighth day of my watch David Graybeard arrived again, together with Goliath, and the pair worked there for two hours. I could see much better: I observed how they scratched open the sealed-over passage entrances with a thumb or forefinger. I watched how they bit the ends off their tools when they became bent, or used the other end, or discarded them in favor of new ones. Goliath once moved at least fifteen yards from the heap to select a firm-looking piece of vine, and both males often picked three or four stems while they were collecting tools, and put the spares beside them on the ground until they wanted them.

18    Most exciting of all, on several occasions they picked small leafy twigs and prepared them for use by stripping off the leaves. This was the first recorded example of a wild animal not merely *using* an object as a tool, but actually modifying an object and thus showing the crude beginnings of tool*making*.

19    Previously man had been regarded as the only tool-making animal. Indeed, one of the clauses commonly accepted in the definition of man

was that he was a creature who "made tools to a regular and set pattern." The chimpanzees, obviously, had not made tools to any set pattern. Nevertheless, my early observations of their primitive toolmaking abilities convinced a number of scientists that it was necessary to redefine man in a more complex manner than before. Or else, as Louis Leakey put it, we should by definition have to accept the chimpanzee as Man.

## REVIEW

### Content

1. Do you like Lawick-Goodall's naming the chimpanzees? If so, why? If not, why not?
2. One quality much needed by the scientist is *patience*. How well does Lawick-Goodall qualify on this point? Can you sense the *excitement*—of discovery and confirmation—that rewards her patience? Relate paragraph 11 of Ritchie-Calder's discussion on the scientific method, which opens this section of the book, to Lawick-Goodall's paragraph 19 here.

### Rhetoric

3. Lawick-Goodall writes up her observations in vividly detailed descriptive prose. How does she help *you* become an observer along with her? Do you feel that you *know* the chimpanzees? Does her kind of scientific reportage make you want to read more of her writing?
4. What is the effect of Lawick-Goodall's short paragraph 7? Does it serve a transitional purpose? A dramatic one?

### Projects

5. Select some animal and characterize it in the way that Lawick-Goodall characterizes the chimpanzees. Give the animal a name, if you like. You might write about a house pet; a yard creature (for example, squirrel, bird, lizard); some animal in a nearby zoo or on a farm. Help your reader get to know your animal.
6. Select an activity in Nature and observe it carefully enough to be able to write about it as Lawick-Goodall writes here. Some possibilities: a flock of birds in flight; a bird building a nest; a squirrel eating a nut; insects collecting food from a flower; ants gathering and storing food; a spider weaving a web. Write so that your reader will feel as if he/she is observing the activity with you.

# Who Is Man?

## LOREN EISELEY

Loren Eiseley (1907–    ) is an anthropologist, a science historian, a naturalist, and a poet, whose professional home base is the University of Pennsylvania. He has led anthropological expeditions both for universities and for
the Smithsonian Institution. Eiseley is a scientist of humanist persuasion,
and his writings reflect a philosophical mind. His many books include *The
Immense Journey* (1957), *The Firmament of Time* (1960), *The Unexpected
Universe* (1969), *The Invisible Pyramid* (1970), and *The Night Country*
(1971). In the following passage from *The Night Country,* the reader hears
Eiseley the poet as well as Eiseley the philosophical anthropologist, as he
muses about the mystery of Man arisen from the elements.

1    . . . As an evolutionist I never cease to be astounded by the past. It
is replete with more features than one world can realize. Perhaps it
was this that led the philosopher George Santayana to speak of men's
true natures as not adequately manifested in their condition at any given
moment, or even in their usual habits. "Their real nature," he con-
tended, "is what they would discover themselves to be if they possessed
self-knowledge, or as the Indian scripture has it, if they became what
they are." I should like to approach this mystery of the self, which so
intrigued the great philosopher, from a mundane path strewn with the
sticks and stones through which the archaeologist must pick his way.

2    Let me use as illustration a very heavy and peculiar stone which I
keep upon my desk. It has been split across and, carbon black, imprinted
in the gray shale, is the outline of a fish. The chemicals that composed
the fish—most of them at least—are still there in the stone. They are,
in a sense, imperishable. They may come and go, pass in and out of
living things, trickle away in the long erosion of time. They are inanimate, yet at one time they constituted a living creature.

3    Often at my desk, now, I sit contemplating the fish. Nor does it have
to be a fish. It could be the long-horned Alaskan bison on my wall.
For the point is, you see, that the fish is extinct and gone, just as those
great heavy-headed beasts are gone, just as our massive-faced and shambling forebears of the Ice Age have vanished. The chemicals still about
me here took a shape that will never be seen again so long as grass
grows or the sun shines. Just once out of all time there was a pattern
that we call *Bison regius,* a fish called *Diplomystus humilis,* and, at this

present moment, a primate who knows, or thinks he knows, the entire score.

4    In the past there has been armor, there have been bellowing out of throats like iron furnaces, there have been phantom lights in the dark forest and toothed reptiles winging through the air. It has all been carbon and its compounds, the black stain running perpetually across the stone.

## "I Am Dead"

5    But though the elements are known, nothing in all those shapes is now returnable. No living chemist can shape a dinosaur; no living hand can start the dreaming tentacular extensions that characterize the life of the simplest ameboid cell. Finally, as the greatest mystery of all, I who write these words on paper, cannot establish my own reality. I am, by any reasonable and considered logic, dead. This may be a matter of concern, or even a secret, but if it is any consolation, I can assure you that all men are as dead as I. For on my office desk, to prove my words, is the fossil out of the stone, and there is the carbon of life stained black on the ancient rock.

6    There is no life in the fossil. There is no life in the carbon in my body. As the idea strikes me, and it comes as a profound shock, I run down the list of elements. There is no life in the iron, there is no life in the phosphorus, the nitrogen does not contain me, the water that soaks my tissues is not I. What am I then? I pinch my body in a kind of sudden desperation. My heart knocks, my fingers close around the pen. There is, it seems, a semblance of life here.

7    But the minute I start breaking this strange body down into its constituents, it is dead. It does not know me. Carbon does not speak, calcium does not remember, iron does not weep. Even if I hastily reconstitute their combinations in my mind, rebuild my arteries, and let oxygen in the grip of hemoglobin go hurrying through a thousand conduits, I have a kind of machine, but where in all this array of pipes and hurried flotsam is the dweller?

8    From whence, out of what steaming pools or boiling cloudbursts, did he first arise? What forces can we find which brought him up the shore, scaled his body into an antique, reptilian shape and then cracked it like an egg to let a soft-furred animal with a warmer heart emerge? And we? Would it not be a good thing if man were tapped gently like a fertile egg to see what might creep out? I sometimes think of this as I handle the thick-walled skulls of the animal men who preceded us or ponder over those remote splay-footed creatures whose bones lie deep in the world's wastelands at the very bottom of time.

9    With the glooms and night terrors of those vast cemeteries I have

been long familiar. A precisely similar gloom enwraps the individual life of each of us. There are moments, in my bed at midnight, or watching the play of moonlight on the ceiling, when this ghostliness of myself comes home to me with appalling force, when I lie tense, listening as if removed, far off, to the footfalls of my own heart, or seeing my own head on the pillow turning restlessly with the round staring eyes of a gigantic owl. I whisper "Who?" to no one but myself in the silent, sleeping house—the living house gone back to sleep with the sleeping stones, the eternally sleeping chair, the picture that sleeps forever on the bureau, the dead, also sleeping, though they walk in my dreams. In the midst of all this dark, this void, this emptiness, I, more ghostly than a ghost, cry "Who? Who?" to no answer, aware only of other smaller ghosts like the bat sweeping by the window or the dog who, in repeating a bit of his own lost history, turns restlessly among nonexistent grasses before he subsides again upon the floor.

## REVIEW

### Content

1. Why does Eiseley say that he is dead? Why does he say that he "cannot establish [his] own reality"? What *is* the "mystery of self" to which he alludes in paragraph 1?
2. Read paragraph 9 very carefully, and try to fantasize yourself into the setting and the mood here. How does it make you *feel*?

### Rhetoric

3. Eiseley often uses the contemplation of some object from Nature as a starting point for his philosophical observations. How well does the fossilized fish serve him toward that end here?
4. Eiseley is known as a master stylist of English prose. Read paragraph 4 again, for his style. What is the *dramatic* effect of the second sentence in paragraph 7? How does the phrasing, "those remote . . . very bottom of time," at the end of paragraph 8, affect you?

### Projects

5. Eiseley's books are usually quite popular with students. If you like his writing, read further in his books, which do not have to be read in their entirety to be enjoyed.
6. Find some object in Nature that sets you to thinking *beyond* simple description and develop your contemplation into a reflective essay. Some possible objects: a particular flower; a rock; a shell; a tree stump; a piece of a meteorite if you can find one; a cocoon; a deserted insect hive.

# Starfolk: A Fable

## CARL SAGAN

Carl Sagan (1934–   ), a specialist in both astronomy and exobiology (the study of life on other planets), is a professor of astronomy at Cornell University. His work has led to the award of both NASA's medal for exceptional achievement and the Prix Galabert, the international astronautics prize. Sagan's books include *Intelligent Life in the Universe* (1966) and *Planetary Exploration* (1970). In *The Cosmic Connection: An Extraterrestrial Perspective* (1973), Sagan attempts to place the planet Earth in relation to the immense cosmos in which he sees her as a relatively miniscule element. The "fable" below is his version of the Creation of the Earth up through the appearance of Man as one—but only one—of the "starfolk."

1   Once upon a time, about ten or fifteen billion years ago, the universe was without form. There were no galaxies. There were no stars. There were no planets. And there was no life. Darkness was upon the face of the deep. The universe was hydrogen and helium. The explosion of the Big Bang had passed, and the fires of that titanic event—either the creation of the universe or the ashes of a previous incarnation of the universe—were rumbling feebly down the corridors of space.

2     But the gas of hydrogen and helium was not smoothly distributed. Here and there in the great dark, by accident, somewhat more than the ordinary amount of gas was collected. Such clumps grew imperceptibly at the expense of their surroundings, gravitationally attracting larger and larger amounts of neighboring gas. As such clumps grew in mass, their denser parts, governed by the inexorable laws of gravitation and conservation of angular momentum, contracted and compacted, spinning faster and faster. Within these great rotating balls and pinwheels of gas, smaller fragments of greater density condensed out; these shattered into billions of smaller shrinking gas balls.

## The First Star

3     Compaction led to violent collisions of the atoms at the centers of the gas balls. The temperatures became so great that electrons were stripped from protons in the constituent hydrogen atoms. Because protons have like positive charges, they ordinarily electrically repel one another. But after a while the temperatures at the centers of the gas

balls became so great that the protons collided with extraordinary energy—an energy so great that the barrier of electrical repulsion that surrounds the proton was penetrated. Once penetration occurred, nuclear forces—the forces that hold the nuclei of atoms together—came into play. From the simple hydrogen gas the next atom in complexity, helium, was formed. In the synthesis of one helium atom from four hydrogen atoms there is a small amount of excess energy left over. This energy, trickling out through the gas ball, reached the surface and was radiated into space. The gas ball had turned on. The first star was formed. There was light on the face of the heavens.

4    The stars evolved over billions of years, slowly turning hydrogen into helium in their deep interiors, converting the slight mass difference into energy, and flooding the skies with light. There were in these times no planets to receive the light, and no life forms to admire the radiance of the heavens.

5    The conversion of hydrogen into helium could not continue indefinitely. Eventually, in the hot interiors of the stars, where the temperatures were high enough to overcome the forces of electrical repulsion, all the hydrogen was consumed. The fires of the stars were stoked. The pressures in the interiors could no longer support the immense weight of the overlying layers of star. The stars then continued their process of collapse, which had been interrupted by the nuclear fires of a billion years before.

6    In contracting further, higher temperatures were reached, temperatures so high that helium atoms—the ash of the previous epoch of nuclear reaction—became usable as stellar fuel. More complex nuclear reactions occurred in the insides of the stars—now swollen, distended red giant stars. Helium was converted to carbon, carbon to oxygen and magnesium, oxygen to neon, magnesium to silicon, silicon to sulfur, and upward through the litany of the periodic table of the elements—a massive stellar alchemy. Vast and intricate mazes of nuclear reactions built up some nuclei. Others coalesced to form much more complex nuclei. Still others fragmented or combined with protons to build only slightly more complex nuclei.

7    But the gravity on the surfaces of red giants is low, because the surfaces have expanded outward from the interiors. The outer layers of red giants are slowly dissipated into interstellar space, enriching the space between the stars in carbon and oxygen and magnesium and iron and all the elements heavier than hydrogen and helium. In some cases, the outer layers of the star were slowly stripped off, like the successive skins of an onion. In other cases, a colossal nuclear explosion rocked the star, propelling at immense velocity into interstellar space most of the outside of the star. Either by leakage or explosion, by dissipation slow or dissipation fast, star-stuff was spewed back to the dark, thin gas from which the stars had come.

## The Planets Evolve

8    But here, later generations of stars were aborning. Again the condensations of gas spun their slow gravitational pirouettes, slowly transmogrifying gas cloud into star. But these new second- and third-generation stars were enriched in heavy elements, the patrimony of their stellar antecedents. Now, as stars were formed, smaller condensations formed near them condensations far too small to produce nuclear fires and become stars. They were little dense, cold clots of matter, slowly forming out of the rotating cloud, later to be illuminated by the nuclear fires that they themselves could not generate. These unprepossessing clots became the planets: Some giant and gaseous, composed mostly of hydrogen and helium, cold and far from their parent star; others, smaller and warmer, losing the bulk of their hydrogen and helium by a slow trickling away to space, formed a different sort of planet—rocky, metallic, hard-surfaced.

9    These smaller cosmic debris, congealing and warming, released small quantities of hydrogen-rich gases, trapped in their interiors during the processes of formation. Some gases condensed on the surface, forming the first oceans; other gases remained above the surface, forming the first atmospheres—atmospheres different from the present atmosphere of Earth, atmospheres composed of methane, ammonia,· hydrogen sulfide, water, and hydrogen—an unpleasant and unbreathable atmosphere for humans. But this is not yet a story about humans.

10    Starlight fell on this atmosphere. Storms were driven by the Sun, producing thunder and lightning. Volcanoes erupted, hot lava heating the atmosphere near the surface. These processes broke apart molecules of the primitive atmosphere. But the fragments reassorted into more and more complex molecules, falling by chance upon clays, a dizzying process of breakdown, resynthesis, transformation—slowly moving toward molecules of greater and greater complexity, driven by the laws of physics and chemistry. After a time, the oceans achieved the constituency of a warm dilute broth.

## Self-Replicating Molecules

11    Among the innumerable species of complex organic molecules forming and dissipating in this broth there one day arose a molecule able crudely to make copies of itself—a molecule which weakly guided the chemical processes in its vicinity to produce molecules like itself—a template molecule, a blueprint molecule, a self-replicating molecule. This molecule was not very efficient. Its copies were inexact. But soon it gained a significant advantage over the other molecules in the early waters. The molecules that could not copy themselves did not. Those that could, did. The number of copying molecules greatly increased.

12    As time passed, the copying process became more exact. Other molecules in the waters were reprocessed to form the jigsaw puzzle pieces to fit the copying molecules. A minute and imperceptible statistical advantage of the molecules that could copy themselves was soon transformed by the arithmetic of geometrical progression into the dominant process in the oceans.

13    More and more elaborate reproductive systems arose. Those systems that copied better produced more copies. Those that copied poorly produced fewer copies. Soon most of the molecules were organized into molecular collectives, into self-replicating systems. It was not that any molecules had the glimmering of an idea or the ghostly passage of a need or want or aspiration; merely, those molecules that copied did, and soon the face of the planet became transformed by the copying process. In time, the seas became full of these molecular collectives, forming, metabolizing, replicating . . . forming, metabolizing, replicating . . . forming, metabolizing, mutating, replicating. . . . Elaborate systems arose, molecular collectives exhibiting behavior, moving to where the replication building blocks were more abundant, avoiding molecular collectives that incorporated their neighbors. Natural selection became a molecular sieve, selecting out those combinations of molecules best suited by chance to further replication.

14    All the while the building blocks, the foodstuffs, the parts for later copies, were being produced, mainly by sunlight and lightning and thunder—all driven by the nearby star. The nuclear processes in the insides of the stars drove the planetary processes, which led to and sustained life.

## Plants Develop

15    As the supply of foodstuffs gradually was exhausted, a new kind of molecular collective arose, one able to produce molecular building blocks internally out of air and water and sunlight. The first animals were joined by the first plants. The animals became parasites upon the plants, as they had been earlier on the stellar manna falling from the skies. The plants slowly changed the composition of the atmosphere; hydrogen was lost to space, ammonia transformed to nitrogen, methane to carbon dioxide. For the first time, oxygen was produced in significant quantities in the atmosphere—oxygen, a deadly poisonous gas able to convert all the self-replicating organic molecules back into simple gases like carbon dioxide and water.

16    But life met this supreme challenge: In some cases by burrowing into environments where oxygen was absent, but—in the most successful variants—by evolving not only to survive the oxygen but to use it in the more efficient metabolism of foodstuffs.

17    Sex and death evolved—processes that vastly increased the rate of

natural selection. Some organisms evolved hard parts, climbed onto, and survived on the land. The pace of production of more complex forms accelerated. Flight evolved. Enormous four-legged beasts thundered across the steaming jungles. Small beasts emerged, born live, instead of in hard-shelled containers filled with replicas of the early oceans. They survived through swiftness and cunning—and increasingly long periods in which their knowledge was not so much preprogrammed in self-replicating molecules as learned from parents and experiences.

18    All the while, the climate was variable. Slight variations in the output of sunlight, the orbital motion of the planet, clouds, oceans, and polar icecaps produced climate changes—wiping out whole groups of organisms and causing the exuberant proliferation of other, once insignificant, groups.

19    And then . . . the Earth grew somewhat cold. The forests retreated. Small arboreal animals climbed down from the trees to seek a livelihood on the savannas. They became upright and tool-using. They communicated by producing compressional waves in the air with their eating and breathing organs. They discovered that organic material would, at a high enough temperature, combine with atmospheric oxygen to produce the stable hot plasma called fire. Postpartum learning was greatly accelerated by social interaction. Communal hunting developed, writing was invented, political structures evolved, superstition and science, religion and technology.

## Man

20    And then one day there came to be a creature whose genetic material was in no major way different from the self-replicating molecular collectives of any of the other organisms on his planet, which he called Earth. But he was able to ponder the mystery of his origins, the strange and tortuous path by which he had emerged from star-stuff. He was the matter of the cosmos, contemplating itself. He considered the problematical and enigmatic question of his future. He called himself Man. He was one of the starfolk. And he longed to return to the stars.

### REVIEW

#### Content

1. Had you thought before about Sagan's point that it was those molecules that replicated themselves best that survived and prospered? Compare Sagan's theory with Darwinian theory. Does this process continue today? Can you give examples?
2. Discuss paragraph 20. Did the first sentence bother you? If so, did you feel better as you read on? Consider this sentence along with the preceding selection by Eiseley: "He was the matter of the cosmos,

contemplating itself." Why does Sagan say this creature who called himself Man—one of the starfolk—"longed to return to the stars"?

**Rhetoric**

3. Evaluate this chapter from *The Cosmic Connection* as a "fable." In what parts does the language sound like what you would expect to find in a fable? Where does it not so sound? Do you ever lose your way while trying to read the piece? And/or does Sagan ever fail to hold your interest? If so, where, and why?
4. The writing here is perhaps most vivid when Sagan uses imagery (word-pictures). The phrase the Big Bang is itself vivid word imagery; what does the phrase refer to? Find other particularly effective instances of imagery. What is the effect of the repetition in paragraph 13?

**Projects**

5. One of the difficulties in talking about events in space is the vastness and the consequent problem of establishing a frame of reference within which to think and envision. Get a well-illustrated book on astronomy from your college library. Bring the book to class for use in a discussion on developing word-pictures to describe the phenomena "out there."
6. Using one of the following sentences from Sagan as the topic sentence of your opening paragraph, write a brief development of that step in creation; use a general reference work, such as an encyclopedia or a good science textbook, to find the factual detail you will need:
   (a) "The first animals were joined by the first plants." (paragraph 15)
   (b) "Some organisms evolved hard parts, climbed onto, and survived on land." (17)
   (c) "Flight evolved." (17)
   (d) "Enormous four-legged beasts thundered across the steaming jungles." (17)
   (e) "Small beasts emerged, born live, instead of in hard-shelled containers." (17)
   (f) "The forests retreated. Small arboreal animals climbed down from the trees to seek a livelihood on the savannas. They became upright and tool-using." (17)

In class you might want to compare your work with those who have chosen the same sentence, or divide into groups of persons who have chosen the same sentence and make as good a single paper out of your several papers as you can. Make the paper read like a fable so that it will be both easy to understand and pleasing to read.

# We Are
# Left-Brained or
# Right-Brained

## MAYA PINES

Maya Pines has been writing on the brain and how it serves us for some time, including *Revolution in Learning: The Years from Birth to Six* (1967). The following selection is adapted from her book *The Brain Changers: Scientists and the New Mind Control* (1973). Here she considers the implications of recent research which suggests that the two halves of our brains have totally differing functions. Apparently the left hemisphere handles our analytic and verbal thinking processes, while the "mute" right hemisphere is more intuitive. Western culture has tended to focus on development of the left side; do we need to be more aware of the advantages of right-hemisphere development?

1    Linked together like Siamese twins right down the middle of our brains, two very different persons inhabit our heads. One of them is verbal, analytical, dominant. The other is artistic but mute, and still almost totally mysterious.

2    These are the left and right hemispheres of our brains, the twin shells that cover the central brain stem. In normal people, they are connected by millions of nerve fibers which form a thick cable called the corpus callosum. If this cable is cut, as must be done in certain cases of severe epilepsy, a curious set of circumstances occurs. The left side of the brain—the speaking half—no longer knows what the right side is doing, yet it insists on finding excuses for whatever the mute half has done, and still operates under the illusion that they are one person.

3    As a result of these extraordinary findings of the past decade, brain scientists have begun to wonder whether our normal feeling of being just one person is also an illusion, even though our brains remain whole. Are the two halves of our brains integrated into a single soul? Is one hemisphere always dominant over the other? Or do the two persons in our brains take turns at directing our activities and thoughts?

4    Theologians are not alone in watching this research with fascination— and some misgivings. It has aroused the interest of many others who are concerned with human identity. As they soon realize, all roads lead to Dr. Roger Sperry, a California Institute of Technology professor of psychobiology who has the gift of making—or provoking—important discoveries.

## Experiments on Cats' Visual Mechanism

5    Sperry was already famous before he began studying people and animals
whose brains had been split in two. In a series of elegant experiments,
he had shown that there exists a very precise chemical coding system
in the brain that allows specific nerve cells—for example, those concerned with vision—to find their way through a tangle of other nerve
fibers, even when obstacles are placed in their path, and somehow connect with the appropriate cells so as to reach specific terminals in the
visual cortex. Next he began to study visual perception and memory.
He wanted to find out what happened when an animal learned certain
discriminations that involved the visual cortex—when it learned, for instance, to push a panel marked with a circle rather than a square. Where
in its brain was that knowledge stored?

6        He put the question to a young graduate student, suggesting that
he investigate how cats that have learned a new skill with only one eye
and one hemisphere transfer this information to the other eye. The
young student, Ronald Myers (now chief of the Laboratory of Perinatal
Physiology at the National Institute of Neurological Diseases and Stroke),
worked with this idea for the next six years. First he developed a method
of cutting through the cats' optic chiasm (the point at which the optic
nerves meet and cross) so as to sever the nerve fibers that normally
cross from left eye to right hemisphere and vice versa, sparing only
those that connect with the same side of the brain. Despite the surgery,
the cats saw quite well. Myers then placed a patch over one of their
eyes and trained the one-eyed creatures to distinguish between a circle
and a square, knowing that the information they acquired would go
to only one hemisphere. When he switched their eye patches to cover
their trained eyes, however, the cats performed just as well as before.
Their memory of this skill was intact. This meant either that the knowledge was stored in the central brain stem, well below the twin hemispheres, or that the knowledge acquired by one hemisphere had somehow been transmitted to the other.

## Testing the Corpus Callosum

7    "Obviously the corpus callosum was the next thing to test," recalls Dr.
Myers. "But from the available evidence, cutting it would have no effect.
If the surgery is properly done, the animals are up the next day and
you see nothing." By all outward appearances, a split-brain cat or monkey is perfectly normal: it can run, eat, mate, solve problems as if nothing had happened to it. When surgeons first split the brain of a human
being in the 1930's (to remove a tumor deep in the brain), they did
so with much trepidation, expecting a terrible change in their patient,

a total deterioration of his psyche. To their amazement, they saw no change at all. The corpus callosum seemed to serve no purpose, despite its large size (it is about 3½ inches long and a quarter of an inch thick in humans). "What is the function of the corpus callosum?" professors would ask their students in the 1940's; as no one knew, they replied facetiously, "It transmits epileptic seizures from one hemisphere to the other." As recently as 1951, Karl Lashley [the neuropsychologist] saw only one other use for it: "To keep the hemispheres from sagging."

8     Nevertheless, Myers proceeded with the next step in the research plan. After cutting through the cats' optic chiasm, he split their corpus callosum as well, separating their left and right hemispheres. Then he trained them as before, with one eye covered. When he removed the cover from this eye and placed it over the other eye, however, there was a dramatic change: the cats reacted as if they had never seen the patterns before. They took just as long to learn the difference between a circle and a square with the second eye as they had with the first. Myers was elated, and the question was finally settled: it was the corpus callosum that transmitted memories and learning from one hemisphere to the other. The thick cable of fibers stood revealed as the sole means of communication between the two halves of the cerebral cortex. Without it, cats could be trained quite separately with each eye. When Myers tried teaching some split-brain cats to select the circle with their left eye and the square with their right, he found that they learned this without the slightest evidence of conflict. They would act in opposite ways, according to which eye was open—as if they had two entirely separate brains.

## Asymmetry in Human Brain

9     In animals, a split brain may prove relatively unimportant. After all, both hemispheres are enclosed in a single head, attached to a single body, and normally exposed to identical experiences. Furthermore, the left and right halves of their brains do exactly the same job. But this is not the case for human beings.

10     Alone among the mammals, man has developed different uses for each half of his brain. This asymmetry, which we all recognize when we say whether we're right- or left-handed, is the glorious mechanism through which man is enabled to speak. It is what separates us from the apes. There are various theories about how it developed and whether it is present right from birth, but it is quite clear that by the time a child reaches the age of ten, one hemisphere—usually the left—has taken over the task of language.

11     For simpler operations, such as receiving sensations from one's hand or ordering movements to one's foot, the human brain remains generally symmetrical. The nerve impulses that carry messages from one side of

the body travel up the spinal column and cross over into the opposite side of the brain, there to form a sort of mirror image of the parts they represent. The nerve connections involved are set at birth in an incredibly precise fashion that allows the brain to know instantly where certain sensations come from and where to aim specific instructions.

12      When tasks become more complex, however, this mirrorlike representation is abandoned. Then the association areas of the brain come into play and each one develops in its own way, according to experience. Since we have only one mouth (unlike the dolphin, which has separate phonation mechanisms on the right and left sides of its body), there is no need for right and left speech centers in the brain. On the contrary, these might conflict with each other and compete for control of the speech mechanisms. In most people, therefore, the speech centers are limited to one side of the brain, usually the left, though about 15 percent of left-handed people have speech on both sides.

## Left Hemisphere Largely Dominant for Language

13   Even among the left-handed, the left hemisphere generally controls speech. This near monopoly of the left hemisphere was recognized in the early eighteenth century, when surgeons examined the brains of people who had lost the power of speech and found severe damage on the left side. Why this should be so preordained is not clear. The left hemisphere tends to become dominant in other ways as well. For example, it controls the right hand, which does most of man's skilled work with tools.

14      Around the age of one, notes psychologist Jerome Bruner, babies suddenly master what he calls "the two-handed obstacle box," a simple puzzle developed by Harvard's Center for Cognitive Studies to study how babies learn the value of two-handedness. The baby will push and hold a transparent cover with one hand, for the first time, while the other hand reaches inside the box for a toy, even though nobody has taught him this skill. To Bruner this seems extraordinary, for it shows that the baby has learned to distinguish between two kinds of grip—the power, or "holding," grip, which stabilizes an object, usually with the left hand, and the precision, or "operating," grip, which does the work, usually with the right. Monkeys and apes also develop a precision grip, says Bruner, but only in man, with his asymmetry, does the power grip migrate to the left hand while the precision grip migrates to the right. This is the beginning of a long road leading to the distinctively human use of tools and toolmaking.

15      If the left hemisphere does all this, why do we need a right hemisphere? Experiments with split-brain cats and monkeys could not shed much light on the differing specialties of man's two hemispheres. The

study of the two personalities in our brain did not really begin until 1961, when Sperry became interested in a forty-eight-year-old veteran whose head had been hit by bomb fragments during World War II.

16    A few years after his injury, W. J. had begun to have epileptic fits; these became so frequent and so severe that nothing could control them. He would fall down, unconscious and foaming at the mouth, often hurting himself as he fell. For more than five years, doctors at Los Angeles' White Memorial Medical Center tried every conceivable remedy, without success. Finally Drs. Philip Vogel and Joseph Bogen cut through his corpus callosum, and the seizures stopped, as if by magic. There was a rocky period of recovery, during which W. J., a man of above-average intelligence, could not speak, but within a month he announced that he felt better than he had in years. He appeared unchanged in personality. He seemed perfectly normal.

17    Meanwhile, Sperry had interested a graduate student, Michael Gazzaniga, in performing a series of tests on W. J., together with him and Dr. Bogen. Gazzaniga soon discovered some extremely odd things about his subject. To begin with, W. J. could carry out verbal commands ("Raise your hand," or "Bend your knee") only with the right side of his body. He could not respond with his left side. Evidently the right hemisphere, which controls the left limbs, did not understand that kind of language. When W. J. was blindfolded, he couldn't even tell what part of his body was touched if it happened to be on the left side.

18    In fact, as the tests proceeded, it became increasingly difficult to think of W. J. as a single person. His left hand kept doing things that his right hand deplored, if it was aware of them at all.

.   .   .

19    Vygotsky [the Russian psychologist] believed that thought is born through words. Without words, he said, quoting a Russian poet, "My thought, unembodied, returns to the realm of shadows." Our earliest memories, too, dwell in a realm of shadows. And yet, something was experienced, and something of its flavor remains to haunt us through the rest of our lives.

20    Perhaps the right hemisphere's functions are too shrouded in shadows to be called thought. According to the Australian physiologist Sir John Eccles, a Nobel Prize winner, the right hemisphere cannot truly think. He makes a clear distinction between the consciousness of sounds and smells, which we share with animals, and the world of language, thought, and culture, which is man-made. Animals can be conditioned, but they cannot create a culture, he claims. Primates leave no constructions, no art, nothing that can live beyond their own time, despite a brain almost as large as man's. In his opinion, everything that is truly human derives from the left hemisphere, where the speech center is, and where interactions between brain and mind occur. When the right hemisphere of

a woman whose brain has been split sees something that makes her smile or blush, it's not correct to say she can'r *report* why she smiled—she doesn't *know* why she smiled. Only the left hemisphere can have true thoughts or true knowledge, through language.

21    "Could the right half of the brain appreciate Chaplin's silent movies?" Eccles was asked at a meeting of the Society for Neuroscience recently. "How would you know?" he shot back, to much laughter in the audience. Both the report of such appreciation and our understanding of it would require the left hemisphere.

## Role of Right Hemisphere

22 Nevertheless, the evidence increasingly favors a generous view of the right half-brain, whose role may be far more important than we know today.

23    When Einstein was asked how he arrived at some of his most original ideas, he explained that he rarely thought in words at all. "A thought comes, and I may try to express it in words afterwards," he said. His concepts first appeared through "physical entities"—certain signs and more or less clear images that he could reproduce and combine. These elements were "of visual and some of muscular type," he added. "Conventional words or other signs have to be sought for laboriously only in a secondary stage, when the mentioned associative play is sufficiently established and can be reproduced at will." This held true only for his creative work in physics; in other activities, he had no trouble with words. He liked to compose limericks, and his letters were both fluent and pithy. Apparently he could make exceptionally good use of both sides of his brain. However, his love of music and his reliance on nonverbal concepts seem to indicate a preference for his right hemisphere.

24    For centuries we have concentrated largely on the verbal side of our brains: the side that produces things we know how to analyze and measure. Our mute half-brain remains uncharted. We know almost nothing about how the right hemisphere thinks, or how it might be educated—and we have just begun to discover how much it contributes to the complex, creative acts of man.

## REVIEW

### Content

1. Had you ever thought about the possibility of "two persons" in your brain before? Consider paragraph 3 in the light of your own experience.
2. A distinction is sometimes made between what is called "vertical"

thinking and "lateral" thinking. Vertical thinking is very logical and sequential, carefully-thought-through, step-by-step thinking; while "lateral" thinking is more flexible, open-ended, subject to free association, receptive to alternate avenues, and so on. Try to remember a problem-solving situation you have confronted. Did you first proceed "vertically," using the left hemisphere of your brain? If you did not arrive at a feasible solution by that route, did one perhaps "come to you" later? Did it consist of any elements you did not recall having *thought* about"? If so, do you think this answer came from your right hemisphere? If you never did arrive at a suitable solution to the problem, could you now try to put it into the right hemisphere, to see if something helpful comes out?

**Rhetoric**

3. Paragraphs 5 through 14 of the Pines excerpt are, for the most part, scientific reporting, including the presentation of experiments. Can you follow the author throughout? What about her writing helps to make this rather difficult material clear and readable for you?
4. Analyze Pines' style in paragraphs 1 through 4 and 19 through 24. How does her writing there differ from her scientific-reportage writing? What reader-involving sentence structures does she use? How does she relate the content about Eccles and about Einstein so as to hold your interest?

**Projects**

5. Be prepared to discuss in class whatever advantages you can think of in having the potentialities of your right hemisphere available to yourself. Then share ideas about how you can increase this availability.
6. Write up your answers to 2 above into a paper. Deal with a problem you are working on currently, if you prefer.

# Cloning

## WILLARD GAYLIN

Willard Gaylin is a professor of psychiatry and law at Columbia Law School and also serves as president of the Institute of Society, Ethics and the Life Sciences at Hastings-on-Hudson, New York. The article from which the following is excerpted originally appeared in *The New York Times Maga-*

*zine*, March 5, 1972, under the title "The Frankenstein Myth Becomes a Reality—We Have the Awful Knowledge To Make Exact Copies of Human Beings." In the article Gaylin reviews scientific experiments in cloning (exact duplication) of, first, carrots and then frogs. He discusses the possibility that cloning of human beings may be next and asks whether we should clone human beings.

1    In the winter of 1971, before a committee of the House of Representatives, the biologist J. D. Watson expressed dismay that the population had been insufficiently alerted to some of the profound implications of new technologies in genetic research. To the uninitiated, the fact that the statement came from a scientist whose own research is in that field may seem analogous to Dr. Frankenstein chastising the Swiss citizenry for failing to storm his laboratories. But this forceful testimony by the distinguished codiscoverer of DNA has been applauded by a growing group of scientists, social scientists and ethicists who sense that the people are shielded, by the complexity of genetic science, from an understanding of the nature and magnitude of threats it poses to their ways of life, their identities and their very existence as a species. The public attention to Watson's testimony—confirming their thesis—was minimal.

2    The Frankenstein myth has a viability that transcends its original intentions and a relevance beyond its original time. The image of the frightened scientist, guilt-ridden over his own creations, ceased to be theoretical with the explosion of the first atomic bomb. The revulsion of some of the young, idealistic men who were involved in the actual making of the bomb or in the theoretical work that led to it, had a demonstrable influence in the scientific community from the nineteen-fifties forward. Some biological scientists, now wary and forewarned, are trying to consider the ethical, social and political implications of their research before its use makes any contemplation merely an expiating exercise. They are even starting to ask whether some research ought to be done at all. With the serious introduction of questions of "ought," ethics has been introduced—and is beginning to shake some of the traditional illusions of a "science above morality," or a "value-free science."

3    Of course, in 1818 when Mary Shelley first created her story, the scientific domination of society was just beginning. The idea of one human being fabricating another was purely metaphorical. The process was presumed to be impossible, a grotesque exaggeration which cast in the form of a Gothic tale the author's philosophical concern about man's constant reaching for new knowledge and control over the forces of nature (the traditional Greek anxiety about *hubris*). It was, to use her words, "a ghost story," a fantasy to frame a poetic truth.

## Artificial Parts

4    But the inconceivable has become conceivable, and in the 20th century we find ourselves, indeed, patching human beings together out of parts. We sew on detached arms, and fix shattered hips in place with metal spikes; we patch arterial tubing with plastic; we borrow corneas from the dead, and kidneys from the living or dead; automatic, rechargeable pacemakers placed under the skin regulate the heartbeat, and radio receivers placed in the brain case may shortly control behavior; there are artificial limbs, artificial lungs, artificial kidneys and artificial hearts; and respected scientific researchers—in a real-life parody of art—are publicly accused of stealing secret and mysterious devices from the laboratories of their rivals.

5    The issue which seemed most worrisome to Watson, and in his opinion called for a campaign to inform the world's citizens so that they might take part in planning possible control measures, was the cloning of human beings. Cloning is the production of genetically identical copies of an individual organism. Just as one can take hundreds of cuttings from a specific plant (indeed, the word *klon* is the Greek word for "twig" or "slip"), each of which can then develop into a mature plant—genetic replicas of the parent—it is now possible to clone animals. The possibility of human cloning seems to produce in nonscientists more titillation than terror or awe—perhaps because it is usually visualized as "a garden of Raquel Welches," blooming by the hundred, genetically identical from nipples to finger nails.

6    To understand the complications and implications of human cloning it is necessary to review some of the "facts of life" and to approach distressingly close to those bromides, the birds and the bees.

## Mendel's Peas

7    Every species of living organism has the capacity to reproduce its own kind. Indeed, this capability is so fundamental to the concept of being "alive" that it is part of the definition distinguishing animate from inanimate. The mechanism whereby species likeness is transmitted from one generation to the other was discovered by the Austrian priest Gregor Mendel in the 19th century, in some of the most amazing research of modern science. While it is not possible to do justice here to Mendel's genetic principles, it is necessary to recall a few of his conclusions. Working with common garden peas, taking such variables as the color of the flower, the size of the plant, the shape and texture of the seeds, Mendel defined the basic laws of heredity. Unlike previous vague conceptions of offspring as some loose amalgam of parental qualities (Darwin's *panmixis*) in which blood lines fused just as blue and yellow water

colors blend to make green, Mendel established that the offspring inherit relatively discrete, independent traits which never mix nor modify each other, but maintain a segregated existence ready to be passed on in pure form to a future generation. He saw the instrument for transfer as a discrete body, later to be called a gene, and recognized that while one gene might dominate another, thus appearing as a particular property, they both existed and were ready to be shipped out to a next generation, again in pure and segregated form. Generally speaking, for example, if you inherit a gene for blue eyes and a gene for brown eyes, you do not usually get the muddy mixture of the two but will have the brown eyes of the dominant gene. Nonetheless, the gene for blue eyes is a part of your genetic potential ready to be handed down intact to your children.

. . .

## Sexual Reproduction and Adaptability

8   The genes in human beings are distributed among 46 chromosomes. These 46 chains of inheritance exist in the nucleus of every single body cell of the organism except for the sex cells. These cells, ova in women and sperm in men, contain only half the normal quantity—23—and are called haploid. When fertilization occurs, the nuclei of the sperm and the egg fuse, forming an egg cell with a full complement of chromosomes. The fertilized egg proceeds to undergo spontaneous division into two, then four, then eight, finally into the billions of cells that comprise the human body. In the meantime, the cells "differentiate," changing drastically in shape and function, thus forming the various tissues and organs of the body. The genetic code, embodied in that chance mixtures of genes from parental chromosomes, guides and contributes in some as yet unknown way to the ultimate form of the adult organism. Sexual reproduction with separate male and female forms guarantees a richness and a variability to the species. This process, combined with Darwinian principles, permits the evolution of individuals with enhanced adaptability and survival values. It is sexual reproduction which mandates continued change—and, therefore, ultimately, improved adaptive capacity.

9     The process of differentiation represents one of the great unsolved mysteries in biology. How can these cells, which are identical in early divisions with each containing the exact same nucleus (meaning the full potential to form the entire creature) evolve so differently? Lung tissue looks different from bone, skin from blood, muscle from cartilage, because the microscopic cells that make up the tissue have evolved into entirely different forms. The individual cell—ignoring most of its potential—becomes a specialist, and takes the form most suited to its function, which also has become specialized. Some cells will become chemical manufacturing units—reproducing for example, insulin; some will

be the wirelike cells of the nervous system that conduct impulses from other cells that have become pain receptors in the skin, to still others that have become "appreciators" of pain in the brain.

10   However it may have occurred, once differentiation develops it would seem that there is virtually no way back, short of regeneration itself. If this is true of an animal, it seems equally true of a vegetable.

## Steward's Carrot

11   If man's heredity mechanism was first understood from common garden peas, it seems only equitable that the mechanism's undoing may be from the common garden carrot. Most of us have had the experience of growing vegetables from seeds. The seed is the equivalent of the fertilized egg ready to go, and, since the earth is its natural womb, the planter is merely a mechanical middleman. In a startling set of experiments during the early nineteen-sixties, Prof. F. C. Steward, a cellular physiologist at Cornell University, began agitating individual cells from carrot root in various nutritive media. Almost any mechanical or chemical stimulus can cause an egg or seed cell to begin dividing—heat, light, touching, shaking, or more exposure to a nutrient medium. Steward used differentiated cells, not seeds, yet amazingly these cells began to proliferate. Eventually, with patience and changing media and techniques, Steward was able to force the individual root cells to form clumps and organized masses: what is more, they began to differentiate again into other kinds of cells.

12   He finally succeeded in carrying one individual cell to the ultimate stage of a full-grown carrot plant—roots, stalk, leaves, flowers, seeds and all. Any cell can, conceivably, be thus forced, once the technology is understood, to grow into a full plant. And what is possible with a vegetable cell is, at least theoretically, just as possible with an animal cell. Animal cells, of course, have already been cultured in the laboratory. Tissue cultures are a basic medical research tool. But tissue cultures are not whole organisms—merely sheets of identical type cells—and the concept of growing a whole organism from one cell asexually in a laboratory would seem impossible. But that Cornell carrot confronts our incredulity. To a scientific mind, the leap from a single cell to cloned carrot is greater than the leap from cloned carrot to cloned man.

## Haldane's Cloning Prophecy

13   Is cloning a man foreseeable in any reasonable time? Years ago, J. B. S. Haldane, the brilliant British biologist and mathematician, confidently assumed the imminence of human cloning and eagerly anticipated its

potential uses. Yet, to most people, such a development was inconceivable. One could imagine taking a single sloughed cell from the skin of a person's hand, or even from the hand of a mummy (since cells are neither "alive" nor "dead," but are merely intact or not intact), and seeing it perpetuate itself into a sheet of skin tissue. But could one really visualize the cell forming a finger, let alone a hand, let alone an embryo, let alone another Amenhotep?

14    There is an entirely different laboratory procedure, known for years, that also offers an alternative to sexual reproduction. When an egg cell is stimulated mechanically or chemically, it will start the division process which leads to the adult form even though it is unfertilized. This virgin birth, or parthenogenesis, occurs in nature, the typical example being the honey bee, whose fertilized eggs produce workers and queens and whose unfertilized eggs develop parthenogenetically into drones or males. Beginning with simple sea forms, laboratory parthenogenesis progressed up the evolutionary ladder to the point that in 1939 a whole rabbit was reported created from an unfertilized egg. However, since in most species the unfertilized sex cell, unlike all of the other cells of the body, is haploid, the individual formed is *not genetically* identical to its mother, or indeed genetically identical to anything.

## Gurdon's Frog

15    It remained for Professor John Gurdon, a biologist at Oxford, to perform the stunning experiment that bridged the technology of parthenogenesis and that of Steward's carrots. In the mid-sixties Professor Gurdon, working with a frog's eggs, devised a technique, employing radiation, that destroyed the nucleus of an egg cell without damaging the body of the egg. Then, by equally complicated mechanisms, he managed to take the nucleus from the ordinary body cell of the frog (with its full complement of chromosomes) and intrude it into the egg cell. Until now, it was an unproved assumption that the nuclei of all cells, regardless of how different they might be, were identical in their genetic inheritance and contained the entire latent potential for reproduction of a differentiated, multicelled adult. If Gurdon's hypothesis was correct, the newly constructed egg cell was now the equivalent of a fertilized egg and should, on stimulation, be capable of producing an adult form. This is precisely what happened. Some of the cells, on division, formed perfectly normal tadpoles, some of which, indeed, became perfectly normal frogs genetically identical to the frog that donated the nucleus.

16    John Gurdon used an intestinal cell. He could have used any other body cell, and the cell could have been from a male or a female. The enucleated egg into which the nucleus was injected was also unimportant, genetically speaking; it was merely the environment. The means

now exist to produce thousands of genetically identical offspring in the laboratory—at least in frogs.

## Can We Clone Humans?

17    What seemed like Haldane's immense and overvalued faith in scientific technology now sounds like a rational prediction. In 1969 Robert Sinsheimer, chairman of the division of biology at California Institute of Technology, stated that he assumed it would be possible to clone human organisms within 10 to 20 years. The way has thus been paved for the production of genetic copies of particularly prized individuals, in enormous quantities if desired—for whatever purposes.

18    There are still major obstacles to the cloning of human beings. Human ova and frog ova are vastly different in some respects—size, for one. Contrary to what one might guess, the frog egg is huge compared to the microscopic human ovum. This is because the frog egg, like a chicken egg, must contain all the nutrient to support the complete development of the embryo; in the human being the egg is implanted in the wall of the maternal uterus soon after fertilization, and a placenta forms which permits direct feeding of the fetus by the mother. The size of human ova, therefore, is incredibly small considering the size of the offspring. H. J. Muller, the great biologist, calculated that all the human eggs from the total population of the earth (then two and one-half billion) would occupy less than a gallon of space. Because of the minute size of human ova, further advances in microsurgery and laboratory techniques will be necessary before cloning becomes possible.

19    Gurdon has already supplied most of the technology for human cloning. Following the method he used on frogs, the nucleus of an egg cell from any donor would be destroyed. A nucleus (they are all alike) from any convenient cell of the person to be "replicated" would be inserted into the enucleated egg by microsurgical techniques (which have not yet been developed). On placing this new egg cell into an appropriate nutrient medium—a number of recipes have been devised—the "normal" process of division would commence. By the time it has divided into the 8- to 32-cell stage—four to six days—it would be ready for implantation.

20    A number of simple implantation devices have already been successfully worked out in animals. The developing egg can be injected directly into the uterine wall at the proper menstrual stage of receptivity. Or, more elegantly, it may be injected into the Fallopian tube and permitted to pass normally into the uterine cavity for self-implantation.

21    Many technical problems still remain, but given sufficient imperative they will be solved. Whether we will actually do human cloning involves other considerations.

# The Ought of Science

22    The types of questions that normally arise about any new and dramatic technological procedure fall into the categories of: can man, will man, and ought man. There is a tendency, particularly in antitechnology treatises, to lump the first two together and to consider the third an independent problem. This kind of reasoning usually assures us that what science can do, it will do. The facts are more complicated, as usual, than the polemics. There is much that man can do which he does not do—because he is aware that he ought not. We do not, for example, perform many behavioral experiments on babies, even though some research would unquestionably contribute to knowledge and the common good. Societal morality has traditionally disapproved of the use of the human beings as research animals. Their humanness protects them from certain kinds of destructive research. But even this rule is being violated in some instances. In at least one recent situation, for example, human fetuses that were about to be aborted were used as part of an experiment to determine the potentially harmful effects of ultrasound.

23    The typical scientist is a product of the culture's ethical system and reacts intuitively to its built-in values—even if he has never thought through its philosophical premises. In general, the culture-value system is one input into the broader psychological forces that drive men toward certain goals and tacitly discourage others.

24    In pure research, however, a goal may be pursued with no advance knowledge of its utility. Thus may a startling technique become available before we are prepared to consider all the implications of its application. Similarly, confusion can arise when the pursuit of one problem leads, accidentally, to the solution of another which, because unanticipated, was insufficiently evaluated. In these circumstances, the experimentalist is often tempted to do what can be done—merely for the excitement of doing it. The work on DNA of J. D. Watson and Francis Crick has opened the way to all sorts of experiments in genetic surgery that may be beyond the intent of the two pioneers.

.   .   .

# A Time To Clone?

25    The technical steps necessary to do human cloning are likely to be inspired not by the quest for a super race but by the need to solve compelling problems. Once developed to a point of predictable success, cloning will first be used as an eccentric application of a standard procedure, for a humanitarian end, as illustrated by a hypothetical case: A couple which has one adored infant and is incapable of having another learns that the child has been mortally injured. What possible harm

would result, it may be asked, if one of the child's cells is taken so that he could be genetically reproduced (with the clone implanted in his mother's womb, or a substitute's) and nine months later "reborn" to the delight and comfort of his mourning parents?

26   Cloning—that most artificial of phenomena—would in this way be exploited to serve the most fundamental of human needs, bearing and raising children. Yet, on the other hand, it would totally cleave that need from related physiological and procreative behavior (sexual passion, tenderness and romantic love) which have traditionally initiated, accompanied and complemented parenthood.

## Other Bioethical Issues

27   Cloning commands our attention more because it dramatizes the developing issues in bioethics than because of its potential threat to our way of life. Many biologists, ethicists and social scientists see it not as a pressing problem but a metaphoric device serving to focus attention on identical problems that arise from less dramatic forms of genetic engineering and that might slip into public use, protected from public debate by the incremental nature of the changes they impose.

28   All the issues have certain common features. The new technology will be motivated by the most humanitarian ends (with the exception of biological war research—another story). Its purpose will be to relieve suffering, to conquer disease, to restore normal capacities (as in conceiving or bearing a child). The difficulties of assessing the worth of this work vs. the cost are compounded because the benefits are immediate, concrete and tend to serve the individual, while the costs, if any, are perceived in abstractions ("humanness," "relatedness" and "quality of life"), are apparent only with time and are paid for by society as a whole or future generations.

29   The human being is the only species capable of systematically altering its "normal" biological system by use of its equally "normal" intellectual capacity. Cloning is but one example of such an intrusion into the reproductive area. The oldest is probably birth control of one sort or another. This capacity, when institutionalized, has a greater impact on a society than merely determining family size. It is a factor in defining the social roles available to women, levels of affluence of the society, and so on and on.

30   Abortion is also on its way to becoming institutionalized, in the sense of becoming accepted, relatively without question, as part of the normal order of things. It, too, will produce broad social effects, particularly when combined with amniocentesis, a technique which permits diagnosis of intrauterine fetal conditions (by withdrawing a sample of the amniotic

fluid with needle and syringe) and would thus give couples the choice of aborting a defective fetus in its early stages.

31    Artificial insemination as a solution for male sterility has been accepted, with some discussion of its psychological reverberations but little of its possible sociological impact.

## In-Vitro Fertilization

32    A parallel problem exists when the husband produces adequate semen, but the wife either fails to produce eggs or has a blocked passageway from the ovary to the uterus. If the woman merely has the blocked passageway, it might indeed be possible to remove an egg from the ovary, fertilize it in a test tube, and replant it at the proper stage of division in her uterine wall. Each clause in that statement represents staggering technical problems—yet each problem has been solved, or is on the verge of solution. Drs. R. G. Edwards and P. C. Steptoe, who have been instrumental in much of the work in this area, are expected imminently to attempt the implantation in a uterus of an in-vitro fertilized egg, with a good chance that it will grow into a normal baby. They may have already tried it, but so far there has been no news about the results if they have. In-vitro fertilization offers an added advantage— or complication, depending on your moral position—over more traditional methods. In the laboratory, during the short interval of days between fertilization and implantation, the sex of the newborn baby will be determinable. There are now selective stains which when applied to a single cell can establish gender without even a chromosome smear and evaluation. Therefore, one could fertilize a number of eggs and offer the parents a choice of gender—as well as other options of genetic composition. On the other hand, it would probably be safer to allow implantation, wait a few weeks and then determine genetic composition by amniocentesis—aborting, if the fetus does not meet parental expectations or standards.

## Substitute Carrying Mothers

33    By utilizing the same technology, a woman with no ovaries but a healthy uterus can borrow an egg from a donor, just as semen may be obtained from a donor. It can then be fertilized by her husband's semen in the test tube and, when ready, implanted in her uterus. By the same token, if a woman has intact ovaries but has had her uterus removed (a not uncommon procedure), she can have a laboratory conceived baby that genetically is hers and her husband's, and ask that it be raised

in the uterus of another woman for nine months. There is no technical problem here at all. It is just as simple to insert the fertilized egg into one uterus that has been prepared for it as another.

34    Once such procedures become accepted, need the reasons for utilizing them be limited to the biological?

35    A professional woman, for reasons of necessity, vanity or anxiety, might prefer not to carry her child. She might gladly pay for nine months' service from another woman. While certain liberationists might applaud the idea of freeing women from the nine-month pregnancy period, they might be appalled at the exploitation of another woman. This should provide the incentive for the development of an artificial placenta—doing away with the need for carrying the fetus in the womb—an undertaking that should not be immensely difficult.

. . .

## Some Questions

36    Who will determine what will be done and what will not? Who will determine what should be done and what should not? What controls should there be? How do we balance private rights and the general good? On what basis will we allocate decisions to either personal conscience or public policy?

37    Are there areas in which control of human development and behavior is bad *per se,* independent of the nature of the controlled things, the intention of the controller or the reasons for control? Are there processes which, once started, will bring irreversible changes so slight as to not be significant in one generation—but may, inexorably and incrementally, bring major changes to successive generations?

38    And if we do attempt human cloning, what will we do with the "debris," the discarded messes along the line? What will we do with those pieces and parts, near successes and almost-persons? What will we call the debris? At what arbitrary point will the damaged "goods" become damaged "children," requiring nurture rather than disposal? The more successful one became at this kind of experimentation, the more horrifyingly close to human would be the failures. The whole thing seems beyond contemplation for ethical and esthetic, as well as scientific reasons.

. . .

## Man as God

39    By the end of the 19th century, technology had surpassed even its own expectations. Man was too arrogant to recognize arrogance. Man did not

have to fear God, he had replaced him. There was nothing that technology would not eventually solve. The whole of history seemed to be contrived to serve the purposes and glorify the name of Homo sapiens.

40    It seems grossly unfair that so short a time as the last 25 years should have produced so precipitous a fall. But then, the way down the mountain has traditionally been faster than the way up. Man has been handed the bill and he is not sure he has enough assets to pay up. We have destroyed much of our environment, exhausted much of our resources and have manufactured weapons of total destruction without sufficiently secure control mechanisms. The biological revolution may offer relief or hasten total failure. Unfortunately, things now move faster, and we are less sure of how to even recognize success or failure.

41    But technology has elevated man—and there is no going back. "Natural man" is the cooperative creation of nature and man. Antitechnology is self-hatred.

42    The tragic irony is not that Mary Shelley's "fantasy" once again has a relevance. The tragedy is that it is no longer a fantasy—and that in its realization we no longer identify with Dr. Frankenstein but with his monster.

## REVIEW

### Content

1. Science is known for saying, "If it can be done, let's do it." Apply this tradition to a discussion of the various biological techniques Gaylin writes about. Consider the last sentence in paragraph 28 here. Compare Gaylin's discussion to the Leach essay entitled "We Scientists Have the Right To Play God," earlier in this section of the book. Think about sentence 1 in paragraph 23 here.
2. Discuss the questions Gaylin poses in paragraphs 36, 37, and 38, specifically in relation to cloning. Should cloning be outlawed?

### Rhetoric

3. Gaylin is writing about serious concerns and complex subject matter. Do you find his wit coming through at points to create a more lively tone and to lighten the heavy reading? Cite particularly effective instances of this. Did you recognize at once the Frankenstein story near the beginning of the article, and did this recognition help to get and hold your attention?
4. Gaylin uses some terms important in discussion of bioethics, which you will no doubt be hearing more and more about. Develop a command of the following, either from their context here or by looking them up: "value-free science" (paragraph 2); *hubris* (3); genetic

code (8); asexually (12); parthenogenesis (14); replicate (19); DNA (24); bioethics (27); in-vitro (32).

## Projects

5. Establish a hypothetical situation in which cloning might be considered. Be prepared to discuss in class the pros and cons of cloning in that situation. Or write a paper on the pros and cons.
6. Write a paper in which you argue for or against one of the following:
   (a) laboratory use of abortive fetuses, either before or after abortion (for example, as in paragraph 22)
   (b) birth control (29)
   (c) abortion (3)
   (d) artificial insemination (31)
   (e) in-vitro fertilization (32)
   (f) use of a substitute mother during gestation period (33–35)

# 9
# Religion

# Man Against Darkness

## W. T. STACE

Walter Terence Stace (1886–1967), born in England, worked for the British Civil Services in Ceylon for 22 years. He came to the United States in 1932 and taught philosophy at Princeton until he retired in 1955. Stace wrote a number of books, among them *The Destiny of Western Man* (1942), *Religion and the Modern Man* (1952), and *The Teachings of the Mystics* (1961). His article "Man Against Darkness" first appeared in *The Atlantic Monthly* in September, 1948. In it Stace maintains that modern man must learn to live without illusions—especially without the "illusion of a good, kindly, and purposeful universe. . . ." In a scientific age, he challenges us to learn to live well for its own sake.

1   No civilization can live without ideals, or to put it in another way, without a firm faith in moral ideas. Our ideals and moral ideas have in the past been rooted in religion. But the religious basis of our ideals has been undermined, and the superstructure of ideals is plainly tottering. None of the commonly suggested remedies on examination seems likely to succeed. It would therefore look as if the early death of our civilization were inevitable.

2   Of course we know that it is perfectly possible for individual men, very highly educated men, philosophers, scientists, intellectuals in general, to live moral lives without any religious convictions. But the question is whether a whole civilization, a whole family of peoples, composed almost entirely of relatively uneducated men and women, can do this.

3   It follows, of course, that if we could make the vast majority of men as highly educated as the very few are now, we might save the situation. And we are already moving slowly in that direction through the techniques of mass education. But the critical question seems to concern the time-lag. Perhaps in a few hundred years most of the population will, at the present rate, be sufficiently highly educated and civilized to combine high ideals with an absence of religion. But long before we reach any such stage, the collapse of our civilization may have come about. How are we to live through the intervening period?

## Facing the Truth

4    I am sure that the first thing we have to do is to face the truth, however bleak it may be, and then next we have to learn to live with it. Let me say a word about each of these two points. What I am urging as regards the first is complete honesty. Those who wish to resurrect Christian dogmas are not, of course, consciously dishonest. But they have that kind of unconscious dishonesty which consists in lulling oneself with opiates and dreams. Those who talk of a new religion are merely hoping for a new opiate. Both alike refuse to face the truth that there is, in the universe outside man, no spirituality, no regard for values, no friend in the sky, no help or comfort for man of any sort. To be perfectly honest in the admission of this fact, not to seek shelter in new or old illusions, not to indulge in wishful dreams about this matter, this is the first thing we shall have to do.

5    I do not urge this course out of any special regard for the sanctity of truth in the abstract. It is not self-evident to me that truth is the supreme value to which all else must be sacrificed. Might not the discoverer of a truth which would be fatal to mankind be justified in suppressing it, even in teaching men a falsehood? Is truth more valuable than goodness and beauty and happiness? To think so is to invent yet another absolute, another religious delusion in which Truth with a capital T is substituted for God. The reason why we must now boldly and honestly face the truth that the universe is nonspiritual and indifferent to goodness, beauty, happiness, or truth is not that it would be wicked to suppress it, but simply that it is too late to do so, so that in the end we cannot do anything else but face it. Yet we stand on the brink, dreading the icy plunge. We need courage. We need honesty.

## Living with the Truth

6    Now about the other point, the necessity of learning to live with the truth. This means learning to live virtuously and happily, or at least contentedly, without illusions. And this is going to be extremely difficult because what we have not begun dimly to perceive is that human life in the past, or at least human happiness, has almost wholly depended upon illusions. It has been said that man lives by truth, and that the truth will make us free. Nearly the opposite seems to me to be the case. Mankind has managed to live only by means of lies, and the truth may very well destroy us. If one were a Bergsonian one might believe that nature deliberately puts illusions into our souls in order to induce us to go on living.

7    The illusions by which men have lived seem to be of two kinds. First, there is what one may perhaps call the Great Illusion—I mean the reli-

gious illusion that the universe is moral and good, that it follows a wise and noble plan, that it is gradually generating some supreme value, that goodness is bound to triumph in it. Secondly, there is a whole host of minor illusions on which human happiness nourishes itself. How much of human happiness notoriously comes from the illusions of the lover about his beloved? Then again we work and strive because of the illusions connected with fame, glory, power, or money. Banners of all kinds, flags, emblems, insignia, ceremonials, and rituals are invariably symbols of some illusion or other. The British Empire, the connection between mother country and dominions, is partly kept going by illusions surrounding the notion of kingship. Or think of the vast amount of human happiness which is derived from the illusion of supposing that if some nonsense syllable, such as "sir" or "count" or "lord" is pronounced in conjunction with our names, we belong to a superior order of people.

8    There is plenty of evidence that human happiness is almost wholly based upon illusions of one kind or another. But the scientific spirit, or the spirit of truth, is the enemy of illusions and therefore the enemy of human happiness. That is why it is going to be so difficult to live with the truth.

## Living Well Without the Great Illusion

9    There is no reason why we should have to give up the host of minor illusions which render life supportable. There is no reason why the lover should be scientific about the loved one. Even the illusions of fame and glory may persist. But without the Great Illusion, the illusion of a good, kindly, and purposeful universe, we shall *have* to learn to live. And to ask this is really no more than to ask that we become genuinely civilized beings and not merely sham civilized beings.

10    I can best explain the difference by a reminiscence. I remember a fellow student in my college days, an ardent Christian, who told me that if he did not believe in a future life, in heaven and hell, he would rape, murder, steal, and be a drunkard. That is what I call being a sham civilized being. On the other hand, not only could a Huxley, a John Stuart Mill, a David Hume, live great and fine lives without any religion, but a great many others of us, quite obscure persons, can at least live decent lives without it.

11    To be genuinely civilized means to be able to walk straightly and to live honorably without the props and crutches of one or another of the childish dreams which have so far supported men. That such a life is likely to be ecstatically happy I will not claim. But that it can be lived in quiet content, accepting resignedly what cannot be helped, not expecting the impossible, and thankful for small mercies, this I

would maintain. That it would be difficult for men in general to learn this lesson I do not deny. But that it will be impossible I would not admit since so many have learned it already.

12    Man has not yet grown up. He is not adult. Like a child he cries for the moon and lives in a world of fantasies. And the race as a whole has perhaps reached the great crisis of its life. Can it grow up as a race in the same sense as individual men grow up? Can man put away childish things and adolescent dreams? Can he grasp the real world as it actually is, stark and bleak, without its romantic or religious halo, and still retain his ideals, striving for great ends and noble achievements? If he can, all may yet be well. If he cannot, he will probably sink back into the savagery and brutality from which he came, taking a humble place once more among the lower animals.

## REVIEW

### Content

1. Does paragraph 4 shock you? Do you agree with Stace, in paragraph 5, that "the universe is nonspiritual and indifferent to goodness, beauty, happiness, or truth"? *Must* one confront "the Great Illusion" and learn to live without it? Why does Stace equate "the scientific spirit" with "the spirit of truth" and why does he say that these are "the enemy of human happiness"? *Can* a person "live virtuously and happily, or at least contentedly," without the Great Illusion? If you do not agree with Stace here, *defend* whatever you do believe, contrary to his position; that is, what you "live by."

2. How do you respond to Stace's definition of "a sham civilized being"? Do you see why Stace proposes that it is more commendable for a human being to be able to live "without the props and crutches"? Do you agree with him?

### Rhetoric

3. Why does Stace capitalize "Great Illusion"?

4. Stace concludes his essay with a number of especially effective sentences structures, an important consideration if a writer wants his thinking to continue to linger in his reader's mind. What is unusual about the way in which each of the last four sentences in paragraph 11 is constructed? What is the effect of the series of short sentences opening the final paragraph? And why does Stace make the middle part of that paragraph all questions?

### Projects

5. To what extent do you believe in the Great Illusion? Think very hard here as you try to check out yourself on this question. Write up your answer into a paper.

6. The theme of an indifferent universe is a popular one in modern literature. Read the very short play "Act Without Words, Part I" by Samuel Beckett (in your college library) and write a paper about how that play reflects this theme. OR Write a paper in which you argue back at the universe, if you can, in response to this poem by Stephen Crane:

> A man said to the universe:
> "Sir, I exist!"
> "However," replied the universe,
> "The fact has not created in me
> A sense of obligation."

# On the Taboo Against Knowing Who You Are

## ALAN WATTS

Alan W. Watts (1915–1973) was a Britisher who became an American theologian, philosopher, lecturer, and writer. Watts was continually concerned with integrating Eastern intuition and mysticism with Western intellect and rationality. His many books reflect that interest, among them *The Legacy of Asia and Western Man* (1937), *The Meaning of Happiness* (1940), *The Way of Zen* (1957), *The Joyous Cosmology* (1962). One of his most popular books is entitled simply *The Book,* with the subtitle *On the Taboo Against Knowing Who You Are* (1966). In the selection here from that book, Watts deplores Western Man's focus on the individual ego, so that he experiences himself and all his fellows as isolated and alienated, inside "separate bags of skin." In such thinking, Nature is also seen as apart from man, so that he feels free to devastate her. We need, rather, Watts says, to realize that we are all "simply the pulses or vibrations of a single and eternal flow of energy," as the Easterner is taught to regard existence.

1   ... The problem of man and technics is almost always stated in the wrong way. It is said that humanity has evolved one-sidedly, growing in technical power without any comparable growth in moral integrity,

or, as some would prefer to say, without comparable progress in education and rational thinking. Yet the problem is more basic. The root of the matter is the way in which we feel and conceive ourselves as human beings, our sensation of being alive, of individual existence and identity. We suffer from a hallucination, from a false and distorted sensation of our own existence as living organisms. Most of us have the sensation that "I myself" is a separate center of feeling and action, living inside and bounded by the physical body—a center which "confronts" an "external" world of people and things, making contact through the senses with a universe both alien and strange. Everyday figures of speech reflect this illusion. "I came into this world." "You must *face* reality." "The conquest of nature."

2    This feeling of being lonely and very temporary visitors in the universe is in flat contradiction to everything known about man (and all other living organisms) in the sciences. We do not "come into" this world; we come *out* of it, as leaves from a tree. As the ocean "waves," the universe "peoples." Every individual is an expression of the whole realm of nature, a unique action of the total universe. Even those who know it to be true in theory do not sense or feel it, but continue to be aware of themselves as isolated "egos" inside bags of skin.

## How We View Nature

3    The first result of this illusion is that our attitude to the world "outside" us is largely hostile. We are forever "conquering" nature, space, mountains, deserts, bacteria, and insects instead of learning to cooperate with them in a harmonious order. In America the great symbols of this conquest are the bulldozer and the rocket—the instrument that batters the hills into flat tracts for little boxes made of ticky-tacky and the great phallic projectile that blasts the sky. (Nonetheless, we have fine architects who know how to fit houses into hills without ruining the landscape, and astronomers who know that the earth is already way out in space, and that our first need for exploring other worlds is sensitive electronic instruments which, like our eyes, will bring the most distant objects into our own brains.)[1] The hostile attitude of conquering nature ignores the basic interdependence of all things and events—that the world beyond the skin is actually an extension of our own bodies—and will end in destroying the very environment from which we emerge and upon which our whole life depends.

4    The second result of feeling that we are separate minds in an alien,

---

[1]"I do not believe that anything really worthwhile will come out of the exploration of the slag heap that constitutes the surface of the moon. . . . Nobody should imagine that the enormous financial budget of NASA implies that astronomy is now well supported." Fred Hoyle, *Galaxies, Nuclei, and Quasars.* Harper & Row, New York, 1965.

and mostly stupid, universe is that we have no *common* sense, no way of making sense of the world upon which we are agreed in common. It's just my opinion against yours, and therefore the most aggressive and violent (and thus insensitive) propagandist makes the decisions. A muddle of conflicting opinions united by force of propaganda is the worst possible source of control for a powerful technology.

5    It might seem, then, that our need is for some genius to invent a new religion, a philosophy of life and a view of the world, that is plausible and generally acceptable for the late twentieth century, and through which every individual can feel that the world as a whole and his own life in particular have meaning. This, as history has shown repeatedly, is not enough. Religions are divisive and quarrelsome. They are a form of one-upmanship because they depend upon separating the "saved" from the out-group. Even religious liberals play the game of "we're-more-tolerant-than-you." Furthermore, as systems of doctrine, symbolism, and behavior, religions harden into institutions that must command loyalty, be defended and kept "pure," and—because all belief is fervent hope, and thus a cover-up for doubt and uncertainty—religions must make converts. The more people who agree with us, the less nagging insecurity about our position. In the end one is committed to being a Christian or a Buddhist come what may in the form of new knowledge. New and indigestible ideas have to be wangled into the religious tradition, however inconsistent with its original doctrines, so that the believer can still take his stand and assert, "I am first and foremost a follower of Christ/Mohammed/Buddha, or whomever." Irrevocable commitment to any religion is not only intellectual suicide; it is positive unfaith because it closes the mind to any new vision of the world. Faith is, above all, open-ness—an act of trust in the unknown.

## Scriptures Are Not Life

6    An ardent Jehovah's Witness once tried to convince me that if there were a God of Love, he would certainly provide mankind with a reliable and infallible textbook for the guidance of conduct. I replied that no considerate God would destroy the human mind by making it so rigid and unadaptable as to depend upon one book, the Bible, for all the answers. For the use of words, and thus of a book, is to point beyond themselves to a world of life and experience that is not mere words or even ideas. Just as money is not real, consumable wealth, books are not life. To idolize structures is like eating paper currency.

7    Therefore The Book that I would like to slip to my children would itself be slippery. It would slip them into a new domain, not of ideas alone, but of experience and feeling. It would be a temporary medicine, not a diet; a point of departure, not a perpetual point of reference. They would read it and be done with it, for if it were well and clearly

written they would not have to go back to it again and again for hidden meanings or for clarification of obscure doctrines.

8    We do not need a new religion or a new bible. We need a new experience—a new feeling of what it is to be "I." The lowdown (which is, of course, the secret and profound view) on life is that our normal sensation of self is a hoax or, at best, a temporary role that we are playing, or have been conned into playing—with our own tacit consent, just as every hypnotized person is basically willing to be hypnotized. The most strongly enforced of all known taboos is the taboo against knowing who or what you really are behind the mask of your apparently separate, independent, and isolated ego. I am not thinking of Freud's barbarous Id or Unconscious as the actual reality behind the facade of personality. Freud, as we shall see, was under the influence of a nineteenth-century fashion called "reductionism," a curious need to put down human culture and intelligence by calling it a fluky by-product of blind and irrational forces. They worked very hard, then, to prove that grapes can grow on thorn-bushes.

## "I" as Vibration of the *Single* Energy

9    As is often the way, what we have suppressed and overlooked is something startlingly obvious. The difficulty is that it is *so* obvious and basic that one can hardly find the words for it. The Germans call it a *Hintergedanke,* an apprehension lying tacitly in the back of our minds which we cannot easily admit, even to ourselves. The sensation of "I" as a lonely and isolated center of being is so powerful and commonsensical, and so fundamental to our modes of speech and thought, to our laws and social institutions, that we cannot experience selfhood except as something superficial in the scheme of the universe. I seem to be a brief light that flashes but once in all the aeons of time—a rare, complicated, and all-too-delicate organism on the fringe of biological evolution, where the wave of life bursts into individual, sparkling, and multicolored drops that gleam for a moment only to vanish forever. Under such conditioning it seems impossible and even absurd to realize that myself does not reside in the drop alone, but in the whole surge of energy which ranges from the galaxies to the nuclear fields in my body. At this level of existence "I" am immeasurably old; my forms are infinite and their comings and goings are simply the pulses or vibrations of a single and eternal flow of energy.

## REVIEW

### Content

1. Do you understand from your own life what Watts means when he says we sense ourselves as "isolated 'egos' inside bags of skin"? Do

you agree with him that this is a "hallucination"? And a *real problem* for the Westerner as he/she yearns to feel at home in the universe? What does he mean by "'I' am immeasurably old . . . flow of energy," at the end of paragraph 9?

2. Discuss paragraph 5, with special attention to Watts' conclusion: "Irrevocable commitment . . . in the unknown." Do you agree with Watts in his definition of faith here?

## Rhetoric

3. Watts is known for his style. What especially characterizes his writing? Can you find particularly good imagery in paragraphs 3 and 9? What makes sentences 2 and 3 in paragraph 2 especially vivid?

4. One of the strengths of Watts' writing is his ability to really involve his reader in his content. How does he do this? He obviously likes to "play around with language." Point to some instances of such informal, "fun" usage.

## Projects

5. Compose a page for The Book Watts says he would like to slip to his children, addressing your page to whatever facet of life you want to think about and basing the page on the view of the world Watts talks about here. Later, compare the page with those others have written and compile the pages into a book. Decide whether you would like to give it to someone you know and/or to use it in your own life.

6. Write a paper in which you relate Watts' discussion to a specific area of ecology, demonstrating how the world view he advocates would help to resolve the issue with which you deal. OR Spend some time contemplating Watts' advice in relation to your own life and write about how adopting this view might affect your own individual life.

# It's the Old-Time Religion

## The Couch Replaces the Church

### MICHAEL T. MALLOY

Michael T. Malloy (1936–   ), a native of Chicago, is a former foreign corre-
spondent who is now a staff writer for *The National Observer,* a weekly
newspaper, from which the following selection is taken (May 26, 1973).
Malloy says that psychiatry is assuming what has been religion's role in
this country, as behavior which would have been regarded as sinful in
the past comes to be seen, rather, as "sick."

1   Psychiatry is well on its way to replacing religion in America. A growing
number of troubled souls give confession to therapists instead of priests.
Millions seek spiritual solace in weekly encounter groups instead of
churches. Most important, "sickness" is replacing sin in our vocabulary,
and "health" is replacing virtue. Society turns more and more to experts
on sickness and health for answers about good and evil.

2      "It is now the law, handed down by the Supreme Court, that alcoholism is a disease; 100 years ago it was quite clear that it was a sin,"
explains Dr. Herbert Modlin, a psychiatrist at the Menninger Foundation
in Topeka, Kan. "Take juvenile delinquency. It used to be obvious: He's
a bad boy. Now he's a sick kid."

## Good and Evil Redefined

3   "In *The Scarlet Letter,* written in 1850, adultery is explained by the minister as due to evil inside the woman," says psychiatrist E. Fuller Torrey
of the National Institute of Mental Health. "In 1972 it is explained
by the psychiatrist as due to the woman's low self-esteem and attempts
to get close to people. In the past 25 years more and more socially
unacceptable behavior is explained in these terms, to the apparent satisfaction of more and more people."

4      The power to define good (health) and evil (sickness) carries with
it the power to change our ideas of right and wrong. The American
Psychiatric Association, for example, is reconsidering the inclusion of

Reprinted by permission from *The National Observer,* copyright Dow Jones & Company,
Inc., 1973.

homosexuality in its official catalog of mental disorders. "We've won the ball game if homosexuality is not an illness," says Ronald Gold, spokesman for the Gay Activists Alliance. "The diagnosis of homosexuality as an illness is used in exactly the same way as when homosexuality was described as a sin or an influence of the devil."

5    The mantle of moral leadership fits awkwardly on the shoulders of the nation's psychiatrists. The indications are that most of them don't want it and feel unqualified to wear it. The majority who do claim to have the moral answers seem to preach ethical codes as much based on faith as is the notion of the virgin birth.

6    People who ask psychiatry for a scientific guide to life may only get a new religion. The new religions are riven with the same theological disputes that split the old ones. The words are different, but the same arguments rage over original sin, the difference between right and wrong, and whether man is indeed made in the image of God.

7    There are many ways to document the tendency of people to turn from religion to psychiatry.

8    "Over the past 25 years . . . the number of primary mental-health personnel (psychiatrists, psychologists, psychiatric social workers, and psychiatric nurses) has increased from 14,000 to 100,000," Torrey and Dr. Scott H. Nelson wrote last year. "Simultaneously the number of ministers and priests has decreased from approximately 250,000 to 200,000.

## Religion Dwindles in Academe

9    So many young people have turned from the study of religion to psychology that mental-health workers are sure to outnumber clergymen in a few years. The two fields were evenly matched as recently as 1961, when about 10,000 degrees each were given in psychology and in religious disciplines. In 1971 students received 44,000 psychology degrees and only 14,500 related to religion.

10    The public hears far more about human behavior from psychologists and psychiatrists than from clergymen. The psychiatrists' advice seems much more popular. Who preaches most often about everything from abortion to adultery on the nightly talk shows? Who writes most of the magazine articles that tell us how to treat our husbands, wives, and children? Who writes the best-selling books on the gut issues of life, love, and death?

11    "That's obviously what's going on, psychological self-help," says Albert Johnston, who forecasts the public taste in nonfiction books for Publishers Weekly. *I'm Okay–You're Okay* and *Games People Play* were both national best sellers. It's very widespread and concomitant with a drop in church attendance."

# From Confessional to Couch

12    "Ten years ago there was a study that found most people with problems went to a clergyman first, about 70 percent," says Dr. Angelo D'Agostino, a psychoanalyst and a Roman Catholic priest. "I don't know the figures now, but they must be significantly less than 40 percent."

13       The journey from confessional to couch may be less a result of psychiatric evangelism than of failure of traditional religion, its authority weakened as science undermines the literal interpretation of one religious myth after another.

14       "Psychiatrists are only falling into a vacuum," says Torrey. "The vacuum used to be filled by priests and ministers. They were always ready to tell you if something was obscene or not, if you should drink or not. Now there are far fewer people who go to ministers asking, 'What should I do?' And there are far fewer ministers who will say: 'The Bible says so-and-so. Therefore you should do it.' "

# Pastors Turn to Psychology

15    Many clergymen have indeed been converted to psychology. Some leave their parish to become pastoral counselors, offering psychotherapy instead of the Ten Commandments to troubled souls. Some stay in the parish and hold encounter groups in the church basement.

16       "Many pastors begin to substitute psychology for theology as their basic science. I think they should stop that," says Dr. Paul Pruyser, a psychologist and professor at the Menninger Foundation. "In thinking so psychologically, aren't they letting down their clients, who came to them to be evaluated morally and ethically? If [parishioners] get a peculiar easiness on moral issues and a lot of psychological material [from pastors], the pastor may leave out precisely the reason why the clients came. Is it any wonder people turn from the pastor to the psychiatrist?"

17       Most psychiatrists probably would deny competing with religion for moral and ethical leadership. On the contrary, most denominations of psychiatry emphasize that the therapist should not impose his own values on a patient.

18       "The best professional answer is that there should not be a moral position; that's the way it is taught in the professional schools," says New York psychoanalyst Bruce Maliver. "But the fact is there is a common morality among most shrinks, and it creeps into their work."

19       "Although I want to believe that I have no visions of how I want my patients to change, I am regularly amazed (and perhaps pleased) to note that my patients gradually move toward value systems that are closer to mine," writes psychiatrist Seymour Halleck in *Politics of Therapy*.

20       Because psychiatrists tend to define religion as a "neurosis," the drift

from theology to therapy should grow by feeding on itself. Even without a reminder that the words were Sigmund Freud's, 55 percent of the psychoanalysts surveyed for a 1970 study agreed with him that belief in God "is so patently infantile, so incongruous with reality, that . . . it is painful to think that the great majority of mortals will never be able to rise above this view of life."

## Psychiatrists' Differing Views

21   If the religious views that underlie traditional Western morality are mere neuroses, what alternative views do psychiatrists project?

22   "There is a big split in the psychological-healing business and, by God, I think it's a theological split," says Dr. Kenneth Mitchell, a Presbyterian minister who heads a Menninger program that trains clergymen in psychology. "Freud believed aggression is inborn. People around here would say the task is to teach people to channel their aggression. That position is so damned close to original sin.

23   "But Carl Rogers' theories are popular because they say you are basically good, basically creative, and if we eliminate the conditions that stifled the goodness and healthiness, then the good in you will come out. It's pretty close to the idea that man is created in the image of God."

24   How does this debate affect you? Take child rearing. If man is essentially good, a parent's task is to avoid warping his child's essential goodness. If he isn't, says Menninger psychiatrist Harold Voth, "part of child rearing is *bridling* the human spirit."

25   "The grand prize of this revolution is ultimate psychiatric authority, the power to impose norms of sanity and insanity upon society," writes Patrick McGrady, Jr., in *The Love Doctors.* "The winners will set standards of behavior, determine medical-school curricula, hire and fire professors, mold upcoming generations of therapists, and be summoned to courts and legislatures to sanctify policies, politics, and policing."

26   This is real power. More people today are locked up in mental hospitals by psychiatrists than in prisons by the courts. No celebrated trial, of a pornographic movie or a Presidential assassin, is complete without platoons of testifying psychiatrists. Torrey notes that psychiatrists were "prominent in almost every case where the [abortion] law was changed."

## Medieval Angels, and Eros and Thanatos

27   The orthodox Freudian position is remarkably similar to the medieval belief that good and bad angels grapple for every human soul; you still see them hovering at the shoulders of comic-strip characters. Freud's

inborn drives even have names: Eros is the tender, constructive, loving life force; Thanatos is the aggressive, destructive death wish.

28    It is a bleak and pessimistic philosophy. Because these angels will always be with us, society will never be fully satisfied. Maliver says Freud defined a well-analyzed man as one with "a mature depression." In his celebrated correspondence with Einstein, Freud offered little hope of stamping out war and other social evils. The Freudian position is more popular with psychiatrists than the general public, and no wonder.

29    The new therapies are connected with Carl Rogers, Fritz Perls, transactional analysis, encounter groups, sensitivity training, T-groups, the human-potential movement, humanist psychology, and other names and slogans. The premise of many is summed up in the title psychiatrist Thomas Harris chose for his best-selling *I'm Okay–You're Okay.*

30    This way of thinking is in sunny contrast to the gray skepticism of Freud. Pruyser says it offers "a proclaimable faith." If man is ultimately good, then all our problems can be solved by removing his frustrations and letting him blossom.

31    In their best-known forms the new therapies run toward openness, touching, liberation, intimacy, sharing, screaming, group confession, spontaneity, "letting it all hang out," and doing your own thing.

32    "They've recognized that the best place to win converts is in the schools," Maliver writes in *The Encounter Game.* "There is no major school system in this country without teachers who have participated in T-groups. . . . In countless numbers of colleges throughout America today, sensitivity training courses are a required part of the curriculum."

33    Yet people who reject the religious basis for morality because it has been undermined by science may find that the Freudian and counter-Freudian world views are equally unscientific. Eros and Thanatos are theoretical constructs, no more proved by science than the angel Gabriel.

## New Gospels as a Faith

34    The "new" psychiatrists seem more certain that they have "the answers" than do their skeptical Freudian brethren. But they often admit that their gospels are indeed based on faith instead of science.

35    "We cannot prove [individuals] are important. We have only the faith to believe they are," writes Harris. "The idea that if you let it all hang out someone will want you is an act of faith," agrees hip psychiatrist Martin Shepard, talking about a basic tenet of his latest work, *The Do-It-Yourself Psychotherapy Book.*

36    Humanism emphasizes love, honesty, tolerance, and a deep regard for the dignity of every human being. Many philosophers would agree it is a basis for a noble system of ethics. But many believe that a combination for their behavior: 'Ah! It's normal. I can do it!' "

37    "Human freedom has never flowered in the midst of screaming crowds," insists Maliver. "Its greatest subversions have occurred when primitive emotion has been encouraged. Most therapists believe that ego development includes the development of impulse control, particularly the control of anger and violence."

## Justifying Any Behavior

38    "Do your own thing, multiple marriage, screw anybody who will lie down for you: It's the worst thing you can do," argues Voth. "But some upstart psychiatrist will come out with a book and people will find a rationalization for their behavior: 'Ah! It's normal. I can do it!' "

39    Few of even the most radical psychiatrists would urge the population to naked, unrestrained license, but anyone who wants to find such promptings in the idea of his own individual worth and the value of spontaneous expression can certainly do so. "I believe it does have an implicit ethic—hedonism," writes Maliver.

40    The new psychological faiths not only duplicate the old theological controversies, but they also quarrel in the traditional manner about whether man should concentrate on his personal salvation or society's. As usual, the faith that thinks it has the answers argues that society can't change until its members are baptized in the new doctrine.

41    Thus Harris argues, along with conservative theologians, that ministers should stay in the pulpit (preferably preaching his brand of transactional analysis) and away from social involvement. "Slums and ghettos and put-downs are not going to disappear in society unless slums and games disappear from the hearts of people. . . . If personal liberation is the key to social change . . . then the church's principal function is to provide a place where people can come to hear the truth."

42    Change "games" to "sin," and "liberation" to "salvation," and you get the idea.

43    "Be yourself, do your own thing, is similar to Nineteenth Century pietism that saving my soul is a personal issue with an utter blindness to the rest of the world," says Pruyser. "It is like Billy Graham's conspicuous silence on the issues of the day. You could say Graham is closer to encounter (than to Freud)."

## The Need for Religion

44    In treating patients most psychological denominations do urge certain moral positions whether they admit it or not. A patient cannot understand and control his own actions unless he is honest with himself and takes the responsibility for what he says and does.

45    "In the past the question of, 'What am I here for?' was usually answered in clear and unequivocal terms," write Torrey and Nelson. "You
are here because it is God's will. The meaning of your existence is to
carry out that will, live a good life, and glorify your Creator."

46    Freud did not pretend to provide a new answer. An individualist humanism that echoes Fritz Perls' dictum—"I please myself first"—gives
us no reason to live when pleasure gives way to pain, tragedy, and the
certainty of death. An altruistic humanism that says we are here to love
our fellow man does not really explain why we should love him as much
as ourselves, or whether man is really worth it.

47    "People do need that fundamental religious ground for their existence, the reason why you can still go on living in the face of tragedy,"
argues D'Agostino. "Psychiatry can't do that. If you can't answer the
questions of, 'Why am I here? What is life for?' then there's no wonder
suicide would seem like a rational option."

48    "It is well known that psychiatry, psychoanalysis, and psychology attract persons who are somewhat troubled within themselves," says Voth.
It is evident that they do not find in psychiatry the answers to the questions that D'Agostino poses. For it is also well known that psychiatrists
commit suicide more than twice as frequently as the rest of us.

## REVIEW

### Content

1. Had you ever thought before of psychiatry as a substitute for religion?
Can you follow Malloy's reasoning on this point? Does he convince
you—even if you do not want to be convinced? Discuss the implications of placing one's faith in first, a therapist, and second, oneself,
versus a more externalized type of faith in an essentially unknown
and unknowable Supreme Being. Do you find organized religion joining hands with psychology more and more? Is this a desirable development, or not?

2. Discuss the implications of sentence 4 in paragraph 1. If many psychiatrists "define religion as a 'neurosis,'" as Malloy states in paragraph
20, then what about the "health" of the religious person? Discuss the
implications of the "new" psychiatry, as reviewed by Malloy in paragraphs 36 through 39.

### Rhetoric

3. Examine how Malloy uses statistics in paragraphs 8 and 9. Do you
see any possibility of fallacious (careless) reasoning here? Consider
the reasoning behind paragraph 48. Does the final sentence necessarily invalidate psychiatry in the way that Malloy suggests here?

4. Why does Malloy use a series of questions in paragraph 10?

**Projects**

5. Write a paper on one of the following topics or arrange a debate in class on one of them:
   (a) psychiatry as a guide to conduct and an aid to living well
   (b) Freudian theories versus the counter-Freudian movement (Perls, Rogers, Harris, et al.), as a basis for improvement of the individual and hence society through psychology/psychiatry
6. Develop a paper out of one of the following:
   (a) some "sin" other than adultery that has now become "sickness," citing specific examples, either as Malloy does through literature (paragraph 3) or from real life.
   (b) Since Malloy's article, the APA has removed homosexuality from its official handbook of mental disorders. Argue whether this is a good or a bad development and why you take the position you do.
   (c) Why is a client's assuming his/her therapist's value system an undesirable development?
   (d) *Is* religion a neurosis?
   (e) Compare aggression with sin, as Malloy begins to do in paragraph 22.
   (f) Discuss the implications of the statement in sentence 2, paragraph 26.
   (g) Compare the medieval good angels and bad angels with Freud's Eros and Thanatos, as Malloy suggests in paragraph 27.
   (h) Argue the first sentence in paragraph 47, with either "do" or "do not" after the first word.

# Why I Am an Agnostic

## CLARENCE DARROW

Clarence Darrow (1857–1938) was admitted to the bar in his home state of Ohio at 21. He went to practice law in Chicago, where he built a reputation as a controversial criminal lawyer. One of his most famous cases was the Scopes Monkey Trial of 1925 in Tennessee, where Darrow defended John Scopes, a young science teacher who had been teaching evolu-

From *Verdicts Out of Court*, edited by Arthur and Lila Weinberg. Quadrangle Books, 1963. Reprinted by permission.

tion in that Bible Belt state. That trial can be related to Darrow's "Why
I Am an Agnostic." This statement was originally part of a 1929 symposium
at which Darrow appeared with a Protestant bishop, a Catholic judge, and
a Jewish rabbi. Darrow argues here against the rationality of literal interpretation of the Bible and goes on to denounce the tendency of orthodox
religion to circumscribe scientific investigation that can better the lot of
man.

1    An agnostic is a doubter. The word is generally applied to those who
doubt the verity of accepted religious creeds or faiths. Everyone is an
agnostic as to the beliefs or creeds they do not accept. Catholics are
agnostic to the Protestant creeds, and the Protestants are agnostic to
the Catholic creed. Anyone who thinks is an agnostic about something,
otherwise he must believe that he is possessed of all knowledge. And
the proper place for such a person is in the madhouse or the home
for the feeble-minded. In a popular way, in the western world, an agnostic is one who doubts or disbelieves the main tenets of the Christian
faith.

2    I would say that belief in at least three tenets is necessary to the
faith of a Christian: a belief in God, a belief in immortality, and a belief
in a supernatural book. Various Christian sects require much more, but
it is difficult to imagine that one could be a Christian, under any intelligent meaning of the word, with less. Yet there are some people who
claim to be Christians who do not accept the literal interpretation of
all the Bible, and who give more credence to some portions of the book
than to others.

## God as Force Is Inconceivable

3    I am an agnostic as to the question of God. I think that it is impossible
for the human mind to believe in an object or thing unless it can form
a mental picture of such object or thing. Since man ceased to worship
openly an anthromorphic God and talked vaguely and not intelligently
about some force in the universe, higher than man, that is responsible
for the existence of man and the universe, he cannot be said to believe
in God. One cannot believe in a force excepting as a force that pervades
matter and is not an individual entity. To believe in a thing, an image
of the thing must be stamped on the mind. If one is asked if he believes
in such an animal as a camel, there immediately arises in his mind an
image of the camel. This image has come from experience or knowledge
of the animal gathered in some way or another. No such image comes,
or can come, with the idea of a God who is described as a force.

4    Man has always speculated upon the origin of the universe, including
himself. I feel, with Herbert Spencer, that whether the universe had

an origin—and if it had—what the origin is will never be known by man. The Christian says that the universe could not make itself; that there must have been some higher power to call it into being. Christians have been obsessed for many years by Paley's argument that if a person passing through a desert should find a watch and examine its spring, its hands, its case and its crystal, he would at once be satisfied that some intelligent being capable of design had made the watch. No doubt this is true. No civilized man would question that someone made the watch. The reason he would not doubt it is because he is familiar with watches and other appliances made by man. The savage was once unfamiliar with a watch and would have had no idea upon the subject. There are plenty of crystals and rocks of natural formation that are as intricate as a watch, but even to intelligent man they carry no implication that some intelligent power must have made them. They carry no such implication because no one has any knowledge or experience of someone having made these natural objects which everywhere abound.

5    To say that God made the universe gives us no explanation of the beginning of things. If we are told that God made the universe, the question immediately arises: Who made God? Did he always exist, or was there some power back of that? Did he create matter out of nothing, or is his existence co-extensive with matter? The problem is still there. What is the origin of it all? If, on the other hand, one says that the universe was not made by God, that it always existed, he has the same difficulty to confront. To say that the universe was here last year, or millions of years ago, does not explain its origin. This is still a mystery. As to the question of the origin of things, man can only wonder and doubt and guess.

## No Evidence for Soul

6    As to the existence of the soul, all people may either believe or disbelieve. Everyone knows the origin of the human being. They know that it came from a single cell in the body of the mother, and that the cell was one out of ten thousand in the mother's body. Before gestation the cell must have been fertilized by a spermatozoön from the body of the father. This was one out of perhaps a billion spermatazoa that was the capacity of the father. When the cell is fertilized a chemical process begins. The cell divides and multiplies and increases into millions of cells, and finally a child is born. Cells die and are born during the life of the individual until they finally drop apart, and this is death.

7    If there is a soul, what is it, and where did it come from, and where does it go? Can anyone who is guided by his reason possibly imagine a soul independent of a body, or the place of its residence, or the character of it, or anything concerning it? If man is justified in any

belief or disbelief on any subject, he is warranted in the disbelief in a soul. Not one scrap of evidence exists to prove any such impossible thing.

## No Such Book as Bible

8    Many Christians base the belief of a soul and God upon the Bible. Strictly speaking, there is no such book. To make the Bible, sixty-six books are bound into one volume. These books were written by many people at different times, and no one knows the time or the identity of any author. Some of the books were written by several authors at various times. These books contain all sorts of contradictory concepts of life and morals and the origin of things. Between the first and the last nearly a thousand years intervened, a longer time than has passed since the discovery of America by Columbus.

9    When I was a boy the theologicans used to assert that the proof of the divine inspiration of the Bible rested on miracles and prophecies. But a miracle means a violation of natural law, and there can be no proof imagined that could be sufficient to show the violation of a natural law; even though proof seemed to show violation, it would only show that we were not acquainted with all natural laws. One believes in the truthfulness of a man because of his long experience with the man, and because the man has always told a consistent story. But no man has told so consistent a story as nature.

10    If one should say that the sun did not rise, to use the ordinary expression, on the day before, his hearer would not believe it, even though he had slept all day and knew that his informant was a man of the strictest veracity. He would not believe it because the story is inconsistent with the conduct of the sun in all the ages past.

11    Primitive and even civilized people have grown so accustomed to believing in miracles that they often attribute the simplest manifestations of nature to agencies of which they know nothing. They do this when the belief is utterly inconsistent with knowledge and logic. They believe in old miracles and new ones. Preachers pray for rain, knowing full well that no such prayer was ever answered. When a politician is sick, they pray for God to cure him, and the politician almost invariably dies. The modern clergyman who prays for rain and for the health of the politician is no more intelligent in this matter than the primitive man who saw a separate miracle in the rising and setting of the sun, in the birth of an individual, in the growth of a plant, in the stroke of lightning, in the flood, in every manifestation of nature and life.

12    As to prophecies, intelligent writers gave them up long ago. In all prophecies facts are made to suit the prophecy, or the prophecy was made after the facts, or the events have no relation to the prophecy.

Weird and strange and unreasonable interpretations are used to explain simple statements, that a prophecy may be claimed.

## Creation of Universe and of Man

13      Can any rational person believe that the Bible is anything but a human document? We now know pretty well where the various books came from, and about when they were written. We know that they were written by human beings who had no knowledge of science, little knowledge of life, and were influenced by the barbarous morality of primitive times, and were grossly ignorant of most things that men know today. For instance, Genesis says that God made the earth, and he made the sun to light the day and the moon to light the night, and in one clause disposes of the stars by saying that "he made the stars also." This was plainly written by someone who had no conception of the stars. Man, by the aid of his telescope, has looked out into the heavens and found stars whose diameter is as great as the distance between the earth and the sun. We now know that the universe is filled with stars and suns and planets and systems. Every new telescope looking further into the heavens only discovers more and more worlds and suns and systems in the endless reaches of space. The men who wrote Genesis believed, of course, that this tiny speck of mud that we call the earth was the center of the universe, the only world in space, and made for man, who was the only being worth considering. These men believed that the stars were only a little way above the earth, and were set in the firmament for man to look at, and for nothing else. Everyone today knows that this conception is not true.

14      The origin of the human race is not as blind a subject as it once was. Let alone God creating Adam out of hand, from the dust of the earth, does anyone believe that Eve was made from Adam's rib—that the snake walked and spoke in the Garden of Eden—that he tempted Eve to persuade Adam to eat an apple, and that it is on that account that the whole human race was doomed to hell—that for four thousand years there was no chance for any human to be saved, though none of them had anything whatever to do with the temptation; and that finally men were saved only through God's son dying for them, and that unless human beings believed this silly, impossible and wicked story they were doomed to hell? Can anyone with intelligence really believe that a child born today should be doomed because the snake tempted Eve and Eve tempted Adam? To believe that is not God-worship; it is devil-worship.

15      Can anyone call this scheme of creation and damnation moral? It defies every principle of morality, as man conceives morality. Can anyone believe today that the whole world was destroyed by flood, save only

Noah and his family and a male and female of each species of animal that entered the Ark? There are almost a million species of insects alone. How did Noah match these up and make sure of getting male and female to reproduce life in the world after the flood had spent its force? And why should all the lower animals have been destroyed? Were they included in the sinning of man? This is a story which could not beguile a fairly bright child of five years of age today.

## Some Other Irrationalities

16    Do intelligent people believe that the various languages spoken by man on earth came from the confusion of tongues at the Tower of Babel, some four thousand years ago? Human languages were dispersed all over the face of the earth long before that time. Evidences of civilizations are in existence now that were old long before the date that romancers fix for the building of the Tower, and even before the date claimed for the flood.

17    Do Christians believe that Joshua made the sun stand still, so that the day could be lengthened, that a battle might be finished? What kind of person wrote that story, and what did he know about astronomy? It is perfectly plain that the author thought that the earth was the center of the universe and stood still in the heavens, and that the sun either went around it or was pulled across its path each day, and that the stopping of the sun would lengthen the day. We know now that had the sun stopped when Joshua commanded it, and had it stood still until now, it would not have lengthened the day. We know that the day is determined by the rotation of the earth upon its axis, and not by the movement of the sun. Everyone knows that this story simply is not true, and not many even pretend to believe the childish fable.

18    What of the tale of Balaam's ass speaking to him, probably in Hebrew? Is it true, or is it a fable? Many asses have spoken, and doubtless some in Hebrew, but they have not been that breed of asses. Is salvation to depend on a belief in a monstrosity like this?

19    Above all the rest, would any human being today believe that a child was born without a father? Yet this story was not at all unreasonable in the ancient world; at least three or four miraculous births are recorded in the Bible, including John the Baptist and Samson. Immaculate conceptions were common in the Roman world at the time and at the place where Christianity really had its nativity. Women were taken to the temples to be inoculated of God so that their sons might be heroes, which meant, generally, wholesale butchers. Julius Caesar was a miraculous conception—indeed, they were common all over the world. How many miraculous-birth stories is a Christian now expected to believe?

## Possession vs. Sickness

20    In the days of the formation of the Christian religion, disease meant the possession of human beings by devils. Christ cured a sick man by casting out the devils, who ran into the swine, and the swine ran into the sea. Is there any question but what that was simply the attitude and belief of a primitive people? Does anyone believe that sickness means the possession of the body by devils, and that the devils must be cast out of the human being that he may be cured? Does anyone believe that a dead person can come to life? The miracles recorded in the Bible are not the only instances of dead men coming to life. All over the world one find testimony of such miracles; miracles which no person is expected to believe, unless it is his kind of a miracle. Still at Lourdes today, and all over the present world, from New York to Los Angeles and up and down the lands, people believe in miraculous occurrences, and even in the return of the dead. Superstition is everywhere prevalent in the world. It has been so from the beginning, and most likely will be so unto the end.

21    The reasons for agnosticism are abundant and compelling. Fantastic and foolish and impossible consequences are freely claimed for the belief in religion. All the civilization of any period is put down as a result of religion. All the cruelty and error and ignorance of the period has no relation to religion. The truth is that the origin of what we call civilization is not due to religion but to skepticism. So long as men accepted miracles without question, so long as they believed in original sin and the road to salvation, so long as they believed in a hell where man would be kept for eternity on account of Eve, there was no reason whatever for civilization: life was short, and eternity was long, and the business of life was preparation for eternity.

## Science and Progress

22    When every event was a miracle, when there was no order or system or law, there was no occasion for studying any subject, or being interested in anything excepting a religion which took care of the soul. As man doubted the primitive conceptions about religion, and no longer accepted the literal, miraculous teachings of ancient books, he set himself to understand nature. We no longer cure disease by casting out devils. Since that time, men have studied the human body, have built hospitals and treated illness in a scientific way. Science is responsible for the building of railroads and bridges, of steamships, of telegraph lines, of cities, towns, large buildings and small, plumbing and sanitation, for the food supply, and countless thousands of useful things that we now deem nec-

essary to life. Without skepticism and doubt, none of these things could have been given to the world.

23    The fear of God is not the beginning of wisdom. The fear of God is the death of wisdom. Skepticism and doubt lead to study and investigation, and investigation is the beginning of wisdom.

24    The modern world is the child of doubt and inquiry, as the ancient world was the child of fear and faith.

## REVIEW

### Content

1. Do you agree with Darrow's argument against a belief in God in paragraph 3; is it *totally* logical? Or is logicality the point here at all? Should one *try* to hold the objects of *faith* up to *logical* scrutiny? Do the questions Darrow poses in paragraph 5 *matter* to you? How do you respond to Darrow's discussion of the soul in paragraph 7?

2. If any of Darrow's discourse on the Bible challenges your own position and/or disturbs you, then prepare to *refute* him where you disagree with him in any of the following paragraphs: 8, 9, 13, 14, 19, 20. How does the last sentence in paragraph 14 strike you?

### Rhetoric

3. Darrow's prose often reads like a lawyer's brief—as if he had prepared it for courtroom presentation. Can you *hear* the lawyer before the bare as you read the above? Point to instances of the following techniques in Darrow's presentation here: informality of tone to appeal to one's listeners; parallel structure; use of the direct question, to involve the hearer/reader; appeals to the *emotions* of one's audience; humor, including sarcasm.

4. Darrow was known to allow his eloquence to overcome his reasoning from time to time. Check out "Why I Am an Agnostic" for this tendency. Note, for example, the generalizations in paragraph 21. Is paragraph 12 *adequately* argued? Does Darrow distort the Biblical meaning of "wisdom" in paragraph 23? Find some other passages in which the content is not as substantial as it should be.

### Projects

5. Edmund R. Leach discusses God in paragraphs 2 and 3 of "We Scientists Have the Right To Play God" in Section 8 of this book. While Darrow rejects an anthropomorphic God, Leach uses the idea of an anthropomorphic God to prove his point that there is something God-like in human beings. In a short paper, have Darrow respond to Leach on this point.

6. (a) Answer the following in a paper: If Darrow's arguments against the Bible are valid, then where *should* one turn for guidance in living? OR

(b) Write a paper about religion as either an aid or a hindrance to scientific progress. OR

(c) Write a paper in which you consider the implications of humankind's "taking over" for God in decisions related to the possible consequences of more and more sophisticated scientific development.

# The Sermon on the Mount

## MATTHEW

Saint Matthew's account of Jesus' Sermon on the Mount is central to Christianity. It contains the Beatitudes, the Lord's Prayer, and a series of admonishments by Jesus about appropriate behavior in keeping with the spirit, versus the ritualistic letter, of the law. The Sermon clearly expresses the altruistic approach to living that has come to be associated with the tenets of Christianity.

1  And seeing the multitudes, he went up into a mountain; and when he was set, his disciples came unto him: and he opened his mouth, and taught them, saying Blessed are the poor in spirit: for theirs is the kingdom of heaven. Blessed are they that mourn: for they shall be comforted. Blessed are the meek: for they shall inherit the earth. Blessed are they which do hunger and thirst after righteousness: for they shall be filled. Blessed are the merciful: for they shall obtain mercy. Blessed are the pure in heart: for they shall see God. Blessed are the peacemakers: for they shall be called the children of God. Blessed are they which are persecuted for righteousness' sake: for theirs is the kingdom of heaven. Blessed are ye, when men shall revile you, and persecute you, and shall say all manner of evil against you falsely, for my sake. Rejoice, and be exceeding glad: for great is your reward in heaven: for so persecuted they the prophets which were before you.

2      Ye are the salt of the earth: but if the salt have lost his savour, wherewith shall it be salted? it is thenceforth good for nothing, but to be cast out, and to be trodden under foot of men. Ye are the light of the world. A city that is set on a hill cannot be hid. Neither do men

light a candle, and put it under a bushel, but on a candlestick; and it giveth light unto all that are in the house. Let your light so shine before men, that they may see your good works, and glorify your Father which is in heaven. Think not that I am come to destroy the law, or the prophets; I am not come to destroy, but to fulfil. For verily I say unto you, Till heaven and earth pass, one jot or one tittle shall in no wise pass from the law, till all be fulfilled. Whosoever therefore shall break one of these least commandments, and shall teach men so, he shall be called the least in the kingdom of heaven: but whosoever shall do and teach them, the same shall be called great in the kingdom of heaven. For I say unto you, That except your righteousness shall exceed the righteousness of the scribes and Pharisees, ye shall in no case enter into the kingdom of heaven.

3    Ye have heard that it was said by them of old time, Thou shalt not kill; and whosoever shall kill shall be in danger of the judgment: but I say unto you, That whosoever is angry with his brother without a cause shall be in danger of the judgment: and whosoever shall say to his brother, Raca, shall be in danger of the council: but whosoever shall say, Thou fool, shall be in danger of hell fire. Therefore if thou bring thy gift to the altar, and there rememberest that thy brother hath ought against thee; leave there thy gift before the altar, and go thy way; first be reconciled to thy brother, and then come and offer thy gift. Agree with thine adversary quickly, while thou art in the way with him; lest at any time the adversary deliver thee to the judge, and the judge deliver thee to the officer, and thou be cast into prison. Verily I say unto thee, Thou shalt by no means come out thence, till thou hast paid the utter-most farthing.

4    Ye have heard that it was said by them of old time, Thou shalt not commit adultery; but I say unto you, That whosoever looketh on a wom-an to lust after her hath committed adultery with her already in his heart. And if thy right eye offend thee, pluck it out, and cast it from thee: for it is profitable for thee that one of thy members should perish, and not that thy whole body should be cast into hell. And if thy right hand offend thee, cut it off, and cast it from thee: for it is profitable for thee that one of thy members should perish, and not that thy whole body should be cast into hell. It hath been said. Whosoever shall put away his wife, let him give her a writing of divorcement: but I say unto you, That whosoever shall put away his wife, saving for the cause of fornication, causeth her to commit adultery: and whosoever shall marry her that is divorced committeth adultery.

5    Again, ye have heard that it hath been said by them of old time, Thou shalt not forswear thyself, but shalt perform to the Lord thine oaths: but I say unto you, Swear not at all; neither by heaven; for it is God's throne: nor by the earth; for it is his footstool: neither by Jerusalem; for it is the city of the great King. Neither shalt thou swear

by thy head, because thou canst not make one hair white or black. But let your communication be, Yea, yea; Nay, nay: for whatsoever is more than these cometh of evil.

6    Ye have heard that it hath been said, An eye for an eye, and a tooth for a tooth: but I say unto you, That ye resist not evil: but whosoever shall smite thee on thy right cheek, turn to him the other also. And if any man will sue thee at the law, and take away thy coat, let him have thy cloak also. And whosoever shall compel thee to go a mile, go with him twain. Give to him that asketh thee, and from him that would borrow of thee turn not thou away.

7    Ye have heard that it hath been said, Thou shalt love thy neighbor, and hate thine enemy. But I say unto you, Love your enemies, bless them that curse you, do good to them that hate you, and pray for them which despitefully use you, and persecute you; that ye may be the children of your Father which is in heaven; for he maketh his sun to rise on the evil and on the good, and sendeth rain on the just and on the unjust. For if ye love them which love you, what reward have ye? do not even the publicans the same? And if ye salute your brethren only, what do ye more than others? do not even the publicans so? Be ye therefore perfect, even as your Father which is in heaven is perfect.

8    Take heed that ye do not your alms before men, to be seen of them: otherwise ye have no reward of your Father which is in heaven. Therefore when thou doest thine alms, do not sound a trumpet before thee, as the hypocrites do in the synagogues and in the streets, that they may have glory of men. Verily I say unto you, They have their reward. But when thou doest alms, let not thy left hand know what thy right hand doeth: that thine alms may be in secret: and thy Father which seeth in secret himself shall reward thee openly. And when thou prayest, thou shalt not be as the hypocrites are: for they love to pray standing in the synagogues and in the corners of the streets, that they may be seen of men. Verily I say unto you, They have their reward. But thou, when thou prayest, enter into thy closet, and when thou hast shut thy door, pray to thy Father, which is in secret; and thy Father which seeth in secret shall reward thee openly. But when ye pray, use not vain repetitions, as the heathen do: for they think that they shall be heard for their much speaking. Be not ye therefore like unto them: for your Father knoweth what things ye have need of, before ye ask him. After this manner therefore pray ye: Our Father which art in heaven, Hallowed be thy name. Thy kingdom come. Thy will be done in earth, as it is in heaven. Give us this day our daily bread. And forgive us our debts, as we forgive our debtors. And lead us not into temptation, but deliver us from evil: for thine is the kingdom, and the power, and the glory, for ever. Amen. For if ye forgive men their trespasses, your heavenly Father will also forgive you: but if ye forgive not men their trespasses, neither will your Father forgive your trespasses.

9      Moreover when ye fast, be not as the hypocrites, of a sad countenance: for they disfigure their faces, that they may appear unto men to fast. Verily I say unto you, They have their reward. But thou, when thou fastest, anoint thine head, and wash thy face; that thou appear not unto men to fast, but unto thy Father which is in secret; and thy Father, which seeth in secret, shall reward thee openly.

10     Lay up not for yourselves treasures upon earth, where moth and rust doth corrupt, and where thieves break through and steal: but lay up for yourselves treasures in heaven, where neither moth nor rust doth corrupt, and where thieves do not break through nor steal: for where your treasure is, there will your heart be also. The light of the body is the eye: if therefore thine eye be single, thy whole body shall be full of light. But if thine eye be evil, thy whole body shall be full of darkness. If therefore the light that is in thee be darkness, how great is that darkness! No man can serve two masters: for either he will hate the one, and love the other; or else he will hold to the one, and despise the other. Ye cannot serve God and mammon. Therefore I say unto you, Take no thought for your life, what ye shall eat, or what ye shall drink; nor yet for your body, what ye shall put on. Is not the life more than meat, and the body than rainment? Behold the fowls of the air: for they sow not, neither do they reap, nor gather into barns; yet your heavenly Father feedeth them. Are ye not much better than they? Which of you by taking thought can add one cubit unto his stature? And why take ye thought for raiment? Consider the lilies of the field, how they grow; they toil not, neither do they spin: and yet I say unto you. That even Solomon in all his glory was not arrayed like one of these. Wherefore, if God so clothe the grass of the field, which to day is, and to morrow is cast into the oven, shall he not much more clothe you, O ye of little faith? Therefore take no thought, saying, What shall we eat? or What shall we drink? or, Wherewithal shall we be clothed? (For after all these things do the Gentiles seek): for your heavenly Father knoweth that ye have need of all these things. But seek ye first the kingdom of God, and his righteousness; and all these things shall be added unto you. Take therefore no thought for the morrow: for the morrow shall take thought for the things of itself. Sufficient unto the day is the evil thereof.

11     Judge not, that ye be not judged. For with what judgment ye judge, ye shall be judged: and with what measure ye mete, it shall be measured to you again. And why beholdest thou the mote that is in thy brother's eye, but considerest not the beam that is in thine own eye? Or how wilt thou say to thy brother, Let me pull out the mote out of thine eye; and behold, a beam is in thine own eye? Thou hypocrite, first cast out the beam out of thine own eye; and then shalt thou see clearly to cast out the mote out of thy brother's eye.

12     Give not that which is holy unto the dogs, neither cast ye your pearls before swine, lest they trample them under their feet, and turn again

and rend you. Ask, and it shall be given you; seek and ye shall find; knock and it shall be opened unto you: for everyone that asketh receiveth; and he that seeketh findeth; and to him that knocketh it shall be opened. Or what man is there of you, whom if his son ask bread, will he give him a stone? Or if he ask a fish, will he give him a serpent? If ye then, being evil, know how to give good gifts unto your children, how much more shall your Father which is in heaven give good things to them that ask him? Therefore all things whatsoever ye would that men should do to you, do ye even so to them: for this is the law and the prophets.

13    Enter ye in at the strait gate: for wide is the gate, and broad is the way, that leadeth to destruction, and many there be which go in thereat: because strait is the gate, and narrow is the way, which leadeth unto life, and few there be that find it. Beware of false prophets, which come to you in sheep's clothing, but inwardly they are ravening wolves. Ye shall know them by their fruits. Do men gather grapes of thorns, or figs of thistles? Even so every good tree bringeth forth good fruit; but a corrupt tree bringeth forth evil fruit. A good tree cannot bring forth evil fruit, neither can a corrupt tree bring forth good fruit. Every tree that bringeth not forth good fruit is hewn down and cast into the fire. Wherefore by their fruits ye shall know them. Not every one that saith unto me, Lord, Lord, shall enter into the kingdom of heaven; but he that doeth the will of my Father which is in heaven. Many will say to me in that day, Lord, Lord, have we not prophesied in thy name? And in thy name have cast out devils? and in thy name done many wonderful works? And then will I profess unto them, I never new you. depart from me, ye that work iniquity. Therefore whosoever heareth these sayings of mine and doeth them, I will liken him unto a wise man, which built his house upon a rock: and the rain descended, and the floods came, and the winds blew, and beat upon that house; and it fell not: for it was founded upon a rock. And every one that heareth these sayings of mine, and doeth them not, shall be likened unto a foolish man, which built his house upon the sand: and the rain descended, and the floods came, and the winds blew, and beat upon that house; and it fell: and great was the fall of it. And it came to pass, when Jesus had ended these sayings, the people were astonished at his doctrine: For he taught them as one having authority, and not as the scribes.

## REVIEW

### Content

1. Jesus' Sermon on the Mount, central to Christianity, has inspired millions over the years. And yet it is replete with paradoxes and subject to widely varying interpretation. For example, *exactly* what does Jesus

mean by "meekness" in paragraph 1? And how is one supposed to be expected to control not only his/her overt actions but even his/her covert responses, as Jesus asks one to do in relation to sex in paragraph 4? What are the implications of trying to comply with Jesus' teaching in paragraph 6, "but whosoever would . . ." through the end of the paragraph; would one not simply be setting himself/herself up to be imposed upon? Why does Jesus reverse Moses' law on divorce? And what happens if teaching scripture of one era in history is accepted without review by a later era, for example, Jesus' divorce law and late 20th-century Western society? Finally, note that Jesus' teachings are heavenly reward-oriented. Do you know how this facet of Christian scripture has been used against the Black, against females, against the poor—to "keep them in their place"?

2. Comparative religionists frequently note that some version of the Golden Rule exists in all the major religions of the world. Some persons argue that the Rule should be interpreted, "Do unto others as they need to be done unto." Do you see any dangers in this reading of the Rule?

**Rhetoric**

3. Jesus is remembered as one of the great teachers of all time. For one thing, he apparently knew how to phrase what he said so that it would be memorable. What sentence structures do you find in the Sermon that help to make his teachings so easy to remember? What passage contains one of the most famous examples of parallel structure in the world? Why did he make frequent use of the direct question?

4. Another reason why what Jesus taught lingers in the mind is that he used a lot of sensory images: for example, tasting salt and seeing light, both everyday experiences that everybody would be familiar with. Note other examples in paragraphs 10, 11, 12, and 13.

**Projects**

5. The translation of the Sermon printed here is from the very popular King James Version of the Bible (1611); therefore it is written in the Elizabethan, or Shakespearean, English of that time. In order to appreciate the richness of the language and to better understand Jesus' points here, compile in class a "glossary" for the Sermon on the Mount. Look up *all* the words that should be included in such a reading aid—not only those you may not know at all, such as "Raca," but also archaisms ("thou," "tittle") and words whose common meanings have changed by now (for example, "ought").

6. Take any passage you like from the Sermon and either support or refute the message in a paper. Make your case more convincing by

applying the particular teaching you choose to an everyday life situation and show how following the teaching would lead to either desirable or undesirable consequences.

# Chief Red Jacket and the Missionary

Chief Red Jacket was an Indian "law giver" whose Indian name (Sagu-yu-what-hah) meant "He Who Keeps Us Alert." A Seneca orator, Red Jacket often spoke for his people, and here we find him responding to a Moravian Church missionary from Massachusetts, the Reverend Mr. Cram, at a gathering called at Cram's request in the summer of 1805. The Council, attended by principal chiefs and warriors of the Six Nations, mostly Senecas, was held at Buffalo Creek in New York State. Red Jacket's words point up the Indians' perception of the conflict between the White Man's Christian teachings and his conduct, as well as the appropriateness of the Indian's religion for the Indian. At the Council, Cram was accompanied by the Agent of the United States for Indian Affairs, who spoke first.

1  First, by the agent:
   "*Brothers of the Six Nations,* I rejoice to meet you at this time, and thank the Great Spirit, that he has preserved you in health, and given me another opportunity of taking you by the hand.
2  "Brothers, the person who sits by me, is a friend who has come a great distance to hold a talk with you. He will inform you what his business is, and it is my request that you would listen with attention to his words."
3  Missionary:
   "*My Friends,* I am thankful for the opportunity afforded us of uniting together at this time. I had a great desire to see you, and inquire into your state and welfare; for this purpose I have travelled a great distance, being sent by your old friends, the Boston Missionary Society. You will recollect they formerly sent missionaries among you, to instruct you in religion, and labor for your good. Although they have not heard from you for a long time, yet they have not forgotten their brothers the Six Nations, and are still anxious to do you good.

From "Indian Speeches; Delivered by Farmer's Brother and Red Jacket, Two Seneca Chiefs," a pamphlet published by James D. Bemis at Canandaigua, N.Y., in 1809.

4    "Brothers, I have not come to get your lands or your money, but to enlighten your minds, and to instruct you how to worship the Great Spirit agreeably to his mind and will, and to preach to you the gospel of his son Jesus Christ. There is but one religion, and but one way to serve God, and if you do not embrace the right way, you cannot be happy hereafter. You have never worshipped the Great Spirit in a manner acceptable to him; but have, all your lives, been in great errors and darkness. To endeavor to remove these errors, and open your eyes, so that you might see clearly, is my business with you.

5    "Brothers, I wish to talk with you as one friend talks with another; and, if you have any objections to receive the religion which I preach, I wish you to state them; and I will endeavor to satisfy your minds, and remove the objections.

6    "Brothers, I want you to speak your minds freely; for I wish to reason with you on the subject, and, if possible, remove all doubts, if there be any on your minds. The subject is an important one, and it is of consequence that you give it an early attention while the offer is made you. Your friends, the Boston Missionary Society, will continue to send you good and faithful ministers, to instruct and strengthen you in religion, if, on your part, you are willing to receive them.

7    "Brothers, since I have been in this part of the country, I have visited some of your small villages, and talked with your people. They appear willing to receive instructions, but, as they look up to you as their older brothers in council, they want first to know your opinion on the subject.

8    "You have now heard what I have to propose at present. I hope you will take it into consideration, and give me an answer before we part."

9    After about two hours' consultation among themselves, the Chief, commonly called by the white people, Red Jacket (whose Indian name is Sagu-yu-what-hah, which interpreted is *Keeper awake*), rose and spoke as follows:

10    *"Friend and Brother,* it was the will of the Great Spirit that we should meet together this day. He orders all things, and has given us a fine day for our Council. He has taken his garment from before the sun, and caused it to shine with brightness upon us. Our eyes are opened, that we see clearly; our ears are unstopped, that we have been able to hear distinctly the words you have spoken. For all these favors we thank the Great Spirit; and Him *only.*

11    "Brother, this council fire was kindled by you. It was at your request that we came together at this time. We have listened with attention to what you have said. You requested us to speak our minds freely. This gives us great joy; for we now consider that we stand upright before you, and can speak what we think. All have heard your voice, and all speak to you now as one man. Our minds are agreed.

12    "Brother, you want an answer to your talk before you leave this place. It is right you should have one, as you are a great distance from home, and we do not wish to detain you. But we will first look back a little, and tell you what our fathers have told us and what we have heard from the white people.

13    "Brother, listen to what we say.

14    "There was a time when our forefathers owned this great island. Their seats extended from the rising to the setting sun. The Great Spirit had made it for the use of Indians. He had created the buffalo, the deer, and other animals for food. He had made the bear and the beaver. Their skins served us for clothing. He had scattered them over the country, and taught us how to take them. He had caused the earth to produce corn for bread. All this He had done for his red children, because He loved them. If we had some disputes about our hunting ground, they were generally settled without the shedding of much blood. But an evil day came upon us. Your forefathers crossed the great water, and landed on this island. Their numbers were small. They found friends and not enemies. They told us they had fled from their country for fear of wicked men, and had come here to enjoy their religion. They asked for a small seat. We took pity on them, granted their request; and they sat down amongst us. We gave them corn and meat, they gave us poison (alluding, it is supposed, to ardent spirits) in return.

"The white people had now found our country. Tidings were carried back, and more came amongst us. Yet we did not fear them. We took them to be friends. They called us brothers. We believed them, and gave them a larger seat. At length their numbers had greatly increased. They wanted more land; they wanted our country. Our eyes were opened, and our minds became uneasy. Wars took place. Indians were hired to fight against Indians, and many of our people were destroyed. They also brought strong liquor amongst us. It was strong and powerful, and has slain thousands.

15    "Brother, our seats were once large and yours were small. You have now become a great people, and we have scarcely a place left to spread our blankets. You have got our country, but are not satisfied; you want to force your religion upon us.

16    "Brother, continue to listen.

17    "You say that you are sent to instruct us how to worship the Great Spirit agreeably to his mind, and, if we do not take hold of the religion which you white people teach, we shall be unhappy hereafter. You say that you are right and we are lost. How do we know this to be true? We understand that your religion is written in a book. If it was intended for us as well as you, why has not the Great Spirit given to us, and not only to us, but why did he not give our forefathers, the knowledge of that book, with the means of understanding it rightly? We only know

what you tell us about it. How shall we know when to believe, being so often deceived by the white people?

18     "Brother, you say there is but one way to worship and serve the Great Spirit. If there is but one religion; why do you white people differ so much about it? Why not all agreed, as you can all read the book?

19     "Brother, we do not understand these things.

20     "We are told that your religion was given to your forefathers, and has been handed down from father to son. We also have a religion, which was given to our forefathers, and has been handed down to us their children. We worship in that way. It teaches us to be thankful for all the favors we receive; to love each other, and to be united. We never quarrel about religion.

21     "Brother, the Great Spirit has made us all, but he has made a great difference between his white and red children. He has given us different complexions and different customs. To you He has given the arts. To these He has not opened our eyes. We know these things to be true. Since He has made so great a difference between us in other things; why may we not conclude that He has given us a different religion according to our understanding? The Great Spirit does right. He knows what is best for his children; we are satisfied.

22     "Brother, we do not wish to destroy your religion, or take it from you. We only want to enjoy our own.

23     "Brother, we are told that you have been preaching to the white people in this place. These people are our neighbors. We are acquainted with them. We will wait a little while, and see what effect your preaching has upon them. If we find it does them good, makes them honest and less disposed to cheat Indians; we will then consider again of what you have said.

24     "Brother, you have now heard our answer to your talk, and this is all we have to say at present.

25     "As we are going to part, we will come and take you by the hand, and hope the Great Spirit will protect you on your journey, and return you safe to your friends."

26     As the Indians began to approach the missionary, he rose hastily from his seat and replied, that he could not take them by the hand; that there was no fellowship between the religion of God and the works of the devil.

27     This being interpreted to the Indians, they smiled, and retired in a peaceable manner.

28     It being afterwards suggested to the missionary that his reply to the Indians was rather indiscreet; he observed, that he supposed the ceremony of shaking hands would be received by them as a token that he assented to what they had said. Being otherwise informed, he said he was sorry for the expressions.

## REVIEW

### Content

1. Does anything in the Agent's and/or the missionary's remarks offend you, either in their content or in their tone? If so, what, and why?
2. Evaluate the Indians' response, through Red Jacket, to the Reverend Mr. Cram. Who comes off as the "sympathetic character" in this little drama? Why? Do you *like* Red Jacket? How did his ending (paragraphs 25 through 28) strike you?

### Rhetoric

3. What is the effect of the short, direct sentences in Red Jacket's discourse?
4. How logically valid is Red Jacket's discussion of religion, in paragraphs 17 through 23?

### Projects

5. In paragraphs 10 and 14, Red Jacket refers to several natural phenomena by word-pictures: e.g., the sunrise (10); the ocean (14). Make a list of a number of other natural phenomena and then create images to make them as vivid as Red Jacket makes the sunrise and the ocean here.
6. Think of a contemporary example of hypocrisy by some institution of "the System" and write a speech exposing it.

# Perfect Joy

## THOMAS MERTON

Thomas Merton (1915–1968) grew up in England, France, and the United States. He worked both as an English instructor and as a book reviewer for the *New York Times,* before coming to social work at a Catholic settlement house in Harlem. In 1938 he converted to Catholicism and in 1948 became a Trappist monk, beginning a life of ascetic physical discipline and contemplation. One of his best known works is *Seven Storey Mountain* (1948), in which he tells of his journey toward and arrival at the inner peace he found as a Trappist. The mystical side of Merton felt a kinship with the East, and in 1965 he published *The Way of Chuang-Tzu,* a collection of parables and poems of the third-century disciple of Lao-Tzu, legendary founder of Taoism, a major Eastern philosophy. (Taoism combined in China with Indian Buddhism to produce Zen, the Japanese name for that form of Buddhism best known in the West.) The following selection is from *The Way of Chuang-Tzu*.

1   Is there to be found on earth a fullness of joy, or is there no such thing? Is there some way to make life fully worth living, or is this impossible? If there is such a way, how do you go about finding it? What should you try to do? What should you seek to avoid? What should be the goal in which your activity comes to rest? What should you accept? What should you refuse to accept? What should you love? What should you hate?

2      What the world values is money, reputation, long life, achievement, What it counts as joy is health and comfort of body, good food, fine clothes, beautiful things to look at, pleasant music to listen to.

3      What it condemns is lack of money, a low social rank, a reputation for being no good, and an early death.

4      What it considers misfortune is bodily discomfort and labor, no chance to get your fill of good food, not having good clothes to wear, having no way to amuse or delight the eye, no pleasant music to listen to. If people find that they are deprived of these things, they go into a panic or fall into despair. They are so concerned for their life that their anxiety makes life unbearable, even when they have the things they think they want. Their very concern for enjoyment makes them unhappy.

5      The rich make life intolerable, driving themselves in order to get more and more money which they cannot really use. In so doing they are alienated from themselves, and exhaust themselves in their own service as though they were slaves of others.

6      The ambitious run day and night in pursuit of honors, constantly in anguish about the success of their plans, dreading the miscalculation that may wreck everything. Thus they are alienated from themselves, exhausting their real life in service of the shadow created by their insatiable hope.

7      The birth of a man is the birth of his sorrow.

8      The longer he lives, the more stupid he becomes, because his anxiety to avoid unavoidable death becomes more and more acute. What bitterness! He lives for what is always out of reach! His thirst for survival in the future makes him incapable of living in the present.

9      What about the self-sacrificing officials and scholars? They are honored by the world because they are good, upright, self-sacrificing men.

10     Yet their good character does not preserve them from unhappiness, nor even from ruin, disgrace, and death.

11    I wonder, in that case, if their "goodness" is really so good after all! Is it perhaps a source of unhappiness?

12    Suppose you admit they are happy. But is it a happy thing to have a character and a career that lead to one's own eventual destruction? On the other hand, can you call them "unhappy" if, in sacrificing themselves, they save the lives and fortunes of others?

13    Take the case of the minister who conscientiously and uprightly opposes an unjust decision of his king! Some say, "Tell the truth, and if the King will not listen, let him do what he likes. You have no further obligation."

14    On the other hand, Tzu Shu continued to resist the unjust policy of his sovereign. He was consequently destroyed. But if he had not stood up for what he believed to be right, his name would not be held in honor.

15    So there is the question, Shall the course he took be called "good" if, at the same time, it was fatal to him?

16    I cannot tell if what the world considers "happiness' is happiness or not. All I know is that when I consider the way they go about attaining it, I see them carried away headlong, grim and obsessed, in the general onrush of the human herd, unable to stop themselves or to change their direction. All the while they claim to be just on the point of attaining happiness.

17    For my part, I cannot accept their standards, whether of happiness or unhappiness. I ask myself it after all their concept of happiness has any meaning whatever.

18    My opinion is that you never find happiness until you stop looking for it. My greatest happiness consists precisely in doing nothing whatever that is calculated to obtain happiness: and this, in the minds of most people, is the worst possible course.

19    I will hold to the saying that: "Perfect joy is to be without joy. Perfect praise is to be without praise."

20    If you ask "what ought to be done" and "what ought not to be done" on earth in order to produce happiness, I answer that these questions do not have an answer. There is no way of determining such things.

21    Yet at the same time, if I cease striving for happiness, the "right" and the "wrong" at once become apparent all by themselves.

22    Contentment and well-being at once becomes possible the moment you cease to act with them in view, and if you practice non-doing (*wu wei*), you will have both happiness and well-being.

23    Here is how I sum it up:

> Heaven does nothing: its non-doing is its serenity.
> Earth does nothing: its non-doing is its rest.
> From the union of these two non-doings
> All actions proceed,

All things are made.
How vast, how invisible
This coming-to-be!
All things come from nowhere!
How vast how invisible—
No way to explain it!
All beings in their perfection
Are born of non-doing.
Hence it is said:
"Heaven and earth do nothing
Yet there is nothing they do not do."

Where is the man who can attain
To this non-doing?

## REVIEW

### Content

1. Can you apply what Chuang-Tzu of third-century China says, through Merton as translator, to contemporary society, considering the last two sentences in paragraph 4, and paragraphs 8 and 16? Does this analysis of "unhappiness in the search for happiness" make sense to you? Is the analysis applicable to *your* life?

2. Do you agree with Chuang-Tzu in paragraph 18 and the first half of paragraph 22? What does he mean by "Perfect joy is to be without joy"? Alan Watts, who was concerned with explaining the East to the West, once wrote, "We do not 'come into' this world; we come *out* of it, as leaves from a tree. As the ocean 'waves,' the universe 'peoples.' " Can you work with Watts' thinking and the Taoist poem above to extend your understanding of how Chuang-Tzu's advice about practicing *wu wei* in one's life would be possible, and could be a good thing?

### Rhetoric

3. Why does Chuang-Tzu compose his introduction entirely of questions?

4. Chuang-Tzu wrote simply and directly. Does it seem likely that his writing style was a reflection of his life-style as a Chinese sage? Might Chuang-Tzu's style, as well as his content, have been particularly appealing to Merton, the ascetic Trappist monk?

### Projects

5. Chuang-Tzu was often known to compose epigrams—pithy and memorable "teaching sayings." "The birth of a man is the birth of his sorrow" is an example. We in the Western world have a number of

well-known epigrams, proverbs, and other famous quotations about the whole question of happiness—finding it, making it, keeping it. Write down as many of these as you can.

6. Write a paper in which you discuss your own search for happiness. What are you looking for? How are you going about the search? Have you already had experiences which suggest to you that the *search* may be a futile one? If so, did you rearrange your *thinking* about "happiness"? If you did not, will you? If not, what does your future look like?

# The Sermon at Benares

## GAUTAMA BUDDHA

Gautama Buddha (563 B.C.?–483 B.C.?) began life as a prince named Siddhartha Gautama, in northern India. At 12 he was sent away for schooling in the Hindu sacred scriptures and four years later he returned home to marry a princess. They had a son and lived for ten years as befitted royalty. At about age 25, the Prince, heretofore shielded from the suffering of the world, while out hunting chanced upon a sick man, then an aged man, then a funeral procession, and finally a monk begging for alms. These sights so moved him that he at once became a beggar and went out into the world to seek enlightenment concerning the sorrows he had witnessed. He wandered for seven years and finally sat down under a fig tree, where he vowed to stay until enlightenment came. Enlightened after seven days, he renamed the tree the Bo Tree (Tree of Wisdom) and began to teach and to share his new understandings. At that point he became known as the Buddha (The Awakened or The Enlightened). The Buddha preached his first sermon at the city of Benares, most holy of the dipping places on the River Ganges; that sermon has been preserved and is printed here. It reflects the Buddha's wisdom about one inscrutable kind of suffering.

1    Kisa Goami had an only son, and he died. In her grief she carried the dead child to all her neighbors, asking them for medicine, and the people said: "She has lost her senses. The boy is dead."

2    At length, Kisa Gotami met a man who replied to her request: "I cannot give thee medicine for thy child, but I know a physician who can."

Reprinted from *The Monist* by permission of Open Court Publishing Company.

3    And the girl said: "Pray tell me, sir; who is it?" And the man replied "Go to Sakyamuni, the Buddha."

4    Kisa Gotami repaired to the Buddha and cried: "Lord and Master, give me the medicine that will cure my boy."

5    The Buddha answered: "I want a handful of mustard-seed." And when the girl in her joy promised to procure it, the Buddha added: "The mustard-seed must be taken from a house where no one has lost a child, husband, parent or friend."

6    Poor Kisa Gotami now went from house to house, and the people pitied her and said: "Here is mustard-seed; take it!" But when she asked, "Did a son or daughter, a father or mother, die in your family?" they answered her: "Alas! the living are few, but the dead are many. Do not remind us of our deepest grief." And there was no house but some beloved one had died in it.

7    Kisa Gotami became weary and hopeless, and sat down at the wayside, watching the lights of the city, as they flickered up and were extinguished again. At last the darkness of the night reigned everywhere. And she considered the fate of men, that their lives flicker up and are extinguished again. And she thought to herself: "How selfish am I in my grief! Death is common to all; yet in this valley of desolation there is a path that leads him to immortality who has surrendered all selfishness."

8    The Buddha said: "The life of mortals in this world is troubled and brief and combined with pain. For there is not any means by which those that have been born can avoid dying; after reaching old age there is death; of such a nature are living beings. As ripe fruits are early in danger of falling, so mortals when born are always in danger of death. As all earthen vessels made by the potter end in being broken, so is the life of mortals. Both young and adult, both those who are fools and those who are wise, all fall into the power of death; all are subject to death.

9    "Of those who, overcome by death, depart from life, a father cannot save his son, nor kinsmen their relations. Mark! while relatives are looking on and lamenting deeply, one by one mortals are carried off, like an ox that is led to the slaughter. So the world is afflicted with death and decay, therefore the wise do not grieve, knowing the terms of the world.

10    "Not from weeping nor from grieving will any one obtain peace of mind; on the contrary, his pain will be the greater and his body will suffer. He will make himself sick and pale, yet the dead are not saved by his lamentation. He who seeks peace should draw out the arrow of lamentation, and complaint, and grief. He who has drawn out the arrow and has become composed will obtain peace of mind; he who has overcome all sorrow will become free from sorrow, and be blessed."

# REVIEW

## Content

1. The Buddha was recognized by those who knew him as "enlightened." What gems of wisdom do you learn from the Enlightened One's first sermon?
2. Does the Buddha's advice in paragraph 10 seem logical to you? Correlate it with Western responses to death. Why does the Buddha, in his sermon, have Kisa Gotami realize, in paragraph 7, the desirability of "surrendering selfishness"? Do you think such surrender is *possible*?

## Rhetoric

3. The Buddha's sermon reads almost like a fairy tale, so simple and direct is its style. What does this suggest to you about the Buddha's effectiveness as a *teacher*? Compare his style with that of Jesus in the Sermon on the Mount, which appears earlier in this section of the book.
4. One reason the teachings of the Buddha are memorable is that he makes frequent use of *similes,* comparing abstractions about the experience of death with everyday events familiar to his hearers; for example, "mortals are carried off, like an ox that is led to the slaughter." Where else in the Sermon do similes vivify his teaching?

## Projects

5. Write a paper in which you compare the Buddha's teachings about death with the common Western view of death. Conclude your paper by stating which approach appeals most to *you,* and why.
6. Someone very precious to a friend of yours has just died, and you want to share what you have learned from the Buddha with your friend to help him/her. Write a letter to your friend.

# Meditation XVII
## No man is an island . . .
### JOHN DONNE

John Donne (1573–1631) was an English poet and clergyman. He became Dean of St. Paul's Cathedral and was the leading voice in English Metaphysical poetry of the seventeenth century. His poetry reflects his passion for both the physical and the spiritual. In addition to his poetry, Donne was known for his sermons and his "meditations," reflections on various religious themes which were gathered in *Devotions upon Emergent Occasions* (1624). The best known of these is "Meditation XVII," which reminds the reader that "no man is an island"—that we are all part of each other.

1    The poet, confined to his bed with a serious illness, hears the bells of the church adjoining, and is thereby reminded of death and the transiency of human life.

2    Perchance he for whom this bell tolls may be so ill, as that he knows not it tolls for him; and perchance I may think myself so much better than I am, as that they who are about me, and see my state, may have caused it to toll for me, and I know not that. The church is catholic, universal, so are all her actions; all that she does belongs to all. When she baptizes a child, that action concerns me; for that child is thereby connected to that head which is my head too, and ingrafted into that body whereof I am a member. And when she buries a man, that action concerns me: all mankind is of one author, and is one volume; when one man dies, one chapter is not torn out of the book, but translated into a better language; and every chapter must be so translated; God employs several translators; some pieces are translated by age, some by sickness, some by war, some by justice; but God's hand is in every translation, and his hand shall bind up all our scattered leaves again for that library where every book shall lie open to another. As therefore the bell that rings to a sermon calls not upon the preacher only, but upon the congregation to come, so this bell calls us all; but how much more me, who am brought so near the door by this sickness. There was a contention as far as a suit (in which piety and dignity, religion and estimation, were mingled), which of the religious orders should ring to prayers first in the morning; and it was determined, that they should ring first that rose earliest. If we understand aright the dignity of this bell that tolls for our evening prayer, we would be glad to make it ours by rising early, in that application, that it might be ours as well as his, whose indeed it is. The bell doth toll for him that thinks it doth; and though it intermit again, yet from that minute that that occasion wrought upon him, he is united with God. Who casts not up his eye to the sun when it rises? but who takes off his eye from a comet when that breaks out? Who bends not his ear to any bell which upon any occasion rings? but who can remove it from that bell which is passing a piece of himself out of this world? No man is an island, entire of itself; every man is a piece of the continent, a part of the main. If a clod be washed away by the sea, Europe is the less, as well as if a promontory were, as well as if a manor of thy friend's or of thine own were: any man's death diminishes me, because I am involved in mankind, and therefore never send to know for whom the bell tolls; it tolls

for thee. Neither can we call this a begging of misery, or a borrowing of misery, as though we were not miserable enough of ourselves, but must fetch in more from the next house, in taking upon us the misery of our neighbors. Truly it were an excusable covetousness if we did, for affliction is a treasure, and scarce any man hath enough of it. No man hath affliction enough that is not matured and ripened by it, and made fit for God by that affliction. If a man carry treasure in bullion, or in wedge of gold, and have none coined into current money, his treasure will not defray him as he travels. Tribulation is a treasure in the nature of it, but it is not current money in the use of it, except we get nearer and nearer our home, Heaven, by it. Another man may be sick too, and sick to death, and this affliction may lie in his bowels, as gold in a mine, and be of no use to him; but this bell, that tells me of his affliction, digs out and applies that gold to me: if by this consideration of another's danger I take mine own into contemplation, and so secure myself, by making my recourse to my God, who is our only security.

## REVIEW

### Content

1. The most famous part of "Meditation XVII" is "No man is an island . . . it tolls for thee." Explain this passage. Do you agree with Donne here? If you do, what are its implications for you?
2. Why does Donne say "affliction is a treasure"? Consider here the last sentence of the Meditation. What does this discussion suggest to you about the teachings of the church when Donne was a dean? How do you feel about all this today? Compare what Donne says about suffering here with what you would expect the Buddha to say about the same situation, based on a reading of his "Sermon at Benares," just preceding this selection.

### Rhetoric

3. Donne wrote in late Elizabethan, or Shakespearean, English: thee for you; doth; perchance; wrought. Do you find him as difficult to read as Shakespeare? If not, why not?
4. Although he writes long, rather involved sentences and although he is concerned with a weighty subject, Donne's writing is not really dense and heavy. What helps to "lighten" the content? How does he help you *visualize* the points he is trying to make?

### Projects

5. Donne wrote religious poetry as well as sermons and meditations. Read his "Holy Sonnet X," which begins "Death, be not proud . . . .,"

and compare his thoughts there with his allusions to immortality in "Meditation XVII."

6. Composing "meditations" is often a good way to "work through" your thinking about things that matter to you. Do some serious contemplating about some concern of yours and then write down a meditation on it. You need not imitate Donne in any way, but feel free to borrow stylistic devices from him if you like.

# 10
# The Future

# One Hundred Technical Innovations Very Likely in the Last Third of the Twentieth Century

## HERMAN KAHN and ANTHONY J. WIENER

Herman Kahn (1922–  ) is associated with The Hudson Institute, a "think tank" at Croton-on-Hudson in New York State. As a futurist, he has helped develop methods for prediction to aid in national decision-making and policy-setting. He has also created strategy games for use by the military, in the classroom, and elsewhere. Kahn's books include *On Thermonuclear War* (1960), *Thinking About the Unthinkable* (1962), and *The Year 2000* (1967). Anthony J. Wiener (1930–  ) is a founder of The Hudson Institute, where he has served as chairman of the Research Management Council, and is coauthor, with Kahn, of *The Year 2000*. The selection below is taken from that book.

1   In order to provide a quick impression of science and technology (with an emphasis on technology) in the last third of the twentieth century, we list (below) one hundred areas in which it is probable that technological innovation will occur in the next thirty-three years. . . .

2   Each item in the list has the following characteristics:

(1)   It is important enough to make, by itself, a significant change in the next thirty-three years. The difference might lie mainly in being spectacular (e.g., transoceanic rocket transportation in twenty or thirty minutes rather than supersonic in two or three hours); in being ubiquitous (e.g., widespread use of paper clothes); in enabling a large number of different things to be done (e.g., super

materials); in a general and significant increase in productivity (e.g., cybernation); or simply in being important to specific individuals (e.g., convenient artificial kidneys).

(2)   A responsible opinion can be found to argue a great likelihood that the innovation will be achieved before the year 2000—usually long before. (We would probably agree with about 90–95 percent of these estimates).

(3)   Each warrants the description technological innovation, revolution, or breakthrough. None is simply an obvious minor improvement on what currently exists.

3      The list is deliberately eclectic and disordered because this communicates a more accurate description of what we know about these future possibilities than the superficial appearance of order and understanding that would be given by a somewhat differently ordered list. Indeed since . . . serendipities and unexpected synergisms play an important role, reading this eclectic and disordered list is almost a simulation of the process of innovation and diffusion.

4      We should also note that the one hundred areas are not entirely randomly ordered. Most people would consider the first twenty-five as (largely) unambiguous examples of progress or human benefit. A few would question even these. The first item, for example, lasers and masers, might make possible a particularly effective kind of ballistic missile defense, and thus, some believe, could accelerate the Soviet-American arms race. Or the expansion of tropical agriculture and forestry, as suggested in the eighth item, could mean a geographical shift in economic and military power as well as a dislocation of competitive industries. Indeed nearly all the areas of innovation could involve adjustment difficulties of this kind. Nevertheless there probably would be a consensus among readers that the first twenty-five areas do represent progress—at least for those who are in favor of "progress."

5      The next twenty-five innovations would clearly have controversial consequences; many would argue that government policy might better restrain or discourage innovation or diffusion here. . . . These twenty-five "controversial areas" raise issues of accelerated nuclear proliferation; of loss of privacy; of excessive governmental and/or private power over individuals; of dangerously vulnerable, deceptive, and degradable over-centralization; of decisions becoming necessary that are too large, complex, important, uncertain, or comprehensive to be left to mere mortals (whether acting privately or publicly, individually or in organizations); of new capabilities that are so inherently dangerous that they are likely to be disastrously abused; of too rapid or cataclysmic change for smooth adjustment, and so on.

6      The last fifty items are included in part because they are intrinsically interesting and in part to demonstrate that it is fairly easy to produce a long list of items of innovation that entail nontrivial consequences.

# One Hundred Technical Innovations Very Likely in the Last Third of the Twentieth Century

1. Multiple applications of lasers and masers for sensing, measuring, communication, cutting, heating, welding, power transmission, illumination, destructive (defensive), and other purposes
2. Extreme high-strength and/or high-temperature structural materials
3. New or improved superperformance fabrics (papers, fibers, and plastics)
4. New or improved materials for equipment and appliances (plastics, glasses, alloys, ceramics, intermetallics, and cermets)
5. New airborne vehicles (ground-effect machines, VTOL and STOL, superhelicopters, giant and/or supersonic jets)
6. Extensive commercial application of shaped-charge explosives
7. More reliable and longer-range weather forecasting
8. Intensive and/or extensive expansion of tropical agriculture and forestry
9. New sources of power for fixed installations (e.g., magnetohydrodynamic, thermionic and thermoelectric, and radioactivity)
10. New sources of power for ground transportation (storage battery, fuel cell, propulsion (or support) by electro-magnetic fields, jet engine, turbine, and the like)
11. Extensive and intensive worldwide use of high altitude cameras for mapping, prospecting, census, land use, and geological investigations
12. New methods of water transportation (such as large submarines, flexible and special purpose "container ships," or more extensive use of large automated single-purpose bulk cargo ships)
13. Major reduction in hereditary and congenital defects
14. Extensive use of cyborg techniques (mechanical aids or substitutes for human organs, senses, limbs, or other components)
15. New techniques for preserving or improving the environment
16. Relatively effective appetite and weight control
17. New techniques and institutions for adult education
18. New and useful plant and animal species
19. Human "hibernation" for short periods (hours or days) for medical purposes
20. Inexpensive design and procurement of "one of a kind" items through use of computerized analysis and automated production
21. Controlled and/or supereffective relaxation and sleep
22. More sophisticated architectural engineering (e.g., geodesic domes, "fancy" stressed shells, pressurized skins, and esoteric materials)
23. New or improved uses of the oceans (mining, extraction of minerals, controlled "farming," source of energy, and the like)

24. Three-dimensional photography, illustrations, movies, and television

25. Automated or more mechanized housekeeping and home maintenance

26. Widespread use of nuclear reactors for power

27. Use of nuclear explosives for excavation and mining, generation of power, creation of high-temperature–high-pressure environments, and/or as a source of neutrons or other radiation

28. General use of automation and cybernation in management and production

29. Extensive and intensive centralization (or automatic interconnection) of current and past personal and business information in high-speed data processors

30. Other new and possibly pervasive techniques for surveillance, monitoring, and control of individuals and organizations

31. Some control of weather and/or climate

32. Other (permanent or temporary) changes—or experiments—with the overall environment (e.g., the "permanent" increase in C-14 and temporary creation of other radioactivity by nuclear explosions, the increasing generation of $CO_2$ in the atmosphere, projects Starfire, West Ford, and Storm Fury)

33. New and more reliable "educational" and propaganda techniques for affecting human behavior—public and private

34. Practical use of direct electronic communication with and stimulation of the brain

35. Human "hibernation" for relatively extensive periods (months to years)

36. Cheap and widely available central war weapons and weapon systems

37. New and relatively effective counterinsurgency techniques (and perhaps also insurgency techniques)

38. New techniques for very cheap, convenient, and reliable birth control

39. New, more varied, and more reliable drugs for control of fatigue, relaxation, alertness, mood, personality, perceptions, fantasies, and other psychobiological states

40. Capability to choose the sex of unborn children

41. Improved capability to "change" sex of children and/or adults

42. Other genetic control and/or influence over the "basic constitution" of an individual

43. New techniques and institutions for the education of children

44. General and substantial increase in life expectancy, postponement of aging, and limited rejuvenation

45. Generally acceptable and competitive synthetic foods and beverages (e.g., carbohydrates, fats, proteins, enzymes, vitamins, coffee, tea, cocoa, and alcoholic liquor)

46. "High quality" medical care for undeveloped areas (e.g., use of medical aides and technicians, referral hospitals, broad spectrum antibiotics, and artificial blood plasma)
47. Design and extensive use of responsive and supercontrolled environments for private and public use (for pleasurable, educational, and vocational purposes)
48. Physically nonharmful methods of overindulging
49. Simple techniques for extensive and "permanent" cosmetological changes (features, "figures," perhaps complexion and even skin color, and even physique)
50. More extensive use of transplantation of human organs
51. Permanent manned satellite and lunar installations—interplanetary travel
52. Application of space life systems or similar techniques to terrestrial installations
53. Permanent inhabited undersea installations and perhaps even colonies
54. Automated grocery and department stores
55. Extensive use of robots and machines "slaved" to humans
56. New uses of underground "tunnels" for private and public transportation and other purposes
57. Automated universal (real time) credit, audit and banking systems
58. Chemical methods for improving memory and learning
59. Greater use of underground buildings
60. New and improved materials and equipment for buildings and interiors (e.g., variable transmission glass, heating and cooling by thermoelectric effect, and electroluminescent and phosphorescent lighting)
61. Widespread use of cryogenics
62. Improved chemical control of some mental illnesses and some aspects of senility
63. Mechanical and chemical methods for improving human analytical ability more or less directly
64. Inexpensive and rapid techniques for making tunnels and underground cavities in earth and/or rock
65. Major improvements in earth moving and construction equipment generally
66. New techniques for keeping physically fit and/or acquiring physical skills
67. Commercial extraction of oil from shale
68. Recoverable boosters for economic space launching
69. Individual flying platforms
70. Simple inexpensive home video recording and playing
71. Inexpensive high-capacity, worldwide, regional, and local (home and business) communication (perhaps using satellites, lasers, and light pipes)

72. Practical home and business use of "wired" video communication for both telephone and TV (possibly including retrieval of taped material from libraries or other sources) and rapid transmission and reception of facsimiles (possibly including news, library material, commercial announcements, instantaneous mail delivery, other printouts, and so on)

73. Practical large-scale desalinization

74. Pervasive business use of computers for the storage, processing, and retrieval of information

75. Shared time (public and interconnected?) computers generally available to home and business on a metered basis

76. Other widespread use of computers for intellectual and professional assistance (translation, teaching, literature search, medical diagnosis, traffic control, crime detection, computation, design, analysis and to some degree as intellectual collaborator generally)

77. General availability of inexpensive transuranic and other esoteric elements

78. Space defense systems

79. Inexpensive and reasonably effective ground-based BMD

80. Very low-cost buildings for home and business use

81. Personal "pagers" (perhaps even two-way pocket phones) and other personal electronic equipment for communication, computing, and data processing program

82. Direct broadcasts from satellites to home receivers

83. Inexpensive (less than $20), long lasting, very small battery operated TV receivers

84. Home computers to "run" household and communicate with outside world

85. Maintenance-free, longlife electronic and other equipment

86. Home education via video and computerized and programmed learning

87. Stimulated and planned and perhaps programmed dreams

88. Inexpensive (less than one cent a page), rapid high-quality black and white reproduction; followed by color and high-detailed photography reproduction—perhaps for home as well as office use

89. Widespread use of improved fluid amplifiers

90. Conference TV (both closed circuit and public communication system)

91. Flexible penology without necessarily using prisons (by use of modern methods of surveillance, monitoring, and control)

92. Common use of (longlived?) individual power source for lights, appliances, and machines

93. Inexpensive worldwide transportation of humans and cargo

94. Inexpensive road-free (and facility-free) transportation

95. New methods for rapid language teaching

96. Extensive genetic control for plants and animals
97. New biological and chemical methods to identify, trace, incapacitate, or annoy people for police and military uses
98. New and possibly very simple methods for lethal biological and chemical welfare
99. Artificial moons and other methods for lighting large areas at night
100. Extensive use of "biological processes" in the extraction and processing of minerals

7    The following are areas in which technological success by the year 2000 seems substantially less likely (even money bets, give or take a factor of five), but where, if it occurred, it would be quite important:

## Some Less Likely but Important Possibilities

1. "True" artificial intelligence
2. Practical use of sustained fusion to produce neutrons and/or energy
3. Artificial growth of new limbs and organs (either in situ or for later transplantation)
4. Room temperature superconductors
5. Major use of rockets for commercial or private transportation (either terrestrial or extraterrestrial)
6. Effective chemical or biological treatment of most mental illnesses
7. Almost complete control of marginal changes in heredity
8. Suspended animation (for years or centuries)
9. Practical materials with nearly "theoretical limit" strength
10. Conversion of mammals (humans?) to fluid breathers
11. Direct input into human memory banks.
12. Direct augmentation of human mental capacity by the mechanical or electrical interconnection of the brain with a computer
13. Major rejuvenation and/or significant extension of vigor and life span—say 100 to 150 years
14. Chemical or biological control of character or intelligence
15. Automated highways
16. Extensive use of moving sidewalks for local transportation
17. Substantial manned lunar or planetary installations
18. Electric power available for less than .3 mill per kilowatt hour
19. Verification of some extrasensory phenomena
20. Planetary engineering
21. Modification of the solar system
22. Practical laboratory conception and nurturing of animal (human?) foetuses
23. Production of a drug equivalent to Huxley's soma

24. A technological equivalent of telepathy
25. Some direct control of individual thought processes

8    We list below ten radical possibilities, some of which hardly make sense. We do not believe that any of them will occur by the year 2000, or perhaps ever. But some of them are discussed today; and such a list does emphasize the fact that some dramatic and radical innovation must be expected. The list may suggest how surprising and exciting (or outrageous) such an event might prove.

## Ten Far-Out Possibilities

1. Life expectancy extended to substantially more than 150 years (immortality?)
2. Almost complete genetic control (but still homo sapiens)
3. Major modification of human species (no longer homo sapiens)
4. Antigravity (or practical use of gravity waves)[1]
5. Interstellar travel
6. Electric power available for less than .03 mill per kw hour
7. Practical and routine use of extrasensory phenomena
8. Laboratory creation of artificial live plants and animals
9. Lifetime immunization against practically all diseases
10. Substantial lunar or planetary bases or colonies

9    And finally there is the possibility—more far-fetched than popular science fiction would have it, but impossible to exclude—of a discovery of extraterrestrial life; or, much more extreme, of communication with extraterrestrial intelligence.

10   These lists make only the obvious point that as a result of the long-term trends toward accumulation of scientific and technological knowledge and the institutionalization of change through research, development, innovation, and diffusion, many important new things are likely to happen in the next few decades. It is worthwhile asking specifically what the consequences of each item—and their synergistic interactions—might be.

———————

## REVIEW

### Content

1. Why do Kahn and Wiener mention both "science *and* "technology" in their opening sentence? Is there a real distinction between the two?

[1]As usually envisaged this would make possible a perpetual motion machine and therefore the creation of energy out of nothing. We do not envisage this as even a far-out possibility, but include antigravity, even though it annoys some physicist friends, as an example of some totally new use of a basic phenomenon or the seeming violation of a basic law.

If so, what? (Refer to Ritchie-Calder's discussion of "The Scientific Method," which opens Section 8 of this book, if you need help here.)

2. Study the first 25 innovations Kahn and Wiener list and consider the "adjustment difficulties" (see paragraph 4) that might be involved in some of them. Then, look at the second 25, and relate some of the issues the authors raise in paragraph 5 to specific items in that list. Apply Alvin Toffler's concept of "future shock" to this whole discussion. (See the selection by Toffler in Section 1 of this book if you do not know about "future shock.")

## Rhetoric

3. Kahn and Wiener make use of a vocabulary rather common among writers about the future—including both already established words that many of us have not heard very often before and other words that have been developed in order to talk about certain concepts in futuristics. Look up, if you do not already know them or cannot decipher them in context here, the following: ubiquitous (paragraph 2); eclectic, serendipity(ies), synergism, simulation (all in paragraph 3).

4. The writing style of futurists often sounds packed and breathless. Analyze Kahn and Wiener's style in these terms. Do you think the style might be related in any way to the content? To the thinking processes of highpowered thinkers about the future?

## Projects

5. If you are particularly interested in this selection, read further in Kahn and Wiener's *The Year 2000*. Or in Alvin Toffler's *Future Shock* or in Buckminster Fuller's intriguing futuristic projections. If you prefer your futurism more in story form, try Kurt Vonnegut's *Cat's Cradle*, Arthur C. Clarke's *Childhood's End* or other science fiction novels by him, or the science fiction of Ray Bradbury or Isaac Asimov.

6. Following their list of the hundred technical innovations they consider "very likely," Kahn and Wiener add 25 "less likely but important" possibilities and ten "radical" possibilities. Some of the items on those two lists have been further developed since 1967 than Kahn and Wiener apparently anticipated. Select one that interests you and research the current status of its development; write up your findings in a paper.

# Why Study
# the Future?

## JOSEPH F. COATES

Joseph F. Coates works with the National Science Foundation in Washington, D.C., in the Office of Exploratory Research and Problem Assessment. Coates is an active member of the World Future Society and conducts courses on the future under the Society's sponsorship. "Why Study the Future?" is taken from an article by Coates, originally entitled "Anti-Intellectualism and Other Plagues on Managing the Future," which first appeared in 1973 in *Technological Forecasting and Social Change*.

## Present State of Futurism

1    The current serious thinking about the future is premised on three propositions:

### (1) There Are Alternative Futures

2    Futurists generally assume substantially different options for new worlds, ranging, in present values, from utopian to dystopian, embracing various economic, social, political, and technological orders, systems, and arrangements. Work of Harmon and Rhyne for the Stanford Research Institute has identified some nine distinctly different futures for the U.S. ranging from oppressive central control to broad, prosperous democratic liberalism.

### (2) Society Can Influence Its Movement Among
### These Alternatives

3    While no serious futurist has argued that we can select our ideal future and move relentlessly toward it, there seems to be a nearly universal feeling among futurists that we can at least collectively take action which will make it more likely that we avoid some of the more dark and hazardous futures. This optimism is premised on two developments: First, technology, while creating problems in the short run or transition period, has also created the mechanisms for moving society, for changing its direction.

4    Second, technology has led to the development of the tools and the

Joseph F. Coates, "Anti-Intellectualism and Other Plagues on Managing the Future," *Technological Forecasting and Social Change*, 4, 245–246. Copyright 1973. Reprinted by permission of American Elsevier Publishing Company, Inc.

techniques which allow us to anticipate advances and alternatives, reliably forecast their likelihood, and identify the factors making them more or less likely. Consequently it is socially and politically possible to elect to select among them.

### (3) Man Both Individually and Collectively Has the Moral Responsibility To Examine the Future and To Exercise His Skill in Navigating Among the Alternatives

5   Russell Rhyne has recently captured these premises in the observation that there is ". . . a quality in man that invites him to shape the world toward his preferences in the belief that he functionally can and morally may do so."

## Characteristics of Current Problems

6   There is a widely felt concern among serious students of the future that the next 30 years is an uncertain and risky period in human development. If this period is successfully weathered, the long range prospects are generally optimistic, at least for the U.S. This uncertainty and anxiety results from our collective failure to grapple with the gross and subtle negative side effects often associated with contemporary technology. While contemporary technology is characterized by its scale, its intensity, its scope, and its interrelatedness, the social and economic control measures over technology have developed in response to simpler technologies more provincially sited, more simply related to each other, and more parochial in scale and impact. Political and social institutions have been conspicuously and infuriatingly slow in producing effective new institutional and personal mechanisms to control and moderate technology.

7   With regard to scale, it is not only within human capability but within human accomplishment to dramatically modify the basic geophysical structure of continents. One does not have to consider the Russian proposal to redirect the major rivers of Siberia, from north flowing to south flowing. The extant hydrologic works of North America now harness a large portion of the free flowing water of the continent for agriculture and power. The high dam at Aswan, designed to transform the economy of Egypt, nicely illustrates the double edge of a well-intentioned, badly planned, poorly thought through technological intrusion. The failure to attend to consequences, foreseeable from knowledge at hand when the project began, is leading to negative side effects which perhaps could have been planned out at the project. Bilharzia, a disease carried by snails, is the fifth major public health disease of the world. The Aswan Dam has given it new impetus. The absence of the annual flooding is modifying the mineral balance in the soil. That may dramatically mod-

ify the fertility of the Nile Valley. The failure to take biological factors into account is also leading to effects on Mediterranean fishing. Together these negative consequences may unnecessarily undercut some economic and social values of the dam. Enterprises on that scale involve long periods of planning, and for all practical purposes they are irreversible. Consequently they provide both the opportunity and implicit demand that secondary and incidental consequences be anticipated and examined. The adverse effects resulting from the inflexibility and irreversibility of large civil work are one major drive to intensively examine the future and future alternatives.

8    Overlaying these considerations is the interrelatedness of technologies and their consequences. Technology has created one society and is rapidly creating one world at least in the sense of a fully integrated system. Unlike simpler societies, where the technology was parochial or small, a modification of the technology in the United States in one place makes change everywhere. For example, the development of a cheap, reliable contraceptive technology is changing marriage and family structure, housing patterns, styles of living, insurance rates, disposable income, leisure, disease patterns, and school construction. Not all major technological changes are recent. The establishment of the land grant college system not only created more effective and efficient farmers and artisans but initiated a broad demand for the finer things in life. Inevitably those demands move far beyond the original narrow, albeit good, intentions and on a generational time scale, change basic values. That stroke of genius in institutional technology has totally altered the life of rural America. The overall effect of college on students and presumably on subsequent adult attitudes has been well studied (Feldman and Newcomb).

## Why Study the Future?

9   Recognizing the above as the merest introduction to the contemporary concerns for the future one can summarize the arguments for studying the future in three simple ways: first, we study the future to prepare for it, second, we study the future to be able to modify and control it, and third, we study the future for sheer delight and out of curiosity.

**REVIEW**

**Content**

1. Were you *surprised* to learn of the possibility of "distinctly different" futures for the United States—and their potential range? Had you considered before the *scope* of change Coates suggests that "cheap,

reliable contraceptive technology" can bring (paragraph 8)? Elaborate some of his thinking in this paragraph. Are you startled by what you arrive at? Do you agree with Coates that we are *morally* responsible— both individually and collectively—for studying the future and for trying to navigate intelligently among the alternatives? Do *you* feel such a moral responsibility? If you do, what are you *doing* about it?

2. Coates refers to how technology is both creating the future and can be used to help us predict and thereby control it. Why do you suppose the latter role for technology is not keeping pace with the former? What can *you* do to encourage more widespread use, by appropriate governmental and other institutions, of technology as a predicting/-controlling "servant" as well as a creating/producing one?

## Rhetoric

3. Coates uses the building of Aswan Dam to exemplify his point about failure to predict as carefully and conscientiously as can be done. How many major negative consequences does he manage to cite in his relatively short development of this example? Does the way he highlights the problems, and the clarity and directness of his prose here, help to convince you of his point?

4. Coates is obviously trying to cover a lot of ground in the article this excerpt is taken from. Do you notice any places in the selection here where the leap from one point to the next is not adequately bridged?

## Projects

5. Find out what *your* college is doing about courses in future studies. If you are not satisfied with your findings, prepare, in class, a statement urging that more be done. Be specific about what you would like to see done, and offer recommendations about how your goals might be achieved. Use some of Coates' arguments—and any support you can glean from other pieces in this section of the book, plus Toffler's article which closes Section 1. Get your completed document to the appropriate officials and plan to stay behind the effort until action occurs.

6. Coates says that one reason for studying the future is "for sheer delight and out of curiosity." Write a paper in which you develop this point, telling how thinking about the future, projecting, fantasizing, could provide delight for *you* and help to satisfy *your* curiosity. Try to make the style and tone of your writing match its content; that is, be funny, satirical, flippant—whatever humorous touch you can make work for *you*.

# What Inventions Will Shape the City of 2010?

## JOHN P. EBERHARD

John P. Eberhard (1927–   ), an architect and educator, became in 1968 dean of the School of Architectural and Environmental Design at the State University of New York at Buffalo. He has a particular interest in futuristics. The Eberhard article from which the "exercise" below is taken, "Technology for the City," appeared originally in International Science and Technology, September, 1966.

John P. Eberhard, architect, holds that seven inventions between 1877 and 1889 made possible the modern city:

### 1877   Telephone
Alexander Graham Bell speaks to his assistant, Thomas A. Watson. Bell calls from Salem. Watson is in Boston, 12 miles away.

### 1880   Skyscraper
William LeBaron Jenney builds the first skyscraper, 10 stories tall, for the Home Insurance Company in Chicago.

### 1880   Incandescent Lamp
The first filaments, made of carbonized sewing threads, burn for 40 hours in Edison's laboratory!

### 1885   Electric Trolley Car
Baltimore replaces the horse—the first American city to do so.

### 1886   Subway
London is the first city to transport people underground, in an electric-powered system, designed by Greathead.

### 1889   Automobile
The Daimler is on the roads traveling at eleven mph!

Reprinted by permission of Com Pub from "Technology for the City," International Science and Technology, September, 1966.

**1889   Elevator**
Otis Brothers install first electric elevator, in Demarest building in New York.

An interesting exercise in futurism is to try to determine the seven—or two—or ten—inventions that will shape the city of 2010.


**REVIEW**
Do the exercise. There is no single "right answer"—but be prepared to defend yours in class discussion.


# The Obsolescence
# of Man

## ARTHUR C. CLARKE

Arthur C. Clarke (1917–   ) was born in England and graduated with First Class Honors in both physics and mathematics from King's College, London. He wrote a technical paper in 1945 which originated communications satellites. In 1969 he coauthored with Stanley Kubrick the screenplay for *2001: A Space Odyssey*. Clarke has written widely, both in the science of the future and in science fiction. His titles include *Childhood's End* (1953), *The Nine Billion Names of God* (1967), *The Promise of Space* (1968), and *Profiles of the Future: An Inquiry into the Limits of the Possible* (1961, revised 1973). In the selection here, from the latter book, Clarke considers the inevitable difficulties that arise when man's brain and energy try to compete with more and more highly sophisticated computer operations, noting that computers are already being used to create yet more complex computers.


1   ... Since this is not a treatise on computer design, you will not expect me to explain how to build a thinking machine. In fact, it is doubtful if any human being will ever be able to do this in detail, but one can indicate the sequence of events that will lead from H. sapiens to M.

sapiens. The first two or three steps on the road have already been taken; machines now exist that can learn by experience, profiting from their mistakes and—unlike human beings—never repeating them. Machines have been built which do not sit passively waiting for instructions, but which explore the world around them in a manner which can only be called inquisitive. Others look for proofs of theorems in mathematics or logic, and sometimes come up with surprising solutions that had never occurred to their makers.

2    These faint glimmerings of original intelligence are confined at the moment to a few laboratory models; they are wholly lacking in the giant computers that can now be bought by anyone who happens to have a few hundred thousand dollars to spare. But machine intelligence will grow, and it will start to range beyond the bounds of human thought as soon as the second generation of computers appears—the generation that has been designed, not by men, but by other, "almost intelligent" computers. And not only designed, but also built—for they will have far too many components for manual assembly.

## Computers May Grow Themselves

3    It is even possible that the first genuine thinking machines may be *grown* rather than constructed; already some crude but very stimulating experiments have been carried out along these lines. Several artificial organisms have been built which are capable of rewiring themselves to adapt to changing circumstances. Beyond this there is the possibility of computers which will start from relatively simple beginnings be programmed to aim at specific goals, and search for them by constructing their own circuits, perhaps by growing networks of threads in a conducting medium. Such a growth may be no more than a mechanical analogy of what happens to every one of us in the first nine months of our existence.

4    All speculations about intelligent machines are inevitably conditioned—indeed, inspired—by our knowledge of the human brain, the only thinking device currently on the market. No one, of course, pretends to understand the full workings of the brain, or expects that such knowledge will be available in any foreseeable future. (It is a nice philosophical point as to whether the brain can ever, even in principle, understand itself.) But we do know enough about its physical structure to draw many conclusions about the limitations of "brains"—whether organic or inorganic.

5    There are approximately ten billion separate switches—or neurons—inside your skull, "wired" together in circuits of unimaginable complexity. Ten billion is such a large number that, until recently, it could be used as an argument against the achievement of mechanical intelligence.

About ten years ago a famous neurophysiologist made a statement (still produced like some protective incantation by the advocates of cerebral supremacy) to the effect that an electronic model of the human brain would have to be as large as the Empire State Building, and would need Niagara Falls to keep it cool when it was running.

6   This must now be classed with such interesting pronouncements as, "No heavier than air machine will ever be able to fly." For the calculation was made in the days of the vacuum tube (remember it?), and the transistor has now completely altered the picture. Indeed—such is the rate of technological progress today—the transistor itself is being replaced by still smaller and faster devices, based upon abstruse principles of quantum physics. If the problem was merely one of space, today's electronic techniques would allow us to pack a computer as complex as the human brain on to a single floor of the Empire State Building.

## New Memory Device

7   Interlude for agonizing reappraisal. It's a tough job keeping up with science, and since I wrote that last paragraph the Marquardt Corporation's Astro Division has announced a new memory device which could store inside a six-foot cube *all information recorded during the last 10,000 years.* This means, of course, not only every book ever printed, but *everything* ever written in *any* language on paper, papyrus, parchment, or stone. It represents a capacity untold millions of times greater than that of a single human memory, and though there is a mighty gulf between merely storing information and thinking creatively—the Library of Congress has never written a book—it does indicate that mechanical brains of enormous power could be quite small in physical size.

8   This should not surprise anyone who remembers how radios have shrunk from the bulky cabinet models of the thirties to the vest-pocket (yet much more sophisticated) transistor sets of today. And the shrinkage is just gaining momentum, if I may employ such a mind-boggling phrase. Radio receivers the size of lumps of sugar have now been built; before long, they will be the size not of lumps but of grains, for the slogan of the micro-miniaturization experts is "If you can see it, it's too big."

9   Just to prove that I am not exaggerating, here are some statistics you can use on the next hi-fi fanatic who takes you on a tour of his wall-to-wall installation. During the 1950s, the electronic engineers learned to pack up to a hundred thousand components into one cubic foot. (To give a basis of comparison, a good hi-fi set may contain two or three hundred components, a domestic radio about a hundred.) . . . At the beginning of the sixties, the attainable figure [was] around a million components per cubic foot; [in the] 1970[s], when today's experi-

mental techniques of microscopic engineering have begun to pay off, it may reach a hundred million.

10    Fantastic though this last figure is, the human brain surpasses it by a thousandfold, packing its ten billion neurons into a *tenth* of a cubic foot. And although smallness is not necessarily a virtue, even this may be nowhere near the limit of possible compactness.

11    For the cells composing our brains are slow-acting, bulky, and wasteful of energy—compared with the scarcely more than atom-sized computer elements that are theoretically possible. The mathematician John von Neumann once calculated that electronic cells could be ten billion times more efficient than protoplasmic ones; already they are a million times swifter in operation, and speed can often be traded for size. If we take these ideas to their ultimate conclusion, it appears that a computer equivalent in power to one human brain need be no bigger than a matchbox.

12    This slightly shattering thought becomes more reasonable when we take a critical look at flesh and blood and bone as engineering materials. All living creatures are marvelous, but let us keep our sense of proportion. Perhaps the most wonderful thing about Life is that it works at all, when it has to employ such extraordinary materials, and has to tackle its problems in such roundabout ways.

## The Human Eye and a Camera

13    As a perfect example of this, consider the eye. Suppose *you* were given the problem of designing a camera—for that, of course, is what the eye is—which *has to be constructed entirely of water and jelly,* without using a scrap of glass, metal, or plastic. Obviously, it can't be done.

14    You're quite right; the feat is impossible. The eye is an evolutionary miracle, but it's a lousy camera. You can prove this while you're reading the next sentence.

15    Here's a medium-length word:—photography. Close one eye and keep the other fixed—repeat, *fixed*—on that center "g." You may be surprised to discover that —unless you cheat by altering the direction of your gaze—you cannot see the whole word clearly. It fades out three or four letters to the right and left.

16    No camera ever built—even the cheapest—has as poor an optical performance as this. For color vision also, the human eye is nothing to boast about; it can operate only over a small band of the spectrum. To the worlds of the infrared and ultraviolet, visible to bees and other insects, it is completely blind.

17    We are not conscious of these limitations because we have grown up with them, and indeed if they were corrected the brain would be quite unable to handle the vastly increased flood of information. But let us not make a virtue of a necessity; if our eyes had the optical performance

of even the cheapest miniature camera, we would live in an unimagina-
bly richer and more colorful world.

18      These defects are due to the fact that precision scientific instruments
simply cannot be manufactured from living materials. With the eye, the
ear, the nose—indeed, all the sense organs—evolution has performed
a truly incredible job against fantastic odds. But it will not be good
enough for the future; indeed, it is not good enough for the present.

## Senses Lacking in Humans

19      There are some senses that do not exist, that can probably never
be provided by living structures, and that we need in a hurry. On this
planet, to the best of our knowledge, no creature has ever developed
organs that can detect radio waves or radioactivity. Though I would
hate to lay down the law and claim that nowhere in the universe can
there be organic Geiger counters or living TV sets, I think it highly
improbable. There are some jobs that can be done only by vacuum tubes
or magnetic fields or electron beams, and are therefore beyond the capability of purely organic structures.

20      There is another fundamental reason living machines such as you
and I cannot hope to compete with nonliving ones. Quite apart from
our poor materials, we are handicapped by one of the toughest engineering specifications ever issued. What sort of performance would you expect from a machine which has to grow several billionfold during the
course of manufacture—and which has to be completely and continuously rebuilt, molecule by molecule, every few weeks? This is what happens
to all of us, all the time; you are not the man you were last year, in
the most literal sense of the expression.

21      Most of the energy and effort required to run the body goes into
its perpetual tearing down and rebuilding—a cycle completed every few
weeks. New York City, which is a very much simpler structure than
a man, takes hundreds of times longer to remake itself. When one tries
to picture the body's myriads of building contractors and utility companies all furiously at work, tearing up arteries and nerves and even bones,
it is astonishing that there is any energy left over for the business of
thinking.

## The Evolution of Intelligence

22      Now I am perfectly well aware that many of the "limitations" and
"defects" just mentioned are nothing of the sort, looked at from another
point of view. Living creatures, because of their very nature, can evolve
from simple to complex organisms. They may well be the only path

by which intelligence can be attained, for it is a little difficult to see how a lifeless planet can progress directly from metal ores and mineral deposits to electronic computers by its own unaided efforts.

23    Though intelligence can arise only from life, it may then discard it. Perhaps at a later stage, as the mystics have suggested, it may also discard matter; but this leads us in realms of speculations which an unimaginative person like myself would prefer to avoid.

24    One often-stressed advantage of living creatures is that they are self-repairing and reproduce themselves with ease—indeed, with enthusiasm. This superiority over machines will be short-lived; the general principles underlying the construction of self-repairing and self-reproducing machines have already been worked out. There is, incidentally, something ironically appropriate in the fact that A. M. Turing, the brilliant mathematician who pioneered in this field and first indicated how thinking machines might be built, shot himself a few years after publishing his results. It is very hard not to draw a moral from this.

## The Challenge of Space

25    The greatest single stimulus to the evolution of mechanical—as opposed to organic—intelligence is the challenge of space. Only a vanishingly small fraction of the universe is directly accessible to mankind, in the sense that we can live there without elaborate protection or mechanical aids. If we generously assume that humanity's potential *Lebensraum* extends from sea level to a height of three miles, over the whole Earth, that gives us a total of some half billion cubic miles. At first sight this is an impressive figure, especially when you remember that the entire human race could be packaged into a one-mile cube. But it is absolutely nothing, when set against Space with a capital "S." Our present telescopes, which are certainly not the last word on the subject, sweep a volume at least a million million million million million million million million million million times greater.

26    Though such a number is, of course, utterly beyond conception, it can be given a vivid meaning. If we reduced the known universe to the size of the Earth, then the portion in which *we* can live without space suits and pressure cabins is about the size of a single atom.

27    It is true that, one day, we are going to explore and colonize many other atoms in this Earth-sized volume, but it will be at the cost of tremendous technical efforts, for most of our energies will be devoted to protecting our frail and sensitive bodies against the extremes of temperature, pressure, or gravity found in space and on other worlds. Within very wide limits, machines are indifferent to these extremes. Even more important, they can wait patiently through the years and the centuries that will be needed for travel to the far reaches of the universe.

28     Creatures of flesh and blood such as ourselves can explore space and win control over infinitesimal fractions of it. But only creatures of metal and plastic can ever really conquer it, as indeed they have already started to do. . . .

29     It may well be that only in space, confronted with environments fiercer and more complex than any to be found upon this planet, will intelligence be able to reach its fullest stature. Like other qualities, intelligence is developed by struggle and conflict; in the ages to come, the dullards may remain on placid Earth, and real genius will flourish only in space—the realm of the machine, not of flesh and blood.

## REVIEW

### Content

1. How does Clarke's conclusion that humans cannot effectively compete with machines make you *feel?* Does paragraph 3 call up an especially acute response in you? If so, why do you think this happens? What "moral" does Clarke expect his reader to draw from his mention of A. M. Turing's suicide (paragraph 24)?
2. Do you agree with Clarke in paragraph 28? Extend his discussion in paragraph 29 to what you can imagine the "fullest stature" of intelligence—in machines—that Clarke refers to might be like.

### Rhetoric

3. Although Clarke is writing here about serious and complex matters, his prose is quite readable. What elements contribute to a certain informality of style and tone? Consider here such things as vocabulary, phrasing, flashes of humor, the use of parenthetical remarks.
4. What is the purpose of Clarke's rather elaborate comparison between the human eye and a camera (paragraphs 13 through 16)?

### Projects

5. Read the short story "EPICAC" by Kurt Vonnegut and tie it in with Clarke's discussion above. With whom do you *identify* in the story; that is, do you find the male mathematician or EPICAC the more "sympathetic character"? If your answer is EPICAC, think about what that suggests. Write a paper about your response(s) to the story. OR If you have seen *2001: A Space Odyssey,* try to recall some of your responses to the part involving Hal the Computer and write about those.
6. Computers with certain humanlike attributes are called "cyborgs." Create a cyborg in your mind and write a short story with some sort of dramatic conflict between your cyborg and a human character.

# The Decline of Sport

## E. B. WHITE

E. B. White (1889–   ), is an American journalist and essayist with a satirical touch. He has become known for his contributions to both *Harper's Magazine* and *The New Yorker* over a long period of years. His collections of personal essays include *Quo Vadimus* (1939), *One Man's Meat* (1942), and *The Second Tree from the Corner* (1953). "The Decline of Sport" is a futuristic scenario of White's satirical predictions for sport in the future, when one can attend a sports event, watch another on TV in the same arena, listen to a third on transistor radio, and so on, all at the same time.

1   In the third decade of the supersonic age, sport gripped the nation in an ever-tightening grip. The horse tracks, the ballparks, the fight rings, the gridirons, all drew crowds in steadily increasing numbers. Every time a game was played, an attendance record was broken. Usually some other sort of record was broken, too—such as the record for the number of consecutive doubles hit by left-handed batters in a Series game, or some such thing as that. Records fell like ripe apples on a windy day. Customs and manners changed, and the five-day business week was reduced to four days, then to three, to give everyone a better chance to memorize the scores.

2   Not only did sport proliferate but the demands it made on the spectator became greater. Nobody was content to take in one event at a time, and thanks to the magic of radio and television noboby had to. A Yale alumnus, class of 1962, returning to the Bowl with 197,000 others to see the Yale-Cornell football game would take along his pocket radio and pick up the Yankee Stadium, so that while his eye might be following a fumble on the Cornell twenty-two-yard line, his ear would be following a man going down to second in the top of the fifth, seventy miles away. High in the blue sky above the Bowl, skywriters would be at work writing the scores of other major and minor sporting contests, weaving an interminable record of victory and defeat, and using the new high-visibility pink news-smoke perfected by Pepsi-Cola engineers. And in the frames of the giant video sets, just behind the goal-posts, this same alumnus could watch Dejected win the Futurity before a record-breaking

crowd of 349,872 at Belmont, each of whom was tuned to the Yale Bowl and following the World Series game in the video and searching the sky for further news of events either under way or just completed. The effect of this vast cyclorama of sport was to divide the spectator's attention, oversubtilize his appreciation, and deaden his passion. As the fourth supersonic decade was ushered in, the picture changed and sport began to wane.

3    A good many factors contributed to the decline of sport. Substitutions in football had increased to such an extent that there were very few fans in the United States capable of holding the players in mind during play. Each play that was called saw two entirely new elevens lined up, and the players whose names and faces you had familiarized yourself with in the first period were seldom seen or heard of again. The spectacle became as diffuse as the main concourse in Grand Central at the commuting hour.

4    Express motor highways leading to the parks and stadia had become so wide, so unobstructed, so devoid of all life except automobiles and trees that sport fans had got into the habit of travelling enormous distances to attend events. The normal driving speed had been stepped up to ninety-five miles an hour, and the distance between cars had been increased to fifteen feet. This put an extraordinary strain on the sport lover's nervous system, and he arrived home from a Saturday game, after a road trip of three hundred and fifty miles, glassy-eyed, dazed, and spent. He hadn't really had any relaxation and he had failed to see Czlika (who had gone in for Trusky) take the pass from Bkeeo (who had gone in for Bjallo) in the third period, because at that moment a youngster named Lavagetto had been put in to pinch-hit for Art Gurlack in the bottom of the ninth with the tying run on second, and the skywriter who was attempting to write "Princeton 0–Lafayette 43" had banked the wrong way, muffed the "3," and distracted everyone's attention from the fact that Lavagetto had been whiffed.

5    Cheering, of course, lost its stimulating effect on players, because cheers were no longer associated necessarily with the immediate scene but might as easily apply to something that was happening somewhere else. This was enough to infuriate even the steadiest performer. A football star, hearing the stands break into a roar before the ball was snapped, would realize that their minds were not on him, and would become dispirited and grumpy. Two or three of the big coaches worried so about this that they considered equipping all players with tiny ear sets, so that they, too, could keep abreast of other sporting events while playing, but the idea was abandoned as impractical, and the coaches put it aside in tickler files, to bring up again later.

6    I think the event that marked the turning point in sport and started it downhill was the Midwest's classic Dust Bowl game of 1975, when Eastern Reserve's great right end, Ed Pistachio, was shot by a spectator.

This man, the one who did the shooting, was seated well down in the stands near the forty-yard line on a bleak October afternoon and was so saturated with sport and with the disappointments of sport that he had clearly become deranged. With a minute and fifteen seconds to play and the score tied, the Eastern Reserve quarterback had whipped a long pass over Army's heads into Pistachio's waiting arms. There was no other player anywhere near him, and all Pistachio had to do was catch the ball and run it across the line. He dropped it. At exactly this moment, the spectator—a man named Homer T. Parkinson, of 35 Edgemere Drive, Toledo, O.—suffered at least three other major disappointments in the realm of sport. His horse, Hiccough, on which he had a five-hundred-dollar bet, fell while getting away from the starting gate at Pimlico and broke its leg (clearly visible in the video); his favorite shortstop, Lucky Frimstitch, struck out and let three men die on base in the final game of the Series (to which Parkinson was tuned); and the Governor Dummer soccer team, on which Parkinson's youngest son played goalie, lost in Kent, 4–3, as recorded in the sky overhead. Before anyone could stop him, he drew a gun and drilled Pistachio, before 954,000 persons, the largest crowd that had ever attended a football game and the *second*-largest crowd that had ever assembled for any sporting event in any month except July.

7      This tragedy, by itself, wouldn't have caused sport to decline, I suppose, but it set in motion a chain of other tragedies, the cumulative effect of which was terrific. Almost as soon as the shot was fired, the news flash was picked up by one of the skywriters directly above the field. He glanced down to see whether he could spot the trouble below, and in doing so failed to see another skywriter approaching. The two planes collided and fell, wings locked, leaving a confusing trail of smoke, which some observers tried to interpret as a late sports score. The planes struck in the middle of the nearby eastbound coast-to-coast Sunlight Parkway, and a motorist driving a convertible coupé stopped so short, to avoid hitting them, that he was bumped from behind. The pileup of cars that ensued involved 1,482 vehicles, a record for eastbound parkways. A total of more than three thousand persons lost their lives in the highway accident, including the two pilots, and when panic broke out in the stadium, it cost another 872 in dead and injured. News of the disaster spread quickly to other sports arenas, and started other panics among the crowds trying to get to the exits, where they could buy a paper and study a list of the dead. All in all, the afternoon of sport cost 20,003 lives, a record. And nobody had much to show for it except one small Midwestern boy who hung around the smoking wrecks of the planes, captured some aero news-smoke in a milk bottle, and took it home as a souvenir.

8      From that day on, sport waned. Through long, noncompetitive Saturday afternoons, the stadia slumbered. Even the parkways fell into disuse as motorists rediscovered the charms of old, twisty roads that

led through main streets and past barnyards, with their mild congestions and pleasant smells.

## REVIEW

### Content

1. Satire is often written to instruct as well as to entertain. Do you think White intended this piece to do so? If so, what do you think he is trying to say?
2. Although this satire was written in the late 1940s, do you see any evidences of what Alvin Toffler calls "future shock" in his book of that same name (1970)?

### Rhetoric

3. Satire works by employing various kinds of humor. Some of the humor is direct, and some more indirect. How does White make direct humor serve him here—in name choices, in the details he chooses to include, and so on? Among the more indirect, or "left-handed" humorous techniques a satirist may employ are irony, exaggeration, and absurdity. How skillful is White with these? Point to several examples.
4. What is the effect of the very long, detail-packed sentences White often writes? How do they strengthen the satirical effect?

### Projects

5. There are a number of American satirists who delight in trying to alert the United States to her weaknesses by spoofing her. If this "teaching method" appeals to you, go to the library and read some in the following writers: James Thurber, Art Buchwald, Harry Golden, more of White himself. Bring in one short passage you especially like and be prepared to read it to the class and explain what makes it effective. Those who prefer movies and television to reading satire might hold a class discussion on current movies and TV programs that work by satire to help America see herself. Can you think of satires on the future? What satirizing devices are used on the screen? What makes these presentations effective? What causes satire to fail when it does?
6. Select some potential source of "future shock" and a write a short satire about it. Use the devices that have been discussed as effectively as you can—and take care not to lose your effect by overdone satire that is too heavy-handed.

# Man-Woman Relationships in the Society of the Future

## HERBERT A. OTTO

Herbert A. Otto, a psychologist, is Chairman of the National Center for the Exploration of Human Potential in La Jolla, California. He has written widely on the family, human sexuality, alternative relationships, and related topics; his books include *The Family in Search of a Future* (1970), *Love Today: A New Exploration* (1972), and *Total Sex: Developing Sexual Potential* (1972). In "Man-Woman Relationships in the Society of the Future," first printed in *The Futurist* magazine for April, 1973, Otto considers some exciting and challenging potential developments in male-female relating beyond those seen as acceptable in the past.

1   Rising employment for women, increasing pressures on both sexes for higher performance, and growing mobility will heighten the man-woman relationship in the society of the future. But many couples will expect more from the relationship than it can yield, so the divorce rate will continue to climb, and serial monogamy will become an increasingly common life-style. For a period of time, the intimate relationships of men and women will tend to become more superficial and artificial.

2   To counteract these tendencies, some alternatives designed to foster intimate relatedness between single men and women are already making their appearance. These organized events are the precursor of what can be expected on a very much more widespread basis in the new society. There are, for example, the numerous Growth Center Workshops for singles, offered by such group facilitators as Betty Berzon and Emily Coleman of the human potentialities movement. The emphasis in these workshops is on helping participants to grow as persons, so that greater warmth, openness and creativity in interpersonal relationships can make their appearance. In the society of the future, such workshops will be very popular with single people as a form of recreation.

3   The society of the future will inevitably develop new modes of creating deeper and more intimate relationships. In the coming years, we can expect increasing experimentation with forms of *instant intimacy*,

From *The Futurist* (April, 1973), published by the World Future Society, P.O. Box 30369 (Bethesda), Washington, D.C. 20014. Reprinted by permission.

both between man and woman and between members of the same sex. Some of today's microlab and small group or dyadic experiences are forerunners of this development.

4    The commune movement and its experimentation with alternative life-styles is rooted, to a large extent, in a desire for greater intimacy in human relationships. During my study of over 30 communes, comments like this were repeatedly heard: "We wanted a greater closeness with people with whom we had something in common," and, "There is a greater feeling of closeness and openness here (in the commune) than there was at home with the family."

5    There is no question that in the society of the future the range of man-woman relationships and alternative life-styles will be expanded. I expect that, within the next decade, as much as 25 percent of the adult population will have experienced a life-style other than dyadic sexual intimacy.

## Marriage Enrichment Programs Will Multiply

6    Coupled with the wider acceptance of alternative life-styles, there will be a strong thrust to develop the potential of monogamy and bring greater fulfillment to this institution. Marriage enrichment programs will replace weekend outings in popularity. Attempts to restructure the framework of monogamy will proliferate. Three contemporary instances which indicate the trend of the future are:

1. Psychologist Sidney Jourard's suggestion of marriage as "serial polygamy to the same person": the participants proceed by reinventing themselves and the relationship.

2. My suggestion of the "New Marriage": i.e., marriage as a framework for developing the partners' personal potential.

3. Nena and George O'Neill's proposal for the "Open Marriage": "an honest and open relationship between two people, based on equal freedom and identity of both partners." From the O'Neill perspective, for a couple with a fully operating and successful open marriage, the marriage will be their primary relationship, while "open companionship" with members of the same or other sex (which *may* involve relating sexually) can be practiced. These, and other forms of revitalizing the monogamous union, will have a place in the lives of the man and woman of the future.

## People Will Be Freer To Choose What They Want To Be

7    New "ideal models" of the man and the woman are in the process of emerging. The new models give men and women greater freedom of

choice in what they can be, and what they want to be. In the choice of wearing apparel, mode of wearing the hair and type of occupation, both sexes will have unparalleled freedom in crossing the gender barriers which exist today. Gender will not be the main component for the recognition and assessment of the person, as is the case today. In the new society, recognition of the uniqueness of the person will be primary, and the gender of a person will not be used as a filter which colors the beholder's perception of that person's unique individuality. The major ideal model in the society of the future will not be marriage, children, and a house in the suburbs, but rather the experiencing of a series of deep and fulfilling relationships and varied environments, viewed as a continuous adventure.

In the intimate area of the sexual relationship, a number of new emphases and shifts can be anticipated.

1. Sex will not be seen as something that man does to woman, or a pleasure that man gives to woman, or vice versa, but will be perceived as a field for mutual responsibility, experimentation and enjoyment.

2. It will be widely accepted that, despite social and technological advances, most people are functioning at only a fraction of their sexual potential, and that the development of sexual potential can play an important role in the actualizing of personal potential.

3. There will be a very rapid increase in the Here-and-Now (i.e., short-term) experiences of sexual relatedness, which will be characterized by great depth and intimacy. These Here-and-Now experiences will be in addition to any ongoing and more permanent man-woman relationship in which the citizen of the future may be involved. In the new society, it will be recognized that loving/caring, sexual and non-sexual relationships are possible within the Here-and-Now framework and that this does not diminish the total flow of love available in a more permanent relationship. It will be recognized that, for some people, this type of Here-and-Now sexual loving relatedness will deepen and revitalize the flow of love in their more permanent relationship.

## Sex Will Become Less Important—But More Highly Valued

8   In the new society, paradoxically, sex and sexuality will be both less important and valued more highly. The power of the puritanical heritage, with its prescriptions, proscriptions, and taboos, is still immense today. As a result of this heritage, a disproportionate amount of importance is assigned to the sexual area of human experiencing. Contrastingly, in the new society, the prevailing attitude will be that sex is a natural, normal part of living, approximately equivalent in importance to food or housing. In short, sex will not be singled out for special emphasis, but since most citizens of the new society will be aware of the vast poten-

tial hidden within the domain of sexual experiencing, this facet of self-discovery and self-unfolding will be valued more highly.

9 In the course of my research in the area of sexual fantasies, I found indications of a considerable fantasy preoccupation by today's men and women with group sex. A marked increase in experimentation with group sex and homophile experiencing as a part of a basically heterosexual pattern can be expected in the new society. Homophile relations will be viewed as a personal or idiosyncratic preference, or as a choice of sexual life-style. The free and open communication of sex fantasies will be generally accepted.

10 The sexual framework will also be increasingly utilized to explore the multiple embryonic selves which are latent within every man and woman. (This is based on the recognition that every individual has the capacity for many rebirths as a basically changed person.) The embryonic selves, among which are "the man in the woman, and the woman in the man," will be more fully explored, within the context of the sexual relationships of the future.

## Spiritual/Existential Questing To Become the Mode

11 Inevitably, the sexual framewrok will be widely recognized, both as a medium for communication and for self-transcendence. Sexual touching will become a part of the accepted public communication and non-verbal language. In the new society, there will be a constant emotional-sexual-mental interchange for the man and woman opting for a close relationship or a relationship of mutual exploration. Both Oriental and Occidental sexual techniques designed for self-transcendence or spiritual communion will be widely employed. The man and woman of the future will be more fully involved in a spiritual/existential quest—the pursuit of the meaning of their existence and all existence. Within the new society, there will be a major thrust for a deeper level of spiritual communion, or to attain the experience of mystical union. Many couples will be committed to helping each other attain this state.

12 An important aspect of the spiritual/existential quest will be the clarification of values and life-goals and their relationship to the total development of the person. The fostering of love and deep caring as a major component (and spiritual force) in the man-woman and same-sex relationships will receive renewed attention. The society of the future will devote some of its energies to the creation of a social climate distinguished by deep caring and love as a basic public health policy. This policy will be based on the widespread recognition that people's mortality and morbidity, the incidence of sickness and dying, are intimately related to the climate of love that surrounds them. The new society will have a renaissance of love, recognizing that this force is the prime mover in humanity's evolution.

# REVIEW

## Content

1. First, do you agree with Otto that our "puritanical heritage" has led to our assigning "a disproportionate amount of importance . . . to the sexual area of human experiencing" (paragraph 8)? Otto then goes on to say that *other* areas of intimacy, having to do with deep caring, loving, and sharing, are becoming more and more important in male-female and other intimate relationships, as our preoccupation with sex, as a separated-off experience, diminishes. Do you agree with him? Would you *like* this to be the case? If so, be ready to explore in discussion *specific* advantages you can foresee. If not, why not?

2. Carry further Otto's discussion of "the spiritual/existential quest" he envisions for the richer relationships he predicts. What does he mean by "spiritual communion"? Does this possibility appeal to *you*? Some persons would view Otto's last three sentences as totally unsubstantiated flights of fancy, bordering on the absurd. How does their content strike *you*?

## Rhetoric

3. Otto uses some vocabulary of the relatively new Human Potential Movement in his article. Be sure you understand the following terms, to help you fully comprehend the points Otto is making: serial monogamy (paragraph 1); human potential (2); microlab (3); dyadic (3 and 5); actualizing of personal potential (7); homophile (9); multiple embryonic selves (10); self-transcendence (11); existential (11); clarification of values (12). In paragraph 8, why does Otto refer to "sex *and* sexuality"; that is, what is the distinction between these two terms?

4. Is any of Otto's phrasing so vague as to render his content unclear to you? If so, what are some of the problems in composition at those points?

## Projects

5. Select some aspect of Otto's discussion that you find especially intriguing and write a brief paper about it. Be prepared to discuss your paper in class.

6. Take a facet of Otto's presentation that *disturbs* you and set yourself to thinking through *why* you are disturbed. Write up how this exercise either broadened your thinking on the subject or left you completely stuck. If the latter occurs, do not view the thinking and writing as a *negative* exercise; you have *begun* to think about a new area. OR Write a paper in which you defend your present life-style of relating, if you are happy with it; or in which you try to think through either how you can improve your present relationship(s) or can move toward more fulfilling relating elsewhere.

# Drugs and the Future

## FRANK J. AYD, JR.

Frank J. Ayd, Jr., a physician, has served as editor of the *International Drug Therapy Newsletter* and the *Medical-Moral Newsletter,* as well as associate editor of *Medical Counterpoint.* "Drugs and the Future" originally appeared in the latter publication in 1969. In this article Ayd discusses some implications of modern man's preoccupation with drugs, for a variety of purposes, and attempts to foresee where that preoccupation may take us in the future. He considers, for example, drugs used to achieve mystical heights, to radically increase intelligence levels, and to temporarily incapacitate a population, among other uses.

1   From the day Eve plucked the forbidden apple from the Tree of Knowledge, man has had an insatiable curiosity about himself—his purpose, his natural and supernatural destinies, his physical and psychological composition, and the causes of his behavior. Man also has had an incessant desire to control and to improve man. Consequently, in the perpetual search for knowledge of man, throughout human history each generation of men has studied man with all the means that were available.

2   Precisely when man first learned that chemicals could affect his mental and physical state favorably or adversely is a secret of history, but ever since, he has sought chemicals to ease pain, to induce pleasure, to preserve and improve health, to enhance his physical and mental powers, to transport himself to mystical heights, to alter and control the behavior of his fellow men, and even to kill his fellow men. Knowing what chemicals can do has impelled man to search continuously for naturally occurring chemicals and, when he became able to do so, to create synthetic ones. The acquisition of the power to produce chemicals which can manipulate man's behavior caused man to strive to learn how these work and where they act in the body so that he could make better and safer substances to alter human behavior. Man's power to do this has been limited until this twentieth century; but technological, biochemical, and pharmacological developments in the past twenty-five years have made it possible for man to discover, synthesize, and study the direct and indirect effects of drugs on the brain and hence on all human behavior.

3   Today we have drugs and chemicals which stimulate and counteract

Reprinted from *Medical Counterpoint,* September, 1969, by permission of the author and the publisher.

fatigue, which are potent pain-easers, which suppress or increase appetite, which induce sleep or cause wakefulness, which enhance or suppress human sexuality, which induce or suppress fertility, which alert or stultify intellectual performance, which can improve mental and emotional illnesses or produce temporary and possibly permanent insanity, which can cause synthetic mysticism, which lengthen or shorten motor performance and endurance, which cause or subdue aggressiveness, or which can produce pleasure or pain. In short, we now have drugs and intoxicants that can affect every facet of man and can ennoble, or debase and dehumanize, man. We have chemicals which enable man to change and control individual and group human behavior. Furthermore, modern Western man is not averse to using drugs and intoxicants to alter his own behavior, as statistics on the use of alcohol, narcotic, and psychedelic drugs like LSD demonstrate. Nor is modern man averse to using drugs and intoxicants to alter and to control the behavior of his fellow men, as evidenced by the use of tear gas, mace, and other chemicals on unruly groups and rioters, by the preparations for chemical warfare, and by the advocacy by some individuals of the compulsory uses of anti-fertility agents to control population size.

4      Cognizant of what can be done today with drugs, scientists are peering into the future to ascertain what compounds they should concentrate on developing to meet the needs of society and to make possible further manipulation and control of human behavior by chemicals. Before discussing the drugs on the horizon or in the planning stage, consideration must be given to the philosophical and cultural climate of today, for these influence the types of drugs sought and their application.

## Scientism and Drug Use

5      Twentieth-century man has become progressively more materialistic and egocentric. A new religion, scientism, has sprung up among some influential scientists and humanists. Many of them have rejected traditional Judeo-Christian morality as obsolete and unworthy of adherence to by man, enlightened and freed as he is by the discoveries of science. They have erected a new hierarchy of values. Ethics, they say, is situational. There is a new morality which holds that every human act—even murder—is good if it is motivated by "love." They champion new sexual mores that permit man to indulge in sexual pleasures in any way he wishes. They advocate new reproduction mores because science has enabled man to be infertile if he wills, and to procreate in new ways. They argue that since man can control the biological makeup of his near and remote descendants, only superior children should be desired and conceived. They tell us that the world no longer needs all the individuals we are capable of bringing into it—especially those who are

unable to compete and are an unhappy burden to others. Hence, they advocate contraception and sterilization to prevent the transmission of unwanted life, abortion or fetal euthanasia to destroy the unborn whose lives have been judged unworthy of preservation and protection, and voluntary euthanasia for the chronically ill whose lives have been declared useless.

6    Many of the high priests of scientism not only endorse an antilife philosophy but also subscribe to the concept that man is the owner of his life and body and therefore can do as he wishes. They have generated a modern foment for man to be totally free and to become the complete master of his destiny and his environment. Paradoxically, they declare that there is no need for self restraint, unless this is dictated by the "superior" objectives of scientism, such as the attainment, through carefully regulated reproduction, of intellectually and physically superior beings who thoroughly enjoy their sexual activities and their leisure time, immune to disease or illnesses, capable of unlimited longevity, and subject only to accidental death or deliberate self-extinction.

7    Scientism promises utopia, a synthetic heaven on earth made possible by chemical, biological, and technological developments. To achieve this objective, scientists believe that many drugs must and will be developed.

8    Among these are:

## Drugs Which Will Curb Human Reproduction

9    Much publicity has been given to the world's population growth. Experts warn that if the growth rate is not soon reduced to zero, the human race will destroy itself by an epidemic of unrestrained breeding. Experts also agree that the oral contraceptives, the intrauterine devices and all other methods of family planning are not the solution to the population crisis. These methods of fertility control depend for their effectiveness on user motivation and this, to the dismay of birth control advocates, is not sufficiently widespread. Hence, scientists are developing and testing birth control methods which require minimum motivation for their successful use. These include:

10    1. Injectable long-acting preparations capable of rendering a woman infertile for months and possibly for as long as twenty years.

11    2. A contraceptive vaccine which would produce indefinite immunologic infertility.

12    3. Abortifacient pills. Scientists have been synthesizing pills which destroy the fertilized ovum before it implants in the womb, which alter the lining of the uterus making implantation impossible, or which terminate the existence of the embryo after implantation. These chemicals are known as post-passion pills, post-coital pills, morning-after pills, week-after pills, or anti- or contranidation pills.

13    There is mounting evidence that good and safe abortifacients are on the way and that more will follow. The advantages of these compounds

over the oral contraceptives will be manifold. They will have to be taken only after intercourse and probably only once in a cycle instead of daily or every day for twenty days in each cycle. Women are more apt to remember to take an abortifacient drug than to forget, as she may "the pill," since these drugs are used retrospectively. They will allow the same, if not more, sexual freedom and abandonment than the oral contraceptives and yet will be less expensive. They probably will not produce the same endocrine and physiologic changes as "the pill" and probably will not require the same medical supervision as takers of oral contraceptives should and must have. These abortifacients, because of their advantages, will appeal to women at all economic and social levels, especially to the economically disadvantaged, the educationally deprived and wherever medical services are in short supply.

### Drugs and the Female Conscience

14      At first some women, because of qualms of conscience, may hesitate to use these drugs. However, since other abortion methods already are used by such vast number of women in the world, it would not be long before oral abortifacients would be preferred by most women. This would be true especially if science supplies an oral abortifacient which would have to be taken only once toward the end of a cycle and which would induce menstruation before the woman knew whether she is pregnant or not. It would be easy for her to rationalize her action and not to feel any guilt at all. Thus, abortifacient drugs may become the mainstay of population-control programs, personal and national, throughout the world.

15      Can you envision procreation being dependent on an antidote for the daily food you eat, or the water you drink?

16      Sound fantastic, ludicrous, unbelievable?

17      Maybe, but it isn't inconceivable. In recent years many who are anxious to defuse "The Population Bomb" and who are impatient with the failure of people to be self-motivated to control their fertility, have been advocating that scientists devise chemicals which would make entire populations infertile so that governments could control at will the rate of its population growth. Such drugs have not been developed, but some scientists are predicting that they will be made and used if necessary.

### New Chemical Aphrodisiacs

18      The search for chemical means to increase sexual appetite, potency, and to maximize the sensual pleasures of sexual relationships is as old as the recorded history of man. In this age of "The New Morality," with its emphasis on sexual freedom and on sensory experiences and the separation of reproduction from conjugal relations, many men and women are using what is available to enhance sexual desire, performance, and enjoyment. Hippies testify that making love under the in-

fluence of a low dose of LSD is "love at its best." Even the elderly are interested in sexual relations—so much so that recently a compound has been marketed as an aid to sexual appetite for the elderly and the impotent. Scientists have located target areas in the brain which can directly and quickly instigate sexual behavior. They have appropriate testing methods and some knowledge of the types of chemicals to examine. Consequently, they predict that chemical aphrodisiacs soon will be available and widely used.

### Drugs To Induce Hibernation and To Ease the Pains of Hunger

19      Although some agricultural experts have abandoned their pessimism and have become optimistic that the world can feed its growing population during the remainder of this century, there are those who insist that famines are imminent. They warn that, if the quantity of people is not limited, the world's food supply will be insufficient to meet the demands for it, and that sometime between 1970 and 1985, because of vast famines, hundreds of millions of people will be starving. These alleged imminent famines, they assert, can be avoided only by a drastic and immediate reduction of the population and the birthrate. Since this may not be achieved, scientists are being exhorted to make better appetite suppressant drugs and compounds which would ease effectively the pains of hunger during periods of food shortages. Furthermore, since the food requirements of hibernating animals are low, Gordon R. Taylor, in his book, *The Biological Time Bomb,* suggests that in times of food shortage, many people might be placed in hibernation. Drugs to achieve this, at least for relatively short periods, exist and some scientists believe that compounds can be developed which could be used for mass hibernation for long periods.

### Drugs To Combat Boredom

20      Futurists confidently forecast that in the next twenty-five years man will have more and more time for leisure and idleness. This, they predict, may become a major problem, for it could, as it has in other historical eras, lead to sloth, boredom, melancholy, despair, and an increase in suicide. Hence, they are pressing scientists to make drugs which could counteract the sloth of the future. In response to these promptings, research is underway to discover and perfect antiennui compounds. Marketing analysts visualize high sales for these products. Such financial incentives may make these drugs realities before the twenty-first century.

### Drugs To Transport Man to Mystical Heights

21      Already many individuals are seeking "instant satori" through the use of psychedelic drugs and other intoxicants. It is expected that this trend will continue and that not only hippies and intellectuals but the most cloistered and unadventurous individuals will demand chemicals which

will speed up transport to pinnacles of emotion and psychological experiences men otherwise would never have known. Hence, scientists say there is a need for new psychedelics. These can and will be produced so that all present "mind expanders" will be obsolete within the next thirty years.

### Drugs To Raise Intelligence to Very High Levels

22    Drugs now are being used to prevent or delay loss of intelligence, but to cope with the demands generated by scientific and technological developments, increased intellectual capacities are deemed imperative. Currently, scientists are studying drugs to raise or lower IQ, to enhance attention span, to improve memory, to increase capacity to absorb knowledge and to heighten verbal, arithmetical, or artistic abilities or talents at will. Experts in this area, such as California psychology professor David Krech, have declared that within five to ten years science will be able to control intellectual capacities with drugs. Since drugs could create geniuses, Gordon R. Taylor warns that we soon may have "a supernaturally intelligent elite with very little ability to find common ground with normal, unimproved men."

23    The advent of chemicals which will influence the development of man's intellectual capacities will raise profound social, legal, and ethical questions. This is why Professor Krech has aptly warned that we must prepare controls over these awesome powers, and not permit them to be exercised indiscriminately.

### Drugs Which Will Increase Longevity

24    The quest for the fountain of youth, immortalized by Ponce de Leon, has never ceased. The conquest of communicable diseases has increased life expectancy phenomenally but there has been no significant change in the maximum life span of man because the degenerative diseases, which are largely responsible for death of the elderly, have been affected very little.

25    Longevity, it seems, is associated both with a stable DNA and with freedom from degenerative diseases which apparently are initiated by mutation in a single cell. If DNA can be stabilized and undesirable mutations controlled, longer life should result. Since a stable DNA could be an ingredient of the legendary elixir of youth, molecular biologists are working to devise chemicals which would stabilize DNA and which would prevent or control cell mutation. These chemicals would alter life expectancy. Futurists are forecasting that these chemicals will be discovered, but at this moment a lengthened life span is only a theoretical possibility.

### Drugs To Produce Temporary Incapacitation of a Population

26    To subdue unruly groups and rioters or the enemy during war, in as humane a way as possible, humanists want scientists to develop chem-

icals which would temporarily incapacitate a population. They envision, for example, the development of very potent substances which, in very minute quantities, could be placed in an aerosol bomb. This would be exploded and its contents inhaled or absorbed through the skin, rapidly rendering people incapable of normal activity. Then the rioters or the enemy could be disarmed, captured, and imprisoned before the effects of the disabling drug have waned. Efforts to create such substances are going on and, according to some scientists, their development is not only feasible but will be a reality in the immediate future. They acknowledge that such drugs will incapacitate everyone exposed to them—the innocent as well as the offenders.

## Comment

27    These are only a few of the drugs in the offing which can and will be used to manipulate and control human behavior. Society must be aware of these trends and give serious consideration to them and to their implications—good and evil—for the individual and society, before they are realities. No one wants to prevent progress but, at the same time, science should not be allowed to forge ahead unsupervised simply on the justification advanced by many scientists, namely, that what science can do, it must. On the contrary, as Sir Theodore Fox aptly remarked to his fellow scientists: "We shall have to learn to refrain from doing things merely because we know how to do them."

28    Desirable as the drugs scientists are contemplating may seem, it is imperative to inquire if this is so. Man is more than a sensate animal. All men have dormant within them capabilities for their physical and spiritual improvement. Should these be germinated by drugs? Can they be? Can man become more virtuous by ingesting chemicals and intoxicants? History testifies that the answer is no. Instead, what has happened when this has been attempted in the past was the achievement of physically sound bodies with morally dulled minds. Whenever individuals or a society concentrated on the betterment of man's physical endowment and on the gratification and enjoyment of the senses, the individual or the society first became debased and then was destroyed.

29    If we ignore the lessons of history, we are doomed to repeat them. Man may know more today but he certainly is no wiser than the Greeks or the Romans whose demise was preceded by debaucheries and the enslavement of thousands of citizens. We are headed in the same direction, using potent drugs and intoxicants to attain hedonistic goals. We are synthesizing compounds, which, if they ever were controlled by fanatical leaders, could be used to control, subjugate and dehumanize men in ways heretofore impossible. Unless we are alert to the dangers of individual and mass chemical bondage and prepare to face the ethical and moral problems posed by scientific developments, then, to para-

phrase Robert Burns, man's inhumanity to man will make countless thousands mourn.

## Current Demand for Freedom of Choice

30    Today the demand for freedom of choice is well established. Many moderns are loathe to discipline themselves. On the contrary, modern man condones and encourages self-indulgence, forgetting that the less demanded of an individual in the way of discipline, observance of rules, and recognition of and respect for authority, the more dispirited and restive he becomes, and paradoxically, the more he wants to control others, since he cannot control himself. Modern man has forgotten also that the fulfillment of one desire is usually the signal for some new wish rather than a cause for contentment.

31    The Greek philosopher, Epicurus, once remarked: "No pleasure is a bad thing in itself; but the means which produce some pleasures bring with them disturbances many times greater than pleasure." Unmindful of this, many people today, especially the young, in seeking pleasure are using products of science and technology that corrupt the body and the mind. The current frenetic pursuit of carnal pleasures and the ingestion of drugs which alter consciousness are producing a harvest of unhealthy minds and bodies. Psychiatrists are seeing an increasing number of apathetic, academically impaired young people without ambition or social involvement and a history of several years of persistent abuse of drugs, including marijuana which is not as innocuous as many misguided physicians and educators claim. These victims of drug abuse are living an aimless, utterly hedonic life style. The growth of such a drug-dependent population would not only destroy many potentially productive young people but also face our society with a growing burden of parasitism.

## Crucial Questions

32    Truly, society must ask itself if the development of more drugs and intoxicants as those I have discussed is desirable and necessary. If they become realities, their use would become fashionable and widespread. Because this could be disastrous, all responsible men must concede that some control over scientific developments is urgently necessary. The issues raised by current scientific trends can only be resolved by true value judgments. These should and must be made by responsible leaders and all citizens. They cannot and should not be made by scientists alone, for they are matters of public welfare, and to delegate to scientists alone social and moral judgments which are the right and duty of every citizen, as history warns, can be very dangerous indeed. If responsible men fail in their duty now, we will have to agree with Homer, who remarked in his *Odyssey:* "What a lamentable thing it is that men should blame

the gods and regard them as the source of their troubles, when it is their own wickedness that brings them sufferings worse than any which Destiny allots them."

## REVIEW

### Content

1. Were you aware of *all* the possibilities for "drug use and abuse" that Ayd cites before reading this article? If not, what *new* thinking did he set off in your mind? Were you able to sort out positive and negative consequences of various uses of drugs as you read and to recognize both advantages and disadvantages; that is, did you suspend any prejudices, positive and negative, about drugs which you may have brought to reading the piece?
2. Be prepared for class discussion on paragraphs 28 through 31. If you disagree with Ayd on any points, be ready to *support* your refutation. If your position coincides with his, be prepared to defend it *beyond* the supprt his discussion provides.

### Rhetoric

3. Why is Ayd's first paragraph effective as an opener for his presentation? What makes his prose *substantial* throughout? Where is his argumentation weak?
4. What do you perceive of Ayd's own biases in paragraphs 5 and 6? What about his diction (word choice), his phrasing, the progression of the development of his discussion, reveals these biases? Should he have exposed his biases *here* or as part of his concluding comments? Does their appearance so early in the piece unduly prejudice the reader ahead of time?

### Projects

5. Select one area of drug use that Ayd cites. Do some research on the *current* known potentialities in that area and be prepared to explain in class the advantages and disadvantages of those potentialities. Decide what recommendations you want to offer to the rest of the class on such drugs and the future.
6. Your best friend, who has moved away recently, has hit "the drug scene" in his/her new town and writes for your advice. Using Ayd's discussion as background or resource, what would you write to him/her? *Can* you write unless you have tried drugs? Compose a letter of practical advice if you feel you can do so. If not, then write a more philosophical letter about such questions as individual freedom and choice vis-à-vis responsibility for one's decisions and actions, or about your own overall views on drugs.

# Conditioning: Babies, Books, and Flowers

## ALDOUS HUXLEY

Aldous Huxley (1894–1963) was an English novelist who later settled in California, where he wrote several movie scenarios. He became interested in the philosophy and mysticism of the East, resulting in a collection entitled *The Perennial Philosophy* (1945). Another interest was hallucinogenic drugs, his experiences in that area producing *The Doors of Perception* (1954), one of the first books on the subject in this country. In addition to these and other nonfiction works, Huxley wrote eleven novels, among them *Antic Hay* (1923), *Point Counter Point* (1928), and *Brave New World* (1932). *Brave New World* was Huxley's dystopian prediction of the society which modern technology would produce. In 1958 he wrote *Brave New World Revisited,* a study of what had actually happened since 1932; the echo title tells the reader that Huxley saw his feared "brave new world" already coming into existence by 1958. In the passage below from *Brave New World,* the reader eavesdrops on a conditioning session in which a particular attitude toward books and flowers is being developed in infants.

1   Mr. Foster was left in the Decanting Room. The D.H.C. [Director of Hatcheries and Conditioning] and his students stepped into the nearest lift and were carried up to the fifth floor.

2   INFANT NURSERIES. NEO-PAVLOVIAN CONDITIONING ROOMS, announced the notice board.

3   The Director opened a door. They were in a large bare room, very bright and sunny; for the whole of the southern wall was a single window. Half a dozen nurses, trousered and jacketed in the regulation white viscose-linen uniform, their hair aseptically hidden under white caps, were engaged in setting out bowls of roses in a long row across the floor. Big bowls, packed tight with blossom. Thousands of petals, ripe-blown and silkily smooth, like the cheeks of innumerable little cherubs, but of cherubs, in that bright light, not exclusively pink and Aryan, but also luminously Chinese, also Mexican, also apoplectic with too much blowing of celestial trumpets, also pale as death, pale with the posthumous whiteness of marble.

4   The nurses stiffened to attention as the D.H.C. came in.

5    "Set out the books," he said curtly.

6    In silence the nurses obeyed his command. Between the rose bowls the books were duly set out—a row of nursery quartos opened invitingly each at some gaily colored image of beast or fish or bird.

7    "Now bring in the children."

8    They hurried out of the room and returned in a minute or two, each pushing a kind of tall dumb-waiter laden, on all its four wire-netted shelves, with eight-month-old babies, all exactly alike (a Bokanovsky Group, it was evident) and all (since their caste was Delta) dressed in khaki.

9    "Put them down on the floor."

10   The infants were unloaded.

11   "Now turn them so that they can see the flowers and books."

12   Turned, the babies at once fell silent, then began to crawl towards those clusters of sleek colors, those shapes so gay and brilliant on the white pages. As they approached, the sun came out of a momentary eclipse behind a cloud. The roses flamed up as though with a sudden passion from within; a new and profound significance seemed to suffuse the shining pages of the books. From the ranks of the crawling babies came little squeals of excitement, gurgles and twitterings of pleasure.

13   The Director rubbed his hands. "Excellent!" he said. "It might almost have been done on purpose."

14   The swiftest crawlers were already at their goal. Small hands reached out uncertainly, touched, grasped, unpetaling the transfigured roses, crumpling the illuminated pages of the books. The Director waited until all were happily busy. Then, "Watch carefully," he said. And, lifting his hand, he gave the signal.

15   The Head Nurse, who was standing by a switchboard at the other end of the room, pressed down a little lever.

16   There was a violent explosion. Shriller and ever shriller, a siren shrieked. Alarm bells maddeningly sounded.

17   The children started, screamed; their faces were distorted with terror.

18   "And now," the Director shouted (for the noise was deafening), "now we proceed to rub in the lesson with a mild electric shock."

19   He waved his hand again, and the Head Nurse pressed a second lever. The screaming of the babies suddenly changed its tone. There was something desperate, almost insane, about the sharp spasmodic yelps to which they now gave utterance. Their little bodies twitched and stiffened; their limbs moved jerkily as if to the tug of unseen wires.

20   "We can electrify that whole strip of floor," bawled the Director in explanation. "But that's enough," he signalled to the nurse.

21   The explosions ceased, the bells stopped ringing, the shriek of the siren died down from tone to tone into silence. The stiffly twitching bodies relaxed, and what had become the sob and yelp of infant maniacs broadened out once more into a normal howl of ordinary terror.

22   "Offer them the flowers and the books again."

23      The nurses obeyed; but at the approach of the roses, at the mere sight of those gaily-colored images of pussy and cock-a-doodle-doo and baa-baa black sheep, the infants shrank away in horror; the volume of their howling suddenly increased.

24      "Observe," said the Director triumphantly, "observe."

25      Books and loud noises, flowers and electric shocks—already in the infant mind these couples were compromisingly linked; and after two hundred repetitions of the same or a similar lesson would be wedded indissolubly. What man has joined, nature is powerless to put asunder.

26      "They'll grow up with what the psychologists used to call an 'instinctive' hatred of books and flowers. Reflexes unalterably conditioned. They'll be safe from books and botany all their lives." The Director turned to his nurses. "Take them away again."

## REVIEW

### Content

1. What you have read here may sound like the fantasy of science fiction to you. But are you aware of the ways in which behavior modification (conditioning) is being employed, with civil and political sanctions, *today* in, for example: (1) prisons; (2) mental hospitals; (3) schools? Can you think of how it is used, in more subtle ways, in advertising, in family life, in the classroom? And, in what yet more subtle ways are we "conditioned" every day by "Society" in all its manifestations?
2. Does anything about paragraph 8 especially bother you?

### Rhetoric

3. Huxley's interest in mysticism comes through in his fiction, often in descriptive passages. Where do you find such prose in the above excerpt?
4. Huxley's fiction is as popular as it is partly because he has a good sense of the dramatic. Analyze how he builds suspense, and involves the reader, in this passage from *Brave New World*.

### Projects

5. A leading contemporary figure in behavior modification is B. F. Skinner. Conditioning plays a major role in the utopia Walden Two which Skinner creates in his novel of that title. Read some passages in the novel that have to do with conditioning and compare how Skinner presents it as a *good* force with Huxley's fictional treatment of it as an evil one.
6. Do some reading in your college library on some contemporary application of conditioning and report your findings in a paper. OR Read some fictional account of behavior modification and write your re-

sponse to the book: for example, *Clockwork Orange* by Anthony Burgess, Skinner's *Walden Two*, more of Huxley's *Brave New World*, or other titles your librarian can suggest.

# I Have a Dream . . .

## MARTIN LUTHER KING, JR.

Martin Luther King, Jr. (1929–1968) was a Southern clergyman and a major leader in the Black civil rights movement. His writings include *Stride Toward Freedom* (1958), *Why We Can't Wait* (1964), and *Strength To Love* (1963). King, a pacifist, believed that equality was to be sought—and won—through nonviolent means. He received the Nobel Peace Prize in 1964. King was a leader in the Freedom March on Washington, D. C., in August, 1963, and his famous "I Have a Dream . . ." speech, delivered at the Lincoln Memorial, became the highlight of the March. King was assassinated in Memphis, Tennessee, in April, 1968.

1   . . . I say to you today, my friends, that in spite of the difficulties and frustrations of the moment I still have a dream. It is a dream deeply rooted in the American dream.

2   I have a dream that one day this nation will rise up and live out the true meaning of its creed: "We hold these truths to be self-evident; that all men are created equal."

3   I have a dream that one day on the red hills of Georgia the sons of former slaves and the sons of former slaveowners will be able to sit down together at the table of brotherhood.

4   I have a dream that one day even the state of Mississippi, a desert state sweltering with the heat of injustice and oppression, will be transformed into an oasis of freedom and justice.

5   I have a dream that my four little children will one day live in a nation where they will not be judged by the color of their skin but by the content of their character.

6   I have a dream today.

7   I have a dream that one day the state of Alabama, whose governor's lips are presently dripping with the words of interposition and nullification, will be transformed into a situation where little black boys and black girls will be able to join hands with little white boys and white girls and walk together as sisters and brothers.

8    I have a dream today.

9    I have a dream that one day every valley shall be exalted, every hill and mountain shall be made low, the rough places will be made plains, and the crooked places will be made straight, and the glory of the Lord shall be revealed, and all flesh shall see it together.

10   This is our hope. This is the faith with which I return to the South. With this faith we will be able to hew out of the mountain of despair a stone of hope. With this faith we will be able to transform the jangling discords of our nation into a beautiful symphony of brotherhood. With this faith we will be able to work together, to pray together, to struggle together, to go to jail together, to stand up for freedom together, knowing that we will be free one day.

11   This will be the day when all of God's children will be able to sing with new meaning

My country, 'tis of thee
Sweet land of liberty,
    Of thee I sing:
Land where my fathers died,
Land of the pilgrims' pride
From every mountain-side
    Let freedom ring.

12   And if America is to be a great nation this must become true. So let freedom ring from the prodigious hilltops of New Hampshire. Let freedom ring from the mighty mountains of New York. Let freedom ring from the heightening Alleghenies of Pennsylvania!

13   Let freedom ring from the snowcapped Rockies of Colorado!

14   Let freedom ring from the curvacious peaks of California!

15   But not only that; let freedom ring from Stone Mountain of Georgia!

16   Let freedom ring from Lookout Mountain of Tennessee!

17   Let freedom ring from every hill and molehill of Mississippi. From every mountainside, let freedom ring.

18   When we let freedom ring, when we let it ring from every village and every hamlet, from every state and every city, we will be able to speed up that day when all of God's children, black men and white men, Jews and Gentiles, Protestants and Catholics, will be able to join hands and sing in the words of the old Negro spiritual, "Free at last! free at last! thank God almighty, we are free at last!"

## REVIEW

### Content

1. King's visionary speech of hope and faith was made in 1963. What fulfillment of that hope and faith can you point to since the speech? What possibilities of additional fulfillment, in both the immediate and

the more distant future, do you foresee? How important do *you* think the concerns King expresses are?

2. Why do you suppose the editor decided to make King's speech the final selection in her book?

## Rhetoric

3. This speech has already become one of the most famous examples of the use of parallel structure in American literature. Discuss what that device contributes to the eloquence of the speech.

4. King was a preacher. How do the style and tone of his speech reflect that training?

## Projects

5. Write a paper in which you describe *your* dream for the future of society.

6. *Later,* after you have had some time to live with your verbalized dream and to think seriously about the implications of *action*—versus mere words—write a second paper about what you are planning to do to help your dream come true.